Early Childhood Development

A MULTICULTURAL PERSPECTIVE

Second Edition

Jeffrey Trawick-Smith

EASTERN CONNECTICUT STATE UNIVERSITY

Merrill,
an imprint of PRENTICE HALL
Upper Saddle River, New Jersey • *Columbus, Ohio*

Library of Congress Cataloging-in-Publication Data

Trawick-Smith, Jeffrey W.
    Early childhood development : a multicultural perspective /
Jeffrey Trawick-Smith.—2nd ed.
      p.   cm.
    Includes bibliographical references (p.) and indexes.
    ISBN 0-13-013565-8
    1. Child development. 2. Early childhood education.
3. Multicultural education. 4. Cognition in children.
5. Observation (Educational method) 6. Handicapped children-
-Education.   I. Title.
    LB1115.T73 2000
    305.23′1—dc21   99-16288
                                        CIP

Cover photo: Tony Stone
Executive Editor: Kevin M. Davis
Developmental Editor: Hope Madden
Production Editor: Julie Peters
Design Coordinator: Diane C. Lorenzo
Cover Designer: Tope Grafix

Text design: John Reinhardt
Production Manager: Laura Messerly
Editorial Assistant: Holly Jennings
Director of Marketing: Kevin Flanagan
Marketing Manager: Meghan Shepherd
Marketing Assistant: Krista Groshong

This book was set in New Century Schoolbook by Carlisle Communications, Inc. and was printed and bound by R.R. Donnelley & Sons Company. The cover was printed by Phoenix Color Corp.

© 2000, 1997 by Prentice-Hall, Inc.
Pearson Education
Upper Saddle River, New Jersey 07458

Photo Credits: Bachman/The Image Works, p. 429; Wayne Behling, p. 52; Paul Conklin/Monkmeyer Press, p. 161; Elizabeth Crews, p. 115; Scott Cunningham/Merrill, pp. 2, 228, 269, 277, 368; Myrleen Ferguson/Photo edit, p. 172; Dan Floss, pp. 198, 234, 290, 307; Tomas D. W. Friedman/Photo Researchers, p. 326; David Grossman, p. 99; Larry Hamill Stock Photography, p. 66; Anthony Magnacca/Merrill, p. 138; Lawrence Migdale, pp. 106, 462; PhotoDisc, Inc., 92; Jacob A. Riis, Museum of the City of New York, 14; Courtesy of Riverside Hospital, p. 85; Barbara Schwartz/Merrill, pp. 4, 16, 36, 44, 180, 186, 354, 442, 454; David Strickler/Strix Pix, p. 204; Julie Tober/Merrill, p. 243; Unicef, p. 77; Anne Vega/Merrill, pp. 10, 27, 112, 118, 132, 144, 154, 165, 191, 209, 256, 302, 315, 390, 403, 414, 469; Eric L. Wheater, p. 332; Todd Yarrington/Merrill, 420.

Printed in the United States of America

10 9 8 7 6 5 4 3 2

ISBN: 0-13-013565-8

Prentice-Hall International (UK) Limited, *London*
Prentice-Hall of Australia Pty. Limited, *Sydney*
Prentice-Hall of Canada, Inc., *Toronto*
Prentice-Hall Hispanoamericana, S. A., *Mexico*
Prentice-Hall of India Private Limited, *New Delhi*
Prentice-Hall of Japan, Inc., *Tokyo*
Prentice-Hall (Singapore) Pte. Ltd., *Singapore*
Editora Prentice-Hall do Brasil, Ltda., *Rio de Janeiro*

Preface

Early Childhood Development: A Multicultural Perspective is a book about the development of all children in the world. It examines the physical, social, emotional, linguistic, and intellectual characteristics of children of diverse cultural backgrounds within and outside of the United States. It discusses both typical and atypical development; children with challenging conditions are profiled.

The book can be used as the primary text for child development or early child development courses in community colleges or four-year programs in education or psychology. It could also be used as a supplementary text in life-span or in graduate-level child development courses where a goal is to promote cultural understanding and sensitivity. Some of my colleagues have used it as a supplement in courses in multicultural education or the anti-bias curriculum. The book is intended to assist future teachers and child care providers in understanding and celebrating the rich diversity of development among children in all neighborhoods in America and around the globe.

TEXT ORGANIZATION AND FEATURES

An initial examination of the Contents will show that the book resembles other texts in child development. All current and important issues and topics are included. The book is organized in a conventional ages-and-stages format. A closer look, however, reveals several unique features. First, every topic is examined from a multicultural perspective. Sections on language development, for example, include descriptions of second-language learning and the linguistic development of non-English speakers. Chapters on intellectual development highlight cultural diversity in cognitive style. Attachment patterns and peer relations among children of diverse backgrounds are explored. Cultural variations in motor play and development are examined.

A second unique feature is that topics in atypical development and special education are smoothly integrated in all chapters. For example, autism and serious emotional disturbance are fully examined in sections on social development, and mental retardation and learning disabilities are extensively described in chapters dealing with cognition. A purpose of the text is to assist future teachers and caregivers, parents, family service providers, and psychologists in understanding and appreciating the characteristics of children with challenging conditions who will be increasingly integrated within regular classrooms.

A final important feature of the book is its real-life, practical orientation. It is intended as a hands-on guide for teachers and caregivers. There is a special assessment feature that helps professionals to interpret the behaviors of children in classrooms. Each chapter ends with a Research Into Practice section which outlines practical classroom and parenting applications. The chapters include numerous stories drawn from diverse cultures within and outside the United States, which bring theory and research to life. A set of activities, including child observations and parent/family interview assignments, is provided at the end of each chapter to guide students in witnessing child development concepts in real life.

WHY STUDY CHILD DEVELOPMENT FROM A MULTICULTURAL PERSPECTIVE?

Why is such a multicultural focus in child development so important? During the twenty-first century, children of traditionally under-represented groups—often called "minorities"—will constitute a new majority within the United States. Because families of historically under-represented groups are younger than those of other cultures, their children will comprise a growing percentage of the preschool and school-age population. Early childhood classrooms will become increasingly diverse, and teachers must be prepared to meet the unique needs of young children of varying backgrounds. Even teachers of monocultural classrooms must assist their students in understanding and appreciating other cultures. A primary goal of teachers today is to provide skills, understanding, and sensitivity which allow children to grow up in a pluralistic society. This textbook is designed to assist teachers in meeting that goal by providing a culturally sensitive account of developmental processes.

NEW FEATURES IN THE SECOND EDITION

This second edition includes many new topics and issues. Exciting new research on infant **brain growth** is presented and interpreted. The importance of a healthy brain for later learning and emotional well-being is examined. The work of **Lev Vygotsky,** a psychologist whose socio-cultural theory is receiving much attention in the field, is examined in great depth. In particular, the practical implications of Vygotsky's research for teachers and parents are considered. The section on artistic development is extended to include an analysis of children's art in **Reggio Emilia, Italy.** Children in this community have been found to develop artistically at an astounding rate. The book explores how this came to be and how teachers and parents can apply strategies and ideas from this Italian region in North America.

The second edition places greater emphasis on the **assessment** of children's development. An assessment feature is provided in each chapter which guides readers in observing and interpreting children's learning and behavior. This feature assists teachers and parents in recognizing atypical development and identifying those children with special needs.

COMPANION WEB SITE

A companion web site has been developed to support readers. The URL of this web site is **www.prenhall.com/trawick**

There are materials on the companion web site for both students and instructors. Students can post messages to other readers on the message board. In addition, they can complete self-checking quizzes for each chapter to test their mastery of concepts and issues. Links to other Web sites are provided to help students find additional information about topics or to assist them in completing research projects.

Instructors can find **cooperative learning activities** to use in their classes. Two or more of these activities are provided for each chapter in the book. These are creative, field-tested, and may be directly printed and copied for classroom use.

ACKNOWLEDGMENTS

A book of this kind is a challenge to write. Such an undertaking is not possible without support and encouragement from many individuals. I would like to thank my family, Nancy, Benjamin, and Joseph, for their patience during my work on this project. They helped me to know when it was time to step away from the computer, put down the manuscript, and take a moment to enjoy fully what is most important in life: their love.

I want to thank my colleagues at Eastern Connecticut State University, particularly Ann Gruenberg, Sudha Swaminathan, and June Wright, who kept me thinking and laughing during the project. I also wish to thank Dick Thompson for his friendship; he encouraged me along the way and even allowed me to postpone a run-a-thon so that I could complete this book! A special thanks goes to Gladys Veidemanis, my high school English teacher, whose influence has endured longer than she can know. She is the person who taught me how to write.

There are three persons who helped me most to begin thinking about child development in a multicultural perspective. Penelope Lisi provided experiences through Project Impact which culminated in this text. I am indebted to her encouragement and many rich insights over the years. Patty Ramsey's work influenced many ideas in these chapters. She was the first to engage my thinking about children and culture, beginning with a conversation during a long ride to the Indianapolis airport. Elizabeth Aschenbrenner has demonstrated an impressive commitment to infusing an anti-bias curriculum in schools in Connecticut. Her stories of local efforts to increase cultural sensitivity have served to inspire and energize my writing.

I would like to acknowledge those individuals who provided the stories, quotes, and cultural descriptions which enrich this book. In particular, I would like to thank Deb Adams, Ingrid Eschholz, Tuala Fitzgerald, Ivy Goduka, Jill Huels, Diana Kimiatek, Hari Koirala, Lirio Martinez, Elsy Negron, Randy Rush, Wilson Soto, and Alwyn White.

Other persons provided technical expertise in the writing of some sections. I want to thank David Trawick for his comments and suggestions on chapters addressing genetics and medical issues. Jeff Danforth provided helpful insights regarding children with ADHD, not to mention a very fine blues tape. June Wright provided materials and ideas on multiple intelligences and brain research, and Ann Gruenberg shared perspectives on atypical development.

I wish to thank Hope Madden, Linda Montgomery, Julie Peters, and Kevin Davis at Merrill/Prentice Hall for keen professional insights, kindness, and tireless patience. They understand well the emotional needs of an author who is writing a complex textbook. The entire editing, production, and marketing staff of Prentice Hall was remarkably helpful and supportive.

The suggestions and comments of the following reviewers of the first edition manuscript were invaluable: Mae P. Arntzen, Mott Community College; Toni Campbell,

San Jose State University; Linda A. Carson, Des Moines Area Community College; Susan Bertram Eisner, Hood College; Kathleen E. Fite, Southwest Texas State University; Rey A. Gomez, Arizona State University; James E. Johnson, Northeastern State University; Jeanne B. Morris, Illinois State University; Sherrill Richarz, Washington State University; Barbara J. Rodrigues, University of Central Florida, and Nancy E. Sayre, Clarion University. I'd like to acknowledge the reviewers of the current edition's manuscript as well: Craig H. Hart, Brigham Young University; Sim Lesser, Miami Dade Community College, Kendall; Cathy Nathan, Texas Tech University; Bobbie H. Rowland, University of North Carolina, Charlotte; and Michelle L. Rupiper, University of Nebraska, Lincoln.

Finally, I would like to thank the children and families whose behaviors and learning serve as the basis for many stories in the book: Benjamin, Joseph, Matthew, Meggie, Brenna, and Haley, and the children and families of the Windham Willimantic Child and Family Development Center in Willimantic, Connecticut; the Temple Early Childhood Education Center and the former John Marshall Elementary School in Louisville, Kentucky; the Christian Center Child Care Center in Bloomington, Indiana; the University of Minnesota Child Care Center in Minneapolis, Minnesota; the Oak Grove Montessori School in Mansfield, Connecticut; and the preschool and kindergarten of the Universidad De Puerto Rico, Colegio Universitario Tecnologico De Bayamon, Bayamon, Puerto Rico.

Jeffrey Trawick-Smith

Discover the Companion Website Accompanying This Book

THE PRENTICE HALL COMPANION WEBSITE: A VIRTUAL LEARNING ENVIRONMENT

Technology is a constantly growing and changing aspect of our field that is creating a need for content and resources. To address this emerging need, Prentice Hall has developed an online learning environment for students and professors alike—Companion Websites—to support our textbooks.

In creating a Companion Website, our goal is to build on and enhance what the textbook already offers. For this reason, the content for each user-friendly website is organized by chapter and provides the professor and student with a variety of meaningful resources. Common features of a Companion Website include:

FOR THE PROFESSOR—

Every Companion Website integrates **Syllabus Manager™,** an online syllabus creation and management utility.

- **Syllabus Manager™** provides you, the instructor, with an easy, step-by-step process to create and revise syllabi, with direct links into Companion Website and other online content without having to learn HTML.

- Students may logon to your syllabus during any study session. All they need to know is the web address for the Companion Website and the password you've assigned to your syllabus.

- After you have created a syllabus using **Syllabus Manager™,** students may enter the syllabus for their course section from any point in the Companion Website.

- Class dates are highlighted in white and assignment due dates appear in blue. Clicking on a date, the student is shown the list of activities for the assignment. The activities for each assignment are linked directly to actual content, saving time for students.

- Adding assignments consists of clicking on the desired due date, then filling in the details of the assignment—name of the assignment, instructions, and whether or not it is a one-time or repeating assignment.

- In addition, links to other activities can be created easily. If the activity is on-line, a URL can be entered in the space provided, and it will be linked automatically in the final syllabus.

- Your completed syllabus is hosted on our servers, allowing convenient updates from any computer on the Internet. Changes you make to your syllabus are immediately available to your students at their next logon.

FOR THE STUDENT—

- **Chapter Objectives**—outline key concepts from the text
- **Interactive Self-quizzes**—complete with hints and automatic grading that provide immediate feedback for students

After students submit their answers for the interactive self-quizzes, the Companion Website **Results Reporter** computes a percentage grade, provides a graphic representation of how many questions were answered correctly and incorrectly, and gives a question by question analysis of the quiz. Students are given the option to send their quiz to up to four e-mail addresses (professor, teaching assistant, study partner, etc.).

- **Message Board**—serves as a virtual bulletin board to post—or respond to—questions or comments to/from a national audience
- **Net Searches**—offer links by key terms from each chapter to related Internet content
- **Web Destinations**—links to www sites that relate to chapter content

To take advantage of these and other resources, please visit the *Early Childhood Development: A Multicultural Perspective,* 2/e Companion Website at
www.prenhall.com/trawick

Brief Contents

Contents

CHAPTER 1

Studying Early Childhood Development in a Diverse World

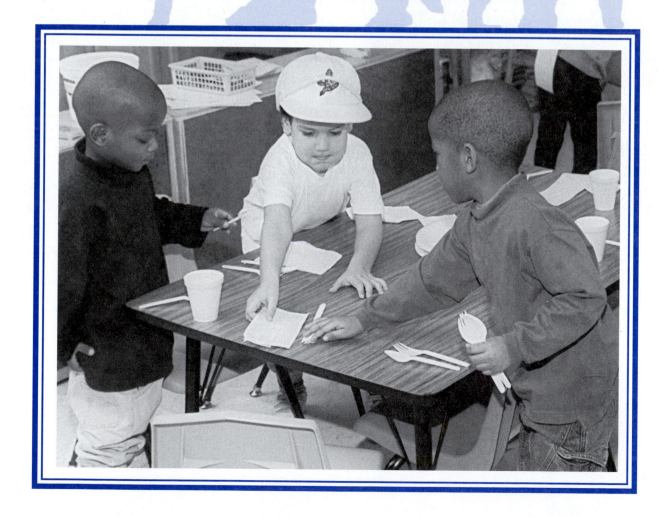

THE PURPOSE OF THIS BOOK IS TO ASSIST PRESENT AND FUTURE TEACHERS OF YOUNG CHILDREN IN USING KNOWLEDGE OF CHILD DEVELOPMENT WITHIN CHILD CARE, PRESCHOOL, KINDERGARTEN, AND PRIMARY-GRADE CLASS-ROOMS. It is a practical guide to what young children are like and how this knowledge can be used to enhance your professional practice. My focus in the book is on diversity and development, and a major thesis is that individual children learn and behave in different ways. Children of diverse cultural and socioeconomic backgrounds, and those with challenging conditions and special needs, will vary in their language, social style, self-perceptions, and physical competence because of unique life experiences. In the following pages I will describe and celebrate this diversity. A significant message I want to convey is that there is not just one way to grow up.

Understanding development and its cultural variations is essential for effective teaching, as the following story reveals:

> Three 4-year-olds—Sarah, Peter, and Alonzo—are working with clay at the art table in a child care center. Their teacher, Ms. Sekar, has placed individual balls of clay on small wooden boards so that each child can select one to work with. Knowing that children at this age have a difficult time sharing, she reasons that dividing the clay into individual portions will avert conflict. She quickly discovers, however, that her careful planning has just the opposite effect.
>
> Peter looks over with an expression of concern at Sarah's clay. "She's got more than me!" he complains to Ms. Sekar. "Oh, no, Peter, she doesn't," she assures him. "I put just the same amount of clay in all the balls. You have just as much as she does." Peter is not satisfied. "No! Hers is fatter!"
>
> Ms. Sekar notices that Sarah's clay ball is pushed flatter, giving it a wide appearance. "Oh! Hers is fatter, you're right. But yours is . . ."—she searches for the right word here—". . . taller." She sees immediately that this argument has gone over Peter's head.
>
> As Peter continues to protest, Alonzo discovers that he needs more clay for a sculpture he is working on. Smiling, he casually leans over and pinches off a large chunk from Peter's ball. Alonzo's actions are more than Peter can bear. "No!" he screams, beginning to cry and trying to grab back some of his clay from Alonzo. Alonzo gives a look of total surprise at Peter's outburst.
>
> After comforting Peter, Ms. Sekar engages all three children in an elaborate negotiation: "Peter seems to be upset because he doesn't have as much clay as

everyone else. What can we do about this?" "Give me back my clay," Peter offers, still angry. "We could put all the clay together," Alonzo suggests. Sarah agrees.

"We could try that," Ms. Sekar responds with enthusiasm. "We could make a huge ball. Then you could tear off the clay you need. What do you think?" "What if I can't have enough?" asks Peter tearfully. "There is so much clay," the teacher answers. "I think you'll have plenty to use. Should we try it?"

Peter finally agrees. They all combine their clay into one large chunk and place it in the center of the table. As the children work, they help themselves to more clay as they need it. This seems to make everyone happy. Ms. Sekar is pleased at how cooperative these young children are in sharing from this "community" lump of clay.

This child care provider has resolved a classroom conflict by applying principles of child development. Because she has read about young children's thinking and social behavior, she is aware that 4-year-olds can be egocentric—that is, so self-oriented that they are unable to fully understand others' perspectives. Because she anticipates difficulties over sharing, she attempts to avoid conflicts by dividing the clay into individual balls. She quickly realizes, however, that she has created more problems than she has prevented.

She knows, again from child development research, that children's thinking is based on the appearance of things: "What you see is what you get." From Peter's perspective, the ball that looks fatter must contain more clay. The caregiver immediately recognizes the futility of trying to convince him that the balls are of equal size.

In resolving the conflict between Alonzo and Peter, the teacher has relied on her knowledge of cultural diversity in child development. She knows that, in Alonzo's family, collective behavior rather than individual ownership is emphasized. Since

Teachers can apply knowledge of child development to curriculum planning and classroom interaction.

joint ownership is the norm in Alonzo's culture, his act of taking clay is simply an innocent effort to share materials.

In involving children in the resolution of this conflict, she has relied on new research showing that very young children can be quite cooperative and can resolve their own conflicts with adult assistance. Her final solution reflects her knowledge of the intellectual and social abilities and limitations of this age group.

This example shows that child development research and theory can be extremely useful in the classroom when applied in concert with careful observation and the wisdom of experience.

WHAT IS EARLY CHILDHOOD DEVELOPMENT?

Anyone who spends time with young children knows that they change in many different ways as they get older. What may not be as obvious is that these changes are qualitative as well as quantitative. Children do not simply acquire *more* knowledge, social ability, or physical proficiency with age; their thinking and behavior become qualitatively *different* over time.

One way to understand qualitative change in development is to reflect on your own life experience. Think back to what you were like 10 years ago. Are you the same person? How have you changed? It is likely that you are quantitatively different—you have more knowledge, a broader repertoire of social skills, or even—like me—a few gray hairs. But you are also likely to be qualitatively different. Your interests have probably changed. You likely solve problems differently or learn things using new methods. You may have a clearer picture of your career goals. Children also become very different human beings with each developmental period, as the following vignette illustrates:

Three-year-old Daisuke shows great anxiety every time the heater blower turns on in his child care center. A caregiver intervenes to help assuage his fears.

DAISUKE: I don't like that thing!

CAREGIVER: Yes. That heater is old and loud. It's just a heater, though. Let me show you. (Leads the child over to the heating unit) See? It's just a machine.

DAISUKE: Just an old machine.

CAREGIVER: That's right. Can you see down inside here? See the parts of the machine in there? That's what makes the noise.

DAISUKE: Yeah. The machine goes r-r-r-r. (Makes a blower noise)

CAREGIVER: Right. So when it comes on, you won't be afraid, right?

DAISUKE: Yeah.

Minutes later, the blower turns on again. Daisuke clings to the caregiver in terror.
Approximately a year later, the caregiver has another conversation about the blower with this same child.

DAISUKE: Remember that heater? (Points to the heating unit)

CAREGIVER: Sure. You didn't like the noise it made.

DAISUKE: I was afraid of it when I was little. I thought it was a . . . monster. (Laughs)

CAREGIVER: I remember that.

DAISUKE: It's just the machine inside that makes that awful racket!

Why is this child, at age 4, no longer afraid of the heater? It isn't just because he has more knowledge of how it works. Indeed, he had learned a good deal of information about the heater from his caregiver when he was only 3. He could even verbalize that it was "just an old machine" that made a frightening noise. Yet his fear persisted. At age 4, he is able to think in a completely different way. His intellectual abilities have changed qualitatively as well as quantitatively. He is no longer fooled by perception (i.e., if the blower sounds like a monster, it must be a monster). He can now use a new kind of reasoning to overcome the misleading appearance of things (i.e., the blower may sound like a monster, but it is really a machine making noise).

In all areas of development, children gradually transform into uniquely different individuals. At each stage, they pose new and fascinating challenges for parents and teachers. What we expect of them, how we interact with them, and what we plan for them to do are all influenced by a knowledge of these qualitative changes in development.

In this book I define "development" as the process by which humans change both qualitatively and quantitatively as they grow older. It is not just the "adding up" of more knowledge or ability with time; it is the process of transforming, of becoming completely new.

WHY STUDY EARLY CHILDHOOD DEVELOPMENT?

This book is intended to be a practical guide for teachers, in particular, on addressing developmental problems and issues in the classroom. It can be used to guide professional practice in at least four ways, as summarized in Table 1-1.

A Guide to Interactions With Children

We know that young children think and act differently from adults. They use a different form of language, interact with other people in distinct ways, and apply unique meanings to social events. The things that make them worry, cry, or laugh are unique and sometimes unpredictable. Their interests and motivations are peculiar to their developmental level. Their need is great to scream and run and play, to throw things, to joke and giggle with peers. Without a deep understanding of what young children are like, adults will have difficulty communicating with and comforting them, challenging their thinking, and helping them solve problems with peers. The following story shows how a thorough and sympathetic understanding of childhood can enhance professional practice:

Janny and Molly are playing together in the block area of a kindergarten classroom. Janny has just knocked down Molly's block structure, causing great upset. The teacher quickly moves over to the area as a loud conflict ensues.

MOLLY: (Crying) Janny, you kicked my building. I'm going to kick yours! (Angrily kicks at Janny's blocks)

TABLE 1-1
Four Ways This Book Can Guide Professional Practice

The book can guide . . .	Example
interactions with children.	A teacher reads in Chapter 12 that the preschool years are a period of magical thinking and irrational fears. So, when a 4-year-old shows anxiety about going onto the playground, she understands the source of the problem and designs a sympathetic, cognitive-based strategy to alleviate the child's fear.
curriculum planning.	A teacher is designing a science activity to teach about seeds in a primary-grade classroom. He reads in Chapter 14 that most children of this age enjoy playing games with rules, so he develops a science board game. He also reads that there are cultural differences in regard to competition, so he designs the game so that all children win and competition is minimized.
identification of children with special needs.	Based on information in Chapter 9, an infant caregiver accurately identifies a 7-month-old who has not become securely attached to her parents. Guided by research, she implements a warmth and responsiveness strategy to help the child bond to others.
appreciation of diversity.	A primary teacher plans to have children read independent research reports to the whole class. However, he reads in Chapter 16 that children of some culture groups express themselves using a storytelling style. So, he gives students an option of telling the group about their projects.

JANNY: No! (Begins to cry and pushes Molly)

TEACHER: (Moving between the two children) Oh! You are both so angry. What's up here?

MOLLY: She knocked down my building. (Screaming at Janny) I hate you!

JANNY: (Crying, speaking to the teacher) She pushed me!

MOLLY: You knocked over my building, Janny!

TEACHER: (To Molly) I know you must be so upset. You worked very hard on that building.

MOLLY: And Janny knocked it down.

TEACHER: Yes. But she wasn't trying to, were you Janny?

JANNY: No. And she just pushed me.

TEACHER: (To Janny) Well, she was very angry. (To Molly) I don't think Janny meant to knock down your building. Sometimes these accidents happen. What can we do here?

MOLLY: Well . . . Janny has to build it.

TEACHER: (To Janny) Can you help Molly rebuild her building?

JANNY: Okay. And maybe we could make a queen's castle.

MOLLY: (In an enthused tone) Alright.

In responding to this conflict, the teacher has applied an understanding of the unique ways children interpret and solve social problems. She knows that young children sometimes assign hostile intent when accidents occur. Molly truly believes that Janny intended to destroy her block structure. Instead of reprimanding Molly for pushing, then, the teacher acknowledges how angry and upset she must be. She also points out to Molly that the toppling of the blocks was accidental. She knows that helping a child to read social situations more accurately will promote positive social development.

This caregiver also applies knowledge of how very young children resolve conflicts. She keeps Janny involved in the discussion, aware that children are often able to settle their own disputes with adult assistance. She also knows that anger toward peers rarely lasts long at this age. Indeed, within a short period of time, the two children have worked out a reconciliation. Had the teacher quickly separated these angry children, a wonderful opportunity for learning conflict-resolution skills would have been missed.

A Guide to Planning Curriculum

The ideas presented in this book can also guide curriculum planning. A full understanding of the thinking and behavior of young children is critical in developing activities and materials that are appropriate for this age group. Overlooking developmental characteristics can lead to an inappropriate curriculum, or what Elkind (1987) calls "miseducation" and Sutton-Smith (1983) refers to as "cognitive child labor." Classrooms still exist that present young children with taxing, passive, and overly abstract academic activities. Such classrooms do not reflect a knowledge of child development.

The following vignette illustrates how a teacher's understanding of typical and atypical child development enhances curriculum:

A preschool teacher sets out trays of cornmeal for children to play with. They can draw in the cornmeal, wipe away their marks, and draw again. A child who is experiencing delayed development of large motor skills is attempting to join another child in this activity. As he tries to draw, he knocks the tray to the floor and the cornmeal spills out. His peer expresses concern.

RUBEY: Look! He spilled it all out!

TAYLOR: (Looks down, says nothing)

TEACHER: Oops! That tray slides off the table so easily.

RUBEY: He knocked it!

TEACHER: It was an accident. I have that problem sometimes. I've knocked things off a slippery table. What can we do to attach the tray so it doesn't slide?

TAYLOR: Glue it, I think.

TEACHER: Well, then the tray would stay stuck forever. How about if I clamp it? (She retrieves a metal clamp from the woodworking area, clamps the tray to the table, and adds more cornmeal.) There. Try that.

The two children draw in the cornmeal for many minutes without further spills.

Here the teacher has provided an appropriate learning material that reflects an understanding of young children's development. The activity is concrete and open-ended, and therefore meets the learning needs of children of this age. The activity also reflects an understanding that end products are not as important to young children as the process of creating. A positive feature of the cornmeal activity is that children can create and re-create many times without concern about finished products.

Based on observations and an understanding of the development of children with special needs, the teacher has quickly assessed that Taylor's motor limitations make this activity inaccessible to him. Her knowledge of motor development has sensitized her to developmental delays and has guided her adaptation of materials to meet his special needs.

A Guide to Observing Children and Identifying Special Needs

Observation is the cornerstone of effective teaching. Teachers and child care providers usually base intervention and curriculum planning decisions on the careful observation of children's developmental needs. This book assists professionals in observing children. It suggests key areas of development to study and describes the diverse behaviors and characteristics that can be expected at various developmental levels. In addition, it guides teachers in identifying children with special needs. Certain behaviors suggest developmental delay or at-risk status. An infant who displays very little motor activity, a preschooler who is limited in language, or an elementary school child who is rejected by peers may require special intervention. Focused observation not only can identify these potential problems, but can also suggest causes and remediation.

In the following example, a caregiver uses child development research to identify a child with special needs.

A 5-month-old has just been enrolled in a child care center. Her caregiver spends much time observing her during her first few days. He notices that the infant is less alert and responsive to adult contact than the other babies. He has read that this is an age when most infants show great interest in other people. He expects to see much smiling, cooing, and other social behaviors.

He knows that social interaction varies across cultures. For example, in some families babies are held or spoken to less often. However, babies of all cultures have some mechanism for making contact with other people, and this infant does not respond at all to his efforts to interact.

The caregiver discusses his concerns with the infant's parents. Together they seek assistance from a medical/social-service team in the community. An assessment reveals that the infant has a hearing impairment. With this information, the caregiver can now adapt interactions to meet the child's special needs. He focuses more on physical and visual stimulation, using physical touch more than language to make contact.

A Guide to Understanding and Appreciating Diversity

This book can also help teachers recognize and appreciate the wide variety of behaviors and characteristics that are typical among a given group of children. A fundamental message of the book is that no two children are alike. Behaviors and characteristics vary because of temperament, culture, gender, socioeconomic status, and a host of other factors. Children are not deficient or at risk because they develop in unique directions. They may display alternative ways of interacting with the world because of their life experience.

Knowledge of child development ultimately helps teachers to be sensitive to typical variations in child behavior, as the following story reveals:

A 5-year-old Japanese-American child, Misaka, has just been pushed off a tire swing. After discussing the event with the aggressor, the teacher attempts to comfort the victim.

TEACHER: Are you alright, Misaka?

MISAKA: (Smiles broadly, says nothing)

TEACHER: It looks like you're okay. Did you get hurt?

MISAKA: (Continues to smile, still does not speak)

TEACHER: Something doesn't seem quite right here. Why don't we sit together for a few minutes and relax. (Pulls the child onto her lap)

After several minutes of sitting together, Misaka begins to speak to the teacher.

MISAKA: (Tears forming in his eyes) He pushed me off.

TEACHER: Yes. I'll bet that hurt.

MISAKA: (In an angry tone) I don't like him!

Initially this teacher misread Misaka's smile as a sign that he was happy and unaffected by the aggression. She then remembers that smiling can mean different things in different cultures. In some Japanese-American families a smile is used to conceal embarrassment, sorrow, or anger. The teacher wisely stays with and nurtures the child until he is ready to express his anger.

Knowledge of child development can help teachers to understand and appreciate diversity.

WHY STUDY EARLY CHILDHOOD DEVELOPMENT FROM A MULTICULTURAL PERSPECTIVE?

During the twenty-first century, children of traditionally under-represented groups—often called "minorities"—will constitute a new majority within the United States. Currently, African Americans, Latinos, Asian Americans, and Native Americans constitute one-third of the U.S. population. Within twenty years, it is expected that they will account for over half (U.S. Bureau of the Census, 1994)! Since families of these ethnic backgrounds are generally younger than those of other cultural groups, their children will represent a growing percentage of the preschool and school-age population. As early childhood classrooms become more diverse, teachers must be prepared to meet the unique needs of young children of varying backgrounds. Even teachers of monocultural classrooms must assist their students in understanding and appreciating other cultures.

Children of different cultures vary in the ways that they communicate and interact with adults and peers, in how they play and learn (NAEYC, 1996), and in how they view teachers and school (Okagaki & Frensch, 1998). Parental socialization practices and beliefs vary markedly across cultures (Chao, 1994). Teachers must come to understand, appreciate, and show sensitivity to these differences as they interact with children in the classroom. They must devise ways to provide their students with knowledge of people of other cultures and positive and significant cross-cultural experiences.

Unfortunately, children of color are often under-represented or misrepresented in child development research (McLoyd, 1990b; M. B. Spencer, 1990). Many studies are conducted with only white middle-class children (Trawick-Smith, 1993). Some textbooks and articles on early childhood have been found to reflect an Anglo-American bias, in which the behaviors and development of white middle-class children are considered typical and those of other cultures are viewed as "abnormal, incompetent, and change worthy" (McLoyd, 1990b, p. 263). Children from non-European cultures or from low socioeconomic backgrounds have often been considered "culturally deprived" (Bereiter & Englemann, 1966) because they speak, learn, or interact with peers in ways that are different from those of white middle-class children. This belief has led some parents and teachers to confuse cultural differences with developmental deficits.

A major purpose of this book is to help teachers appreciate that many developmental variations are, in fact, differences that can be explained by life experience. These differences are quite often adaptive. Unique behavior, language, and learning patterns of children of a particular cultural group are acquired for a reason (McLoyd, 1990b; Trawick-Smith & Lisi, 1994). They assist the child in getting along in his or her family and community and are valued, expected, and encouraged by parents, other adults, and peers. Behaviors that vary from those of children in mainstream society may be very typical within the child's own cultural milieu.

In this book, I have taken great care to differentiate between developmental deficits—real special needs that can and should be addressed through intervention—and cultural differences—variations in development that are part of the rich cultural history of children. The following definitions of key phrases used in this book will help to clarify distinctions among different sources of diversity:

- *Unique/Diverse Needs.* These phrases refer to the social, emotional, and learning needs of all individuals regardless of gender, ethnicity, or intellectual ability.

Each individual within a classroom will have unique ways of learning or interacting with others, and in no group of students will all individuals be alike.

- *Special Needs.* This refers to the needs of children with social, emotional, intellectual, or physical delays or disabilities. The term "special" is borrowed from the field of Special Education. This terminology should not be confused with "cultural needs." You should not assume that children of some ethnic groups necessarily have special needs.

- *Cultural/Ethnic Diversity.* These phrases refer to variation in the needs or play and learning styles of children of various cultural groups. For example, children of different cultures have different styles of communicating. "Diversity" must not be confused with "deficit." Differences across cultures are just that—differences to be celebrated, not deficits to be remediated.

- *Socioeconomic Status.* This refers to variation in children's needs due to family economic and educational levels. Children of poverty, for example, will have unique needs; those of extremely wealthy families will as well. "Socioeconomic status" must not be confused with "cultural or ethnic diversity." Children of color, for example, are not necessarily of low socioeconomic status. These phrases also must not be associated with "special needs"; children of poverty do not automatically have developmental delays.

- *Children of Color, Children of Historically Under-Represented Groups.* These phrases will be used in this book to replace the traditional word "minority" to describe children of non-European, non-Caucasian ethnic background. Although cumbersome, these phrases are more accurate, since persons of color could soon represent a majority of the populations in some sections of the United States. Also, these terms are viewed as more positive. All too often, "minority" is construed as a negative term.

RESEARCH INTO PRACTICE

CRITICAL CONCEPT 1

Development is defined as the process by which humans change as they grow older. This change is not just quantitative in nature; humans do not just acquire *more* knowledge and ability, but change qualitatively as well. At each stage, humans think, behave, and perceive the world very differently.

Application #1

Teachers should assess qualitative changes in their students over time, not just quantitative increases in knowledge as measured by achievement or IQ tests. Observing how a child solves a math problem or thinks through a scientific experiment, for example, will yield more information about development than determining whether the child has given a right answer.

Application #2

Teachers should provide classroom experiences that enhance how children think, interact with peers, and feel about themselves. Activities that merely lead to acquisition of facts may not promote qualitative aspects of development.

CRITICAL CONCEPT 2

A wealth of research exists on what children are like and how they develop in the early years.

Application #1

Child development research can guide teachers and parents in interacting with children in ways that promote positive behavior and learning.

Application #2

Child development research can assist teachers in creating a developmentally appropriate curriculum.

Application #3

Child development research can help teachers and parents to observe typical and atypical development and identify children with special needs.

Application #4

Child development research can assist teachers in appreciating cultural and developmental diversity and distinguishing cultural differences from developmental deficits.

SUGGESTED ACTIVITIES

1. Observe two children of very different age levels (e.g., a 3-year-old and a 5-year-old or a 6-month-old and a toddler). Take notes on your observations, focusing on qualitative as well as quantitative differences, as described in this chapter. Later, write an analysis of how the two children are alike and different, guided by the following questions:

   a. How are the two children alike or different in the ways they interact with peers?

   b. How are their methods of communication/language alike or different?

   c. How are the two children physically alike or different?

   d. How are they alike or different in their thinking?

   e. What emotional states did you observe? To what degree do you attribute these differences to development?

2. Observe two children of the same age who are from different cultural groups. Take notes on your observations. Later, write an analysis of how the two children are alike and different, guided by the following questions:

   a. In what ways are the two children alike in their behavior and abilities? How are they different?

   How might culture or family life explain observed differences?

   b. How do observed differences between the children enrich and enliven the classroom? What unique contributions does each child make to the social life of other children?

3. Interview a director of a child care center or preschool. Ask questions about the diversity of children and families served by the program, relying on concepts presented in this chapter. Ask about methods for accommodating diversity in the classroom. Write a report on your interview, based on the following questions:

   a. To what degree do children served by the program have unique/diverse needs, as defined in this chapter?

   b. Are children with special needs served? Which disabilities or delays are represented?

   c. Is there cultural/ethnic diversity among children and families served? Which ethnic groups are represented? Are children of historically underrepresented groups enrolled in the program?

   d. Are families of diverse socioeconomic backgrounds served by the program?

   e. What strategies are used to accommodate the needs of all individuals served?

CHAPTER 2

Historical Perspectives and Research in Early Childhood Development

THIS CHAPTER WILL EXAMINE THE ROOTS OF CHILD STUDY. We will explore historical views of childhood, as well as research methods of both past and present. Not only are these topics of scientific and historical interest, they are of practical importance as well. Ideas about child rearing and development from long ago are still reflected in many current caregiving and teaching practices. Research findings can also directly influence adult-child interactions in the home and classroom. The following story shows how historical views and early research affect a novice teacher's classroom practice.

> A student teacher, Stephen, has planned a small-group activity for a preschool class. However, as he begins he encounters an unanticipated difficulty. One of the children will not stay seated in the circle he has created. She continues to jump up, talk in a loud voice, and stand in front of other children so they cannot see.
>
> "Susan, you need to sit down," he says. She sits quietly for a moment or two, but as he continues she jumps up again.
>
> "Look!" she cries out. "There are monkeys up in the tree! My other teacher read this!"
>
> "Susan, if you can't sit quietly, I'll have to move you away from the group," warns Stephen sternly. He has read about the time-out strategy in an introductory psychology text. When he was young, his own teachers used this technique to deal with misbehavior. When the child interrupts again, Stephen takes quick action: "I'm sorry, Susan. You'll need to sit on a chair at the back of the room. I warned you." With this, he tries to lead the child to the chair, but she resists vigorously.
>
> "No!" she screams. "I won't!" Other children begin to laugh, and the student teacher senses that he is losing control. Recognizing that he is in trouble, he looks to his supervising teacher, Ms. Laiti, who has just entered the classroom. This experienced teacher comes to the rescue. "Susan, why don't you sit on my lap while we hear the rest of the story?" This seems to satisfy the child. Stephen struggles to regain his composure and continues with his activity.

Stephen, an inexperienced student teacher, has made an error in judgment; his responses to this child are ineffective. Threats and time-outs are not useful in dealing with this dilemma. These strategies have fallen out of favor among most in the profession, as new research has emerged on children's emotional development. Ms. Laiti, who is more experienced, handles the problem more smoothly. She bases her actions on what she knows about this child and about the characteristics of 4-year-olds, generally.

Why did Stephen act as he did? Novice teachers often rely on the thinking and practices of their own teachers or parents. Some of the strategies he tries—giving a warning and then issuing a time-out, for example—may have been acceptable practices two decades ago when he was growing up. There could be something of the old view, "Children should be seen and not heard," reflected in his response to this child. His insistence that students sit quietly, listen, and display absolute deference during his story reading may also reveal an attitude—prevalent in years past—that children are simply little grown-ups who can learn and behave as adults if properly trained. In studying the history of childhood, Stephen might be surprised to discover the roots of those beliefs and dispositions which led him to react as he did.

There is usually a lag between the emergence of new ideas about child development and their implementation in professional practice. It takes a long time for new research findings and innovative theories to find their way into the classroom. This is because research is often reported in scholarly journals or in papers that are presented only to other researchers. It is critical for teachers of young children to stay up-to-date, but to do so takes time and an ability to decipher "research-ese."

This chapter has several purposes. The first is to present a brief history of thinking and research in child development. I hope you will see how perspectives in child-

Some current classroom practices are rooted in outmoded historical beliefs about how children should learn and behave.

hood have changed over time, and will come to see that some lingering classroom practices are really grounded in the thinking of the past. A knowledge of the historical roots of child study may assist you in reflecting on your own classroom practice and identifying those strategies that reflect dated notions of childhood.

A second purpose for this chapter is to familiarize you with research methodology, so that scientific journals will not appear so imposing. My intent is not to turn you into a researcher, but to assist you in reading and interpreting studies that have practical classroom implications. My focus will be on critical analysis of research, since all studies on human subjects are necessarily flawed. In particular, I will raise concerns about whether current and past research have adequately reflected the cultural diversity within our society.

A HISTORY OF CHILD STUDY

Western Perspectives on Childhood

Up until the Middle Ages, there was no concept of "childhood" in the minds of most adults in Western society. Up until 6 or 7 years of age, children were considered "infants"—nonpersons who were sometimes uncared for and unwanted (Aries, 1962). They died in great numbers during this time, many at birth. Infanticide was not uncommon through the seventeenth century; healthy and unhealthy infants were drowned or abandoned. Clearly, little value was placed on the early years of child development in Europe during this period.

Once children reached the age of 7, they were viewed as little adults. This perspective is reflected in the paintings of earlier centuries. Children are often shown with mature adult faces, sitting calmly and piously alongside adult family members (deMause, 1974). With this perception came the expectation that children would behave as adults. This attitude lingers to this day.

During the Renaissance in Western society, perspectives on childhood began to change. Children were gradually viewed as distinctly different human beings. Parents became preoccupied, however, with rooting out "inherent evil" (Pollack, 1983). Children were believed to have been born "bad," and it was the role of adults to train them in the teachings of the Church and to "beat the devil out of them" when they strayed. This view that children are innately immoral persisted through the eighteenth century. Harsh training and a focus on "breaking the will" of children can be seen even today among some misguided parents and teachers (deMause, 1974).

In Europe and the United States, the nineteenth and twentieth centuries were periods of relative enlightenment in regard to the treatment of children. A new emphasis was placed on socialization. "The raising of a child became less a process of conquering . . . than of training" (deMause, 1974, p. 52). When the Industrial Revolution brought about the need for a large labor force, concern about the welfare of children whose parents were at work began to be expressed. Public schools and eventually child care programs were established to socialize children in every aspect of development. Improvements in health care led to a drastic reduction in childhood mortality. The late twentieth century, generally, brought a growing concern for children's physical, emotional, social, and intellectual needs.

Western perspectives on childhood throughout history are presented in Figure 2-1. The figure shows that caring and concern for children have been relatively recent historical phenomena in Europe and America. These historical trends have led historian deMause (1974) to predict a period of "helping" in Western society in which adults will at last come to recognize children's needs and nurture and guide early development. Unfortunately, research on those in poverty and on traditionally under-represented ethnic groups in Europe and America suggests that not all children have enjoyed these advances in care and understanding (Children's Defense Fund, 1998; Huston, McLoyd, & Garcia Coll, 1994). Up until the mid-twentieth century, for example, children in poverty were sometimes economically exploited by employers and even by their own parents. Some were forced to work long hours under horrendous conditions in factories and farms (Kessen, 1965). To this day, children of color, in particular, live in poverty in disproportionately high numbers (Children's Defense Fund, 1998).

Zigler and Finn-Stevenson (1993) have suggested that the 1970s ushered in a shift away from concern about children and families. They cite increases in the reporting of child abuse and neglect cases, accompanied by decreases in family services to address these problems. They point to complex family stressors which may put children's development in new jeopardy: divorce, substance abuse, domestic violence, and parental depression. A new concern is children's exposure to violence; a growing number of children witness violent acts in their homes and neighborhoods (Garbarino & Kostelny, 1996). Children in poverty are significantly more likely to ex-

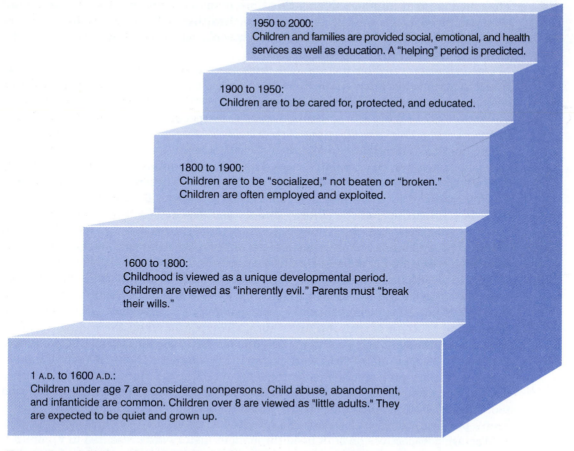

1950 to 2000:
Children and families are provided social, emotional, and health services as well as education. A "helping" period is predicted.

1900 to 1950:
Children are to be cared for, protected, and educated.

1800 to 1900:
Children are to be "socialized," not beaten or "broken." Children are often employed and exploited.

1600 to 1800:
Childhood is viewed as a unique developmental period. Children are viewed as "inherently evil." Parents must "break their wills."

1 A.D. to 1600 A.D.:
Children under age 7 are considered nonpersons. Child abuse, abandonment, and infanticide are common. Children over 8 are viewed as "little adults." They are expected to be quiet and grown up.

FIGURE 2-1 A history of perspectives on and treatment of children in the Western world is presented. The figure shows that care of and concern for children is a relatively recent historical occurrence in the United States and Europe.
SOURCE: deMause, 1974; Pollack, 1983.

perience the violent death of a family member or friend (Children's Defense Fund, 1998). It must be concluded that not all children in modern Western society are receiving the care and support that they deserve. The needs of families and young children are still not being fully met in contemporary America, and it is important for teachers of young children to serve as advocates.

Non-Western Perspectives on Childhood

Historical information on attitudes and care of non-Western children is scarce. Historical work that is most often cited in child development texts focuses on European and, later, American perspectives (Aries, 1962; deMause, 1974). What have been the viewpoints and approaches in Native American, African, Puerto Rican, and Asian societies toward children over the centuries?

African History. Historical views on children of some non-Western societies can be traced through descriptions of family life of centuries ago. Accounts of the strong kinship and tribal bonds of early African families, for example, suggest that adults showed a high degree of concern and caring toward children, as they did toward members of their families and communities (Hale-Benson, 1986; Nsamenang, 1992). Mother-child relationships were especially strong in early Africa. Nobles (1974) has suggested that this special bond preceded the slavery era, and that the strong role of the mother is "deeply rooted in our African heritage and philosophical orientation" (p. 15).

Native American History. Early descriptions of Native American families also portray close familial and tribal ties. Although great diversity exists among tribes, a theme woven through the ancient stories, family histories, art, and music of most Native American cultures is the interdependence among and respect for all living things. Children were a significant part of the natural order, and so were highly cherished and protected. Communities and families adopted a clear division of labor and a sense of social responsibility. Child rearing was a collective endeavor performed by mothers and fathers, older tribal members, and older and even same-age children. Children were socialized from the earliest days to become part of a group, yet were afforded much opportunity for individual expression through art and music. Individual differences were accepted as part of the natural scheme. The high value placed on both social relationships and individual expression is fundamental to Native American life to this day (Blanchard, 1983).

Ancient stories portray the very humane treatment of Native American children in centuries past. Training "occurred in close contact with many people who praised, advised, guided, urged, warned, and scolded, but, most importantly, respected children" (Blanchard, 1983, p. 118). Although infant mortality may have been viewed as necessary for population control in early centuries, the birth of a healthy child was the cause for tribal celebration.

Chinese and Japanese History. Early attitudes toward children in China and Japan were influenced by the writings of Confucius (551–479 B.C.). Confucianism's focus on interpersonal harmony led to the belief in both societies that children are inherently good—a perspective that did not emerge in Europe until many centuries later. A respect for children can be found in descriptions of early Chinese and Japanese life. The education of children was a concern even in ancient times (Ho, 1994). Between the sixteenth and nineteenth centuries, Japanese and Chinese children were encouraged to learn through observation and imitation; question-asking was valued. In the eighteenth century, Kibara (1710) wrote that children should be guided in self-directed learning. He recommended only moderate amounts of punishment or reinforcement.

In China as early as the thirteenth century, infancy was recognized as a unique period in development. According to Chinese philosopher Wang Zhong-yang, the first 60 days of life were a "sensitive period." The emergence of smiling and walking represented milestones in human growth. It was proposed that the strength of parent-child bonds could lead to a successful transition from infancy to childhood.

Slavery and Colonialism. The experience of childhood in some non-Western cultures from the eighteenth to twentieth centuries was strongly influenced by slavery and colonialism. Ogbu (1992) has argued that the experience of oppression added a new dimension to the lives of non-dominant cultural groups generally, and to children in particular. As families were enslaved or tribes and communities conquered, new parental values and child-rearing practices emerged by necessity.

Ethnic studies scholars have identified several ways that the lives of children and families have been affected by oppression (Garcia Coll, 1990; Greenfield, 1995). These are presented in Table 2-1. As shown in the table, families of subjugated cultures became more collective and collaborative in their thinking and action. Family and nonfamily members banded together, often pooling resources and sharing care-

TABLE 2-1
The Influences of Oppression on the Lives of Children and Families

Characteristics of Historically Oppressed Families	Example
Collectivism	Persons of historically oppressed groups have more often lived in extended families, which include parents, grandparents, and even aunts and uncles.
	Family members have often pooled resources and sacrificed individual goals for the good of the family. Collective child care has been common.
	Neighbors and "friends who are like family" have banded together in the face of adversity.
	Children have been taught "enmeshment"—a strong attachment to family and culture.
Firm and directive parenting	Parents of historically under-represented groups have often directly regulated children's behavior in an effort to protect them from the dangers of racism and physical violence.
	Children have been encouraged to be obedient and not "talk back" to those in authority—particularly slaveholders or powerful members of dominant culture.
Valuing or devaluing Western education	Some children of historically oppressed groups have been urged to "exceed white children" in their achievement in Western schools.
	Some children of historically oppressed groups have been taught to reject the learning and values of Western schools.

giving tasks. Puerto Rican families of the late nineteenth century, for example, are described as close-knit and mutually supportive. Strong kinship bonds were considered an important adaptation to the conditions of social and economic injustice of the time (Sanchez-Ayendez, 1988). These bonds have historically extended beyond family lines in Puerto Rican culture. Early practices such as *compadrazgo* (co-parenting by relatives and nonrelatives) and *hijos de crianza* (informal adoption of children by nonfamily members) reflect a commitment to shared child rearing among all community members. Close friendships among individuals living in proximity to one another were common. The phrase "como de la familia" ("like one of the family") is used to this day to refer to these special mutually supportive nonfamily relationships.

Similar kinship and "para-kinship" relationships have been described in early African-American culture as well (Hale, 1994). The experience of slavery led to powerful family bonds. It was through the family that "the slave received affection, companionship, love, and empathy . . . and some semblance of self-esteem" (Staples, 1988, p. 305). Nonfamily adults also played a role in child rearing, particularly when families were separated by the sale of parents or a slaveholder's death. To this day, "a strong desire exists among Black people to be related to each other" (Hale-Benson, 1986, p. 16).

As shown in Table 2-1, child-rearing techniques also changed as a result of oppression (Garcia Coll, 1990). Parents often adopted firm and directive socialization practices in order to protect their children from dangers inherent in slavery or colonization. African slave parents, for example, would play the vital role of restricting children's actions so as to avoid their harsh punishment by slaveholders. They encouraged self-sufficiency at an early age; children needed to get along on their own, especially in cases where parents were sold or the family was split up in other ways. Survival demanded that children become mature before their time. They were urged to work hard, complete required tasks, and never complain (Staples, 1988). Slave parents did not hesitate to use the "switch" when children became dangerously insolent (Hale, 1994).

Among the Plains Indians during Western expansion, parents taught young children—even infants—not to cry. This was an adaptive practice designed to keep children from giving away their location to the enemy. Keeping children under control was, again, a necessity for survival among Native American cultures (John, 1988).

Firm and directive parenting, which may be observed to this day among some families of traditionally oppressed peoples (Hale-Benson, 1986), has historical roots. It is important to point out that such child-rearing styles are not wrong or deficient; such directive interactions have allowed children to survive over the centuries. In neighborhoods where violence and drug use are common, it is still imperative for parents to closely scrutinize and direct children's activities. Doing so leads to positive child development among some groups (Baumrind, 1994).

Beliefs about children's education and success in the dominant culture were also affected by colonization and slavery, as shown in Table 2-1. In some cultures, oppression led to a striving for educational achievement within the dominant society. In others, withdrawal from and rejection of Western paths to success were common. Both attitudes may be viewed as adaptive; both represented the best thinking by parents in how to help their children develop in positive directions. Hale-Benson (1986) has noted a strong achievement orientation among African-American families. Since the time of emancipation, parents have encouraged their children to be ambitious and hard-working, and to "exceed white children's behavior and performance" (p. 48). This has not meant that parents wish children to abandon their African heritage. Many families focus on striving for success in the dominant culture while maintaining pride in one's African traditions.

In contrast, for centuries some Native American families have encouraged children to actively reject the values and practices of the dominant culture (Wise & Miller, 1983). Some parents have emphasized schooling less, and focused instead on teaching competencies that are more highly valued in Native American tradition. In such families, children may come to judge their self-worth not on success as defined in Western terms, but on achievements related to their own culture. Lefly (1976) found that children of Seminole and Miccosukee tribes in Florida had significantly higher self-esteem when they had not been acculturated into the dominant society. Generally, traditional modes of interaction have enhanced positive development in some groups.

In summary, children of the world have diverse histories that explain variations in development and parenting. Understanding and appreciating children's unique historical roots is important for teachers of young children in interpreting classroom behavior and family relationships today.

RESEARCH ON YOUNG CHILDREN

Much of the information in this book has been drawn from research on young children's development. Because research on human subjects is necessarily flawed, research findings merely provide good guesses about the relationships between children's behavior, learning, or other characteristics and their experience and genetic makeup. As a result, teachers of young children should be guided by research findings but not enslaved by them. They must be able to weigh the results of a particular work and to judge its relevance to classroom practice, based on the methods used or the sample selected.

For centuries, scientists and philosophers have been interested in children's development. The aim of early work in child study was to describe "normal" development and determine its causes. What was considered normal, however, was often what society *at the time* defined as acceptable thought or behavior. John Locke (1632–1704) and Jean-Jacques Rousseau (1712–1778), who were among the first Western writers to recognize the importance of environment in children's development, wrote about the origins of "goodness" and "sinfulness" in childhood. Goodness, from their perspective, was adherence to the teachings of the Church and the mores of industrialized society. Any deviation from mainstream thought or behavior of this historical period likely would have been viewed as aberrant.

Pioneers in the field of child study conducted descriptive observations of children in an effort to plot the course of normal development. Johann Heinrich Pestalozzi (1746–1827) and Charles Darwin (1809–1882) published biographies of their own children in an attempt to capture milestones of human growth. Obviously, the study samples of these scientists were limited. What these authors were, in fact, observing were the behaviors of children from privileged European families at that time. Diary studies often reflected the biases of a particular era. Diarists often emphasized or exaggerated information that supported current norms, systematically omitting information that might be deemed "shameful" by the community (Pollack, 1983).

G. Stanley Hall (1844–1924), an eminent psychologist at the turn of the twentieth century, was the first to test child development theories using larger and more representative samples of children. Hall invented a now-common research tool, the questionnaire, to gather data. Later researchers extended Hall's scientific methodology in

TABLE 2-2

Example of a Normative Chart for Motor Development in Infancy

Age	Motor Development Milestone
1 month	Raises chin up off the ground
2 months	Raises chest up off the ground
4 months	Sits with adult support
7 months	Sits alone
9 months	Stands holding onto adults or furniture
10 months	Creeps
14 months	Stands alone
15 months	Walks alone

SOURCE: Ames, 1937; Gesell & Ilg, 1949; Shirley, 1933.

the study of children, selecting even larger samples and utilizing more formal, controlled, and objective observation techniques (Gesell & Ilg, 1949; Shirley, 1933). The results of these studies were often reported in **normative charts,** which presented milestones in physical, mental, or social development for each age level of childhood. A sample normative chart for motor development is presented in Table 2-2.

A problem with these studies was that they usually included only white middle-class children. For example, Shirley's (1933) study of motor milestones in infancy—sometimes cited in child development textbooks today—was conducted with babies of white families in Minnesota. Would these same findings have been obtained if the study included children from other cultural groups within the United States, or in the world as a whole?

Recent research on young children has become exceedingly sophisticated. Much of the information shared in this book has been derived from these more modern studies. Several types of research designs are commonly employed to investigate specific aspects of young children's development, including correlational, experimental, qualitative, and ethnographic studies. We will discuss these in the following sections.

Correlational Studies

One approach is the **correlational study,** in which two or more behaviors or developmental characteristics are observed for a particular group of children and an effort is made to determine whether relationships exist among them. Is infants' babbling related to the amount of time parents spend talking with them? Is achievement in first-grade reading related to self-esteem? These are the kinds of questions asked and answered in correlational studies. In each case, groups of children are observed, tested, or otherwise assessed, first on one factor and then on another. The scientist then determines whether relationships exist between the two factors.

I conducted a correlational study in which I examined relationships between children's overall social competence and their ability to persuade their peers (Trawick-Smith, 1992). First, teachers rated a group of preschool children on social ability. Later, the subjects were observed playing with peers. A coding system was used to determine whether or not these children were effective in persuading playmates to do things. A relationship was found between overall social competence and persuasiveness. Children who were rated as competent could more effectively get peers to perform tedious tasks for them (e.g., "Will you pick up my blocks for me?"), to accept new play themes (e.g., "Do you want to play circus?"), or to give over desired objects (e.g., "Can I have one of your long blocks?").

Some correlational studies are **cross-sectional.** In these investigations, factors of interest are examined by observing a group of children of many different ages only once or a small number of times. An example is a study by Brownell and Carriger (1990) on the relationship between age and cooperative behavior in the early years. In this investigation, researchers selected children of ages 12, 18, 24, and 30 months and observed them playing with same-age peers in a special play area. The only toy available in this area was one that would not work unless children collaborated with one another. It was found that 12-month-olds virtually never cooperated and that 18-month-olds cooperated only sporadically. In contrast, 24- and 30-month-olds were found to be highly cooperative in their play. The authors concluded that a relationship exists between age and cooperation: the older children are, the better they are able to cooperate with peers.

Some correlational research is **longitudinal.** In this type of study, a group of children is followed over a period of time in order to observe changes in their behavior and development at various age levels. One such study focused on early peer relationships and later social adjustment (Hymel, Rubin, Rowden, & LeMare, 1990). A group of second graders was assessed on a number of measures related to making friends and being accepted by peers. These same children were evaluated again in the fifth grade. Those who were rejected by peers at age 7 were found to be more aggressive at age 10 than children who had positive early relationships. Those who were withdrawn when in the second grade were more likely to be so in the fifth grade. The authors concluded that a relationship exists between early social experience and later social adjustment.

A caution must be issued about correlational studies: just because two characteristics or behaviors are found to be related does not mean that one causes the other. If amount of parent language is related to infant babbling, can we assume that the former caused the latter? Or could infants' babbling have, instead, caused parents to speak to them more? It seems plausible that highly vocal babies would elicit increased response from adults. Teachers must be careful in interpreting and applying correlation research. Although scientists often conclude that one factor causes another, many alternative explanations are possible.

Experimental Studies

Another type of research design is the **experimental study.** In this method, the researcher intervenes in some way in children's lives and observes what happens. Will teaching parents to respond to babies when they cry lead to healthy emotional development? Will reading books to preschoolers promote their language and literacy? These are the sorts of questions an experimental study attempts to answer. In each case, the researcher causes something to occur in the lives of children and then measures the outcome. Often the goal of such investigations is to determine whether an intervention causes a positive change in children's learning or behavior.

Experimental studies can be quite short in duration. In an investigation of separation anxiety, for example, mothers were trained in special ways to say good-bye to their toddlers in a laboratory play area (Lollis, 1990). Some of the mothers were instructed to prepare their children before leaving them by talking with them extensively about toys available in the play environment and helping them to get involved in play activities. Mothers in the second group were told not to interact with their children within the play space unless approached. After this training, the mothers were asked to leave their children for a short period. The effects of the departure methods were immediately observed. Children whose mothers had interacted with them were less likely to exhibit upset during the brief separation period. Children whose mothers did not prepare them for departure were more likely to show anxiety. The researchers concluded that, through preparation, parents can reduce the anxiety of separation.

Experimental studies can also be longitudinal. In a study of impoverished children in Columbia, researchers provided a group of families with food supplements for children and parents, beginning at mid-pregnancy (Super, Herrera, & Mora, 1990). Another group was provided with both food supplements and twice-weekly visits from a parent educator to promote cognitive development. A third group, which did not have access to these services, was used as a control. All children were followed until age 6. Those who received food supplements fared better on physical and intellectual growth measures than those who did not receive the supplements. The group that received both food supplements and home visits was even better off in these areas. The researchers concluded that nutritional and educational intervention can, over time, reduce the physical and intellectual risks of impoverished environments.

The results of experimental studies often lead researchers to conclude that one factor has caused another to occur. If the children who were provided with nutritional and educational services are better off than those who did not receive these services, it is likely that the intervention caused positive outcomes. This interpretation of findings is illustrated in view (a) of Figure 2-2. Caution must still be used in interpreting the results of experiments, however. Other interpretations are possible, as depicted in views (b), (c), (d), and (e). Child and family characteristics, positive parent interactions, or even biased research may explain positive outcomes, rather than the services themselves.

Multicultural Critique of Traditional Research

Multicultural scholars (Banks, 1995; Ogbu, 1992) have raised concerns about traditional research methods, particularly in the study of children of diverse cultural backgrounds. They argue that modern researchers have systematically excluded subjects of traditionally under-represented groups (McLoyd & Randolph, 1985; Trawick-Smith, 1993). Further, when children of non-dominant cultural groups are included in studies, they are regularly compared to their white middle-class peers on measures or behaviors that reflect the dominant culture's values. Children who speak Spanish as their primary language, for example, have been compared to their Anglo peers on measures of standard English competence. In such comparisons, children of traditionally under-represented groups are often portrayed as less competent.

Professionals must use care not to assume that conclusions and recommendations of researchers always apply to all individuals or ethnic groups. Some scholars have advocated qualitative and ethnographic studies which are more sensitive to and appreciative of cultural differences (Cizek, 1995; Ogbu, 1992).

Qualitative/Ethnographic Studies

Traditional correlational or experimental studies make extensive use of **quantitative methods** in which children are observed and their behaviors are tallied or rated numerically. The numbers that are obtained are then entered into sophisticated computer programs, and in-depth statistical analyses are performed. An alternative

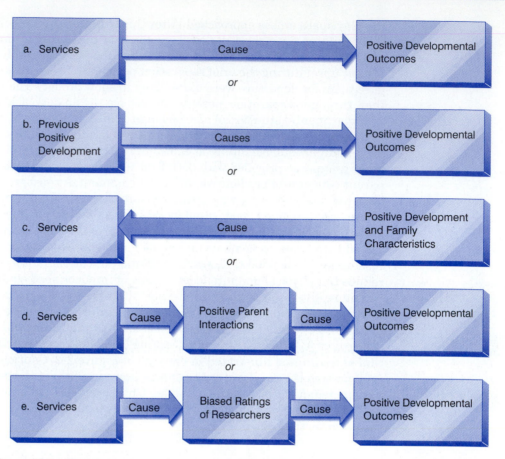

FIGURE 2-2   There are many ways to interpret the findings of an experimental study. Several alternative explanations are possible for the outcomes of a nutritional services study, for example: (a) The services themselves caused positive development. (b) The children selected for the study were more advanced in their development *before the study even began.* (c) Families who volunteered their children for the study were more concerned and caring. These positive family characteristics enhanced development. (d) The nutritional services caused parents to change in some way—to become more positive or nurturing with their children, for example. These changes resulted in positive outcomes. (e) Researchers who were studying the effects of nutritional services subconsciously rated children higher in development if they received these services.

methodology is gaining support among researchers in the field: **qualitative research.** This method involves open-ended observations of children, usually in natural settings. The purpose is to provide a "thick description" (Denzin & Lincoln, 1994) of children's development that captures all aspects of their lives: classroom environment, friendships, parents and family life, and community.

The results of qualitative studies are usually presented as rich and detailed narratives that illustrate children's development. A qualitative study of how preschool children learn to read, for example, could include in-depth descriptions of how individual subjects used books over a long period of time. The researcher reviews and interprets these descriptions. Qualitative researchers do not often draw sweeping, universal conclusions about all children in the country (or the world) from their findings. Instead, their purpose is to describe individual behavior or development

In an ethnographic study, the researcher attempts to write a "thick" description of all that children say and do.

within a particular environmental context. This methodology, then, moves away from an effort to identify what is "normal" for all children.

In one descriptive study of play behavior, 12 preschool children were observed interacting during make-believe in a natural classroom setting (Trawick-Smith, 1998a). The purpose was to ascertain what children do during "metaplay"—that is, when they temporarily stop their make-believe, step out of their pretend roles, and argue or negotiate about what will happen next. In the study, detailed descriptions of children's metaplay negotiations were given. The following is one excerpt:

ROSITA: (Holding up a wooden dowel) This will be my magic witch wand.

AIDA: That stick?

ROSITA: It's a witch wand to . . . um . . . cast the spell, alright?

ROSITA: What's it do?

AIDA: Let's say if the princess goes like this (makes noises, waves the dowel) then it makes things into gold, alright Rosita?

Researchers examined the transcriptions for patterns or trends in behavior and identified several distinct metaplay negotiations.

Another type of qualitative research is **ethnography.** This method utilizes the traditional procedures of the anthropologist to study children's development within cultural context. Researchers who follow this methodology spend a great deal of time as participants in the culture of subjects being studied. (Ethnographic researchers might even live in the same community as subjects!) In so doing, they come to more fully understand and appreciate the culture within which children grow and develop.

Some newer studies have been done within the culture of the preschool or child care classroom. Here the researcher spends a long period of time with students, teachers, parents, and administrators, coming to know the environment as a "participant observer." The researcher takes field notes of experiences and observations and gathers other forms of information about subjects. For example, in an effort to chronicle the emergence of writing, a researcher spent a long period of time within a preschool classroom—interacting with teachers, parents, and children of diverse cultural backgrounds (S. Harris, 1986). She interacted informally with children in the classroom and, while doing so, took field notes and gathered samples of children's work. Later she reviewed the materials and narratives she had accumulated and wrote a qualitative description of how the classroom environment affected children's literacy.

Ethnographic investigations capture the rich complexity of culture and context. Good ethnographers fully understand and appreciate the diverse histories, life experiences, worldviews, competencies, and socialization practices of cultural groups, and they describe these within their reports. Ethnographic research probably provides the fullest picture of child development from a multicultural perspective.

Studying Children in Your Own Classroom

Teachers of young children can conduct child development research themselves. Whenever they observe children in the classroom in a thoughtful and organized way, they are engaged in **action research**—informal research used to answer pressing questions related to classroom life. Some action research methods resemble those used in correlational or experimental studies, while others are equivalent to methods used in qualitative and ethnographic research.

Quantitative Classroom Observation. Sometimes teachers want to gain a quick understanding of children's growth and development in particular areas. In these cases, quantitative observation methods may be useful. One of the most common is the developmental checklist. This is a listing of developmental milestones or behavioral characteristics of interest to a teacher. Children are observed and rated on each item on the checklist according to a predetermined coding system. Sample items from a checklist that assesses preschoolers' social development are presented in Table 2-3.

Teachers using this checklist would determine whether children can perform each of these social tasks independently, with adult assistance, or with direct adult guidance. Results would reveal those students who need support in social interactions and the areas in which they require such assistance. Data from a developmental checklist can also provide parents with an overview of development.

Other quantitative research methods can be adapted for use in the classroom. For example, a child care provider may want to determine how frequently a particular child engages in literacy activities during the day, or a kindergarten teacher may wish to record the number of contacts students make with peers. In these instances, a coding system (similar to those researchers use) can be developed to tally how often these behaviors are performed.

Several types of coding system procedures are used. In **event sampling,** teachers make a check or notation on a coding sheet every time a particular behavior is observed. For example, a teacher who is interested in how frequently children exhibit ag-

TABLE 2-3

Checklist Assessing Social Development of Preschoolers

Social Skill	Teacher Rating
Interacts with peers	I
Uses language with peers to express needs or ideas	I
Plays cooperatively with peers	AA
Shares toys and materials	AA
Enters peer groups effectively	DG
Elicits and maintains the attention of peers	AA
Resolves conflicts with peers	DG

Coding System:

I = Can perform the skill independently

AA = Can perform the skill with some adult assistance

DG = Needs direct guidance from adults in performing the skill

gressive behavior will carefully observe all aggressive interchanges and make a tally or checkmark whenever these occur. Over time, data may be collected on which children are most aggressive or how prevalent aggression is within the whole classroom.

In **time sampling,** teachers observe children at regular intervals and record interactions that occur within that time frame. For example, a teacher might observe a child's interactions every 10 minutes during a free-play period in the classroom. At the moment of the observation, the teacher might note whether the child is playing alone or with other children. Over the course of a morning, the teacher would continue gathering data on the child's social contact at 10-minute intervals and place a checkmark under "playing alone" or "playing with peers" on a coding sheet. Over time, the teacher would get a picture of how frequently children interact with others. More elaborate time-sampling systems can be developed. Table 2-4 presents a coding sheet that allows the teacher to code, at once, the level of social involvement and the type of play that a child is exhibiting. At some regular interval—say, every 5 minutes—a teacher using this system would make a checkmark corresponding to the type of play (e.g., construction play) and the level of social participation (e.g., cooperative play) the child exhibited.

Teachers can design their own observation systems to study behaviors of interest or concern. Great care must be taken, however, to clearly and objectively define behaviors to be studied. In a coding system for aggression, for example, should name-calling be considered an aggressive act? Should a checkmark be made when a child physically resists a peer's attempt to snatch a toy? These issues must be resolved before observation begins. In designing observation systems, teachers must also be cautious not to select behaviors that are valued only by the dominant culture. For example, a social interaction rating scheme would be considered culturally biased if it included the item "establishes eye contact with peers and adults." Although looking directly at a speaker is a part of typical communication within Euro-American society, eye contact is viewed as a sign of disrespect in other cultures (Irujo, 1988).

TABLE 2-4
Sample Coding
Sheet for
Observing Social
Participation and
Type of Play

Level of Social Participation	Functional Play	TYPE OF PLAY		
		Construction Play	Dramatic Play	Games
Solitary play	///	/////		
Parallel play		//	//	
Associative play		////	/	
Cooperative play		////		///

"/" indicates an observation of that play category during a 5-minute period.

SOURCE: Parten, 1932; Piaget, 1962; Rubin, Maioni, & Hornung, 1976.

Qualitative Classroom Observation. Qualitative methods of classroom observation may be most useful to teachers because they are relatively easy to administer and because they provide rich descriptive information about children which can be shared with parents and other professionals. Also, they avoid the cultural bias that can exist in coding systems. Consider the following comparison of qualitative versus quantitative observations of aggression:

OBSERVATION #1 (QUANTITATIVE):

A teacher uses a coding sheet to tally the frequency of aggressive acts by a particular child. A total of 5 tally marks are made on the sheet during a single morning of observation.

OBSERVATION #2 (QUALITATIVE):

A teacher writes the following descriptions of classroom events that took place during a morning observation:

> Nader builds with blocks, stacking them higher and higher until the structure teeters. Laticia enters the play area and comments to Nader, "I can do a taller one! That's not a very good one." Nader does not look up and continues to build. "That's a stupid one!" Laticia says in a loud voice.
> Laticia moves to Nader's building and kicks it, toppling the blocks. Nader screams in anger and pushes Laticia backwards, before I can move over to intervene. Laticia falls and is crying loudly as I enter the area.

In a previous quantitative observation it was found that Nader frequently engages in aggression. However, that finding does not give a full picture of the circumstances surrounding these aggressive acts. Nor does it provide information to assist in solving this classroom problem. In the qualitative description, events leading up to aggression can be studied. Nader has been provoked; many observations of this kind may suggest that he is actively rejected by peers and may be the target of negative social behaviors. In the description, Nader's reaction to the provocation is revealed. Actually, he displays quite remarkable restraint when the first taunts are made. It is only after a severe offense has taken place that he strikes out. From this information, intervention strategies can be designed to address Nader's peer rejection or to help him learn nonviolent ways to react to his classmates' negative behaviors. Such qualitative descriptions may also help the teacher in promoting Laticia's social development.

There are many types of qualitative observation methods. Two that are commonly adopted for use in classrooms are anecdotal records and case studies.

Anecdotal Records. The **anecdotal record** is the qualitative observation method most often used by teachers. In this method, notes are taken on classroom observations and then rewritten later in a more full and descriptive way. An example of the steps that are followed in writing anecdotal records is presented in Figure 2-3.

1. *Selecting a child or children to be observed.* Sometimes an individual student is the focus of the study. At other times, whole-classroom observations are conducted. Observations in a particular play area or center are also common.

2. *Selecting the focus of the observation.* Teachers often focus their observations on a particular behavior or area of development. In most instances, the observation is structured to gather information to solve a particular classroom problem. However, sometimes teachers will watch classroom interactions generally and record whatever seems noteworthy. This can lead to important unanticipated discoveries about classroom life.

3. *Taking notes during observations.* The teacher takes brief notes during the observation, jotting down key events and behaviors and the names of the children involved. An effort is made to record dialogue. Even writing short phrases can remind the observer later of conversations that took place. The observer carefully records the setting and time of day for all entries. Taking notes while teaching is a difficult task. Experienced teachers often carry a small notepad and make brief observations and notations when a break in classroom activity occurs.

FIGURE 2-3
Five steps are followed when writing anecdotal records.

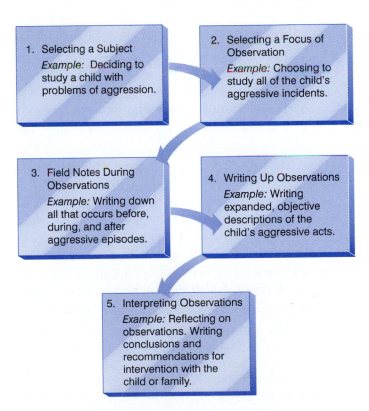

1. Selecting a Subject
   Example: Deciding to study a child with problems of aggression.

2. Selecting a Focus of Observation
   Example: Choosing to study all of the child's aggressive incidents.

3. Field Notes During Observations
   Example: Writing down all that occurs before, during, and after aggressive episodes.

4. Writing Up Observations
   Example: Writing expanded, objective descriptions of the child's aggressive acts.

5. Interpreting Observations
   Example: Reflecting on observations. Writing conclusions and recommendations for intervention with the child or family.

4. *Writing up observations.* When time allows, teachers write up their anecdotal records in a more descriptive form. It is important to reconstruct observations as soon as possible after they take place. Although these descriptions are rich and detailed, they are accurate and objective. They describe behavior rather than interpret it (e.g., instead of writing, "Sonia was angry this morning," a teacher would write, "Sonia had a frown on her face and spoke to everyone in a loud voice.")

5. *Interpreting anecdotal records.* After several records are written, teachers will begin to reread and interpret them. They may look for patterns of behavior across observations, or search for solutions to problems revealed in these narrative descriptions. They may use excerpts from these records to share at parent conferences or with teams of intervention professionals.

Case Studies. On occasion, a teacher will wish to do a more comprehensive study of a particular child. It may be that classroom observations do not provide all the information that is needed. A child intervention team—comprised of teachers, social workers, school psychologists, or other professionals who are working together to address the needs of an individual child—may require in-depth information on the child's family and community life as well as school-related behaviors. In such instances, a case study may be written.

A **case study** is an accumulation and interpretation of information from many different sources across time. A good case certainly includes anecdotal records; however, other sources of information are also used. Summaries of interviews with parents or descriptions of visits to a child's home may be incorporated. Data on the community or the child's neighborhood can be added. The following information is commonly included in a case study:

1. Anecdotal descriptions of classroom behavior.
2. Information on peer relations, classroom friendships, and interactions with teachers.
3. Descriptions of previous school experience (i.e., records from other child care providers, attendance records, developmental checklists from earlier years).
4. Physical descriptions/health and medical information.
5. Interests and activity patterns in school (i.e., data on what the child does frequently during free play and which materials he or she uses, results of interviews with the child about his or her interests).
6. Informal observations of the competence (i.e., language samples, collections of drawings, photographs of block structures).
7. Formal assessments of the competence (i.e., results of developmental screenings, clinical interviews).
8. Descriptions of the child's family life and culture (i.e., summaries of parent interviews, descriptions of home visits, socioeconomic information).
9. Descriptions of the child's neighborhood.
10. Descriptions of what the child does outside of school (titles of favorite books, diaries of television viewing, checklists of nonschool activities).

After this information has been assembled, a descriptive narrative is written to summarize and interpret the findings. Conclusions and recommendations are often included. The case study may be shared with other professionals or parents, adhering to rules of confidentiality. It may be included as part of the teacher's ongoing classroom record of the child's development.

RESEARCH INTO PRACTICE

CRITICAL CONCEPT 1

Perspectives on what children are like have changed throughout history. Historical accounts in Western society portray children as being treated poorly in early centuries, but cared for more compassionately in modern society.

Application #1

Teachers should become historians in their own field by studying how viewpoints on learning and development have evolved over time. In so doing, they can borrow from the rich traditions of great thinkers and early practitioners, and can discover and better understand the historical roots of many current classroom beliefs and practices.

Application #2

Teachers can reflect on the historical origins of their own perspectives and classroom methods and can identify any strategies that are based on outdated beliefs about children. Traditional practices such as time-out and the "sit still and listen" approach, for example, are based on old views of childhood and should be modified or abandoned in favor of newer strategies.

CRITICAL CONCEPT 2

In spite of improvement in the treatment of children in recent times, services and educational opportunities are still not available to all children. Some children are in great need, even in modern America.

Application #1

Teachers should assist families in accessing social, nutritional, and health care services in a time of scarce community resources. Without support in these areas, children cannot learn and develop in classrooms.

Application #2

Teachers should become advocates for policies and programs that provide children and their families with adequate services. Political action is an important role of modern early childhood educators.

CRITICAL CONCEPT 3

Non-Western cultures have a different history. Many of the socialization practices of children and families of these cultures are related to the experiences of slavery and oppression.

Application

Teachers should accept and appreciate cultural differences in parenting that stem from historical experiences of oppression. More directive and protective parenting and an emphasis on obedience are examples of logical adaptations in parenting that result from cultural adversity.

CRITICAL CONCEPT 4

Much of the research cited in this book involves quantitative methods. Although quantitative studies of children yield important information, flaws and biases are inherent.

Application #1

Teachers and parents need an understanding of research methods in order to critically evaluate new information on child development.

Application #2

Because of common flaws in research methods, teachers and parents must be cautious in interpreting findings. Study findings must not be viewed as truths, but as "good guesses" about what children are like.

CRITICAL CONCEPT 5

Qualitative research is gaining favor among child development researchers. It is viewed as less culturally biased and more useful for practicing classroom teachers.

Application #1

Teachers should use anecdotal records as a means of describing and assessing children's learning, behavior, and overall development.

Application #2

Teachers should write case studies of individual children and families, particularly those with special needs.

SUGGESTED ACTIVITIES

1. Interview two parents, one who currently has young children living in the home and one whose children are adults. Ask questions about child rearing: Which kinds of behavior do (did) you expect of your children within the home? How would you characterize your relationship with them? How important is it that young children respect and obey adults? Are (were) your children allowed to disagree with you? How loud and active are (were) your children allowed to be in the home? What should be done about misbe-havior in the preschool years? Take notes during your interview; later, write an analysis, guided by the following questions:

   a. In what ways were the answers of the two parents different? How were they alike?

   b. To what degree do answers reflect historical perspectives described in this chapter (e.g., children should be "little adults"; they must be taught to be "good"; they must be ruled with a "firm hand")?

c. What can you conclude from your interview about changes in parenting beliefs and practices over the last several decades?

2. Interview two parents of young children who are of distinctly different cultural groups. Ask questions about what children are like and how they should be educated. The following questions might be considered: What learning and behaviors should be expected of preschoolers? Of early elementary children? What should teachers and parents do to assure that these two age groups learn and behave in these ways? What should classrooms for these two age groups be like? What should teachers and parents do when children of these two ages misbehave? Take notes on your interview. Later, write an analysis guided by the following questions:

a. How were the two parents' answers different? How were they alike?

b. Which sources of information does the adult use to answer these questions? For example, does this adult rely on research? On systematic observation? On personal opinion?

c. To what degree do answers reflect family background, culture, or other life experiences? For example, does this adult rely on beliefs passed down from parents or other family members? Does this adult refer to conditions in the neighborhood or community that influence thinking about children?

d. What can you conclude about cultural differences in parenting beliefs and practices?

3. Perform a quantitative study: Observe a child between the ages of 2 and 8 for two 20-minute periods in a classroom. In the first observation, simply count the number of other children with whom your subject makes contact during this period. Each time the child speaks to or makes nonverbal contact with a peer, make a tally mark on a sheet of paper.

Perform a qualitative study: On the second observation, write notes on everything that the child does during the time period. Describe in precise detail the child's interactions with peers. Later, reconstruct this observation, writing an anecdotal record as described in this chapter.

Write an analysis of both observations, guided by the following questions:

a. What conclusions can be drawn from each observation?

b. In what ways were these two observation methods different?

CHAPTER 3

Theories of Child Development

RESEARCHERS AND EDUCATORS HOLD SEVERAL DISTINCT SETS OF BE-LIEFS, or theories, about how children grow and develop. One theory holds that children simply mature as they grow older. Another is that the environment shapes what children become. In some theories, genetics and environment are believed to interact to influence learning and behavior. In this chapter, we will review five theories of child development. The major tenets of each theory will be demonstrated by applying them to the following real-life classroom dilemma:

Four-year-old Adam moves into the block area of his Head Start classroom, where two other children have built a make-believe car out of large blocks. One of the two children announces loudly as he enters, "Adam can't play!" Adam ignores this statement and sits down on the pretend car beside his two peers. He snatches a plastic firefighter's hat from the head of the child who has just called out. The child protests loudly, "No, Adam! Give it back!" Adam pushes him off the car with great force. His victim begins to cry and call for a teacher's assistance.

The teacher, Ms. Rodriguez, moves into the area quickly. She is very familiar with the problem she now faces; Adam has been hitting, kicking, and pushing other children since he began the Head Start program 3 months ago. Adam's aggression seems to have increased lately. Talks with Adam's mother have not helped. She is very concerned about his classroom behavior but is having great difficulty coping with the problem. As an unemployed single parent, she is struggling to make ends meet. She has suffered from depression and is receiving mental health services. She is 20 years old and has three other children.

Ms. Rodriguez now stands before Adam and the child he has just assaulted. She must make an on-the-spot decision about how to respond. What specific steps should she take? What should she say to Adam? To his victim? What long-term strategies should she adopt to help Adam learn less aggressive ways of interacting with peers?

How this teacher will respond will depend, in part, on what she believes about why Adam behaves as he does. If she believes that he is aggressive because he has learned these behaviors from watching violent models in the neighborhood or on television, she will select one kind of intervention. If she believes that he has severe underlying emotional challenges that must be addressed, she will attempt a different strategy. If she believes that he lacks knowledge about how to interact positively with others, she will consider a third approach. Perhaps she perceives that some combination of these conditions is at the root of Adam's difficulties, in which case she will decide on yet another intervention. In other words, the teacher's decision about how to deal with Adam's aggression will depend on her theory about his development.

A theory is a system of beliefs about something. A child development theory is an integrated collection of beliefs about why children behave, think, and feel as they do. A theory might include beliefs about the nature of learning and development, the role of heredity and environment, and how adults, other children, schools, and communities contribute to the development process. Adam's teacher will base her decisions about Adam on a complex system of beliefs pertaining to these issues.

TABLE 3-1

Theories of Child Development

Theory	Prominent Theorists	Assumptions About Child Development
Maturationist theory	Gesell	Human traits are determined primarily by genetics. Children simply mature with age; environment plays a minor role.
Behaviorist theory	Skinner, Watson, Bandura	Human traits are acquired through experiences within the environment. Adults can purposefully shape desired learning and behavior through positive reinforcement.
Psychoanalytic theory	Freud, Erikson	Emotional development stems from an ability to resolve key conflicts between desires and impulses and pressures from outside world. Adults can promote children's emotional health by providing appropriate opportunities for the gratification of drives.
Cognitive-developmental theory	Piaget	Intellectual development is internal and personal. Knowledge is constructed actively by learners, who struggle to make sense out of experience. Learners assimilate new ideas into what they already know, but also adjust previous thinking to accommodate new information.
Sociocultural theory	Vygotsky	Adults and peers can "scaffold" children's learning by asking questions or challenging thinking. Through social interaction and verbalization, children construct knowledge of the world.
Ecological systems theory	Bronfenbrenner	Development is influenced by the personal, social, and political systems within which children live. Interactions between the family, school, community, social and political system, and the individual child will determine developmental outcomes.

Several prominent, contrasting theories about child development can be identified. These are presented in Table 3-1. Each is based on research and a set of assumptions about the nature of human experience. No single, universally accepted theory exists. Researchers and practicing teachers may hold one perspective or another, or they may hold an eclectic view that attempts to blend the beliefs of several distinct viewpoints. Some theories are interrelated and complementary; others offer conflicting perspectives on childhood.

Theories about children are extremely practical. It is a myth that a theory is abstract and esoteric and holds little value in the real world. A theory can guide professional practice by ensuring that there is an underlying purpose for classroom routines and that the process of educating young children is carried out consistently. A theory can help a teacher solve a problem like Adam's. Very specific and useful strategies can be derived from each major theoretical perspective.

MATURATIONIST THEORY

One of the oldest theories of development holds that children learn and behave as they do because they have inborn predispositions to do so. From this perspective, most of what we become as humans is genetically predetermined. Some children are talented in the arts, for example, because of inherited, genetically derived traits. Some are aggressive due to inborn temperament. From this view, all children, regardless of background or culture, acquire the same basic abilities and knowledge—how to walk, talk, and read, for example—at around the same age and in a relatively fixed order because the emergence of each of these skills is predetermined at birth.

This theoretical perspective—often called **maturationist theory**—assigns relatively little importance to the child's environment (Gesell, 1933). For example, to the maturationist, parenting and teaching are far less important than genetics. Social class and culture are not particularly emphasized. In its purest form, this theory suggests that children simply mature as they get older; they will turn out as they will, with little influence from the outside world.

A predominant metaphor used by maturationists is that of a growing plant. Children's development is seen to be like the blossoming of a flower or the growth of a seed. Given the basic nutrients of life—loving care, safety, and a healthy diet—children will grow and flourish in a predetermined way, just as a plant does. Major environmental obstacles may slow down the path of this growth, just as a plant is impeded by a lack of water or sun. Once essential needs are restored, the child will continue to flourish, just as a plant recovers from a drought.

Early research by maturationists (Gesell, 1933; G. S. Hall, 1893) sought to identify how social, physical, intellectual, and personality characteristics unfold as children mature. The focus was on providing a profile of "normal" maturation. Gesell conducted controlled observations of thousands of children in order to identify developmental "milestones"—that is, specific characteristics that could be expected to emerge in children at various age levels (Gesell & Ilg, 1949). His work was made available to parents, who used his developmental time schedules to assess their own children's growth. His research, thus, served to relieve anxiety in some parents and intensify it in others. According to Gesell and his colleagues, major developmental and behavioral problems stem from an environment that restricts maturation (Ilg & Ames, 1965). Children who are placed in rigidly academic classrooms or are expected to perform difficult tasks before they are ready are likely to exhibit problematic behaviors.

Modern maturationists have focused more directly on how genetics contributes to development (Plomin, 1995; Scarr, 1993). Although the research methods of these scientists vary considerably, their assumptions about child development are generally the same: genetics and maturation have a more powerful effect on behavior and learning than the environment. These authors provide evidence that at least some developmental characteristics, particularly physical ones, do seem to emerge in a fixed order and at around the same age. A classic study by Dennis and Dennis (1940) of walking in Hopi Indian children is a good example. These researchers found that infants who were strapped to cradleboards—rigid boards that held children upright and greatly restricted their movement—learned to walk at the same time as infants whose parents had given up this old custom. Gesell himself conducted an experiment in which one infant twin was taught to climb up and down stairs and the other twin was not. The trained infant showed advanced stair-climbing ability only for a short time; the untrained twin quickly caught up, once given experience with stairs (Gesell & Thompson, 1929).

Other studies of twins also lend credence to a maturationist view. Identical twins raised apart have been found to show surprisingly similar characteristics in many different areas of development, including activity level, sociability, attention span, impulsivity, introversion/extroversion, and propensity to mental health problems such as schizophrenia or alcoholism (Gottesman & Goldsmith, 1994; Plomin, 1995). Other studies have shown that personality traits such as boldness or timidity can be identified in infancy and that these persist into adulthood (Kagan, 1994). One well-known longitudinal study identified several infant personality types—"easy," "difficult," and "slow-to-warm-up"—and showed that these personality characteristics could still be observed in subjects through adulthood (A. Thomas & Chess, 1977). Of special interest to parents and teachers are studies showing that "difficult" personality characteristics (e.g., harsh and negative reactions to new or frustrating situations, irregular patterns of sleeping or eating, and numerous adjustment problems) present at birth continue to be observed in later childhood (Huffman et al., 1994). From a maturationist perspective, these traits are genetically determined and will unfold regardless of environmental intervention.

Working With Adam

How would maturationists explain Adam's aggressive behaviors? What strategies would they recommend to address the problem? This theoretical perspective suggests two overall causes of Adam's difficulty. First, Adam could be acting as he is simply because he is immature. From this perspective, positive social behaviors unfold over time with maturation, so less mature children are not able to interact effectively with peers. It is possible that Adam is not developmentally ready for participation in such a large Head Start group. One very controversial strategy that is often suggested by maturationists is to postpone Adam's enrollment in a preschool setting until he is more mature. In a year's time, he may gain social abilities that will allow him to function more positively. This strategy often has been called "buy a year."

Another maturationist explanation for Adam's behavior is that he may have been born with a "difficult" personality. If Adam's challenging interactions are displayed across all play settings or times of day, and if he seems truly unable to gain control of these negative behaviors, he may have inherited a "difficult" temperament. How can teachers and caregivers respond if Adam's problems are purely genetic? It is recommended that classroom and home environments be restructured to accommodate these personality traits. Since children like Adam may have difficulty with transitions and new situations, these should be carefully planned and minimized. Establishing a regular, predictable routine, maintaining constancy in the physical play space, and making other efforts to create a sameness in Adam's experiences will be helpful, from this viewpoint. Since children with difficult temperaments often react severely to being held or restrained, great effort should be made to avoid these behaviors in interactions.

Adults should also practice tolerance and acceptance, from a maturationist view. Teachers might "ignore the little things" in Adam's classroom behavior and tolerate minor oppositional behaviors without reaction. Challenging interactions are viewed simply as part of Adam's personality. The following vignette shows the maturationist theory in practice:

Adam has just entered the art area where a group of children are cutting with scissors. All the available scissors are being used. He tries to snatch a pair away from Samantha, a child who is working there. A teacher witnesses the incident from a distance.

ADAM: (Pulling on the scissors) Give me these!

SAMANTHA: (Clinging to the scissors) Adam! No! (Looks to the teacher for help)

TEACHER: (In a calm voice) Adam, Samantha is using those scissors.

ADAM: (Still pulling on the scissors, says to Samantha in a threatening voice) You better give me those!

TEACHER: (Retrieves another pair of scissors from a cupboard) Here's another pair. Why don't you use these? I'll sit with you and you can tell me about what you're working on. (Gently guides Adam to his own seat and sits next to him)

In this interchange, the teacher shows understanding and tolerance for Adam's severe outburst. Rather than using harsh or punitive methods, he has calmly resolved the dilemma by redirecting Adam's activity. With maturation, Adam may eventually be able to regulate his own social behaviors.

Critique and Multicultural Analysis

Many studies do not support a pure maturationist perspective—even Gesell (1933) found that environment plays an important role. Research on twins has shown that a significant portion of behavior and development can be explained by life experience. For example, follow-up studies on temperament show that personality can change over time as a result of environmental factors (Kagan et al., 1994). Research on IQ shows that there exists a **heritability ratio**—a mathematical estimate of the role of genetics in determining intelligence. By most researchers' estimates, over half of "innate" intelligence can be explained by environment (Plomin, 1995).

In addition to the challenges to maturationism presented by research, a growing number of professionals are raising concerns about the educational and political implications of such a theory (Charlesworth, 1989). Concern has been expressed that a maturationist perspective could lead some parents or teachers to give up on children like Adam, reasoning that if challenges are predetermined, it is fruitless to intervene. If problems are to be solved by pure maturation, then a "wait and see" approach would be taken for even the most severe problems of child development. Some have suggested that the "buy a year" strategy might better be phrased "lose a year," since opportunities to address the child's difficulties would be lost (Shepard & Smith, 1989). Detractors of maturationist theory contend that, although its messages of tolerance and acceptance of differences are valuable, care should be taken not to assign too great a role to genetics. Doing so could lead to a pattern of inaction in the classroom when children are in need of support.

The staunchest opponents of maturationism argue that it leads to cultural bias (Ogbu, 1994; Padilla et al., 1991). These authors point with alarm to the early work of Arthur Jensen, a prominent educational psychologist who created a furor in 1969 with an article entitled "How Much Can We Boost IQ and Scholastic Achievement?" In the article, Jensen argues that African-American children have lower IQs than white children because of genetically derived intellectual deficiencies. He proposes that educational programs for these lower-IQ students be focused on simplistic thinking processes and that they be guided toward professions that do not require abstract reasoning or problem-solving. The dangers of a maturationist theory are obvious from Jensen's work: the argument of genetic determinism can be used, as it has been for centuries, to advance a belief that some races are inferior.

Ogbu (1994) argues that racial differences in children's behavior and learning are just that—differences, not genetic deficits. These differences stem from the unique experiences, histories, and worldviews of particular cultures. Cultural variations— diverse languages and dialects, learning styles, or patterns of interaction, for example—are derived from social experience. Such variations should be understood and appreciated, not remediated.

True deficits in competence do exist among individuals of all cultures, and these also can be traced to life experiences—experiences such as oppression, poverty, poor health care, or inadequate schools. These factors can be successfully ameliorated through intervention. From Ogbu's perspective, environment, including culture, is the most critical element in child development.

BEHAVIORIST THEORY

The **behaviorist theory** offers a very different perspective on child development. Behaviorists contend that all that children are and will become is derived from experience. At birth, from this view, a child's mind is a "blank slate" or an "empty vessel" to be gradually filled by the environment. Development in all areas—from personality type, to ability to read, to career preference—is a result of environmental influence. Behaviorist theory assigns great importance to the role of adults, and holds that parents and teachers must purposefully shape children's learning. Although most behaviorists believe that children are born with certain rudimentary facilities—for example, a fundamental ability to learn and a nervous system that allows perceptual and motor growth—they argue that maturation and genetics are relatively unimportant in human development. One of the first behaviorists in America, John B. Watson, summarized this theoretical perspective in its purest form when he described the newborn baby as merely "a lively bit of squirming flesh, capable of making few simple responses" (1929).

A critical tenet of behaviorist theory—and one from which the theory's name originated—is that all learning is really observable behavior. From this perspective, even such complex tasks as reading, talking, or solving a mathematics problem are considered to be behaviors that can be observed and measured. Reading, for example, may be viewed as the behavior of saying aloud or to oneself the sounds and words represented on a printed page. From a behaviorist view, advancement in any area of learning is simply a change in behavior. Becoming a more competent reader, for example, is the process of being able to say new sounds, bigger words, or longer sentences as they appear on the page. The job of the teacher or parent is to present new skills in small and logically sequenced units and then to shape children's acquisition of these in special ways.

Classical and Operant Conditioning

Watson was the first to apply one form of behaviorism, **classical conditioning,** to children's learning. His now-famous experiment with an 11-month-old child, Albert, illustrates his method. At the beginning of the experiment, Albert had shown no fear of rats. During the conditioning period he was presented with a rat, but at the same moment a loud noise sounded. This created great upset. (This experiment was conducted before the American Psychological Association had written modern rules of research ethics!) Over time, Albert became afraid of rats, because he learned to associate their presence with the loud noise. Even when the noise was no longer made, he cried when rats (and later other furry objects) were presented to him. He had learned a conditioned response, albeit a useless and perhaps troublesome one: to cry in the presence of rats and similar stimuli. This proved, according to Watson, that through environmental conditioning a child could be shaped, behavior by behavior, to become almost any type of person (J. B. Watson, 1929).

A more modern application of behaviorism has been provided by B. F. Skinner (1948), who developed a system of **operant conditioning** based on the work of Watson and others. Skinner attempted to show that if children's desirable behaviors are rewarded systematically by adults, children are more likely to perform those behaviors. Children who are rewarded for using the toilet independently, for example, will do so more often. If parents wish children to sit quietly at the dinner table, they should reward them for this behavior after it occurs. Skinner maintained that operant conditioning works with academic learning tasks as well. If teachers want children to read new words in a lesson, they can reward them for successfully doing so.

A principle of operant conditioning is that children's behavior can be shaped only gradually. When a toddler is just starting to use the toilet, for example, rewards should be given for small steps—say, just trying to get to the bathroom on time. Breaking down learning into manageable units and rewarding small steps forward are key features of operant conditioning.

Skinner (1948) wrote at length about the kinds of responses adults should provide to children's behavior. Reinforcers such as verbal praise and tangible rewards (i.e., snacks, toys, stickers) should be given only after positive behaviors have been performed. Punishment should not be used; undesirable behavior should simply be ignored. A good deal of patience is required, then, in carrying out Skinnerian parenting or teaching!

Social Cognitive Learning Theory

If reinforcement should not be provided until after desirable behaviors are performed, how do teachers or parents induce children to act in positive ways to begin with? A teacher could wait a long time for a child to share a toy or speak a new word by mere accident. Albert Bandura (1989) has provided an additional tool to the behaviorist: imitation. He argues that children acquire new behaviors merely by observing others perform them. For example, children will learn to share by watching others do so, and will learn how books work by observing parents or teachers reading them. Bandura's work lends support to the adage, "Children are more likely to do what we do than what we tell them to do"!

Children are most apt to learn behaviors they observe if they see these being reinforced. In his classic **social cognitive learning** study, Bandura (1965) found that children were more likely to behave aggressively if they watched a model punch a doll and then receive rewards for this. Much positive social behavior, Bandura contends, is learned by witnessing others perform positive acts and then seeing them praised or rewarded. A practical application of Bandura's work is that a teacher can help one child to interact positively by openly praising another who is behaving appropriately.

Working With Adam

From the perspective of Skinner or Bandura, Adam's problems are behavioral, as are all aspects of child development. So, strategies need to be implemented to change Adam's social interactions in the classroom, to induce him to perform kind or cooperative behaviors. A systematic reward system should be established in which Adam's positive social behaviors—no matter how fleeting—are reinforced with stickers, special privileges, or snacks. Later, the teacher might move to social reinforcers, such as praise. Such strategies have often been called "catching children being good," since prosocial behaviors in a child like Adam may be very infrequent. While implementing these strategies, misbehavior should be ignored. This will ensure that Adam is not inadvertently rewarded for his aggression by adult attention. If Adam's behavior becomes too disruptive or dangerous, a time-out might be given, in which Adam would be asked to sit away from the group. Skinner argues that time-out is

Behaviorists believe that adults should praise desirable behavior while ignoring disruptive or antisocial behavior.

not a punishment. (Many practicing teachers, however, who have witnessed children's negative emotional responses to this practice disagree.)

Behaviorists would also suggest that positive models of prosocial behavior be provided. Teachers or parents might go out of their way to model kindness and cooperation themselves, and to avoid harsh responses such as shouting or physical punishment. Also, adults could purposefully praise the positive interactions of Adam's peers in his presence. This would show that such behaviors are rewarded. The following vignette illustrates behaviorist theory in practice:

Two children are playing cooperatively in the sandbox on the playground. Adam moves in, shouting and snatching sand toys away from them. His peers initially ignore him and keep playing. A teacher quickly intervenes.

TEACHER: (Speaking to the two children who are playing cooperatively) Samantha and Stuart, I like how nicely you are playing together. You are sharing your toys and being kind to each other.

SAMANTHA: (In a proud tone) Yeah. We're nice friends.

TEACHER: Yes. (Presenting several new digging toys) Would you like to play with these?

ADAM: (Shouting at his peers) You can't play with those. You get out of here!

TEACHER: (Ignores Adam's outburst and continues to talk to the two other children) Maybe I'll play with you. (Sits down and begins to work in the sand with the two children)

ADAM: (Throws a handful of sand out of the sandbox and screams) I'm going to get all this sand out of here! (Now throws a bucket out of the sandbox)

TEACHER: (Ignores Adam, speaks to the two others) What are you working on here, a castle?

STUART: Yeah. It's a castle for . . . pirates, I think.

ADAM: (Watches a moment, then speaks in a quieter tone) I'll help pile the sand. (Scoops sand into a bucket and offers it to his peers) Here. You put this on.

TEACHER: Adam, great! You're helping us out. (Hands a digging toy to him) Would you like to use this to help us with our castle?

In this situation, a teacher has ignored Adam's misbehavior and, in his presence, rewarded two children who are cooperating. She patiently ignores Adam's undesirable behaviors. Adam finally displays positive social interaction. The teacher then quickly praises and rewards these prosocial acts.

Critique and Multicultural Analysis

Behaviorism has come under harsh criticism in recent years (R. A. DeVries & Kohlberg, 1990). A major concern has been that modeling and reinforcement do not fully explain learning. The case of language development illustrates this clearly. The behaviorist view is that language learning is shaped through reinforcement—that is, when very young children imitate adult utterances, these are praised or rewarded

(Skinner, 1957). Research suggests that this is simply not how language is acquired (K. Nelson, 1988). Children invent their own unique utterances when they learn to talk. For example, children might first use the correct form of "took" and then, out of the clear blue, use their own version: "taked" or even "takeded." Is it likely that this new, "incorrect" form was imitated from an adult model? Would adults systematically praise this "misstatement"? Another example is the child's invention of new words. Could the child who refers to a bald adult as having a "barefoot head" possibly have heard this from an adult model?

In fact, parenting studies show that adults do not praise the correctness of children's language (Owens, 1994). For example, if a child were to declare, "I pushed Sarah," it is unlikely that an adult would respond with, "I like the way you used the past tense correctly." Instead, adults usually reply to the content of children's utterances.

Children demonstrate countless novel behaviors and learning in other areas that cannot be explained by an imitation and reinforcement theory. Why do very young children believe that a cow is a "doggie"? Why will they argue that 10 cookies spread out in a long line are more than 10 cookies that are bunched together on a plate? Can these ideas possibly be observed or reinforced by adults? Many researchers argue that learning is more complex than a mere change in overt behavior (R. A. DeVries & Kohlberg, 1990). They contend that development is internal and personal; it more often involves the mental action of children than any external behavior by adults.

Multicultural critiques of behaviorism abound. Serious questions have been raised about the practice of excessively praising or rewarding children's behavior (Hitz & Driscoll, 1988), particularly children of ethnically diverse backgrounds (M. S. Steward & Steward, 1973). Some families or cultural groups virtually never use **positive reinforcement,** yet their children grow and learn (Garcia Coll, 1990). Stars, stickers, and verbal praise do not appear, then, to be a necessary ingredient for positive development. Children whose family experiences do not include constant praise may be overwhelmed, in fact, by teachers who rely on tangible rewards or lavish accolades. Research suggests that for some children, praise may actually inhibit learning, creativity, and even self-esteem (Hitz & Driscoll, 1988).

A number of other questions about behaviorism have been raised by multicultural scholars: Which behaviors should be reinforced? Who should decide? Upon whose values, histories, and worldviews should these decisions be based? Can and should all children's behavior be shaped to conform to standards of mainstream America? Boykin and Toms (1985) have argued that tenets of behaviorism have been used "to promote Anglo-Saxon ideals" (p. 35). Problems arise, they suggest, when adults reward behaviors that are not valued by a child's cultural group. Worse yet, some behaviors that are reinforced in school may be in conflict with the values of one's own family. For example, in one commonly used language development kit, children are rewarded for establishing eye contact and talking in a group. These are not behaviors that are valued or appreciated in all cultures. In some families, eye contact is a sign of disrespect and quietness is highly valued (Irujo, 1988). Behaviorism, then, can lead to "mixed socialization messages" (Boykin & Toms, 1985, p. 36) which create conflict and confusion for children of historically under-represented groups.

Early educational programs designed around behaviorist principles generally do not have a good track record in meeting socialization or learning goals, particularly for children of low socioeconomic status or those of traditionally under-represented groups. A number of longitudinal studies have found, for example, that African-American children—particularly boys—fare less well in behaviorist classrooms (Hart, Burts, & Charlesworth, 1997; L. B. Miller & Bizzell, 1983; Schweinhart & Weikart, 1996).

PSYCHOANALYTIC THEORY

The **psychoanalytic theory** varies from other child development perspectives in that it focuses exclusively on the formation of personality. Psychoanalysts contend that children's emotional health stems from an ability to resolve key conflicts between their internal desires and impulses and pressures from the outside world. For example, infants feel an urgent need for pleasurable oral stimulation and experience great tension until this desire is satisfied. However, in the real world, babies cannot eat all of the time, so they must control their urges to some degree until an appropriate opportunity presents itself.

From a psychoanalytic perspective, a healthy child is one who learns to walk a fine line between immediate need fulfillment and the control of urges. Parents and teachers play a critical role in the process. They must provide just the right amount of nurturance. If they allow too little or too much gratification, according to the psychoanalytic theory, a child may fail to mature emotionally.

The best-known psychoanalytic theorist was Sigmund Freud (1938), a physician, who formulated a perspective of personality development based on his observations of neurotic adult patients. He postulated that needs and desires—such as the need for oral pleasure—are located in the **id,** a significant part of the mind. According to Freud, the id creates a constant pressure to satisfy basic drives; many of these derive from sexual feelings. If the id were the only aspect of personality, humans would seek to gratify their needs without delay. However, the **ego** emerges in early infancy to keep the id in check. The ego, another fundamental component of the mind according to Freud, redirects the demands of the id so that need fulfillment is sought only at appropriate times. At the end of early childhood the **superego** appears within the personality. This component of the mind comprises the conscience; all the values and mores of one's culture are included.

Here's how these three systems of the mind interact, according to Freud: A 5-year-old has an urge to obtain a toy that another child is using. The id drives her to snatch the toy and run off. The ego redirects her, however, to delay this behavior because the moment is not right; the child using the toy is older (and bigger!) and might resist. Also, a teacher hovers nearby. At the same time, the superego informs the child of important societal rules. The superego reminds her that being a "good girl" means sharing and taking turns, so the child refrains from taking any action at all.

Erikson's "Ages" of Emotional Development

Erik Erikson (1963, 1982), another psychoanalyst, elaborated on and extended Freud's theory. He proposed eight "ages" through which humans must pass from birth to adulthood if they are to feel competent and self-fulfilled. These stages are presented in Table 3-2.

Like Freud, Erikson proposed that healthy personality growth is characterized by a resolution of inner conflicts. Each stage of emotional development, from Erikson's view, involves a struggle between two opposing emotional states—one positive, the other negative (see Table 3-2). These polar states push and pull at the individual, creating tension and posing unique interpersonal problems. For Erikson, the individual's primary psychological work at a particular stage is to resolve this emotional conflict in a positive direction. The role of teachers and parents in this process is to assist children in striving toward positive emotional states, which are critical to their particular stage of development.

TABLE 3-2

Erikson's Eight "Ages" of Emotional Development

Stage	Approximate Age	Description
Trust vs. mistrust	Birth to 18 months	Children must come to trust that basic needs will be met by caregivers and that the world is a predictable and safe place. Otherwise, they will develop feelings of mistrust in others and the world.
Autonomy vs. shame/doubt	18 months to 3.5 years	Children must acquire a sense of independence from parents and a belief that they can do things on their own. If children are overly restricted when asserting their independence, they will develop feelings of shame and doubts about their individuality.
Initiative vs. guilt	3.5 to 6 years	Children must feel free to act, to create, to express themselves creatively, and to take risks. Children who are inhibited in these pursuits can become overwhelmed with guilt.
Industry vs. inferiority	6 to 12 years	Children must come to feel competent in skills valued by society. They need to feel successful in relation to peers and in the eyes of significant adults. If they experience failure too often, they will come to feel inferior.
Identity vs. role confusion	Adolescence	Adolescents must develop a clear sense of self. They must acquire their own unique roles, values, and place in society. If they are unable to piece together these elements into a coherent view of self, role confusion results.
Intimacy vs. isolation	Young adulthood	Young adults must be willing to risk offering themselves to others. An inability to give to another can lead to feelings of isolation.
Generativity vs. stagnation	Mature adult	Adults must gain a sense that they have contributed to the world in some lasting fashion. Through child rearing, civic deeds, or paid work they must come to feel they have in some way given to others. Those who do not achieve this sense may suffer stagnation—a sense that there is no direction or purpose to one's life.
Integrity vs. despair	Older adult	Older adults must come to feel great satisfaction with the events and accomplishments of their lives. They must look back on their experiences with pride and acceptance. Those who cannot feel this satisfaction as life draws to an end suffer great despair.

SOURCE: Erikson, 1963.

As shown in Table 3-2, four of Erikson's stages involve conflicts in early childhood. The first of these conflicts—between trust and mistrust—occurs in infancy. Emotionally healthy babies, according to Erikson, come to trust that they have nurturing, responsive caregivers who meet their basic needs. They come to view the world as safe and predictable. They enter into trusting relationships, first with primary caregivers and later with other human beings. "Security" is another word that describes this emotional state. Although humans will always experience feelings of mistrust about their relationships or the security of the world, from Erikson's view, the emotionally healthy baby is essentially trusting of the world and the people within it. Children who are abused or neglected, whose caregivers do not respond to their needs, or who for other reasons come to doubt the trustworthiness of the world will not resolve this emotional conflict in a positive way. They may be impaired from entering into relationships with others and may be unable to advance to later stages of emotional development.

The second of Erikson's conflicts—between autonomy and shame and doubt—occurs during the toddler years. Once children are trustful of adults and know that their basic needs will be met, they are willing to venture out away from the safety of parents and family. They now wish to become individuals apart from those with whom they have bonded. In their striving for individuality, children often assert themselves, rebel against rules, and assume a negative affect when confronted with adult control. Erikson argues that the emotionally healthy toddler gradually acquires a sense of **autonomy**—a feeling of individuality and uniqueness apart from his or her parents. Children who are overly restricted or harshly punished for attempts at becoming individuals will come to doubt their individuality and suffer shame. Gradually, such children can become timid, lack confidence in their abilities, and assume identities as mere extensions of their parents.

Erikson contends that children who develop a strong sense of autonomy as toddlers will desire to take action and assert themselves during their preschool years. They will wish to create, to invent, to pretend, to take risks, and to engage in lively and imaginative activities with peers. Erikson (1963) calls this urge to make creative efforts **initiative.** If adults encourage these efforts, a sense of initiative will flourish. However, when adults criticize children or in other ways lead them to believe their efforts are wrong, feelings of guilt arise. Moderate feelings of guilt can play a positive role in development, of course. These can lead children to assume responsibility for their own behaviors, for example. Overwhelming guilt, however, inhibits emotional growth.

Preschool children are content to make many creative attempts, regardless of the outcome. However, during the early elementary years, from Erikson's viewpoint, children wish to master real skills—the skills of older children and adults. They want to read and write like grown-ups, to excel at sports and other games, and to be strong and smart. Erikson maintains that children who have genuine successes in the early years and whose accomplishments are accepted and appreciated by adults and peers will develop a sense of "industry." Conversely, those who consistently experience failure and lack of acceptance will develop a sense of inferiority.

Working With Adam

Psychoanalysts would view Adam's difficulties as primarily emotional. They would search for solutions to his problems by exploring his early life and, in particular, his mother's socialization practices. (Recall that his mother is very young, has four children, and suffers from depression.) Was Adam's mother warm and nurturing? Did she promote trust? Did she allow him to become autonomous and to take initiative? Or did she inhibit his efforts at self-expression? Answers to these questions would guide decisions about intervention.

Aggressive children like Adam very often have not formed secure attachments to parents or other adults (Mitchell-Copeland, Denham, & DeMulder, 1997). They may, in Erikson's words, "mistrust" their environment and the people in it. A first step in working with Adam, then, might be to create for him a safe, predictable classroom environment and a strong bond with a teacher. An orderly classroom with stable enrollment and staffing and a consistent routine could help establish trust. A certain teacher might be assigned to spend time with Adam, giving warmth and nurturance and responding with enthusiasm to his accomplishments. Over time, Adam might come to trust this teacher. This attachment could facilitate positive relationships with other teachers and peers. Since bonds take time, this adult might continue to work with Adam for an extended period. The staff might rethink the practice of "graduating" children to a new classroom and teacher each year, for example.

Because a lack of trust is at the root of Adam's difficulty, from a psychoanalytic standpoint, great care would be taken to avoid harsh, punitive discipline, which is so common in the lives of aggressive children. Punishments for aggression (even Skinner's time-out) would, at best, control short-term behavior; at worst, they would engender further hostility and mistrust in Adam.

Once Adam has become attached to one or a small number of adults, he could be encouraged to be autonomous in his play and learning. He should be allowed to make choices, express himself, take risks, and explore his environment with minimal restriction. This is not to say that he should be allowed to do whatever he wishes. Psychoanalysts believe that adults must provide limits; need-gratification must be controlled and redirected, or children become too egocentric and demanding.

Later, if Adam shows a healthy sense of autonomy, he could be encouraged to take initiative. From a psychoanalytic viewpoint, play and art activities that allow interpersonal expression would be most important during this period. These experiences would allow Adam to make creative attempts and to become bold and confident. They would also provide him with an opportunity to "work through" troublesome life experiences.

In the primary grades, Adam would need to experience success. According to Erikson, it is real achievement that nurtures a child's sense of industry. If Adam were to fail constantly in school or with friends and family, he would develop a sense of inferiority.

Critique and Multicultural Analysis

A growing number of concerns have been raised about the psychoanalytic theory and its usefulness in teaching and parenting. The most commonly cited weakness is that it does not explain development of the whole child, but only a narrow range of emotional states (R. M. Thomas, 1992). How can a psychoanalytic perspective inform the teaching of early literacy or mathematics in the classroom? What implications does it hold for enhancing motor development? The theory does not seem to appreciate the interrelatedness of intellectual, physical, social, and emotional growth.

Another common criticism has been that the entire theory is based on personal observations of a small sampling of individuals. Freud, for example, drew his conclusions from case studies of nineteenth-century Viennese adult psychiatric patients, most of whom were white, upper-middle-class women. There have been recent charges that some of his case studies were of composites rather than real people! Although Erikson observed children in a variety of cultures, his work is also based on the subjective interpretation of a small number of cases (R. M. Thomas, 1992).

Multicultural and feminist scholars have elaborated on these limitations. Boykin and Tom (1985) have argued that some psychoanalytic stages of personality development, such as autonomy, reflect Anglo-Saxon ideals that are not appreciated in all cultures. Some ethnic groups value collective thought and action, so they emphasize behaviors such as relying on other people, checking with others before taking action, and sharing possessions. In some Japanese-American families, for example, a sense of belonging and collectivism—not individual autonomy—are goals in child rearing. Similar values of collectivism have been reported in African-American, Puerto Rican, and Native American cultures (Harrison, Wilson, Pine, Chan, & Buriel, 1990).

Gilligan, Brown, and Rogers (1990) further suggest that psychoanalytic theories tend to view the development of male children as normal or ideal and thus portray unique features of female development as deficient. For example, from Gilligan's view, separating from parents and becoming an autonomous person are uniquely important to the personality formation of boys, while attachment and intimacy are the norm for girls. Yet psychoanalytic theorists interpret separation as healthy and intimacy as a sign of overdependence.

Taken together, these criticisms suggest that not all children can be expected to develop through stages of emotional growth as Erikson and Freud have described them. Some children will form stronger bonds with family and community than others. Some will display less autonomy and initiative, others more.

COGNITIVE-DEVELOPMENTAL THEORY

The **cognitive-developmental theory** holds that mental growth is the most important element in children's development. Cognitive-developmentalists argue that almost all aspects of human life—even making friends, feeling happy or depressed, or enjoying a sunny day—are directly influenced by thinking and language. Making friends, for example, is determined in part by one's knowledge of peers and how they behave. Feeling sad often stems from one's mental interpretation of events or personal predicaments.

Intellectual functioning is extremely complex and internal, from a cognitive-developmental perspective. A skill such as reading or performing a new math operation is not learned merely by a change in behavior, as behaviorists might contend. Nor do these skills simply unfold, as maturationists might argue. Learning such skills involves intricate and internal mental actions; the learning occurs through elaborate processes inside the learner's mind, not outside of it.

One of the most influential of the cognitive-developmentalists, Jean Piaget (1896–1980), integrated elements of psychology, biology, philosophy, and logic into a comprehensive explanation of how knowledge is acquired. A fundamental principle of his theory is that knowledge is *constructed* through the action of the learner (Piaget, 1971). (Students of Piaget have often used a carpentry metaphor to describe this action; thus, his theory is often referred to as "constructivism" [R. A. DeVries & Kohlberg, 1990].) The action to which Piaget refers might be physical. For example, a baby comes to know about a rattle by banging it and listening to the noise it makes. Learning also involves mental action: the learner must do something mentally with new information in order to really learn it.

Piaget's idea that learning involves action is illustrated by the following example: A toddler who lives in the city takes a ride in the country with her father. She sees a cow and calls out "doggie!" The father responds, "That's a cow." They pass another cow, and another, and eventually the child calls it by its correct name. What has happened here appears simple, but is actually quite complex. When the child came across this strange new animal, she had to fit it into something she already knew about; that is, she had to make sense of her experience, based on previous understandings. She

Jean Piaget is the most noted cognitive-developmental theorist.

knew about dogs, so she decided that this must be an example of a dog. She had fit this large animal with horns into her mental category "dog." Piaget (1971) calls this step in the learning process **assimilation.** The child has assimilated this new phenomenon into something she already knows about.

However, the child would still not have learned much had assimilation been the only step. Another mental action was necessary. As the child looked at the cow, noticed its size and horns, and heard it say, "moo," she became puzzled. Puzzlement is critical for learning, according to Piaget. "This is a little different from a dog," she may have thought. So, she had to adjust her previous conception of animals a bit. Piaget calls this process of modifying previous understandings **accommodation.** The child may have created two categories of animals, perhaps "doggies" and "great big doggies with horns." (A child in one research study actually invented the name "biggiedoggie" for cows!) Conveniently, this child's father provided a label for this new category: "cow."

Both assimilation and accommodation are needed for learning. If accommodation did not occur, learners would never modify their thinking about things; in the example, the child would go on calling cows "dogs." If assimilation did not occur, there would be no previous understanding to rely on; the child in the example would be so confused about the appearance of the cow and what it might be that she could make no sense of it whatsoever. The ideal learning arrangement, according to Piaget, is one in which the child is confronted with a conflict or dilemma that is personally meaningful but which causes puzzlement and requires a modification of previous thinking. Learning experiences should have elements of both familiarity and novelty.

Through assimilation and accommodation, Piaget argues, humans advance through stages of intellectual—or **cognitive**—development. These stages are presented in Table 3-3. Each stage of the child's life is marked by qualitatively different kinds of thinking, according to Piaget. Babies are in the **sensorimotor stage;** they rely purely on action and the senses to "know" things. Knowledge, to a baby, is getting the things he or she needs through movement and perception. Preschoolers are in the **preoperational stage;** they are able to use internal thought, including symbols, but still rely on perception and physical cues in the immediate environment for learning. Children in the elementary years are in Piaget's **concrete operational stage;** their thinking and learning have become more internal and abstract. Still, young elementary students need the support of concrete objects in order to learn. First- or second-grade children will better learn a math concept, for example, if they are able to discover it by acting on concrete materials. It is not until children reach the **formal operational stage,** according to Piaget, that they can engage in purely abstract thought which is not tied to the physical world. This may not occur until adolescence or early adulthood.

Working With Adam

Cognitive-developmentalists would believe that Adam's difficulties with peers stem from a lack of **social cognition**—that is, an inability to understand social situations or the outcomes of social behaviors. They would cite research showing that highly aggressive children often inaccurately interpret their peers' actions and motives (Crick & Ladd, 1987) and are usually not aware of alternative strategies for solving social problems (Trawick-Smith, 1990). From the cognitive-developmental perspective, Adam may lack important social knowledge. An intervention should be aimed at teaching him how to interpret social situations.

One strategy would be to have Adam view videotapes or observe real-life interactions of peers playing in a variety of social situations. Teachers would then ask questions to guide his interpretation: What happened when Lawanda pushed Miko? How

TABLE 3-3
Piaget's Stages of Cognitive Development

Stage	Age	Description
Sensorimotor	0 to 18 months	Infants rely solely on action and the senses to "know" things. Intelligence is an ability to get what one needs through movement and perception.
Preoperational	18 months to 6 or 7 years	Preschool children can use symbols and internal thought to solve problems. Their thinking is still tied to concrete objects and to the here and now. They are fooled by the appearance of things.
Concrete operational	8 years to 12 years	Elementary school children are more abstract in their thinking. They can use early logic to solve some problems and are less fooled by perception. They still require the support of concrete objects to learn.
Formal operational	12 years to adulthood	Adolescents and adults can think abstractly and hypothetically. They can contemplate the long ago and far away. Their thinking is free from the immediate physical context.

SOURCE: Piaget, 1952b, 1954, 1959, 1965.

did Cheryl get Ahman to play with her? How did Hannah feel when Nemah yelled at her? In each case, the teacher would be trying to help Adam learn about social behaviors and situations. Teachers could also intervene in Adam's own conflicts to achieve this same goal. Interventions such as asking "What happened when you pushed Seth?" would guide Adam in interpreting the less-than-positive outcomes of aggressive behavior.

Teachers could also assist Adam in generating alternative solutions to social problems. When angry conflicts come up, for example, the teacher could ask the child to consider non-aggressive strategies: "What else can you do, besides hitting, if you're angry?" or "Can you think of a better way to get the blocks than just grabbing them?"

Besides these focused interventions, cognitive-developmentalists would propose creating a classroom environment for Adam that facilitates general cognitive development (R. A. DeVries & Kohlberg, 1990; Schweinhart, Weikart, & Larner, 1986). A program that encourages children to play, solve problems, and make sense of novel objects and situations would enhance general intellectual ability and, in turn, social cognition.

Critique and Multicultural Analysis

Because Piaget relied upon observations of a small number of typically developing children to formulate his theories, some have asked whether he has described accurately the understandings and behaviors of all children at each stage of development. Research indicates, for example, that children may be more intellectually competent than Piaget has suggested (Flavell, 1992). Also, some have argued that his observations reflect the development only of children of his particular culture. For example, studies of Mexican children who had had extensive experience with pottery-making at an early age showed an understanding of quantity at a much earlier age than Piaget's theory would have predicted (Price-Williams, Gordon, & Ramirez, 1969). Other of Piaget's ideas—his emphasis on autonomy in thinking and learning, for example, or the value he placed on games in childhood—have been criticized as Western- and male-oriented (Gilligan, Brown, & Rogers, 1990; Harrison et al., 1990). These elements of his theory, it is argued, reflect the competitive, individualistic society in which he lived and worked.

In spite of these criticisms, many multicultural scholars view cognitive-developmental perspectives as quite sensitive to cultural and gender diversity (Ogbu, 1992; R. M. Thomas, 1992). Miller-Jones (1988) advocates a cognitive-developmental theory, for example, because it focuses on developmental processes—such as assimilation and accommodation—and because it does not emphasize the acquisition of specific knowledge or skills which can vary in importance across cultures. She argues that not all children will learn to tie shoes or use a spoon at a particular age, as Gesell would suggest. Nor will all acquire certain, specific academic or social skills which are "shaped" by dominant culture, as Skinner would propose. But, all children of the world will learn—through assimilation and accommodation—the skills, knowledge, beliefs, and values important to their own family and culture.

SOCIOCULTURAL THEORY

The **sociocultural theory** is also concerned with intellectual development. Theorists of this group, however, believe that thinking and learning are not as internal and individual as Piaget proposed, but rather are highly influenced by language, social interaction, and culture. The originator of this theory is Lev Vygotsky (1896–1934), whose work is currently receiving much attention in the field of education. Vygotsky's personal history is quite fascinating. A prolific writer from the former Soviet Union, his most significant work was written in only a 10-year period. He died of tuberculosis at age 38. His work was suppressed by the Soviet government for a long time, and it was not until the early 1960s that his writings were translated into English. Yet his impact on recent thinking in child development has been profound.

Vygotsky's views are similar to Piaget's in a number of areas. He argues that children construct knowledge through action. When children solve problems with concrete objects, from Vygotsky's perspective, they acquire new concepts (Vygotsky, 1962). He describes stages of intellectual development, as Piaget has done. His theory differs from Piaget's in one fundamental way: he assigns greater importance to external influences—language, social interaction, and the larger society.

Vygotsky's theory is illustrated in Figure 3-1. As shown in the figure, he proposed that children engage in two distinct and independent mental activities in the earliest months of life—nonverbal thought and nonconceptual speech. In **nonverbal thought,** children observe objects or events or perform actions without using language. An example would be an infant pounding a rattle and attending to its sound. In **nonconceptual speech,** a child utters words or phrases without thinking about what they mean. Examples are playful babbling or the rote recitation of a song.

To Vygotsky, language and thinking are, at first, separate processes. Intellectual development involves connecting language and thinking. A toddler gradually associates the sound of a rattle, for example, with verbal labels—"rattle," "noise," or "loud." Only when language and thought are related in this way can children think in more complex ways.

During the preschool and primary years, according to Vygotsky, children engage in much **verbal thought,** in which language and thinking are integrated and mutually supportive. Verbal thought allows the acquisition of complex concepts. An understanding of size, for example, is enhanced when children can use words like "small" or "smallest" and "big" or "biggest." **Self-directed speech** is a behavior that shows that young children are using language to guide learning. Five-year-olds frequently talk to themselves, naming objects or narrating their actions—particularly as they solve problems. When playing a number game, for example, a kindergartner might be overheard counting out loud. Vygotsky notes that the more difficult a problem is, the more frequent a young child's self-directed speech. Until 7 or 8 years of age, there is still much isolated nonverbal thought and nonconceptual speech. Young children continue to engage in rote verbalizations or perform actions without using language.

In adolescence and adulthood most thinking is accompanied by language, as shown in Figure 3-1. When solving problems or learning new concepts, adults essentially speak to themselves. Of course, much of this language is internal. Adults will sometimes still engage in out-loud self-directed speech when learning tasks are difficult. It may be that readers of this book are muttering these passages aloud as they struggle to understand Vygotsky's theory!

According to Vygotsky, then, language is not merely a mode of expression—a reflection of what children already know, as Piaget described it—but a fundamental tool for constructing knowledge. Needless to say, a quiet classroom where children must just sit and listen is not optimal for learning, from this view. When teachers use language and encourage children to do the same, they are enhancing thought, as well as speech.

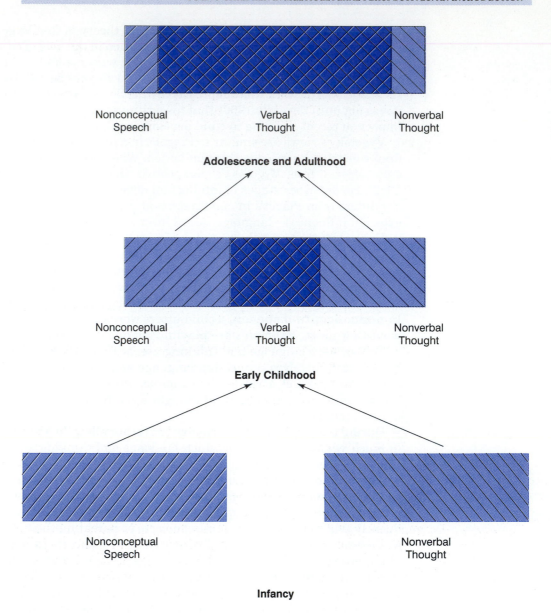

FIGURE 3-1 According to Vygotsky, speech and thought are separate processes in the early years. As children get older, they integrate the two into verbal thought. By adolescence, most mental activity involves verbal thought.

Vygotsky's theory contains practical ideas for promoting intellectual development. He proposes that teachers and parents **scaffold** children's learning—that is, use language and other social interactions to guide thinking. Here is how scaffolding works: When children are faced with problems they can solve on their own, adults should not interfere. Independent thinking is an ultimate goal of teaching or parenting, from Vygotsky's view. On the other hand, if tasks are so challenging to a child that they are insurmountable, adults should offer direct solutions. There are times, however, when problems or tasks are only slightly above a child's ability level.

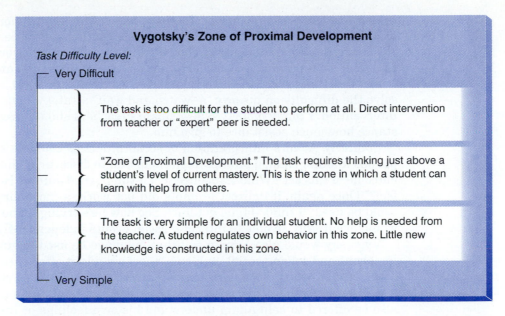

FIGURE 3-2 The zone of proximal development is a period during problem-solving when a task is just beyond a child's level of mastery. This is a time when an indirect prompt or question can help children solve the problem independently.
SOURCE: Vygotsky, 1978.

Here adults can ask questions or give hints that allow the child to solve problems independently. When adults indirectly guide children's own thinking and learning in this way, intellectual growth occurs. Parents and teachers should watch, then, for moments when indirect guidance can be given. Such periods are in what Vygotsky calls the **zone of proximal development.** This zone is represented in Figure 3-2.

An example of learning to read illustrates Vygotsky's ideas of scaffolding and the zone of proximal development: A 6-year-old is reading a picture book and becomes stuck on a word. If she is completely stumped, her parent should assist her very directly. He might read the text for her or even guide her to an easier book. If, on the other hand, the child quickly figures out the word and continues on with the story, the parent should not interfere at all. Independent reading is the ultimate goal. But what if the child is close to figuring out the word on her own? This would be a situation within the zone of proximal development. It would be a moment when an adult might be most effective in promoting literacy. The parent might give a hint or ask an interesting question in order to guide the child in solving her own problem. "Look at the picture," the parent might suggest. "What is the wolf doing? Does that help you figure out the word?" Or the parent might offer the sound of the word's first letter: "P-p-p. What word in your story would start with that sound?" To Vygotsky, such interactions are most powerful in promoting learning.

Working With Adam

Vygotsky's ideas for helping Adam would be similar to Piaget's. He would propose intellectual interventions—strategies to help Adam think about social problems and solve them independently. Following Vygotsky's framework, scaffolding would be the primary tool to accomplish this. Teachers might watch for a moment when a question or suggestion would help Adam resolve a conflict with a peer on his own: "You both want the same riding toy? What would be a good way for you both to use it?" Of course, if such prompts did not help Adam, a more directive intervention could be tried: "One thing you could do is take turns." On the other hand, if Adam was able to solve the difficulty on his own, a "watch and wait" strategy could be chosen with no intervention. From Vygotsky's view, Adam's teachers should decide in each circumstance how much assistance to give him.

Similarly, Adam's interpretation of social problems could be scaffolded. If Adam pushed another child, a prompt might help him to discover, on his own, the negative outcome of this act: "What happened when you pushed Jamal? How did it make him feel?" Once again, if indirect prompts did not work, a more directive intervention could be used: "I think Jamal got hurt. See how he's crying?" The hope is that Adam would eventually be able to interpret social events independently.

Vygotsky would also recommend that language be used to guide Adam in thinking about and solving social problems. Teachers might offer phrases to help him remember appropriate social responses. After an aggressive interchange, for example, a teacher might say, "If you're mad, you should say, 'I don't like that!'" Words might also be offered to help Adam understand his own feelings or his classmates': "He's very sad that you pushed him," or "I can see you're very angry." Encouraging Adam to talk through conflicts out loud would assist him in thinking in more complex ways about social relationships.

Critique and Multicultural Analysis

Due to Vygotsky's untimely death, his work is considered to be incomplete and sketchy (R. M. Thomas, 1992). Much of his writing has only recently been available to Western scholars, so it is relatively new to mainstream psychology. A small but growing cadre of modern researchers are now extending and testing his theory (Berk & Winsler, 1995; Rogoff, 1990). Although some have criticized his ideas as merely reflecting the Marxist-Leninist thinking of his time and culture (Bruner, 1984), much research supports his perspective (Rogoff, 1994). Vygotsky's theory has been viewed as particularly practical, with direct applications to teaching (Bodrova & Leong, 1996) and parenting (Freund, 1989). This is likely due to a tradition among Soviet psychologists to seek solutions to community problems or to improve the well-being of disadvantaged groups within society (R. M. Thomas, 1992).

The sociocultural theory receives high marks from multicultural scholars because it views development as social and collective, rather than purely individual (Rogoff, 1994; Rogoff, Mistry, Goncu, & Mosier, 1993). Vygotsky's concepts of collaborative learning and joint problem-solving relate well to the collective orientation of many non-Western families. His beliefs about testing and assessment, for example, are viewed as particularly sensitive to other cultures. He argues that scores on individually administered tests are not good measures of competence for most children. What a child is able to do with help from others is what is most indicative of intelligence. Thus, banding together with others to solve problems—as is common in many non-Western families—is more significant than individual achievement.

Vygotsky's is one of the few theories to appreciate the influence of culture on development. From his view, teachers and parents impart to children not only specific social skills and academic knowledge but also the values and customs of the larger society. Further, individual learners can have an impact on culture. The zone of proximal development is said to be a "transaction" in which students and teachers influence one another's thinking (Rogoff et al., 1993).

ECOLOGICAL SYSTEMS THEORY

The **ecological systems theory** focuses most directly on child development within the larger world. Unlike the perspectives previously reviewed, this theory emphasizes the influence of the many institutions and settings—the community, the school, the political system—within which children live. Urie Bronfenbrenner (1979), the leading proponent of this theory, has been critical of psychologists and educators who focus only on individual growth and behavior without regard for the social, political, or economic conditions in which children grow up. He maintains that the family, local social service agencies, schools, state and federal governments, the media, and the current political thinking of the time all must be considered in a comprehensive explanation of human development.

Bronfenbrenner uses the word *ecology* to refer to the settings and institutions that influence the growing human being. He suggests that there are multiple ecologies—that is, many different settings—which affect development. Further, he proposes that these ecologies lie in distinct layers or ecological systems around the developing human. Figure 3-3 illustrates graphically how these ecological systems interact with one another and the individual child.

As shown in the figure, the first layer, the **microsystem,** most directly affects child development. The microsystem is comprised of all institutions, experiences, and influences within the child's immediate environment. These include the family, pediatric services, the school, teachers or child care providers, and peers. The child both influences and is influenced by these persons and institutions. For example, a child's social behavior is enhanced by certain teacher interventions, and the teacher interventions are affected by the child's behavior.

Institutions within the microsystem influence one another; for example, parents are affected by schools and schools by parents. A teacher may provide information to a pediatrician about a medical problem; the pediatrician may, in turn, make recommendations for in-class adaptations to address the problem. Bronfenbrenner has argued that these interconnections comprise the second ecological layer—the **mesosystem.** When strong, supportive linkages exist between persons or organizations in the microsystem, according to ecological systems theory, positive child development is enhanced.

Additional ecological systems affect children indirectly. As shown in the figure, the **exosystem** is comprised of institutions or persons that do not actually touch children's lives but which indirectly affect their experiences. For example, the legal services system, a friend of the family, or the welfare department may not directly promote social or intellectual growth of children. However, they may enhance the mental or physical health of the family, provide resources needed for adequate nutrition or shelter, or improve the effectiveness of parents. These positive influences will, in turn, promote healthy child development.

The final ecological system shown in Figure 3-3 is the **macrosystem,** which contains the overarching values, ideologies, laws, worldviews, and customs of a particular culture or society. Although institutions of the macrosystem seem far removed from individual child development, they are extremely influential. An example of this

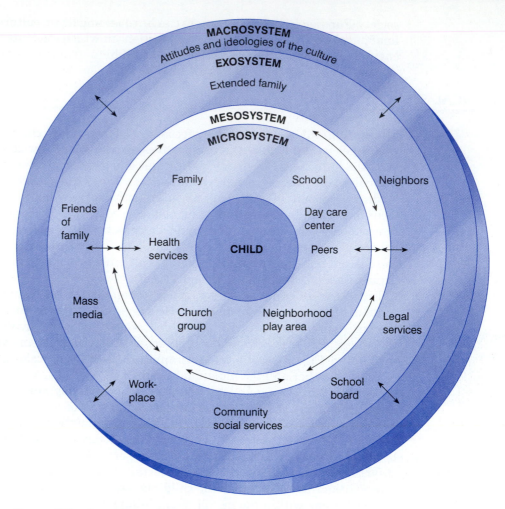

FIGURE 3-3   According to Bronfenbrenner, various ecological systems interact with each other to influence child development.

SOURCE: Kopp, C. B., & Krakow, J. B. *Child Development in Social Context.* Copyright 1982 by Addison Wesley Publishing Co., Inc. Reprinted by permission.

is provided by Berk (1997), who reports that child abuse is more prevalent in societies where the use of physical punishment or force in child rearing is accepted. In cultures where values of respect and caring for children are the norm, abuse is less common.

Working With Adam

In previous sections we have identified a number of classroom interventions based on theories of child development. These strategies would be viewed as too narrow by ecological systems theorists. To merely address individual behavior, feelings, or social understandings within the school setting would affect only one small element within Adam's microsystem. From an ecological systems perspective, a much broader social intervention would be needed.

A first step in addressing Adam's challenging behaviors would be to create supportive linkages among the microsystem institutions in his life. Teachers, social service professionals, medical personnel, and Adam's mother would need to collaborate in finding solutions to his difficulties. For example, the teacher might arrange for a planning meeting with Adam's mother and other significant family members, social and mental health service providers, and other professionals working with Adam and his family. A collaborative intervention—to be implemented in the home, the classroom, the community center, or home-visiting program—might be devised. For example, the psychoanalytic approach of promoting attachment could be implemented collaboratively across settings in Adam's microsystem. Individuals in each setting would provide predictable, nurturing, and responsive environments that enhance emotional bonds. Regular meetings could then be held between the parent and teacher to discuss problems and successes in implementation.

The teacher might visit Adam's home, and his mother might be invited into the classroom. Parent-education programs might be planned. The purpose of these initiatives would be to increase interconnections between school and family—that is, to strengthen the mesosystem. Following ecological systems theory, the teacher might adopt strategies to address other ecological systems. Assistance might be given to Adam's mother to obtain mental health services or to access resources to feed and clothe her family. The teacher might even assist in crisis management, helping the mother obtain legal services or career counseling when needed. Although such support activities are viewed by some as exceeding the limits of a teacher's role, they are absolutely crucial exosystem interventions from an ecological systems perspective; without them, no amount of in-class intervention will have a lasting impact.

Finally, the teacher might even launch a campaign to alter problematic elements in Adam's macrosystem. Political action against elected officials who threaten to cut child and family services might be undertaken. Lobbying activities to promote the regulation of television violence might be initiated. Advocacy would be a regular professional responsibility of teachers, from this perspective. These efforts would be based on a fundamental principle of ecological systems theory: child development problems are best addressed within a compassionate and caring society that values and protects its children.

Critique and Multicultural Analysis

Few research studies have examined child development from the perspective of ecological systems theory. Such work is exceedingly time-consuming and challenging (M. B. Spencer, 1985). Identifying all of the macrosystem, exosystem, mesosystem, and microsystem variables that affect children's social or intellectual development would be a formidable, if not impossible, undertaking. Studies have been conducted to determine some of the microsystem and exosystem causes of childhood problems. Certain **risk factors**—conditions that may lead to poor development—have been identified. These include poverty, lack of social services, violence in the community, poor housing, family disharmony, and child abuse (Rutter, 1987; Werner, 1990). Conversely, **protective factors**—conditions that may insulate children from the negative effects of poverty or community violence—have been studied (Garbarino, Dubrow, Kostelny, & Pardo, 1992). Among these are a positive home environment, attachment to parents, adequate housing and safe neighborhoods, and a positive preschool experience. Very few theorists of any field would deny the importance of these factors in shaping children's development.

The ecological systems theory has been viewed as culturally sensitive. It not only accepts cultural differences, but also fully integrates these differences into an explanation of human development. Customs, language, worldviews, and histories of particular ethnic groups—all part of the macro-, exo-, and microsystems—are viewed as fundamental aspects of the developmental process. For example, from this perspective, the learning and behavior of African-American children should not be studied in isolation from the social and political world. The historical roots of slavery, experiences of oppression, conditions in the immediate neighborhood, and economic hardship would be considered integral aspects of the developmental process (M. B. Spencer, 1985).

Because ecological systems theory focuses on the social, political, and economic contexts in which development occurs, it is believed to be most useful in identifying social issues concerning children in poverty or those of historically under-represented groups. Unlike perspectives that focus on individual development, ecological systems theory informs policy-making and advocacy activities. In fact, Bronfenbrenner's model has been a favorite among child development advocates and activists (Garbarino & Kostelny, 1992; M. B. Spencer, 1985; Zigler & Weiss, 1985).

RESEARCH INTO PRACTICE

CRITICAL CONCEPT 1

A theory of child development is a belief system about how and why children grow, learn, and behave as they do. Theories are very practical; they can guide adults in making decisions about teaching and caring for children.

Application

Teachers and parents should clarify their own theories about children and how they develop. A clearly articulated theory leads to thoughtful and consistent parenting and teaching.

CRITICAL CONCEPT 2

Five predominant theories of child development can be identified in the literature. All hold some value in resolving classroom dilemmas. Each provides useful guidance to parents and teachers.

Application

Teachers should become familiar with alternative theories of child development. They should borrow critical concepts and strategies from each theory in their professional practice.

CRITICAL CONCEPT 3

The maturationist theory holds that most of what children become is inherited at birth; behaviors and abilities simply unfold as children mature.

Application #1

Teachers and parents should understand that some characteristics of children are genetically determined at birth. They must come to appreciate diverse interpersonal styles or temperaments that are part of children's biological heritage.

Application #2

Teachers should adapt classrooms to meet the unique inborn traits of individual children, rather than expect children to adapt to classrooms.

CRITICAL CONCEPT 4

Behaviorist theory holds that the child is a "blank slate" at birth and is simply "filled in" over time by experience. From this perspective, adults can use rewards, praise, modeling, and other tools to shape children's development in any desired direction.

Application #1

Teachers and parents can use positive feedback and other rewards to influence children's behavior.

Application #2

Teachers and parents should behave as they wish children to behave, thereby modeling desirable behavior. Children are more likely to do what adults do than what adults tell them to do.

CRITICAL CONCEPT 5

The psychoanalytic theory is concerned mainly with personality formation. Psychoanalysts characterize psychological growth as a process of resolving emotional conflicts between instinctual desires and the demands of the real world.

Application #1

Teachers and parents should be nurturing and responsive to the needs of their infants and toddlers so these young children of this age will acquire feelings of trust.

Application #2

Teachers and parents should encourage autonomy, initiative, and the acquisition of new skills in order for preschool and primary children to resolve emotional conflicts in a positive direction.

CRITICAL CONCEPT 6

Cognitive-developmental and sociocultural theorists view mental growth and language as most critical; they view development as the active, internal construction of knowledge. These theories are often viewed as more culturally sensitive than other perspectives on child development.

Application #1

Teachers and parents should provide interesting experiences, ask questions, and pose challenges that lead young children to actively solve problems and construct understandings of the world.

Application #2

Teachers and parents should "scaffold" children's learning by asking questions, prompting, or giving hints when a child is within the "zone of proximal development"— that is, when the solution to a problem is just beyond the child's level of ability.

CRITICAL CONCEPT 7

Ecological systems theories hold that developmental processes do not occur in a psychological vacuum, but rather that individual child development is influenced by factors in the immediate environment as well as society and culture as a whole. Ecological systems theories are thought to be most useful in defining social issues and guiding social policy decisions.

Application #1

Teachers must realize that classroom intervention alone will not ensure positive child development. Family, community, and societal factors must also be optimal for children to learn and be healthy.

Application #2

Teachers must help parents and families access community resources. They should become knowledgeable about and establish relationships with local service agencies, and should ensure that parents have access to these agencies.

Application #3

The role of the teacher must be expanded to include advocacy. Teachers must lobby their local, state, and federal legislators, organize community or parent advocacy groups, and in other ways work to ensure a child-caring community and society.

SUGGESTED ACTIVITIES

1. Observe a group of children playing in a classroom or on the playground. Take careful notes on any incidents in which children perform negative or inappropriate behaviors (e.g., breaking classroom rules, using physical or verbal aggression, displaying oppositional behavior with adults). Write down what happens before, during, and after these events. Later, write an analysis explaining these situations, based on ideas from this chapter and guided by the following questions:

   a. Why have these children behaved as they have, according to maturationist theory?

   b. Why have the children behaved as they have, from a behaviorist perspective?

   c. Why have the children behaved as they have, from a psychoanalytic perspective?

   d. How would a cognitive-developmentalist explain these behaviors?

   e. How would these behaviors be interpreted from a sociocultural perspective?

2. Observe a teacher of young children and take notes on classroom interactions. Later, write an analysis of your observations, guided by the following questions:

   a. What elements of a maturationist perspective did you see in the teacher's interactions with children (e.g., tolerance of immature behavior, postponing tasks or activities for some children until they are "ready")?

   b. What elements of a behaviorist perspective did you see (e.g., using praise or rewards, ignoring misbehavior, "catching children being good," modeling positive behaviors)?

   c. What elements of a psychoanalytic theory did you observe (e.g., promoting attachment, encouraging autonomy and initiative)?

   d. What elements of a cognitive-developmentalist perspective did you see (e.g., encouraging children to construct their own learning through action, helping children to interpret/understand social situations)?

   e. What elements of sociocultural perspective did you see (e.g., "scaffolding" children's problem-solving)?

CHAPTER 4

Cultural Perspectives on Genetics, Prenatal Development, and Birth

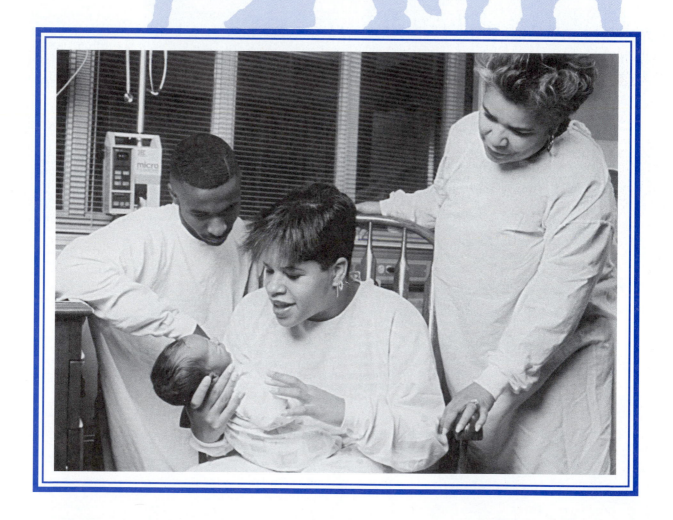

I N THIS CHAPTER, WE WILL CONSIDER GENETICS, PRENATAL DEVELOPMENT, AND CHILDBIRTH FROM A MULTICULTURAL PERSPECTIVE. Following a brief overview of each of these topics, I will present a more extensive discussion of cultural variation. A full understanding of child development before and during birth requires knowledge of the unique histories, worldviews, and family practices of diverse cultural groups, as the following story reveals:

Mr. Salazar, the director of a social services program, has just learned that a young Native American mother he is working with, Rose, has become pregnant. Since Rose's first child has had a variety of developmental and health problems, he tries to invite her to a free health clinic offered by his program. He has difficulty contacting her, though. When he calls her home, Rose's grandmother—who speaks mainly Chippewa—answers the phone. She has difficulty understanding him. Although he leaves messages, Rose does not return his calls.

Mr. Salazar makes the decision to go to Rose's home to tell her about the health clinic. When he finds no one there, he sits on the front porch of the family apartment, waiting. One hour passes, then another; but his resolve grows. He will continue to wait, because he believes the well-being of a new and developing human is at stake. If he can arrange for prenatal health care and nutrition services, this new child will get off to a much better start than Rose's first child did.

When Rose finally arrives, Mr. Salazar tries to explain his visit: "I want to invite you to a clinic, so your new baby will be healthy." Rose looks down and does not answer. "Good health and nutrition are very important for a developing fetus," he persists. The mother still does not reply, but quietly excuses herself and walks into her apartment, closing the door behind her. He stands a moment on the front steps, puzzled over what has just transpired.

Later, Mr. Salazar complains to a friend, a Midewiwin who is a social service worker: "I can't believe she cares so little about her unborn fetus. Will this new child stand a chance if Rose doesn't get decent prenatal care?" His friend laughs. "Oh, she cares a great deal for her children, I'm sure. You have a lot to learn about our culture. It's just very difficult for her to come to your clinic; there are barriers that you don't know about." "Barriers? The clinic is free!" Mr. Salazar responds. "Why can't she come just this one day, for her child?"

"There are cultural barriers," his friend explains. "This is one reason for the high mortality rate of Native American newborns in our country." He goes on to describe the traditions and values of many Native American families. He explains that they often have a great need for privacy; most Native

Americans, particularly women, have a tradition of personal modesty. The crowded, public setting of a health clinic and the intrusive examinations that are likely may be too intimidating. Even Mr. Salazar's unexpected visit to her apartment must have caused great consternation, he suggests.

He goes on to explain that Native Americans have a rich history of health care and medical treatment that is overlooked and often denigrated by Western doctors. The herbal remedies and tribal ceremonies used by Native Americans to prevent illness reflect a worldview in which humans must be in harmony with nature. Medical care is an extended family matter; all close relatives are often involved in treatment. Western medical experts have not recognized the value of these practices until recently, the director's friend asserts. Doctors are finally appreciating that Native American and Western techniques can be integrated to effectively address health issues.

Mr. Salazar, with the help of his friend, eventually arranges for Rose's family—including her grandmother—to receive medical and prenatal care at a nearby clinic, where staff are sensitive to cultural traditions. The director is pleased to learn several months later that Rose has given birth to a healthy baby.

This story illustrates how culture can influence development in the very earliest stages of life—even before birth. Such seemingly physiological processes as fetal health and birth weight can be affected by cultural beliefs and practices.

GENETICS: AN OVERVIEW

What children become is determined, in part, by what they have inherited biologically. There is much debate about how much influence genetics has on development, but most researchers agree that genetics and experience interact to affect how children turn out (Scarr, 1993).

Genes and Chromosomes

The process of child development begins at conception (although parental lifestyles even before conception may influence children's growth!). Following sexual intercourse, millions of sperm cells from the father travel up the fallopian tubes in the mother's body toward the egg, or **ovum.** Only one cell can successfully penetrate the ovum; once this penetration occurs, the egg becomes immediately resistant to other sperm cells. A remarkable chemical reaction then occurs: the nuclei of these two tiny cells combine and share information that will determine the traits of a new and unique person.

Information on the characteristics of parents and their ancestors is carried in the sperm and egg in **genes;** these are comprised of molecules of deoxyribonucleic acid, or **DNA.** Genes are ordered along larger bodies called **chromosomes,** which are contained in the nucleus of all human cells. Chromosomes carry all the genetic information necessary for the development of a unique individual; they help to determine such diverse traits as eye color, temperament (Chess & Thomas, 1987; Kagan et al., 1994), and even—some have claimed—political orientation (Eaves, Eysenck, & Martin, 1989).

Typical cells in the body contain 46 chromosomes. Sperm and egg cells are unique, however, in that each contains only 23 chromosomes. How did these cells come to contain only half the typical number of chromosomes? They were formed within the father's testes and the mother's ovaries by a special cell-division process called *meiosis*. When the sperm and egg combine during conception, so do the chromosomes in their nuclei. The result is a fertilized egg, or *zygote,* that has a full complement of 46 chromosomes. These chromosomes determine what the developing person will inherit from both parents.

The zygote begins to divide almost immediately after conception through a process called *mitosis*. At the same time, it begins a journey of several days down the mother's fallopian tube. It eventually becomes imbedded in the soft tissue of the mother's uterus. Here it continues to divide and grow at a remarkable rate into what will eventually become a new person.

When the egg and sperm join, the mother's and father's genes combine to determine the characteristics of this unique person. What happens when the mother's genetic information leads to a particular trait and the father's leads to just the opposite? In most cases the gene for one of these traits will be **dominant**—that is, it will win this genetic tug-of-war and express its characteristics in the developing human. If the mother contributed a dominant gene for tallness, for example, the child would become tall. The gene for shortness—the **recessive gene**—would not express itself. A recessive gene only expresses itself when it is paired with another recessive gene.

In actuality, genetics is not quite so simple. Most traits involve a combination of several genes, and sometimes traits are blended. The environment plays a role in whether genetic information inherited by the child will actually be expressed. A good example is the inheritance of general intelligence. IQ is determined, in part, by genetics; however, most geneticists believe that there is no such thing as a "smart" gene. What a person inherits from parents at conception is a "heritability range"— that is, a range of potential intellectual abilities (Scarr, 1993). For example, a child might inherit the potential to be of moderate to high intelligence, but achieve only moderate intelligence because of a limited environment. Another child might inherit a potential for only low to moderate ability, but achieve the same, moderate level of ability because of a more supportive environment. In each case, the level of intellectual capacity depends on both genetics and life's opportunities.

Of all the human traits determined at conception, perhaps none is as significant as gender. All human cells contain a special pair of chromosomes: an XX pair in females and an XY pair in males. This single pair of chromosomes—one contributed by the mother, the other by the father during conception—determines the gender of the developing person. The mother's egg can only contribute an X chromosome, while the father's sperm cell can contribute either an X or a Y. If a sperm cell containing an X chromosome penetrates an egg (which always has an X), a female is conceived. If an egg is fertilized by a sperm cell with a Y chromosome, a male is conceived. It is the genetic contribution of the father, then, that determines gender.

Twins can result from one of two genetic processes. Sometimes, at the time of conception, two separate eggs are released from the mother's ovaries and are fertilized by two different sperm cells. The result is that two genetically distinct siblings are born at the same time. These "fraternal" twins (not exclusively fraternal, of course, because they could be sisters or a brother and sister!) are no more alike than other siblings. They have developed from separate zygotes containing different genetic information. "Identical" twins occur in the rare instance when a fertilized egg divides immediately after conception into two separate zygotes. Both zygotes travel down the fallopian tube into the uterus and grow separately into genetically identical persons. Identical twins are necessarily of the same gender, since they have developed from the same sperm cell and egg. Twins occur in about 2% of births, and about two-thirds of these are fraternal.

Hereditary Diseases

Some problems in development before birth can be attributed to genes and chromosomes. Sometimes these can lead to physical malformations, mental retardation, or poor health. One condition caused by chromosomal abnormalities is Down syndrome. Individuals with this condition have received three number 21 chromosomes instead of the typical pair. Moderate to severe mental retardation, problems with the heart and other organs, and unique physical features such as reduced stature and somewhat flattened facial features are common characteristics of a child with Down syndrome. The condition occurs in 1 out of 500 to 1 out of 700 births; the possibility increases with the age of the mother.

In Rh disease, another genetically related problem, the infant inherits blood from the father that is incompatible with that of the mother. If the **fetus** inherits Rh-positive blood from the father and the mother is Rh-negative, the mother's body will produce antibodies that can become toxic. The result can be fetal anemia, jaundice, mental retardation, and death. A family's firstborn child is not at great risk, since not enough time has elapsed for antibodies to form before the child is born. Subsequent children are most affected. Fortunately, through careful screening of the mother's blood before birth, the problem can be avoided. A special serum can be administered to destroy Rh-positive blood cells as they enter the mother's body during her first delivery. This inhibits the formation of antibodies that can affect the development of subsequent children. Prenatal health screening is critical, then, to avoid the damaging affects of this condition.

Some genetically derived problems afflict only males or females; these derive from abnormalities of the X and Y chromosomes that determine gender. Diseases that affect only males include hemophilia, a condition that leads to internal bleeding, and Klinefelter's syndrome, which can result in sterility, physical malformation, and mental health problems. Only females are afflicted with Turner's syndrome, a condition that leads to physical malformation and sterility.

GENETICS FROM A MULTICULTURAL PERSPECTIVE

How are genetics and culture interrelated? Are some cultural variations in child development inherited biologically? Can culture actually influence how some genes are expressed in the developing person? These are questions debated by geneticists and multicultural scholars. Sandra Scarr (1993) has summarized the relationships among genetics, culture, and individual variation in this way: "Becoming human is one matter. Becoming French, Mongolian, or African-American is another. Becoming George Sand, Genghis Khan, or Martin Luther King, Jr. is still another" (p. 1333). Her point is that there are at least three significant sources of variation in human development: the biological evolution of the species, the cultural heritage, and the genetic makeup of the individual human being. All of these factors interact with and support one another. Scarr rejects the notion that one factor is predominant: "For too long, psychologists have argued nature *versus* nurture, biology *versus* culture, as though one cause excluded the other" (p. 1335). A full understanding of human genetics requires an understanding of the complex ways all three factors interact.

Becoming Human

Genetics regulates most directly the process of becoming human. All children inherit certain "species-specific" characteristics—for example, language, smiling, general intelligence, and emotionality—that can be observed across all cultures and in all individuals. All cultural groups provide opportunities for children to acquire such traits. However, these opportunities tend to differ from one culture to another. For example, all societies have some mechanism for teaching language, but they differ in their teaching methods. That so many fundamental characteristics can be observed across cultures suggests that human beings are really more alike than they are different, regardless of where they grow up or what their individual circumstances may be.

Becoming an Individual

There are, of course, individual differences in development. To use Scarr's example, Martin Luther King, Jr., and Genghis Khan were clearly unique and different human beings! These individual variations may be partly determined biologically, from Scarr's view. A child may suffer from a hereditary disease that will contribute to lifelong atypical development or poor health. Another may inherit genetic information that will partially explain a pleasant temperament or difficulty learning math. Experience plays a key role, however, in determining how these inherited traits will actually be expressed as the human develops. According to Scarr (1993), environments provide a "range of opportunities" for development (p. 1336). A child with Down syndrome may become more or less intellectually competent, depending on environment. A child born with a predisposition to be of pleasant temperament may be less positive if the environment does not nurture this inborn trait.

Scarr (1993) has argued not only that environment can shape the way children turn out, but also that children can "create their own environments" (p. 2). Using the previous example, a child who has inherited biologically a pleasant temperament may elicit positive behaviors from parents or peers. When adults respond to a pleasant manner with support and nurturance, the child may become even more positive in interactions. Thus, it is the child's temperamental disposition that leads to a nurturing environment, not the other way around!

Becoming an Individual Within a Cultural Group

How does culture influence development? How do African Americans become African American and Mongolians become Mongolian? Within a particular cultural group there is vast individual variation in development which stems from the genetic and environmental influences we have discussed. Japanese-American children, for example, vary greatly in social competence, temperament, and learning style (Yamamoto & Iga, 1983). Given such variety within cultures, can one conclude that there are no cultural differences? Are all individuals so unique that it is pointless to think about cultural diversity in development? Derman-Sparks (1989) has described a "denial of differences" view in which the rich cultural diversity within our society is not appreciated. Differences among cultural groups do exist, of course. Some of these differences are genetically derived, while others are rooted in the unique experiences of groups throughout history.

Cultural Differences Related to History and Experience. Most cultural differences have evolved, from Scarr's (1993) perspective, as groups have adapted to the unique challenges of their surroundings. Cultures have defined what is important for children to know, believe, and be able to do, based on what is needed for survival of the group. Although genetics has provided the raw materials to acquire these abilities, it is cultural experience that defines the specific behaviors and knowledge that children will learn.

Ogbu (1992) gives an example of how challenges from the outside world have led some cultures to adopt unique child-rearing practices. Some African-American parents have adopted a directive parenting style that has evolved to keep children from harm in an inhospitable, biased society (Baumrind, 1994; Hale, 1994). This parenting style has been found to lead to positive development for African-American children, even though it may be viewed as authoritarian by those in the dominant culture. In some Native American families, the maintenance of cultural values is critical. Sometimes traditional public schooling is seen as a threat to this. As a result, success in school is not always a highly valued goal for parents; this may explain the high drop-out rate in some Native American communities (Slonim, 1991; Wise & Miller, 1983). An important point to remember is that such cultural differences are logical, purposeful, and directly related to experience. They are not genetically derived deficits, as some writers have asserted (Herrnstein & Murray, 1994).

Differences Related to Genetics. Some cultural variations can be related directly to genetics. For example, differences have been found across ethnic groups in the motoric activity of infants (J. E. Brown et al., 1986; Lester & Brazelton, 1982; Malina, 1982). Stature and weight vary across cultures; children of Asian ancestry have shorter stature, broader hips, and shorter arms and legs, while those of African descent are relatively taller and have longer limbs.

Certain hereditary diseases are more prevalent within particular ethnic groups (Milunski, 1977). African-American children are more likely to suffer from **sickle-cell anemia,** a disorder that causes heart and kidney problems and early death. In some African communities, 30% of newborns carry the gene that causes this disorder (Zigler & Finn-Stevenson, 1993). Asians are more likely to inherit thalassemia, a red blood cell disorder that causes damage to vital organs. Children of European or Pueblo Indian ancestry are more often afflicted with cystic fibrosis, an enzyme disorder that causes mucus to form in the lungs and intestinal tract. Tay-Sachs disease, an enzyme-related condition that causes the brain and nervous system to deteriorate, more often strikes Jews of Eastern European descent.

Although these diseases are purely genetic in origin, anxieties about children's afflictions and parents' responses when these occur have become a part of cultural heritage. The story of Randy illustrates this point:

Randy is a 36-year-old African-American professor at a small eastern university. He has just been released from the hospital, where he had fought a life-threatening bout with pneumonia. This is not the first time he has had to cope with serious illness; his "crises" are numerous and come on quickly and without warning. "Another battle is won for now," he comments to well-wishers at a faculty meeting.

One day, at age 13, after choir practice at church, Randy sat down in a pew next to his grandmother, resting his head against her shoulder. She had always been there for him, he was thinking; at that very moment, his stomach began to hurt. His abdominal pains grew over the next few days, and his mother's usual remedies didn't seem to be working. Randy was eventually admitted to the hospital. He remembers his mother crying and recalls being confused at her sadness. This was just a stomachache, after all; surely he would get better. Only later would he learn that he'd been diagnosed with a genetic disease, sickle-cell anemia, which meant he had little chance to live a full life. "It is pretty hard to deal with at age 13," Randy recalls. "I was young and looking forward to life. And now I was being told that I would die."

The stomach crisis finally passed, but in no time another challenge arose. Randy developed sores around his ankles which grew and became more and more painful. These were leg ulcers, he was told, the first of many he would suffer. They would last 30 to 60 days. He remembers having trouble walking to school because of the pain. Some days he could not put on his shoes.

But Randy survived. He finished high school and went off to college. Here, stress, financial worries, and poor diet led to numerous visits to the campus infirmary. He joined ROTC, hoping to become an officer in the Air Force. He suffered a devastating blow when he underwent a routine physical examination and was told the Air Force would not commission him because of his disease. Yet Randy persevered. He became a certified teacher, earned a master's degree, and then completed a Ph.D. program at a prestigious university. He had certainly beaten the odds.

When asked why he has survived for so long, Randy answers without hesitation: "Religion. My family has always been deeply religious. I have a strong mother, a strong father. They were strong believers, and I was brought up in the church." Randy believes it is not a coincidence that his ailment first began in church with his grandmother nearby; that early experience represents for him how religion and a supportive extended family have gotten him through.

Randy is clearly aware of what the future might hold. He could die suddenly of a stroke or organ failure. "Sometimes I ask, 'Why me?' 'What would life be like if I did not have the disease?' But then I ask, 'Would I value life as much if I didn't have it?'"

Randy's observations mirror Hale's (1994) view that the strength of black families and their religious orientation have allowed survival of the culture in adversity.

Cultural Differences Versus Genetic Deficits. We can conclude that cultural differences in child development—which surely do exist—stem mostly from the unique experiences and histories of various ethnic groups. For centuries, however, biology has been used to perpetuate racism. For example, a genetic argument has been used to espouse the intellectual superiority of one culture over another. Although few modern-day social scientists assert that some cultures are inferior, work suggesting this continues to be published. One such book, *The Bell Curve,* by Richard Herrnstein and Charles Murray (1994), received much recent attention in the popular press. Its authors note that a disparity exists between the IQs of certain ethnic groups and white Americans. They hint that the IQ advantage for whites is explained, in large measure, by genetics. Many criticisms have been raised about this work. Some have challenged the statistics reported. Others have raised questions about whether measures of IQ favor persons of white middle-class background. Still others point out that individuals from under-represented groups lack the resources and opportunities enjoyed by the dominant culture. The IQ disparity, they argue, is really a disparity of access (Ceci, 1991).

Unfortunately, such books tend to revive archaic beliefs about "cultural deficits." They suggest that individuals within a particular cultural group are deprived because their unique values, socialization practices, or competencies do not match those of the dominant culture. Such perspectives are extremely dangerous from a public policy and education standpoint. I will argue throughout this book that cultural differences are just that: differences. They may be explained by experience or genetics or an interaction of these, but they are always to be appreciated as part of the rich diversity that makes up our world.

PRENATAL DEVELOPMENT: AN OVERVIEW

How does development proceed once the sperm and egg and the zygote, or fertilized egg, travels down the fallopian tube? The zygote becomes imbedded in the uterine wall and begins to grow rapidly. Three distinct stages of **prenatal development** can be identified. These are described in Table 4-1.

The *period of the ovum,* which lasts about 2 weeks after conception, involves the rapid growth of a shapeless mass of cells. However, *cell differentiation* has already begun during this period. As described in the table, specialized cells are created that will grow into all of the important tissues and organs of the developing human. The period of the ovum is one of risk for development; *miscarriages*—that is, spontaneous abortions—occur most often during this early stage (Tanner, 1990).

The second period of prenatal development, the *period of the embryo,* begins around 2 weeks after conception and extends to approximately the eighth week. Amazingly, almost all major organs and structures of the human body are formed during this stage, and many begin to function. Also during this period, important organs begin to form outside of the **embryo.** These include the **placenta,** a soft mass that allows the flow of nutrients from the mother to the embryo, and the **um-**

TABLE 4-1
Stages of Prenatal Development

Stage	Age	Significant Developments
Period of the ovum	Conception to 2 weeks	Cell differentiation occurs. Embryoplast cells form; these will become the developing person. Trophoblast cells are differentiated; these will develop into the placenta and other important external tissues. Miscarriage is most common during this period.
Period of the embryo	2 weeks to 8 weeks after conception	The heart, brain, lungs, digestive system, kidneys, and liver all are formed. The heart begins to beat. Facial features—eyes, nose, ears, mouth, tongue, tooth buds, and upper and lower jaws—develop. The placenta, umbilical cord, and amnion form. The length of the embryo is about 1.5 inches.
Period of the fetus	8 weeks to birth	Further development and growth of organs and limbs occurs. Brain growth is especially rapid. The fetus begins to open and close eyes and even suck a thumb. This is often considered a period of less risk. However, poor maternal health and nutrition still put the fetus at risk.

bilical cord, the "lifeline" that transports these nutrients. An important, protective fluid-filled sack, the **amnion,** has now formed around the developing organism. The rapid growth of the embryo makes this a period of some developmental risk. Environmental influences such as maternal drug use or illness can have a devastating effect during this stage. Maternal nutrition is critical for the embryo's development.

The final prenatal stage, the *period of the fetus,* is marked by continued development of the organs and rapid growth. Since many of the organs have already formed, the fetal stage is often considered a less critical period in development. It is important to point out, however, that important development occurs at each prenatal stage. For example, brain growth is extremely rapid in the final 3 months of prenatal development (and for many months after birth!). Maternal nutrition is extremely important, then, during this time. Most doctors urge a healthy maternal lifestyle during all 9 months of pregnancy to ensure positive fetal development.

The three stages of prenatal development and the significant physical growth that occurs in each are presented in Figure 4-1. The figure also shows periods of risk in the formation of various organs and systems.

ENVIRONMENT, CULTURE, AND FETAL DEVELOPMENT

Environmental agents can negatively influence fetal development. These include poor nutrition, drugs, and maternal illness during pregnancy. Due to some of these factors, children of color have a rockier road to travel from conception to birth. On almost any measure of fetal development or neonatal health, African Americans, Puerto Ricans, Native Americans, Mexican Americans, and Asian Americans do not fare as well as Caucasians. For many traditionally under-represented groups, the infant mortality rate is almost twice as high as that for whites (Children's Defense Fund, 1998; Garcia Coll, 1990).

Why are such problems more common among certain ethnic groups? One explanation is poverty. Poverty rates are higher for almost all under-represented populations (Garcia Coll, 1990; Huston, McLoyd, & Garcia Coll, 1994; U.S. Bureau of the Census, 1998). Poverty is among the most debilitating of conditions in prenatal development (Pollitt, 1994); it contributes to a range of hazards.

Drugs

Substance abuse by a pregnant mother can have catastrophic effects on the developing fetus. Heroin use, for example, has been associated with premature birth, physical malformations, respiratory difficulties, lower birth weight, and greater risk of death at birth (Robins & Mills, 1993). Further, newborns of heroin-addicted mothers become addicted because they have ingested the drug through the placenta since conception. These babies begin their lives suffering withdrawal symptoms. Long-lasting negative effects may result from early exposure to heroin (Stechler & Halton, 1982), although the lasting impact of *in utero* exposure to drugs is still debated (Griffith, Azuma, & Chasnoff, 1994; Robins & Mills, 1993; Schutter & Brinker, 1992).

Cocaine use has caused growing concern in recent years. An inexpensive form of this drug, "crack," is so accessible that its abuse has become the fastest-growing drug problem in our country. Crack-addicted mothers have a greater chance of miscarriage or premature delivery. Their newborns are more likely to suffer brain damage,

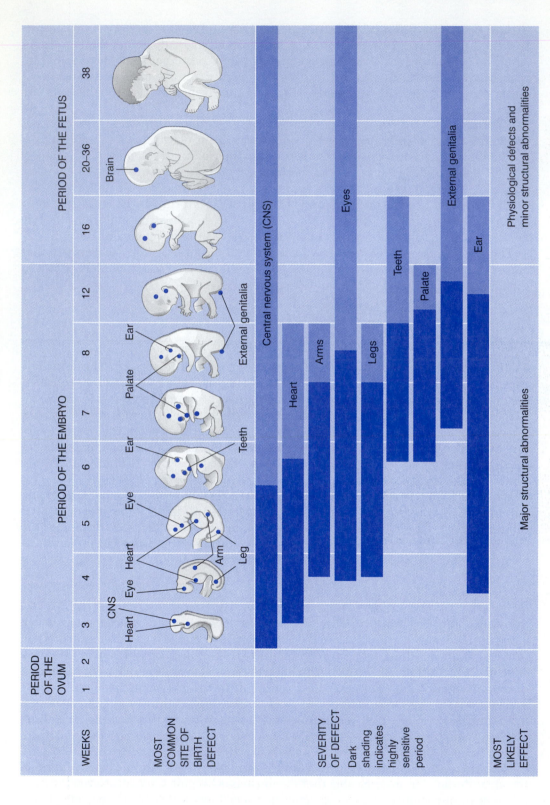

FIGURE 4–1 Organs and systems form at different periods in prenatal development. Darkly shaded lines indicate sensitive periods during which specific organs or structures are at risk. Environmental agents can negatively affect development during these periods.

SOURCE: Moore, K. L. (1989). *Before We Are Born: Basic Embryology and Birth Defects*, 3rd ed. W. B. Saunders. Reprinted by permission.

Poverty and cultural barriers to health care may lead to poor prenatal development.

low birth weight, and other physical malformations (Griffith et al., 1994; Hawley & Disney, 1992; Robins & Mills, 1993). These "crack babies" must suffer a withdrawal period that is significantly longer than that for children born to heroin-using mothers (Wallis, 1986).

Mothers who use illegal drugs are more likely to smoke and use alcohol as well, compounding the risk (S. F. Johnson, McCarter, & Ferencz, 1987). Maternal smoking has been linked to miscarriage, premature delivery, and low birth weight (Floyd, Rimer, Giovino, Mullen, & Sullivan, 1993). Even smoking by fathers has been associated with genetic abnormalities (H. J. Evans, 1981). Evidence suggests that effects of smoking may be long-term. Children of smoking mothers have been found to be less responsive, fussier, and more sluggish during infancy, and to perform poorly on attention and picture-recognition tasks in the preschool years (Streissguth et al., 1984). Children whose mothers smoked during pregnancy have been found to be less competent readers and to have social adjustment problems in later childhood (Fergusson,

Horwood, & Lynskey, 1993; U.S. Department of Health, Education, and Welfare, 1979). In 70% of cases of **sudden infant death syndrome (SIDS)**—a condition that causes healthy babies to suddenly die in their sleep—mothers smoked during pregnancy (H. J. Hoffman & Hillman, 1992).

Alcohol use during pregnancy has also been related to physiological difficulties in newborns. Mothers who drink heavily during pregnancy may give birth to babies with **fetal alcohol syndrome,** a condition that can lead to nervous system impairment, mental retardation, hyperactivity, and deficiencies in weight, height, and brain size. Even one drink a day may have negative effects on fetal development (H. C. Olson, Sampson, Barr, Steissguth, & Bookstein, 1992). Most doctors recommend that pregnant women abstain from alcohol completely.

Commonly used over-the-counter or prescription drugs may also threaten prenatal development. Such diverse medications as aspirin, tetracycline, and Valium have been found to lead to complications and health problems. Sometimes so many drugs are used by a mother during pregnancy that when fetal problems arise, it is difficult to pinpoint which drug is the cause (Robins & Mills, 1993).

Sometimes the effects of drugs are not clearly known for many years. For example, in the case of diethylstilbestrol (DES), a drug prescribed between 1945 and 1970 to prevent miscarriage, no discernible consequences were observed immediately after birth. It was only when the female offspring of mothers taking the drug reached adolescence that its effects became known. The daughters were found to have a higher rate of vaginal cancer and to be more likely to have miscarriages when they became pregnant. Male offspring of DES users were discovered to be more likely to develop cancer or to be infertile (Rosenblith, 1992).

Mothers in poverty are more likely to abuse illegal drugs, probably due to the stress associated with being poor. Poor mothers obviously have fewer resources and are more likely to be unemployed. They are also more likely to become victims of violence and to live with other persons who abuse drugs. Not surprisingly, poor mothers suffer a higher rate of depression and psychiatric disorders (Amaro, Zuckerman, & Cabral, 1989; Robins & Mills, 1993). Drug abuse may reflect a struggle to find some comfort in a difficult life. Unfortunately, it can lead to disastrous effects for a developing fetus.

Poor mothers of all cultures abuse drugs. However, mothers of historically underrepresented groups are more likely to use highly addictive drugs, heroin and cocaine in particular. Data have also suggested that drug use in large cities is more prevalent among young mothers of color (Anthony & Petronis, 1989). Hence, newborns of poor mothers or those of under-represented groups are somewhat more likely to suffer the negative effects of *in utero* drug exposure. These statistics demonstrate a need for enhanced education and prenatal health care, particularly among younger women of these populations. The statistics also suggest that programs to end poverty and support low-income mothers can contribute to positive child development.

A word of caution must be issued about ethnicity, class, and drug use. Just because some forms of substance abuse are more prevalent among those in poverty or those of under-represented groups, this does not mean that all, or even many, individuals in these populations will use drugs. Among all women of childbearing age, for example, only 5% use cocaine; when women under age 22 are excluded, the rate drops to 3% (Robins & Mills, 1993). So drug use cannot be considered common in any class or culture.

Nutrition and Health

Poor nutrition and maternal illness can influence fetal development. Since the developing fetus receives nutrients from the mother through the placenta, a malnourished mother is likely to give birth to a malnourished baby. It is a myth that a fetus can miraculously extract needed nutrients from the mother even when she is not eating well. Babies of malnourished mothers are often born prematurely or die soon after birth; those who survive are likely to suffer from low birth weight (Brozek & Schurch, 1984). Children born to malnourished mothers may suffer cognitive delays later in life (Barrett, Radke-Yarrow, & Klein, 1982). This may be due in part to the fact that malnutrition during important periods of fetal brain growth can impede nervous system development (Winick, 1981).

Maternal illnesses can have a serious effect on prenatal development. Rubella—a relatively mild disease for the mother—can cause a range of disorders in the developing fetus, including congenital heart disease and central nervous system disorder, as well as death (Moore & Pursaud, 1993). The human immunodeficiency virus (HIV), which causes the fatal disease AIDS, can be transmitted from an infected mother to her fetus (Pizzo & Wilfert, 1994). The virus can even be passed from mother to child through breast milk (Landau-Stanton & Clements, 1993)!

Newborns of traditionally under-represented groups may be less healthy than those of Euro-American ancestry. As described above, they are more often of low birth weight and are more frequently born prematurely (Garcia Coll, 1990; U.S. Department of Health and Human Services, 1996). African-American newborns show a greater incidence of general nutritional deficiency; anemia among poor African-American and Latino babies is as high as 20 to 40% (Pollitt, 1994). Southeast Asian babies also are more often impaired by iron deficiency (Nutritional Status of Minority Children, 1987).

These cultural gaps in health status are primarily due to poor prenatal care for some groups (Children's Defense Fund, 1998; Garcia Coll, 1990). A major barrier to adequate health care for many mothers is economic; good nutrition and regular medical visits can be expensive. A number of government programs have been established to address this problem. An example is the WIC program (Special Supplemental Food Program for Women, Infants, and Children), which is designed to provide low-income pregnant mothers with high-protein and iron-fortified foods, nutritional education, counseling, and regular medical evaluation. Research over several decades has shown that the program has had positive effects on families who participate, both in the United States and in developing countries (Kotelchuck, 1984; Pollitt, 1994). Children whose mothers received this prenatal support were found to have advanced cognitive abilities at age 5 (Hicks, Langham, & Takenaka, 1982).

These findings suggest that such comprehensive social programs are a powerful way to bolster the health status of our nation's children. Unfortunately, the real cash value of many government programs for children and families has declined in the 1970s and 1980s (Huston et al., 1994). Advocates of young children must regularly remind policy makers that investments in prenatal health care now will lead to long-term savings as children continue to grow and develop in healthy ways throughout their lives.

There are non-economic cultural barriers to prenatal care as well. Spanish-speaking pregnant mothers have been found to be reluctant to go to clinics or other medical care facilities where only English is spoken (R. M. Anderson, Giachello, &

Aday, 1986; L. R. Chavez, Cornelius, & Jones, 1986). Cultural beliefs and practices create obstacles to health care and social services. John Red Horse (1983) tells a story that illustrates this point:

> Margaret is a single, Native American mother with a newborn baby. When she was hospitalized for an extended period with a heart problem, her child was placed in a foster home and a caseworker was assigned to monitor family needs. Margaret came to be friends with the foster parent over time; in her culture, friendships are like family relationships.
>
> There came a time when Margaret's health had deteriorated and she became preoccupied with her own medical problems. During this period she did not ask to see her baby. Neither the caseworker nor the foster parent took the initiative to arrange for a visit; however, both became angry that Margaret did not demand one. They wondered why she did not wish to see her own child. When Margaret was eventually released from the hospital, she received a hostile greeting from the foster parent and discovered that the caseworker had initiated court action to terminate her parental rights.
>
> Both the caseworker and the foster parent had completely misunderstood Margaret's behavior because they did not understand her culture. In some Native American families, child care is a collective family and community affair. Since the foster mother was like a relative, Margaret had no concern about leaving her child in her care for a long period. She knew her baby would be well taken care of. Margaret, in fact, had wanted very much to see her child; however, demanding to do so was not part of her cultural communication style.
>
> It was only after many interviews that Margaret's motives were finally understood in cultural context and her family life restored.

This story raises an important issue: What would happen if Margaret became pregnant again? This would certainly be a high-risk pregnancy; her health status and low income would suggest a need for rigorous health and nutritional intervention. But after the experience described above, would Margaret be willing to visit a clinic or hospital for prenatal care? Her introduction to Western health care and social service systems nearly led to a disastrous outcome for her family. Lack of cultural sensitivity and understanding by some medical and social service professionals can be a very real barrier to prenatal care (Boyce et al., 1986).

Teen Pregnancy

It has long been argued that teenage mothers have an increased rate of complications in pregnancy and childbirth because their young bodies are not yet ready to provide for optimal fetal development. One theory is that a young girl's body, which is undergoing a growth spurt itself, will compete with the developing fetus for nutrients. Indeed, babies of teenage mothers may be at risk; they suffer a higher incidence of infant mortality and a greater likelihood of mental deficiencies after birth. It is now believed, however, that these risks are not associated solely with the age of the mother. Teenage mothers are more likely to live in poverty, and hence have poor medical care and fewer nutritional resources. These factors likely account for many of the problems of fetal development among teenage mothers. When adequate prenatal care is provided, teenage mothers are more similar to older mothers in the outcomes of their pregnancies (Fraser, Brockert, & Ward, 1995; Roosa, 1984).

Teenage pregnancies occur in all cultures and socioeconomic groups. However, the newborns of low-income teenage mothers from historically under-represented populations may be most at risk. Because poor health care and nutrition are a major threat to fetal development in teenage pregnancy, the economic and cultural barriers to medical and nutritional services for some cultural groups create special problems for poor young mothers and their fetuses.

There is a need to provide education about human sexuality, birth control, pregnancy, health care, and nutrition well before young women are at risk of becoming pregnant. (Potential young fathers also need these programs!) Some experts have advocated extensive health programs in late elementary or early middle school (Rodriguez & Moore, 1995). Not only would such programs address health and nutrition concerns, but they are likely to reduce the incidence of teen pregnancy altogether (Mauldon & Luker, 1996). In addition, culturally sensitive health clinics within middle and high schools and community centers may help to break down barriers to prenatal care for teenagers who do become pregnant.

Although teenage pregnancies more often result in medical complications for poor and under-represented cultural groups, there may be greater support within families for young mothers of these populations. Several generations often live together in families of traditionally oppressed peoples (Harrison, Wilson, Pine, Chan, & Buriel, 1990). For example, three to four times as many African-American children as Anglo children have grandparents living in their homes (U.S. Bureau of the Census, 1998). Grandparents of historically under-represented groups have been found to be more involved than their white counterparts in the lives of their grandchildren (Cherlin & Furstenberg, 1986). Grandmothers in some cultures provide special support in prenatal, perinatal (during birth), and postnatal care (Pearson, Hunter, Ensminger, & Kellam, 1990). They may guide young mothers in eating well and preparing for childbirth. Teenage mothers and their newborns suffer fewer problems of development when they live with their parents before, during, and after birth (Sahler, 1983). Grandmothers not only contribute to positive experiences during pregnancy and birthing for their teenage daughters, but play a critical parenting and parent educator role within extended families (Pearson et al., 1990).

CHILDBIRTH

After 9 months of prenatal development, a series of complex physical reactions takes place and the birth process begins. Muscular contractions in the mother's body work to thin and open the cervix—the lower part of the uterus—so that the baby can be pushed into the birth canal. Eventually, the baby is expelled through the vagina; shortly after, the placenta is expelled as well. There are three distinct stages in the childbirth process: dilation, expulsion of the fetus, and expulsion of the placenta.

The longest stage of **labor** is dilation, in which continuous contractions prepare the cervix for delivery. The contractions begin at regular intervals, perhaps 15 to 20 minutes apart, and become more frequent and intense. The increasing intensity of contractions can cause significant discomfort to the mother. As the cervix dilates, the amnion—the fluid-filled sack surrounding the fetus—ruptures, letting out the fluid. When this occurs, it is said that the mother's "water has broken."

Contractions continue for an average of 12 to 14 hours for first births and 4 to 6 hours for subsequent deliveries. Near the end of this stage, mothers experience a particularly intense period of labor called transition, during which the cervix is stretched around the baby's head.

Expulsion of the fetus is a much shorter stage of labor, usually less than an hour for first births and half an hour for subsequent deliveries. During this stage, the mother experiences the infamous "urge to push," an involuntary and unrelenting need to push the baby out with abdominal muscles. The mother's pushing, coupled with continued contractions, moves the baby down the birth canal and out of the vagina into the world.

The moment they are born, babies immediately exhale and often begin to cry. Once they are breathing, their dependence on nutrients through the placenta has ended. The placenta is cut and clamped and they begin their lives independent from the mother's body.

The arrival of a new baby distracts most parents from the shortest and final stage of labor: expulsion of the placenta. During the 5- or 10-minute wait for the placenta to detach from the uterine wall and be expelled, new parents are usually holding and caressing their baby. Perhaps they are also engaging in friendly disputes about family resemblances and name choices.

The entire birthing process is illustrated in Figure 4-2.

Western Childbirth Procedures

Modern technology has given rise to a set of standard medical procedures used frequently in hospital births in Western societies. These include the fetal monitor, which measures fetal heart rate and detects distress, and anesthesia, medication to ease the mother's discomfort. During many Western births, an episiotomy is performed just before the expulsion of the fetus. This involves making a small incision in the vagina to avoid tearing during delivery. **Forceps** are sometimes used to assist in difficult labors during the expulsion of the fetus; these are large metal tongs that are fitted around the newborn's head to gently ease the baby from the birth canal. A vacuum extractor—a device that pulls the baby from the birth canal by applying a suction to the scalp—is being employed more frequently, as it is believed to be safer for the newborn. In some instances, a cesarean section is performed, in which the newborn is surgically removed from the uterus through the abdomen. The usual reason for a cesarean is fetal distress, although some physicians routinely perform these for mothers who have previously given birth in this manner.

Concern has been raised about whether some of these procedures are needed. There is some evidence that anesthesia or forcep deliveries can lead to complications after birth (Rosenblith, 1992). The use of a fetal monitor may result in more cesareans, as medical personnel may misread typical fluctuations in heart rate as signs of distress (Quilligan, 1995). This is a problem because a cesarean is major abdominal surgery which carries risks and may greatly impede the mother's recovery and ability to parent during the period directly following birth. These concerns have led some parents to demand more "natural" approaches to childbirth.

The "natural childbirth" movement has flourished in the United States over the last few decades. More and more parents are asking that birthing be comfortable, family-oriented, and non-medical. A number of specific "innovations" have found their way into American hospitals. Many of these have actually been practiced across many cultures for centuries. Western hospitals are now providing "birthing rooms"— cozy, home-like spaces where mothers and family members can feel more at ease dur-

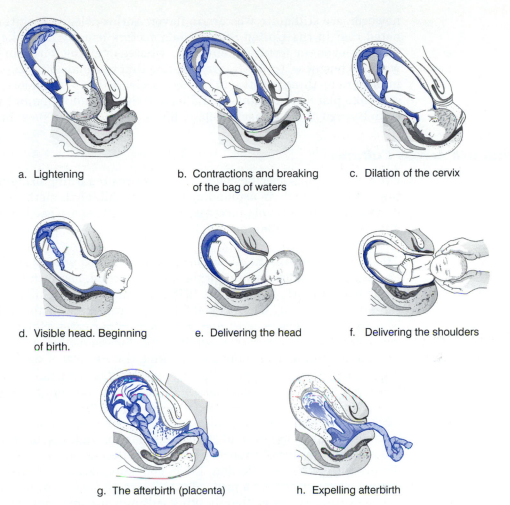

a. Lightening

b. Contractions and breaking of the bag of waters

c. Dilation of the cervix

d. Visible head. Beginning of birth.

e. Delivering the head

f. Delivering the shoulders

g. The afterbirth (placenta)

h. Expelling afterbirth

FIGURE 4–2   Labor and delivery advance in steps. Labor involves processes shown in views a, b, and c. The stages of birth are shown in views d through f.

SOURCE: Schiamberg, L. B. (1988). *Child and Adolescent Development.* Upper Saddle River, NJ: Macmillan. Reprinted by permission.

ing the birth process. Most have adopted policies that allow—and often encourage— fathers to observe and participate in labor and delivery.

Two physicians whose writings have directly influenced natural childbirth practices in this country are Ferdinand Lamaze and Frederick Leboyer. Lamaze (1958) first introduced the notion that mothers be prepared for birth through education and exercise. He suggested a series of breathing techniques to use during labor which would at once relax and focus the mother and "oxygenate" the baby. He also was one of the earliest Western writers to advocate that fathers or other companions play a key role in the birth process. Leboyer (1975) was most concerned about treatment of the newborn immediately after birth. He noted that delivery rooms were traditionally loud and bright, and proposed dimming lights, reducing sound, and providing newborns with warm baths and much skin-to-skin contact with parents.

Many of these ideas resemble childbirth beliefs and traditions of non-Western cultures or those of earlier eras. Some of these recent natural childbirth trends, however, are still quite Western in flavor. Anthropologist Brigitt Jordan (1983) has noted that in the United States, male doctors usually make key decisions in the process, even in natural deliveries, whereas "giving birth in most societies is women's business" (p. 3). (It is interesting that two male physicians are the pioneers in modern birthing practice in Western society!) The vast majority of natural births still take place in hospitals in the United States and in many European countries (U.S. Bureau of the Census, 1994). This is not the case in most other societies.

Childbirth Across Cultures

Every culture has specific beliefs and practices regarding bringing new babies into the world. Although an astounding variety in childbirth methods exists, all cultures provide a common set of processes and supports that are needed to ensure a healthy and joyous delivery (Jordan, 1983).

The Joy of Childbirth. All cultures value the birth process as a momentous event. Reasons reported for celebrating the birth of a child, however, vary from one cultural group to another (L. W. Hoffman, 1975). In some families, children are seen as future caretakers for elderly mothers and fathers, so parents view the birth of a baby as the beginning of lifelong comfort and security. In other cases, childbirth has special religious significance or carries a certain status for the mother in the community. Sometimes a newborn may be hailed as ensuring the survival of the family lineage. Childbirth is a joyous event in all cultures; a new baby is almost always seen as a source of happiness and affection, regardless of the associated economic or emotional challenges.

Childbirth Support. In all cultures, some person (or persons) is responsible for educating the new mother and supporting her through the birth process. The background and training of support persons vary, depending on how a particular culture defines the birth event (Jordan, 1983). For example, in the United States, childbirth is most often considered a medical process, so physicians or medically trained practitioners support the mother. In other cultures, non-medical personnel are primary supports. These may include "non-specialists" such as family members, neighbors, or friends. The United States is one of the few countries in the world where non-family, non-medical support persons have not been regularly included in the birth process (Lieberman & Ryan, 1989). However, this trend is changing.

In many cultures, births are attended by **midwives,** childbirth specialists (usually women) who, by virtue of their own experience and perhaps some medical training, have been assigned this role in the community. In the Yucatán, midwives are responsible for assisting with almost all births. Midwives are well respected in Yucatán towns, as Jordan (1983) describes: "There is no particular deference in her interactions with medical doctors. She acknowledges their expertise in certain areas . . . but she is also aware of her own special expertise" (p. 14). Other support persons are always present during delivery in the Yucatán: the mother and father, family members, neighbors, and friends of the woman giving birth. These individuals come and go during labor, taking turns providing support.

A growing number of American births include a midwife, although attending physicians generally maintain direct control over the process (Eskes, 1992). In some subcultures of the United States, childbirth support comes exclusively from family or community members because of a lack of resources. Onnie Lee Logan (1991), a "granny midwife" in Mobile, Alabama, until 1984, delivered countless babies in her

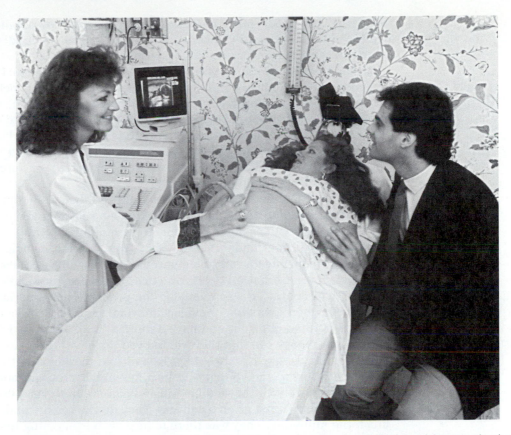

In all cultures, there is a person who is responsible for educating a new mother and supporting her through the birth process.

low-income African-American community without any medical support, because none was available: "Let me tell you about white doctors at this time. I don't think they paid too much attention to black families then, because the spirit of white people didn't go out for the black people. They didn't care" (p. 56). In this case, a non-medical childbirth support system emerged in the community as a result of poverty and prejudice. It appears to have been an effective system; since granny midwifery was outlawed in Alabama in 1984, maternal and infant death rates have climbed in the state (Logan, 1991). One reason could be that mothers in rural towns are now required to drive hours to reach hospitals for obstetric care.

Childbirth Education and Preparation. All societies have some provision for preparing mothers for childbirth, although the length and nature of this preparation vary. In the United States, preparation for childbirth is formal and extensive. Not only do obstetricians and hospitals provide education, but many families participate in Lamaze classes or other programs of childbirth preparation. In these classes, mothers are taught about nutrition and the physical stages of labor. They practice breathing exercises that will assist with the discomfort of contractions. Education is critical, according to Lamaze (1958), because knowledge of the process reduces fear and helps the mother to relax during labor. Fathers or other "birthing coaches" are sometimes trained in childbirth classes as well. Such childbirth classes are attended primarily by middle-class parents. Twenty percent of pregnant mothers in the United States—primarily those in poverty—receive no childbirth preparation (or prenatal care) at all (Jordan, 1983; Klerman, 1991a).

In the Yucatán, childbirth preparation is brief and informal. It usually takes place during labor (Jordan, 1983). This may be partly because of a belief that childbirth is necessarily frightening and painful. Extensive preparation aimed at convincing mothers otherwise would be pointless. In fact, women come to believe, through stories passed down for generations, that pain is an expected and normal part of bringing children into the world—the experience that sets women apart from men. Fathers are encouraged to attend the delivery, primarily to appreciate the suffering required to bring a child into the world.

The Yucatán midwife may make several pre-labor visits to the pregnant mother to ascertain the due date and give a *sobada*—a soothing abdominal massage. However, most instructions about birthing are given during childbirth itself. Lessons are provided by all in attendance: midwife, family, friends, or neighbors; no one person is solely responsible for informing parents about what is occurring.

When Onnie Lee Logan (1991) practiced midwifery in Mobile, virtually no formal childbirth preparation was available for poor African-American families. Granny midwives, when available, provided informal childbirth preparation methods: "In those days I had to go out and have a meetin' with 'em befo' I delivered their baby. When they engage you that they wanted you to deliver their baby, you in turns would have to make from two to three trips to visit that mother to outline things, to see how the situation was goin' on, and to he'p her make preparations" (p. 92). Midwives' preparations went far beyond birthing education, however: "When they go on a delivery, they didn't just go on a delivery. They do the cookin' and washin'. It wasn't so much the midwifin'. They was there to he'p with everything they could" (p. 52).

Childbirth Procedures. Delivery practices also vary by culture. In a typical American birth, parents are provided with a pleasant, home-like birthing room in a hospital, where they will stay throughout labor and delivery (Lieberman & Ryan, 1989). This is in contrast to earlier practice, whereby mothers were moved from a labor room into a sterile, bright delivery room to give birth. Today the typical American mother strives to take as few medications as possible during labor, although some do request anesthesia if contractions become too painful. Others receive pitocin, a drug to stimulate labor, if the cervix is not dilating quickly. American hospitals place a great value on speed of delivery. Doctors often administer pitocin after what would be judged a very short period of time in some cultures (Jordan, 1983).

During labor, the mother is accompanied by a "coach." This is usually the father, although sometimes it is a childbirth educator or friend. Hospitals usually limit the number of persons in attendance. The coach guides the mother in breathing exercises during contractions and serves as an advocate. During the birth itself, mothers are usually asked to assume the flat-on-the-back "lithotomy" position. The United States is the only country in the world where mothers historically have been asked to lie down to give birth (Jordan, 1983). Some hospitals now use birthing chairs or allow the mother to squat (Lieberman & Ryan, 1989).

During birth, an episiotomy is likely to be performed and forceps or a vacuum extractor may be used. These practices may be other signs of time urgency on the part of American medical personnel (Jordan, 1983). In many cultures, such procedures are virtually never performed. Delivery takes longer in these communities, but healthy babies are born.

After birth, American parents are allowed a "bonding" period with the newborn which lasts 20 minutes to an hour. The baby is then taken to the hospital nursery, examined, and washed. A number of medical procedures are followed. Many American hospitals now allow "rooming-in," in which the mother (and father) may keep the baby with them in their hospital room. When parents sleep, the newborn is usually returned to the nursery.

In the Yucatán, mothers give birth in their own homes surrounded by neighbors and family and a community midwife. A blanket screen is provided for privacy, but this does not isolate the mother completely from the ongoing activities of the household. The mother is in control of decision-making during labor and delivery; attendants are there only to support her. Medications are not administered to control pain, nor are breathing or relaxation techniques utilized. Mothers are taught to accept that childbirth is painful and are expected to express their discomfort in an outpouring of emotion.

At the time of delivery, the Yucatán mother lies semi-upright in a hammock. In most societies, mothers are upright in delivery; this position is reportedly more comfortable and the baby is expelled more easily (Jordan, 1983). During delivery, one of the support persons is positioned at the mother's head so that she can wrap her arms around this person for comfort and support. Other attendants gather around her. The midwife assists in the delivery, easing the baby out after the head has appeared. No modern tools or technology are used. Occasionally the midwife will bring medical instruments, such as a thermometer, a suction for mucus, or surgical scissors to cut the placenta. The midwife never performs episiotomies or forcep deliveries.

After birth, the Yucatán midwife does not treat the newborn in a particularly delicate way. The baby is passed from person to person, and the grandmother often holds and caresses the baby while the midwife sponges the mother. The baby stays with the family from this time on. Any formal medical evaluations are conducted within the family's home by a visiting physician or nurse (Jordan, 1983).

Onnie Lee Logan's (1991) midwife experiences were similar. With no medical instruments, medications, or medical personnel in attendance, childbirth among the poor in Mobile was natural by necessity. Birthing often took place in homes with no running water or heat. Usually the mother and her own mother attended. The father was only occasionally involved. During labor, the granny midwife's role was one of giving emotional support: "I'll tell you one thing that's very impo'tant that I do that the doctors don't do and the nurses doesn't do because they doesn't take time to do it. And that is I'm with my patients at all times with a smile and keepin' her feelin' good with kind words" (p. 32).

The childbirth techniques Logan describes, which were passed down from her mother, are only now finding their way into modern obstetric practice in hospitals: "During labor I keep them on their feet where in the hospital they buckle them down. I'd let my mother stay on her feet until she'd have to lay down" (1991, p. 141). About episiotomies, Logan writes, "I do all my work keepin' 'em from having lacerations and havin' to have stitches. That doctor would've took her in there and give her a long laceration to get the baby" (p. 142). Logan's strategy was to apply hot compresses, a technique that "I didn't get in class at the bo'd of health neither. It was given to me by God . . . and they dilate so good without me doin' any lacerations at all" (p. 142).

Logan writes about the advantages of an upright birthing position and hints at why the flat-on-the-back method is so popular among obstetricians: "There are so many women that want to have babies in that sittin' position. It's not unusual. It feels good. The mother gets mo' relief. Now it might not be mo' relief for you but it will be for her" (1991, p. 151). After birth, Logan's babies would stay with their parents at home. However, the poor conditions of the family residence were often cause for concern. She would clean the house and stoke the wood stove, even tear sheets to use as baby blankets if the family had none.

Sometimes Logan found herself playing unusual roles to support the newborn and the family. On one cold morning after a birth, representatives of a stove company arrived to repossess a wood stove—the family's only source of heat. Thankfully, she was there to intervene: "I said, 'You move that stove outa here I'm gonna have you arrested. . . . This lil infant just been born. . . . I'm gonna have you arrested for takin' all the heat from these po' people that they got" (1991, p. 107). The men agreed to leave the stove and return when the weather was warmer.

RESEARCH INTO PRACTICE

CRITICAL CONCEPT 1

Child development begins long before birth. Genetic information is passed on from ancestors through a miraculous series of chemical processes.

Application

Caregivers and parents should accept and appreciate some differences in temperament, physical growth, sociability, and intellectual competence as part of individual children's biological inheritance.

CRITICAL CONCEPT 2

Genetics alone does not explain how children will turn out; environment plays a role, even before birth. Environmental hazards can negatively influence prenatal development. Health of the mother is critical.

Application #1

Mothers should abstain from alcohol, tobacco, and other drugs during pregnancy. Even common over-the-counter or prescription drugs should not be used without guidance from a physician.

Application #2

Mothers should eat healthy foods during pregnancy. The developing fetus acquires nutrients directly from the mother's diet. A poorly nourished mother will give birth to a poorly nourished baby.

Application #3

Caregivers should assist low-income and teenage mothers in accessing adequate health care and nutritional services during pregnancy. They should maintain relationships with the local WIC office and other social service agencies that provide prenatal care and support.

CRITICAL CONCEPT 3

The childbirth process itself can influence growth of the newborn. Complications at birth can lead to poor infant development.

Application #1

Parents and families should become knowledgeable about the birthing process. Childbirth preparation classes or other childbirth education activities are important. Most societies have some form of birthing preparation.

Application #2

Arranging for support during labor and delivery will assist the mother physically and emotionally. In most societies, a spouse, parent, friend, or village midwife attends the birth of a child.

Application #3

Giving birth without the use of drugs is a goal in many societies. Using Lamaze techniques or other relaxation and natural pain-reduction methods will reduce the need for medication during labor and delivery.

CRITICAL CONCEPT 4

There is cultural variation in genetics, including the prevalence of genetic diseases. Some genetic disorders, such as sickle-cell anemia and Tay-Sachs disease, are more prevalent in certain cultural groups.

Application #1

Prenatal genetic tests, such as amniocentesis or chorionic villus biopsy (to be described in the next chapter), are recommended for parents within high-risk cultural groups. Findings of these tests can determine the presence of disorders.

Application #2

Genetic counseling will assist parents of high-risk families. In such counseling, professionals help parents to determine the odds of transmitting genetic diseases to their offspring. Such counseling can also prepare parents whose developing fetus has been diagnosed with genetic disorders.

CRITICAL CONCEPT 5

For certain cultural groups, prenatal development and childbirth are influenced by barriers to medical care.

Application #1

Social service workers, teachers, and caregivers must advocate for adequate and culturally sensitive health care and nutritional services for pregnant mothers.

Application #2

Medical personnel must be sensitive to alternative medical beliefs and practices among cultural groups, including diverse childbirth preparation and practices.

Application #3

Medical personnel must be sensitive to the anxieties and unique emotional needs of pregnant mothers of diverse cultural backgrounds.

Application #4

Medical institutions must provide personnel who can speak the native languages of families in the community.

Application #5

Caregivers, other professionals, and family members should be encouraged to accompany pregnant mothers on health care visits or during delivery.

SUGGESTED ACTIVITIES

1. Interview a mother or couple who are expecting a baby. Ask about childbirth preparations and plans for childbirth itself. Write an analysis of your interview, guided by the following questions:

   a. What plans do these parents have for childbirth preparation, birthing support, and childbirth procedures?

   b. In what ways do these plans reflect traditional Western childbirth practices? In what ways are these less typical of American birthing methods?

   c. To what degree do culture, family background, and socioeconomic status influence their childbirth plans?

2. Make arrangements to visit a nursery at a local hospital. Observe, through the viewing window, how newborns are cared for. Write an analysis of your experience, guided by the following questions:

   a. What procedures did you observe for the care of newborns? What would you guess is the purpose of each?

   b. Contrast the experiences of newborns in a modern American hospital which you have observed with those of newborns in the Yucatán and rural Alabama, as described in this chapter. What advantages did you see to hospital births? What disadvantages?

3. Interview a physician or nurse working in a community health clinic to ask about cultural and socioeconomic barriers to health care. Write an analysis, guided by the following questions:

   a. What does the interviewee see as the major barriers to health care among the population served?

   b. To what degree do answers reflect the interviewee's sensitivity to diverse cultural beliefs and health practices?

   c. How would you assess the interviewee's commitment to and strategies for reducing cultural barriers to adequate health care?

CHAPTER 5

The Newborn

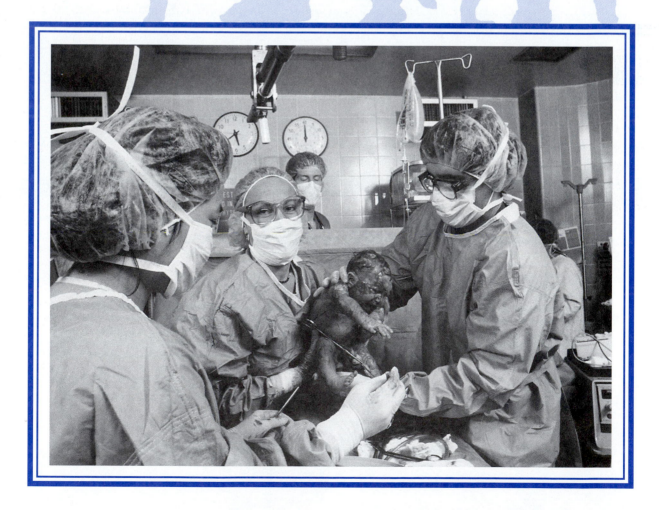

THIS CHAPTER EXAMINES THE CHARACTERISTICS AND DEVELOPMENT OF NEWBORN BABIES. During the first few weeks after birth—sometimes called the neonatal period—infants have a unique look, sound, and feel. They are more helpless, fragile, and dependent than they will ever be again. Their needs for nurturance and sustenance seem endless. Some new parents are not fully prepared for life with a neonate, as the following story illustrates:

Yolanda, a 16-year-old, is about to become a new mother. Throughout pregnancy and during a rough labor and delivery, all she can think about is how wonderful her life will be as a parent. Her son will be the smartest, happiest baby, she asserts. He will love her and care for her as he gets older; she is his mother! Her friends will come by to admire him as he smiles and coos. She and her son will play games and spend all waking hours outside of school together.

When Yolanda is discharged from the hospital, she goes to her parents' home, where she and her son will live until she finishes high school. On the first day out of the hospital, her son just sleeps. She is disappointed that he is not awake and playful. She wants him to get to know her; she wants to tickle, rock, and hold him. These are the things that mothers and babies should do together, she thinks. However, he just sleeps. "Don't worry, girl. You'll have plenty of time to be together," her mother says with a knowing look.

In the late afternoon, her baby wakes but only cries. He is inconsolable. Yolanda tries feeding and rocking. Nothing seems to work. He is crying so hard now that his tiny chin begins to tremble. She thinks surely this is a sign of some serious illness. She looks to her mother for help. "Some babies just cry like that," her mother says with a comforting smile.

The nighttime is even worse. Her son awakens many times. By morning, Yolanda is tired, worried, and disbelieving that this is now her life. The romantic images of motherhood have vanished. Then, her son gazes into her eyes as she feeds him. Holding her warm little son somehow makes up for all the hours of anxiety and fatigue.

This young mother has learned that newborns have unique needs and dispositions. Their repertoire of play activities is extremely limited; they mostly sleep, cry,
and eat. As this young mother found out, life with a newborn is a challenging yet
emotionally satisfying experience.

NEWBORN APPEARANCE

Newborn babies are quite striking in appearance. They are remarkably small. Great
poets and essayists have for centuries attempted to capture in rhyme and verse the
absolute tininess of newborns—their minuscule fingers and toes, their delicate, wee
bodies. The sheer smallness of a newborn can be quite startling to unprepared parents. Some perfectly healthy babies can weigh as little as 5 pounds, so small they
could be held in one hand!

Most **neonates** have puffy facial features; their eyes may look particularly
swollen. One parent who is fond of sports analogies suggested that his newborn baby
looked like a prize fighter who had just gone 12 rounds. This puffiness is due to an
accumulation of fluids in the head when the baby assumed a head-down position before and during birth. The puffiness fades in the first few days after birth.

Contributing to the newborn's interesting appearance is a condition called *molding,* in which the head is squeezed and misshaped during the trip through the
mother's relatively small birth canal. Some babies' heads are so distorted in the
process that parents become alarmed. However, babies' heads resume their usual
rounded shape very quickly within the first few days after birth. How can this
squeezing occur without causing damage to the newborn? Before and after birth, babies' bones consist mainly of cartilage and hence are very soft. A newborn's head also
has an open space between the bone tissue called the **fontanelle.** This allows the
baby's head to safely compress during birth. Babies whose heads are even an inch or
two larger than the mother's pelvis can be born without complication.

At birth, newborns are often covered with a white, waxy substance called vernix
caseosa. This is secreted from glands around hair follicles and forms a protective
coating and lubricant that smooths the baby's passage down the birth canal.

The body of the newborn is oddly proportioned. The relative size of neonatal body
parts reveals growth patterns that will guide development throughout early childhood.
One of these growth patterns is the **cephalocaudal growth gradient,** which refers
to the tendency of human development to proceed from the top down. Infants' and children's heads (and brains!) grow more rapidly than their legs and feet. Nowhere is this
more obvious than in the newborn. At birth, babies' heads are disproportionately huge.
Because of this, when parents hold newborns they must give careful support to the
head, which wobbles on less-well-developed neck muscles. The top-heaviness of newborns as compared to older children and adults is illustrated in Figure 5-1.

Another growth pattern which is obvious in the newborn is the **proximodistal
growth gradient,** which refers to a growth trend that proceeds from the center of
the body out. Infants' and children's trunks develop more rapidly than their ap-
pendages; large movements precede refined use of fingers or toes. Newborns' "pot-
bellied" appearance is due to this proximodistal pattern. Their trunks and internal
organs grow most rapidly while their legs, arms, hands, and feet remain relatively
small and less developed.

The way newborns look may play a critical role in their development. Their tiny,
disproportionate features suggest helplessness and vulnerability, which could prompt
human parents to nurture and protect them. Lorenz (1971) has proposed that "baby-

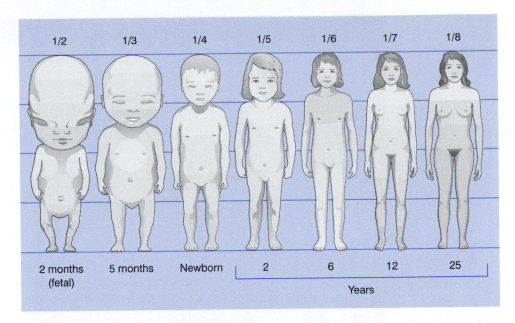

| | | | | | | |
| 1/2 | 1/3 | 1/4 | 1/5 | 1/6 | 1/7 | 1/8 |

| 2 months (fetal) | 5 months | Newborn | 2 | 6 | 12 | 25 |

Years

FIGURE 5-1 The cephalocaudal growth gradient—the tendency to develop from the top down—is obvious in the body proportions of newborns, children, and adults.
SOURCE: Schiamberg, L. B. (1988). *Child and Adolescent Development*. Upper Saddle River, NJ: Macmillan. Reprinted by permission.

ish features" trigger a "nurturing impulse" in both human and nonhuman adults. His theory is stated most pragmatically by an exhausted father who had been up all night with his crying newborn: "She was asleep, then she was awake. Asleep, awake. If she hadn't been quite so cute, I never would have put myself through this ordeal."

DIVERSITY IN NEWBORN STATES

Newborns engage in a relatively limited number of experiences during their first days of life; they watch the world go by, cry on occasion, and sleep a great deal. These various experiences have been categorized into what child specialists call psychological states (J. C. Harris, 1995; Michelsson, Rinne, & Paajanen, 1990). These states are listed in Table 5-1. Each is described in relation to how aroused and alert the infant is. As can be seen in the table, three of these are sleeping states. How much time newborns spend in specific states and how rapidly, predictably, and good-naturedly they shift from one state to another will vary from one infant to another. Significant differences in infant state patterns exist across cultures.

Sleeping

Newborns spend a significant portion of their lives sleeping. Excited first-time parents or grandparents, eager to get to know a little newcomer, will express disappointment at how few waking hours there are to talk or play. In the first weeks of life, a baby may sleep between 16 and 20 hours in each 24-hour period (Bamford et al., 1990; Whitney & Thoman, 1994). Unfortunately for tired parents, these hours of sleep are not continuous; in fact, new babies usually take brief naps of about 4 hours,

TABLE 5-1
Newborn
Psychological
States

State	Characteristics
Sleep	Newborns' eyes are closed. They are not aroused or stimulated by moderate noise or other sensations. Newborns are in a sleep state for the vast majority of a 24-hour period.
Regular Sleep	Newborns exhibit no movements; their eyes are still. Breathing is regular, slow, and quiet.
REM Sleep	Newborns twitch, whimper, and grimace. Their eyes can be seen moving beneath closed lids. The brain is particularly active during this state.
Drowsiness	Newborns are in a state between sleep and wakefulness. They are still and quiet; their eyes open and close. They can be roused into full wakefulness by stimulation. Newborns are often in this state before sleep.
Alert	Newborns are quiet and attentive to stimuli. They intensely study persons and objects around them. It is believed that in this state newborns come to learn about their world.
Awake and active	Newborns are highly active. They flail their limbs and turn their heads in gross, global movements. It is believed that in this state newborns acquire motor abilities.
Crying	Newborns emit loud, distressing sounds. They flail limbs; their faces are often contorted. Different cries have been identified—those which communicate hunger, pain and anger.

SOURCE: Michelsson, Rinne, & Paajanen, 1990; Wolff, 1966.

followed by periods of wakefulness. Needless to say, full nights of sleep are a thing of the past for parents of newborns.

Sleep may be one way that infants take breaks from the barrage of overwhelming stimuli in their new worlds. In one study, researchers found that infant stress is reduced during sleep (Larson, Gunnar, & Hertsgaard, 1991). Babies in this research were found to have less cortisol—a chemical produced under stressful conditions—in their saliva following nap time. (Interestingly, this lower level of cortisol was also found in babies after a long car ride, even if they did not sleep during the trip!) Environmental conditions that prohibit sleep, such as loud noise or a lack of adequate space or time for naps in child care, may put young babies at risk.

As infants get older, they tend to sleep for longer continuous periods and remain awake for more extended intervals as well. By 6 or 7 months, many babies begin sleeping for a full night. Not all infants are aware that this is how they are to behave, however; my son, for example, did not quite master the art of sleeping through the night until age 5! In fact, an "average" infant may not truly exist with regard to sleep patterns. Tremendous individual variation in sleeping routines exists within all cultures (Bamford et al., 1990; J. C. Harris, 1995). Some children sleep for long periods right after birth; some sleep infrequently, even into childhood.

What causes sleep pattern variation? Babies may be born with "biological clocks" that regulate cycles of eating and sleeping. Evidence of this comes from studies showing that day-night rhythms can be identified in early infancy and remain constant through the first year of life (Bamford et al., 1990). Although pediatricians or grandparents may offer advice on sleep problems (e.g., "Let her cry it out when she wakes up at night," or "Respond quickly during the first 6 months, then he'll sleep securely during the second 6"), no amount of strategizing can dissuade a newborn from following his or her genetically wired time clock.

Another source of variation in newborn sleep patterns is culture. Parents of diverse ethnic backgrounds adopt very different practices in regard to sleeping arrangements. In many families in Africa, India, Okinawa, the Philippines, and Mexico, for example, babies sleep with a mother or grandmother for over a full year after birth (Goldberg, 1977; B. B. Whiting & Edwards, 1988). This is true of several under-represented ethnic groups within the United States, as well (Bornstein, 1995; Chisholm, 1983; Powell, 1983). Some Korean-American children, for example, will sleep with their mothers until age 5 (Yu & Kim, 1983). Although these sleeping practices are sometimes misunderstood by people of Euro-American cultures, they are quite typical of other cultural groups around the world. Sleeping situations may have an impact on infant sleep-wake patterns. Infants who sleep next to their mothers, for example, may have their needs for comfort or hunger met immediately without significant arousal from sleep. Those who sleep in another room or whose parents hold back from responding to nighttime crying may be more likely aroused from sleep.

It is interesting to note from Table 5-1 that there is not just one kind of sleep; infants experience several different sleep states. Perhaps the most fascinating and puzzling of these is irregular sleep, during which **rapid eye movement (REM)** sleep occurs. REM sleep is one of life's great mysteries. In this sleep state, the brain is especially active; adults often dream during REM. Infants in REM sleep twitch, whimper, and grimace, while in regular sleep they are passive and motionless. Even more mysterious is the fact that babies are in REM sleep for much longer periods than adults; over 30% of a newborn's life is spent in this sleep state (J. C. Harris, 1995; Roffwarg, Muzio, & Dement, 1966; Whitney & Thoman, 1994).

Why do babies spend so much time in REM sleep? The *autostimulation theory* holds that REM sleep exercises the nervous system. Newborns need stimulation but spend very little time awake; therefore, their brains provide much-needed internal stimulation while they are in REM sleep. Research supports this theory. One study found that when babies spent more time awake, their REM sleep periods were reduced (Boismier, 1977).

Alert and Waking Activity States

Most child psychologists agree that alert and waking states are most critical for infant development. It is during these periods that babies explore their world and exercise their senses and motor abilities. One argument for soothing crying babies very quickly is that in calmer waking states they are able to learn more about their new world and the people in it (Moss, Colombo, Mitchell, & Horowitz, 1988). In order to spend useful time in alert and waking states, then, babies must be able to soothe themselves or be soothed by parents when they are upset. Infants who are in a crying state for inordinate amounts of time or who are easily drawn from quiet, alert activity to extreme upset may not benefit from the same level of cognitive and social stimulation.

The length of time babies spend in waking and alert states and their ability to return to these states quickly after upset varies across cultures. Biological factors as well as differences in parenting practices may account for these variations (Garcia Coll, 1990). Chinese-American, Japanese-American, Puerto Rican, and Navajo infants have been found to spend particularly long periods of time in quiet, alert states (Chisholm, 1983; Freedman, 1974; Garcia Coll, Meyer, & Brillon, 1995). Infants of these ethnic groups have also been found to be more easily soothed or better able to console themselves when upset, and they are less easily perturbed when alert and active.

In one study, babies of diverse backgrounds were presented with a variety of objects, pictures, and sounds. Puerto Rican babies were more alert when these stimuli were presented. They could more easily follow the direction of both moving objects and sounds. In contrast to other subjects in the study, Puerto Rican babies virtually never cried, even when stimulation was increased (Garcia Coll, Sepkoski, & Lester, 1981). In other research, Caucasian newborns have been found to be more easily perturbed and excitable, and African-American babies have been observed to spend more time than babies of other cultural groups in motor activities during waking states (Freedman, 1974; Garcia Coll et al., 1981).

What is the importance of these cultural comparisons? Differences in state patterns may explain why parents of different cultures interact with their babies in different ways. Navajo children are quiet and alert much of the time, and their parents are passive and less verbal in their interactions with them (Chisholm, 1983; Garcia Coll, 1990). Euro-American babies may become upset more easily during waking periods; mothers of these cultural groups are found to respond more quickly and often to crying and fussiness (Richman, Miller, & Levine, 1992). African-American babies are more motorically active during waking hours, and their mothers spend much time in physical play with them (Garcia Coll, 1990; Hale, 1994). Adults must strive for a good fit between these unique state patterns and their interactions with babies.

Crying

Crying is the universal way that babies communicate their needs. Adults of both genders, of all ages, and of all cultural groups—whether or not they have children of their own—become troubled or agitated by infant crying (Humphry & Hock, 1989; Murray, 1985). Even newborn babies become upset at the cries of other infants (Murray, 1979; Reich, 1986). It may be that concern about crying is a part of human biological heritage.

Parents report that they can accurately determine what their baby is communicating through crying. Unique cries to communicate hunger, anger, pain, and a need for attention have been identified by parents and researchers (Wolff, 1969). However, parents may be relying more on context than the features of crying to determine what babies need. When an infant hasn't eaten in a long while and cries, a parent is likely to accurately guess that hunger is the problem. In one study, when parents were played a tape recording of various infant cries, they were far less able to identify which needs were being communicated (Green, Jones & Gustafson, 1987). What parents can do very well is distinguish their own infant's cries from those of other infants (Wiesenfeld, Malatesta, & DeLoache, 1981). They can also very accurately distinguish urgent cries, which are loud and long, from less urgent ones (E. F. Zeskind, Sale, Maio, Huntington, & Weiseman, 1985).

How do parents respond to infant cries? Parents in all cultures take action in some way when their babies are upset. The outdated belief that responding too often to babies' cries will spoil them has been refuted by research. In a classic study by S. M. Bell and Ainsworth (1972), children were actually found to cry less in the second 6 months of life if their mothers responded consistently during the first 6 months. These authors suggest there may be a later payoff for early responsive parenting.

Perhaps the most fascinating finding of this research was that infants of responsive mothers were more advanced in communication abilities at age 1. This finding

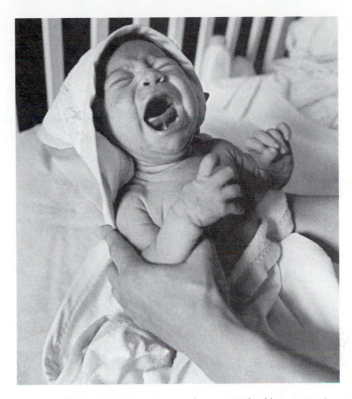

Crying is a universal way that newborns communicate needs. How parents respond to crying varies across cultures.

supports the notion that crying is communication; if mothers respond to cries, their babies may more often experience the power of vocalization. This research has led some professionals to urge parents to always respond to babies' cries quickly. However, this formula for infant care may be too simple. Bell and Ainsworth (1972) reported great variation within their "responsive" parent group in regard to how quickly and by what method mothers soothed their babies. Some mothers were immediate in picking babies up or feeding them; others waited a few minutes to respond. Their babies all cried less and communicated more effectively at age 1. In a replication of this study, Tavecchio and Izendoorn (1987) found that mothers who responded to some kinds of cries but not others (such as "fussy" cries) had babies who were equally well adjusted and communicative later in life. Further, responding was found to take many forms among the parents studied. They discovered that some important reactions to crying that had not previously been studied (e.g., talking to a baby from across the room) were useful parent responses.

Cross-cultural studies have suggested that patterns of responsiveness and crying vary significantly across families and ethnic groups. In some societies, for example, quick responding does not always lead to less crying, as Bell and Ainsworth (1972) have proposed. In research on Bedouin tribespeople in Israel, babies whose parents responded immediately to even minor whimpers or fussiness were found to cry a great deal during the first year of life (Landau, 1982). Constant crying and quick responses to it were viewed as part of cultural tradition within this society. This study raises questions about whether "responding quickly" to newborn cries means the same thing in all cultures. It also suggests that excessive crying may not be viewed as an altogether bad thing within some societies.

Infant crying can serve as a tool for diagnosis of newborn health. Babies' cries have certain common acoustical properties—that is, typical crying has a certain pitch, volume, and duration. Variations in these properties may indicate problems. For example, unusually high-pitched crying and cries that are short in duration have been associated with Down syndrome, encephalitis, undernutrition, and various forms of brain damage (Huntington, Hans, & Zeskind, 1990; Lester, 1987).

BREASTFEEDING AND CULTURE

When babies are not sleeping, crying, or gazing out at the world, they are eating. Newborns eat frequently, consuming small "snacks" as often as every 2 hours. Before pasteurization of cow's milk, babies in all societies of the world were breastfed. Mothers of wealthy families who chose not to breastfeed their infants would hire wet nurses to do so (Zigler & Finn-Stevenson, 1993). Only in recent times has bottle feeding become an option.

Most newborn babies in the world still breastfeed (Ryan, Rush, Krieger, & Lewandowski, 1991). Breastfeeding is most prevalent in less-developed countries. In Papua, New Guinea, for example, breast milk substitutes are only available by prescription. In Iran, breastfeeding is considered one of the "rights" of infancy (Hull & Simpson, 1985). It is also true that children from non-Western countries are likely to be breastfed for longer periods before weaning (Levine, 1977). Babies in rural Africa are usually not weaned until after age 2.

In industrialized societies, mothers began using bottle-fed formula around the turn of the century. By 1966 only 18% of American mothers were breastfeeding; bottle feeding was viewed as a sign of modernization (Guthrie, 1986). There has since been a revival of breastfeeding in the United States, with over half of mothers in recent years choosing to breastfeed their newborns (Ryan et al., 1991). Breastfeeding in America varies by culture and socioeconomic status. Middle-class Euro-American mothers are most likely to breastfeed; poor mothers of African-American or Latino backgrounds, less likely (MacGowan et al., 1991).

New evidence suggests that breastfeeding can be beneficial to newborns' health. Mothers are believed to become attached to their babies through breastfeeding interactions (R. Lawrence, 1991). Also, mother's milk and, particularly, colostrum—a clear yellow fluid that is produced before breast milk during the first days after birth—are believed to retard the growth of certain bacteria and to serve as an important immunological agent for babies (J. E. Brown, 1995). Many pediatricians now recommend breastfeeding, even if only for the first few months after birth.

Concerns have been raised in recent decades about increases in the use of formula feeding in underdeveloped countries. Formula companies, facing shrinking Western markets, had begun to market their products in impoverished countries, touting bottle feeding as a modern alternative to breastfeeding. This tactic has had serious consequences. Not only is formula feeding costly to mothers with scarce resources, but it brings a risk of infection due to use of contaminated water and lack of proper sterilization (A. S. Cunningham, Jelliffe, & Jelliffe, 1991). Under pressure, companies have changed these marketing practices. However, bottle feeding has continued at a high rate in some of these impoverished communities (J. F. Steward et al., 1991).

REFLEXES

Babies engage in unique movements during the first few months of life. They often exhibit global wiggles, in which their whole body quivers even when only one part is stimulated. For example, tickling a newborn's big toe may cause the whole body to wiggle. This suggests that a newborn's movements are not differentiated; the infant cannot purposefully move just one body part or another. Some believe that the act of swaddling—wrapping the baby's entire body snugly in a blanket—is comforting because it stills these active, uncontrollable, whole-body movements.

Newborns engage in a variety of **reflexes**—involuntary movements that are built in to a baby's nervous system. A list of common reflexes, including descriptions and the course of their development, is provided in Table 5-2. These reflexes are part of human biological heritage; they are identical in newborns of all cultures.

As you can see in the table, some reflexes simply disappear with development. For example, the moro reflex—a movement in which the arms are thrown outward and hands clenched when there is a loud noise or sudden loss of support—diminishes between 4 and 6 months. Other reflexes may develop into purposeful actions as babies gain control over their bodies. For example, the rooting reflex, in which a

TABLE 5-2

Newborn Reflexes and Their Developmental Course

Reflex	Description	Developmental Course
Grasping	Newborn grasps tightly any object—such as a parent's finger—that is placed in the palm.	The reflex becomes less strong at about 4 months when the baby gains voluntary control over grasping. Grasp movements develop into fine motor abilities in later life.
Moro	The arms are outstretched and then pulled into the body in response to a loud noise or sudden loss of support.	The reflex disappears by 5 months.
Rooting	When a finger or nipple is rubbed against the cheek, the head is turned in that direction. The newborn opens the mouth and often sucks.	The reflex becomes less strong at 3 months when the baby gains voluntary control over head turning and searching for nourishment.
Sucking	The newborn sucks when an object comes in contact with the mouth. Sometimes the reflex is exercised in sleep, even without external stimulus.	The reflex becomes less strong at 3 months; the baby gains voluntary control over sucking. Sucking movements become refined; babies learn to adapt their mouths to various-size nipples and eventually to a cup.
Walking	The newborn takes steps when placed on a surface or against a step.	The reflex disappears at about 3 months. It is debated whether the reflex comprises important early practice for later walking.

baby involuntarily turns the head toward the source of a tickle on the cheek, and the sucking reflex, a rhythmic sucking that occurs when the mouth is stimulated, develop into complex voluntary acts necessary for eating. Babies learn quickly to voluntarily turn the head and accurately seek and find a nipple. They learn to suck more efficiently and to coordinate sucking with swallowing. Some reflexes, then, are absolutely crucial for survival.

Besides the survival functions of some reflexes, they can be an important diagnostic tool for pediatricians. Absent reflexes or those that persist when they should normally disappear are associated with a variety of problems, including brain damage. Premature infants have weaker reflexes at birth and are slower to lose them in later infancy (Beckwith & Rodning, 1991). Children living in poverty will often have weaker reflexes because of poor health status and low birth weight (Garcia Coll et al., 1988).

Reflexes may also serve as the basis for important early parent-infant play, as the following vignette reveals:

A father from the Yucatán has spent little time with his newborn; his wife, her mother, and a midwife have chased him from the room again and again. "The baby's going to sleep," they scold. "Don't bother her." At last the mother and others have stepped over to the cooking area, and he has a moment alone with the baby. He reaches down tentatively and anxiously strokes his tiny daughter's hand. She grasps on tightly to his finger with surprising quickness and strength. This sudden connection to his daughter is startling and wonderful. As he begins to gently wave his hand back and forth, the baby clings on. A huge grin crosses his face. "Little girl! Little girl!" he coos and laughs. This game continues for several minutes. At last his mother-in-law returns. "No!" she says. "Go away! You'll bother her!"

Here the grasp reflex has allowed an uncertain parent to have a unique play interaction with his daughter. Since newborns have a limited range of social behaviors, reflexes provide parents with an early, enjoyable, though perhaps primitive, interpersonal contact.

EXPLORATION AND HABITUATION

The word *exploration* often connotes the active and thoughtful study of the world. An explorer is a person who physically travels to new frontiers or into outer space. A scientist is said to explore complex phenomena using sophisticated knowledge and technology. Can newborns, who are unable to purposefully move and who have limited power to interpret the world, engage in exploration? Infant research suggests that they can. When a young baby gazes out at a parent or a mobile dangling over the crib, she is exploring the world. When another listens intently to the sounds of the family dog barking, he also is exploring the world. Not only do newborns perceive sights and sounds; they can recognize and distinguish among them. They have preferences for what they listen to and see. They get bored staring at objects or listening to sounds that are very familiar.

We know that babies are able to explore because of a phenomenon called **habituation.** When newborn babies study an object or a sound for a period of time, they appear to become familiar with it. The stimulus becomes less interesting and exciting to them; they may choose to look away at something else or they may show less excitement in their body movements. When this occurs, babies are said to have habituated to a particular stimulus. The occurrence of habituation means that very young infants can "know" about something; they become so familiar with its properties that they become disinterested. This explains why an infant's new toy may be exciting for a short period but then loses its appeal. It may also explain why a new noise, such as a dog's bark, may be upsetting to newborns at first but later go almost unnoticed.

Psychologists have taken advantage of habituation to study what babies know and are able to do. For example, much of what we know about newborn perception is based on a research technique that relies on habituation. Here's how it works: Let's say a group of researchers is eager to learn whether babies can distinguish their mother's voice from other adult voices. First, they provide newborns with a special nipple that records the frequency of their sucking. They discover that newborns suck especially rapidly when they are exposed to new sounds. Next, they play a tape of an unfamiliar female voice for each of their subjects. They find that babies initially suck wildly in response to this new stimulus. Over time, however, the infants become familiar with the voice; it no longer excites or captivates them, so their sucking slows down. In the middle of the experiment, the voice of each infant's own mother is suddenly played on the tape. The babies' sucking, which had significantly slowed, now increases sharply. In fact, they suck more rapidly in response to their mother's voice than to the stranger's. What can the researchers conclude? That babies must have been able to tell the difference between these voices, that they must "know" the unique features of their mothers' speech. This habituation research method has also been used to determine babies' abilities to see, touch, smell, taste, and feel motion.

Newborns of some cultural groups habituate faster to new sights and sounds. In several studies, for example, Chinese-American, Japanese-American, and Navajo infants were found to habituate more quickly than Euro-American babies (Freedman, 1974). In another investigation, African-American and Euro-American babies were found to habituate more rapidly than Puerto Rican babies (Garcia Coll et al., 1981). Puerto Rican infants of this study remained alert and active for longer periods of time when presented with both visual and auditory stimulation.

How can this information be useful? It shows that some infants can be expected to adjust more quickly to new experiences and events than other infants. Some newborns will show sustained interest in, but also become upset at, new sights and sounds. In these cases, caregivers and parents should introduce new toys or play environments more slowly. Other newborns may become more quickly accustomed to stimuli, in which case they may enjoy a more frequent change in environment. Given cultural variations in the rate at which babies adapt, caregivers working in multicultural settings should be particularly sensitive to the habituation patterns of newborns when making changes in the play environment.

NEWBORNS WITH SPECIAL NEEDS

Thus far in this chapter we have discussed typically developing newborns. Vast variations exist, however, in neonatal behavior and development. Some newborns have special needs caused by unfavorable conditions before, during, or after birth. Some special needs may be the result of genetics, others of environmental influences. Many challenging conditions are a function of socioeconomic status and culture.

Genetic Disorders

Some children are afflicted with genetic disorders that affect development. Sometimes these can be detected before birth through **amniocentesis**—a procedure by which genetic information is obtained from a small sampling of amniotic fluid as early as the twelfth week of pregnancy. In a newer procedure, **chorionic villus biopsy,** tissue is drawn from the outer membrane of the amniotic sac; this procedure allows detection of genetic disorders as early as the ninth week of pregnancy. Conditions that are commonly detected before or right after birth include Down syndrome, Tay-Sachs disease, and cystic fibrosis (these are described in Chapter 4).

Some disorders escape detection during pregnancy. In these cases, a neonatal assessment by a pediatrician will often indicate problems. Perhaps the most comprehensive and widely used test of newborn functioning is the **Neonatal Behavioral Assessment Scale (NBAS),** developed by Brazelton, Nugent, and Lester (1987). In this assessment, the pediatrician observes or tests the newborn baby's repertoire of behaviors, including reflexes, states, responses to stimuli, and soothability. When NBAS scores are combined with other medical information, many neurological impairments can be detected within the first few weeks after birth (Amiel-Tison, 1985).

Environmental Risk Factors

Developmental problems at birth are sometimes the result of **teratogens**—harmful agents in the environment. An example of a teratogen is the drug thalidomide, which was found to cause physical deformities in newborns. New teratogens continue to be identified as risk factors. For example, fathers' and mothers' exposure to Agent Orange during the Vietnam War and to chemical weapons during the Gulf War have been found to threaten healthy fetal development.

Newborns of mothers who smoke, drink, or abuse drugs during pregnancy may show signs of developmental problems at birth, including birth defects and brain damage. For example, newborns who suffer from **fetal alcohol syndrome** (described in Chapter 4) have been found to be more irritable and less easily soothed almost immediately after birth (Janzen & Nanson, 1993). Even one drink a day by the pregnant mother can lead to delays in motor functioning (Larroque et al., 1995). Newborns whose mothers smoked during pregnancy have been found to be less responsive to stimuli and to cry more intensely during neonatal assessments (Milunsky, 1989). Even nonsmoking mothers who are exposed to secondhand smoke will give birth to lower-birth-weight babies (Eskanazi, Prehn, & Christianson, 1995).

Poor Health Status and Prematurity

The infant mortality rate in the United States is alarmingly high. Although the incidence of neonatal deaths has declined in recent years, almost all industrialized nations have lower rates of infant death than the United States (Wegman, 1994). What is more disturbing is the disproportionately high percentage of neonatal deaths among babies of historically under-represented cultural groups in this country. In 1995 the infant mortality rate for Euro-Americans was 6.3 deaths per 1,000 births. For this same year, African-American infant deaths were over twice as high, at 15.1 per 1,000 (Children's Defense Fund, 1998). Similar trends are found among Native American, Latino, and some Asian groups (Dowling & Fisher, 1987; U.S. Department of Health and Human Services, 1996). It is important to note that infant mortality rates are high for these under-represented groups at all socioeconomic levels (Markides & McFarland, 1985). Apparently, poverty alone does not explain cultural differences in infant mortality.

Illness. Some infants who survive the first year suffer from serious illness resulting from poor health status or genetics. Severe health problems are more common among babies from families of low socioeconomic status. Historically underrepresented ethnic groups are also more likely to be afflicted (Children's Defense Fund, 1998). A high incidence of bacterial meningitis, for example, has been found among Navajo and White Mountain Apache Indian babies (Losonsky, Santosham, Sehgal, Zwahlen, & Moxon, 1984). Cystic fibrosis is more common in Pueblo Indians, and sickle-cell anemia among African Americans.

Impoverished babies, particularly those of African-American and Latino cultural groups, also suffer more frequently from milder, common illnesses. Although these affect development less severely, chronic poor health in infancy may have a long-lasting impact on intellectual and social development (Pollitt, 1994). The incidence of mild illness among children of color or those in poverty has probably been underestimated. Families with limited resources cannot afford medical visits for less serious health problems, and many have no health insurance (Children's Defense Fund, 1998).

Anemia. Why do some newborns fail to survive? Why are others chronically ill? One reason is poor nutrition. Iron-deficiency anemia is especially prevalent among newborns in this country (Children's Defense Fund, 1998; Yip, 1990). Chronic anemia has been associated with infant death, poor health, and a broad range of developmental problems in later life (Lozoff, 1990). Anemia is especially prevalent among infants of African-American and Latino families in America; a rate as high as 25% has been found for these groups (Pollitt, 1994).

Prematurity and Low Birth Weight. Premature birth and low birth weight contribute to infant mortality. **Low-birth-weight infants** who survive are at risk of poor developmental outcomes. **Premature births** are those in which a child has been born at least 3 weeks before the end of the full 38- to 42-week gestational period. Babies who are less than 5.5 pounds (2,500 grams) at birth are also sometimes considered premature. Premature babies are extremely vulnerable; their mortality rate is quite high (Perlman et al., 1995). Since their biological systems are not fully developed, they often suffer breathing difficulties, problems with temperature regulation, and jaundice. Premature infants behave differently; they are often less alert and responsive and are more difficult to feed. They can also be less predictable in sleep patterns and hypersensitive to stimuli. For these reasons, parents' reactions to them may be less positive. In one study, parents were found to touch, hold, or talk less frequently to premature babies than to full-term infants during feeding (Goldberg, Brachfeld, & DiVitto, 1980).

Although some premature babies have developmental problems later in life, many fare extremely well, gaining weight quickly and showing no signs of difficulty in later childhood (Easterbrooks, 1989). Positive parenting and other forms of early intervention may make a difference in these outcomes. Premature babies who are held, touched, and talked to frequently gain weight more quickly and are more developmentally advanced than those who do not receive this special intervention (Hack, Klein, & Taylor, 1995; Spiker, Ferguson, & Brooks-Gunn, 1993).

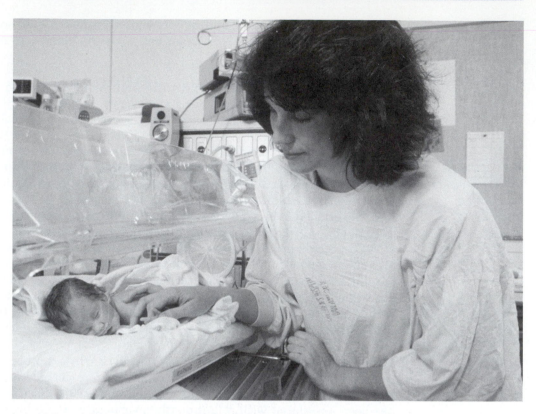

Low birth weight and premature birth contribute to infant mortality and put infants who survive at risk.

Rates of prematurity and low birth weight vary across cultural and socioeconomic groups in the United States, as shown in Figure 5-2. African Americans have an exceedingly high incidence of low birth weight (16.1%). Other groups are also at greater risk. Puerto Rican babies are more likely to be born prematurely (9%) (Garcia Coll, 1990; Paneth, 1995). Rates of prematurity are particularly high for babies born to teenage mothers of historically under-represented groups (R. M. Goodman, 1986). Euro-American, Cuban-American, Mexican-American, and Asian-American babies have significantly lower rates of low birth weight (around 5.5%). These trends may be explained in part by socioeconomic status; high-risk groups tend to live in poverty at higher rates (Beckwith & Rodning, 1991; Paneth, 1995). However, culture may also play a role. Linguistic and cultural barriers may keep mothers of some groups from accessing health care or nutritional services (Children's Defense Fund, 1998).

In addition to increasing the likelihood of prematurity and low birth weight, poverty contributes to developmental risks for such infants after birth. In fact, socioeconomic status is the best predictor of how premature babies will turn out; the lower the families' income and education, the more likely babies are to fare poorly (Paneth, 1995).

Sudden Infant Death Syndrome. Sudden infant death syndrome (SIDS) strikes fear in the hearts of parents around the world. One out of 360 infants dies of this mysterious condition (Wegman, 1994). Families of all countries and ethnic groups

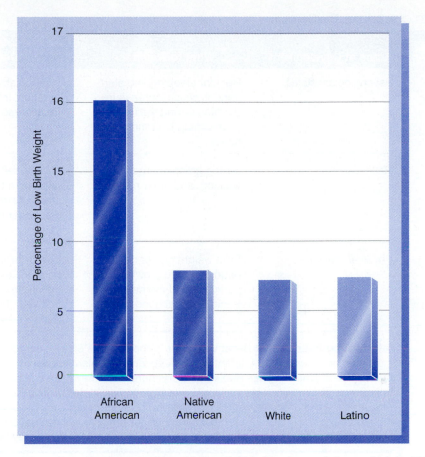

Figure 5-2 Percentage of low-birth-weight babies is over twice as high in African American families as in Euro-American and other cultural groups.

SOURCE: Adapted from Children's Defense Fund. (1998). *The State of America's Children.* Washington, DC: Author.

can be affected. What is frightening about SIDS is that babies simply stop breathing and die silently, for no apparent reason, usually at night. Most new parents have spent more than one sleepless night constantly checking their infant's breathing in fear of this silent killer. The causes of SIDS are unknown. Some pediatricians suspect that SIDS is a generic label used to describe a range of life-threatening conditions. Babies born to mothers who are heavy smokers or who abuse cocaine and heroin are more likely to die from SIDS (Haglund & Cnattingious, 1990; E. A. Mitchell, Ford, & Steward, 1993). Siblings of babies who have died of the condition are also at greater risk (Guntheroth, Lohmann, & Spiers, 1990). Other research has focused on the position in which babies sleep. SIDS is more common among those who sleep on their stomachs (H. J. Hoffman & Hillman, 1992). When infants are routinely put down to sleep on their sides or backs, the risk of SIDS is reduced by 50% (Spiers & Guntheroth, 1994).

Although babies of all cultural and socioeconomic groups can be stricken by SIDS, those in poverty and of African-American and Native American backgrounds are at greatest risk (H. J. Hoffman & Hillman, 1992). Babies of some countries are more likely to be afflicted—those in Australia and New Zealand, for example. In other countries, such as Japan and Sweden, the incidence is quite low.

ASSESSING YOUNG CHILDREN: The Newborn

Areas of Development	What to Watch for	Indicators of Atypical Development
Psychological states	Regular sleeping and alert periods which increase in duration during the first half-year. Crying to communicate needs.	Inconsolable crying of long duration. Infrequent alertness. Peculiar-sounding cries.
Reflexes	Strong grasping, rooting, sucking, and other reflexes.	Certain reflexes are not present in the early days of life. Reflexes do not disappear during the first year.
Physical growth	Birth weight of 5 or more pounds. Rapid growth, particularly of the head and trunk. General good health.	Low birth weight. Poor pediatric evaluation on NBAS. Failure to grow rapidly in the first year. Frequent illness and poor nutritional status.

Interpreting Assessment Data: Variations in these areas of development may be a result of individual or cultural factors. Infants may sleep longer at night because they sleep with their parents during the first year. Babies who cry more often may have a less positive inborn temperament. Unpredictable variations in psychological states or peculiar-sounding crying may indicate a challenging condition, however. Low birth weight and poor nutrition could be the result of poverty or poor prenatal care. Further professional evaluation is needed when such indicators are present. Nutritional and educational intervention may be recommended.

RESEARCH INTO PRACTICE

CRITICAL CONCEPT 1

Newborns spend their time in a narrow range of psychological states. They sleep for many hours. When awake, they cry and eat. Two particularly important states are the alert and waking periods, during which newborns visually explore the world and the people within it.

Application #1

Infant caregivers and parents should be able to identify and understand the importance of each newborn psychological state. Babies should be afforded opportunities to spend meaningful time in each state; for example, a soothing, quiet space for uninterrupted sleep and a visually stimulating environment for alert looking should be provided. Caregivers should respond appropriately to infants' cries for food and nurturance.

Application #2

Parents and caregivers should learn to read newborn states and adjust interactions accordingly. Babies learn most during the active and waking states; these are important times for moderate stimulation. The drowsy state, in contrast, is a time when babies should not be disturbed.

CRITICAL CONCEPT 2

During waking states, newborns habituate to familiar sights and sounds; that is, once they come to know something, they grow disinterested in it. They become excited when new objects appear and new events occur.

Application #1

Caregivers and parents can observe habituation processes in newborns as a way of assessing perceptual and intellectual development. For example, when a baby is observed studying a new mobile, and then showing disinterest in it over time, it can be concluded that the child has perceived and learned about the mobile and is now ready for new stimulation.

Application #2

Parents and caregivers should provide a moderate amount of stimulation for newborns. If the environment does not include interesting events or objects, babies will have nothing to study and habituate to. If too much stimulation is provided, babies may not be able to study and become familiar with any one object or person. They may become overwhelmed by the bombardment of perceptual stimuli.

CRITICAL CONCEPT 3

The time newborns spend in various states and how quickly they habituate to new stimuli vary from one ethnic group to another. This may be partly due to genetics. However, parents of diverse backgrounds respond in unique ways to newborn states. For example, some parents respond quickly with warmth and feeding when babies cry; others are slower in responding or use distracting techniques. These differences in interactions may explain some of the diversity in infant states and behavior.

Application #1

Caregivers should understand and be sensitive to cultural differences in newborn states and habituation. Care should be taken not to misconstrue neonatal differences as deficits.

Application #2

Caregivers should adjust their interactions to the unique state patterns of individual babies. Babies who are easily upset and cry more often should be soothed and nurtured more. Those who are often awake and active should receive more social stimulation. Babies who habituate more slowly should not be overwhelmed with too many novel objects or people. Slow-habituating babies may warm up slowly to new people, new room arrangements, and new experiences.

CRITICAL CONCEPT 4

Some newborns may be at risk of poor development. Low-birth-weight infants can suffer poor developmental outcomes, particularly within families living in poverty.

Genetic disorders and illness may also threaten healthy development in the earliest days of life. Some problems stem from barriers to health care for families of historically under-represented groups.

Application #1

Caregivers should provide special support for babies in high-risk categories and their families. Low-birth-weight infants, for example, would benefit from greater social and intellectual stimulation in child care. Parent education programs can be provided to help families of high-risk babies provide positive interaction in the home.

Application #2

Caregivers should serve as advocates for families of children in high-risk categories. Helping parents gain access to nutritional and health care services is an important role of the infant care provider in modern life. Actually accompanying family members to a clinic or a public assistance office may be necessary to overcome cultural and linguistic barriers to family services.

SUGGESTED ACTIVITIES

1. Observe a newborn baby in a home or child care center for at least 20 minutes. Write a narrative description of all behaviors you see, guided by the following questions:

   a. How would you describe the baby's general appearance (i.e., skin coloration, hair or lack of it, body proportions)?

   b. How would you describe this newborn's movements? What kinds of "global wiggles" or other whole-body actions did you observe? What caused the baby to wiggle in these ways?

   c. What single body-part movements did you see (e.g., kicking a single leg, grasping with a hand)? What caused these movements to occur?

   d. How attentive was this newborn to you and the outside world? Did the baby look at you or other objects? Did the baby turn toward noises or in other ways show that he or she could hear well?

   e. Based on these observations, what can you conclude about newborn appearance, movement, and perception?

2. Obtain parental permission to test the reflexes of a newborn and a 4- to 8-month-old baby. Check the grasp reflex by placing a finger in each baby's palm. Check the rooting and sucking reflexes by stroking the baby's cheek near the mouth or gently rubbing a pacifier or bottle across the baby's lips. Check the plantar reflex—an automatic flexing of the toes—by running a finger along the sole of the baby's foot. Write descriptions of each baby's reflexes, guided by the following questions:

   a. How did each baby respond to your stimulation?

   b. How strong were the reflexes of each baby? What differences did you observe between the two age groups?

   c. What surprised or puzzled you about the differences in the two babies' reflexes? What can you conclude about changes in reflexes over the first few months of life?

3. Watch a young infant sleep at home or in a child care center for at least 20 minutes. Write a description of everything you see. Write a report on the experience, guided by the following questions:

   a. What kinds of wiggles did you observe? How would you characterize the activity level of the sleeping baby?

   b. Which of the sleep states described in this chapter did you observe? Did you see evidence of REM sleep? If so, describe the activity level and movement patterns of the baby during REM.

   c. If you observed the baby fall asleep, describe the process. Were there a few minutes of calm, drowsy wakefulness before sleep? Did the baby fall asleep quickly? Did he or she have trouble getting settled or comfortable? Did the baby need help from parents or caregivers in getting to sleep?

d. If you observed the baby wake up, describe the process. What kind of state followed sleep? How would you characterize the baby's actions and activity levels following a nap?

4. Observe a classroom of infants in a child care center for at least 30 minutes. Watch for evidence of infant psychological states among all the children present (i.e., crying, alert, and waking and active behavior). Write a report describing each state that you observe, guided by the following questions:

a. Which states were you able to observe among these babies? Which specific behaviors and expressions were associated with each infant state?

b. How long did babies remain in the states you observed? Did some babies remain longer than others in a single state? Did some move from one state to another quickly?

c. What events caused babies to change from one state to another?

CHAPTER 6

Infant Physical Growth and Brain Development

INFANCY IS THE PERIOD FROM BIRTH TO AGE 2. In this chapter we will explore trends in infant physical and motor growth and examine the remarkable growth of the infant brain. We will also see how cultural differences in child-rearing practices or beliefs can lead to variations in these areas of development. We will consider atypical patterns of development, as well as interventions to support children with challenging physical conditions.

The following story shows why information on infant physical growth is essential for both new parents and teachers:

"Why isn't Ding Fang walking yet?" a parent suddenly asks Ms. McBride, a child care provider, when he brings his infant daughter into her center early one morning. Ms. McBride is taken aback; this baby is only 13 months old, can already stand alone, and shows no signs of motor delay. She is surprised that the father would have this concern. She understands, however, that he—like so many other first-time parents—is anxious about his child's development. Because few infants have arrived yet, and Ms. McBride has two assistants, she is able to leave the play area for a few minutes. She invites the father into her office, where she shows him developmental charts of typical infant motor development.

"If you look here," she says, "you can see that Ding Fang is right on track in terms of her motor abilities. She can stand up already; you can see from the chart that many babies her age are not able to do this yet."

The father explains, "I see other babies about Ding Fang's age in our apartment complex who are walking already. Some have been walking for quite awhile. I wondered if something was wrong. Ding Fang seems very quiet . . . relaxed, you know? She doesn't try to get up and run like the other children."

Ms. McBride responds in a reassuring tone. "Babies are all different. Some walk early, some a bit later. Some are more active than others. Some babies are very bold, very eager to get up and be on their own. And run away from their parents," she adds with a laugh. "Other babies seem to be in no rush to move on their own. All of these patterns are typical. Ding Fang is just following her own path to being a grown up child. She will walk very soon, I know."

The caregiver in this story has demonstrated sensitivity to a parent's need for reassurance about his child's development. She knows that parents compare their babies' growth patterns to those of other babies. When an infant who lives next door is showing advanced motor development, parents make comparisons . . . and worry.

In supporting this particular father, the caregiver has relied on knowledge of infant motor development. She is aware of the normative data—information on how babies develop on the average. She also knows that there is typical variation in infant motor growth, and that physical development and activity level vary across families and cultures. Because of temperament or family life experience, children of some ethnic groups are more bold and active, while others are less so. Recognizing that Ding Fang's quieter, less active style may be part of her cultural heritage, she conveys to the child's father that diverse patterns of motor activity are common.

PHYSICAL GROWTH AND MOTOR DEVELOPMENT

Infants grow very rapidly between birth and age 2. By the second year, many children are four times as heavy and over a foot longer than they were at birth. Babies' bodies change structurally as well. Although they remain top-heavy, their legs and trunk grow rapidly and begin to catch up with the rest of the body during the second year. A layer of subcutaneous fat, commonly called "baby fat," gives the young baby a plump appearance. This layer of fat cushions and provides a source of nutrition to the very young infant. By age 2 toddlers have lost some of this subcutaneous fat and, with it, their roundish appearance.

During infancy, muscle and bone tissue grows rapidly, explaining the remarkable increase in strength, coordination, and stamina that occurs during this period. A brain growth spurt also takes place, causing babies to gain physical competence by leaps and bounds. These rapid changes invariably cause unexpected mishaps: a 6-month-old may suddenly roll off a changing table, or a 9-month-old may stand for the first time and, without warning, pull a plate off the table. Before parents can adjust to one new stage of motor development, babies may have acquired even more sophisticated modes of locomotion that pose additional challenges. Keeping up with infant motor development requires vigilance and great energy!

Descriptions of "typical" physical growth are often based on observations of white middle-class infants from the United States (McLoyd, 1990b). However, there is much variation across cultures in babies' size and the pace of their physical growth. For example, Southeast Asian infants and toddlers tend to be shorter than Euro-American babies (J. E. Brown et al., 1986). Many African and African-American infants are advanced in motor development and physical growth (Super, 1981). Some children living in poverty are smaller due to malnutrition (Children's Defense Fund, 1998). Even within cultures, tremendous variation in size and motor ability exists among typically developing children.

Motor Abilities

Motor abilities emerge in a relatively fixed order in infancy. Babies creep before they walk. When they begin to walk, they hold onto a hand or a piece of furniture until they can manage alone. They swipe at objects before they can accurately reach out and grab them. They grasp objects by trapping them between their fingers and palm

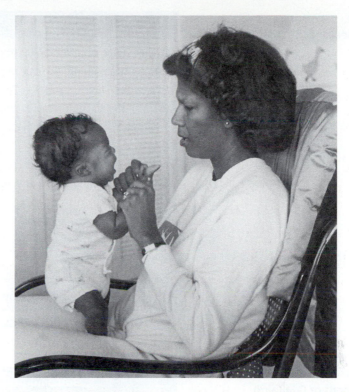

There is cultural variation in infant motor development. African and African-American babies tend to be advanced in physical abilities.

before using the thumb and index finger in a more sophisticated **pincer grasp.** The order in which these abilities are acquired is the same among most children around the world.

Early child development researchers have studied the emergence of these infant motor behaviors and have created developmental charts—called **normative charts**—that show the average age at which certain behaviors first appear (Gesell, 1933; Shirley, 1933). These charts are still used by pediatricians and parents to judge developmental advancement. A chart depicting general motor milestones in infancy is shown in Table 6–1, and the progression of infants' grasping abilities is shown in Table 6–2.

Caution must be used in interpreting these developmental profiles, however. Although the sequence of motor development is relatively fixed, not all children acquire motor abilities at the same pace. Individual differences in creeping, for example, can vary by 7 or 8 months for typically developing children (Bertenthal & Campos, 1990). The age at which babies walk also varies significantly among individuals (Thelen & Ulrich, 1991). Developmental charts can cause undue anxiety among parents if misinterpreted. Some parents may even attempt direct training of motor skills, causing frustration for both themselves and their children.

Motor development profiles are often created from observations of white middle-class children. Children of other cultural groups may acquire physical abilities at a much different pace than indicated on these charts. African and African-American babies, for example, have been observed to be advanced in motor competence (Brazelton, Koslowski, & Tronick, 1971; Rosser & Rudolph, 1989).

TABLE 6-1
Motor Milestones in Infancy

Milestone	Average Age
Raises head; can lift chin up from floor or bed	1 month
Raises chest up off the floor or bed	2 months
Sits up with adult support	2.5 months
Bats at objects; cannot accurately grasp them	3 months
Reaches for and grasps objects	6 months
Sits alone steadily	6.5 months
Stands with adult support	8 months
Stands up holding onto furniture	9 months
Creeps	10 months
Walks when led by an adult	11 months
Stands alone	11 months
Walks alone	12 months
Climbs stairs	13 months
Walks down stairs with both feet on each step	26 months

SOURCE: Bayley, 1969; Shirley, 1933.

TABLE 6-2
Development of Grasping in Infancy

Grasping Ability	Average Age
Swipes at objects; makes no contact	16 weeks
Swipes at objects; makes contact. Does not grasp.	20 weeks
Makes primitive grasping movement with fingers; object still not accurately held.	20 weeks
Squeezes and holds object between fingers and palm. Thumb is not used.	24 weeks
Squeezes object between fingers and thumb.	28 weeks
Picks up objects between thumb and index finger (pincer grasp)	52 weeks

How can cultural and individual differences in motor development be explained? Some believe that these differences are the result of biological inheritance (Freedman, 1974). There is research to support this claim. In Dennis and Dennis's (1940) study of Hopi Indian infants, those who had been tightly swaddled and strapped to a cradleboard walked at about the same age as those who were not confined in this way. In a study by Gesell and Thompson (1929), a child who was trained to climb stairs displayed better stair-climbing ability than her twin sister. However, her sibling quickly caught up. These researchers concluded that babies will ultimately follow their own unique maturation patterns regardless of environmental influences.

Others argue that environment and culture explain this diversity in motor functioning. Chisholm (1983), for example, offers an explanation for why infants who are strapped to cradleboards during the day are as advanced as those who are not so confined. He observed that Navajo infants were more active and interacted very frequently with parents when off the board. He proposes that these babies received adequate practice in motor activities during evening periods. Garcia Coll (1990) has provided evidence that African-American babies are advanced in motor skills because of the way they are handled by parents and other family members. She cites research that interactions between African-American parents and babies are more active, less likely to involve quiet toys, and more likely to involve physical touch (Brill, 1986; Hale, 1994; Rosser & Rudolph, 1989). Garcia Coll's research suggests that the babies of middle-class African-American parents who have adopted more Westernized parenting styles are less motorically advanced. Cultural variations in development may, then, be the result of a unique blend of parenting values and practices, family life, and genetic contributions from ancestors.

Toddler Motor Development and Self-Help Skills

During the last half-year of infancy—from approximately age 18 months to 2 years—children enter a new period of development called toddlerhood (some child specialists do not consider toddlers to be infants anymore). Changes in intellectual, language, and motor growth mark this as an especially challenging and fascinating period. Toddlers, for the first time, move primarily in an upright position. This ability opens new worlds for them. High surfaces are now accessible; they can reach for and pull down family heirlooms or favorite furnishings. Child-proofing homes and teaching babies not to touch become critical parenting issues. Toddlers can walk and even run—and this includes running away. Toddlers hold powerful aspirations to be on their own and to explore without adult intrusion. Parents must be very vigilant with children at this age.

Toddlers are much stronger than younger infants. A parent from the American West has described diapering a toddler as an experience very similar to roping and branding a calf. Many toddlers do not wish to be confined for the endless period—in child time—that it takes to change a soiled diaper. They will wiggle and struggle, jump up half-clothed, and make a break for the door.

Toddlers cut most of their teeth between 18 months and 2 years. This allows them to eat meats and other foods that were difficult before. It also allows them to bite—including, unfortunately, siblings and peers. Teething also creates the challenge of dental care; pediadontists ask parents to rub or brush babies' teeth, procedures that require risky sojourns into the mouths of babies just learning the power of their jaws.

In toddlerhood, fine motor abilities that require the coordinations of fingers and thumb are acquired. Once they master the pincer grasp, toddlers can engage in fine motor play: they can make simple puzzles, work with modeling clay, or tear paper. They can also open cabinets, take the tops off of household cleaners, or pick up (and usually place in their mouths) small objects such as pennies or an older sibling's marbles. Child-proofing is especially important in toddlerhood, as choking is a major concern at this age.

Child-Proofing From a Multicultural Perspective. Child-proofing takes many forms and is influenced by cultural values and practices. In some families, home environments are fully redesigned during toddlerhood so that babies can touch anything they wish. The goal is to encourage autonomy and reduce reprimands and restrictions. In other families, toddlers are required to learn rules for what may be touched or played with. Infractions are met with hand-slapping or firm reprimands.

Toddlers move quickly and hold powerful aspirations to be on their own and explore without adult intrusion.

It may be that this early form of discipline has a goal of "toughening" children or protecting them from dangers in their neighborhoods (Hale, 1994).

A classic study by Levine (1977) shows the diversity of child-proofing strategies used in the world. He observed that in a village in western Kenya, babies were reared outdoors for the most part. The risks to these toddlers were great, including danger of burns from cooking fires and falls off cliffs or into rivers, lakes, and dye pits. In this case, the challenge was not child-proofing the home, but child-proofing the whole world! The solution? Parents of this village carried their toddlers on their backs from the time they could walk until they were old enough to understand rules and the dangers around them. This represents an interesting reversal of the common trend of carrying babies only until they can walk on their own. In this Kenyan village, carrying became necessary only when babies learned to move about.

As children become more advanced motorically, they are expected to perform certain self-help tasks. Which tasks are to be learned and how quickly children are expected to learn them are defined by particular cultures. In some cultural groups, early independence and self-care are highly valued (Hale, 1994); in others, children are expected to rely heavily on parents until quite late in childhood (Powell, 1983; Yu & Kim, 1983).

Eating. Eating with a toddler is a fascinating experience in any culture. As a father, I've made many enlightening observations of toddlers' eating habits: the creative mixing of foods, experiments with the aerodynamics of breakfast cereals, and tests to determine how persistent parents will be in retrieving dropped spoons. In one fascinating observation, my oldest son was seen holding his spoon in a particularly mature manner with his left hand while shoveling food into his mouth with his right.

Such experiences vary across cultures. In some families, toddlers are expected to sit for meals and eat with a spoon or another eating implement as early as age 2. Such behaviors as throwing food or using one's hands to eat are discouraged. In white working-class families in America and Europe, self-control and neatness are often expected at an early age (L. W. Hoffman, 1984). In other cultures, rules at mealtime are not so rigid, nor are they imposed so early. In Nyansongo, Kenya, toddlers eat off the plates of others, including their younger siblings (B. B. Whiting & Edwards, 1988). Variation in how toddlers eat is a function of the foods eaten in a particular culture and the implements used. It is easy to see how much less challenging it would be to learn to use a spoon than to use chopsticks, for example.

The following story, told to me by an American researcher working in an East African village, illustrates how eating expectations vary drastically from one culture to another:

> A researcher sits on the ground to eat an evening meal with a large family. There are no eating implements; food is eaten with the fingers. The researcher studies a toddler who has invented a novel system of raising his bowl to his lips and pouring rice into his mouth as if drinking from a cup. Much rice spills onto the ground; at most half of the food actually reaches his mouth. The father takes the child's hand and shows him how to pick up food with one's fingers. The young toddler imitates this behavior. The researcher and father speak in the family's language:

> RESEARCHER: So, you teach your child to use fingers to eat?
>
> FATHER: He wastes too much food when he eats like this (demonstrates the child's original eating method). He eats like an animal and wastes food.
>
> RESEARCHER: (Laughs) So, you tell your child, "Be sure to eat with your fingers."
>
> FATHER: (Looks puzzled, doesn't understand the joke)
>
> RESEARCHER: (Laughing still) Well, see, in my family my mother was always telling me, "Don't eat with your fingers. Use a spoon or fork." I just think it's funny that you tell your child just the opposite.
>
> FATHER: How do you feel your food that you eat? Part of enjoying a meal is feeling the foods, running your fingers over vegetables or the grains of rice. (He demonstrates) It is a pleasure to eat in this way.

It is important for caregivers and teachers to consider cultural variations when pursuing goals of teaching table manners or proper eating habits at snack time. American eating styles are not necessarily valued in all cultures.

Toileting. Toddlerhood is often a time when American parents decide to train their children to use the toilet independently. Brazelton (1962) has suggested that children at this age are both psychologically and physiologically ready to learn this new skill. Many parents, however, view toilet training as a trying experience. Often they feel a sense of urgency about their child's accomplishing bladder and bowel control. Anxieties are exacerbated by the fact that many child care centers will not admit children who do not use the toilet independently. From a friend I heard the following story that highlights the frustrations of toilet training:

> Two-year-old Nathan's parents decided to encourage independent toileting by giving him a small plastic dinosaur every time he successfully used the toilet. This seemed to work for a while, but Nathan began to have an increasing number of "accidents." During one such event, Nathan's mother asked him what the problem was: "You've been going in the toilet, and I give you a dinosaur each

time. But now you're going in your pants again." The toddler responded with a sly smile, "I want two dinosaurs, Mommy."

His mother reflected: Nathan may not use the toilet, but he has certainly learned how to negotiate!

In the United States, parents take many different approaches to toilet training. White middle-class parents often adhere to a "child-oriented approach" suggested by baby experts (Brazelton, 1962; Spock & Rothenberg, 1985). In this method, parents wait until they are absolutely certain the child is ready, then use gentle reminders, modeling, and positive guidance to help children achieve independent toileting. Some middle-class American parents have adopted behaviorist strategies (Azrin & Foxx, 1974), in which rewards and praise are used to shape independent toileting behaviors, as illustrated in the story of Nathan.

It is important to note that these strategies are used primarily in white middle-class families in America. African-American parents and grandparents more often use reprimands and punishments for bowel or bladder "accidents." They also are more likely to expect independent toileting at an early age (Hale, 1994). These practices reflect cultural values of early self-sufficiency and autonomy. In Korean-American and Japanese-American families, parents are more likely to be casual in their approaches to toileting and tolerant of later mastery (Yamamoto & Kubota, 1983; Yu & Kim, 1983). One early study of Japanese Americans found that the longer a family had lived in the United States, the more urgency parents felt about toilet training (De Vos, 1954). Middle-class American beliefs about the need for early training appear to become integrated over time into traditional Japanese-American family life.

In other parts of the world, parents report that toileting of toddlers is not a problem or even a goal of socialization. After extensive observations in many non-Western countries, J. W. M. Whiting (1977) reported that toileting was seldom mentioned by parents in discussions of child-rearing issues. He found that in some warm climates, babies often run unclothed for most of the day and urinate or defecate where they wish. The extent of parents' efforts in these communities may be to gently lead them farther away from important living areas, such as places of food preparation.

In a classic study of toileting practices in East Africa, M. W. DeVries and DeVries (1977) describe a process where babies at 3 weeks old are taken to a special place outdoors to urinate or defecate. This occurs day and night. At the phenomenally early age of 5 months, many babies of this community begin to communicate a need for elimination with noises or body movements.

Despite the varieties of routines for toilet training in the world, all typically developing children acquire the procedures unique to their culture, and often at about the same age. Regardless of whether harsh reprimands, rewards, or modeling is used, or even when no conscious effort to train is made at all, most children achieve bladder and bowel control by age 3. Parents' selection of toileting techniques, then, may be more a function of family and cultural beliefs than of any real advantage one strategy has over another.

PERCEPTUAL DEVELOPMENT

Long ago it was believed that babies were born into a confusing world of fuzzy shapes and strange, garbled sounds. Most parents and even researchers thought only older infants could see faces, recognize voices, or distinguish among tastes and smells.

New techniques for studying infant perception have shown, however, that babies have quite remarkable perceptual abilities right after birth.

Vision

Newborns see quite well objects that are between 7 and 15 inches away (Bronson, 1994). Interestingly (and perhaps not coincidentally), this is approximately the distance a parent's face is from an infant who is being held. Babies' visual acuity increases over the first few months of life; it is estimated that by age 1, they see as well as they ever will (Haith, 1990).

One way we know that young babies can see clearly is that they like to look at some patterns or objects more than others. Infant visual preferences are illustrated in Figure 6–1. It is has been discovered that newborns prefer patterns over solid shapes (Fantz, 1963), moderately complex patterns over either simple or complex ones, curved lines over straight ones, and large squares over small ones (Fantz, Fagan, & Miranda, 1975). By 4 months, babies can also distinguish among colors and prefer blue and red to yellow—the same color preferences as adults (Bornstein, 1992).

One thing that newborn babies may prefer to look at are human faces (Fantz, 1961). In fact, in one study newborns looked longer at drawings of faces with features displayed in typical order than at face-like drawings in which features were randomly arranged (Fantz, 1963). Later studies have not replicated these findings, however (Small, 1990). It may be that very young infants do not recognize faces per se,

FIGURE 6–1

Infants show preferences for what they look at. The human face appears most interesting to them.

SOURCE: Fantz. R. L., "The origin of form perception." *Scientific American,* 204. Copyright 1961 by Scientific American. All rights reserved. Reprinted by permission.

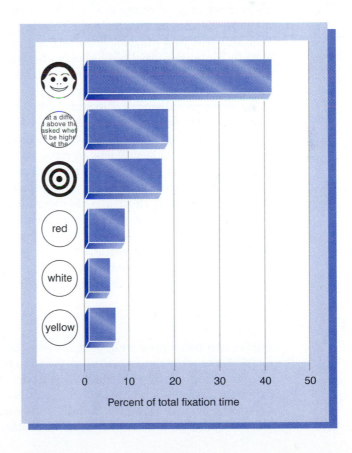

Percent of total fixation time

but look at them intently because they are such interesting visual patterns. A 6-week-old baby's smile at the appearance of his mother's face, for example, may merely be a response to a high-contrast image. Parents aren't aware of this, however; they report that the infant's gaze is a sign that "my baby knows me." Thus, newborns' innate visual interests, present at birth, may promote parent bonding.

Tracking and scanning are two special abilities that assist babies in viewing the world. **Tracking** is the ability to visually follow a moving object with one's eyes. Newborn babies make attempts to move their heads and readjust their eyes to keep interesting objects in their field of vision (Aslin, 1987). Their efforts are jerky, inefficient, and poorly controlled, however. They must turn the entire head and then refocus every few inches as an object moves in front of them. They only follow objects moving side-to-side in their field of vision. They rarely look up and down. Tracking rapidly becomes smoother and more accurate during the first 6 months of life (Bronson, 1990).

Tracking ability varies by culture. Puerto Rican babies, for example, have been found to track objects more efficiently than babies of other cultural groups (Garcia Coll, Sepkoski, & Lester, 1981). This might be due to biological inheritance. Unique cultural experience might also play a role, since tracking ability can be influenced by practice (Aslin, 1988). Babies may learn to track more efficiently in larger, extended families, for example, where there is much movement and there are many interesting persons to observe.

Scanning is a visual ability to look over all the features of an object and get a complete picture of what it is like. When adults examine an unfamiliar painting or an artifact in a museum, they quickly scan its visual details and get a sense of it as a whole. Newborns cannot do this. Instead, they tend to look at only one feature of a stimulus—at just one corner of a triangle or one ear of a teddy bear, for example. Within 3 months after birth, babies become much more competent in scanning an entire object (Bronson, 1994). They quickly look at one feature and then another until they have processed the whole object.

Another visual ability of infants is depth perception. In a classic study, Gibson and Walk (1960) discovered that babies as young as 6 months would not crawl out over a **visual cliff** even when they were encouraged to do so by their mothers. (The cliff, of course, was a perfectly safe surface covered with clear glass which only gave the appearance of being a deep abyss.) Babies' refusal to venture out over the cliff provided clear evidence that they could perceive depth at this young age. In a more recent study, 10- and 12-month-olds were found to have quite sophisticated distance perception—a form of depth perception (McKenzie, Skouteris, Day, Hartman, & Yonas, 1993). In this research, babies were found to more often reach for objects that were close to them, but less often for those that were far away. Even newborns—only days old—have been found to widen their eyes, pull back their heads, and hold up their hands when they view objects moving toward them (Bower, 1975).

Hearing

Babies can hear quite well, perhaps even before birth. In one study, fetuses as early as 26 weeks after conception were found to respond to sounds with accelerated heart rates and increased movement (Kisilevsky, Muir, & Low, 1992). Newborns can distinguish among sounds of different kinds—high and low pitches or loud and soft noises (Olsho, Koch, Carter, Halpin, & Spetner, 1988). Certain sounds, such as lullabies, singing, or heartbeats, tend to soothe them. Others, such as sudden, high-pitched noises, agitate them (Sansavini, Bertoncini, & Giovanelli, 1997). Newborns tend to cry at the sound of other infants' crying (Sagi & Hoffman, 1976). An implication of this finding is that humans may be born with an innate propensity to become upset over human cries. Parents may more readily respond to the cries of their own babies because they are naturally predisposed to be disturbed by this sound.

Babies are more attentive to certain sounds. They prefer singing and women's voices (Glenn, Cunningham, & Joyce, 1981), and they are especially attentive to the voice of their own mother (DeCasper & Fifer, 1980). They can discriminate among individual consonant sounds (Eimas & Tartter, 1979), even those of other languages (Trehub, 1976)! Babies as young as 2 days old can distinguish adult-to-child speech (which is characterized by especially exaggerated, higher-pitched intonation) from adult-to-adult speech (Cooper & Aslin, 1990). Five-month-olds are able to discriminate between intonations indicating approval (i.e., "Very good!") and disapproval (i.e., "No!"), even when uttered in different languages (Fernald, 1993).

Abilities to locate the direction of sounds, search for and track their sources, and selectively listen to one sound over another are acquired as early as 5 months (Lewkowicz, 1996; Pickens, 1994). Cultural differences in these abilities have been observed. For example, Puerto Rican infants have been found to track sounds more accurately than Caucasian or African-American infants (Garcia Coll et al., 1981). Again, such differences may be partly due to genetics and partly due to unique family or community experiences.

Taste and Smell

Taste and smell develop early among the senses. The ability to discriminate among smells and tastes may be acquired well before birth (R. M. Bradley, 1972). Newborns can distinguish among five tastes: sour, bitter, salty, sweet, and neutral (Rosenstein & Oster, 1988). They have clear taste preferences, sucking on a sweet solution more continuously and slowly, as an adult might savor a gourmet meal (Crook, 1987). Readers who have a sweet tooth may find it interesting to know that their cravings may be part of biological inheritance present at birth. In contrast, newborns do not appear to like salty solutions: they suck these in short bursts and for only brief periods (Crook, 1987). The craving for salty snacks prevalent in some American cultures, then, may be an acquired taste.

Newborns can distinguish between pleasant and unpleasant smells (Lipsitt, Engen, & Kaye, 1963). They also can detect where an odor is coming from. When an unpleasant smell comes from one direction, they rapidly turn their heads the opposite way (Reiser, Yonas, & Wikner, 1976).

Taste and smell are critical for neonatal survival. Infant preferences for certain sweetish, nonsalty solutions will facilitate early nursing. A series of fascinating studies has suggested that odor guides newborn feeding as well. Babies only a few days old prefer the odor of their own nursing mothers' breast pads to the smells of those of unfamiliar lactating women (Cernoch & Porter, 1985; Schaal, 1986). These authors conclude that odor may attract babies and direct their search for the nipple. A fascinating finding is that these odor preferences do not exist among bottle-fed babies. This suggests that such preferences arise from early experience with maternal smells (Balogh & Porter, 1986). Another study has found that female babies are more likely to show these preferences than are males, suggesting a genetic cause (Makin & Porter, 1989). Again, a complex interaction of heredity and experience may be at work in infants' acquisition of perceptual abilities.

Touch

The sense of touch develops before birth and plays a critical function in human development throughout life. Parental touch has a positive effect on infant emotions and health. Babies are soothed by being stroked or patted (Korner & Thoman, 1972). Parental touching has been found to elicit smiles, gazes, and increased attention from very young babies (Stack & Muir, 1992). A routine of warm touching can lead to positive developmental outcomes for at-risk babies (Scafidi et al., 1986). Touch may be a primary way that parents communicate with their babies or initiate play (A. S. Carter, Mayes, & Pajer, 1990). Touch also serves as a medium for learning about things. For example, 8-month-olds have been found to recognize and remember the shapes and textures of objects (Catherwood, 1993).

Even newborns can distinguish among tactile stimuli and discriminate between touches to one part of the body or another (Kisilevsky & Muir, 1984). Touch is often used in conjunction with other senses to interpret the world (Lockman & Wright, 1989). For example, looking and touching may be utilized together to recognize a toy.

PERCEPTUAL-MOTOR CHALLENGES IN INFANCY

Genetic disorders and complications before or during birth can adversely affect infant motor development and perception. Some disabilities are detected early in infancy or even before birth. However, their full impact on babies' ability to move about and explore objects and people may not be fully realized until the middle of the first year. A baby with a particular challenge may interact quite typically in the early weeks of life. Only later, when smiling, grasping objects, and sitting up are expected, do the adverse effects of the disability become obvious.

Visual Impairment

Babies with visual impairment but with no other disabilities will develop early motor skills at a typical pace (Adelson & Fraiberg, 1974). However, at a point when sighted infants begin to reach for and grasp objects, blind babies will not. At an age when most typically developing babies are beginning to crawl or walk, blind babies remain relatively stationary (Bower, 1975). Several theories have been offered to explain such motor delays (Adelson & Fraiberg, 1974). In typical homes or child care centers, babies' movements are often guided and motivated by vision. Blind babies move less because they are not visually inspired to get somewhere. They don't reach as often, because they are not motivated to obtain an object which they cannot see (Bower, 1975). An important implication is that rich auditory experiences must be created for infants with visual impairments. Providing toys that have interesting tactile and sound qualities has been found to promote the motor abilities of blind infants (Fraiberg, 1977).

Hearing Impairment

Hearing impairment can also influence infant development. As with visual impairment, this challenging condition may not be obvious in the early weeks of life. Babies with poor or no hearing may acquire motor abilities and even babble much like unimpaired infants. When they have acquired motor skills that allow them to respond to auditory stimuli, however, their challenging condition becomes obvious (Meadow, 1980). The vast majority of research on hearing disability in infancy focuses on delays in language development. Hearing-impaired babies show significant problems in learning language (Marschark, 1993). Concerns that hearing-impaired babies will fail to form positive relationships with parents have also been raised (Schlesinger & Meadow, 1972). However, more recent research suggests that when parents are warm and responsive in their interactions, their hearing-impaired babies become as securely attached as hearing babies (Lederberg & Mobley, 1990).

Many other disorders can hamper perceptual and motor development. Down syndrome can produce motor delays that are observable in infancy. Physical malformations resulting from the disorder can also affect perception. Eye cataracts, for example, are prevalent in babies with Down syndrome. Cerebral palsy, a condition caused by brain damage from oxygen deprivation or trauma before or during birth, often leads to blindness, deafness, or permanent impairment of motor abilities.

Early intervention can significantly affect the degree to which disabilities interfere with motor development. In one study, children with severe motor impairments, including those with Down syndrome, were provided with intensive services, including home-based intervention, parent support, and social services (Shonkoff, Hauser-Cram, Krauss, & Upshur, 1992). During the 12 months of the study, infants achieved an 8-month gain in motor development, with some advancing by as much as 12 months. These outcomes are remarkable given the motor delays these babies exhibited before the study. The researchers concluded that a multidisciplinary, family-based intervention can significantly enhance motor skill among babies with disabilities.

BRAIN GROWTH

One of the most significant physical changes in infancy is brain growth. A baby's brain develops at an astonishing rate; by age 3 it is as complex as it will ever be (Shore, 1997)!

How the Brain Works

The brain is comprised of billions of brain cells, called **neurons,** that are designed to send and retrieve information across organs or muscles. A neuron is illustrated in Figure 6–2. Each neuron is made up of a cell body that is surrounded by **dendrites,** elongated tissues that receive messages. A very long thread of tissue, the **axon,** extends out from the cell body toward other nerve cells. The purpose of the axon is to send messages. If an infant decides to reach out and grasp a favorite toy, a signal is sent from one neuron to another—from the axon of one cell to the dendrite of the next. In this way, the message is passed along to the muscles and perceptual organs that are needed for this movement.

The message in one cell is transmitted to another via chemical secretions called **neurotransmitters.** These travel out of the axon of one cell and pass into the dendrites of the next. The place where the axon and the dendrite meet is called a **synapse.** The number of synapses in the brain increases rapidly during infancy and accounts for the remarkable intellectual growth during this period. Another tissue that helps neural messages to travel efficiently from one cell to another is **myelin.** This is a fatty sheath that surrounds the axon and ensures that signals travel efficiently, quickly, and accurately.

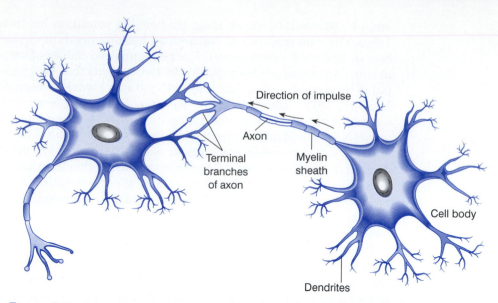

FIGURE 6–2 A message is sent from the brain to the body via neurons. The message is passed across cells through neurotransmitters which travel from the axon of one cell to a dendrite of another. This occurs at a juncture called a synapse. Myelin, an insulating sheath around the axon, ensures that the message travels accurately from cell to cell.

The brain is organized into regions. Each of these is responsible for specific functions. *Sensory* regions send and receive information regarding the sense organs. *Motor* regions regulate movement. *Association* regions are responsible for complex thought processes. One important area of the brain is the frontal cortex, which develops rapidly beginning at around 8 months. This area is associated with the ability to express and regulate emotions. (Note that 8 months is around the age at which most babies become securely attached to their parents!)

The brain is also organized into right and left hemispheres. In right-handed individuals, the left hemisphere governs analytical thinking and language and the right hemisphere governs spatial and auditory perception. The left hemisphere controls the right visual field and the right controls the left visual field. This specialization of left and right sides of the brain has been referred to as brain lateralization.

The "Super-Dense" Infant Brain

The number of neurons and the connections among them—the synapses—increase at a startling rate in the early years. By age 2, the number of synapses reaches an adult level. By age 3, a child's brain has 1,000 trillion synapses—twice that of any reader of this textbook (Shore, 1997)! Infants' brains have been referred to, then, as super-dense. They contain more complex neural connections and have a higher metabolic rate (i.e., they use more energy) than at any other period of life (Chugani, 1997)!

Babies acquire more synapses than they will need. So, after age 3 some of these connections are eliminated. In the elementary years, as many synapses are lost as are added. By adolescence, the loss of synapses far outpaces their acquisition. Typical 18-year-olds, then, have lost roughly half of their infant synapses. After infancy,

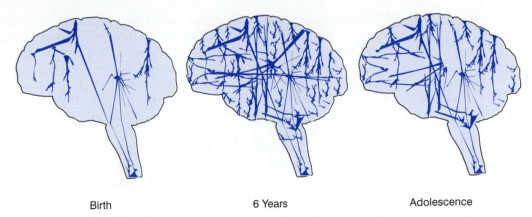

Birth   6 Years   Adolescence

FIGURE 6–3   Synapses in the brain increase rapidly in the early years. The number of synapses actually decreases in adolescence and adulthood as neural connections are "pruned."
SOURCE: Chugani, 1997.

then, brain growth is a pruning process in which brain connections that are not used or needed disappear. Figure 6–3 shows this trend (Chugani, 1997).

Which synapses are kept and which are discarded? Shore (1997) argues that it is a "use it or lose it" process. Synapses that have not been used often enough disappear, while those that have been reinforced through experience become permanent. For example, if babies exercise synapses in the cerebral cortex that are responsible for thinking and language, these will be maintained. Babies will, thus, become more competent in these areas. Children who do not use these synapses, however, may be hampered in language or thinking.

Shore (1997) argues that this pruning and reinforcing of synapses explains, in part, why there are cultural variations in skills and thinking. Children growing up in hunter-gatherer societies might, at an early age, acquire neural connections needed for efficient hunting. For such children, synapses that promote perception and motor coordination might be used and maintained. Growing up in crowded, urban apartment buildings, she suggests, might reinforce synapses that allow children to filter out certain kinds of stimuli. Brain growth is an interaction, then, between biology and cultural experience.

Promoting Infant Brain Growth

How can parents and caregivers nurture the brain growth of babies they care for? One obvious way is through early stimulation. Providing perceptual, motor, and language experiences for babies will enhance the formation of dendrites and increase the number of synapses (Chugani, 1997). Of course, overstimulation—a constant bombardment of sights and sounds—would work against healthy brain growth. Such experiences might cause stress, leading to interference in neural development (Gunnar, 1996).

The most powerful influence on infant brain growth, however, is attachment—the process by which infants bond emotionally with significant adults in their lives. When babies receive warm, responsive care from parents and other caregivers, they come to know and trust these adults. The resulting bond literally protects the human brain from stress or trauma (Gunnar, 1996). Here's how it works:

When babies experience stressful events, levels of a hormone called cortisol are elevated in the body. Cortisol threatens brain development by reducing the number of synapses and leaving neurons vulnerable to damage. Babies who suffer great trauma—as in the case of child abuse or neglect, for example—are at risk of poor brain growth because of these high cortisol levels. In particular, areas of the brain that regulate emotions are affected (Perry, 1996). Infants under great stress are more likely to suffer anxiety, impulsivity, hyperactivity, and poor control of their emotions later in life.

Babies who are securely attached to caregivers, however, are less likely to produce cortisol under stressful conditions. When they do, the levels of this hormone are far lower than those for children who are not attached. Thus, a warm bond with parents and other caregivers—so important for security and happiness—also has a positive impact on physical brain development (we will consider specific strategies for promoting infant attachment in Chapter 9).

ASSESSING YOUNG CHILDREN: Infant Physical and Motor Development

Areas of Development	What to Watch for	Indicators of Atypical Development
Large motor abilities	Large muscle skills: grasping, creeping, and standing in the first year; walking, running, jumping, and climbing in the second.	Typical motor development only until a time when grasping, sitting up, or walking are expected; then, significant delays.
Perceptual and fine motor abilities	Increasing ability to hear, see, touch, taste, and smell stimuli during the first months of life. Increasing skill in coordinating senses and fine motor actions (e.g., looking at and picking up a small object).	Failing to respond to visual or auditory stimuli. An inability to coordinate perceptions (e.g., failure to turn one's head in the direction of a sound).
Self-help or family life skills	An ability to eat with a spoon and sit at a table during meals by age 2. An ability to take off or put on some items of clothing by this age. An ability to use the toilet independently by age 3.	An inability to perform such simple self-help functions as feeding oneself or using the toilet by age 3.

Interpreting Assessment Data: Variations in these areas of development may be due to differences in cultural practices or family life experience. Infants whose parents play with them actively will show more advanced motor abilities. Children of some cultural groups will not acquire specific self-help skills because these are not stressed within their families. An inability to attend to stimuli or to perform simple motor activities may be the result of challenging conditions, such as visual or auditory impairment. Significant delays may also be common for children with cerebral palsy or Down syndrome. Early intervention in infant care centers or homes can enhance the perceptual development of infants with these special needs.

"Prime Time" for Brain Growth

Since the brain grows so rapidly in infancy, this period is considered a prime time for neural growth. Shore (1997) argues that a primary responsibility of parents and infant care providers is "the day-to-day care of young children's brains" (p. 26). Even infants with severe brain-related disabilities—autism or mental retardation—can benefit from early intervention programs. Both home-based and center-based programs for infants have been found to significantly reduce cognitive, social, and health problems.

This prime time is also a period of great vulnerability. Brain development is significantly impaired by *in utero* exposure to drugs, child abuse, maternal depression, and other factors (Dawson & Fischer, 1994; Shore, 1997). Even in these cases, however, early intervention can offset such negative influences if provided in the first 3 years of life (Ramey & Landesman-Ramey, 1996).

RESEARCH INTO PRACTICE

CRITICAL CONCEPT 1

New techniques for studying infant perception and motor competence show that babies have remarkable abilities to explore and move about. Their physical and perceptual skills are acquired in a relatively fixed order; for example, babies sit up before they can stand, and toddle before they can walk.

Application #1

Caregivers and parents should become familiar with the order in which motor abilities are acquired. Using this information, they can assess progress in physical growth and identify babies with physical challenges.

Application #2

Caregivers and parents can create infant play environments that promote large motor development. In child care, equipment should be provided to meet the needs of a variety of levels of competence. Mats or carpeting would allow younger infants to wiggle, scoot, roll, and crawl. Cushioned stairs and platforms, ramps, and low climbing equipment are useful for older babies and toddlers.

Application #3

Caregivers and parents should provide interesting and safe toys for babies to look at, bang on, chew, throw, listen to, and explore in other ways. Toys that stimulate several different senses, such as objects that are visually interesting and also make noise, are particularly useful in infant perceptual and motor development.

CRITICAL CONCEPT 2

There is great individual variation in the age at which perceptual and motor abilities are acquired. Culture may be one factor that influences the pace of motor development. The games parents play with their babies, carrying practices, and the kinds of toys available can affect physical competence. How quickly toddlers learn self-help skills such as toileting also can be influenced by cultural beliefs and practices.

Application #1

Caregivers should be aware of cultural differences in motor development. Care should be taken not to misconstrue such physical differences as deficits.

Application #2

Caregivers can create a multicultural motor curriculum for babies by interviewing parents about what games are played in the home. The traditional chants, songs, finger plays, and games of diverse cultural groups can be introduced to babies of all cultures in infant care.

Application #3

Caregivers and parents should discuss family expectations for children's learning of self-help skills such as toileting and eating. Consensus should be reached on finding goals for independence that reflect cultural beliefs and traditions but do not cause stress in children.

CRITICAL CONCEPT 3

Perceptual and motor development are affected by challenging conditions. Genetic disorders or environmental trauma before or during birth can significantly impair physical growth. Intervention programs that provide services to babies and their families can offset the negative effects of these disorders.

Application #1

Communities should offer home-based and center-based early intervention programs that provide services to infants with special needs and their families.

Application #2

Child care providers can adapt play environments to meet the needs of babies with challenging conditions. Infants who are blind, for example, can be provided with toys that are rich to the touch or create interesting sounds.

Application #3

Families of infants with special needs can be given emotional support. Caregivers can encourage parents to express frustrations and anxieties. Parent support groups can be organized within infant care centers.

CRITICAL CONCEPT 4

The brain grows and develops at a remarkable rate in infancy. A typical 3-year-old has twice the number of synapses—connections among brain cells—as adults. After age 3, children lose synapses they do not use. Stimulation and warm, responsive caregiving are needed to ensure that important brain cell connections are created and maintained.

Application #1

Parents and caregivers should provide intellectual and language stimulation—talking, singing, reading to, and playing with infants. Care should be taken not to overstimulate babies, however, since overstimulation can lead to stress and impede neural development.

Application #2

Parents and caregivers should provide nurturing and responsive care in order to facilitate attachment. Using warm, physical touch and responding quickly to needs, adults can create positive emotional bonds with babies. These bonds not only enhance feelings of security, but will protect infants' brains from damaging environmental influences.

SUGGESTED ACTIVITIES

1. Observe a group of babies of varying ages in a child care setting. Select two children who are at least 4 months apart in age. Write descriptions of the motor activities of each, contrasting the two infants in regard to sitting up, standing, walking, running, grasping, throwing, or other abilities described in this chapter. Write a report on your observations, guided by the following questions:

   a. What specific differences did you observe in motor ability between the two infants?

   b. What can you conclude about changes in motor abilities during these periods of infancy?

2. Observe two babies in a child care center who are at least 4 months apart in age. Spend time with the infants and conduct simple tracking activities with each (e.g., dangling an interesting toy across their fields of vision). Write a description of infants' responses, guided by the following questions:

   a. How smoothly do babies turn and focus on the objects that are moved in front of them?

   b. To what degree do babies reach for toys? How accurate are they in grabbing them?

   c. What can you conclude about differences in infant visual perception between these two ages?

3. Visit an infant care center that serves children with special needs. Observe two children of roughly the same age who have very different developmental characteristics (e.g., an infant with Down syndrome and a typically developing infant). Write a comparison of the two babies, guided by the following questions:

   a. How are the babies alike in their motor activities, in their activity levels, and in the psychological states they exhibit?

   b. What are some "universal" physical and motor traits that are present in both babies?

   c. How do the two infants differ in their motor activities? To what do you attribute these differences? Do you suspect individual differences in competence or maturation? To what degree do challenging conditions contribute to motor differences?

4. Visit an infant care center that serves children of diverse cultural backgrounds. Observe two infants of roughly the same age who are of distinctly different cultural groups. Write a comparison of the two babies, guided by the following questions:

   a. How are the babies alike in their motor activities, in their activity levels, and in the psychological states they exhibit?

   b. What are some "universal" physical and motor traits that are present in both babies?

   c. How do the two infants differ in their motor activities? To what do you attribute these differences? To what degree does culture or family life contribute to these motor differences?

   d. What conclusions can you draw about cultural diversity and infant motor development?

CHAPTER 7

Cognitive Development in Infancy

IN THIS CHAPTER WE WILL DISCUSS THE INTELLECTUAL DEVELOPMENT OF CHILDREN FROM BIRTH TO AGE 2. Researchers and child specialists use the term *cognition* to refer to mental abilities. In this chapter, we will see that infant cognition differs markedly from that of older children or adults. The following story illustrates why cognitive development of babies is fascinating and important. The problem-solving of the two infants in the story shows the remarkable cognitive changes that children go through as they develop during this 2-year period.

A Bedouin Arab mother works busily in the kitchen, one of only two "rooms" in the tent where her family lives in the Negev desert in Israel. Her two infants are nearby. She is continually shooing her oldest, a 16-month-old, away from the cooking fires. Her 4-month-old lies next to her on a pile of blankets. When this youngest infant begins to fuss, the mother hangs a piece of rope over a pole so that it dangles just inches from her baby's face. (There are virtually no toys in this home; anything that is available—pieces of cloth, wood, furniture, and even animals that wander through the tent—becomes a plaything for the children.)

The strategy works. The 4-month-old wiggles with excitement. As he does, he accidentally bats the rope with his hand and makes it swing. This causes much smiling and additional wiggling; once again, his hand sends the rope swinging. All of this activity captures the attention of the 16-month-old, who stops playing and studies carefully this interesting toy. After a moment, she toddles over to her brother, draws back an arm, takes aim, and smacks the rope. This sends it swinging violently, so much so that it comes loose and falls on her brother. "Uh-uh," she says looking anxiously toward her mother. The 4-month-old is smiling, however, and wiggling more actively than ever. He appears to believe that his wiggles and this interesting new result were somehow related. The mother scolds her oldest, replaces the rope toy, and resumes her work.

The Arab mother in this story has demonstrated the seemingly universal understanding that dangling an interesting object is an excellent way to divert infant upset. More importantly, the story illustrates the differences in cognition between babies of different ages. The 4-month-old performed only random actions that created accidental results. From his playful activities, it is obvious that he does not understand clear connections between flailing arms and the swinging rope. In contrast, the 16-month-old was very purposeful and reflective in her action. She studied the rope, moved closer to it, carefully measured the length and speed of her swing, and accurately sent the rope swaying. She planned to swat the toy and then carried out her plan in an impressive manner—too impressive, perhaps. She quickly realized that her action caused a problem, one that could lead to a scolding from her mother. She used vocalizations and sophisticated facial expressions to communicate her anxiety. In general, the story shows the phenomenal difference in thinking between two infants who are just a year apart in age!

PIAGET'S VIEW OF INFANT INTELLIGENCE

The most well known and elaborate description of infant cognitive development is provided by Jean Piaget (1952b). He refers to the developmental period between birth and age 2 as the **sensorimotor stage.** In Piaget's view, thinking at this age involves getting things done physically by using the senses. There is no infant thought without action, he argues. Babies' cognition is in sharp contrast, then, to the internal, reflective thought processes of adults. Whereas adults contemplate, analyze, infer, or imagine, babies just act.

An illustration will clarify these ideas: Imagine that a highly desirable object is out of your reach, say on a high shelf. How would you go about getting it? You would probably hesitate a moment and think through the problem, picturing alternative strategies in your mind. If a chair was nearby, you might envision dragging it close to the shelf to stand on. In no time at all you would have formulated a plan, carried it out, and retrieved the object. According to Piaget's theory, young babies would follow a very different process in retrieving a toy that is out of reach. With little hesitation, they would swat at the object. Or, they might cry for an adult to get it for them. They would do these things without a clear understanding of what the results might be. Before a certain age, babies would not engage in careful reflection or thoughtful planning; they would simply take action.

Over the course of 2 years, babies' thinking gradually becomes more internal. When faced with this same problem, 2-year-olds would contemplate more thoroughly the steps they might take to get the toy. They might try several different techniques, perhaps even inventing very novel approaches. They might try to climb the bookshelf like a ladder, for example. (Such creative problem-solving poses many challenges for parents!) To Piaget, it is this shift from simple action to more internal thinking that marks infant cognitive development.

Piaget's Substages

Piaget plotted intellectual advancement from pure sensorimotor action to internalized thinking. He described six substages through which infants develop on their way to becoming more sophisticated thinkers. These steps are presented in Table 7-1.

TABLE 7-1
Piaget's Substages
of Infant Cognitive
Development

Substage	Age	Description
Reflexes	0 to 1 month	Infants perform simple, involuntary reflexes.
Primary circular reactions	1 to 4 months	Infants engage in circular actions with their bodies. A movement or vocalization is made; this creates an interesting sensation and is repeated. There is yet no understanding of cause and effect.
Secondary circular reactions	4 to 8 months	Infants engage in circular reactions that involve other objects. They may shake a rattle, note an interesting result, and shake it again. There is still no understanding of cause and effect.
Coordination of secondary circular reactions	8 to 12 months	Infants can perform a series of actions that have been performed in previous substages. They may shake, then bang, then chew a rattle. They understand that certain actions cause certain consequences. So, they engage in goal directed behavior—they set out to cause something to happen.
Tertiary, circular reactions	12 to 18 months	Infants can perform novel, never-before-tried actions to solve problems, e.g., they may use trial and error to obtain an interesting object placed high on a kitchen counter.
Mental combinations	18 to 24 months	Infants can solve some problems using mental images. They can think through their actions without actually performing them. They can study and later imitate the behaviors of others.

SOURCE: Piaget, 1952b.

Substage 1. In the first substage, from birth to 1 month, babies have a very limited repertoire; they do little more than wiggle reflexively, according to Piaget. Significant development occurs during this short period, however. Reflexes are refined and organized. For example, newborns must adapt their sucking reflex in order to retrieve nutrients from the nipple of a bottle or their mother.

Substage 2. During the second substage, between 1 and 4 months, babies begin to engage in **primary circular reactions.** These are actions involving babies' own bodies which are performed by accident but then repeated because they produce interesting sensations. For example, a baby may flail arms and legs about, notice the fascinating feel of this, and continue to perform these actions. A less positive example of a primary circular reaction was performed by my son when he was only 2 months old: By chance, he had reflexively grasped hold of a clump of his own hair and pulled. The initial sensation was interesting enough and the pulling continued. In no time, however, this action began to hurt. I eventually had to rescue him, interrupting the circular reaction by helping him loosen his grasp on his hair. These are called **circular reactions** because the infant as yet has no clear understanding, from Piaget's perspective, of what causes what. The wiggles and the sensation simply go together. A circular reaction is illustrated in Figure 7-1.

FIGURE 7-1

A primary circular reaction in early infancy. Cooing causes interesting sounds; these sounds cause continued cooing. The reaction goes round and round, with no understanding of beginning or end.

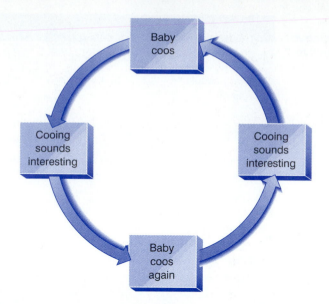

Substage 3. In substage 3 of infant cognitive development, between 4 and 8 months, babies engage in **secondary circular reactions.** These are actions that involve other objects: toys, clothing, even parents. For example, a baby might grasp a rattle, wiggle it by accident, notice the interesting noise it makes, and keep wiggling. As another example, I attached a mobile to the sleeve of my 6-month-old son's shirt with string. He swung his arms wildly as he watched the butterflies on the mobile fly about. This went on and on, and over time the butterflies fell off, one by one. The toy manufacturer clearly had not built a toy sturdy enough to survive the rigors of secondary circular reactions!

I have found that banging things is a prevalent secondary circular reaction among infants at this age. In fact, I've named this "the period of incessant pounding," since my own children seemed to take such pleasure in loud, headache-producing bangs that tended to go on and on. It is hard to say how long a baby might persist in creating this repetitive racket. Few parents have the stamina to find out. They are often observed creating distractions or redirecting babies to quieter toys. A consolation for a parent enduring many minutes of spoon-banging is that this is an important intellectual activity.

Substage 4. In substage 4, between 8 and 12 months, significant advancements occur. A new kind of action emerges at this substage—the coordination of secondary circular reactions. Babies combine several behaviors they have practiced in earlier stages. They may reach out, grasp a rattle, shake it, then bang it against a table. More important, babies of this period are, for the first time, able to understand that certain actions cause certain consequences. For example, they can tell the difference between the act of banging a rattle and the noise that results from this action.

Piaget invented a research method for studying this new causal thinking. He presented babies with an interesting toy which was placed out of their reach on a blanket. The blanket was within their grasp, and they were shown how to pull it toward themselves to get the toy. After infants had retrieved the objects several times by pulling the blanket, the toy was again placed out of reach. This time, however, it was placed next to the blanket, not on it. The infants were then allowed to solve the problem on their own. Before 8 months, babies were confused by the task. They would pull on the blanket again and again, even though the toy was not sitting on it. Thus, they were not able to think carefully about cause and effect. Their blanket-pulling was, likely, a secondary circular reaction.

After 8 months, however, babies were quite shrewd in solving the problem, showing they understood cause and effect more clearly. They could recognize that pulling the blanket only worked when the toy was sitting on top of it. When the toy was not on the blanket, they would abandon blanket-pulling and try completely different strategies. They might attempt to climb over the table, for example, or look to their parents for help.

Another kind of thinking that emerges in substage 4 is **object permanence**—an understanding that objects exist even if they cannot be seen or heard. Piaget has proposed that very young babies are unable to think about things they cannot perceive. When a favorite toy is hidden away in a toybox, for example, it simply does not exist in the mind of a 4-month-old. By 8 months, however, babies begin to contemplate objects that are not present. They may look around for misplaced toys or missing family members. Piaget developed a research method to study the development of this kind of thinking, as well. He showed babies of different ages a toy; just as they reached for it, he hid it behind a screen. Infants in substages 1, 2, or 3 no longer reached or searched for the object after it was hidden. When they could no longer see it, they acted as if it did not exist. In contrast, babies in substage 4 and later substages did search for and find the missing object.

Substage 5. Substage 5, from 12 to 18 months, is characterized by increasingly novel actions. According to Piaget, infants at this age not only combine previously mastered strategies, but try new ones to achieve their goals. If the old methods for getting an object that is out of reach—say, standing on tiptoes, reaching, or grasping—do not work, a brand-new, never-before-tried action might be attempted. A child might pull a chair over to the kitchen counter to retrieve a plate of brownies. If that fails, the child might try using a tool—perhaps a broom—to knock the brownies off onto the floor. It is clear that toddlerhood is a time of significant experimentation. One challenge of caring for children of this age is their powerful desire to accomplish things through active trial and error.

Children of substage 5 make further progress in causal thinking and object permanence. Although they become more and more competent at distinguishing between actions and consequences or determining what causes what, they still experience confusion. Flaws in causal thinking are common at this age and can create challenges for parents, as the following story reveals:

A father from a small village in Guatemala is puzzled over the fact that every time he wears an old straw hat, his 15-month-old daughter shows great upset. What is particularly odd is that he has worn the hat often from the time his daughter was born; never until now has she shown this strong reaction. He tries to think of every possible reason for the problem. Does the hat look like something frightening? Does it represent a bad experience for her? It is only as he is preparing for a trip to visit relatives in another village that he discovers the source of the difficulty. He realizes that he wears the hat when he travels.

His last two trips, he recalls, were to take his daughter to a clinic in nearby Guatemala City—once to have her immunized and a second time to have her treated for an illness. It is clear that his daughter is associating his hat with frightening and, in one case, painful visits to the nurse.

Other examples abound of how early causal thinking creates challenges. In American homes, some toddlers cry at signs of their parents' departure, such as when a sitter arrives or a mother puts on her coat. Others may climb into a highchair in the middle of the afternoon because they see parents working in the kitchen and assume it is dinner time.

Substage 6. Substage 6, from 18 to 24 months, is characterized by internalized thought. The older toddler can, for the first time, solve problems by thinking them through using mental images. At this substage a child studies a problem before acting, and engages in less physical trial and error. One parent's story provides a good example: Her child simply studied an adult unclasping a "child-proof" safety lock on a kitchen cabinet, and then later unclasped it on the first try to obtain a yummy snack of dog biscuits. So, this substage can also be a challenging period due to toddlers' intellectual as well as physical development!

By substage 6, babies can find objects that were hidden hours or even days earlier. I learned this in real life when one of my sons, as a toddler, hid his own shoes in a grocery bag in the kitchen one evening. The next day, his mother and I panicked as

Between 18 and 24 months, infants begin to solve complex problems, often studying objects or people first, before acting.

we tried to find the shoes while dressing him for child care. The shoes were nowhere to be found. He smiled as he watched us search frantically. When this grew tiresome, he toddled into the kitchen, pulled the shoes from their hiding place, and offered helpfully, "Here y'go, Daddy."

Although many advancements take place by substage 6, there are still many limitations in thinking. One characteristic that persists into toddlerhood is **egocentrism.** This is a type of thinking in which children are unable to understand that there are other viewpoints in the world besides their own. People at every age show some egocentrism, but infants are especially egocentric. Some child specialists have even suggested that babies view the entire world as being simply a part of themselves.

One difficulty that arises because of egocentrism is a tendency for toddlers to erroneously believe that their own actions have caused completely unrelated consequences. A child who has just been scolded for running toward a busy road, then later stumbles and skins a knee, may believe the naughty act caused the fall. The following is another example:

> A 23-month-old has been diagnosed with an ear infection and is required to take a nasty-tasting antibiotic. Her father has a difficult time getting her to swallow the medicine; she turns her head, spits, and cries. Eventually, she gives in and swallows. When every drop is gone, her father soothingly says, "There ya' go."
>
> After a number of days of this routine, the toddler begins to say, "de go," "de go," every time she sees her father approach with the full medicine spoon. These verbalizations become more urgent as he places the spoon near her mouth. He eventually realizes that his daughter has associated the phrase "there ya' go" with the end of an unpleasant experience. It is clear that she is saying this phrase because she believes this will cause the medicine-giving to stop. Persistent flaws in her causal thinking, as well as her egocentrism, have led her to misinterpret which event is the cause and which the effect.

In this example, the child is making a superb effort to interpret the world. However, she is still confused about which event causes the other and about her own power to make things happen. It is important for parents and child care providers to understand such limitations in toddlers' thinking. Adults need to be very explicit in discussing causes and effects. Simply saying "No!" when a child touches something dangerous, for example, may not clarify which action caused the reprimand. For example, if the child happened to be rubbing an eye at about the same time, the unintended message would be: if you rub your eye, you will get a stern admonishment.

A Multicultural Critique of Piaget's Theory

Piaget's descriptions of infant development have been found to be quite accurate. Researchers have tested his theories for decades and have found that babies appear to acquire cognitive abilities in precisely the order that Piaget described (Kaye & Marcus, 1981). The primary challenge to Piaget's work has come from researchers who note that infants have greater cognitive competence than he suggested. For example, studies have shown that object permanence may be present quite early in life (Braillargeon, Graber, Decops, & Black, 1990; Flavell, 1985). Babies appear to understand the existence of some objects earlier than others. They show upset at the disappearance of a parent even before they are able to search for missing toys in Piaget's task (S. M. Bell, 1970).

One reason for Piaget's underestimation of babies' cognitive abilities may be the lack of sophisticated research technology available when he was formulating his theory. His observations were done with smaller numbers of subjects in naturalistic settings without the complex laboratory equipment available today (Flavell, 1992). Also, his studies were limited to children of European background.

In spite of Piaget's misjudgment about the pace at which babies develop cognitive competence, his work continues to be viewed as the definitive account of infant cognition. The most important part of his theory—his descriptions of how and in what order cognitive skills emerge—has held up extremely well over time.

Multicultural scholars (Hale, 1994; Ogbu, 1992) have argued that Piaget's view of cognitive development is more sensitive to cultural diversity than other theories of human development. They point out that Piaget's framework focuses on universal thought processes, such as causal thinking and object permanence, rather than emphasizing the content of knowledge, which is shaped by culture. From a Piagetian perspective, exactly what babies know or are able to do—whether they can recognize a grandmother, turn the pages of a book, or speak the word "doggie," for example— is not as important as general mental functioning. The ability to recognize a particular object is not as critical as being able to retrieve, explore, search for, or solve problems with it within the environment. This culture-neutral element of Piaget's work has led Hale-Benson (1986) to conclude that "major aspects of his theory can be applied to all human societies and groups, and differences in performance can be accounted for without imputing inferiority or deficiency" (p. 24).

If multicultural scholars are correct, Piaget's descriptions of infant cognitive development must be accurate for babies of any cultural group. Research has, for the most part, found this to be so. For example, in one study, middle-class Euro-American infants were compared with those from two small villages in Guatemala in their performance on such Piagetian tasks as object permanence (Kagan, 1977). "Remarkable concordance" (p. 278) was discovered among these infants in the sequence with which they acquired cognitive skills. Small differences in the ages at which certain skills emerged were found. Babies from the isolated and impoverished Indian villages were slightly delayed in learning some skills. Nonetheless, the similarities between the two groups of babies were marked. Findings support Piaget's idea that cognitive development proceeds, for all babies, in predictable steps. Similar results have been obtained in studies of many other cultural groups (Dasen, 1984).

OTHER COGNITIVE SKILLS IN INFANCY

Besides the cognitive abilities that Piaget identified, several other aspects of infant mental functioning have been explored by researchers, including memory and pretend play.

Memory

Babies can remember persons, actions, and objects at a very early age. In one remarkable study, 8-week-olds were found to remember a learned behavior for up to 2 weeks (Rovee-Collier, Griesler, & Early, 1985). In this investigation, a ribbon was attached from a mobile to the legs of infant subjects. At first, these young babies did not seem aware that they could make the mobile move by kicking; they were taught to do so by researchers. Two weeks later, babies were again attached to the mobile. Without hesitation they began to kick their legs, suggesting they had remembered the situation and the actions from previous experience. At periods beyond 2 weeks, however, babies no longer kicked when the ribbon was attached.

Other studies found that babies didn't remember how to kick unless the entire setting was exactly the same as it was when the first experience occurred (Borovsky & Rovee-Collier, 1990). For example, if babies were trained to kick a mobile in one setting—say, in their crib at home—and were later placed in a different crib or provided with a different kind of mobile, they were not able to reenact the original behavior. This suggests that young babies may not remember specific events. Instead, they may recollect whole situations, or "spatiotemporal maps," as these authors call them. A baby's thinking might go like this: "I recognize this place, the softness of the pad I'm laying on, this person standing nearby, that set of floating butterflies, this funny ribbon attached to my leg; the whole scene is familiar. So I remember that kicking and butterfly wiggling go together." If anything is out of place, though, if things look or feel different, the whole experience vanishes from the baby's memory.

In many studies, babies have been found to acquire impressive visual memory skills by the age of 6 or 7 months (McCall & Carringer, 1993; Rose, Feldman, & Wallace, 1992). Visual memory is an ability to recognize objects that were seen at an earlier time. In these investigations, babies were shown various stimuli—abstract patterns, faces, or three-dimensional objects—until they became fully familiar with them. Later the babies were shown each picture or object again, along with a new, dissimilar one. The babies were observed to stare longest at the new, dissimilar object. It was concluded in these studies that they remembered the original stimulus—so well, in fact, that it had become very familiar and was no longer as interesting as a new object or picture.

By age 13 months, children have been found to recall complex actions after significant delays. In one study, children of this age could reproduce a series of actions (e.g., making a track and rolling a toy car down it) even a week after they had observed these actions performed by an adult (Bauer & Hertsgaard, 1993). A significant finding of this study was that adult verbal cues (e.g., "Remember when we made the car go down the track?") increased the accuracy of infant memory. An implication is that parents and caregivers can use language to help even preverbal 1-year-olds learn and remember important behaviors, such as "Don't touch!" or "That's very hot!"

How long do these memories last? Will babies recollect experiences in later childhood? Astounding results of one study (Perris, Myers, & Clifton, 1990) show that 2 1/2-year-olds could reenact a task they had performed just once at age 6 months! Thus, early experiences appear to stay in children's memories a long time. These findings reaffirm the importance of providing positive home and classroom environments for babies. The experiences parents or caregivers provide during this age will have a lasting influence.

Is infant memory related to later cognitive abilities? In one study, babies' visual memory was found to be associated with language and reading ability, quantitative competence, and general intelligence at age 6 (Colombo & Mitchell, 1991). In a summary of 23 studies of infant memory, McCall and Carringer (1993) concluded that infants' ability to remember is associated with IQ scores at age 8. In fact, these authors suggest that infant memory tasks are a better way to predict later cognitive functioning than traditional infant intelligence tests.

Infant Pretend Play and Cognitive Development

Play is a common activity in infancy. One sophisticated form of playing—pretend play—is particularly useful in enhancing intellectual abilities before age 3. The following story provides an excellent illustration of pretend play in the early years:

Alonzo, an 18-month-old, is playing in a barren courtyard outside his apartment in a housing project in an urban neighborhood. His mother sits on the front steps, keeping a watchful eye on her son. She is saddened that he doesn't have a nice space to play in or toys to use. The playground in the project is in disrepair and unsafe.

She notices that Alonzo has created a play environment for himself. He has found the only object in the area, half of a clay brick, and is pushing it along the cracked sidewalk leading up to their front door. He displays an impressive repertoire of car noises: engine roars, fire sirens, and an occasional tire squeal. His mother smiles. She is fascinated and amazed by his ingenuity.

People from all cultures engage in play from the time they are very young. Play has been defined as any behavior that is nonliteral, intrinsically motivated, self-chosen, and pleasurable (J. E. Johnson, Christie, & Yawkey, 1999). Thus, play can include dress-up, playing checkers, rolling down a hill on the playground, or swinging on a swing. These activities make childhood fun, but they are also critical for cognitive development.

One early form of play is the spontaneous, repetitive motoric activity of early infancy. An infant's circular reactions (described earlier in this chapter) are usually quite playful. Rhythmically banging a rattle, for example, is enjoyable and intrinsically rewarding, so it can be considered playing. Cooing and babbling are really spontaneous play with sounds. Several examples of infant motor play are presented in Table 7-2.

Some early motor play is social; babies play with other people even in the earliest months of life. In many cultures, parents are the first playmates; they initiate or respond to playful infant behaviors. When they do this, they are not only making warm contact with their children, but are also promoting intellectual growth. For example, when an African-American father plays "faces" by letting his baby touch his face and then putting his own hands on hers, he is promoting early causal thinking. The baby learns that her action—touching—causes the father to respond in kind (Hale-Benson, 1986). When a mother in a Euro-American family plays peekaboo, she is teaching her infant a lesson in object permanence. If the mother's face disappears, does it still exist? The solution to the riddle is sudden and thrilling as the mother's face reappears, accompanied by the high-pitched vocalization, "Peeeeek-a-booooo." When a mother in India plays the Bengali game *Kan Dol Dol,* in which she and her baby hold one another's ears and sing, she is facilitating imitation. In the game, the baby emulates the mother's actions and intonations (Roopnarine, Hossain, Gill, & Brophy, 1994).

In some cultures, young babies have non-parent playmates as well. In one small Italian village, infants were observed playing as often with extended family members and even neighbors as with parents (New, 1994). Older siblings, cousins, or neighbor children were particularly frequent playmates; they would engage babies in games of practice walking or *batti, batti, le, manini,* a version of patty-cake. These experiences with other playmates are important, and not just socially. All of the noisemaking and pounding, laughter and surprise, wiggling and bouncing that char-

TABLE 7-2
**Examples of Infant
Motor Play**

Type of Play	Examples
Primary circular reactions	An infant accidentally makes a "raspberry" noise with tongue and lips. This creates an interesting sound. He playfully repeats this vocalization again and again.
	A father tickles his infant daughter. She shrieks with delight. He tickles her again. She responds with another giggle. They continue with the game in an endless chain of tickles and shrieks.
Secondary circular reactions	The sleeve of an infant's shirt is attached by a thread to a mobile dangling over his crib. He wiggles accidentally and causes the butterflies on the mobile to flutter about. He shows a brief expression of surprise, then wiggles again.
	An infant playfully pounds a toy plastic hammer on the tray of her high chair. She pounds for a minute or more, then stops, smiles, and looks at her father. Then she pounds again. The game continues until her father distracts her with a quieter toy.
Imitation games	An Indian mother and her infant son play a traditional Bengali game, *Kan Dol Dol*. The mother gently holds the baby's ears and begins to sing. The baby reaches out and grabs her mother's ears; he vocalizes in unison with her song.
	A father claps his hands in a playful gesture. His baby smiles, wiggles, and imitates the gesture.
Simple pretense	A baby lays her head on a pillow and closes her eyes pretending to sleep. "Night, night," her father says. A smile crosses her face. She opens her eyes and laughs.
	A baby pretends to drink from an empty cup. Then she holds the cup to her mother's mouth; the mother makes noises to indicate she is drinking. The baby places the cup to her own mouth again and imitates her mother's sounds.

acterize early social motor play provide unique opportunities for babies to construct their understanding of the world.

Pretend play is a very useful form of play that emerges in later infancy. In this activity, babies transform themselves into make-believe people, animals, or objects. They may pretend to be a parent feeding a baby or a doctor giving immunizations. They often change real objects into imaginary ones. They might use an old gourd, for example, as if it were a real cup filled with juice, or hold a toy telephone as if it were a real one. Often, infants carry out increasingly complex make-believe enactments in such play. For example, a child who is pretending to be the village blacksmith will pound a rock as if it were real metal and create noises that simulate the sounds of metal being plunged into cold water.

Vygotsky (1976) argued that this kind of play is practice at symbolizing. Symbolizing is a mental activity in which an abstract symbol is used to stand for an idea or an object that is not present. The words on this page are symbols, as are spoken words. When a child pretends to drink juice from a gourd, the gourd is a symbol that

During later infancy, some children begin to play with peers.

represents a real cup that is not present. So, early pretend play is important practice at using **symbolic thought.**

Pretend play emerges as early as age 1 and becomes more complex and frequent through toddlerhood (Trawick-Smith, 1991). The earliest form of infant make-believe play involves the pretend use of familiar objects to enact customary routines associated with those objects in real life (M. M. Watson & Jakowitz, 1984). A 14-month-old might take a cup and pretend to drink; another might lie on a pillow and pretend to sleep. In the second year, babies begin to use two or more objects in these simple pretend enactments (McCune, 1995). A pillow and a blanket might be used to pretend to sleep, or a toy pitcher might be used to pour pretend liquid into a toy cup. It is easy to see that these activities involve early symbolic thought; objects are being used to play out events that are not really occurring. The objects and actions are symbols, not unlike words and text.

In the second year, play takes a significant leap forward. For the first time, children use objects in their play to represent things that are completely different. A wooden rod might be used as a spoon, or a cylinder-shaped block as a cup. This sort of play involves sophisticated symbolizing. For example, it is intellectually challenging for Alonzo, the 18-month-old in the story at the beginning of this section, to imagine that a brick is a car, since these two things are so totally different.

VARIATIONS IN INFANT COGNITIVE DEVELOPMENT

Cognitive development varies among individual infants. This variation arises from numerous sources. Some children may simply have unique developmental time clocks that cause them to follow their own idiosyncratic paths toward healthy, typical childhood. Others have family or community experiences that lead to unique patterns of intellectual growth. Some suffer debilitating conditions, such as illness, genetic disorder, or poverty, that influence their cognitive development. For these reasons, a group of infants in any given child care setting will likely represent a rich diversity of cognitive styles and abilities.

Culture and Infant Cognition

Cultural experience can influence cognition in infancy. The pace at which babies acquire cognitive skills sometimes varies across cultures. In a study in Botswana, for example, !Kung babies were found to be significantly advanced in their performance on various cognitive tasks as compared with Euro-American babies (Konner, 1977). Although infants of both cultures were found to acquire cognitive skills in the same order, !Kung babies were several months ahead of their American peers in the acquisition of these skills.

How can these cultural differences be explained? It may be that some cultural traditions or socialization practices lead to advancement in certain intellectual abilities. For example, in the Botswana study, the advanced mental abilities of !Kung infants were attributed to the high frequency of social and cognitive stimulation in !Kung family life. A typical day for a !Kung baby includes a phenomenal degree of parent-infant play. Toys are provided, and mobiles and other objects are hung from cribs. !Kung mothers wear elaborate ornamental necklaces which babies play with as they sit in their mothers' laps. !Kung babies also spend an extensive period of time each day in a vertical posture, which may facilitate alertness and sensorimotor exercise.

Such parenting practices are culturally derived, a part of !Kung tradition. These interactions are encouraged and expected in that part of the world, and community life is structured to allow parents to care for babies in this way. A word of caution is in order: These same child care practices might be impossible to carry out within another culture; in fact, these practices may not even be desirable for babies from other ethnic backgrounds. The point of cross-cultural research is not to identify successful practices from one culture in order to transfer them to another, but rather to gain an understanding and appreciation of rich cultural variation in cognition among babies.

Researchers may find cultural differences in infant cognition for other reasons. Nyiti (1982) proposes that, in some research, problems in the way cognition is tested cause babies of one culture to be found less competent than those of another. He points out that researchers are often of different ethnic backgrounds than babies of the particular cultural group being studied. Babies may have difficulty relating to and understanding these culturally different adults. For example, when Euro-American researchers use English to ask bilingual Puerto Rican toddlers to play with certain objects, they may confuse, distract, or otherwise inhibit them from showing what they can really do.

Nyiti (1982) also suggests that findings of cultural differences may be explained by poor estimates of age in some communities. Within many cultures, birth dates and precise ages are not considered important. Parents simply do not think about infant development in terms of months beyond birth. Hence, they tend to make inaccurate guesses about the ages of their children and inadvertently provide researchers with flawed data.

Finally, some cultural differences in infant cognition may result from babies' unfamiliarity with the toys or objects used in studies. Native American babies may not be drawn to or interested in looking at the same objects as Euro-American babies. For example, if a toy holds no personal or cultural meaning to an 8-month-old Navajo infant, the infant may not eagerly search for it in an object permanence task. In one study, babies from Zambia, who rarely played with objects or toys in their homes, were found to show little interest in looking at or pursuing objects of any kind (Goldberg, 1977).

Although real cultural differences do exist, they may be highly distorted when research techniques are not culturally sensitive. Care must be taken not to interpret diversity in infants' pace of intellectual development as an indicator of cultural deficiency.

Poverty

Poverty is one of the most debilitating conditions for children (Werner & Smith, 1992). Infants from impoverished homes are more likely to suffer delays in cognitive development and language. The longer babies live in poverty, the more severe these delays (Dowling & Fisher, 1987). Being poor in infancy can have lasting effects. In one study, children who lived in poverty as infants were found to be less competent in school-related cognitive tasks at age 10 (D. Walker, Greenwood, Haret, & Carta, 1994). However, being from a low-income family does not automatically mean that a baby will have cognitive deficiencies. Some infants who live in poverty develop quite typically (Huston, McLoyd, & Garcia Coll, 1994). A range of family and neighborhood factors will determine the developmental impact that poverty will have. These are presented in Figure 7-2.

Babies of low-income families who live in safer and less crowded homes are more likely to acquire typical cognitive and language competence (R. H. Bradley et al., 1994). On the other hand, babies who do not receive adequate nutrition or who are not well cared for—two sadly common consequences of impoverished family life—may show intellectual delays.

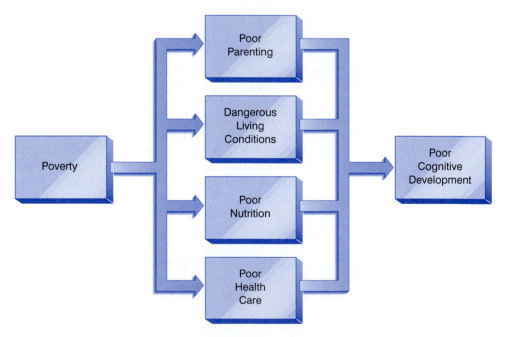

FIGURE 7-2 Poverty leads to poor developmental outcomes by increasing family stressors and creating unhealthy home and community environments.

Nutritional Deficiency. Poor nutrition is common among low-income families. Iron-deficiency anemia and protein deficiency are especially prevalent among poor African-American and Latino babies, and among those from economically under-developed countries. Babies suffering these conditions perform poorly on measures of infant cognitive development (Pollitt, 1994). One explanation for the devastating effects of malnutrition is that during the crucial period when babies are experiencing rapid brain growth, a lack of nutrients can seriously inhibit neurological development.

Parenting. Parents in poverty are often under a great deal of stress. This can negatively influence parent-child relationships. Parents who are suffering either chronic poverty or sudden economic decline become increasingly punitive and coercive and less supportive and warm over time in interactions with their children (McLoyd, 1990a). This has a particularly devastating effect on infants. Babies in poverty who receive less responsive, accepting, stimulating, or organized care have been found to display poor cognitive functioning (R. H. Bradley et al., 1994). Babies whose parents are more positive survive experiences of poverty with little cognitive delay. In low-income Haitian-American families, for example, warm and positive parenting was found to significantly enhance the intellectual functioning of high-risk 1-year-olds (Widmayer et al., 1990).

Challenging Conditions and Infant Cognition

Other sources of variation in infant cognitive development include illness, injury, genetic disorder, and other challenging conditions. For example, children with **Down syndrome** are often significantly delayed in mental development. Cognitive difficulties of infants with Down syndrome are less apparent in the early months of life. By the second year, however, these babies show significant delays in the acquisition of cognitive, language, and play skills (Cicchetti & Beeghly, 1990). The degree to which the disorder affects cognitive growth in infancy is related, once again, to parenting. Babies who receive significant social, intellectual, and motor stimulation from parents or other adults will show substantially more advanced cognitive development than babies who do not receive this care (Kaplan, 1996).

Challenging conditions are also caused by problems during birth. Sometimes babies have trouble getting enough oxygen during the birth process. Blood vessels may break in a baby's head during a difficult labor, restricting oxygen flow, or a baby may become tangled in the umbilical cord. In some cases, babies have trouble breathing right after birth and require neonatal oxygen intervention, in which an oxygen face mask or even a ventilator must be provided. These experiences may affect brain development and thereby cause cognitive delays in infancy. For example, babies who suffered oxygen deprivation or hemorrhaging at birth have been found to perform less well on learning tasks at 13 months of age (Millar, Weir, & Supramaniam, 1992).

Low birth weight can also affect cognitive development in infancy (Behrman, 1995). Since babies born in poor families and those from historically under-represented cultural groups are more likely to be afflicted by this condition, it is difficult to distinguish the effects of this health indicator from those of poverty or racial barriers to health care. It is now believed, however, that low birth weight in itself can create cognitive difficulties noticeable in the first 2 years (Bhushan, Paneth, & Kiely, 1993; Brooks-Gunn, Klebanov, Liaw, & Spiker, 1993). Home environment and health care greatly influence the outcomes for low-birth-weight babies. Medical and social support before, during, and after pregnancy can greatly reduce the negative effects of low birth weight on infant cognition (Paneth, 1995).

Families, Culture, and Infants with Special Needs

Families of infants with special needs can suffer great stress (Shonkoff, Hauser-Cram, Krauss, & Upshur, 1992). The identification of cognitive delays, neurological impairment, or Down syndrome in infancy can create feelings of guilt, frustration, or anxiety among parents (Beckman, 1991). Mothers of infants with special needs have been found to suffer especially high levels of stress, particularly when the causes of the challenging condition cannot be clearly identified (Goldberg, Markovitch, MacGregor, & Lojkasek, 1986).

One study found that fathers of exceptional infants also experience anxiety. They worry about different things than mothers do, however (Shonkoff et al., 1992). Mothers more often suffer global stressors such as depression, anxiety about day-to-day parenting, or feelings of incompetence. Fathers are more narrowly concerned about poor attachment; they are most likely to worry that they will not come to love or bond with their child because of challenging conditions.

A number of factors have been found to reduce stress in families of infants with special needs. Extensive child and family services, including early educational intervention, home visitation by professionals, and parent support groups, can reduce parent anxiety (Shonkoff et al., 1992). Informal social support from relatives and friends is also related to family adjustment; parents who are aided by grandparents or caring neighbors will cope more successfully (Beckman, 1991). Families of infants with milder conditions will experience less stress.

Cultural traditions and values may help some families to cope with the stresses of raising an infant with special needs. Parents of historically under-represented groups more often live in extended families. African-American, Puerto Rican, Asian-American, and Native American households, for example, are likely to be multigenerational. Friends and neighbors commonly assist in child rearing and family problem-solving within these cultural groups. Informal social support networks—groups of relatives and friends who support one another emotionally and financially—are formed as an adaptive strategy for surviving the challenges of poverty or racial bias (Harrison, Wilson, Pine, Chan, & Buriel, 1990). Such support networks have been found to significantly reduce stress among parents who have infants with special needs (Beckman, 1991). A neighbor might provide a regular respite for a weary single mother. An experienced grandmother might assist a young father in learning to meet an infant's unique needs. Such informal social support might be as psychologically helpful to some families as formal intervention (Shonkoff et al., 1992).

In cultures that accept and appreciate diversity of development, the anxiety associated with special needs might be lessened. For example, in some Native American families, less importance is placed on the timing of children's development (Blanchard, 1983). Parents of such families may believe that babies will walk and talk when they will. Individuality is not only tolerated but encouraged (John, 1988). Such acceptance reflects historical perspectives on the natural order of things. All that exists is good and right, according to ancient Native American beliefs (Red Horse, 1983). There are no abnormalities, from this view. Differences are to be appreciated because they are part of nature.

Parents in some societies have little concern about developmental delay in infancy because the issues of basic survival are so overriding. In his classic research in West Africa, for example, Levine (1977) reports that mothers in communities facing starvation and high infant mortality had very little interest in their infants' cognitive development. Neurological impairments or mental retardation would likely go unnoticed in such communities. Keeping one's baby alive might be the only measure of positive developmental outcome in such families. Impairments that would draw great attention in one society, then, would receive scant notice in another.

Early Intervention

The negative influence of some of the factors we have described may be reduced through early intervention. Babies who are at risk of intellectual delay may be provided with nutritional, educational, or family interventions that can greatly offset the damaging effects of poverty, malnutrition, poor health, or genetic disorder (Shore, 1997).

Nutritional Intervention. A number of studies have shown that the negative effects of poverty, malnutrition, and low birth weight are significantly reduced by providing nutritional guidance and resources to mothers during pregnancy and food supplements to their infants after they are born (Pollitt, 1994). In one study, when poor Guatemalan mothers and children were provided nutritional supplements, the children showed advanced cognitive abilities throughout infancy (Pollitt, Gorman, Engle, Martorell, & Rivera, 1993). An important finding of this study was that these cognitive advantages lasted for a long period of time. Even in adolescence, these children were found to have advanced intellectual abilities! In a study in the United States, prenatal nutrition and health care were found to reduce preterm deliveries and low birth weight, as well as the cognitive difficulties associated with these conditions (G. R. Alexander, Weiss, & Hulsey, 1991).

Unfortunately, there has been less interest in the United States in recent years in implementing health- and nutrition-related interventions. Instead, greater emphasis has been placed on intellectual and social interventions in the home or classroom (Pollitt, 1994). The power of early nutrition has been often overlooked, yet it may be the most effective intervention for supporting the development of babies in poverty.

Family and Parent Interventions. As we discussed, poor parenting and a less supportive home environment are among the negative effects of poverty. Effective parent interactions are associated with positive infant cognitive development, especially among babies with special needs. Family and parent intervention is a powerful method, then, of providing early support for babies' development. Home-based programs have been designed to assist parents, grandparents, siblings, and other caregivers in learning to perform nurturing and cognitively stimulating interactions. These programs can have a profound influence on babies. Such interventions have been found to significantly enhance the intellectual abilities of babies with Down syndrome and of those in poverty (F. A. Campbell & Ramey, 1994; Landry & Chapieski, 1989).

These studies illustrate how important parent support and education are in child development. Caregivers can make a difference by assisting families in providing nurturing environments for their babies. It is important to point out, however, that parent programs should be culturally sensitive. Parent education programs must recognize that there are many ways to show warmth, provide stimulation, and respond to babies' needs, and must appreciate the wide range of approaches to caregiving found across cultural groups (Lally, 1994).

Educational Interventions. Infant education programs have been found to be especially effective for at-risk children. In such home- or center-based programs, professionals provide direct intellectual or social stimulation. In one program, a home visitor might play causality or object permanence games with babies right in the family home. In another, a caregiver might stimulate the language of toddlers in a child care center. These programs have been found to produce long-term positive re-

ASSESSING YOUNG CHILDREN: Infant Cognitive Development

Areas of Development	What to Watch for	Indicators of Atypical Development
General cognitive abilities	Increasingly complex circular reactions: first repetitive actions with one's own body, later actions performed on other objects. An ability, by 8 months, to search for objects when they are not in view. By this same age, making frequent attempts to cause events to occur through physical action. An ability, by 18 months, to study and think about problems internally before trying to solve them.	Failure to progress beyond primary circular reactions (e.g., simple actions with one's own body). An inability, at 8 months, to retrieve toys, signal for help from an adult, or solve other problems that require causal thinking. A tendency to solve all problems by physical trial and error after 18 months.
Specific intellectual skills	An ability, by 6 months, to remember familiar persons or objects for short periods. An ability to perform simple make-believe enactments with one's own body by age 1 year (e.g., pretending to sleep). Skill in pretending with other people or dolls by 18 months.	Showing poor memory of familiar persons or objects. Continuing to engage in simple, repetitive motor play without make-believe beyond 18 months.

Interpreting Assessment Data: Variations in these areas may be due to culture and family life experience. Cognitive abilities such as object permanence or remembering specific objects will vary depending on the availability of toys within the home. The types of play children engage in—make-believe, active motor play, or quieter pursuits—will be determined by culture and family preference. Children who cannot solve problems of cause and effect or who *never* engage in make-believe may be at risk, however. Illness, injury, or genetic disorders may be a cause; further evaluation is needed. Nutritional, family, and educational intervention can often offset the negative effects of these conditions.

sults for children with Down syndrome or other genetically derived challenging conditions (Bricker, Carlson, & Schwartz, 1981). Furthermore, children in severe poverty have been found to make significant intellectual gains when such programs are combined with health care and nutritional supplements (Grantham-McGregor, Powell, Walker, Chang, & Fletcher, 1994). The positive effects of early intervention are greater if begun in early infancy (F. A. Campbell & Ramey, 1994).

High-quality child care alone can lead to gains in infant cognition. In one study, in fact, poor children who began a center-based program before their first birthday performed better on later school-related cognitive tasks than children who had entered centers later in life (Caughy, DiPietro, & Strobino, 1994).

One source of variation in infant cognitive development, then, is the availability of nutritional, family, and educational services. In the United States, infants of middle- or upper-middle-class backgrounds are more likely to have access to nutritional and health resources and to high-quality educational programs (Phillips, Voran, Kisker, Howes, & Whitebook, 1994). Infants who live in poverty often do not have these resources and services.

RESEARCH INTO PRACTICE

CRITICAL CONCEPT 1

Infants make impressive strides in cognitive development. In 2 short years, they acquire abilities to find objects, cause events to occur, imitate others, and remember objects and people. They learn to put things into categories and play make-believe games.

Application #1

Caregivers and parents can initiate hiding games to promote children's conception of object permanence. Peekaboo and "drop the spoon" are examples for younger infants. "Hide and seek" and "hide the object" are appropriate games for toddlers.

Application #2

Caregivers and parents should provide experiences that help babies understand cause and effect. Toys involving an action that produces an interesting result are ideal. Examples are a squeeze toy that makes an interesting noise, or a pull toy that makes popping sounds when it is dragged along the floor.

Application #3

Caregivers and parents can play imitation games with older infants and toddlers. These include games with actions, such as patty-cake or rubbing faces. As children acquire language, simple songs and rhymes are appropriate.

Application #4

A dramatic play area can be provided for toddlers. Children can be encouraged to play out simple make-believe enactments with realistic props. Drinking and eating, pounding with a plastic hammer, and talking on a toy telephone are examples.

CRITICAL CONCEPT 2

Children of different cultures may show different cognitive abilities or may acquire these abilities at different rates. For example, in societies in which babies are stimulated by adult contact throughout the day, advanced infant cognition may be observed. Generally, variations in infant development reflect the rich cultural, developmental, and socioeconomic diversity of our country and our world.

Application #1

Caregivers should understand and appreciate variations in cognitive development in infancy. Care should be taken not to confuse cultural differences with deficits.

Application #2

Caregivers can interview parents to learn about the games and activities that are used to promote cognitive development at home. This information can be used to infuse rich cultural play traditions in infant care.

CRITICAL CONCEPT 3

Poverty, malnutrition, and genetic disorders can interrupt cognitive development in infancy. Early intervention can offset some of these negative influences.

Application #1

Caregivers must be able to identify challenging conditions in the babies they care for. This requires that they understand the behaviors and intellectual characteristics that indicate atypical development. Identifying special needs and accessing services to address those needs are among the most important responsibilities of infant care providers.

Application #2

Caregivers and parents must be aware of the devastating effects of poverty and poor health care on infant development. They must become advocates for early education and for nutritional, health, and family support services.

SUGGESTED ACTIVITIES

1. Observe two 6- to 12-month-old babies in child care who are of different ages. Write down descriptions of interesting behaviors they perform that show thinking or problem-solving, as described in this chapter. Write a report on your observations, guided by the following questions:

   a. What kinds of circular reactions were observed? Did babies perform these using their own bodies? Objects or toys? Vocalizations?

   b. Generally, how would you characterize the babies' causal thinking? Did either baby set out to cause something to happen?

   c. What did babies do with objects? Did you see behaviors that show object permanence (e.g., searching for a toy that was out of sight, or dropping a toy and retrieving it)?

   d. What kinds of problems did you see babies solve? How did they get basic needs met? How did they retrieve toys or other desired objects?

2. Obtain permission from parents of two babies between the ages of 4 and 8 months to perform several Piagetian tasks. With each baby, show an interesting object, then hide it under a towel or box just as he or she reaches for it. Note what the baby does. If the baby can find the toy several times in one hiding place, try placing it under a second towel or box. Note what happens.

   Next, perform three or four simple behaviors such as clapping or gently pounding the table or floor. Note what the baby does in response. Then, demonstrate several more complex behaviors—say, clapping and then touching your nose. Note whether the baby imitates these behaviors. Write a report on the experience, guided by the following questions:

   a. To what degree does each baby understand object permanence? Discuss what you can conclude from the object-hiding experience.

   b. How well does the baby imitate? Does the baby imitate some behaviors more accurately than others? Does the baby attempt to imitate the more complex behaviors? What can you conclude from the imitation task?

3. Complete a half-hour observation in a child care center or home. Observe a child who is over 4 months old and has a challenging condition (e.g., Down syndrome, hearing impairment). Take notes on this child's interactions in the play environment. Write a report on your observations, guided by the following questions:

   a. How would you characterize the baby's use of objects? Does the infant reach for, grab, manipulate, look at, or mouth objects? Did you observe circular reactions? Did the baby imitate peers or adults during your observation?

   b. How well does the baby appear to hear, see, and touch? Does the infant appear to accurately perceive the world, or are there perceptual limitations?

   c. To what degree does the baby's challenging condition affect learning?

   d. What interventions do caregivers use to stimulate cognitive and perceptual development?

CHAPTER 8

Infant Language and Literacy

IN THIS CHAPTER WE WILL EXAMINE INFANT LANGUAGE AND LITERACY DEVELOPMENT. Babies use language at a surprisingly early age. They can understand words and phrases before adults are even aware that they can. They display an impressive repertoire of verbalizations to convey needs or express ideas. Sometimes these language behaviors are not easy for adults to recognize and interpret, as the following story reveals:

A mother has brought her 10-month-old son to a parent conference in her older daughter's elementary school. As the teacher and mother chat, the young toddler plays with toys in the classroom. Suddenly the child blurts out, "huh-duh, huh-duh!" and points to the door. The teacher is puzzled. What could the child be trying to communicate? She is even more surprised by the mother's response: "No, sweetie. You can't go out now. We'll go in a few minutes." The baby doesn't seem satisfied. "Huh-duh," he says in an angry tone. "No. You can't go right now," the mother responds gently. The baby finally goes back to playing, and the mother and teacher resume their discussion. Later, the teacher comments on the mother's remarkable ability to understand her baby's messages. The mother explains: "I've just gotten to know his little language. I'm pretty good at figuring out what he's trying to say."

Is the baby in this story really using language, as his mother thinks? Are such garbled utterances really words? What is real language, and when does it first emerge in human development? How is language development affected by the type of language spoken or the number of different languages to which one is exposed? These are questions that language specialists—known as psycholinguists—ask as they observe linguistic abilities unfold in the early years.

RECEPTIVE LANGUAGE

Language understanding is often called **receptive language** by psycholinguists. Babies understand words long before they can actually speak them (Fenson et al., 1994). This means that parents and teachers should begin talking to babies even before the babies begin to talk. At what age will babies benefit from adult conversation? No one knows the answer to this question. Before age 1, babies can show us they understand words. When asked "Where's Mommy?" a baby may point or smile. It may be that babies can comprehend even earlier in life but lack the motor skills to show what they know. To be safe, it is advisable to speak to babies at birth (if not before; some mothers make it a practice to have long conversations with their fetuses while pregnant!). Even if babies don't clearly interpret our messages in their early months, such conversations are good practice for parents.

Speech Perception

Evidence suggests that hearing language even in early infancy is useful. Newborns perceive and process language differently than they do other sounds. For example, in brain-wave studies, newborns display more activity in the left side of their brains when they hear language and more activity in the right side when they hear music (Molfese, Freeman, & Polermo, 1975). Since language is believed to originate in the left hemisphere of the brain, hearing speech may exercise the early linguistic functions of the nervous system.

Psycholinguists have found that babies are quite competent in perceiving speech sounds. Within the first few months of life, they can distinguish among some consonant and vowel sounds (Eilers & Minifie, 1975; Trehub, 1976), intonations, pitch (Fernald, 1993), and loudness (Bench, 1969). In a controversial study, W. S. Condon and Sander (1974) reported that babies wiggle in concert with the rhythms of human voices. All of this research suggests that infants are "wired" for language learning at birth. In fact, babies may be better able to distinguish among speech sounds of different languages than adults are (Fernald, 1993; Jusczyk, Cutler, & Redaz, 1993). Trehub (1976) found that English-speaking babies were able to distinguish between two Czech sounds, even though their parents could not. Japanese babies have little trouble discriminating between the English sounds for the letters "l" and "r," even though Japanese adults are unable to do this (Eimas & Tartter, 1979). These findings suggest that babies may be born with a capacity to learn any language, but their speech perception narrows over time to include only the speech sounds of their own culture's language.

Understanding Words

Sometime in the second half of the first year, babies come to understand words (Fenson et al., 1994). The first words they can interpret are usually labels for objects (e.g., ball, door, mommy). There are a variety of theories about why this is so. Parents may use object words more in their talk to babies (Bridges, 1986). It is also possible that babies believe, at first, that all words are names of objects (Markman, 1992). The first words babies learn are influenced by culture: Spanish babies learn Spanish words, English babies learn English words, and so on. More than this, however, different types of words may be emphasized more in one culture than another. For example, in a culture in which compliance and directive parenting are the norm, the word "no" may be learned earlier (Shatz, Grimm, Wilcox, & Niemeier-Wind, 1989). Babies in Italy understand quite early in life the names of different kinds of pasta (Tomasello & Mervis, 1994).

PRODUCTIVE LANGUAGE

Productive language is language that babies can actually speak. An infant's early words are often considered the first instances of productive language. However, there is evidence that gestures, noises, and even crying constitute the earliest forms of productive communication. The baby in the story at the beginning of this chapter was expressing an idea with his "huh-duh" comment. Psychologists consider communication to be any symbolic expression that holds meaning. So, the infant's garbled babble might rightfully be considered true productive language.

Crying

Crying is perhaps babies' earliest form of productive communication. Through cries, newborns communicate upset, and they show the intensity of their disturbance by varying the pitch and duration of their cries and the number of pauses between bursts of crying (D'Odorico, 1984). Debate continues about whether very young infants can communicate specific needs, such as hunger, pain, anger, or fear, by altering the acoustical properties of their cries. Most parents swear that this is so. Some studies have shown that parents and trained professionals can differentiate among various kinds of cries. Other investigations have found that even experienced parents are not accurate in reading the precise meaning of their own babies' cries (Muller, Hollien, & Murry, 1974). What is clear from these crying studies is that babies can vary their vocalizations right after birth.

Crying varies significantly among individuals. Temperament and family circumstances may influence amount of crying. Babies of different ethnic groups show different crying patterns. Among many Euro-American babies, for example, crying is a preferred method of communication, while Navajo, Chinese-American, and Japanese-American babies cry less often (Chisholm, 1983; Freedman, 1974).

If crying is communication, is it somehow linked to later language development? A classic study by S. M. Bell and Ainsworth (1972) indicated that babies whose parents responded quickly to their cries were less likely to cry in the second year of life and were more advanced in communicative competence. It may be that responding to crying shows the power of vocalization, and that babies with responsive parents graduate more quickly from this early form of communication to actual language. Parents of different cultures will, of course, respond in different ways to infant crying. Some offer a pacifier, others play or talk, and others snuggle and nurse (P. S. Zeskind, 1983). There is no one correct way to respond to crying. All of these methods may enhance infants' communicative competence.

Noises and Gestures

As babies get older, they make noises and gestures to communicate. By age 1, infants of most cultures understand when others point to things and will themselves point to refer to objects (Bates, O'Connell, & Shore, 1987). At about the same time, culturally defined gestures emerge: a Japanese baby might demonstrate early bowing (Ogura, Yamasjota, Murase, & Dale, 1993), a Euro-American baby might wave "bye-bye" or clap in excitement, and a Mexican infant might make the movements of *tortillitas,* a version of patty-cake (Jackson-Maldonado, Thal, Bates, Marchman, & Gutierrez-Clellan, 1993).

Noises are also used to communicate ideas. A child may make a "r-r-r" noise to refer to a car, a moaning sound for cows, or a "sh-sh-sh" sound to show running water (Reich, 1986). A frightening and dismaying example is offered by a father living in an urban housing project in America. He relates that his 1-year-old daughter says "puh-puh-puh" to indicate gunshots in the neighborhood.

Babbling

Babbling is repetitive vocalization that babies perform during much of the first year of life. Most psycholinguists do not think that babbling is true communication, but rather that the infant is playing with noise. Much early babbling involves a primary circular reaction, as described in the previous chapter: the baby accidentally makes a noise, which creates an interesting sensation, which causes the baby to repeat the vocalization. Babbling becomes more and more elaborate with age, as babies' vocal systems mature. Stages of babbling are presented in Table 8–1.

Early coos contain only open vowel sounds. By 4 or 5 months, more consonants are added. Near the end of the first year, long strings of vowel-consonant-vowel patterns are uttered (P. R. Mitchell & Kent, 1990). By 10 or 11 months, babies' babbling is an **expressive jargon** that is so similar to adult speech in complexity and intonation that it sounds as if the baby were speaking in full, albeit incomprehensible, sentences.

Early babbling includes a wide variety of speech sounds, many of which are not used in the baby's native language. During the second half of the first year, however,

TABLE 8-1

Stages of Babbling

Stage	Description
Pretend crying stage	Infants produce fussy, cry-like sounds which are not true cries.
Vowel cooing stage	Infants produce long strings of open vowel sounds (e.g., "oooooooh," "aaaaaah").
Consonant cooing stage	Infants produce strings of consonant-like sounds (e.g., "raspberry" noises with lips and tongue or drawn-out "k" and "g" noises emitted from the back of the throat).
Lallation stage	Long consonant-vowel-consonant strings (e.g., "mamamamama," "babababab").
Shortened lallation stage	Shorter consonant-vowel-consonant utterances (e.g., "mama," "lala").
Expressive jargon stage	Long, complex babbles that sound identical in intonation to adult speech.

babbling appears to be somewhat influenced by the language or languages spoken in the home. Babies of diverse cultural and linguistic groups babble in noticeably different ways. In one study, even untrained listeners could guess the native languages of babies from distinct linguistic backgrounds (de Boysson-Bardies, Sagart, & Durand, 1984). Family dialect, however, does not appear to influence babbling; African-American and Euro-American babies use roughly the same English sounds and intonations in their babbling (Irwin, 1952). Arnberg (1987) suggests that infants from bilingual or multilingual homes may demonstrate a broader repertoire of babble sounds, reflecting their exposure to more than one language. Research has not yet been conducted to confirm this possibility.

If babbling is not a form of communication—that is, if it is not used to express needs or ideas—then is it useful for later language learning? One function it does have is to induce conversations with parents. When a baby engages in expressive jargon, for example, a parent is likely to respond verbally. Often complex conversations, involving turntaking and lively intonation, follow (Pine, Lieven, & Rowland, 1997). Babbling is a playful behavior that allows babies to make verbal contact with others.

First Words

Between 8 months and 18 months, babies speak their first words. It is very difficult to tell exactly when this occurs, as a baby's early words are often unintelligible and their meanings unclear to adults. Eventually, new words can be understood. It is important to know, however, that babies' meanings for the words they speak may be very different from adults' meanings for those same words. Just because a baby can utter a word does not mean that he or she understands its full meaning. The following story illustrates this:

> A father is playing with his 1-year-old daughter in the backyard of their apartment building. "Pelota!" ("Ball!"), he calls out as he throws her a large rubber ball. To his astonishment, she tries to throw the ball back. It flies into the air, almost behind her. "Pelota!" she calls as she does this. The father becomes truly excited—his daughter has not spoken this word before.
>
> Later, in the apartment, the father tries to show his wife and his mother that their toddler has learned a new word. He hands the ball to her, but she will not name it. He rolls it to her and says "pelota." No success. The wife and grandmother laugh, thinking that surely parental pride has gotten the best of him.
>
> As his wife leaves for work, he tries again to show her that her daughter has learned a new word. He rolls the ball to her across the lawn. She smiles, picks it up, but says nothing. With a laugh the mother leaves. The moment she is gone, the daughter flings the ball back toward her father. "Pelota!" she calls out.

This father has just received a practical lesson in language development. He finally understands why his 1-year-old daughter would not speak this new word in the apartment: to her, "pelota" does not simply mean "ball," but "throw the ball in the backyard." Only later, through much experience with balls of various kinds in many different contexts, will the baby gradually come to understand the full, adult meaning of the word.

Two kinds of errors are typical when toddlers begin to use words. The first is **overgeneralization.** Babies often overgeneralize a new word so that it refers to many more things than it should. For example, a baby will use the word "car" to mean cars, trucks, tractors, and even strollers. Another will use the word "papa" to refer to any adult male: the mailman, a tribal elder, a doctor at the clinic. (This, of course, leads to many jokes and questions of paternity!) As children hear a word and use it in many contexts, they gradually construct a more accurate meaning and reduce the various generalizations of the word.

A second common error is **overrestriction.** Toddlers will often use a word to refer to a narrower range of things than an adult would. The story above is an example: the child uses "pelota" only if she is throwing the ball in the backyard. Egocentrism at this age contributes to overrestriction. The word "shoes" may be restricted to the meaning "my own shoes," and the word "cup" might mean only "my own red cup." In these cases, babies need to broaden the meaning of words. Through experience with language, they gradually construct a fuller definition.

Which words do babies speak first? Two types of words that are likely to emerge early are names of things, such as ball, dog, and daddy, and social expressions, such as "bye-bye," "no," and "want" (Gleitman & Gleitman, 1992). Children who first acquire names of things are referred to as *referential,* while those who initially use social expressions are called *expressive.* Many factors determine which category a child will fall into. Temperament may lead some children to be more wary of people and less likely to use social words. Children who are exposed to few toys and objects and many people in their homes or neighborhoods may learn social words initially.

Culture may influence whether children will be referential or expressive. Euro-American babies, for example, speak more nouns as first words. They are more referential than Japanese-American babies, who tend to be more expressive (Fernald & Morikawa, 1993). These tendencies may reflect culturally derived parenting practices and socialization beliefs. Euro-American mothers tend to emphasize object labeling and direct language teaching in their interactions with their babies. These mothers are regularly observed playing a labeling game, in which they quiz their children on the names of things: "What's this? It's a book." Japanese-American mothers, in contrast, focus more on social behaviors in their interchanges with babies. This trend reflects *omoiyari,* a traditional concept that emphasizes harmony in human interactions (S. White, 1989). These mothers have been observed using toys or other play objects primarily to engage their babies in social interaction.

The structure of language itself may also influence first word use. English has been referred to as "noun-dominant," so English-speaking children may more often be referential (Gopnik & Choi, 1990). In languages such as Japanese and Korean, nouns are less frequent and are often deleted, so expressive language styles may more often emerge among children speaking these languages.

Culture, of course, determines precisely which words will first be uttered. In a large study of word acquisition, Tomasello & Mervis (1994) discovered that words referring to animals and sounds, childhood games, and food and drink were very frequent among toddlers' first 50 words. It is easy to see that words in these different categories would vary significantly across cultures and across ethnic groups within the United States. Families eat different foods, have different pets or other experiences with animals, and have their own traditional games. These unique experiences will determine early words.

Early Words in Bilingual Families. At least half of all children in the world are bilingual or multilingual (Reich, 1986), including a growing number of children in the United States (U.S. Department of Education, 1995). How does the experience of bilingualism influence word learning?

Toddlers from bilingual families learn the names for some objects in one language and the names for other objects in the second language.

In the earliest stages of word acquisition—before 18 months of age—babies acquire new words from both languages as if they were all part of a single vocabulary (Arnberg, 1987). For example, a child from a farming family that speaks both English and German might use the German word for horse ("pferd") as well as the English word for pig. In an English-Spanish speaking family, a child might refer to some foods in English and others in Spanish, such as "apple" for apple and "platano" for banana.

It is rare for toddlers to use words from both languages to describe the same concept or object. Children almost always opt to name something consistently in one language or the other (Saunders, 1988). By 18 months of age, infants begin to use some "mixed speech"; a baby might learn the names of a few especially important items in *both* languages. This is more common in homes where one parent speaks one language and the other a different language. In this case, a toddler might say "ball" to one adult and "pelota" to another (Arnberg, 1987). This ability to figure out which adult speaks which language and to adapt speech accordingly is really quite remarkable at such a young age!

In some instances, toddlers will combine the words of two languages into a single utterance (e.g., "kittygato" for cat). Whether babies will use one language more than another, use some words of both languages to describe concepts, or engage in mixed speech will be determined by the nature of the bilingual environment in which they grow up (Saunders, 1988). Steps in bilingual word acquisition are depicted in Figure 8–1.

There are infinite varieties of bilingual family settings. Consider the following possibilities:

- A baby lives with a Spanish-speaking grandmother and an English-speaking mother.
- A baby grows up in a home where only Cherokee is spoken. At age 1, she attends a child care center where only English is spoken.

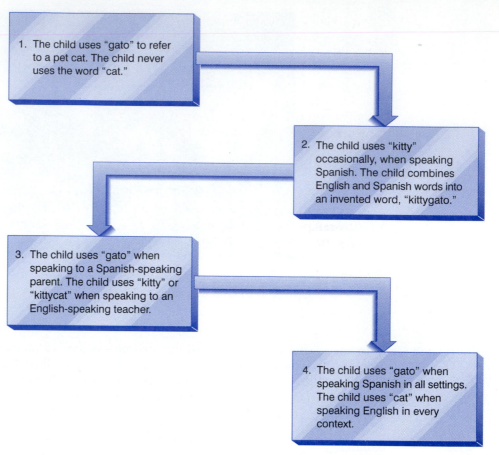

1. The child uses "gato" to refer to a pet cat. The child never uses the word "cat."

2. The child uses "kitty" occasionally, when speaking Spanish. The child combines English and Spanish words into an invented word, "kittygato."

3. The child uses "gato" when speaking to a Spanish-speaking parent. The child uses "kitty" or "kittycat" when speaking to an English-speaking teacher.

4. The child uses "gato" when speaking Spanish in all settings. The child uses "cat" when speaking English in every context.

FIGURE 8–1 The learning of a word in two languages follows a series of steps. Shown here are the steps a preschooler follows in learning the English word "cat" and the Spanish word "gato."

- A baby grows up with parents and older siblings who speak an African-American dialect at home and in the neighborhood but standard Euro-American English in more formal settings.
- A baby grows up in a home where parents speak Spanish as their native language but wish to speak only English around their children to help them assimilate into American life.

Diversity in language environments explains the rich variation in communication style and competence during the early years.

A question frequently asked by parents and teachers is whether babies living in a bilingual environment will suffer delays in vocabulary growth. It would seem that bilingual babies might experience complex and perhaps confusing verbal environments. In a bilingual home, for example, every object would have at least two words to describe it. This concern has arisen from early studies that only looked at bilingual children's ability to learn English. Not surprisingly, babies who grow up in homes where both Spanish and English are spoken have been found to have smaller usable English vocabularies (J. V. Jensen, 1962).

It is easy to see why such studies do not reflect the best ways to look at bilingual vocabulary development. Bilingual babies learn some of their words in one language and others in another language. Measuring vocabulary by looking only at words of one of the languages does not provide a complete picture. When the vocabularies for all languages spoken in the home are added together, virtually no difference is found between monolingual and bilingual children in number of words learned in the early years (Arnberg, 1987). In fact, children of bilingual homes might be somewhat advanced in both verbal and nonverbal intelligence (Padilla et al., 1991).

Two-Word Utterances

Between 18 months and 2 years, babies begin putting words together. Although their first sentences are only two words long, they can express amazing numbers of ideas or relationships between objects and actions. The following English toddler utterances, for example, are likely to get immediate attention from adults:

"All broke."

"Kitty bye-bye."

"Book flush."

"Me bite."

"Oh-oh paint."

"All wet."

Using just two words, toddlers comment about objects or events, announce actions, and even confess to all manner of misadventures. To express ideas with two words is a significant intellectual achievement. For the first time, toddlers must contend with word order, or what psycholinguists refer to as **syntax.** To appreciate the complexity of combining words, consider the sentence "Car go," which a baby uses to mean "The car went down the street." In this utterance, the baby has provided a stripped-down version of an adult sentence. This is the simplest utterance possible that will still have meaning. All but the most important words necessary to convey the message are left out. Some psycholinguists have referred to this as **telegraphic speech** because of this economy of expression. Babies speak as though they were paying for every word!

In a two-word utterance, babies must make challenging decisions about word order. In "Car go," the baby places the agent, "car," before the action, "go," thus following the basic rules of sentence construction in English. Even very young toddlers make few word-order errors (e.g., "Go car"). Most psycholinguists believe that babies apply simple rules of their native language to construct their early sentences. Of course, they don't consciously think about rules as they speak. Children, generally, have a **tacit knowledge of language;** it is an "I can do it, but I can't tell you how I do it" form of thinking.

Two-Word Utterances in Bilingual Families. Bilingual babies progress to two-word utterances at about the same age as monolingual babies. For those learning two or more languages, however, putting words together poses special challenges, especially if the languages are very different. Every language has a unique word order. Verbs appear at the ends of sentences in some languages and in the middle in others. Adjectives follow nouns in some languages and precede them in others. So, babies growing up in bilingual families have two sets of rules to learn and apply as they create simple sentences.

How do toddlers put two-word utterances together when faced with contrasting rules about word order? They work out quite ingenious solutions to the problem. Some babies simply select one of the languages they hear around them and apply only its rules. A baby that speaks both Spanish and English, for example, may rely just on the rules of Spanish word order, even when speaking English (Reich, 1986). For example, in Spanish adjectives often follow nouns, as in "el gato blanco," so a toddler might apply this rule to English utterances as well and say "the cat white" instead of "the white cat." Other babies have been found to actually invent their own unique word-ordering system that is a combination of the languages spoken in the home (Saunders, 1988).

Bilingual babies also face challenges in picking just the right words to create simple sentences. One problem is that words work differently in different languages. In Chinese, for example, many words can act as both a noun and a verb. This is less frequent in English (the word "plan" is one example) (Aaronson & Ferres, 1987). So, a child that speaks both Chinese and English is more likely to create a simple English sentence such as "I noising" to mean "I am making noise."

Because of the complexity of two-word sentence construction, babies from bilingual homes often engage in language switching, in which words from two languages are blended in a single utterance. For example, a baby that speaks both Swedish and English may say "Titta, bunny" for "Look, bunny" or "Horsie sova" for "Horsie sleep." In some cases, babies will take words with the same meaning from each language and combine them into a two-word utterance, such as when a baby that speaks both German and English says "bitte please." It has been well documented that parents and other adults grow anxious hearing these early language mixtures; many believe these constructions to be confusing and damaging to language learning (Arnberg, 1987). A temptation is to correct toddlers, but this tactic is counterproductive. In their preschool years, bilingual children will be able to separate the two or more languages which they hear.

TODDLER LITERACY

Babies in some cultures are exposed to written as well as oral language. In American families, adults and toddlers of all cultural groups spend time together reading stories or browsing other written materials. When parents read with babies, they promote early literacy skills, such as how to handle books or turn pages. Such experiences show that reading is interesting and worthwhile. In shared reading activities, babies learn that stories are read with a certain pacing and intonation. Schickedanz (1999) has observed that even fairly young babies who have been read to often will babble in a unique way, called **book babble,** during a reading session.

When reading to their toddlers, parents have been found to **scaffold** early literacy learning. Scaffolding, an idea drawn from Vygotsky's (1978) work, is the process by which adults give support or guidance for some parts of a task or activity, and then gradually give over regulation of the experience to children. In so doing, adults help children to become more and more independent in their thinking and actions. Parents have many ways of scaffolding children's learning during a reading session. The parent might first turn pages of a book and then ask the child to do so. The parent might point to pictures and ask the child to name them, and then later encourage

When adults read to toddlers, they often "scaffold" early literacy learning.

the child to do so independently. Or the parent might ask children to guess what happens next—for example, a father might ask, "What do you think she saw?" and the child might respond "Bunny!" (Teale, 1984). The following vignette illustrates adult scaffolding of a child's early literacy:

A grandmother and a 2-year-old sit in the kitchen of their apartment looking at a department store catalog. The child sits in the grandmother's lap holding the reading material in front of him.

GRANDMOTHER:	(Pointing to a picture on a page) What's this, Terry?
CHILD:	Man.
GRANDMOTHER:	That's a man isn't it?
CHILD:	Yeah. Man.
GRANDMOTHER:	But what about over here? (Points to another part of the page)
CHILD:	Man . . . mans.
GRANDMOTHER:	Yeah. That's two men, right Terry? Two men.
CHILD:	Two men.
GRANDMOTHER:	That's right. (Turns page. Waits without speaking.)
CHILD:	Wa dis?
GRANDMOTHER:	What is that?

CHILD: Shush caysh.

GRANDMOTHER: (Laughs) Yeah. Suitcase. (Waits again)

CHILD: (Turns page on his own) Wa dat?

The reading continues with the toddler turning the pages, asking and then answering his own questions about the pictures.

This grandmother is scaffolding her grandchild's reading experience. At first she directly manages the page-turning and question-asking, but soon she gives over regulation of the activity to the child, first by pausing to allow him to ask the questions and later by allowing him to turn the pages himself. This vignette illustrates another important point: not all infants have their earliest print experiences with storybooks (Pellegrini, Perlmutter, Galda, & Brody, 1990). Magazines, signs, and the text on cereal boxes may be more prevalent in some families or cultural groups.

LANGUAGE DEFICITS VERSUS LANGUAGE DIFFERENCES

Some children have language delays or challenges. Typically developing 1-year-olds babble in highly expressive jargon, acquire first words, then create two-word utterances. Babies with challenging conditions often do not. The absence of these language features usually prompts parents or caregivers to suspect that the child has a challenging condition. Several conditions that affect language development are presented in Table 8–2.

Hearing Impairment and Infant Language

Some language delays in toddlerhood have clearly specified causes. Hearing impairment is an example. In the early months of life, babies with hearing impairments vocalize in much the same way that hearing babies do. In fact, their babbles are so typical that many parents do not even suspect problems at this age. By 6 months, however, the vocalizations of these infants decrease significantly. They often do not progress to complex babbles and expressive jargon as typically developing babies do (Goldin-Meadow, Mylander, & Butcher, 1995).

TABLE 8-2

Some Challenging Conditions That Affect Infant Language

Condition	Effects on Infant Language
Hearing impairment	Babbling is typical until age 6 months, but vocalizations begin to decrease in the second 6 months of life. More complex babbling and expressive jargon do not appear.
Down syndrome	Babbling and early words are delayed. Babies respond less often to others' language, make fewer requests, and initiate conversations infrequently.
General language delay	Babbles or words resemble the vocalizations of much younger, typically developing children. Language may or may not "catch" up with that of non-delayed peers over time.

A traditional view has been that, from this point on, hearing impairment severely disrupts all aspects of language development. However, several remarkable studies suggest that babies with hearing impairments do, in fact, continue to progress in communicative ability, but use a different kind of system of communication (Goldin-Meadow et al., 1995; Goldin-Meadow & Morford, 1985). Babies with such impairments who have not been exposed to sign language often invent a system of gestures to communicate. Amazingly, this system develops following a pattern that is similar to typical language development. Around the age at which first words emerge, babies who cannot hear will begin to use single gestures to stand for objects or actions. For example, a baby might use a twisting motion to express a desire for a certain container to be opened. At the age when typically developing toddlers are using two words, babies with hearing impairments will combine two gestures to express elaborate ideas. It is evident that they have the same strong need to communicate and will construct a way to do this in the absence of hearing and speech abilities.

Research has also shown that babies who are exposed to American Sign Language (see Figure 8–2) early in life learn this communication system in precisely the way that hearing babies learn oral language (Goldin-Meadow & Morford, 1985). In one study (Petitto & Marentette, 1991), young babies with hearing impairments were found to babble in sign language using gestures in a playful, repetitive manner, just as hearing babies might repeat consonants in babbling. For example, one infant used the sign for "ba" repeatedly, much like a speaking baby's typical consonant-vowel voice play, "ba, ba, ba."

Down Syndrome and Infant Language

Another example of a clearly identified source of language delay is Down syndrome. Babies with this condition show significant disruption in language development within the second half of their first year. In addition to experiencing oral language delay, babies with Down syndrome show difficulty in general communication with parents (Landry & Chapieski, 1989). They may pay less attention and give fewer verbal responses when parents speak to them. Also, they make fewer requests and initiate fewer conversations.

General Language Delay

Some language delays have no apparent cause. Toddlers have been found to acquire language more slowly even when they suffer no obvious perceptual or cognitive problems. These children have limited vocabularies or do not begin to use words un-

FIGURE 8–2
Infants who are exposed to American Sign Language have been found to babble with hand signs.

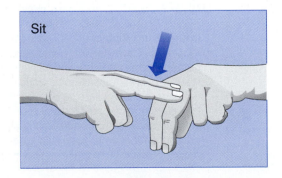

Sit

til very late. Some have trouble understanding words spoken to them. Although a variety of terms have been used to describe this phenomenon, the phrase **general language delay** is probably most common. Language delays are believed to be just that: general delays in typical speech acquisition. Most researchers find that the language of children with delays is identical to the speech of younger, typically developing children (Ratner, 1989). The term "delay" causes some confusion, however. It implies that such children will simply catch up with their peers in language competence over time. This is not always the case, however. Many children with general language delays in toddlerhood or in the preschool years are more likely to have academic problems and to be identified as having learning disabilities later in life (Tallal, 1987).

Toddlers with language delays are usually defined by what they are not rather than by what they are. They are *not* mentally retarded. They do *not* have genetic disorders. It is likely, then, that this category of disorder represents a whole range of different and perhaps unrelated conditions which have diverse causes. Many experts

ASSESSING YOUNG CHILDREN: Infant Language and Literacy Development

Areas of Development	What to Watch for	Indicators of Atypical Development
Oral language abilities	Uses crying, gestures, and babbling to communicate needs or make contact with others. Babbles speech sounds which are found in the child's family's language. Understands some words by 1 year. Utters single words by this age. Speaks two-word utterances between 18 months and 2 years.	Failure to cry or in other ways communicate needs. An inability to understand or respond to language by age one year. Failure to use one-word utterances by 18 months. Use of only one-word utterances beyond 2 years.
Literacy skills	Responds to children's literature or other adult reading material with smiles, coos, or animated babbling by age 2. By this same age, shows an understanding of how books work (e.g., how pages turn).	An inability to attend or respond positively to shared reading experiences with an adult.

Interpreting Assessment Data: Variations in language and literacy are due to the specific languages spoken in the home and cultural differences in reading preferences. Children will babble different sounds and will utter one or two words less early in life, if they are trying to learn two languages simultaneously. They may be more attentive to magazines or mail-order catalogs than to children's books if these are more common in their home. Significant delays in understanding and production of simple one- or two-word utterances, however, may indicate challenging conditions, such as hearing impairment or general language delay. Further evaluation and early language intervention may be needed.

believe that minimal brain dysfunction—minor and undetectable damage to the brain—is responsible for much language delay (Tallal, 1987). Other causes have also been suggested, such as poverty, family stress, and poor health (Leonard, 1982; Reich, 1986). There is no one profile of a child with language delay, then, and no single intervention that is successful in all cases.

Unfortunately, some children have been identified as having language delays merely because they are from families of different cultures or because they speak different dialects or languages (Reich, 1986). Great care must be taken not to assume that **language differences** are deficits. Child care providers should not, for example, expect infants from bilingual homes to speak English as quickly as native English speakers. Differences in communicative styles must also be appreciated. For example, quietness may not be a sign of delay, but rather of a culturally derived communicative style (Irujo, 1988). A quiet style might also be a common response to the overwhelming experience of learning a new, second language (Arnberg, 1987).

RESEARCH INTO PRACTICE

CRITICAL CONCEPT 1

Infants begin to understand language long before they can talk. At birth they can distinguish speech from other kinds of sounds and recognize the voices of significant adults. In the second half of the first year, they are able to understand words and phrases.

Application #1

Caregivers and parents should talk to babies starting at birth, even though babies are not yet talking themselves. Rich conversation directed toward infants will stimulate language centers in the brain and promote later communicative competence.

Application #2

Since it is not known precisely when infants understand words, caregivers and parents should be careful about what they say around them. Toddlers who are not yet speaking may still comprehend a sensitive or confidential topic discussed by adults in their presence.

CRITICAL CONCEPT 2

Early in life, babies communicate through crying, making noises, smiling, gesturing, and pointing.

Application

Parents and caregivers should watch for and respond to infants' nonverbal communication. Responding quickly to signals such as crying and smiling will show babies the pleasure and the power of social interchanges and will encourage them to refine their communicative abilities.

CRITICAL CONCEPT 3

Near age 1, babies can speak words. Vocabulary grows exceedingly quickly during the first 2 years of life. The first words babies learn are often names of things they can act upon, such as "ball," or words that have social meaning, such as "bye-bye."

Application #1

Caregivers and parents should provide a language-rich environment for babies, since language grows so quickly during the first 2 years of life.

Application #2

Caregivers and parents should label objects for children. For example, the adult can point to an object and say, "What's that?"; when the infant says "ball" the adult responds, "Yes! That's a ball."

Application #3

Caregivers and parents should use social words with infants, such as "bye-bye," "night-night," and "hi." They can encourage babies to use these words, as in "Say bye-bye to grandma."

CRITICAL CONCEPT 4

Bilingual children learn words in two different languages and combine these into one large mental dictionary. Sometimes they become confused about which language to speak at which time, and sometimes they combine words from the two languages into a single utterance.

Application #1

Caregivers and parents should appreciate the challenge of learning more than one language and be patient with children who show confusion in word learning.

Application #2

Labels for objects and social words should be spoken to bilingual infants in both languages. Caregivers must learn enough words in a baby's native language to be able to name important objects or events in their lives, such as "lunch," "nap time," and "good-bye."

Application #3

In assessing language development, caregivers must consider the size of children's full mental dictionary, not just their English vocabulary. Asking bilingual children to name objects or pictures in both their native language and the language being learned will give a true picture of semantic development.

CRITICAL CONCEPT 5

Two-word utterances are constructed in toddlerhood. At this point, children must learn early rules of word order. They must place the agent before the action, as in

"Daddy throw" rather than "throw Daddy." Bilingual infants have a harder time learning word-order rules, since they often must acquire two very different sets of language rules.

Application #1

Caregivers and parents can talk with toddlers using simple sentences that clearly identify the agent, action, and object. They can overlay these statements across children's activities, as in "You're throwing the bean bag" and "Jamal took your block."

Application #2

Caregivers and parents must understand how challenging it is to learn the syntax of two different languages. They must be patient when children use the word-order rules of one language when speaking in another. Such "errors" are a fundamental part of bilingual development.

SUGGESTED ACTIVITIES

1. Observe a group of babies of any age in child care. Write down every example of infant communication that you observe. Include vocalizations, pointing, body language, crying, or any other method a baby uses to send a message. Write a report on your observations, guided by the following questions:

   a. Which gestures did babies use to communicate?

   b. Describe vocalizations that you observed.

   c. Did babies babble? Did this appear to be communication or play with sound?

   d. What was the most effective method of communication you observed?

2. Observe a group of babies in child care. Take notes on all instances of crying. Write a report on what you observe, guided by these questions:

   a. Which types of cries did you observe? Could you distinguish urgent cries from non-urgent ones? Could you tell precisely what babies were expressing in their cries?

   b. What did adults do when babies cried? Did they respond quickly? Did they treat crying as communication?

   c. What did the other babies do when one would cry?

3. Observe a toddler between 18 months and 2 years who is growing up in a bilingual home. Write down every utterance he or she makes within a 10-minute period. Write an analysis of your observations, guided by these questions:

   a. Which words did the toddler use? Are the words in one language or both? Which language did the baby appear to favor? Which types of words (i.e., object names or social expressions) did the toddler use most?

   b. Did the toddler construct two-word sentences? What ideas were expressed? Describe any telegraphic speech you heard, based on ideas from the chapter. Did you hear any language switching?

4. Visit a child care center or home-based intervention program that serves children with special needs. Select a typically developing baby and one with a challenging condition (e.g., visual impairment or mental retardation). Observe each child for 20 minutes and write a report contrasting their interactions in the classroom, based on the following questions.

   a. How were communications of the two children alike? How were they different?

   b. Did both children use a variety of words? Did both construct two-word sentences?

   c. Contrast the two children's abilities to communicate. Could both effectively convey messages?

   d. What can you conclude about the influence of the challenging condition on communication?

CHAPTER 9

Infant Social and Emotional Development

IN THIS CHAPTER WE WILL EXAMINE INFANTS' SOCIAL AND EMOTIONAL RELATIONSHIPS. Infants form strong bonds with caregivers very early in life. They come to know, become attached to, and show a desire to be with a small and very select group of people in their lives. The wonderful emotional bonds formed with infants are among the greatest rewards of parenting or caregiving. These strong bonds also pose challenges, as the following story reveals:

> A mother and father are saying good-bye to their 18-month-old on her first day in child care. The mother squeezes the little girl tightly and for a long time; she seems reluctant to let go. Next, the father gives a hug. The toddler smiles and appears to be enjoying the attention. They stand together for many minutes, and the parents appear to grow increasingly anxious.
>
> "We need to go now, sweetie," the father finally says. The toddler still smiles. "We'll be back, though, okay?" he reassures her as the two start to move toward the door. Their daughter toddles after them, giggling as if they are playing a game. "Bye-bye, Sarah," the mother says in a shaky voice. The toddler's smile quickly disappears. "Bye-bye?" This phrase holds a great deal of meaning.
>
> "No!" the child screams, at last understanding what is happening. "No go, Mommy!" She is crying now. The mother and father cease their retreat. The mother approaches the upset child and gives her another hug. "We'll be back," she soothes. This has no effect. The child's screams intensify.
>
> A caregiver moves in quickly, carrying a picture book. She hugs the little girl and tries to distract her. "Would you like to come over and read with me?" The toddler calms a bit, but as her parents move closer to the door, she begins to wail again. As the parents walk out, her upset is most intense. All day long at work, the parents are haunted by the sounds of their child's screams. They will replay this nightmarish experience in their heads for years to come.
>
> The toddler, on the other hand, stops crying within a few minutes after their departure. She now sits in the caregiver's lap, happily turning the pages of a storybook.

This vignette shows the strength of early attachments. It also illustrates that bonds are bidirectional. Parents are as fearful of separating from their infants as their infants are about being separated from their parents.

Babies can form such close relationships with many different people—parents, grandparents, siblings, child care providers, neighbors (Teti & Ablard, 1989). Whom babies become attached to is not so important as that they have at least one person in their lives whom they care about and who cares about them deeply. These relationships in infancy are crucial for later healthy development. Forming a bond with others in the early years has been found to protect children emotionally from the negative effects of poverty, domestic and community violence, parental substance abuse, and other stressors that threaten mental health (Werner & Smith, 1992).

TRUST AND ATTACHMENT

The work of Erik Erikson (1963), which we discussed in Chapter 3, is very useful in examining infant social and emotional development. According to Erikson, a critical emotional struggle in infancy is between trust and mistrust. Emotionally healthy babies come to understand that they have nurturing, responsive caregivers who meet their basic needs. They come to view the world as safe and predictable. They enter into trusting relationships with caregivers and later other human beings. *Security* is another word to describe this emotional state. A degree of mistrust is also healthy and important for survival. For example, it causes an infant to hesitate from crawling away from a parent to explore a dangerous set of cellar stairs. Humans will always experience some feelings of mistrust in which doubts about their relationships or the security of the world emerge. The emotionally healthy baby, however, is, for the most part, trusting of the world and the people within it.

Babies who are abused or neglected, who do not have caregivers that respond to their needs, or who for other reasons have come to doubt the trustworthiness of the world will not resolve this emotional conflict in a positive way. They may be impaired from entering into relationships with others and may be wary of new situations or people. They may be unable to advance to later stages of psychosocial development, and so are more likely to suffer mental health problems later in life.

Attachment Formation

A critical part of achieving trust, from Erikson's view, is the ability of babies to come to know and bond with caregivers. Forming an emotional bond with others in infancy is called **attachment.** In his classic work on infants, John Bowlby (1969) described attachment as a bidirectional process in which babies and parents (or other caregivers) make contact with each other in ways that lead to emotional bonds. Babies perform social behaviors—smiling, making eye contact, cooing—that capture adults' attention and elicit strong feelings of caring and concern. Caregivers respond to these behaviors with warmth and social contact. Thus, babies and significant adults become attached to one another.

A traditional view has been that infants form attachments only with their mothers. Extensive cross-cultural research has shown, however, that this is not the case. Babies most often form attachments to multiple caregivers. In one study, only 10% of infants were still attached to a single adult at 18 months of age (Schaffer & Emerson, 1964). Babies form attachments to fathers that are as strong and secure as those formed with mothers (N. A. Fox, Kimmerly, & Schafer, 1991; Lamb, 1987). In most two-parent families, babies become attached to both father and mother at approximately the same time (Lamb, 1981). In cultures in which grandparents, aunts and uncles, or other relatives live in the home, attachment to non-parent caregivers is common. In these cases, babies form attachments to these adults at the same time that they bond with the mother. In many cultural groups, older siblings have caretaking responsibilities, so bonding with siblings is common (Ainsworth, 1977; Teti & Ablard, 1989).

Bowlby (1969) identified stages that infants go through in the formation of bonds with caregivers. In the early months, babies show great interest in all people. They smile and babble at others and grasp onto their fingers or hair. This is an important stage. Babies who do not show interest in responding to others or who do not have opportunities to do so may be at risk for later emotional difficulties. Bowlby observed that babies between 4 and 6 months of age begin to prefer interacting with certain familiar people. They smile and coo more intensely at caregivers and show puzzlement or wariness around strangers. By 6 months of age, they show an intense desire to be with just these familiar caregivers and show concern when they are not present.

Separation Anxiety and Stranger Anxiety

Between 6 and 8 months of age, babies show **stranger anxiety,** a fear of unfamiliar persons that often results in great upset. The following story highlights the problems that occur during this period:

> A Puerto Rican woman is saddened when her son, his wife, and her beloved 4-month-old grandson leave the island to live in New York City. She has become very close to her grandchild. He always smiles so brightly when she enters the room, and he seems to enjoy being held and carried by her. When she hugs and kisses him good-bye at the airport, he responds by flashing a big smile and pulling her hair.
>
> Two short months later, the family decides that the grandmother should come live with them on the mainland. She is thrilled, in part because she will be with her grandchild again. During the long flight, she thinks about nothing but him. She anticipates his smiling face at their reunion. Upon arriving, she excitedly rushes into the airport waiting area, where she spots her daughter-in-law cradling her cherished infant grandson. She scoops up the tiny baby in her arms, hugs him, and then holds him away from her so she can see his beautiful face. She is confronted with a look of terror. The baby bursts into trembling sobs, bends away from her, and reaches toward his mother. The grandmother is crushed. What could have occurred to sour their wonderful relationship after only two months?

After 6 months of age, babies begin to show **separation anxiety,** a fear of being separated from caregivers. They show upset when their parents leave them. Sometimes only a brief departure to another room will trigger distress. Separation anxiety is very familiar to caregivers who work with infants and toddlers. The first days of school can be challenging when lots of new babies are enrolled.

Stranger anxiety and separation anxiety vary from infant to infant and situation to situation. A baby who is with a parent or caregiver—preferably sitting securely on a familiar lap—is less likely to become upset over the appearance of strangers. In the airport story above, then, the grandmother would have done well to allow her grandson's parents to hold him while they became reacquainted. Early experiences with being away from caregivers and meeting strangers will reduce both types of anxiety (Thompson & Limber, 1990). Some babies are cared for by extended family members and neighbors from the time they are born. This type of collective child rearing is an adaptive strategy among parents of historically under-represented groups (Harrison, Wilson, Pine, Chan, & Buriel, 1990). Babies in such families tend to show less upset at the appearance of strangers and at the departure of parents.

Other cultural practices and beliefs influence stranger anxiety and separation anxiety. Babies in Uganda were found to display greater upset at separation from parents than those in the United States (Ainsworth, 1977). This difference was explained by variations in departure patterns of parents in these cultures. In Uganda, parents rarely leave their babies, but when they do are gone for long periods. For example, a mother might stay with her baby every waking moment until it is time to harvest garden vegetables. When this time comes, however, an extensive separation is necessary. African babies in this study had had little practice at separating. Also, they had come to understand that a parent's departure meant a long separation, so their separation anxiety was great. Figure 9-1 shows similarities and differences in separation anxiety patterns across cultures.

Cultural beliefs about infant care may affect separation anxiety and stranger anxiety in infants. Fathers and mothers of some ethnic groups believe that babies should never be cared for by non-parent providers. When these parents are forced to separate from their children because of work obligations, they tend to suffer severe anxiety. They may have strong negative feelings about leaving their babies in child care.

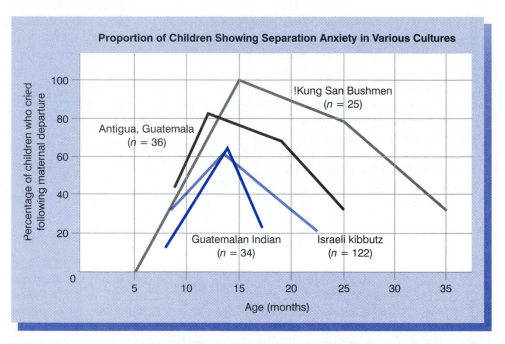

FIGURE 9-1 Frequency of separation anxiety in infancy varies from one culture to another. In all cultural groups, such anxiety becomes most intense in children at 13 to 15 months of age.
SOURCE: Kagan, J. Kearsley, R. B., & Zelazo, P. R. (1978). *Infancy: Its Place in Human Development*. Cambridge, MA: Harvard University Press.

Korean-American parents are an example. They often report a reluctance to have their children cared for in centers, by baby-sitters, or even by relatives (Yu & Kim, 1983).

How do negative parental attitudes and feelings affect infant anxiety? Parents may inadvertently communicate their worries to children at the time of departure. Mothers or fathers leaving their children in infant care, for example, can express upset through language or facial expression. Such behaviors may increase infant distress (Hock, McBride, & Gnezda, 1989; Thompson & Limber, 1990).

A number of studies have addressed practical solutions to the problems of separation anxiety and stranger anxiety. Research by Weinraub and Lewis (1977) and Lollis (1990) found that 2-year-olds showed less upset at parents' departure in child care when the separation was explained to them clearly ahead of time. Separation was also found to be smoother if the departing parent suggested activities for the child to engage in during separation. An important practical finding of these studies was that toddlers cried more upon separation if the parent sat and actually played with them for a time before leaving them. The most effective strategy for parents, then, may be to point out play activities to their children, but without playing along with them.

Types of Attachment

Mary Ainsworth has engaged in extensive research to refine understandings of infant attachment. She devised a research method for examining the nature of attachment which she called the **strange situation procedure** (Ainsworth, Blehar, Waters, & Wall, 1978). In this procedure, babies are placed in a playroom. First, the baby plays with toys in the presence of the mother. Next, the mother leaves and an unfamiliar person enters. The mother returns briefly, then leaves again, and the baby plays alone. Many babies in this situation cry when their mothers depart, but this reaction isn't the important point of the procedure. What is significant, according to Ainsworth, is what babies do when the mother returns. Some babies greet their mothers joyously; others do not. It is the nature of the reunion, from Ainsworth's perspective, that reveals the quality of the mother-child bond.

Using this technique, Ainsworth discovered that several types of attachment exist. These are summarized in Table 9-1. Babies can be categorized as demonstrating either **secure attachment** or **insecure attachment.** Roughly 70% of babies in the United States form secure attachments (Ainsworth et al., 1978; van Ijzendoorn &

TABLE 9-1
Types of Attachment

Attachment Type	Description
Secure	Plays happily within a strange play setting, if a parent is present. May cry when the parent leaves the room, but will greet the parent joyously at their reunion.
Insecure/avoidant	May or may not cry at a parent's departure from a strange play area. Ignores and even moves away from the parent when he or she returns.
Insecure/ambivalent	May show great upset when a parent leaves a strange play area. Continues to be inconsolable when the parent returns. Will alternate between desperate clinging and angry rejection during the reunion.

Kroonenberg, 1988). A securely attached baby will play happily with toys during the mother's presence in a strange situation. Upon her departure, the baby may cry, but the reunion will be a happy one. The baby may hug or cling to the mother for a time, but will quickly stop crying.

Insecurely attached babies behave differently in a strange situation. Ainsworth et al. (1978) identified two distinct behavioral patterns among insecure babies. *Insecure/avoidant* babies may or may not show upset when their mothers leave. However, they will completely ignore them when they return. Such a baby may actively move away from the mother or ignore her efforts to make contact when she comes back into the play area. *Insecure/ambivalent* babies alternate between extreme upset and angry rejection when the mother returns to the playroom. Such a baby may first cling to the mother during their reunion, and then push her away or even strike her. Insecure/ambivalent babies are often inconsolable upon the parent's return.

Attachment, as determined by Ainsworth's strange situation paradigm, appears to affect development in later childhood. Securely attached infants tend to be more friendly and competent and to have more positive views of themselves in later childhood (Sroufe, 1985). In contrast, insecure/avoidant babies tend to become more aggressive, more impulsive, and less cooperative (M. F. Erikson, Sroufe, & Egeland, 1985; Turner, 1993). Insecure/ambivalent infants tend to become timid, dependent, and whiny in later childhood (Sroufe, Fox, & Pancake, 1983). They are also more inhibited in their exploration and play with peers (Cassidy & Berlin, 1994). In the elementary years, they are more likely to be identified as having social and emotional problems (M. Lewis, Feiring, McGuiffog, & Jaskir, 1984).

Cultural Variations in Infant Attachment

Babies of many cultural groups around the world fall into secure or insecure categories of attachment at approximately the same rates as American infants: 70% are securely attached, 20 to 25% are insecure/avoidant, and 5 to 10% are insecure/ambivalent (N. A. Fox et al., 1991; Sagi, van Ijzendoorn, & Koren-Karie, 1991). Several studies raise questions, however, about whether babies' behavior in Ainsworth's strange situation paradigm is a universal indicator of attachment. In a study of Japanese babies, over 40% showed insecure/ambivalent attachment, compared to 5 to 10% in other cultural groups (Miyake, Chen, & Campos, 1985). The Japanese babies in this study were so upset at the mother's departure that they could not be consoled during the reunion phase of the procedure. Similar findings were obtained in a study of Chinese-American infants in a child care setting (Kagan, Kearsley, & Zelazo, 1978). When placed in several strange situations, Chinese babies showed less secure attachment, staying closer to their mothers and playing less. Studies of infants in northern Germany indicate a higher rate of insecure relationships, particularly insecure/avoidant attachments (Harwood, Miller, & Irizarry, 1995). Is it plausible that so many babies in these cultural groups are at risk of poor attachment to parents?

Several explanations have been offered for these cultural differences. Japanese-American and Chinese-American babies spend far less time away from their mothers than babies of other cultures; the resulting upset at separation may have been so severe that reunion behavior was negatively affected (S.-J. Chen & Miyake, 1986). In this case, the research method may simply not be valid for these babies. In fact, nonstop crying for long periods after separation may be an expected and culturally correct response for babies in societies where infant-mother bonds are sacred. Anything but great anxiety on the part of the baby—or the mother—during and after time apart could be interpreted as a sign of a less strong relationship.

The high rates of insecure/avoidant attachment in German communities could be the result of cultural values and socialization practices as well (Harwood et al., 1995). North German mothers are found to engage in independence training in which children at a young age are encouraged to separate and closeness and dependence are discouraged. It is understandable, then, that babies of these cultural groups would be more likely to ignore mothers upon reunion in the strange situation procedure.

Caution must be used, then, in relying on separation and reunion behaviors to measure attachment. More culturally sensitive methods of observing infant-caregiver bonds may be needed.

Parenting Behaviors, Attachment, and Culture

Parenting behaviors influence attachment formation. The two examples that follow show contrasting styles in parent interactions. Which style is more likely to support strong emotional bonds?

EXAMPLE 1

As a woman in a small village in India works in the garden outside her home, her 4-month-old granddaughter sleeps in a basket nearby. The baby awakes and begins to cry. The grandmother scoops the baby up, hugs and comforts her, then straps the baby to a sling across her abdomen. She then returns to her gardening, stooping over the vegetables and pulling weeds in a rhythmic motion. The baby falls asleep, cradled securely against her grandmother, gently rocking with her movements.

EXAMPLE 2

A mother in a city in Kenya has just acquired a crib for her 5-month-old son. Enthused about what she perceives to be a modern European child care method, she places her sleeping baby in the crib in his room and leaves to run errands. After a time, the infant awakes and cries in hunger and anxiety. No one is in the home to comfort him. Even when the mother returns home, she does not respond to her baby's cries. She wishes to train her baby to stay in the crib while she does her work.

Two dimensions of parenting, illustrated in the first example above, have been found to lead to secure attachment in babies: responsiveness and warm physical contact (Isabella, 1993; Isabella & Belsky, 1991; Pederson et al., 1990; Thompson & Limber, 1990). Responsiveness involves carefully interpreting babies' signals—the cries, whimpers, eye contact, noises, or other behaviors that express their needs—and responding in appropriate ways. Quickly picking up and rocking a baby who is crying for contact is an example of responsiveness. Reacting slowly and then giving a baby a bottle when that is not what is desired would be a less responsive interaction. The grandmother in Example 1 is a responsive caregiver. She accurately reads her granddaughter's crying as a desire to be held, and then she reacts quickly.

Warm, physical contact is a separate dimension of parenting. Nurturing parents spend lots of time in physical contact with their babies, holding them, bouncing

Infants and toddlers become attached to adults who are warm and responsive.

them, playing with them, or simply gazing into their eyes. The grandmother in Example 1 manages to provide warm, physical contact while continuing with her work. When she straps her granddaughter close to her body, the baby falls immediately back to sleep.

Do warmth and responsiveness lead to attachment in all cultures? Some cross-cultural research suggests that these basic attachment processes are universal. However, variation exists in the exact ways that parents respond or provide nurturance. In Ainsworth's (1977) classic study in Uganda, nursing a baby during upset was found to be an important behavior for promoting attachment. African mothers who nursed in response to infant crying were more likely to have securely attached babies. In the United States, however, where nursing was less common at the time, nursing was less important to the attachment process. In fact, babies in U.S. homes were found to frequently become attached to parents or other adults who were not responsible for feeding them. Other methods of warm contact, such as snuggling or rocking, were discovered to be more likely to promote bonds.

Ainsworth concluded that responsiveness and warmth are important caregiving behaviors in all cultures, but how these are expressed varies greatly. Each family, she argues, has a unique "cluster of attachment behaviors" that are necessary for strong emotional bonds. The behaviors of one culture may be irrelevant in another, so there may be no one, best way to create positive relationships with babies.

Looking through the lens of one's own cultural values and customs, it is easy to form an opinion that the attachment practices of another culture are deficient.

Levine (1977) provides an example of this in his observations of impoverished families in Africa. Babies in the communities he visited were held and fed with very little affection. He notes that most Westerners would consider this a negative pattern of interaction. After all, in European and Euro-American families, warmth and responsiveness include smiling, stroking, and hugging. The absence of these nurturing behaviors might be construed as a sign of poor relationships. A careful and unbiased look at these interactions suggests just the opposite, however. Levine describes how babies' cries for food or contact receive immediate response in these communities. Children rarely have to wait to have their needs met. They become attached to adults as securely as in any other community. The lack of affect in parenting is a part of the tradition in this cultural group, Levine explains. It represents a kind of emotional distancing from children that is common in communities where infant mortality rates are very high.

Child care providers and teachers must remember that the attachment behaviors valued in their own families may be different from those of families they work with. Great care must be taken not to misinterpret cultural expressions of warmth or responsiveness. A parent may respond to a baby's signals with rough-and-tumble play or humor. Warm contact may include being carried in a backpack or being bounced on a knee. Some attachment behaviors may be delivered without a great deal of affection or enthusiasm, but these are effective parenting interactions, nonetheless.

Attachment and Infants with Special Needs

Many people assume that infants with special needs will have difficulty forming secure bonds with their caregivers. The following story illustrates this:

A single mother has been attending a support class for parents of infants with Down syndrome. The focus of this class is on initiating play and responding to infant cries. She grows more and more irritated as she listens to her instructor talk about risk factors and concerns about attachment. "You'll need to make a special effort to form an attachment with your baby," he tells the class. "Children with Down syndrome may not become attached to you easily. And some of you may have trouble forming bonds to your baby. Has anyone felt that this has been a problem?"

The mother can stay quiet no longer. "No. I never feel that way. Are you saying we won't love our babies as much? That they won't love us? I can't believe that. I'm offended, in fact."

The instructor is startled, but he tries to maintain composure. "I'm not saying you won't love your baby. I'm just saying that sometimes parents and children have a hard time connecting with one another, so it makes sense to try extra hard to create bonds. That's the nature of this condition."

The mother is not satisfied. "I don't buy it. Not at all. I know my baby and he knows me. Down syndrome or no, he and I already have this attachment you're so worried about. Quite honestly, I think you underestimate the love we have inside of us."

The instructor nods humbly and moves on to another topic. At the end of the session, he thinks about the experience. Perhaps he has underestimated what parents know and feel about their own babies. He pledges that in the future he will not to jump to conclusions so quickly about parents' relationships with their children.

It is not surprising that this parent educator worries that infants with challenging conditions will not become securely attached to caregivers. Folk wisdom suggests that infants with various cognitive and social disorders create stress for parents, and that parents' responsiveness or warmth might be negatively affected. Infants with certain challenges might have poor relationships with parents because they have impaired communication systems. Babies with hearing impairments, for example, might have poor verbal interactions with parents, and this could disrupt attachment. All of this makes perfect sense. For the most part, however, research does not support these assumptions. Parent-infant bonds have been found to form in the most trying of circumstances. Children with profound disabilities will still become attached to caregivers.

There are a few exceptions. A few studies report some interruption of attachment behaviors in interactions between parents and infants with facial deformities (Barden, Ford, Jensen, Rogers-Salyer, & Salyer, 1989). Although parents of babies with cleft palates or more severely disfiguring syndromes report that their interactions are positive, they tend to hold their babies less often, interact with them less frequently, and provide less warmth. Such interactions could affect attachment, although no studies have been done to determine this.

Cross-cultural studies have shown that severe infant malnutrition negatively affects attachment (A. Chavez & Martinez, 1979; Valenzuela, 1990). It may be that malnourished babies are more irritable and recover less quickly from upset than well-nourished children. It could also be that their parents have emotional difficulties that affect their parenting.

In a study on responses to atypical crying, parents and non-parent adults rated cries of brain-damaged infants as sounding less pleasant, and in some cases ignored them (Frodi & Senchak, 1990). If these findings can be generalized to other types of impairments, then it could be that the atypical crying of infants with special needs might fail to elicit the warm parental responses that Ainsworth believes are so important.

Beyond these few studies, the majority of research suggests that infants with special needs form bonds with parents that are as secure as those formed by typically developing children. Infants with hearing impairments, for example, have been found to form secure attachments to parents in exactly the same way that babies with normal hearing do (Lederberg & Mobley, 1990). It appears that verbal communication is not a necessary condition for positive relationships with caregivers. Very similar findings are reported in studies of low-birth-weight babies and of babies who experienced complications during birth (Easterbrooks, 1989). In spite of the stresses and challenges associated with these conditions, both mothers and fathers were found to form healthy, positive attachments to their babies, and vice versa.

In a major summary of many different studies of attachment and infant problems, children with such diverse challenging conditions as Down syndrome and low birth weight were found to form secure attachments at the same rate as typically developing infants (van Ijzendoorn, Goldberg, Kroonenberg, & Frenkel, 1992). However, these authors did find significant attachment problems when the parents themselves faced challenging conditions. Problems such as substance abuse or psychiatric disorder among caregivers are linked to insecure attachment among all babies, not just those with special needs. These researchers conclude that the mental health and functioning of *adults* is far more critical in the process of attachment than are childhood disorders.

Mental health problems make it difficult for parents to respond quickly and with warmth to infant initiatives. In one study, depressed mothers with typically developing babies were more likely to experience attachment difficulties than emotionally healthy mothers of infants with special needs (Lyons-Ruth, Connell, Grunebaum, & Botein, 1990). Social and mental health services can significantly improve these mother-infant relationships.

Interventions That Affect Attachment

What can be done when insecure attachments begin to form? Can professionals intervene with high-risk groups (e.g., depressed mothers) to enhance infant-parent relationships? As I mentioned, one problem with the idea of attachment intervention is that different cultures have different ways of securing infant bonds. A responding behavior in one culture may not be effective in another. In such cases, efforts to teach specific parenting behaviors may be fruitless.

These concerns have been borne out in research. In a program designed to teach high-risk mothers attachment-related interactions, a curriculum of games and activities was implemented during home visits and classes at a child development center (Spiker, Ferguson, & Brooks-Gunn, 1993). The effects of the intervention were minimal, though positive. However, white parents showed more positive outcomes than African-American parents. It may be that the procedures and parenting techniques being taught were geared primarily to the dominant Euro-American culture.

In contrast, a number of very effective attachment interventions are more culture-neutral. One of the most unique of these involved simply giving mothers front carriers resembling the homemade slings used in African villages. When mothers used these, they were in close, continual physical contact with their babies (Anisfeld, Casper, Nozyce, & Cunningham, 1990). Parents were not taught to interact with babies in any special way; they simply were given the carriers when their babies were 3 months old. At 13 months, babies of all cultural groups—white, African-American, and Latino—were more securely attached to their mothers than those whose mothers did not receive the carriers. An important finding was that precise parenting interactions did not seem to make a difference. Breastfeeding, for example, did not lead to more positive attachment. Close body contact led to positive findings, regardless of how mothers interacted with their babies as they carried them.

In another culture-neutral intervention (Lieberman, Weston, & Pawl, 1991), Mexican-American and Central American mothers with insecurely attached babies were provided informal, open-ended support sessions designed to "respond to the affective experiences of mother and child" (p. 202). No direct teaching was involved, although professionals would make suggestions or provide developmental information when it was helpful. At the end of the program, babies were more securely attached, and mothers displayed more frequent interactions and greater empathy.

Taken together, these studies highlight the importance of culturally sensitive intervention. Parent education or support efforts will be ineffective if parents are advised to perform behaviors inconsistent with the values or socialization practices of their cultural group.

Infant Care and Attachment

In the United States, as a growing percentage of mothers enter the workforce, more and more infants are being cared for outside the home. Concerns are being raised about the effects of infant care on the attachment process. Will babies who spend long hours in child care become insecurely attached? How can parents be responsive and warm, provide regular physical contact, and in other ways foster strong emotional bonds when they are away from their babies all day? Early research assuaged parents' fears. Babies in child care centers were found to be as securely attached as those who were cared for by parents at home (Brookhart & Hock, 1976).

A more recent study, however, rekindled fears about infant care. Belsky and Steinberg (1988) found that babies who spent 20 or more hours a week in care outside the home during the first year of life were less likely to become securely attached to parents. These findings, which were published extensively in both the popular and professional literature, staggered those in the infant care profession. Responses to this study from child specialists and caregivers were immediate and spirited. Some pointed to many earlier studies that did not show insecure attachment among child care babies (Clarke-Stewart, 1988).

Others challenged the research methods, particularly the strange situation procedure. One researcher argued, for example, that in a society in which infants now separate and reunite on a daily basis, reactions to the strange situation procedure may mean something very different than they did when Ainsworth was first conducting her studies (Thompson, 1988). The following vignette illustrates this possibility. Is the baby in this story insecure/avoidant in his attachment to his mother, or is some new process at work that reflects modern life in child care?

When a mother says good-bye to her toddler in a child care center, he becomes more upset than usual. He did not sleep well the night before, and she had to get him up early because she has a morning meeting. He was cranky in the car all the way to the center, and when she leaves him he cries and becomes angry. She feels extremely guilty at work for many hours afterward.

During her lunch hour, she decides to visit the center to see how her son is getting along. Perhaps a little bonding time might make him feel more loved and make her feel less guilty. When she enters the center, her son is absorbed in play at the water table. He and another child are laughing and splashing. When her son sees her, his smile disappears. "No! No!" he calls out, assuming that she is picking him up for the day. He completely rebuffs her overtures. She backs away and watches.

Her son's caregiver offers comforting words. "He's having a lot of fun there. I don't think he wants to go home just yet." She returns to work relieved that her son is in good hands and enjoying the day.

Most caregivers and parents who have babies in child care centers have observed similar interactions. In the early morning, children might prefer to stay at home, but by the end of the day they don't want to leave the center. The behaviors of the child in the story above are apt to give the misimpression that he is insecurely attached. However, the true feelings underlying these interactions indicate otherwise. The child's behaviors may simply show that he has adapted to a life filled with separations and reunions, alternate caregivers and new situations, early mornings and late nights. A new way of observing attachment may be needed, one that is sensitive to the modern, complex lives of working parents and their children (Thompson, 1988).

AUTONOMY

Marked changes in social behavior occur during the second year of life. Consider the following examples:

- A baby who has enjoyed playing quietly outside her urban apartment building suddenly shows great interest in a busy parking lot nearby. The more her mother scolds her for going close to this dangerous area, the more interested she seems. Before long, on every trip outdoors, she makes at least one attempt to run to the parking lot.
- A baby of pleasant temperament suddenly begins to say "no" to almost anything. He screams "no" when it is bedtime, dinner time, or even time to go out to play. At one point his mother offers ice cream. "No!" he shouts as he simultaneously reaches for the bowl and spoons ice cream into his mouth.
- A father always dresses his daughter for child care. One morning, the toddler insists on dressing herself. She struggles with the task, trying to put her shoes on before she has put on her pants. "No! I do it," she protests when her father tries to help. Because of this, the father is over an hour late for work.

What has occurred to bring about such changes? When toddlers become more intellectually competent, they tend to be more curious and eager to explore—even dangerous parking lots. When they discover that "no" is a powerful social word that has great impact on family members, they want to use it. When they acquire new motor abilities, they want to exercise them.

Significant social and emotional changes lead babies to behave in new and challenging ways in the second year of life. Erik Erikson's work is helpful in describing these changes. Erikson argues that once children are trustful of adults and know that their basic needs will be met, they are willing to venture away from the safety of parents and family. They now wish to become individuals apart from the adults with whom they have bonded. With this striving for individuality, children often assert themselves, rebel against rules, and assume a negative affect when confronted with adult control. According to Erikson (1963, 1982), these challenging, though necessary, behaviors are explained by the next emotional conflict which humans encounter: autonomy versus shame and doubt.

The emotionally healthy toddler, according to Erikson, gradually acquires a sense of autonomy—a feeling of individuality and uniqueness apart from parents. It has been argued that autonomy in both thinking and behavior is the most important disposition for later learning and development (Kamii, 1982). Children who are overly restricted in their attempts to become individuals (e.g., incessant hand-slapping when they try to explore forbidden objects around the home) will come to doubt their individuality. They will eventually suffer shame for their efforts. Such children can become timid and lack confidence in their abilities. They may assume identities as mere extensions of their parents.

How do children become autonomous? Erikson has proposed that creating environments in which children can become independent in thought and action will contribute to children's autonomy. Parents should encourage children to assert themselves. They should hold back from harshly reprimanding their children's initiatives, according to Erikson.

Cultural Variations in Autonomy

During a recent meeting of a parent support group, a mother spoke at length about the frustrations of living with a toddler. She described negative and defiant behaviors which she attributed to "the terrible twos." Another mother remarked that she had experienced none of these challenging interactions. Her son was pleasant, quiet, and compliant; there were no strains whatsoever on family relationships. Yet another mother commented that her son had shown early defiant behaviors, but she had acted swiftly to counteract them. Through firm discipline, she explained, she had kept her toddler from developing negative attitudes and conduct. From discussions such as these, it is easy to see why autonomy is expressed differently by different toddlers. Cultural beliefs, methods of discipline, or infant personality may explain why each family faces unique experiences in toddlerhood. Behaviors during this period are so diverse across cultures and sexes, in fact, that some have concluded that Erikson's descriptions of autonomy are inaccurate (Boykin & Toms, 1985; Gilligan, 1982).

In many cultures, toddlers are discouraged from separating from parents. In these families, children are carried and breastfed, and sleep with adults throughout infancy and even into older childhood (Garcia Coll, Meyer, & Brillon, 1995; Super & Harkness, 1982). Toddlers of these cultural groups may not display the extreme separation behaviors that Erikson described (Tobin, Wu, & Davidson, 1989). In other cultures, self-sufficiency is encouraged very early in life (Hale, 1994). Children of these groups may demonstrate expressions of independence that are stronger than even Erikson would have predicted (Slonim, 1991).

Other cultural beliefs and practices may affect the degree to which children will seek autonomy. Native American parents have been found to emphasize restraint

In some families, toddlers are discouraged from separating from their parents; instead, dependence and "enmeshment" are encouraged.

and control in toddlerhood, not independence and self-expression. From birth, bonds with family are emphasized and individualism is scorned (Blanchard, 1983; Garcia Coll et al., 1995). Likewise, in many Japanese-American and Chinese-American families, dependence is prolonged; children never do completely separate from families and parents (Kelly & Tseng, 1992; Sue & Chin, 1983; Yu & Kim, 1983).

Puerto Rican mothers have been found to value physical closeness, respect for and obedience to adults, tranquil behavior, and good manners in toddlerhood (Harwood et al., 1995). Although many mothers of this group report a need to instill some degree of autonomy to ensure survival, they do so reluctantly. One Puerto Rican mother justifies giving some amount of independence in this way: "Maybe the moment will come when they won't need me because I will be too old, and then I will be sure that they are going to be able to face their problems" (p. 115). It is clear that this parent is concerned with autonomy only because a separation might be necessary someday, not because it is a positive step toward emotional well-being, as Erikson proposed.

Gender may influence whether babies are encouraged to be autonomous. Some have speculated that in Western society, independence is a characteristic of males, not females (Gilligan, 1982). In contrast, B. B. Whiting and Edwards (1988) report that in a number of non-Western cultures, independence increases with age only in girls. It is likely that boys and girls of all cultures will eventually come to recognize themselves as unique individuals. However, it cannot be assumed that all toddlers will assert their individuality in flamboyant ways, strike out on their own, or shun their parents in the process. So, caregivers should not attempt to shape all children to conform to Erikson's ideal.

TEMPERAMENT

Parents often report that infants exhibit unique personality types, even in the earliest months of life. A mother might exclaim, "He just smiles and coos all the time. He's just a good baby. He always has been!" A father might say, "She's so different from my first child. Right from the day she was born, I could tell she'd be a feisty one." Sometimes these unique personality types are surprising and puzzling to parents, as the following story reveals:

> A child care provider has been caring for babies for many years. He has also studied child development extensively through formal coursework and independent reading. He believes he is well prepared to meet the emotional needs of his own daughter when she is born.
>
> Knowing the research by Mary Ainsworth, he and his wife try hard to be responsive to their daughter's crying. Even when she cries in the middle of the night, they take turns getting up to comfort and feed her. Though they find this to be exhausting, they believe it's what their daughter needs for healthy emotional growth. They keep waiting for the payoff that Ainsworth describes in her work: that babies whose parents are responsive will cry less in later infancy.
>
> But this predicted reduction in crying never occurs. His daughter shows negative reactions to her world as intensely at age 2 as she did at birth. "This is simply the way she is," the father concludes.

A scientific term for "the way she is" is **temperament.** Babies are born with basic temperaments that will influence their social relationships and emotional health

TABLE 9-2
Infant
Temperaments

Temperament	Characteristics
Active	Shows a need for constant motion. Wiggles and bangs objects. Constantly seeks interaction and stimulation.
Bold	Takes initiative in interactions with parents and, later, peers. Is relatively fearless in exploration and play.
Difficult	Erupts in powerful outbursts of upset. Shows negative reactions to new situations or people. Cries often and is not easily consoled.
Easy	Shows a sunny disposition and frequent smiling. Adjusts smoothly and happily to new situations or caregivers.
Fearful	Becomes more easily afraid of new or puzzling situations. Will show greater wariness or upset when confronted with the "visual cliff" experiment, for example.
Shy	Shows a reticence to interact with others. Is quieter and less vocal around strangers.
Slow-to-warm-up	Exhibits wariness of new situations or people. Is less positive in affect and more likely to cling to caregivers.
Timid	Takes less initiative. Is wary of strangers. Shows caution in exploration and play.

SOURCES: Goldsmith & Campos, 1990; Kagan, Reznick, & Gibbons, 1989; Kochanska & Radke-Yarrow, 1992; Chess & Thomas, 1990.

for years to come. A number of these temperament types have been identified by infant researchers. These are summarized in Table 9-2.

Alexander Thomas and Stella Chess (1977) were among the first to conduct studies of infant temperament. In a famous longitudinal investigation, they found that babies could be categorized into three personality types that could be identified at birth: **easy, difficult,** and **slow-to-warm-up.** "Easy" babies have sunny dispositions, are friendly around strangers, and are easily consoled. Parents of newborns with easy dispositions tend to describe parenting as "a piece of cake" or "a breeze." They may not understand why other parents suffer such stress raising their newborns.

Babies in the "difficult" category cry easily, show less positive affect, and react negatively to new circumstances and unfamiliar people. They may show powerful outbursts of upset which can include inconsolable crying, spitting food, and pulling hair. Parents of difficult babies often ask themselves, "What am I doing wrong?" The caregiver in the story above, for example, has learned that no amount of good parenting will change some aspects of a baby's fundamental disposition. A third temperament type is called the "slow-to-warm-up" personality. Babies with this disposition are very wary of strangers and reluctant to separate from parents. They may show less overt emotion, positive or negative.

Among the babies that Thomas and Chess studied, 35% could not be classified. Some babies, then, will have clearly identifiable and persistent personality traits and others will not. Also, it is important to note that within each category there are babies who have various degrees of a particular personality trait. Among difficult babies, for example, some are extremely negative, others less so.

An amazing finding of Chess and Thomas's (1990) research is that subjects still showed roughly the same personality types in adolescence! It is easy to imagine how children of various personality types might behave as they get older. Readers have likely met "easy" adults who have friendly, easy-going personalities; difficult adults who respond less positively and get upset easily at change or new circumstances; and slow-to-warm-up individuals who are shy, timid, and reserved. Jerome Kagan (1994) has also found that in-born infant temperament types persist into later childhood and adolescence. A high rate of mental health disorders and conduct problems in school have been found among those born with difficult temperaments (Caspi, Henry, McGee, Moffitt, & Silva, 1995). This suggests that personality type can predispose children to risks.

Temperament and Attachment

Does temperament affect the quality of parents' or caregivers' relationships with babies? The infant in the following vignette has a difficult temperament that has caused stress and sleeplessness for his parents. Will his negative interactions, over time, interfere with family bonds?

> Two young parents are trying to wash clothes at the laundromat, but their 10-month-old seems determined to keep them from doing their work. He cries out in high-pitched, ear-splitting screams. Other people at the laundromat give disapproving looks and move away. The father rocks and bounces his son, then gives him a pacifier, but the baby spits it out and resumes his angry wail. Now the mother takes a turn. She rattles her keys in front of his face. This tactic works for half a minute. The baby studies and grasps the keys, then loses interest and throws them forcefully to the floor. After much effort, the parents give up trying to console their angry baby. They throw their half-clean wash into a basket and head for home.

Surely these interactions will take a toll on infant-parent relationships. How can these parents provide the warmth and responsiveness necessary to promote attachment? How can this baby, in a perpetual state of upset, bond with them? Amazingly, attachment does occur! In study after study, babies of all temperaments—including personalities as difficult as that illustrated in the story above—are found to become securely attached to their parents at exactly the same rate (Belsky & Rovine, 1987; B. Vaughn, Lefever, Seifer, & Barglow, 1989). It makes no difference whether babies are grouchy and unsmiling, timid and quiet, passive and unplayful; parents find ways to create positive interactions and foster warm bonds. This fact speaks to the powerful, loving urge of parents and babies to form relationships with one another.

Temperament and Culture

Within all cultures, some babies are difficult and others are easy; some are shy and others bold. There are, however, some personality trends that can be observed within specific cultural groups. These are likely the result of biological heritage. For example, very early in life, babies of Chinese-American and Japanese-American families have been found to be less irritable and excitable and more easily calmed, or, in a word, easy (Kagan et al., 1994; Freedman, 1979). These temperamental traits persist at least through infancy. Although very early experience could explain some of these unique personality differences, researchers conclude that genetics is most influential (Garcia Coll, 1990).

In other studies, Navajo babies also were found to cry infrequently and to be more easily consoled and less perturbable (Chisholm, 1983; Freedman, 1974). It is interesting to note that parents in these cultural groups also tend to be quieter and less excitable (Fajardo & Freedman, 1981). Do these parents and children have similar traits because of genetics? Or do parents adapt their interactions to meet the temperamental needs of their babies? It is difficult to answer these questions. However, it is clear that a "goodness of fit" in personality traits exists among family members in Navajo culture. The quiet, easy temperaments of infants and the less excitable personalities of parents are a good match.

In a cross-cultural comparison, Puerto Rican babies were found to be less upset and to cry less often in new situations than Caucasian and African-American babies (Garcia Coll, Sepkoski, & Lester, 1981). African-American newborns were more active. Garcia Coll et al. (1995) interpret these differences as evidence of biological contributions to personality. They suggest, however, that maternal health and nutrition during pregnancy and later parent interactions contribute as well. For example, if a baby has a difficult temperament, suffers poor intrauterine development, and has a parent who responds more negatively, an extremely challenging personality type may emerge. If any one of these variables is changed, however—say, a baby enjoys healthy prenatal development or has parents who respond more positively—a less difficult temperament pattern may result.

A difficult temperament is viewed in most cultures as a risk factor. In a classic study in Africa, however, difficult temperament was actually found to promote survival and healthy development. M. W. DeVries and Sameroff (1984) found that Masai Kenyan babies with difficult temperaments were more likely to thrive during a 10-year drought because their fussiness and crying ensured that they would be adequately fed by their mothers. These findings demonstrate that certain personality types may be more highly valued in one culture than in another (Harwood et al., 1995). Would Masai mothers even use the somewhat pejorative term "difficult" to describe this powerful temperament that assures survival?

EARLY EMOTIONS

Early infant emotions both shape and are shaped by relationships with others. Babies express contentment when they are nurtured; they show distress when an unfamiliar adult picks them up. An intriguing question is whether infants feel the same way about things as adults do. To examine this issue, researchers have conducted studies in which they have observed and rated infant expressions. Babies have been found to make certain facial contortions when angry and others when surprised. Contentment is easy to spot: babies smile and even laugh. Figure 9-2 illustrates several of these infant expressions. Researchers study these expressions and their development and speculate on what babies feel. They also plot the ages at which particular emotions emerge in human development.

Parents appear to play a critical role in teaching babies emotions. They demonstrate various emotional states through exaggerated facial expressions or intonation. Babies can discriminate among these different expressions only days after birth (Izard & Harris, 1995). By 10 months of age, they can distinguish among facial expressions that look similar but represent very different emotions (Ludeman, 1991).

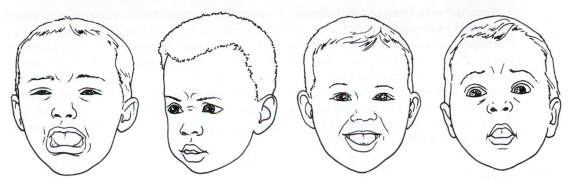

FIGURE 9-2 Distinct infant facial expressions have been identified and studied in order to learn about the development of early emotions.

SOURCE: Krantz, M. (1994). *Child Development: Risk and Opportunity.* Belmont, CA: Wadsworth.

For example, they show different reactions to happy and sad faces, even when these look very much the same.

Visual cues may not be the only way babies notice emotions in parents. In one study, touch, in the absence of facial expression, was effective in communicating feelings of excitement or comfort to 3- to 6-month-olds (Stack & Muir, 1992). In another study, vocalization was found to play a role in imparting feelings (Caron, Caron, & MacLean, 1988). When mothers read stories to babies using various emotional intonations (e.g., happy, sad, angry), babies as young as 5 months could differentiate among these vocalizations.

Babies rely on adult expressions to guide their own feelings. For example, babies who see mothers displaying positive facial features show less distress in the presence of a stranger (W. D. Rosen, Adamson, & Bakeman, 1992) and are more likely to explore an unusual object (Svejda & Campos, 1982). In one study, babies were persuaded to cross a visual cliff if their mothers showed an encouraging expression (Sorce, Emde, Campos, & Klinnert, 1985). In a process called **social referencing,** babies refer to adult emotional reactions to determine how they should feel.

Adults teach children emotions through the use of exaggerated facial expressions.

Another way that adults transmit feelings is through their responses to infant emotional expressions. Adults are quite accurate in interpreting infant expressions of happiness, sadness, surprise, interest, fear, contempt, anger, and disgust (Izard & Harris, 1995). So, they may be sensitive to infant emotions, allowing them to respond appropriately (Malatesta, Culver, Tesman, & Shepard, 1989). Interestingly, abusive parents were found to misread their infants' emotional states (Kropp & Haynes, 1987). They could not pick up on their children's distress signals, for example. This might explain, in part, their devastating reactions to their children and the poor developmental outcomes that result.

Culture and Emotions

Does culture influence the expression of early feelings? Cross-cultural research suggests that basic human emotions are universal (Ekman, 1994). Such feelings as fear, happiness, and anger are part of human interactions within all cultural groups and are expressed through similar facial expressions. What may vary by culture, however, are the times and places when certain emotions may be expressed. In which situations are smiling or laughter appropriate? When may anger be openly communicated? Rules about the expression of emotions vary by culture and are learned even by very young children.

Children of Japanese and Chinese families are often taught—through direct guidance or example—to avoid outward expressions of anger (Slonim, 1991). African and African-American children, in contrast, are encouraged to express feelings openly. Euro-American children display a moderate amount of emotional expression. Hale-Benson (1986) warns that teachers and caregivers must take into account the feelings orientations of the cultural groups they work with and not insist that children express emotions (e.g., "Tell Susan how angry you are!") when this is not culturally appropriate. Nor should they deny children these expressions when they are culturally meaningful (e.g., "Calm down, Jamal. You're getting too excited and loud.")

INFANT RELATIONSHIPS AND EGOCENTRISM

An infant trait that influences social relationships is egocentrism. **Egocentrism,** which we discussed in Chapter 7, is a kind of thinking in which young children have difficulty understanding the perspectives of other people. Infants and toddlers have trouble, for example, understanding that others have needs and feelings, as the following examples illustrate:

- A pregnant mother, suffering from morning sickness, slumps in the bathroom with terrible nausea. Her toddler son pulls on her shirt from behind, begging to have his favorite book read "right now."
- A toddler becomes enraged when another child comes to the child care center with shoes identical to her own. "Mine!" she screams. Even though she has her own shoes on, she insists that her peers' shoes are hers as well.

It is clear from these examples that babies often think their needs are most important and that everything in the world belongs to them. It is easy to see how this kind of thinking influences social interactions. Such displays of egocentrism have led some to label this period of development the "terrible twos."

Research shows that while toddlers are egocentric, they can also be very kind and sociable. They share objects with their parents and other toddlers without being asked, give spontaneous hugs (Rheingold & Hay, 1976), and interact quite well with peers—smiling, laughing, and offering toys as they play (Eckerman, Whatley, & Kutz, 1975). How can these behaviors be reconciled with the view that these babies are unable to understand the perspectives of others? It may be that there is an ongoing struggle in the second year of life between the needs of self and the desire to be with others. The following story illustrates this idea:

A toddler and her father walk along a city sidewalk in Manhattan. The father holds on tight to his daughter's hand. In her other hand she holds a bagel,

ASSESSING YOUNG CHILDREN: Infant Social and Emotional Development

Areas of Development	What to Watch for	Indicators of Atypical Development
Emotional health	By age 6 months, shows a strong attachment to parents or caregivers through smiling, clinging, and in other ways showing a desire to be near these persons. Shows temporary upset during separation from parents or other caregivers. By age 18 months, exhibits some willingness to separate from parents and other caregivers. Demonstrates an ability to work and play alone some of the time.	Shows a lack of interest in or caring for other human beings by age 6 months. Expresses an inordinate amount of upset or anger when separated from parents or family. Completely ignores parents when reunited with them after child care. Remains clingy and dependent on parents after 18 months.
Relationships with others	Shows an interest in other children and non-family adults. Shows early empathy and kindness toward peers.	Shows no interest in peers or adults. Does not respond to and even becomes troubled by social contact from others.
Specific social skills	Makes contact with others through verbalization, playful behavior, smiling, gesturing, or sharing objects.	Performs few social behaviors. Verbalizes little and makes no contact with others.

Interpreting Assessment Data: Variations in social behavior may be due cultural and family practices. Babies of some cultures will be more wary or less social because of unique styles of parenting and family interaction. Children whose family values dependence and discourage autonomy may show greater upset during separation from parents. These children may be less independent in toddlerhood. If babies avoid *all* contact with adults and peers, however, or show poor attachment to parents, further evaluation is recommended. Family stressors such as poverty and substance abuse can interfere with positive family relationships. Mental health services for the whole family may be helpful.

which she chews vigorously as they walk. After a number of blocks, the bagel is quite wet from the toddler's saliva. She accidentally drops it onto the dirty sidewalk. "Oh-oh," she says, scooping the bagel back up.

"Dirty," the father says. "You can't eat that. Don't eat that dirty bagel." "No eat," the toddler responds, shaking her head but clinging to the bagel. She looks over at a man sitting on a bench, a complete stranger. She pulls free from her father and toddles over to him. "Here. You have this," she says, offering her filthy, saliva-soaked bagel to the stranger. Her father grabs hold of her hand again and guides her away.

Here, the elements of egocentrism and kindness are blended. It is a relatively egocentric idea that someone else would wish to eat a spoiled food item that the child has been eating. On the other hand, the toddler wishes to offer it to someone else; no one asked her to do this. The child's thinking probably went something like this: "I have been eating this yummy bagel and *I* like it, so someone else might want to eat it too." Such acts of spontaneous kindness are common at this age.

RESEARCH INTO PRACTICE

CRITICAL CONCEPT 1

Infants form important relationships with caregivers, relatives, neighbors, and peers. Healthy babies in all cultures—even those with challenging conditions—form early attachments to significant adults. These bonds are critical to later relationships.

Application #1

Caregivers and parents should be very nurturing in their interactions with infants. Behaviors such as warm physical touch, smiling, and being close helps babies become attached to adults.

Application #2

Caregivers and parents should respond to infants' cries or bids for attention. Babies become attached to adults who respond to their initiatives predictably and in interesting ways.

Application #3

Caregivers must be culturally sensitive in showing warmth and responsiveness. In some cultures, warm physical touch is not the norm. Parents respond in different ways to crying. A good match must be found between caregiver interactions and the cultural experiences of infants.

CRITICAL CONCEPT 2

In the second year, children who have become attached will begin to strive for a sense of autonomy. They will wish to become individuals separate from their parents. Whether children will become fully independent, however, depends on culture. In some families, dependence is highly valued and individualism is discouraged.

Application #1

Caregivers and parents should understand and appreciate some toddlers' need to become independent. Tolerating assertive and sometimes negative behaviors and allowing a degree of freedom and choice are critical for many children at this age.

Application #2

Caregivers must learn why some parents encourage dependence in their children. Historical experiences, immediate dangers in the neighborhood, or a need for families to band together in the face of adversity may lead parents to discourage independence in their toddlers. Caregivers should not adopt autonomy as a goal for all children in their care.

CRITICAL CONCEPT 3

Infants' social relationships are also influenced by inborn temperament. Some babies have inherited "difficult" dispositions, others "easy" ones. Bold and timid babies can also be differentiated.

Application #1

Caregivers and parents must be aware of the role of biology in determining the basic dispositions of some infants. Guilt-ridden parents must be helped to understand that a negative or wary temperament may not be due to poor parenting, but to inborn characteristics.

Application #2

Caregivers and parents must accept and appreciate the inborn traits of babies. For example, working with or raising "difficult" children may require a great deal of patience and tolerance.

CRITICAL CONCEPT 4

Babies acquire a range of emotions and facial and vocal expressions to represent these. Interactions with family members will assist babies in emotional development. For example, a parent's own expressions of sadness or surprise will help infants to differentiate these feelings.

Application #1

Infant care providers and parents can use exaggerated facial expressions and gestures to transmit emotions to babies. They can engage in up-close, face-to-face interactions in which they show surprise, happiness, or puzzlement.

Application #2

Caregivers and parents can use facial expressions to show caution or fear when infants are in jeopardy. Displaying an exaggerated look of concern when a toddler wanders toward a busy road or climbs too high on a climber will transmit the message that there is danger.

CRITICAL CONCEPT 5

Egocentrism—an inability to understand others' perspectives—is a cognitive characteristic that influences social relationships in infancy. Babies tend to believe that the whole world centers on them. Egocentrism does not seem to inhibit kindness and sharing among toddlers, however. Infant social relations are marked by fascinating blends of self-centeredness and empathy.

Application #1

Caregivers and parents should understand that egocentrism is a cognitive trait, not a personality flaw. They should be tolerant of egocentric behavior and not attempt to insist on cooperative interactions.

Application #2

Children's egocentrism should not prevent adults from trying to instill altruism. Caregivers and parents should model or prompt kindness and sharing. Even highly egocentric infants will perform these behaviors if encouraged.

SUGGESTED ACTIVITIES

1. Observe the arrival of infants at an infant care center in the early morning. Based on the ideas about attachment presented in this chapter, write a report on your observations, guided by the following questions:

   a. What signs of separation anxiety did you observe? Of stranger anxiety? How did parents or other caregivers and child care providers respond to these fears?

   b. Describe the various strategies parents used to say good-bye to their babies. Describe the strategies caregivers used to assist in the departure. Are some methods of separation smoother than others? Which lead to upset? Which lead to happier separations?

   c. Do adult and child separation behaviors differ from one family to the next? To what do you attribute these differences? Does culture contribute? Infant temperament? Does it make a difference who is dropping the baby off (e.g., grandparent, father, mother, neighbor)?

2. Observe as parents or other caregivers pick up their babies from child care at the end of the day. Write a report on your observations, guided by the following questions:

   a. How would you characterize adult-child reunions? To what degree were these happy occa-sions? What did parents, other caregivers, or the child care providers do to make this so?

   b. Did you see signs of avoidant behavior, as observed in the strange situation procedure described in this chapter?

   c. Did you see signs of ambivalent behavior?

   d. To what degree did these reunions differ across families? To what do you attribute these differences? Culture? Temperament? Does it make a difference who picks the child up (e.g., mother, father, grandparent, neighbor)?

3. Observe as child care providers interact with infants or toddlers. Take notes on their responsiveness and warmth, as described in this chapter. Write a report on these behaviors guided by the following questions:

   a. What specific responding behaviors did you observe? What effect did these responses have on babies?

   b. What warm or nurturing behaviors did you see? What effect did they have?

   c. If you observed more than one caregiver, did you see differences in how each interacted with babies in these areas? To what would you attribute caregiver differences in warmth or responsiveness?

4. Observe babies in a child care center and identify two babies with distinct temperaments. Write a report in which you contrast the two babies, guided by the following questions:

   a. In which key personality dimensions did the two babies differ (e.g., activity level, negative or positive disposition, timidity or boldness)?

   b. To what do you attribute these differences? Do you believe these personality traits are inborn or learned? Does the baby show these same traits in all situations? With all people?

5. Observe two toddlers between the ages of 18 months and 2 years in a home or child care center. Describe behaviors that show each child is striving for autonomy, as Erikson described. Write a report in which you contrast the autonomous behaviors of the two children, guided by the following questions:

   a. What behaviors did you observe which showed that both toddlers were struggling for autonomy?

   b. Were there differences in how strongly the two asserted their independence? If so, to what do you attribute these differences?

   c. How did adults in the environment react to expressions of autonomy? Did their reactions to the two children differ? To what do you attribute these differences?

6. Observe a newborn and an older infant (between 4 and 8 months of age). During each observation, write down each distinct emotion that you observe (e.g., happiness, anger, fear). Record the facial expressions that indicate each emotion as well. (Review the infant emotions identified by researchers, as listed in this chapter.) Write a report in which you contrast the emotions of these two infants, guided by the following questions:

   a. Which distinct emotions did you observe in the newborn? Which facial expressions were associated with each emotion?

   b. Which emotions did you observe in the older infant? Which facial features were associated with each emotion?

   c. Did the babies differ in the types or numbers of different emotions they demonstrated?

   d. From your observations, what can you conclude about infant emotional development?

CHAPTER 10

Preschool Physical and Motor Development

THE PRESCHOOL YEARS—FROM AGE 2 TO AGE 5—ARE MARKED BY SIGNIFICANT PHYSICAL GROWTH AND DEVELOPMENT. This chapter profiles the extraordinary motor advancements that occur during this period. Preschoolers are more coordinated, show surprising strength and speed, and display tireless energy. However, great diversity in these physical changes exists among individuals. The following vignette shows how variations in motor activity and physical play preferences can be seen within a single child care center.

A university child care center in a large Midwestern city serves a culturally diverse group of children. A caregiver, Ms. Shapiro, is challenged to create activities that meet the diverse needs and interests of all the children in her care. She creates a new science center, which includes objects from nature that she feels relate to the lives of children and their families. This center contains not only items from the woods, but also those from urban environments, such as wasp nests and bird feathers. She asks families to help her collect things for the center; they contribute items that hold cultural meaning. One family offers different types of beans and grains, another brings in a sampling of vegetables from the family garden.

Ms. Shapiro plans for children to sit in the center and feel, weigh, and examine the items under a magnifying glass. However, what they actually do with the items is quite different. Two children do spend time quietly examining objects. Two others, though, seem far more enamored with the new screen divider that the caregiver has put up to separate the science center from the rest of the classroom. These children begin a spontaneous, raucous game of peekaboo, taking turns ducking down behind the divider and then popping back up with shrieks of laughter. Soon the game evolves into chasing; the two children pursue one another round and round this interesting screen. Another child takes items off a table and tosses them into the air. She studies these objects as they fall to the floor and break apart. Other children soon join her.

As the students continue with these activities, working together to ensure the demise of her carefully planned center, Ms. Shapiro ponders what has gone wrong.

The caregiver in this vignette has been very careful to provide materials relating to children's interests. She has demonstrated sensitivity to the unique community and cultural experiences of the families she serves. The problem is, she has failed to recognize another important area of diversity in children's development: *movement*. Individual children move through the world differently. Some are very active, others prefer quiet solitude and reflection. Some children explore objects by acting on them; they must throw, swing, bang, or bend them to fully understand their properties.

Movement styles and preferences, activity levels, and motor abilities vary across cultures (Hale, 1994). In some cultural groups, quietness and stillness are valued. In others, animated interaction is the norm. Physical activity also differs by age; younger children have a harder time sitting still for long periods. Perhaps there is a poor match between the activities this caregiver has planned and the motor needs of this particular group. The caregiver in this story might have included in her new center some choices involving greater movement. An object drop area, a pendulum swinging game, or nutcrackers to break open designated materials have been recommended as appropriate science experiences for more active young learners (Trawick-Smith, 1994).

An important message of this story is that a culturally sensitive preschool classroom must include more than a multicultural curriculum. Simply providing materials or topics that reflect diverse backgrounds is not enough. Teachers and caregivers must adapt space and activities to meet cultural and developmental differences in motor activity as well. Teachers must engage children in appropriate levels and types of physical activity. Among some groups of children, an active classroom not only feels more comfortable, but leads to greater learning (Hale, 1994).

PHYSICAL GROWTH

Some patterns of physical and motor development are universal. Children of all cultures grow physically in certain similar ways during the preschool years. First and foremost, all children of this age do grow. Actually, growth rate slows during this developmental time period in contrast to the astounding pace of physical development during infancy. The preschool years are a time of slow but steady increase in height, weight, and muscle tone. A look at a 3-year-old and a 5-year-old will reveal the significant physical development that occurs in early childhood.

Preschoolers' bodies grow faster than their heads. The huge-headed appearance of infancy and toddlerhood gradually disappears as torsos grow longer and stomach muscles stronger. These changes give preschoolers a flatter stomach; the endearing potbelly of infancy gradually fades. A pronounced physical change that occurs during the preschool years is arm and leg growth, although preschoolers remain short-legged in contrast to adults.

These growth patterns lead to a shift in the center of gravity, the point at which body weight is evenly distributed. Babies' centers of gravity are high in the body, somewhere in the area of the chest. This makes them very top-heavy and thus more awkward on their feet, unable to make sudden movements without toppling over (Lowrey, 1986). A preschooler's center of gravity is nearer the belly button. This lower weight distribution allows children of this age to perform actions that were impossible only a year or two before. Physical changes in the preschool years are also evident in weight increases: a typical preschooler weighs 31% more at the end of this period than at its beginning. (It is interesting to note, however, that in infancy weight increases 300%!)

Preschoolers' height and weight vary significantly, even within single cultural groups. A study of children within the United States, for example, showed that height among 4- and 5-year-olds ranged from under 90 centimeters to over 115 centimeters (Lowrey, 1986). The weight of these same children was even more variable, with a range of 30 to 50 pounds. All children studied were developing in healthy, typical ways. A child's simply being small in the preschool years is not a cause for concern.

Cultural variations in the size of preschool children have been found to exist. Children of Asian ancestry, for example, tend to weigh less and be of shorter stature than those from other groups (Lowrey, 1986). Genetically derived body structure accounts for most of this variation, but environmental factors may be a factor. For example, the short stature of Southeast Asian children living in poverty has been linked to iron deficiency (Nutritional Status of Minority Children, 1997). In contrast, African and African-American preschoolers tend to be taller and heavier. Differences in home and family environments have been cited as one reason for higher weights among these cultural groups. For example, more active play in the early years has been linked to greater muscle tone among African-American children (Garcia Coll, 1990). Higher weight and height among children of African descent is also the result of an inborn body type.

Euro-American and European preschoolers fall somewhere between Asian and African cultural groups in stature. This has led researchers to refer to such children's height and weight as "typical," African children's as "precocious," and Asian-American children's as "delayed." These are value-laden words that suggest physical anomalies. In truth, what is typical growth in one culture is very different from that in another. No one cultural growth pattern is the norm.

GROSS MOTOR DEVELOPMENT

Children of all cultures acquire **gross motor abilities**—skills that require the use of large muscles in the legs or arms, as well as general strength and stamina. Examples of such skills include running, jumping, throwing, climbing, and kicking. A number of gross motor abilities that are acquired in the preschool years are presented in Table 10-1.

Advancement in these areas often appears to be so rapid that adults come to believe these abilities are acquired overnight. One preschool teacher describes the high-speed, death-defying tricycle-riding prowess of a 5-year-old who only several days before was unable to get the trike to move at all. A parent reports that his 4-year-old, who just weeks before was unable to swing herself, had suddenly begun to perform sophisticated aerial acrobatics on the swing set. How did these abilities emerge so quickly?

Actually, motor development is characterized by a gradual refinement in abilities. Steps toward mastery of a particular skill are many, although each step is not always easily observed. Although a child might demonstrate sudden accuracy in throwing, for example, this skill actually was acquired in small steps. The process began in infancy, with primitive swiping and grasping. In toddlerhood, the child may have begun throwing underhanded. In the early preschool years, the child may have begun to throw overhanded, but with awkward body movements (i.e., stepping forward with the same foot as the throwing arm). From the earliest days of life, the child may have practiced the timing of the release of objects. In infancy, the child had to overcome reflexive grasping. In toddlerhood the child had to learn to let go of an object

TABLE 10-1
Gross Motor Abilities Acquired in the Preschool Years

By the end of the preschool years, children usually can . . .
walk up and down stairs, alternating feet.
walk in straight and circular lines.
balance while walking on tires or balance beams.
climb ladders and climbers alternating feet.
run with both feet leaving the ground.
stop, start, and change directions quickly when running.
leap off a hill or climber and land squarely on both feet.
jump over blocks, tires, or other obstacles leading with one foot.
hop on one foot for 10 or more repetitions.
gallop, using one lead foot.
ride tricycles or other riding toys, using the pedals.
stop and start riding toys and steer around barriers.
throw balls and other objects using the whole body and stepping forward with the leg that is opposite the throwing arm.
catch objects using only the hand and arms and bending the elbows to absorb the impact of a throw.
kick objects using a bent knee and a back and forward swing.
swing on a swing independently.

at the just right time when throwing (Cratty, 1986). It was only after many of these small, unnoticed advancements that the child's throwing competence would become suddenly apparent to adults.

Locomotion skills, such as walking and running, progress in the same way. Although parents or teachers may have suddenly noticed that preschoolers are difficult to keep up with, the speed, balance, and coordination at this age took a long time to develop. In toddlerhood and the early preschool years, their steps were unsure. They stumbled often, tipped over when changing directions or stopping suddenly. They rarely moved directly in a straight line. They did not engage in true running; both their feet would not leave the ground at the same time when they would lope along (Cratty, 1986). Gradually, they become more competent in their locomotion. By age 3 they could walk in a straighter line, and at 4 in a circular path. They became better at climbing up and down stairs. At around age 4 they could alternate steps for the first time when stair-climbing. At this age they could also leap, gallop, and hop. Their running at last became controlled and coordinated. So, by the late preschool years most children would be off and running, with their parents chasing behind and wondering, "When did they learn to move so quickly?"

There are two distinct kinds of movement abilities: movement consistency and movement constancy (J. Keogh, 1977). **Movement consistency** refers to basic movement skills such as running or catching. **Movement constancy** refers to an ability to adapt these movements to meet varying environmental challenges (e.g., being able to catch balls of different sizes or being able to run uphill and down as well as on flat surfaces). Both are critical for play and everyday life in all cultures. A child in Chicago learns not only to run, for example, but to run up and down ramps, over tires, and along balance beams on the playground. A child in rural

Guatemala must not only run, but change directions and stop and start quickly when herding farm animals.

Not only must children learn to coordinate the movements of their own bodies, they must often adapt these in relation to what other children are doing (J. Keogh, 1977). In a game of tag, for example, children must do more than simply run. They need to start and stop, shift direction, or speed up in relation to the actions of peers who are pursuing them. **Reaction time** is also important in many childhood games. Traditional American pastimes such as musical chairs, "red light, green light," and slapjack require quick motoric reactions to stimuli.

Cultural Variations in Motor Skills

Since physical growth is most often governed by genetics and maturation, preschoolers across cultures are more alike than they are different in motor development (Goldsmith, 1987). Some cultural variations do exist, however, in the pace with which skills emerge. Children from tribes in Central and South America appear to acquire specific motor skills earlier than Euro-American preschoolers. Similar, advanced development was discovered among Asian children (Lester & Brazelton, 1982). African and African-American preschoolers were also found to acquire certain large motor abilities earlier than their Euro-American peers (Morgan, 1976; Super, 1981). Again, both genetics and experience explain these differences. Garcia Coll (1990) speculates that the way children are held and played with by parents and other family members contributes to differences in motor development. Diet and nutrition can also produce variations.

Cultural Variations in Activity Level

Anyone who has spent time in a preschool or child care center is aware of individual differences in children's activity levels. Some preschoolers are quiet, others are extremely active. Activity level generally increases during the first 2 years of life and then, for most children, decreases significantly through age 5 (Eaton & Yu, 1989). Not all children become less active in the preschool years, however (Goldsmith, 1987). A good deal of evidence suggests that needs and preferences for movement are biologically inherited. For example, studies have shown that identical twins have very similar activity levels, whereas non-identical twins do not (Saudino & Eaton, 1989). Boys have been found to be consistently more active than girls, suggesting that high activity level is a sex-linked genetic trait (Eaton & Yu, 1989).

Children's need for movement varies by culture. This is partly the result of unique biological inheritance (Gandour, 1989; A. Thomas & Chess, 1984). It is also affected by differences in home and family environments (Garcia Coll, 1990). A study of Puerto Rican and Euro-American mothers, for example, has shown how values can influence children's activity levels (Harwood, Miller, & Irizarry, 1995). Puerto Rican mothers were discovered to be more likely than Euro-American mothers to rate active play as undesirable. In contrast, Mexican-American and African-American parents report that action and rhythmicity are a central part of child rearing and family communication (Hale, 1994; Mejia, 1983). Because of differences in parental beliefs and interactions, children of these cultural groups are likely to develop very distinct movement patterns.

The activity levels of individuals of one culture are sometimes misunderstood by those of another. A case in point is the response of some Euro-American teachers to the active styles of African-American preschoolers (Hale, 1994). Some teachers have been found not only to misinterpret the active play of children of this cultural group, but to try to quiet or slow it down (Hale-Benson, 1986; Morgan, 1976). Preschool teachers must understand and appreciate diversity of activity level and provide activities that meet the wide range of movement needs in a given classroom.

MOTOR PLAY AND CULTURE

Preschoolers of different cultures use motor abilities in different ways as they play. Some may use kicking skills to play a game with a ball, others may use these to kick rocks into the cooking fire. Some may refine kicking to enact pretend martial arts battles, others might skillfully kick a can along the sidewalk all the way back home from the grocery. This section will provide examples of preschool motor play across cultures.

Running and Walking

Running and walking are observed in children of all cultures as they engage in free play. American preschools or child care centers afford many opportunities for varied walking experiences, including tiptoeing quietly to the bathroom, climbing up and down steps, and keeping up with older children on a field trip. All of these activities require adaptation in walking behaviors.

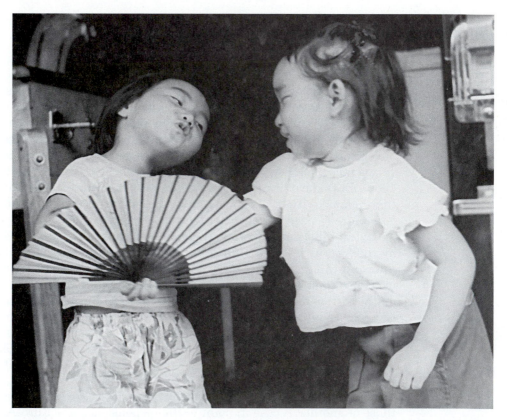

Preschoolers of all cultures acquire the same motor abilities but use them very differently in their play.

It is impossible to keep children from running, as even teachers in "sit quiet and listen" classrooms learn quickly. Simply letting children move uninhibited about the classroom or on the playground will result in much running practice.

Open-ended chasing is a common running game played on American preschool playgrounds. Distinct from organized games of tag with clearly defined rules, chasing involves wild, chaotic running about as one or several children chase after others. Sometimes the chasers and chasees reverse roles without warning. The following is an example of such a chasing game:

Three children are playing a make-believe game in which one is a giant who chases and captures people.

JENNA: (In a gruff, make-believe voice) Oh, I'm tired, alright? I'm a tired giant. I am going to sleep now. But no one better throw leaves on me during my nap.

EDGAR: (Laughs. Takes a handful of leaves which have been raked up on the playground and throws them on the sleeping "giant.")

JENNA: (Doesn't stir; continues to snore loudly)

Rosita: (With eager anticipation in her voice) Oh, oh. Throw some more leaves on.

EDGAR: (Giggling) I'll do it. (Throws more leaves)

Suddenly Jenna rises up and emits a roar. She darts after one of her classmates, then quickly shifts direction and chases another. At first, the children being chased run quickly; then they slow down, eager to be captured. Jenna grabs hold of Edgar and pulls him back to the leaf pile.

JENNA: (To the captured child) Now you stay there while I take my nap. And I hope no one else throws leaves on me.

The game continues for many minutes. Slight variations occur: children come to the rescue of peers who are captured, the giant keeps sleeping for many minutes while the children throw leaves, the giant runs in slow motion during the chase.

In this chasing game, children acquire running consistency—that is, basic running skill. However, they also show running constancy as they vary their running movements to meet all kinds of circumstances and in response to the actions of peers. For example, they must anticipate the direction and speed with which the giant pursues them and vary their own speed accordingly. They run over or under obstacles and up and down a hill on the playground.

Running games are common in other cultures. In Taiwan, children at a very young age fly kites (Pan, 1994). One child or an adult might pull the string while other children run alongside. Children might gather and run about underneath the flying kite. Although this game is very different from American chase, it also develops children's running abilities. Children must run hard and adapt their running to the conditions of the field and quickly change direction as the wind blows the kite.

In Polynesia, children play a game along the boat ramps near their homes. As the waves rise and break, children run away from them so as not to get wet (Martini, 1994). Teasing is another childhood favorite in this culture. In this game, one child or a group of children teases a younger or same-age peer or sibling and then runs away with whoops and laughter. Many Euro-Americans do not consider this to be the most positive form of social play, but it certainly causes children to exercise their running abilities. Polynesian preschoolers also engage in active make-believe which includes imaginary hunting expeditions. They charge after and pretend to kill valley goats, pigs, or dogs. Kepelle village children in Sierra Leone also engage in hunting play, called *Sua-Kpe-pele,* in which chasing of animals is common (Bloch & Adler, 1994). Each type of play poses challenges that require running adaptation; changing directions to outrun a wave or pursue a goat are examples.

Climbing and Jumping Down

Climbing competence requires large motor development as well as a positive disposition toward taking risks. For example, when climbing a net ladder, children must not only have strength and coordination, they must also overcome the anxiety of being up so high. Adults often reassure children who are fearful (e.g., "I'm right here if you need help" or "The ladder is very safe. You won't get hurt climbing up there"). When adults acknowledge children's risk-taking (e.g., "Oh, my! Look how high up you are! You're way over my head! How did you climb so far up!"), they instill confidence and a desire for more adventurous play (Gallahue, 1982).

Once children have climbed up on something, they generally jump down. Jumping is a complex action that develops gradually in stages. Young preschoolers step off from surfaces rather than jump down from them. As they get older, they begin to actually leap, landing first on one foot and then the other. In these early jumps, children awkwardly throw their arms back and fail to lean forward for balance (Schickedanz, Schickedanz, & Forsyth, 1982). The consequence is often a lopsided landing. Children in the early preschool years usually leap from the lower platforms of a climber or bottom rungs of a ladder until their jumping abilities improve. Girls and boys differ in their jumping skill: girls are more precise in their jumps, while boys can leap higher (Cratty, 1986).

Games involving climbing up and jumping down are common in any culture. Middle-class American children often have access to innovative playground equipment. A growing number of playgrounds at preschools and child care centers—and even the backyards of private homes—include elaborate playscapes that allow safe climbing and jumping. Such sophisticated equipment is not a part of child play experiences in all cultures. In Puerto Rico, preschoolers might climb on low walls or leap from banks into shallow streams, under the watchful eye of a parent or older sibling (L. D. Soto & Negron, 1994). Wall and fence climbing are common in urban neighborhoods as well, as the following vignette illustrates:

Two 4-year-old cousins play together in an urban park. The play area is a grass surface with several broken swings and half-buried concrete sewer pipes. The children are drawn to the periphery of the area, where a three-foot-high brick wall surrounds the park. They climb up and walk along the wall. Soon they begin a game in which they leap from the wall to the ground. "Look at me, Mama!" one child announces from atop the wall, then he screams and leaps. He lands on both feet but then drops to the ground and rolls over dramatically.

"Be careful now, Jamal," his mother warns. "You're way high up. Don't want skinned knees, now." She says this with a smile, knowing the wall is low enough and the ground is soft enough that there is no real danger.

"Yeah. I can get up high too," says Latonia, trying to best her cousin. She climbs to the top of the wall. "Look at me, Auntie Sarah, I'm jumping!" she screams out in mock horror, sailing through the air and landing on both feet in the grass. The game continues for over an hour.

Catching and Throwing

Balls predominate in children's play in Western societies (Kaplan-Sanoff, Brewster, Stillwell, & Bergen, 1988). Children acquire throwing and catching abilities gradually. Only in the elementary years will they display highly coordinated ball-handling skills (H. G. Williams, 1983). In the early preschool years, children begin to throw overhanded. Their early attempts lack any control, however. Where a thrown object will land is difficult to predict at this age; sometimes it will actually fly backwards behind a child. During the course of the preschool years, children's arms become more fluid and less rigid when they throw, and they are better able to time the release of objects. Eventually they begin to use their whole bodies, not just their arms. Near the end of the preschool years, some children learn to step forward with the foot opposite the throwing arm and to shift their weight to get behind a throw. At this point, throws become longer and more accurate (Cratty, 1986).

Catching ability also progresses during the preschool years. Initially, children are rigid, passive targets. They simply put out both arms and wait for the object to strike them. If a thrown object happens to come directly between their arms, they may trap it against their chest to make the catch. More often than not, however, the object goes wide, and they make no effort to move their arms or adapt their movements to catch it. Sometimes a ball or beanbag will bounce off of their outstretched arms. Their reaction time is simply not quick enough to grab an object as it strikes them. Older preschoolers begin to catch more effectively. They move their arms more quickly and bend them to absorb the impact of the object as they catch it. They become very competent at catching large objects (e.g., a beach ball) by age 5, but still struggle with small balls or other catching toys.

Children will practice throwing without great coaxing from adults. Spontaneous throwing games predominate during free play. Any kind of material might become an object to be thrown. Without warning, very young children are apt to lay hold of inappropriate objects and invent indoor throwing games that threaten life and limb! In American preschools and child care centers, beanbags or balls of different sizes are provided to stimulate throwing and catching behaviors (Kaplan-Sanoff et al., 1988). In other cultures, balls may not be available, but throwing still predominates in children's play. In Polynesia, children throw rocks (Martini, 1994). Preschoolers of this culture can be observed standing for long periods on a bridge tossing large and small stones into the water below. They also throw rocks at cans or toss sticks for a dog to retrieve. A favorite game, even at this young age, is dashing glass soft-drink containers against rocks or throwing them into the water. In another popular game, young children in Polynesia throw lemons at one another. Although these activities may seem unusual and perhaps inappropriate to adults of Western cultures, they are marvelously inventive and reflect the unique play environments of children.

Balancing

When preschoolers grow taller, their center of gravity becomes lower and their balance improves (Lowrey, 1986). Balance is required for many games. Children often engage in play in which they deliberately cause themselves to become off-balance

(Aldis, 1975); examples are spinning around and around and then trying to walk, or sliding down a particularly slippery slide then trying to regain balance at the bottom. Low balance beams and other equipment are useful for balance play. Preschool playground equipment in America is often designed to encourage balancing games, as the following story illustrates:

> Two children stand and bounce on one of several old tires that lie horizontally on the playground. One child begins to walk around the tire rim. When she comes to the point where her peer is standing, she stops and says, "Hazel, move!"
>
> "Oh, that's easy," her friend responds and begins to walk around the tire in the same direction. They circle round and round together many times.
>
> "And let's say if you fall off," the first child announces, "you get eaten by . . . um . . . sharks, alright? Oh, and let's say we switch directions now, okay?" The two children stop and turn; as they do, they wobble a bit but do not touch the ground. "Those sharks coulda got us!" the first child laughs.

Balancing activities are not limited to games on play equipment. In many cultures playgrounds are not available, so balancing activities must be improvised from available household or outdoor materials:

> A 5-year-old girl in a village in Senegal invites a slightly younger sibling to play a make-believe balancing game. She fills two large cans with water and balances one of them on her head, demonstrating how it is to be carried. "Don't spill a single bit or the food will be wasted," she instructs in an adult tone. The younger girl places the second can on her head. As the older child begins to walk a winding path, holding herself erect and supporting the can on her head with one hand, her sister follows after. With one careful step after another, they make their way through the village in single file.

This is a typical form of "work-play" among girls of Senegal, performed as preparation for adult responsibilities (Bloch & Adler, 1994).

Rough-and-Tumble Play

Children of all cultures engage in wild, silly roughhousing that looks, from outward appearances, like fighting or aggressive behavior. This form of play is forbidden in many American schools and households out of concern that it might lead to real fighting. A growing body of research suggests that rough-and-tumble play, which includes wrestling, play-fighting, rolling around, or chasing peers—all accompanied by screams, laughter, and noise-making—is useful for motor development and social learning. Such play likely relieves tension, exercises many different muscles simultaneously, leads to close physical contact with peers, and is generally great fun. Rough-and-tumble play with nurturing adults may contribute to greater competence in peer interactions (MacDonald & Parke, 1986). Contrary to what would be expected, this form of play does not lead to aggression, nor does it result in unruly or uncontrollable behavior (Pellegrini & Perlmutter, 1988).

Rough-and-tumble play may be the ideal context for acquiring motor abilities in early childhood. Children who are less active might be enticed into activity by such open-ended, humor-filled interchanges. Children who do not care for organized games or who prefer make-believe activities might be attracted to the competition-free, highly

Children of all cultures engage in rough-and-tumble play.

symbolic features of rough-and-tumble play. Wrestling, running, and shouting on the playground are appropriate and powerful ways to practice motor skills. Very few activities that an adult could invent would lead to the same levels of exercise (Myers, 1985).

Do children of all cultures engage in rough-and-tumble play? Multicultural studies suggest so. Research on Polynesian children shows that pretend-fighting is prevalent in the early years. Groups of multiple ages have been observed waging "war" with one another by wrestling, punching, calling names, and throwing rocks, lemons, or pretend spears (Martini, 1994). Japanese children play a traditional game that resembles sumo wrestling. However, such rough, active play has declined in the past few decades within Japanese society as television and video games have become popular pastimes (Takeuchi, 1994). B. B. Whiting and Edwards (1988) observed rough-and-tumble play in six very distinct cultures. In some of these societies, parents were observed teaching young children how to distinguish between rough play and true aggression. At an early age, then, some preschoolers may be tutored in how to modulate their brute force, to hold back from hurting others, or to show clear signs of playfulness, such as smiling or laughing.

FINE MOTOR DEVELOPMENT

The ability to coordinate smaller muscles in the arms, hands, and fingers is referred to as **fine motor development.** Remarkable advances in the development of fine motor skills occur during the preschool years. At this age children begin to use these smaller muscles to perform a variety of self-help skills, as the following story illustrates:

A 4-year-old arrives at a Midwestern child care center in winter. He is wearing a new "snowmobile suit," a miniature version of the full-body outfit that an ice fisherman or snowmobile rider might wear in subzero temperatures. His suit is covered with elaborate zippers, buttons, snaps, clasps, and velcro attachments. One caregiver chuckles at its resemblance to a costume from a science fiction movie.

The child is enormously proud of his new suit and rushes about the center showing friends and teachers. "It's like my Dad's, you know. It's a real one. It's for snowmobiles. It's got all this neat stuff. See?" The children are duly impressed. The teachers, who are a bit more practical, are imagining the time it will take to dress this little boy for outdoor play.

Now comes the challenging task of taking the outfit off. It's nice and warm in the center; if the child leaves on his wonderful suit, he will perish from the heat. His teacher reminds him of this and offers help. "Why don't you let me give you a hand. Can I get some of these zippers started for you?"

"No!" the child responds vigorously, "I can do all this." It is clear that part of the thrill of wearing the new suit is demonstrating how all the various snaps and zippers work. He sits on the floor beside his cubby and sets to work getting out of the outfit. A small group of admirers, including both teachers and peers, gathers around to watch. He struggles with some parts of the suit, but perseveres. It takes him a full 20 minutes to remove it. Everyone applauds when he finishes. He smiles and holds up the suit one last time for all to see before hanging it on a hook.

At this moment, the director pokes her head into the classroom. "Just wanted to remind you that today is our monthly fire drill. We'll be going outside in a few minutes."

Although children may struggle a bit with self-help skills such as buttoning, zipping, or eating with utensils, these are mastered, for the most part, by age 4 or 5. Some children, like the preschooler we just met, show surprising command over small muscles. They are able to tie their shoes or remove elaborate clothing independently. A great deal of variation in fine motor competence will exist, however, among children in a typical child care or preschool setting.

Fine motor abilities are supported by advancements in perception. Preschoolers can see, hear, touch, taste, and smell as well as adults can (Siegler, 1986). Further, they are much better at interpreting what they perceive than they were during infancy. For example, 4-year-olds have been found to be quite sophisticated in noticing details in pictures and making accurate interpretations about what they see (Jones, Swift, & Johnson, 1988). They scan visual stimuli much more completely than infants, fixating less on just one feature of a picture or object (Davidoff, 1975). They begin to coordinate these newly acquired perceptual abilities with body movements. A 4-year-old can now skillfully use vision to guide hands in drawing. A 5-year-old can turn the pages of a small book while looking at pictures and print. This ability to integrate movements and perception has been called **perceptual-motor coordination.** Examples of specific fine motor abilities that develop in the early years are presented in Table 10-2.

As with gross motor development, adults are surprised by what they perceive as sudden spurts in their children's fine motor control. A Head Start teacher tells of a child who seemed to struggle with fine motor tasks, then announced one day that she could now tie her own shoes. The teacher watched in amazement as the child successfully demonstrated her newfound skill. A parent describes how a young preschooler suddenly began to draw people—primitive heads with long legs below them. Until this moment, the child had only scribbled. Although adults might marvel at

TABLE 10-2
Fine Motor Abilities Acquired in the Preschool Years

By the end of the preschool years, children usually can . . .
eat with a fork and spoon.
spread food with a knife.
put on clothing and shoes independently.
button large buttons on clothing.
zip and unzip clothing.
finger paint.
sculpt with clay.
cut with scissors.
manipulate with accuracy the small pieces of a puzzle or pegboard.
grasp a writing implement or paintbrush using the thumb and fingers.
create representational drawings, including human heads and facial features.
write some primitive, conventional letters or one's name.
coordinate hand and arm movements with vision, hearing, touch, and other senses.

how quickly children gain control over small muscles, this is actually a gradual and complex process.

ARTISTIC DEVELOPMENT

Children of all cultures engage in quiet games that involve the use of small muscles. The types of games vary according to the available toys and cultural traditions. Making puzzles, molding clay, cutting and stacking objects, and building with blocks are common fine motor activities in some cultures. Drawing and other forms of artistic expression are perhaps the most universal form of fine motor play.

Drawing Development: A Traditional View

Children's drawing illustrates fine motor development as well as intellectual growth in the preschool years. Traditional theorists have described stages of drawing through which children progress, beginning with the scribbling stage and advancing to more representational drawing levels (Di Leo, 1982; Lowenfeld, 1947). Descriptions of these stages are presented in Table 10-3.

In toddlerhood and the early preschool years, children often scribble. Over time, these scribbles become more controlled, often containing more circular strokes and discrete shapes. Children achieve even greater control when they learn to hold the drawing implement in their fingers instead of gripping it in their fist, and to place their arms down on the table as they draw. Their scribbles become smaller and more discrete. Eventually, children name their scribbles or tell stories about them. Even in the early preschool years, then, children exhibit an awareness that art can be used to symbolically represent the real world. Children must advance through the scribbling stage before they are able to produce more representational work. Even after they have moved on to more elaborate drawing, older preschool children will revisit scribbling for enjoyment or comfort.

TABLE 10-3
Stages of Drawing in Early Childhood

Stage	Approximate Age	Description
Scribbling stage	15 months to 3 or 4 years	Large zigzagging lines give way to more controlled and circular markings later in this stage. Eventually, discrete shapes appear. Children begin to name their scribbles as they approach the next stage.
Preschematic stage	3 or 4 years to 6 or 7 years	Early representations are drawn. For the first time, adults can recognize what children have created. Names of drawings stay the same over time. Early drawings are comprised of heads with basic features. Over time, arms, hands, legs, arms, and detailed facial features emerge.
Schematic stage	6 or 7 years to 9 or 10 years	Whole scenes which include houses, trees, a sun, and people are created. Figures "float in space" and are out of proportion early in this stage. Later, figures may be anchored to a ground line with a shading of blue at the top of the page representing the sky.

Adapted from Di Leo, 1982; Lowenfeld, 1947; and Seefeldt, 1987.

In the later preschool years, children often begin to create simple representations of the people and things that are important to them. Heads predominate in their drawings during this period. As children progress, they draw stick arms and legs which at first protrude from the heads of their figures and later are attached to bodies drawn below the heads. Other representational figures—trees, houses, animals, clouds, the sun—emerge in children's drawings as they develop into the early primary grades, although these are often drawn out of proportion or may be shown floating through space. In the elementary years, elaborate scenes are created which reflect a greater degree of correspondence to the real world. At this stage, the figures often are anchored to a ground line, and a patch of blue sky may be added above. Samples of children's drawing representing several of these stages of development are presented in Figure 10-1.

An interesting feature of children's drawing is repetitive practice. Once children begin making small, circular scribbles, they draw these over and over again on paper. Once they begin to draw heads, they fill pages with them. Teachers begin to worry about the supplies budget as children go through reams of paper, drawing identical heads on each sheet. This repetitive practice may be an effort to gain mastery over newly acquired abilities.

Representing life on paper requires more than skill at controlling a marker or crayon or being able to see the object one is drawing. Drawing also has a cognitive component. Piaget has argued that children are more likely to draw what they know than what they see (Piaget & Inhelder, 1963). For example, children draw transparent houses with visible people. Such a drawing represents not what they actually see when they look at a house, but what they know occurs inside: family members sleeping, eating, and playing. Drawing development involves, then, a complex coordination of perceptual, motor, and cognitive skills.

FIGURE 10-1 Drawing ability develops rapidly during the preschool years. Children first scribble (a), then draw heads (b). Arms, legs, and other body details emerge soon thereafter (c). Some children draw full figures by the end of the preschool period (d).

Is drawing a good indicator of fine motor skill in all cultures? In societies where drawing, writing, and other forms of graphic representation are essential, drawing may be an excellent, natural context for observing development (Gandini, 1997a). It is important to note that not all cultural groups use Western writing implements such as pencils, markers, or crayons. For example, to assess drawing development among Yup'ik Eskimo children in southwestern Alaska, one would need to observe "storyknifing," an activity in which children draw symbols in mud as they tell traditional stories (deMarrais, Nelson, & Baker, 1994). Even preschoolers (called "tag-alongs" by older Yup'ik children) learn to knife stories along the riverbank.

Some cultures do not value or emphasize drawing or writing at all. In one study, British and Zambian children were asked to copy two-dimensional figures (Serpell, 1979). British children were more competent in reproducing the figures with pencil and paper. This result could lead to the erroneous conclusion that Zambian children are delayed in motor or cognitive abilities. In fact, Zambian children were advanced in their ability to accurately form these shapes with strips of wire. Simple sculpturing with wire is more prevalent within this culture than Western forms of drawing.

Drawing Development: The Reggio Emilia Perspective

An excellent example of how culture influences artistic development can be found in Reggio Emilia, a region in Italy. Over the past several decades, researchers and educators from all over the world have flocked to schools in this area to study the remarkable artistic achievements of very young children who live there (Gandini, 1997b). Preschoolers as young as age 3 have been observed creating highly representational works of art. An example of the extraordinary drawing of children in Reggio Emilia is shown in Figure 10-2. From a traditional view, such complex drawings should not emerge until children were well into the elementary years (Lowenfeld, 1947).

Why are children in this part of the world so advanced? Within their culture, the arts are highly valued. Parents and teachers in Reggio Emilia believe that artistic expression is more than just a way of expressing feelings. Drawing, painting, sculpting, and singing are fundamental ways in which children reflect on their learning (Gandini, 1997a). In contrast to many American schools, artistic efforts take center stage in Reggio Emilia classrooms. They may be more highly valued even than traditional mathematics or reading.

These cultural values lead to specific classroom practices that enhance children's artistic expression. The following are characteristics of Reggio Emilia classrooms for children through age 6 (Gandini, 1997a). Readers might reflect on how these could be implemented in American schools.

1. *Art is used as a representation of learning.* The arts are more than simple outlets for personal, creative expression in Reggio Emilia classrooms. Art media are used to help children represent and reflect on their discoveries. If children conduct pouring experiments with water, they then draw, paint, or sculpt what they have discovered. After a field trip to a museum, children use art materials to represent their observations. Art is integrated into meaningful, interdisciplinary projects; it is not considered a separate part of the curriculum.

2. *Art and all other learning experiences are collaborative.* Although there are opportunities for children to work alone with art media, most artistic representations are completed in groups. Further, parents are often involved in their children's artistic efforts. They are encouraged to study, reflect upon, and even contribute to their sons' or

FIGURE 10-2 Children in Reggio Emilia, Italy, create highly realistic artwork at an early age. Such complex drawings are not made by American children until the later elementary years.

SOURCE: Edwards. C., Gandini, L., & Forman, G. (1994). *The hundred languages of children: The Reggio approach to early childhood education.* Norwood, NJ: Ablex Publishing Corporation. Reprinted by permission.

daughters' representations. Teachers are considered "partners" (Gandini, 1997a, p. 19). During representational activities, they ask questions, make suggestions, and guide children's work. This is in marked contrast to the traditional "hands-off" approach to art—common in American schools—in which children are simply left alone to create.

3. *Time and space are devoted to artistic representation.* Large spaces are provided in Reggio Emilia classrooms for artistic expression. A special art studio—called an *atelier*—is often provided for use by both children and teachers. There are no time constraints on children's representational activities, so a project may go on for days or even weeks. Children are encouraged to revise earlier drafts of drawings or paintings. In contrast, American schools do not provide such time and space. Children might spend 15 minutes at a small art table, for example, and then place their completed drawing in their cubbies to take home.

4. *A teacher who is trained in the visual arts is available in each school.* Schools in Reggio Emilia have an *atelierista*—a resident artist who guides children in their representations. This teacher works closely with other teachers in the school to integrate the arts into all learning experiences. This is quite a different role from that of the American art teacher who pulls children out of classes to conduct brief lessons in arts and crafts.

5. *Learning experiences are displayed in the classroom using documentation panels.* The works of children, along with writing and photographs, are displayed on beautiful panels throughout the classroom. These are more than decorations. They show children's development and learning. For example, several drafts of a child's self-portrait may be presented—each showing a new, more sophisticated understanding of self. These panels allow teachers and parents to assess children's development. They also allow children to review and reflect on learning and artistic representation.

These unique classroom features represent the value that this community places on the arts. Children's advanced artistic development in Reggio Emilia may be more a result of unique cultural traditions and worldviews than of specific teaching practices. Still, many American teachers are implementing Reggio Emilia techniques, with great success, in their own classrooms (D. C. Williams & Kantor, 1997).

GENDER AND MOTOR DEVELOPMENT

Researchers have observed gender differences in motor development during the preschool years. Boys have been found to lose baby fat and acquire muscle tone more quickly than girls. They tend to be larger and stronger throughout the early years. Girls are more competent at fine motor activities. This may be because some areas of the brain—those responsible for perceptual-motor abilities—are more fully developed in females during this period (Tanner, 1990). Boys are generally found to be more active; they engage in more rough-and-tumble play than girls (P. K. Smith, 1997). Boys tend to take more risks and to be more adventuresome in play (Sanders & Harper, 1976).

Research on gender and motor development has been conducted mainly with white middle-class children. For this reason, findings of gender differences are not surprising; this cultural group tends to socialize boys and girls to behave very differently motorically (Jacklin, 1989). In middle-class America, boys are given more practice and encouragement in acquiring large motor skills, and adults hold stereotyped expectations of children's motor abilities (Caldera, Huston, & O'Brien, 1989). Parents buy different kinds of toys for boys and girls, and these toys accentuate different motor skills (Kacerguis & Adams, 1979).

It is possible that gender differences are not so great outside Euro-American culture. For example, in studies of children of color in six different societies, including the United States, B. B. Whiting and Edwards (1988) found fewer differences in activity level or rough-and-tumble play between boys and girls. It must also be pointed out that even in societies in which boys show greater motor competence, individual differences are great. Many individual boys are less competent than many individual girls. Data on "average" children will not give a full picture of differences among preschoolers.

PERSONAL AND FAMILY LIFE SKILLS

Advances in motor development allow preschoolers to take better care of themselves and to take on simple household responsibilities. In middle-class homes in America, young children perform such self-help tasks as dressing themselves, picking up their toys, bathing, brushing their teeth, and eating with utensils. As early as age 3, many children can accomplish self-help skills with some help from adults. For example, assistance is needed in tying shoes, buttoning small buttons, or coordinating a fork and table knife to cut food. Children master most of these self-help skills by age 5.

In many families in the United States, preschoolers are assigned chores related to family life, such as straightening their rooms or helping to wash dishes. Some assist in the preparation of family meals. As they develop their motor abilities, they are able to take on more complex tasks, such as drying dishes with a towel or zipping up a coat, with less adult assistance.

Family chore assignments are more extensive in some cultures than in others. Young children from non-industrialized countries are often more involved in household work than those in European and American families. Preschoolers in communities in India, Okinawa, the Philippines, Mexico, and Kenya, for example, were observed to perform a range of jobs that most American children would never be assigned (B. B. Whiting & Whiting, 1977). Such chores included collecting firewood, fetching water, herding and tending livestock, grinding grain, and harvesting vegetables. Children were also found to perform universal household tasks, such as preparing food, at an earlier age than would be expected in American families. A 2-year-old in India, for example, was observed cutting vegetables with a knife alongside an older sibling (B. B. Whiting & Edwards, 1988).

Child care is a family chore that is commonly assigned early in life in some cultures. Very young children have been observed carrying, feeding, or in other ways tending to the needs of their infant siblings (B. B. Whiting & Edwards, 1988). A woman from Lebanon recollects the child care duties that were assigned to her when she was only 3 years old, growing up in a small village outside of Beirut:

> I was asked to sit on my bed with my baby brother—only a year younger than me—while my mother went out. "Don't let him go to the bathroom on the bed," my mother would warn. "Make sure he goes right in the pot." So, I would sit for hours watching and playing with him. I would guide him to the pot by the bed when he would need to go. I would play I was a mother and that my brother was my very own baby. This game would continue until my mother returned home.

Child care tasks are regularly assigned to preschoolers in non-industrialized communities. In the United States, young children of historically under-represented groups are also more likely to be given caregiving responsibilities (Powell, 1983). In almost all cultures, young girls are more often assigned child care duties (Morelli, 1986; B. B. Whiting & Edwards, 1988).

It is easy to see how motor abilities are exercised as young children care for their siblings: they must chase after, hold, carry, and sometimes confine their younger brothers or sisters. The following vignette illustrates the large motor abilities required in infant care:

> A 5-year-old girl in a small village in Kenya is up early. She has been assigned as the child nurse to her infant brother. Her mother and father have already gone to work in the garden, and she is left in full charge of her young sibling. When he awakes and cries, she picks him up and holds him close. As he calms down, she holds on with one arm and reaches with the other for a bottle to feed him. She must grip him tightly as she does this; he is 8 months old and very big for his age.

After feeding him, she places him into a sling. Her brother wiggles and kicks—he does not seem eager to be confined. She then straps the sling to her back. She stands up, maintaining her balance, then walks off to play with friends in another part of the village.

This young girl exercises the same large muscles a child of another culture might when climbing on a playscape. She uses large upper-body muscles; she walks and balances. Her play activities, such as a game of tag, will be particularly challenging with her sibling strapped to her body!

PHYSICALLY CHALLENGING CONDITIONS

Some children have challenging conditions that affect their motor development, including neurological and perceptual disorders, attention deficit/hyperactivity disorder, and malnutrition.

Neurological and Perceptual Disorders

Cerebral palsy, a disorder that can be caused by oxygen deprivation before or during birth, affects motor coordination and muscle strength. Young children with cerebral palsy vary greatly in the extent of impairment; some are quite competent in motor skills and can acquire typical play and self-help abilities, while others suffer severe multiple handicaps, including visual and hearing impairments. These children may require significant support in play or daily life needs. **Down syndrome,** another challenging condition, can cause delays in gross motor abilities, fine motor abilities, and language abilities in preschoolers.

Some preschoolers show general motor delay that has no specified cause. In some cases, this is accompanied by delays in language or cognition. This condition may be due to minimal brain damage, perhaps occurring in fetal development or during the birth process, which is imperceptible to physicians in neonatal tests.

Visual and hearing impairments often affect motor ability. It is clear that many of the motor play games described above, such as climbing, jumping, and balancing, will be more challenging for children who cannot see or hear well. However, motor play differences between perceptually impaired preschoolers and their peers are minimal when play environments are adapted to accommodate visual or hearing challenges. Teachers and parents can adapt play equipment, provide sensory-rich materials, and guide children in their motor activities. When these accommodations are made, virtually no differences are observed in the play of perceptually impaired and non-impaired children (Esposito & Koorland, 1989; Frost & Klein, 1979). The following story illustrates how slight adaptations in materials in a preschool program can enhance play experiences for a child with visual impairments:

Cedric, a child who has a visual impairment, tries to join peers who are creating a large mural with markers in the art center. He knocks over a can holding the markers as he reaches for one. Grasping the marker in his fist, he now begins to make marks on the mural.

TADESSE: (In an angry tone) No, Cedric! You're making a mess. That's just scribbling.

MICHAEL: (Speaking at the same time as Tadesse) You can't help. You're messing up our mural. (Now complaining to the teacher, who is approaching) Cedric's messing up our mural!

CEDRIC: (Says nothing; looks confused)

TEACHER: (To the other children) Cedric has trouble drawing because he can't see well. (To Cedric) Is it hard for you to find the paper and markers, Cedric?

CEDRIC: (Nods. Still does not speak.)

TEACHER: You know, we have templates that help you draw shapes. (Offers metal templates. Takes Cedric's fingers and helps him locate and feel the templates.) See? You can trace inside these and make shapes.

MICHAEL: Yeah. Like triangles. Can I try one?

TEACHER: Sure. Shapes would look nice on the mural. (To Cedric) Cedric, let me help you get started.

The teacher takes Cedric's hands and shows him how to trace with markers inside a template. All three children begin to work together on the mural.

Here the teacher has quickly assessed that a perceptual limitation has made a useful activity inaccessible. By adapting the materials, she has remedied the situation. Teachers can monitor activities throughout the classroom and make adaptations to meet special needs (Musselwhite, 1986).

Attention Deficit/Hyperactivity Disorder

One motor-related condition which is occasionally identified within the preschool years is **attention deficit/hyperactivity disorder (ADHD).** Children with this disorder are extremely active and impulsive and are more easily distracted (American Psychological Association, 1994). Debate about what causes this disorder is ongoing; most researchers believe that minimal brain dysfunction is the source of the problem (Wender, 1987). The behaviors of children with ADHD are more problematic during their school years, when long periods of sitting and paying attention are expected (Wicks-Nelson & Israel, 1997). However, even children in Head Start, child care, or kindergarten are sometimes identified with ADHD. Occasionally, controversial measures have been taken to reduce the activity levels of preschoolers believed to have ADHD, as the following story reveals.

A young single mother living in poverty has just given birth to her third child. She suffers from depression and is receiving counseling and parent support services from a community social service agency. Her oldest son, Bobby, has just been enrolled in kindergarten in the elementary school near her home. On the first day of school, Bobby's mother warns the teacher, "Watch out for Bobby. He's a real terror!" She describes the damage Bobby has done to her apartment and the difficulty she has had controlling him. She speaks loudly and within hearing range of Bobby, who stands, staring blankly. As his mother leaves, she explains that Bobby has been prescribed Ritalin, a drug used to control hyperactivity. "That keeps him from being so off-the-wall," she explains. Bobby takes in the whole conversation.

Over the next few days, the head teacher consults with Bobby's family services team. She learns that Bobby has been identified as suffering from ADHD
and has been prescribed Ritalin by a physician. She is quite shocked, since she
has observed that Bobby is lethargic and sluggish—far from hyperactive. The
teacher convinces social service providers, the physician, and Bobby's mother
to try a few months without medication. Bobby's behavior changes markedly.
He is alert, focused, and involved in classroom activities. He is also remarkably
active, yet his behavior is manageable. After several days, the teacher recommends that Bobby no longer be medicated.

Much later, the school psychologist comes to suspect that Bobby has been
overmedicated by his mother. In fact, Ritalin was prescribed initially because
his mother complained to a physician about Bobby's behavior at home.

This story illustrates the complexity of addressing the special needs of preschoolers. Parenting and home environment, family mental health problems, and poverty
interact to compound Bobby's emotional and educational difficulties. Strategies such
as prescribing Ritalin can be effective in controlling the challenging behaviors of
some children with ADHD (DuPaul & Barkley, 1993). However, there are no simple
solutions; often elaborate family intervention is also necessary.

One concern raised about ADHD is that it is an overdiagnosed condition. Any typically active preschooler may be labeled hyperactive by an uninformed parent or professional. Great care must be taken in the preschool years not to confuse high activity
level with ADHD. It has been argued that children of historically under-represented
groups are at risk of being mislabeled (Hale-Benson, 1986). For example, the African-
American children's preference for high activity has been misinterpreted as an early
sign of ADHD (Morgan, 1976). What some professionals have called "hyperactivity,"
"overstimulation," or "uncontrollable behavior" among African-American children,
Boykin (1978) refers to as "verve." A typical high activity level and authentic ADHD
are very different things.

Malnutrition

Malnutrition can have a devastating effect on motor development in the preschool
years. Protein energy malnutrition affects approximately half of the world's children
(Lozoff, 1989). Limited growth and poor skeletal formation have been found in those
suffering from this condition. Malnourished young children have been found to be ap-
athetic, listless, and inactive (Pollitt, Gorman, Engle, Martorell, & Rivera, 1993).
Problems of malnutrition are not limited to non-industrialized countries. Over 5 million children in the United States do not have enough food to eat (Children's Defense
Fund, 1998). Although American children are not as likely to experience severe malnutrition, they suffer stunted growth and limited perceptual and motor development.

The negative effects of malnutrition can be offset by dietary supplements and
medical intervention. These are especially effective when provided early in life and
when they are coupled with other kinds of support, such as educational programs or
family services (Pollitt et al., 1993). Sadly, children who are extremely malnourished
in the early years may never reach their full developmental potential.

Early Intervention

Generally, the motor development of young children with special needs is greatly enhanced by early intervention programs that provide classroom or home-based edu-

cation and parent support (Casto & Mastropieri, 1986). Early identification of special needs is critical. Some studies suggest that if intervention programs are begun in infancy, children will show fewer delays in later years (K. White, Bush, & Casto, 1985). However, a summary of a large number of studies has shown that even when educational programs are not provided until the preschool years, some children show remarkable improvement in motor and cognitive abilities (Shonkoff, Hauser-Cram, Krauss, & Upshur, 1992). It is never too late for intervention, then.

ASSESSING YOUNG CHILDREN: Preschool Physical and Motor Development

Areas of Development	What to Watch for	Indicators of Atypical Development
Large motor abilities	Large motor skills, such as walking, running, climbing, throwing and catching, and balancing, by age 4. An ability to start and stop movements quickly and to coordinate actions with those of others. Play abilities such as riding tricycles or kicking balls.	Lack of coordination, balance, and muscle strength. Poor eye-hand coordination. Highly active, impulsive, uncontrollable play behaviors.
Perceptual and fine motor abilities	An increasing ability to perform small muscle tasks, such as molding clay, making puzzles, cutting with scissors. An ability, by age 6, to draw recognizable figures—heads and stick bodies, for example.	An inability to handle scissors, puzzle pieces, or drawing implements by age 4. Remaining in the scribble stage of drawing and representing no heads or other recognizable shapes by age 6.
Self-help or family life skills	An ability to perform most self-help tasks: feeding, bathing, toileting and dressing oneself by age 4. An ability and interest in household chores, such as simple cleaning, caring for one's own toys, and attending to the needs of younger siblings.	Poor self-help skills; dependence on others for dressing or toileting beyond age 4. An inability to perform simple household tasks.

Interpreting Assessment Data: Culture and individual variations in development will affect these motor abilities. Children will acquire the motor skills emphasized in their particular community and culture. Those who grow up in cultures where there are no games may not acquire throwing, catching, or kicking skills. In families where artistic expression is highly valued, drawing abilities may develop more quickly. In communities where children must contribute to household work for the survival of the family, life skills will emerge at an early age. Significant delays in *all* large and small motor skills may indicate challenging conditions, however. Children who are exceptionally impulsive and active might be referred to for evaluation. A motor-based, stress-free preschool program can benefit children with these challenges. Nutritional intervention with families can also address some motor problems at this age.

Do typical American preschool programs offer adequate opportunities to exercise motor abilities? A study by Poest, Williams, Witt, and Atwood (1992) suggests that they do not. Preschoolers were not found to engage in adequate physical activity, at school or at home, regardless of the season. Even in summer, physical activities were limited in many programs. One interesting finding of the study was that teachers who had more extensive training in early childhood education were more active in promoting motor development in preschoolers. Trained teachers' knowledge of the importance of motor development in the early years may explain this finding.

RESEARCH INTO PRACTICE

CRITICAL CONCEPT 1

Significant changes in physical growth and motor development occur in the preschool years. Children get taller, stronger, and more coordinated. They acquire gross motor skills (abilities to use the large muscles) and fine motor skills (small muscle abilities) in a predictable sequence.

Application #1

Teachers, caregivers, and parents should provide opportunities for preschoolers to exercise large muscles every day. Areas should be created in classrooms to ensure active play even in inclement weather. These might include low climbers, tossing games, a balance beam, and any other equipment that will fit well in a classroom.

Application #2

Preschool children should be engaged in games that involve running and walking, such as open-ended chasing on the playground, tag, follow-the-leader, and "giant steps."

Application #3

Climbing equipment should be provided on preschool and child care playgrounds. Safe playscapes with platforms children can jump off will promote important motor skills.

Application #4

Preschool children should be provided toys for catching and throwing, such as soft, large balls, beanbags, and other objects, both in the classroom and on the playground.

Application #5

Balance materials should be available for preschool-age children. Low balance beams, tires, and lines on the sidewalk or classroom floor are examples.

Application #6

Teachers and caregivers should appreciate the importance of rough-and-tumble play. Safe areas for rough play, such as soft mats and grassy hills, can be identified. Rules for rough-and-tumble play, such as taking your shoes off when wrestling on the mat, can be instituted. Careful monitoring will ensure that rough play does not lead to injury.

Application #7

Teachers and caregivers can offer preschoolers a range of small motor experiences in the classroom. Fine motor development is promoted by art activities such as drawing, painting, sculpting, cutting, and making collages, and materials such as blocks, puzzles, books, stringing beads, and felt boards.

CRITICAL CONCEPT 2

Research on early childhood programs in Reggio Emilia, Italy, suggests that children can express themselves artistically at a very early age. Children from this community have been found to use art media in very sophisticated ways to represent what they have learned.

Application #1

Teachers and caregivers should integrate the arts—including drawing, painting, and sculpture—into all learning activities and projects.

Application #2

More time should be given for the completion of art projects. Children should be encouraged to work on some representational activities for days or even weeks. Making many drafts of a single artwork should be encouraged.

Application #3

Collaborative artistic experiences should be provided. Children should be encouraged to engage in collective representations with peers, parents, and teachers.

Application #4

Panels documenting children's artistic representations should be displayed attractively on classroom walls. Children and parents should be encouraged to study these panels in order to assess development and learning.

CRITICAL CONCEPT 3

Children's motor development varies across cultures. Children in some cultural groups acquire certain abilities quickly, others more slowly. How newly learned motor behaviors are used also differs significantly across cultures. Motor play reflects differences in family life and historical tradition; some children play tag, others fly kites, still others chase sheep or chickens. All of these activities promote the same basic motor abilities.

Application #1

Teachers and caregivers must understand and appreciate cultural differences in motor development. They must recognize that some children will be more rough or active and that others will be quieter or less motorically advanced. Care must be taken not to construe these differences as deficits.

Application #2

Teachers and caregivers can create a multicultural motor curriculum in the classroom by interviewing families about motor activities and games played in the home. This information can be used to integrate traditional games of diverse cultural groups into classroom play activities. Children will gain motor skills as well as cultural understanding when playing such games.

CRITICAL CONCEPT 4

Girls and boys show different patterns of physical growth and motor activity. Some of these differences are related to genetics, others to experience.

Application #1

Teachers and caregivers must understand and appreciate gender diversity in motor play. Differences in activity level, accuracy or strength in movement, and play preference must not be construed as deficits that need to be remediated.

Application #2

Girls and boys must be afforded the same motor play opportunities. All children should be encouraged to be active in the classroom and on the playground. Care must be taken not to unintentionally promote stereotypic play.

CRITICAL CONCEPT 5

Some preschoolers have challenging conditions that impair motor activities. Malnutrition can have a devastating effect on development, resulting in physical delays. Poor motor development can be remediated by nutritional and health services and early intervention.

Application #1

Teachers and caregivers must be aware of the characteristics of children who have physically challenging conditions and who suffer from malnutrition. Early identification of exceptionalities is one of the most important responsibilities of professionals working with young children.

Application #2

Teachers can support the motor play of children with special needs. They can adapt classrooms, equipment, and materials so that all children have access to games and activities. They can guide children with physical challenges in exercising small and large muscles.

CRITICAL CONCEPT 6

Early childhood education programs hold promise for ameliorating poor motor development. However, teachers and caregivers need to do more to enhance the quality and frequency of physical activity in school.

Application #1

Teachers must ensure that preschoolers get exercise every day. It is an incorrect assumption that children will get all of the exercise they will need after school at home or child care.

Application #2

Many organized games must be redesigned so that all children are moving all of the time while playing them. Games in which less competent children are quickly eliminated and have to sit out (e.g., "musical chairs") or in which only one child at a time gets to run or play (e.g., "duck, duck, goose") can be modified so that all players are exercising at once.

SUGGESTED ACTIVITIES

1. Observe two preschool children of different ages (e.g., a 3-year-old and a 5-year-old) but of the same gender as they play in a Head Start or child care center. Take notes on their physical characteristics and motor activities. Later, write a report comparing the two children, guided by the following questions:

   a. How do the two children differ in stature and body proportions? Are their facial features different? What other physical differences did you note? What can you conclude about change in physical appearance in the preschool years?

   b. How would you characterize differences in motor competence? What specific motor abilities did you observe in the two children? What similarities and differences did you see in their running, jumping, climbing, throwing, or balancing?

   c. How would you describe the activity levels of the two children? Did you observe differences between them in this area?

   d. Describe any rough-and-tumble play that you observed. Did the two children differ in the amount or the quality of this type of play?

2. Observe two preschool children of distinct cultural groups, but of the same gender, within a kindergarten or child care center. Take notes on the kinds of motor games and activities each child plays. Write a report contrasting play preferences of the two children, guided by the following questions:

   a. Which types of play did you observe that were common to both children (e.g., climbing games, throwing, running)?

   b. What differences did you observe in the two children's play preferences?

   c. Did you observe differences in activity level or rough-and-tumble play?

   d. Did you see motor activities that appeared to be influenced by culture? Generally, to what degree do you think cultural background explains differences in motor play of the two children?

3. Observe a preschool boy and girl of approximately the same age as they engage in motor play in a child care center or preschool. Take notes on their motor activities. Write a report comparing their play, guided by the following questions:

   a. What types of play did you observe that were common to both children (e.g., climbing games, throwing, running)?

   b. What differences did you observe in the two children's play preferences?

   c. Did you observe differences in activity level or rough-and-tumble play?

   d. Did you see motor activities that appeared to be influenced by gender? Generally, to what degree do you think gender explains differences in motor play of the two children?

4. Observe a child with special needs (e.g., a child with Down syndrome, mental retardation, hearing impairments). Take notes on the child' play activities. Write a report on your observations, guided by the following questions:

   a. What kinds of motor play activities did the child appear to prefer?

   b. To what degree did you see the child exercise motor skills outlined in this chapter (i.e., climbing, running, balancing, catching and throwing)? Were any of these activities missing in the child's motor play?

c. To what degree did the child's challenging condition affect motor activities?

d. How did teachers interact with the child to promote motor growth?

5. Ask a preschool, kindergarten, or child care teacher to collect children's drawings for you. (Children are often eager to draw for adults, and teachers are usually pleased to gather drawing samples for study.) Ask that the ages of the children be written on the back. Look over the drawings and write an analysis of them based on the following questions:

a. How do the drawings differ from one another? How are they alike?

b. Which drawings show the greatest control over the marker or crayon? Which show less competence in controlling the drawing implement?

c. What can you conclude about fine motor development during the preschool years from comparing drawings of different age groups? What can you conclude about cognitive development from studying the drawings?

CHAPTER 11

Cognitive Development in the Preschool Years

BETWEEN THE AGES OF 2 AND 5 YEARS, CHILDREN BECOME QUITE SOPHISTICATED IN THEIR THINKING. Gone are the primitive circular reactions and the trial-and-error problem-solving of infancy. Preschool-age children think problems through before acting. They engage in a new form of reasoning that is both impressive and fascinating. In this chapter we will explore these cognitive advancements in the preschool years.

So remarkable are young children's intellectual abilities that adults sometimes forget that preschoolers are still in the early stages of cognitive development. Parents, caregivers, and teachers need to remember that preschoolers think in a way that is qualitatively different from the way adults think. The following vignette shows both the new sophistication of young children's thinking and the cognitive limitations of this age level:

Three 4-year-olds have just completed a traditional card game, "Concentration," in their preschool classroom. "I won!" one young player announces. A teacher approaches and asks, "How do you know?" "Easy. I got the most cards," the child answers proudly.

The teacher continues to question the winner. "Great. How did you figure that out?" "Well, because!" exclaims the child, placing his pile of cards next to each of his playmates' piles in comparison. "See? I've got more!" "So, you have more because your pile is taller?" the teacher asks. "Yep. Got more cards," he answers confidently.

"Wait a minute!" another child protests. "Let me look at something." He spreads his cards end-to-end on the floor in a line. This line contains so many cards that it extends from the math area out into the center of the classroom. He makes similar lines next to his own with his playmates' cards.

The teacher, observing this, says, "Now, this is interesting. What are you doing?" "Checking to see if Seth won," this second child responds. "Now look. See? His line is longer. You did win, you creepo," he says with a laugh.

The teacher asks, "Does everyone agree? Did Seth win?" There are no more challenges or disputes, so the teacher asks no more questions.

"Let's play again," another child offers. They continue playing, and determining the winner of each round in this unique way, for the rest of the morning.

It is easy to see from this story how far these preschoolers have advanced intellectually since infancy. They invent a very reasonable method of solving the problem of who won the card game. Coming up with two different ways to determine the winner took complex thought. Even so, these children did not solve the problem as an adult would; they did not think to count the cards. They solved the problem by relying on perception: if a pile of cards *looks like* more, it must *be* more. So, preschoolers' thinking is more internal and sophisticated than in earlier years, but is still very much tied to concrete objects in the real, observable world.

PIAGET'S THEORY OF PRESCHOOL COGNITION

To Piaget, the preschool years are a period of transition in cognitive development (1952b). Young children gradually leave behind the very early thought processes of infancy, which were tied to the concrete world. They can now think beyond objects or people that are immediately before them and are able to reflect on things they cannot see, hear, touch, or act upon. They can imagine objects or people that are not present, contemplate future events, and recall past ones.

On the other hand, preschoolers do not use logic as adults do, according to Piaget. Their reasoning is hampered by several mental limitations. They still rely too heavily on their senses in their thinking. They are easily distracted by the appearance of things; what they see, hear, or touch can actually hinder their problem-solving. The following story illustrates this:

A father is driving his 4-year-old son to child care. He introduces a game to make the long drive fun.

FATHER: Let's play "I'm thinking of something." I'll go first . . . let me see . . . ah. I've got one. I'm thinking of something green.

CHILD: Christmas trees?

FATHER: Nope. Great guess, though.

CHILD: (Begins to look around the car) Oh, I know. (Digs through his lunch bag) This apple in my lunch?

FATHER: Please don't take your lunch out, David. I'm afraid you'll lose your apple. You won't have it for lunch, then.

CHILD: (Appears to ignore his father's comment) Well?

FATHER: (Becomes distracted by his driving; appears to forget about the game) Um . . . oh! No. Not the apple.

CHILD: Give me a hint.

FATHER: It's got wheels . . .

CHILD: (With great excitement) The car! It's green!

FATHER: (Also enthused) Got it! Okay, now it's your turn.

CHILD: (Begins to look obviously around the car) Oh, I know!

FATHER: Got one?

CHILD: (Stares intently at the steering wheel) You'll never get this one. I'm thinking of something black.

The father begins to guess, intentionally not naming the steering wheel although the child looks right at it. As they pull into the parking lot of the child care center, the father gives up. With much laughter, the child reveals that he was thinking of the steering wheel. His father feigns absolute surprise.

In this story a 4-year-old has displayed quite sophisticated thinking. In his "Christmas trees" guess, he shows he can contemplate things that are not present and events that have occurred in the past. However, in making the apple his second guess, he shows that he is still quite reliant in his thinking on what he can see and touch. He looks around the car and through the lunch bag in his hands in search of possible solutions. When it is his turn, he chooses something for his father to guess by scanning his immediate physical environment only. His thinking in this case seems limited to what he can see around him.

Because preschoolers' thinking is still based so much on perception and action, Piaget argued that learning at this age requires an environment that is rich in sensory experience and provides much activity with objects. Through active manipulation of play materials, preschoolers gradually construct an understanding of the world. Passive models of learning, in which children are instructed directly by adults, are useless at this age, from Piaget's perspective.

Characteristics of Preoperational Thought

Piaget (1952b) provides rich descriptions of preschoolers' thinking, or what he calls **preoperational thought.** He identifies several fundamental ways that children of this age think differently from adults. These differences are summarized in Table 11-1.

Perception-Based Thinking. Often young children are fooled by what things look or sound like, as the following story reveals:

A 4-year-old child lies in bed on a hot night, unable to sleep. His two brothers are sound asleep next to him. He begins to feel alone and afraid. He wiggles and kicks, hoping to rouse one of his older siblings, but they sleep on.

He suddenly spots the curtains blowing in the window. He is certain that he sees a puma climbing in to eat him, so he cries out. Not only do his brothers wake up, but his mother and grandmother as well. They rush in to his room to determine the problem. "It's a puma!" he cries.

"No. You're frightened by the curtains, silly boy," his grandmother says, turning on the light. "See? Just curtains." The preschooler smiles sheepishly. "Just curtains. Yeah. I saw the curtains."

The mother sits on his bed, stroking his head. "Go to sleep," she softly urges. His grandmother turns the lights off, then on, then off again to show him that things look different in the dark.

Finally, the child and his brothers fall asleep and the adults leave the room. A short time later, the preschooler wakes again. "Puma! Puma!" he calls out, and the family comes to the rescue once more.

Why does the child's fear continue? He seems to know that what he sees is a curtain blowing in the window. When the light is on, he can laugh and say, "Just curtains." When the light is off, however, his fear returns. Piaget would suggest

TABLE 11-1
Characteristics of Preoperational Thought in the Preschool Years

Characteristic	Example
Perception-based thinking	A child sees two bowls which each hold exactly 10 mango kernels. In one bowl the kernels are spread out. The child reports that that bowl holds more.
Unidimensional thinking	A father who is building a wall asks his daughter to find him a large, square stone. The child goes off and returns with a small square one. "Too little," the father responds. "I need a *large* square." The child goes off again, this time returning with a huge round stone.
Irreversibility	A young preschooler gets her hands on her older brother's science project for school. She completely disassembles it. Her angry father discovers her handiwork and insists she put all the pieces back together. However, she hasn't a clue how to reverse her efforts and place items back the way they were.
Transductive reasoning	A child pushes his younger brother in order to get a straw doll. As he plays with the doll he begins to sniffle. All at once, his angry mother is upon him. She snatches the doll away and gives it back to the younger sibling. The child believes he has been punished for sniffling.
Egocentrism	A child who is wearing a new pair of moccasins comes across another child who is wearing an identical pair. He becomes terribly upset. "Those are mine," he wails, even though he can see his own moccasins on his own feet.

that this is due to perception-based thinking. If the curtain appears to be a mountain lion, then it must be a mountain lion. To a preschooler, "what you see is what you get."

Unidimensional Thought. Preschoolers tend to focus on only one characteristic of an object or one feature of a problem at a time. They are said to *center* on a single phenomenon and have difficulty coordinating more than one idea or activity. This is called **unidimensional thought.** What would occur if a child care provider were to say to a classroom of 4-year-olds, "I want you to put your paintings in your cubbies, wash your hands, and get ready for lunch, just as soon as we are finished with our story"? It's unlikely the caregiver would even finish this sentence before children were racing to their cubbies. They would center on the caregiver's first instruction and miss the rest of the message.

Following are two other examples that illustrate this kind of thinking:

EXAMPLE 1

A kindergarten teacher is reading a book about a circus to a group of children. When she turns a page, the children see an illustration of a clown that looks vaguely like a local television character.

HANNA: Oh, look! Chuckles! It's Chuckles the Clown.
TEACHER: (Smiles and nods) It looks like Chuckles, doesn't it? (Tries to resume reading)

ALONZO: Know what? I saw the real Chuckles at the mall.

RHONA: Chuckles is really a man.

ALONZO: Yeah, but he's a clown too.

TEACHER: Okay. Well, let's see what happens next at the circus. (Quickly turns the page and attempts to move on with the story)

ALL CHILDREN: (In unison) Chuckles!

TEACHER: (Looks at the book, sees that the same clown is depicted on this next page, as well. Tries to reengage the children in the story.) Let me ask you this: Will the clowns from Clown Town ever find the rest of the circus?

MALCOLM: Chuckles can do magic. He did tricks at my brother's school . . .

The teacher finally gives up reading the book and encourages children to discuss Chuckles the Clown.

EXAMPLE 2

A teacher asks children in her Head Start class to clean up at the end of the morning. She watches in amazement as two children straighten up the block area. They work for many minutes, placing together blocks that are alike. However, they have come up with a very different categorization scheme than an adult would select. When they have finished, she notices that one shelf contains only triangular blocks and is nearly empty. The other shelf is overflowing with the rest of the blocks. She comments on this to the children:

TEACHER: (Pointing to the shelf with the triangular blocks) So why did you only put a few blocks here?

LEVI: See, this is where we put all the triangles. That's how we did it. Triangles right in here. (Pats the shelf proudly)

TEACHER: (Looking at a second shelf) Oh, this is so full of blocks. They're just falling out. Should we put some of these on the emptier shelf? We could put all the small blocks over there, maybe. (Begins to demonstrate, moving blocks from the full shelf to the nearly empty one)

GABRIEL: No! This is for the blocks that aren't triangles. See? Only the triangles go over there.

YANNIS: (Speaking at the same time as Gabriel) That's how we did it. Triangles (points to the nearly empty shelf) and blocks (points to the full shelf).

The teacher does not intervene further. During the next free-play session, other children decide to reshelve the blocks. This time they use a different categorization scheme, so the blocks are more evenly distributed across shelves.

In both examples, the children have centered on one idea or feature of a phenomenon. In Example 1, children are so centered on ideas about a local television character that they have trouble focusing on a story. In Example 2, children are centered on just one feature of blocks: "triangleness." Their categorizing is based simply on whether or not a block is a triangle. They have much difficulty thinking about other dimensions of blocks at the same time.

Irreversibility. Piaget (1952b) noted that children have difficulty reversing the direction of their thinking. This is called **irreversibility.** Here is a simple test to show this: Take a group of preschoolers for a walk on the playground. Along the way, stop at eight different spots. At the end of the walk, ask the children, "Can you take me back exactly the way we came?" You will find that they have a very difficult time reversing their steps. They might revisit the various stopping points out of order. Or they might simply walk back to the starting point without stopping at all. The problem is that they cannot reverse their thinking. Here is another example:

Two Puerto Rican preschoolers—a 4-year-old and a 5-year-old—sit at the dinner table, watching as their aunt pours a ladleful of beans onto each of their plates. Each receives one large ladleful; the aunt is careful to be equitable. But an argument erupts nonetheless. The children's plates are of different sizes, causing the amounts of beans to look different. The 4-year-old insists that she has fewer beans. "See? He has more!" she cries. The exasperated aunt tries to reason with her. "I put one ladle of beans on each plate! See?" She demonstrates by pouring a ladleful on her own plate. This does not appear to help. To the 4-year-old, the other child appears to have more beans, so he must have more.

Preschool children have trouble reversing operations. When taking a walk, they cannot easily retrace their steps back to the starting point.

It is easy to see how perception-based reasoning plays a role in this controversy. But irreversibility in thinking is also a source of difficulty. Why can't this upset preschooler understand her aunt's logical explanation that each has received the exact same amount? One problem is that she cannot reverse the process of ladling in her mind. If she could, she would mentally transport her plateful of beans back into the ladle. She would do the same with her sibling's plate. She could then visualize that both would equally fill the same utensil and so would be the same amount.

Transductive Reasoning. According to Piaget (1952b), preschool-age children are much better able to sort out cause and effect than are infants. However, they are still limited in their causal thinking. They tend to put one immediate event into relationship with another immediate event and leap to an assumption that one causes the other. For example, if a child is running about his apartment at the same moment a plant near a window blows over in the wind, the child may associate the two events and assume that his running caused the plant to fall. Piaget called this faulty causal thinking **transductive reasoning.**

Transductive reasoning can cause stress and guilt in young children. For example, if a child is misbehaving just as police arrive at the apartment door to arrest a relative, she could assume that she caused the arrest and feel guilty (Garbarino, Dubrow, Kostelny, & Pardo, 1992). Or, if a child is scolded for being too active and loud, and then moments later is informed that his parents are separating, he is likely to feel guilt at causing the separation (Hetherington, 1989). Adults must be very careful, then, to clarify for preschoolers the nature of relationships between negative life events.

Egocentrism. Piaget believed that preschool-age children are still quite egocentric—they continue to have difficulty understanding others' perspectives. Piaget devised an experiment to show this (Piaget & Inhelder, 1963). Children were asked to sit at a table and look at a model of three mountains arranged in a particular design. A doll was positioned across from each child. The child was asked to "draw a picture that shows what the doll sees." Piaget found that children under 6 years of age would usually draw the scene not from the doll's perspective but from their own. Not until the elementary years would they understand that the doll's perspective is different from their own and represent this in their drawings.

Of course, **egocentrism** can have its challenges. A child may have difficulty understanding that others have needs and desires, as the following story illustrates:

A 5-year-old Indian child in a barrio in Mexico busies himself all morning breaking rocks apart in the courtyard of his family's home. He is so fully engrossed that he does not notice all of the activity around him. This is the day that everyone takes their produce to the market to sell. His grandparents, parents, older siblings, an aunt, and several close friends who live in the same complex have just finished packing vegetables to carry to town and are now ready to go.

The child's mother calls to him, asking him to follow along. The preschooler refuses. "No! I have to finish my rocks," he insists. Ignoring the fact that his entire family is packed and waiting, he picks up another rock and begins to pound on it. His mother grasps him by an arm and tries gently to pull him away from his work. He resists. "One more," he compromises. So, while the entire family waits, he pounds the rock for several more minutes until it breaks apart. Satisfied, he joins his family on their trip to the market.

Symbolic Thought. One of the most significant advancements in the preschool years, according to Piaget, is the acquisition of **symbolic thought.** This is a form of thinking in which symbols are used to stand for things that are not present. Language is a good example of symbolic thought. When speaking, children use words as symbols to stand for things. Symbolic thought also occurs in play. A toy telephone is used to make a pretend call, or an empty cup is used to drink pretend milk. Simple words are spoken to represent actions, persons, or objects. In the later preschool years, children begin to use even more abstract symbols, or what Piaget called *signs.* Sophisticated sentences are constructed to stand for whole ideas. Drawing and scribbling are used to "write" stories. Young children engage in complex make-believe in which they use gestures, objects, or their own bodies to stand for things that are completely different.

Piagetian Tasks

Piaget invented fascinating experiments to show some of these unique aspects of young children's thinking. In these experiments, children would be asked to perform problem-solving tasks that highlight specific cognitive processes. The tasks and children's responses to them are described in Table 11-2.

Conservation. Piaget proposed that preschoolers lack **conservation,** an understanding that properties and amounts stay the same even when physical appearances are changed. Adults have acquired conservation. They know, for example, that if orange juice is poured from a small into a large cup the amount remains constant. Young children do not understand this; their lack of conservation can lead to faulty problem-solving.

Piaget devised an experiment to show that young children lack *conservation of number.* The steps of the experiment are shown in Figure 11-1. Sitting with individual children, Piaget would spread out two sets of eight objects—say, red and black checkers—on a table. The checkers would be lined up in one-to-one correspondence: each black checker was lined up with a red one (see Step a). Piaget would ask the child, "Are there more red checkers, more black checkers, or are there the same

TABLE 11-2
Piagetian Tasks That Show Preoperational Thought

Task	Description and a Preoperational Child's Performance
Conservation of number	A child is shown two sets of objects that are equivalent but are arranged in different patterns. The child will report that one set has more than the other.
Conservation of continuous quantity	A child is shown two differently shaped containers that hold equal amounts of water. The child will report that one container holds more than the other.
Categorization	A child is presented with objects that have multiple attributes; they vary by size, color, and shape. A child is asked to put "the things that are alike together." The child will use only one attribute—say, color—to categorize. For example, all yellow, green, or blue shapes will be placed together, regardless of shape or size.

FIGURE 11-1

In Piaget's experiment on conservation of number, children are shown an arrangement of checkers, as shown in Step a. Then, the checkers are rearranged in different ways, as shown in Step b. After the rearrangement, preschoolers often report that one group of checkers now has more than the other.

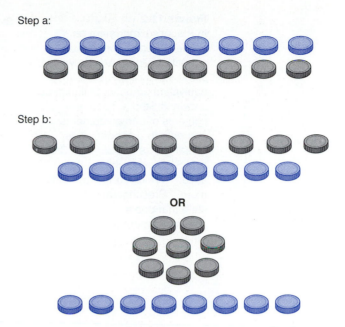

Step a:

Step b:

OR

amount of black and red?" Preschool-age children would invariably announce that the sets were equivalent.

Next, Piaget would reconfigure one line of checkers (see Step b). He might bunch the black ones together or spread them out farther than the red ones. The important thing was to make the two sets of checkers *look* different. Preschoolers were then asked, "Are the sets of checkers still the same, or are there more black ones or red ones?" Children would now argue that the spread-out set (or possibly even the bunched-up one) had more. Piaget would challenge children's thinking at this point, asking, "You said before that there were as many red as black checkers. Are you saying now that there are more red ones?" or "Another child told me she thought there were still as many black as red ones. What do you think?" Piaget would even ask children to count the checkers. No matter how many hints were given, however, children under age 5 or 6 would hold to their belief that one set or the other had more.

Why? Because of all the limitations in thinking described above. Children are fooled by perception. If one set *looks* like more, it must *be* more. No amount of logic will dissuade a young child from believing this. Also, children of this age center on only one dimension of the problem. They might focus on the length of the line and say, "This one has more because it's longer." Or they might center on thickness of the collection of checkers and claim, "This one has more because it's thicker." They cannot consider both length and thickness at the same time.

Children also struggle with this experiment because they lack reversibility. They cannot mentally rearrange the checkers back into a line after they have observed them being pushed together. Elementary-age children can do this; they can say, "This is the same because if you spread the checkers back out again, they would be just the same as the other set."

Piaget designed a similar task to show how children lack *conservation of continuous quantity*. This experiment is illustrated in Figure 11-2. In this experiment, Piaget had children watch as he poured the same amount of water into two identical

FIGURE 11-2

In Piaget's experiment on conservation of continuous quantity, children are shown two same-sized containers with equivalent amounts of liquid, as shown in Step a. Then, the contents of one container is poured into a shorter, wider container, as illustrated in Step b. In Step c the child is then asked, "Which container holds more?" Preschoolers regularly state that one of the containers now holds more liquid than the other.

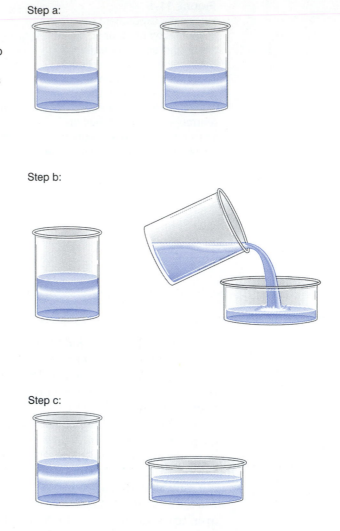

Step a:

Step b:

Step c:

containers (see Step a). Next, he would pour the water from one container into a much wider one (Step b). The child would watch as this was done. Now the water levels would be very different, as depicted in Step c. When preschool children were now asked which container had more, they might say the narrow container had more because the water was "higher," or that the wide container had more because the water was "fatter." Only after age 6 or 7 did children respond that the quantity of water was equivalent in both containers. Even with repeated hints ("I didn't take any water out; I just poured it into another container"), younger children were fooled.

Again, this task shows perception-based thinking. To the child, one container looks like it has more water, so it must have more. Unidimensional thinking is evident as well. Children center on the height or wideness of the water, but cannot think about both concepts at the same time. Finally, the task demonstrates irreversibility in children's thinking. They cannot mentally reverse the operation. That is, they cannot imagine the water in the new container being poured back into the original one.

FIGURE 11-3
In Piaget's experiment on categorization, children are asked to sort objects of different colors, shapes, and sizes. Preschool children usually select only one attribute to use in sorting the shapes. For example, they may put all green objects in one pile and all red objects in another. In this figure, a child has sorted only by shape, ignoring the size and color of the objects.

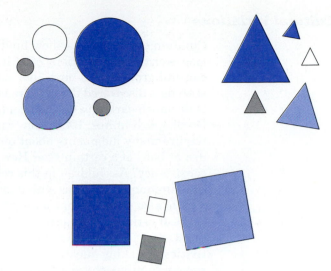

Categorization. In a very different experiment, Piaget demonstrated unidimensional thinking by asking children to categorize objects. In this **categorization** task, children were presented with items of different colors and shapes and asked to "put the things that are alike together." Preschoolers would often sort by color (e.g., putting all yellow objects together and all blue objects together); by shape (e.g., putting all triangles together and all squares together); or by size (e.g., putting all large objects together and all small objects together). Rarely did they rely on two or more dimensions at the same time (e.g., putting all large yellow triangles in one pile and all small blue triangles in another). A typical categorization scheme used by preschoolers is presented in Figure 11-3.

Piaget noticed that young children would sometimes shift from relying on one property to relying on another when categorizing. A child might, for example, start out by putting one blue triangle down, then a red one, and then a green one, relying first on shape. But since the last item was green, the child might shift suddenly to the property of color and put down a green square, a green circle, and green rectangle. Next, the child might switch to rectangles in categorizing. In the end, a child might place all shapes into a single category! Only in the elementary years did Piaget find that children were able to use multiple properties to categorize. After age 6 or 7, children would put blue triangles in one pile, green triangles in a separate pile, and so on. This experiment shows how young children center on one property or another, but not more than one, in problem-solving.

CRITICISMS OF PIAGETIAN THEORY

Piaget studied children of Western backgrounds without the benefit of the sophisticated laboratory techniques available today. In spite of this, recent studies have shown that his general descriptions of young children's thinking are quite accurate. Some research findings, however, indicate that he may have underestimated preschoolers' intellectual abilities. There are several major reasons for Piaget's misjudgment about preschoolers' cognitive abilities: (1) cultural variations, (2) faulty research methods, and (3) the role of language and social interaction in learning.

Cultural Variations

Children of all cultures show fundamental characteristics of preoperational thought. However, minor variations exist in performance on specific Piagetian tasks from one cultural group to the next. In a classic study of cognitive development in Mexico, researchers discovered that children of families who make pottery acquired conservation skills much earlier in development than Piaget would have predicted (Price-Williams, Gordon, & Ramirez, 1969). How can this be explained? Pottery making would seem to require many judgments about quantity: How much clay should be used to make an urn or bowl of a certain size? How much water should be added to obtain the correct consistency? As children in this community assist their parents in making pots, they have unique experiences with quantity that their European peers do not have.

It is also possible that parents in pottery-making families value more highly the skills of estimating quantity and emphasize these skills subconsciously in everyday life (Ogbu, 1988). They might guide children's attention to amounts in all family activities by asking questions (e.g., "Can you get enough water to fill the urn?"). In European families, these abilities are not so essential for a successful adult life.

Children of some cultural groups are found to acquire Piagetian cognitive skills more slowly than children in Euro-American cultures (Cole & Scribner, 1974). Does this mean that children of these societies are intellectually inferior? Certainly not. As in the pottery-making example, these findings may simply reflect differences in the particular skills that are valued or emphasized. Abilities needed to succeed in Piagetian tasks may not be as important in some families. For example, quantifying objects may be a less significant aspect of daily life in a community in which sharing and collective ownership are the norm (Wise & Miller, 1983). When everything is shared, there is little need for making judgments about amounts.

Nyiti (1982) has suggested that deficits found in young children of some cultures may be due to cultural bias in research. When Western researchers present Piagetian tasks to children of very different cultures, they may not get a full picture of cognitive competence. Cultural or linguistic barriers may impede performance. Nyiti found that Micmac Indian children of Nova Scotia showed lower levels of functioning if they were tested in English instead of their native language.

Flaws in Research

Research flaws of other kinds have been cited to explain Piaget's underestimation of preschoolers' abilities. Some researchers have changed Piaget's experiments slightly or designed new ones, using more sophisticated technology. Resulting findings indicate that children may be more competent than Piaget has proposed. For example, Borke (1975) altered Piaget's "three mountains" experiment (discussed earlier) and found that even 3-year-olds could represent what a doll is looking at if provided with appropriate means for reporting this. Unlike Piaget, Borke did not ask children to draw the doll's view of the mountains—a very difficult task at this age. Instead, she placed the three mountains on a turntable and asked children to *show* what the doll was looking at by turning it. Even very young preschoolers could turn the turntable one way and say, "I'm looking at this," and then turn it the other way and say, "The doll is looking at this." So, children may be less egocentric than Piaget's original experiments indicate.

Several researchers invented new methods for studying children's unidimensional thinking (N. H. Anderson & Cuneo, 1978; Cuneo, 1980). In these studies, preschoolers were shown rectangular cookies that varied in height and width. They were asked which cookies would make them most happy. The overall mass of the cookie was the characteristic that influenced children's answers. Thick, narrower cookies or thin, wide ones were equally likely to be chosen, whereas cookies that were both narrow *and* thin were not selected. So children seemed to be able to take into account both thickness *and* width in solving this problem. Why do children show unidimensional thinking on Piaget's tasks but not on this one? The task may be more interesting when cookies are used instead of checkers. Motivation may be higher when more meaningful (and tasty!) objects are used.

Researchers have shown that when Piaget's conservation tasks are altered, results are quite different. In one study, the conservation of number task was conducted again in a unique way. Instead of a researcher, a "naughty teddy bear"—a puppet—spread out one row of the checkers (Dockrell, Campbell, & Neilson, 1980). Amazingly, more 4-year-olds could solve the problem under this condition than in Piaget's original experiment. How can the addition of a make-believe animal cause such an improvement in children's thinking? The researchers concluded that the playful atmosphere of the test allowed children to focus on the problem itself, rather than on what the adult experimenter was doing and saying. In the original experiment, children may have been distracted by the fact that a very serious grown-up had altered one set of checkers. They may have come to believe that one set of checkers had more than the other because an adult had done something to it. The manner, language, and appearance of adult experimenters might influence children's performance on one-on-one tests.

Vygotsky's Perspective: The Role of Language and Social Interaction

One concern raised about Piaget's theory is that it does not fully recognize the contributions of language and social interaction in development. Many of Piaget's observations were of individual children, and his tasks were designed to be completed by one child at a time. Piaget did not emphasize the role of adults in his work. In his descriptions of his own children at play, references to parents were so rare that some readers have humorously asked, "Where was Mrs. Piaget?"

Vygotsky (1978) has argued that children's thinking is highly influenced by interactions and conversation with other people. If we want to know how children think and learn, he proposes, we need to observe them in natural interchanges with others. The following vignette illustrates how real-life interactions influence children's problem-solving:

A kindergarten teacher has placed objects from nature, boxes, markers, and labels on a large table in the science center of his classroom. Children are invited to make a museum here by putting things that are alike together and labeling them, "just like in a real museum." Two children are hard at work, creating categories and making labels.

ELORA: I think we should put these nests (holds up a bird's nest) and the bee things (points to a wasp's nest) together, alright, Sean?

SEAN: No, 'cause the bee nests are too small. Small ones go here (points to a pile of small objects of different kinds that he has assembled).

ELORA: (In an annoyed tone) That's not how you do it, Sean. You don't put little things all together at museums. You put nests together and

	rocks together, like this. (Demonstrates these ideas by moving objects from Sean's pile)
SEAN:	(In an angry voice) No! You're messing it up. You're making a mess with my museum!
TEACHER:	(Moving over to the science center) What's up here? You both sound angry.
SEAN:	(Loudly) Elora moved all my stuff. I made a pile and she says I can't. See? She moved my things all around.
ELORA:	But he's not making a museum. He's just getting the little stuff and putting it here.
TEACHER:	So, he's making a pile of little objects. And you want to make different kinds of piles. Is that right? So, what can we do about that?
SEAN:	(In a calmer tone) Make Elora put my pile back.
ELORA:	We could make a nest pile with big things and a nest pile with little things. Alright, Sean? See? (Begins to move objects around the table again)
SEAN:	(Shows interest but says nothing)
TEACHER:	(To Sean) See what she's doing? She's putting all the nests together, but then you can put the small nests in one place and the bigger nests in a different place.
ELORA:	(Already categorizing objects) See, Sean? This is a pile for little nests. And you can make a pile for little rocks and . . . little stuff. (Laughs)
SEAN:	Okay, but I do all the little stuff. (Joins Elora in categorizing)

The children in this story are categorizing. Initially, Sean uses a simple feature, size, to create a pile. Elora has a different scheme in mind. The resulting dispute, including intervention by an adult, leads to a very complex, multidimensional categorization strategy. The children sort objects first by their origin in nature and then by size. What led to this advanced mode of thinking? Sean's thought processes were challenged by Elora and by the kindergarten teacher. Would Sean have developed such a sophisticated museum had he not been playing with a peer?

Vygotsky (1978) has argued that young children cannot show their highest levels of thinking when they are alone. He suggests that when children get support from a more competent peer or an adult, they are far better at solving problems. When Elora says, "You put nests together and rocks together," she provides a structure for Sean's categorization. At the same time, she encourages his independent problem-solving. In other words, she **scaffolds** his problem-solving without performing the task for him.

Parents and teachers are also found to naturally scaffold children's learning (Freund, 1989). They ask questions or give hints while at the same time giving children as much responsibility as possible. The teacher's statements in the story demonstrate scaffolding: "So, he's making a pile of little objects. And you want to make different kinds of piles. Is that right? So, what can we do about that?" Again, a supportive structure is provided for problem-solving; the actual solution, however, is left up to the children.

Vygotsky proposed that language plays a particularly critical role in learning. He noted that preschooler's **self-directed speech**—the inner-directed language described in Chapter 3—helps children to guide their own attention and to organize ideas internally. When they talk to themselves, children think at higher levels. Where does private speech come from? To Vygotsky, it originates from verbal instructions and other messages from adults and peers. When a parent says to a child in a mosque, "Sit still and pray," the child may be heard repeating this phrase quietly to guide self-control. When a Head Start teacher says, "Use words when you're angry, don't hit," children may be heard uttering this statement to direct social problem-solving. Contrary to Piaget's position, Vygotsky believed that such direct verbal instructions from adults contribute significantly to cognitive development.

To Vygotsky, then, preschoolers would solve problems more competently than Piaget proposed if they were able to talk and socialize. How would Piaget's preschool subjects have performed on his tasks if they had been encouraged to work on these with peers or had had an adult scaffolding their activities?

Culture and Social and Language Interactions

For preschoolers of some cultures, social and language interaction are especially critical for learning. Children of Euro-American cultures have been described as **field independent** (Rodriquez, 1983); that is, they have a unique cognitive style that allows them to solve problems without much outside assistance. They can focus on the specific steps of a task without being distracted by the full external environment, or the field. They are better able to work alone (Figueroa, 1980).

Children in other cultures tend to be **field sensitive.** This means that they rely on the entire environment and everything and everyone within it to solve problems. Mexican-American, Puerto Rican, and African-American children tend to display this cognitive style. When field-sensitive children perform a Piagetian task, they will not just look at the checkers or the container of water. They will attend to everything around them: the whole room, the noises and voices coming from outside, and even the expressions of the experimenter. Such a child might search the adult's face, for example, for clues in solving a problem. The most important characteristic of field-sensitive children is a need for social interaction and language in order to learn. This need arises from unique cultural experiences. In particular, the collective behavior

Children of some cultures are very reliant on social interaction and conversation with others in solving problems.

and action of family members within some cultures tends to nurture a field-sensitive cognitive style. It is clear that field-sensitive children, more than others, require the kind of social scaffolding that Vygotsky describes (Rodriquez, 1983).

Unfortunately, the vast majority of preschool and elementary school teachers are from field-independent cultures. They tend to develop learning activities that are geared to their own cognitive style, such as puzzles to be completed by just one child or easels with space for just one painter at a time. Field-sensitive preschoolers perform less well on some of these tasks (Kalyan-Masih, 1985). Later in life, in a typical test-and-drill elementary school, they are at special disadvantage (Rodriquez, 1983). An implication of this research for teachers of young children is that classroom environments should be created to allow extensive social interaction and conversation. Cooperative projects and play activities must be designed to meet the needs of preschoolers with diverse cognitive styles.

COGNITIVE DEVELOPMENT AND PRESCHOOLERS WITH SPECIAL NEEDS

A variety of challenging conditions can affect cognitive development. Preschoolers with **mental retardation,** for example, will not solve problems or learn concepts as typically developing children do. Mental retardation is defined as a condition leading to general intellectual impairment. It may either have clearly identified organic causes (e.g., **Down syndrome** or other genetic disorders discussed in earlier chapters) or be of unknown origin (Kaplan, 1996). Children with mental retardation progress through the same stages of cognitive development, but significantly more slowly than others. Further, they may never reach the highest levels of cognitive development in adulthood. Figure 11-4 illustrates these variations in the development of categorization. Retardation has been found to affect symbolic functioning. Delays in language, literacy, and play behavior are common (Odom & Bricker, 1993).

Piaget's descriptions of sensorimotor and preoperational stages of development may still be quite useful in observing the play and learning of young children with mental retardation. Since skills will be acquired in a sequence—if not at a pace—that is similar to typical development, Piaget's framework can reliably guide teaching and parenting of children with this condition. For example, 4- or 5-year-olds with mental retardation may have the characteristics typical of the late sensorimotor period that Piaget described. Their thinking and problem-solving may be tied exclusively to perception and physical action. It is possible that they have not fully acquired the symbolic thought and pre-logical problem-solving of their typically developing peers. For this reason, a multimodal learning environment rich in texture and visual and auditory stimulation is recommended (Odom & Bricker, 1993). Children with retardation may need more direct guidance in exploring, playing, and interacting with peers (Musselwhite, 1986).

THEORIES OF THE MIND

One of the most remarkable cognitive advancements in the preschool years is an early formation of a **theory of the mind** (C. S. Rosen, Schwebel, & Singer, 1997). At a surprisingly young age, children begin to understand—or form a theory about—what the mind is, how it works, and how it might be controlled. Such a theory sounds extremely sophisticated—far too complex, it would seem, for preschool-age children

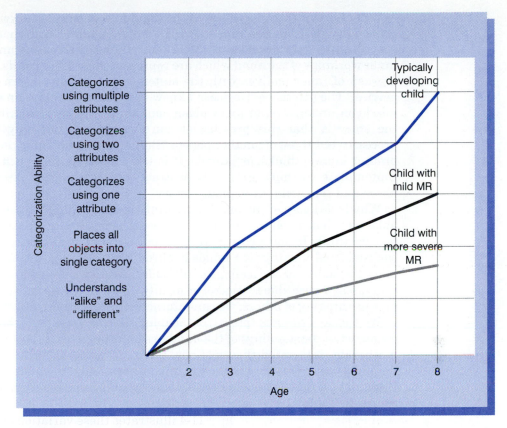

FIGURE 11-4 The figure shows development of one Piagetian ability—categorization—for three hypothetical children. A typically developing child will acquire an ability to categorize by two attributes by age 6 and by more than two attributes by age 8. Children with mild or more severe mental retardation may progress more slowly in this area or may never reach the multiple categorization stage.

to understand. Yet there is evidence that children as young as age 2 do form such a theory. Signs of this can be observed within simple play activities, as the following story reveals:

> A 4-year-old child plays with her 18-month-old brother in her family's small house in rural Kenya. She is playing a chasing game: she taunts her sibling, then runs away from him. He toddles after her, shrieking with delight. At one point she climbs into an enormous basket, and her brother loses sight of her for a moment. "He doesn't know I'm in here," she whispers to her mother who is working in the kitchen. "He thinks I ran out the door." Sure enough, her brother toddles out the front door looking for her. His mother brings him back in.
>
> The chasing game continues and becomes more wild. Because the house is so small, the noise and activity begin to annoy the mother, who is busy preparing food. At one point the toddler bumps a table, tipping a bowl and sending berries rolling onto the floor. This is all the mother can tolerate. "No more running!" she scolds. "Stop it now!" Her daughter appeals: "He didn't mean to knock over the berries. It was an accident." The mother is not moved by the argument, however, so the girl and her brother find a quieter game to play.

Where is evidence of a theory of the mind in this story? The young girl's language gives one clue. She uses words such as "know," "think," and "mean to"—terms that describe internal mental states. More important, she shows an understanding of the inner workings of the mind which are represented by these words. She demonstrates a grasp of inner motives with the statement, "He didn't mean to knock over the berries." The utterance "He doesn't know I'm in here" displays an awareness that the mind can understand or know about something. The most significant revelation in the story is that this preschooler can comprehend not only her own thinking processes but those of another person. She can guess, and quite accurately, what her brother knows, thinks, or intends. It is truly amazing that such a young child can contemplate the mind—a highly abstract concept that has puzzled adult philosophers and scientists throughout history!

Why is a theory of the mind important? It is one thing to just think; doing so enables us to learn, solve problems, or make decisions. It is quite another to think about *how* we think. In doing so, we attend to our inner mental processes. For example, we can reflect on the steps our minds go through in learning something, or can contemplate the source of our feelings or attitudes. When we are aware of our own thought processes, we are able to control or modify them. When we can contemplate the feelings or thinking of others, we can interact with them more effectively.

We speak of *theories* (plural) of the mind here because many believe that children construct understandings of the mind in separate pieces. It is only in adulthood that a coherent, integrated theory of how the mind works is formulated. At least three distinct types of theories of the mind have been found to emerge in early childhood. Each plays a function in children's cognitive and social development. These are presented in Table 11-3.

Theories About Internal Emotional States

Theories about internal emotional states are particularly useful in social interactions—even in the preschool years (C. S. Rosen et al., 1997). Children who can read emotions are better able to decide how to interact with adults and peers. They can

TABLE 11-3

Theories of the Mind That Emerge in the Preschool Years

Theory	Description
Internal emotional states	Preschool children can accurately interpret their own emotions and those of others. Further, they know that emotions come from within and may be hidden from other people.
Motives and intentions	Preschool children can interpret others' motives, so long as they are obvious. They can also accurately identify the intentions behind actions. Statements such as "He was trying to be mean" and "He didn't mean to; it was an accident" show these theories of the mind.
Knowing and remembering	Preschool children have a general understanding of internal thought processes. They know that "know," "remember," "guess," "forget," and "pay attention" are things that occur in the mind, though they have trouble differentiating among these concepts.

make judgments about when a peer is grumpy and should be left alone or when another is happy and in the mood to play. In some cases, a child's very survival can depend on the theory of the mind, as the following story illustrates:

A 4-year-old is playing in her apartment when her father bursts into the room. She has not seen him in a long time because he and her mother separated after a long period of fighting. She wants very much to talk and play with him and to get a hug, but she can tell by the way he has entered that he is angry and drunk. The child knows that when he gets this way, he can be mean and even physically abusive. So she says nothing to her father, but backs quietly out of the room. As she exits, her mother enters from the kitchen, yelling at her father. She escapes to the front porch, where she sits with her hands over her ears to muffle the sounds of their argument.

Theories of Motives and Intentions

Another theory of the mind relates to motives. Preschool children are able to interpret, to some degree, their own motives as well as others' (Lillard, 1995). Children as young as age 3 have an understanding of what motives are and can distinguish between those that are positive or negative. They might report that a peer knocked down a block structure because she was "being mean," or that another shared a snack because he was "being nice." They can analyze their own motives for behavior as "bad" or "good." By the end of the preschool years, they can even identify whether behaviors are intentional or unintentional. By the time children reach age 4 or 5, teachers can help them reflect on social problems by noting that "He didn't mean to" or "It was just an accident."

Theories of Knowing and Remembering

Preschoolers reveal theories of knowing and remembering when they play. When a child announces, "We're the police, remember?" or "I know who you're pretending to be," he or she is showing a knowledge of these thinking processes. The exact meanings of some of these concepts may not be fully acquired until later childhood (Lovett & Pillow, 1991). Young children have been found to define "know" or "remember" as "getting the right answer," for example (Misciones, Marvin, O'Brien, & Green, 1978). Still, preschoolers are aware of and have some control over knowing and remembering processes. They understand that "know," "remember," and "pay attention" involve doing something special in the mind. When a parent says "Now remember," or a teacher says "Try to learn this," children give special attention to the information that follows. They are more likely to retain it than if they were not given these cues (Flavell, Green, & Flavell, 1995).

Variations in Theories of the Mind

Children begin to formulate theories of the mind at about the same time and in similar ways across cultures or ability levels. Theories of the mind appear to be fundamental, universal understandings that are not influenced by individual circumstances.

Challenging Conditions. Even challenging conditions may not significantly impede theories of the mind from being formed. In one study, 4-year-olds with Down syndrome were found to be as capable as typically developing preschoolers at solving tasks that require guessing what others are thinking (Barron-Cohen, Leslie, & Frith, 1985). In another investigation, language-delayed children were found to perform similarly to typically developing peers on tasks where they were to anticipate others' thoughts (Perner, Frith, Leslie, & Leekam, 1989).

Autism is the one significant exception. Autism is a condition characterized by a lack of awareness of others, a preference for objects to people, and an intense desire for sameness. Other symptoms include language delays, self-destructive behavior, and repetitive, ritualistic body movements (Barron-Cohen, 1997). Integrating multiple stimuli is a problem for autistic children; they have trouble putting together multiple sources of information to form a coherent whole. For example, they tend to have difficulty interpreting the many visual and auditory cues of a person talking, so the full message is often missed.

Autistic preschoolers perform very poorly on tasks related to theories of the mind. They have difficulty interpreting others' motives, beliefs, and thoughts (Perner et al., 1989). In fact, some researchers hypothesize that autistic children's poor social and emotional functioning may be attributed, in large degree, to a failure to form accurate theories of the mind (Leslie, 1987; Leslie & Frith, 1987). If autistic children are not aware of the internal feelings of others, they may become less interested in or committed to relationships, and less likely to understand the emotional impact of their social behaviors. If they are not aware of the mental processes involved in paying attention, they may be less likely to guide their minds to focus on relevant stimuli.

Culture and Theories of the Mind. Long ago, a prevalent theory in anthropology was that sophisticated understandings of mental states existed only in modern, Western societies where there was a high level of formal education. Early writers noted that in some cultures dreams are considered predictions about the future and that memories are thought to be imposed by outside, spiritual forces (Lienhardt, 1961). How could people with such beliefs possibly form accurate theories about mental states?

A fascinating study was conducted in one such culture—a Baka village in the rainforests in Cameroon (Avis & Harris, 1991). People of this village hold spiritual beliefs that would appear to contradict an accurate theory of the mind. They believe, for example, that dreams predict the future. Would preschoolers in this community come to understand internal mental states as Western children do? In the study, 3- and 4-year-olds were presented with theories of the mind tasks in a culturally sensitive way. Two Baka experimenters played a hiding game with subjects, using the foods and implements of the culture. First, children were asked to sit with the two experimenters around a cooking fire. One experimenter, Mopfana, would begin to cook mango kernels, but then get up and leave for a moment. The other experimenter, Mobissa, who by virtue of age was of higher status, would then ask the children to play a trick and hide the kernels. (Note the importance of culturally sensitive research methods!) Once the kernels were hidden, Mobissa would ask the children several questions: "When Mopfana comes back, where will he look for the kernels? Before Mopfana opens the lid to the bowl where the kernels are, will his heart feel good or bad? After he lifts the lid, will his heart feel good or bad?" By age 4, the Baka children were very good at accurately predicting thoughts and feelings. The authors conclude that spiritual beliefs in no way limited children's understandings of intentions, thinking processes, and emotional states. Other studies from other parts of the world have verified that, in spite of diverse worldviews, all children acquire theories of the mind at around the same time in development (Flavell, Zhang, Zou, Dong, & Qi, 1983; D. Gardner, Harris, Ohmoto, & Hamazaki, 1988).

Theories of the Mind and Play. Where do theories of the mind originate? Most researchers believe that interactions with others, particularly other children, enhance these understandings. When children play together, they sometimes argue. As they do, they are likely to reflect on intentions, motives, feelings, and thought processes. Siblings may provide the first opportunities for children to engage in play arguments that lead to theories of the mind (Perner, Ruffman, & Leekam, 1994). Parents with more than one child are no stranger to these intense disputes, which may include such taunts as "You're doing that just to be mean," "You meant to hurt me," or "I know

ASSESSING YOUNG CHILDREN: Preschool Cognitive Development

	Areas of Development	What to Watch for	Indicators of Atypical Development
	General cognitive abilities	An ability to solve problems using more internal thought. Using private speech—talking to oneself—to guide learning. An ability to solve more complex problems with support from peers or adults. An ability to use symbolic thinking in pretend play, artwork, or storytelling.	Inability to solve problems—such as puzzles or matching games—using concrete objects. Difficulty distinguishing between actions and their outcomes. Delays in symbolic abilities, such as language, drawing, or make-believe.
	Specific intellectual skills	An ability to solve simple number problems, with occasional errors by age 5. By this same age, an ability to identify objects that are "alike" and "different" and to put similar objects into a single category. An ability to distinguish among simple internal states and mental processes, such as knowing and remembering and feeling happy or sad.	Signs of confusion or frustration when asked to perform number, categorization, or matching tasks. Difficulty in interpreting others' beliefs, feelings, motives, and thoughts.

Interpreting Assessment Data: Cognitive development varies across families and cultures. Problem-solving abilities with concrete objects, for example, will depend on whether toys and other objects are available in the home. Family life will influence the understanding of quantity. Children in pottery-making families, for example, may be advanced in their ability to judge amounts. *Significant* delays in general problem-solving may indicate challenging conditions, however, such as mental retardation and general language delay. A lack of pretend play or an inability to interpret the feelings or intentions of peers may suggest other developmental problems, including autism. Children showing these deficits should be recommended for further evaluation. A preschool program that includes concrete problem-solving activities and pretend play may enhance their cognitive development.

something you don't." It is easy to see the contributions of these interchanges, both to children's theories of the mind and to the stress level of their parents!

Certain kinds of sibling play or play with peers may enhance theories of the mind. When children engage in make-believe, they reflect regularly on their own thought processes (Trawick-Smith, 1998a), as the following statements made by children during play reveal:

- "Let's say you don't know the princess has magic power."
- "I'm real mad at you, alright? And pretend you cry and then you say you're sorry. Then we go to the show, okay?"
- "I'm the mean witch and I steal your purse to get your money."
- "No, Eleana, you don't call the fire department, 'cause you don't think it's a fire yet, alright?"

In each statement, preschoolers demonstrate that they are contemplating motives, intentions, feelings, and thought processes.

RESEARCH INTO PRACTICE

CRITICAL CONCEPT 1

Young children make rapid intellectual advancements during the preschool years. They now engage in what Piaget has called preoperational thought, a new form of thinking that allows them to solve problems using some internal reflection. They can now think about objects or people that are not present, and can reflect upon things they cannot see, hear, touch, or act upon. They can imagine objects or people and represent them in make-believe, and can contemplate future events and recall past ones.

Application #1

Teachers and caregivers should provide preschoolers with problem-solving activities in classrooms. Puzzles, simple scientific experiments, quantifying and counting games, blocks, and cooking experiences are examples of learning experiences that enhance cognitive development.

Application #2

Teachers and caregivers should create elaborate dramatic play centers in classrooms. These should include realistic and non-realistic props that allow children to play out real experiences in their lives. Typical home-related play materials such as dolls, toy dishes, and plastic tools are important. Props that relate to special events or topics in the curriculum can be provided. A toy store, post office, or hospital will allow children to expand their make-believe themes.

Application #3

Teachers and caregivers should ask distancing questions—questions that encourage children to think about persons, objects, or events that are not immediately present. Examples are "What did you do yesterday?" "How is a cow different from a person? From a dog?" and "What are you going to do after child care today?" Concrete experiences that help children to think about the long ago or far away are useful. For example, showing children tools used long ago and tools used in other cultures helps them begin to think in historic and global perspectives.

CRITICAL CONCEPT 2

Piaget has proposed that preschoolers are still limited cognitively. They think in qualitatively different ways than adults. Their thinking is still perception-based, meaning that they rely heavily on the feel, touch, smell, taste, sound, and appearance of things in solving problems.

Application #1

All learning experiences for preschoolers should involve use of the senses. Children must touch, examine, and experiment with concrete objects in order to learn.

Application #2

Highly abstract learning experiences, such as rote-memory math or reading exercises or "sit still and listen" instruction, should be avoided in the preschool years. Children cannot learn if they cannot handle and explore real objects.

CRITICAL CONCEPT 3

Piaget has described preschoolers' thinking as marked by fascinating errors in logic. Young children often conclude, for example, that inanimate objects that move are alive. Their thinking tends to be unidimensional: they often center on just one object or aspect of a problem at a time. They have trouble reversing activities or operations mentally. Their causal thinking, while more sophisticated than in infancy, is still faulty. They engage in transductive reasoning, in which two unrelated events are placed into a causal relationship. Finally, they are still quite egocentric; they have trouble understanding the perspectives of others.

Application #1

Teachers and caregivers should understand and appreciate that misconceptions and unreasonable fears are common in the preschool years and stem from cognitive limitations. "Errors" and misinterpretations of the world should be accepted as necessary and positive steps toward more advanced reasoning.

Application #2

Teachers and caregivers should take great care in explaining phenomena to children. They should engage children in discussions about which things are alive and which are not. They should provide experiences in which children contemplate things made by humans and things that result from natural causes. Opportunities to observe natural phenomena should be provided.

Application #3

Simple problems should be posed to help preschoolers think about more than one object, event, or person at a time. Categorization activities are an example. Children can be encouraged to "put things that are alike together" at the museum table in the classroom. They might be invited to categorize differently shaped blocks in the math center. As children work, caregivers or teachers can ask questions or make comments that induce children to think about more than one attribute at a time: "You put all the triangles here? Can you make two piles of triangles, so that the triangles that are alike are together?"

Application #4

Teachers and caregivers can provide activities that prompt children to reverse their activities. A small group might be taken for a walk on the playground and then asked, "Can you walk back the same way we came?" Children can be asked to take block structures down one block at a time, essentially reversing the building steps. Children can be asked to tell stories or rhymes backwards.

Application #5

Children can be provided with activities that allow them to act upon objects and observe results. Activities such as blowing balls through a maze, rolling toy cars down a ramp, swinging a pendulum to knock over bowling pins, and pouring water into different kinds of tubes allow children to experience cause and effect. As children play in these ways, teachers can ask causal questions: "What happened when you. . . ?" "What would happen if you . . . ?" "What can you do to make . . . happen?"

Application #6

Teachers and caregivers can plan classroom experiences in which preschoolers take the perspectives of others. Guessing games that require children to give clues to help other players guess an object or person promote perspective-taking. There is no more helpful perspective-taking activity than dramatic play, in which children must assume the roles of others.

CRITICAL CONCEPT 4

Piaget's research methods have come under criticism. Children have been found to be more competent than his early work has suggested. Piaget may have underestimated the role of language and social interaction in thinking and problem-solving. His work was based on observations of children of European background; children of other cultures have been found to differ in cognitive development.

Application #1

Caregivers and teachers must understand and appreciate diversity in preschoolers' cognitive development. Children of some backgrounds will acquire concepts earlier than others. Some will depend on social interaction and language to solve problems. Care must be taken not to interpret cultural differences in cognition as deficits.

Application #2

Caregivers and teachers should plan a curriculum that matches the cognitive styles of children enrolled in the classroom. In particular, children of collective cultures, who tend to rely heavily on other people for thinking and learning, should be given opportunities for cooperative and socially active problem-solving.

CRITICAL CONCEPT 5

An intellectual advancement in the preschool years is the emergence of a theory of the mind. Young children have been found to acquire early understandings about what the mind is and how it works. They develop theories about emotions, motives and intentions, and knowing and remembering. These early theories are formulated by children of all cultures, and even by some children with challenging conditions.

Application #1

Teachers and caregivers can assist preschool children in reflecting on their own feelings and those of others. Interventions in real social problems are particularly helpful, such as "How did you feel when Jonah said you couldn't play?" or "How do you think Emur felt when you pushed her?"

Application #2

Teachers and caregivers can help children think about intentions and motives. In real-life conflicts, they can ask, "Why do you think he knocked over your blocks? Do you think he meant to be mean?"

Application #3

Teachers and caregivers can provide activities that encourage children to remember objects or events. One example is a game in which children are asked to recall objects that are displayed and then hidden. As the game is played, an adult can ask questions that help children focus on how the mind works: "How many do you think you will remember?" "What is something you could do to help you remember these?" and "If it's too noisy, is it easier or harder to remember?"

SUGGESTED ACTIVITIES

1. Perform conservation tasks with two preschoolers of different ages (e.g., a 4-year-old and a 5-year-old) in a child care setting or home. Each child should be individually tested away from distractions. Descriptions of these tasks are found in the chapter; the following is a brief overview of procedures:

   Conservation of Number: Line up eight to ten red and black checkers in one-to-one correspondence so that it is easy to see there are as many red as black ones. Point to each line and ask the child, "Are there more red checkers, more black checkers, or the same amount of red and black checkers?"

   After the child says aloud that the two lines have the same number of checkers, gather one line of checkers into a pile while leaving the other arranged in a line. Ask the same question given above. Does the child state now that one set has more checkers? If so, ask the child to count both sets, then ask the question again. Challenge the child in other ways:

   "You said they both had the same number of checkers before, remember? And I didn't add any or take any checkers away. So . . ." Then repeat the question.

   Conservation of Continuous Quantity: Fill two identical clear containers (tall, thin laboratory beakers work very well) with water so that both contain the same amount. Point to each container and ask, "Does this container have more water, or does this container have more water, or do they both have the same amount of water?" If the child says one container has more, pour a little out of that one until the child states that the two containers hold the same amount of water.

   Once the child says that the two containers hold equivalent amounts, pour the water from one of the containers into another, wider container. The new container should be wide enough that the water levels are now very different. Now ask the child the questions given above. If the child indicates that one now holds more than the other, ask challenging questions, as in the previous experiment: "You said they had the same amount before, and I didn't add any water. So, does this container really have more?"

Write a report on your experiments, guided by the following questions:

a. Did children perform on these tasks as Piaget would have predicted? In what ways were the two children different in their problem-solving?

b. How was each child's performance influenced by perception-based thinking? By unidimensional thought? By difficulty reversing an operation?

c. What can you conclude about young children's thinking? In what ways were you impressed with these children's problem-solving? In what way was their thinking limited?

2. Perform the same two experiments described in activity number 1 with children of two different ages. This time, however, have them complete the tasks together. Allow them to discuss and argue about the problem as you conduct the two experiments. Take notes on their interactions. Later, write a report on your experiences, guided by the following questions:

a. How did the performance of the two children differ from activity number 1?

b. What role did each child play in the problem-solving process? How was the older child different from the younger one in these interactions?

c. Did you see signs of scaffolding by the older child?

d. What role did language play in the process? Did either child instruct the other verbally? Did you hear any self-directed speech?

3. Observe a group of preschool children of diverse cultural backgrounds in a classroom. Watch them as they interact in different kinds of play and learning activities (e.g., dramatic play, puzzles, blocks, art, and group time). Attempt to identify a child whom you believe to be field independent, based on descriptions in this chapter. Then identify a child whom you believe to be field sensitive. Later, write a description of the two children, guided by the following questions:

a. What behaviors led you to believe that one of the children you selected was field independent? What led you to conclude the other was field sensitive?

b. Contrast the social interactions of the field-independent child with those of the field-sensitive child. In what ways were their problem-solving strategies (e.g., making puzzles, building with blocks) different?

4. Observe a preschool child for at least one hour in a classroom. As you observe, record any evidence of a developing theory of the mind, as described in this chapter. Watch for indicators of the child's theories about emotional states, intentions and motives, and knowing and remembering. Pay special attention to the words the child uses. Later, write a report on your observation, guided by the following questions:

a. What language or social behaviors did you observe, if any, which indicate that this child understands internal emotional states?

b. What indicators were there, if any, that the child was aware of motives and intentions?

c. What behaviors did you observe that showed the child was aware of internal processes of learning, remembering, and knowing?

CHAPTER 12

Symbolic Thought: Play, Language, and Literacy in the Preschool Years

PRESCHOOL-AGE CHILDREN ARE HIGHLY IMAGINATIVE. They tell elaborate stories, interpret and reinvent their lives in their drawing and writing, and create fanciful worlds through make-believe. They are able to do all of these things because they possess **symbolic thought:** the ability to use symbols—whether words, scribbles, toys, or inventive make-believe actions—to represent ideas. The following vignette illustrates the many symbolic abilities of preschoolers:

> Two 4-year-olds are playing in a pretend post office that has been created in the dramatic play area of their Head Start center. They write on stationery and envelopes and then place their completed letters in a make-believe mailbox provided by the teacher.

OLIA: (In a pretend, adult-like voice) Well, I need to write to my daughter now. She has moved away and I need to write her. Come on, Marcie. Let's write to our daughters, okay?

MARCIE: How old are they?

OLIA: Let's say they're . . . um . . . teenagers.

MARCIE: Okay. 'Cause teenagers can read 'em. We can write . . . they can read 'em. Tell 'em to come home, alright? Come home right now. (Makes scribbles on the stationery, as if writing this message in a letter)

OLIA: And write them not to have a baby. (Scribbles intently on her letter)

MARCIE: (Laughs and continues to write) No. The daughters don't have babies.

OLIA: They can have a baby. My sister has a baby. Now look. (Holds up her letter) It says, "Don't have a baby, 'cause that's not . . . something . . ." I can't remember what this part says.

MARCIE: Well, I'm going to tell 'em to come home right now.

> The two children write and discuss their letters. Finally, they place them in envelopes, address these with scribbles, and mail them at the post office.

OLIA: Let's say I'm the daughter now, and I get your letter, okay? (Takes an envelope from the mailbox and assumes a different make-believe voice) Oh. A letter! What does this say?

MARCIE: (Takes the letter from the other child and runs her fingers along the scribbles) "Dear Daughter. Please come home now. Aren't you scared by yourself? Love, Mommy."

This play episode is filled with examples of symbolic thought. The two children use vocal intonations, gestures, and announcements of make-believe to transform themselves into other characters, and the real world into a pretend situation. They use scribbles on paper to stand for ideas that fascinate and perhaps worry them. A play mailbox is transformed into a real one. In these interactions, the children talk, write, read, and pretend. In this chapter we will examine the importance of these activities in young children's development.

SOCIODRAMATIC PLAY

With advances in cognition, preschoolers' play becomes more complex. The simple pretenses of toddlerhood—repetitive, make-believe acts with objects (e.g., pretending to drink from cup)—have given way to much more complex enactments. These involve other children and include more intricate themes and story lines. Such pretend play, called **sociodramatic play,** predominates children's leisure activities during the preschool years. The following is an example of this play form:

> A 5-year-old girl hums to herself as she builds a platform out of large hollow blocks. She suddenly notices a classmate standing nearby and invites her to play: "Lauren, let's go! The car's ready. You ride in my car too, okay?"
>
> The younger girl, clearly eager to join the play, moves over the block structure and asks, "Is this a car or a truck? I think it's a truck."
>
> "No, a car." her older playmate responds. "Now I'll be the mother. Hurry, we'll be late! It will never do to be late!" She says this in a particularly serious, adultlike tone. "It's a truck," the younger girl persists.
>
> At this point the older child puts her hands on her hips and exhales, seemingly exasperated. "Now honey, you get in here!" she commands, using her adult voice again. "Okay," her playmate responds, "but it's a truck."
>
> "Yeah, but let's say it's, like, a car-truck, alright?" the older child offers as a compromise. This seems to satisfy her playmate, who now sits down on the blocks.
>
> "Now I'm the mommy and you're the baby," the older girl directs. Predictably, the younger child responds, "No! I'm not the baby! Let's say we're both mothers and this will be our baby." At this point she retrieves a doll from the nearby dramatic play area. "This is our baby, Rachel." She speaks now to the doll in a gentle, parental tone: "Rachel, you need to lie down and be good in our truck, 'cause we can't drive when you make all that noise."
>
> The discussion now turns to their destination. "We're going to New York City, okay sweetie?" the older girl says in her grown-up voice. "Oh, no," counters her playmate. "It's so crowded there today! Let's go to McDonald's instead."
>
> The older child responds, "Well, we'll go to McDonald's first and get our food. Then we better go to New York to the show."

It is easy to see in this story how sociodramatic play and cognitive development are related. The two girls engage in much high-level thinking as they plan and later embark on a make-believe trip. They must use much language to negotiate the pretend elements of their play. They announce verbally what various play objects represent ("The car's ready") and what will happen next on their make-believe journey ("We're going to New York City"). They also use language to define make-believe roles ("I'm the mommy and you're the baby"). Without language, children would have a very hard time agreeing upon a shared meaning for the many symbols and pretend situations that make up this form of play (Garvey & Kramer, 1989).

In sociodramatic play, children try out adult-like phrases and intonations as they enact their make-believe roles. Much representational thought is required, as objects are used to stand for things that are not actually present (such as using blocks to represent a car). Overall, the sociodramatic play setting is a safe and noncritical arena for exercising mental skills. Research has demonstrated that this form of playing contributes to children's development in many ways (J. E. Johnson, Christie, & Yawkey, 1999).

Sociodramatic Play and Cognition

A circular relationship exists between play and each of three fundamental areas of development: intelligence, creativity, and language. These three intellectual areas contribute to play ability, and play, in turn, contributes to development in these areas. These complex relationships are illustrated in Figure 12-1.

Children who are intellectually competent tend to be expert players. Their play themes are more complex and their pretend enactments are more symbolic. They use more language and interact more fully with peers (J. E. Johnson et al., 1999). Furthermore, the very act of playing appears to enhance intellectual growth. Expert players may be skilled, in part, because they play so often. A number of studies have

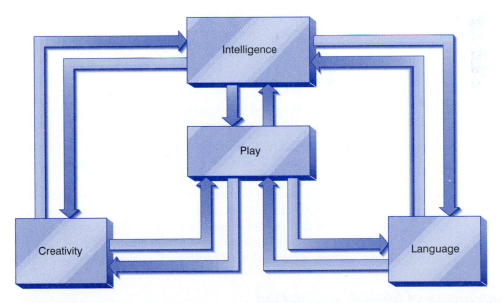

FIGURE 12-1   The complex web of relationships between play and cognition is illustrated. Arrows indicate the direction of effects. Play influences intelligence, for example, and intelligence influences play. More intricate relationships can be seen: play enhances language, language increases intelligence, and the intellectual growth that occurs results in even greater play skills.

found that children who frequently engage in sociodramatic play or are encouraged to do so by adults score higher on IQ tests and perform more competently on Piagetian tasks (Christie, 1983; Rubin, Fein, & Vandenberg, 1983). Others have found relationships between sociodramatic play and problem-solving (Pepler & Ross, 1981) and creativity (Dansky, 1980).

Strong connections have been discovered between sociodramatic play and language or language-related abilities such as reading (Christie, 1994; Dickinson, 1994). Vygotsky (1978) has explained these language-play connections by noting that both involve symbolic thought. He has proposed that sociodramatic play is an important step between the concrete thought processes of early childhood and the more abstract thinking of adulthood. This kind of play allows children to practice using symbols. For example, when children pretend that a wooden rod is a broom or make noises to represent a tornado, symbols are being used: the rod stands for the broom and the noises stand for the wind, much like words stand for ideas. By age 5, these symbols become very abstract, as the following vignette reveals:

Three 5-year-olds are pretending to be firefighters in a street near their home in Mexico City. They run from one side of the street to the other, making loud siren noises.

OMAR: The fire's burning up. But pretend the fire guys can't get through, cause of the earthquake.

CARLOS: (Talking at the same time as Omar) Yeah. The earthquake is shaking the place.

LOURDES: No. Let's say we have to put out the fire now. The earthquake stopped, alright? (Speaking in an adult tone) Spray on the fire! (Makes more siren noises)

OMAR: Where is the burning building?

CARLOS: (Looks down the street. Points to the wall of a large apartment building.) There. It's burning there.

OMAR: It's pretty bad. It's all burned up, I think.

LOURDES: It's burning up. We need to stop it.

CARLOS: We need our hoses. (Looking puzzled, turns to his peers) But we don't have hoses.

OMAR: Like this. (Makes a gesture to show he is holding a fire hose, and makes noises that sound like spraying water)

In this play episode, objects and gestures are used to represent things that are completely different. A wall of an apartment complex becomes a burning building. A movement of the hands becomes a fire hose squirting water. A siren noise represents an entire fire truck. These transformations of reality require significant "symbolic leaps" between the real world and an imagined one (J. E. Johnson et al., 1999).

Components of Sociodramatic Play

Sara Smilansky, a pioneer in play research, has conducted in-depth observations of children's play in Israel and the United States. She has identified several critical components of sociodramatic play that can be observed in most children between 2

TABLE 12-1
Sara Smilansky's
Sociodramatic Play
Quality Elements

TABLE 12-1
Sara Smilansky's
Sociodramatic Play
Quality Elements

Quality Element	Description
Role playing	Children assume a make-believe role of another person, animal, or object and perform appropriate actions through gestures and verbalizations. *Example:* A child pretends to be a firefighter putting out a pretend fire.
Make-believe (Actions)	Children announce make-believe actions and perform these with gestures. *Example:* A child says, "I'm squirting out the fire," and makes a gesture and noises to show this.
Make-believe (Objects)	Children use real objects to represent make-believe ones. *Example:* A child uses a wooden rod as if it were a fire hose.
Make-believe (Situations)	Children announce make-believe situations. *Example:* A child shouts, "The house is burning and there are people trapped inside!"
Social interaction	Children coordinate make-believe roles and actions with peers. *Example:* A child helps another to pull the fire hose up to the burning house.
Verbalization	Children interact with one another verbally both inside the make-believe play and outside of it. *Example:* A child states, "Help! The fire's got me!" from inside a make-believe situation. *Example:* The child says, "Let's say you're another fireman, alright?" from outside a make-believe situation.
Persistence	Children maintain their play themes for over 5 minutes. *Example:* A child engages in firefighter play for 20 minutes without significant interruption.

SOURCE: Smilansky, 1968; Smilansky & Shefatya, 1990.

and 5 years of age: role playing, make-believe, social interaction, verbalization, and persistence. These are described in Table 12-1. Smilansky has proposed that when children display deficits in any of these areas, adults should target these for intervention. She has shown that through informal play interactions, adults can enhance children's performance of these specific play skills (Smilansky, 1968; Smilansky & Shefatya, 1990).

Play, Class, and Culture

Smilansky and other play researchers have reported that children of low socioeconomic status or those from non-technological societies play less often and less well. In many play studies, children of color in the United States are found to have specific play deficits. McLoyd (1986) has argued that findings of play deficits among some groups may be the result of culturally insensitive research methods. She points out that toys used in play studies often hold little cultural meaning for some children. When research is conducted within classrooms, some children may be inhibited from showing their true play abilities. In a study I conducted, for example, children from Puerto Rico were found to engage in their most elaborate play outdoors on the playground (Trawick-Smith, 1998a). Others have discovered that naturalistic neighborhood play may be a better context for assessing play skills (Malone, Stoneman, & Langone, 1994).

In a study where deficits were found among African-American kindergartners, subjects were asked to play a "mommy and daddy" role-playing game. In a critique of this investigation, Hughes (1995) notes that 83% of the children in this study lived in single-parent homes. Hale-Benson (1986) suggests that the broad range of play activities of African-American children cannot be fully captured by narrow tests of sociodramatic play. Teachers and researchers should broaden their definitions of play, then, to appreciate a wider range of in- and out-of-classroom play activities.

Play-Work. Children of low socioeconomic status are likely to be assigned household tasks at an earlier age than middle-class children (B. B. Whiting & Edwards, 1988). Obviously, family chores will limit the amount of play time in children's lives. Does this mean that children of poor families do not enjoy the same play opportunities as their middle-class peers? Research suggests that children cleverly integrate work and play during the day into what has been called **play-work.** Descriptions abound of children of many different cultures playing while they work. Often, they carry out their household tasks in a make-believe adult manner. Bloch and Adler (1994) describe how West African boys carry sticks as pretend spears while they tend livestock. Their fathers provide them with small tools—replicas of real adult implements—to use in the garden. Girls are observed pretending to carry water in miniature pots as they follow along behind their mothers, who carry real water vessels.

Children who are assigned child care responsibilities also play as they work (B. B. Whiting & Edwards, 1988). The following story shows how a young child plays a sophisticated make-believe role while contributing in important ways to family life.

> A 5-year-old plays on the living room floor with a neighborhood peer and her 17-month-old sister while her mother works in another part of the apartment. The girl feeds her younger sibling a dry breakfast cereal, one flake at a time, while crooning, "Here ya' go, honey. That's a good girl to eat it all up." Her friend makes a play suggestion: "Let's say these are carrots and vegetables and we try to get our baby to eat them."
>
> "Alright," says the 5-year-old. She commands her sister, "Eat those vegetables so you can grow up right, baby." The toddler enjoys the game and gobbles up the cereal. Then the older sister suggests to her friend, "But now let's say it's time for bed, alright?" She scoops her sister up into her arms and carries her to the couch. The baby begins to protest loudly. Her mother calls in from another room. "Samantha, you watch the baby, now."
>
> The child and her friend soothe the crying toddler. They make a pretend bed out of a comforter on the couch and lay the toddler on it. "Night, night," they say in unison as the younger child feigns sleep.

Here a child plays an important caregiving role while carrying on an elaborate make-believe theme with a friend. Would the child show the same level of play ability in an artificial research room or classroom setting?

Non-Toy Play. Play studies often involve presenting realistic toys—small replicas of adult-sized implements—for children to play with. Such toys are commonly found in Euro-American households in the United States. However, not all children play with realistic toys. Hale-Benson (1986) describes African-American children's play as less object-oriented and more people-centered. She suggests that African-American homes are not as likely to contain intricate toys. Instead, play more commonly involves physical interaction with peers, siblings, and parents. She contends that this feature of family life has led some Euro-American educators to erroneously conclude that African-American home environments are deficient. Her belief is that toys would only interfere with the play styles of such families. This orientation toward people reflects an African heritage, she contends. She notes that "African children don't play with dolls, they play with their mother's babies" (p. 70).

Commercially made toys are not available in many other cultures. In East India, children play with discarded paper, wood, and clay (Roopnarine, Hossain, Gill, & Brophy, 1994). Parents sometimes fashion toys out of available objects, such as rattles made from gourds and stones, play tortoises made from coconut shells, and paper snakes. In sharp contrast, the most popular toys of children in some Japanese families are computer and video games. These are found in more than a fifth of all households in Japan. Such play is alarming to educators who value traditional sociodramatic play activities. However, research suggests that when Japanese children use certain kinds of computer games, they engage in many of the same play processes as children who use traditional toys (Takeuchi, 1994). Wright and Samaras (1986) have shown that when children play with certain kinds of software, they pretend, socialize, and verbalize with computers at the same rates as when they engage in traditional sociodramatic play!

An educational implication of cross-cultural play research is that classroom environments must be planned with great sensitivity to cultural differences. Children of different cultural backgrounds use different kinds of toys, choose different types of play themes, and sometimes integrate work and play. Traditional housekeeping centers with realistic props may not be sufficient to meet all children's play needs in preschool or child care. Simply filling up classrooms with realistic toys in order to compensate for perceived deficits in children's home environments is ill-advised (Hale-Benson, 1986).

Play and Children with Special Needs

Children with special needs engage in play. Their activities are similar to those of typically developing children, but certain play limitations are evident. Sometimes children with special needs require extra adult support or modifications in the classroom or home environment in order to play. Without assistance, their sociodramatic play can be less symbolic or less verbal.

Play and Visual Impairments. Preschoolers with **visual impairments** begin to engage in sociodramatic play at around the same time as typically developing peers (Fraiberg, 1978). However, they perform fewer make-believe enactments and are less imaginative in their themes (Tait, 1973). How can visual impairments inhibit the frequency of make-believe? Hughes (1995) hypothesizes that children who cannot see or who see poorly are challenged in their ability to distinguish fantasy from reality in play. The following play situation illustrates the problem:

> A child who has a visual impairment is playing with peers in the dramatic play area. One of her playmates announces, "The phone is ringing," and holds up a toy telephone. His smiles and body language indicate that this is a pretend enactment.
> Other children, without visual impairments, immediately understand that he is playing, because they can interpret his visual cues. The visually impaired child, however, appears confused. She relies only on his tone of voice to interpret his statement, and is not sure whether he is pretending or has actually heard a phone ringing.

Play in preschool is often stimulated by novel play objects. Interesting toys or raw materials suggest particular play ideas (Trawick-Smith, 1990). A blind child would not be visually stimulated by these. Teachers can facilitate play in children with visual impairments by giving regular tactile "tours" of the classroom, helping them "rehearse" play with new toys, or assisting them in interpreting the make-believe of their peers (Hughes, 1995).

Play and Hearing Impairments. Children with **hearing impairments** are also less likely to engage in make-believe. They symbolize less with objects and participate less often in joint make-believe with peers (Esposito & Koorland, 1989). A problem for hearing-impaired children is an inability to engage in the sophisticated communication necessary to carry out elaborate pretend play themes (Trawick-Smith, 1994). Preschoolers regularly use language to announce make-believe (e.g., "This is a broom, alright?" or "Let's say we go to the circus but nobody's there"). Often other playmates disagree with these play suggestions and offer alternatives (e.g., "No. That's not a broom, it's a gun!" or "No, the clowns are there, alright?"). Thus preschool play involves elaborate verbal negotiations among players, and children with hearing impairments have trouble participating in such negotiations. Not only are they less able to understand their peers' comments, they are also likely to have communicative challenges that make self-expression difficult.

Teachers can facilitate hearing-impaired children's play with peers by assisting them in communicating ideas clearly and interpreting the play suggestions of others. These interventions will be more successful in integrated classrooms where hearing and hearing-impaired children play together. In one study, less sophisticated play was observed in self-contained classrooms containing only children with hearing impairments (Esposito & Koorland, 1989).

Play and Cognitive Challenges. In spite of intellectual challenges, children with **mental retardation** have been observed performing highly imaginative and abstract make-believe roles with peers (C. C. Cunningham, Glenn, Wilkinson, & Sloper, 1985). However, their play abilities—as is true of other areas of their development—may be somewhat delayed (Kaplan, 1996). The sociodramatic play of children with mental retardation is very similar to that of typically developing children who are several years younger (Li, 1985). The following story contrasts the play of a 5-year-old who has mental retardation with that of a typically developing peer:

> Thomas, who has mental retardation, joins Keisha, a typically developing child, in a cooking play activity in the dramatic play center of his kindergarten classroom.

THOMAS: (Moves over to the toy stove, takes a toy kettle, and bangs it on the stove) The pot is banging. (Laughs)

KEISHA: (Takes the toy kettle away from Thomas. Speaks in an adult tone.) No. Don't bang in our house. Too noisy for your father to sleep. Get me some cups to pour the coffee.

THOMAS: (Grabs another pot and a spoon and bangs them together, laughing) I can bang these. (Repeatedly takes the top off the pot and puts it back on again)

KEISHA: No. You need to set the table 'cause you're the youngest boy. You're the brother.

THOMAS: (Says nothing. Sits down at the table where dishes have been placed. Begins to drink from a toy cup.)

KEISHA: Good coffee. Now I'm going to put out the dessert. But you better not eat any 'til after the lunch, alright? (Begins to bring various additional plates and pots from the toy stove over to the table) Mmm . . . smell the spaghetti sauce. (Holds a pot under Thomas's nose)

THOMAS: (Takes a plastic fork and pretends to eat) Mmm . . . Good spaghetti.

KEISHA: Didn't I tell you no dessert! (Exhales in pretend exasperation) Well, eat the pie then. It's the lemon kind with sprinkles.

THOMAS: (Pretends to eat with a plastic fork)

The children in this episode are of two different levels of play development. Thomas's activities resemble those of younger preschoolers. He engages in much **functional play:** repetitive action, such as banging dishes or removing and replacing the top to a pot. He uses less language. His pretend enactments are confined to eating or drinking with toy dishes. He does not fully join in the Keisha's elaborate play themes, which are typical for children of this age. The story illustrates how children with cognitive challenges and those who are developing typically can enter into meaningful joint play interactions in classrooms.

Play and Autism.   Unlike the challenges previously described, **autism** appears to severely limit sociodramatic play. Most children with autism engage in very little make-believe. They are more likely to use toys or objects in repetitive motor actions (e.g., banging a pan) and less likely to symbolize with them (Baron-Cohen, 1997). Their unique play preferences exacerbate their already fragile relationships with peers.

Why don't children with autism play? Hughes (1995) identifies two distinct perspectives on the question. One view is that children with autism lack a **theory of the mind** (described in the previous chapter). Imagine how an inability to think about the thought processes of others would impede make-believe. To pretend, a child needs to ask, "How would the character I am playing think, feel, and behave?" Further, a child would need to regularly assign beliefs, feelings, and thought processes to others in order to sustain elaborate play themes (e.g., "Let's say you don't know I'm hiding in the box, okay?"). From this perspective, children with autism don't play simply because they can't.

Another view is that children with autism can play but choose not to. In one study, these children were found to engage in as much pretend play as typically developing children and those with mental retardation when they were encouraged to do so by adults (V. Lewis & Boucher, 1988). This has important implications for teachers and parents. Children with autism, who may not be naturally drawn to play activities, may need much support to initiate and sustain their play.

FIRST- AND SECOND-LANGUAGE ACQUISITION

Children's language grows in four fundamental ways during the preschool years:

1. Their speech becomes clearer; pronunciation, fluency, and articulation all improve. These areas of language development are often referred to as **phonology.**
2. Preschoolers use many words, and come to understand word meanings more fully. These aspects of language are sometimes called **semantics.**
3. Preschoolers' sentences grow in length and complexity. They begin to use clauses and complex word endings to extend and enhance their self-expression. Such language features are referred to as **syntax.**
4. Finally, preschoolers become quite adept at using language to get things done socially. Social communication is often called **pragmatics.**

These developments vary depending on whether children are learning one, two, or more languages. Most children in the world are **bilingual.**

Phonology

Children acquire speech sounds gradually in the early years. Some preschoolers are hard to understand because they have not mastered key sounds, as the following story illustrates:

A teacher, Ms. Sorenson, is listening attentively to Martin, a 3-year-old, tell about a movie he went to see with his family. Martin's retelling is difficult to understand. In his excitement, he uses many misstarts or stutters (i.e., "and then . . . and then . . . and then, know what happened?"). He has trouble pronouncing certain sounds. At an important point in the story, Ms. Sorenson is having special difficulty understanding him:

MARTIN: (Says something incomprehensible in a passionate tone)

MS. SORENSON: I'm sorry, I didn't quite understand you. Could you tell me again?

MARTIN: (Repeats the same garbled message)

MS. SORENSON: I'm sorry. I just didn't catch it. Say it one more time, sweetie.

MARTIN: (Shows frustration, repeats his utterance)

MS. SORENSON: Oh! I see! How interesting! (The teacher shows enthusiasm, even though she still has not understood a word)

Such interchanges are common in the early preschool years. Children have not yet acquired all the sounds of language. Their intonation and fluency are less sophisticated than those of adults. **Phonology** develops gradually in early childhood, and preschoolers can be expected to struggle with speech sounds throughout much of this period. Harsh correction or insistence that children start over again will not be useful, and may even be damaging, to language learning.

It is understandable that children learn speech sounds slowly; each sound requires a complex manipulation of various parts of the body responsible for speech, called **articulators.** These are illustrated in Figure 12-2. Articulators include the front and back of the tongue, the teeth, the lips, the roof of the mouth, the vocal chords, and even the lungs. All of these must be used in harmony to make a single sound. I invite you to engage in an experiment in order to appreciate the complexity of phonology. Paying great attention to all the parts of your body that are in motion, speak the following sounds: *s, v, t, p, o, h, g.* Which different body parts were used? How did the sounds differ from one another in terms of the articulators that were needed? Did you notice that the *v* sound requires use of the vocal chords, whereas the *t* sound does not? Did you discover that in making the *p* sound, air is obstructed fully and then allowed to burst out of the mouth, but that when making the *s* sound, the air seeps out slowly?

Typical and Atypical Phonology. Speech problems worry parents and teachers. When a child cannot pronounce an *l* or *r* sound by age 5, or stumbles over words in stutter-like misstarts, a great deal of anxiety arises. However, the vast majority of preschool articulation errors are typical. Researchers have identified the approximate ages at which various speech sounds are first spoken accurately (Ingram, 1976). This information often is presented in developmental charts which teachers

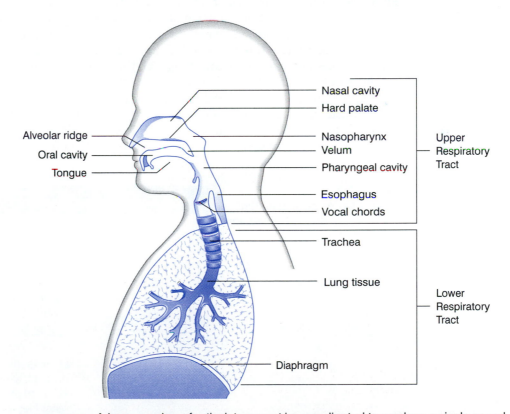

FIGURE 12-2 A large number of articulators must be coordinated to produce a single sound.

or parents use to assess phonological development. A sample phonological chart is presented in Table 12-2. As shown in the chart, some sounds emerge early in development; these sounds may be easier for children to pronounce (R. G. Schwartz & Leonard, 1982). Others, such as certain consonant sounds and blends, are extremely difficult. It might be not be until age 7 or 8 that these sounds are mastered.

Sometimes children have phonological challenges that can be identified and addressed in early childhood. There are a number of indicators of serious speech delay. Children who at an older age cannot pronounce many early-acquired speech sounds may be at risk. For example, if a 5-year-old cannot articulate the sounds *d, b,* or *g*—shown in Table 12-2 to be acquired by age 3—a formal speech evaluation may be recommended. Children who are not stimulable in these early speech sounds may be most in need of intervention. Children are said to be **stimulable** for a particular sound if they can accurately imitate it when it is presented to them by an adult. It is common for children to mispronounce a sound in natural speech but to accurately imitate the sound during a stimulability test. Children who cannot accurately produce early sounds under these controlled circumstances are more likely to require some intervention.

Children who make unpredictable substitutions for speech sounds they cannot pronounce are likely to be recommended for formal evaluation. Typically developing children make regular, logical substitutions when trying to speak sounds they cannot articulate. Readers who are familiar with children's language will recognize some of these regular substitutions: *w* used instead of *r,* as in "wabbit" for "rabbit"; *d* substituted for *th,* as in "dat" for "that." These substitutions somehow sound right. They are close enough to the correct sounds that listeners can understand what is being said. Some children do not make these regular substitutions, however. They may use many different sounds in place of one they cannot pronounce. For example, the child pronounces "rabbit" as "abbit" one time and then as "dabbit" the next. These substitutions may not sound anything like the correct pronunciations, so communication is impeded. Children who make irregular substitutions are at greater risk of later speech delays (Menn, 1989).

Children who show single-sound stuttering, accompanied by tension or facial grimaces, may also be at risk of later phonological difficulties. All preschoolers are **disfluent** in that they stumble over words and restart sentences (e.g., "the ball . . . the

TABLE 12-2

Typical Order of Acquisition of Specific Speech Sounds for Boys and Girls

Age of Acquisition	Girls	Boys
3 years	p, b, m, w, d, n, k, g, h, ng	p, b, m, h, w, d, n, k, t, g
4 years	l	ng
5 years	j, y	y
6 years	sh, ch, r, zh, f, wh	zh, wh, j
7 years	s, z, th, v	f, l, r, ch, sh, s, z, th, v
7 to 9 years	bl, br, dr, fl, dl, kr, pl, skw, sl, str, tr, pr, other blends	bl, br, dr, fl, dl, kr, pl, skw, sl, str, tr, pr, other blends

ball . . . the ball . . ."). Asking children to slow down or start over is not recommended, since such disfluencies are typical and will disappear with age. Occasionally, a child will show a single-sound disfluency (e.g., "b-b-b-b-ball"), with great strain being displayed on the child's face. In such cases, further evaluation may be recommended.

Preschoolers are most likely to be recommended for evaluation and speech therapy when teachers, parents, and peers cannot understand them. The bottom line in deciding whether a speech challenge should be addressed is the degree to which a child can communicate. If a child is communicating well, intervention is often postponed (Ratner, 1989).

Phonology in Second-Language Acquisition. When children learn two or more languages, they must acquire several completely different sound systems (Arnberg, 1987). Needless to say, it is challenging to coordinate the phonological rules of distinct languages. Children often use the sounds of one language—usually the one that is used in the home—to speak in a second. For example, in Spanish, *v* sounds are pronounced as *b,* so Spanish-speaking preschoolers may say "bisit" instead of "visit" when speaking English.

Examples also can be found in the language of young children who speak **Black English Vernacular (BEV)** (Labov, 1971). BEV is a form of English spoken by African Americans in many communities in the United States. It is a rule-governed language that is as complex and expressive as standard English. BEV has its own unique phonology. Children speaking BEV will pronounce the standard English sound *th* as *d,* saying, for example, "dis" instead of "this." The standard English suffix *-ing* is pronounced "in" in BEV, as in "singin" instead of "singing."

Children who are acquiring a second language often substitute the speech sounds of their native language for those of the language they are learning.

It is important to remember that these are language differences, not deficits. The unique phonological features of children's language are to be understood and appreciated. They represent the creative efforts of children to acquire more than one language.

Semantics

Preschoolers' **semantics**—their knowledge of word meanings—develops quickly. Early studies of word acquisition show that children advance from a usable vocabulary of 272 words at age 2 to 2,289 words at age 5 (M. E. Smith, 1926). Children know even more words than they actually speak. Reich (1986) estimates that 5-year-olds understand over 8,000 words—significantly more than early studies had indicated. Furthermore, just because children speak a particular word does not mean that they know its complete meaning. Psycholinguists now study how children construct the meanings of words. In particular, they investigate how children learn challenging words, such as opposites or kinship terms, and word endings.

Young children have been found to construct the meanings of particular words very gradually (Fenson et al., 1994). They may at first **overgeneralize** a word, using it to stand for far more things than an adult would. For example, the word "car" might be used to name all vehicles, including trucks, vans, and motorcycles. Later, children actively and gradually refine the meaning of the word. As another example, a 3-year-old, dressing to go outside, might announce to her child care class: "I'm putting my coat off." Is the child completely confused about the meaning of "off"? Not at all. She knows it is a spatial term that refers to the relationship of the coat to her body. Her definition of the word might be simply, "where the coat is right now." Gradually she will sort out the subtle differences between "on" and "off" and use the words appropriately.

Semantics and Children With Special Needs.
Occasionally, children will show serious difficulties in learning words. Sometimes these challenges are identified early by teachers and parents. Often they are linked to other challenging conditions. Children with mental retardation have been found to understand and produce words at a level comparable to that of much younger children (Layton & Sharifi, 1979). Children with general language delays often have difficulty retrieving words in speech and are slow to learn the full meanings of new ones (Rice, 1987).

Children show difficulty retrieving words in a variety of ways. They may stutter or pause for long periods while trying to recall simple names or descriptions. They may use the word "thing" with great regularity to name objects. One child who had difficulty with names of things was reported to refer to a spoon as "what you eat breakfast with," and a zipper as "what's on my brother's pants" (Ratner, 1989). In these cases further evaluation may be necessary.

Semantics and Second-Language Acquisition.
Children who grow up in bilingual or multilingual homes must learn more than one vocabulary. In the early preschool years, children do not easily distinguish between languages. Often they treat all words they have learned in both languages as part of the same mental dictionary. Evidence of this may be found in young bilingual preschoolers' common practice of inserting words of one language into sentences spoken in another. For example, a 5-year-old who speaks both Swedish and English says "en block" for "the block" or "Ar det ducks?" for "Is that ducks?" (Arnberg, 1987). These utterances show that children are not clearly discerning which words go with which language.

Another sign that younger bilingual preschoolers generate one big mental dictionary is that they use words of either one language or another, but rarely both, to name certain items or activities (Saunders, 1988). For example, children who speak both Spanish and English may use "gato" for "cat," since they have a cat in their Spanish-dominant home, but use "mouse" rather than "raton" to refer to a pet in their English-dominant classroom.

When assessing very young bilingual children's semantic development, it is very important to test competence in both languages. When making a tally of the number of words a child uses, words from both languages must be counted. Tests in which children name pictures or objects are only valid if children are allowed to respond in either language. Otherwise, the assessment will not provide a full picture of a child's vocabulary (Arnberg, 1987).

One of the most important advancements in preschool bilingual development is discovering the distinction between words of different languages (Warren-Leubecker & Bohannon, 1989). By age 5, children recognize that the words used in one language are somehow different from those in another. They rely on concrete cues in the environment to assist them in making these early distinctions. They notice, for example, that peers or non-family adults may not understand certain words which they speak. They may observe that certain words are spoken in the home but never in child care or kindergarten. In fact, they may experience a "language shock" in which they speak in the "wrong language at the wrong time" at school and are derided or ignored (Arnberg, 1987). Over time, they may begin to speak the words of just the dominant language in school and words of their family's language only at home.

It is not until the later preschool years—when children begin to understand their bilingualism—that they show a desire to learn words for new objects or ideas in both languages (Saunders, 1988). At this point, interesting inquiries arise in the home or classroom:

Molly, a 5-year-old English-speaking child, is taking a walk with her bilingual class and teacher. A large bird flutters up.

MOLLY:	What's that?
TEACHER:	(Laughs) You know what that is, I think.
MOLLY:	(Shakes her head "no")
TEACHER:	That's a bird. You know birds, right?
MOLLY:	(Shows an annoyed expression) No, silly. I know birds. What is it in Wilson's language? (Wilson is a Spanish-speaking peer in her class)

Older bilingual preschoolers also begin to test out the impact of different words for the same object. They may say a word in one language and, if the response is not adequate, say the word in the second language. One child was found to ask for treats or toys in one language, and, when his parents did not comply, to make the request again in the second (Saunders, 1988). Sadly for him, his parents caught on to the scheme and persisted in saying no!

The kinds of words spoken in a particular language are determined by culture. Values, customs, and even climate determine which words are important in a particular cultural group (Bryen, 1986). For example, the Eskimo language has 40 different words to represent the various states of snow (Dale, 1976). Since English is a noun-dominant language, it contains many labels for things (Fernald & Morikawa, 1993).

Some speculate that this is because English-speaking societies are object-oriented (Gopnik & Choi, 1990). In contrast, Korean and Chinese languages have fewer nouns; these societies are believed to be more people-oriented.

Children of one culture who are trying to learn the words of another are faced with many challenges. Some words in the second language may have no equivalent in their own. Words that hold important cultural meaning for children may not even exist in another language. The following story shows how even the differences in the semantics of two distinct forms of English can create challenges:

A readiness test is being administered to a group of African-American kindergarten children living in an urban southern neighborhood. The teacher has come to the language section of the test that requires him to read words and ask his students to put an "X" on corresponding pictures in the test booklet.

The teacher comes to the word "toboggan," for which children are expected to place a mark on a sled shown in the picture. An uproar occurs, however. A young spokesman for the group complains, "There ain't no toboggan here!" Almost all other children agree. The testing session collapses into chaos.

It turns out that in this school and neighborhood, a "toboggan" is a ski cap worn by older males. It is an important part of self-expression on the street. Using "toboggan" to mean a sled makes no sense to these kindergartners.

Syntax

Syntax refers to the rules that govern the formation of sentences. Children's sentences grow longer during the preschool years. There are several reasons for this. Unlike toddlers, who speak in short, telegraphic utterances, preschoolers use full sentences. The child who said "Move chair" at age 2 now says "I moved the chair" at age 5. All the parts of speech are now present: the agent ("I"), the action ("moved"), and the object ("chair"). In addition, new features emerge. The child begins to use **morphemes**—small words or parts of words that hold meaning. Morphemes include endings such as the past tense -*ed* or the plural -*s,* and articles such as "a" and "the." Most of the important English morphemes are learned by age 4 and are acquired in a surprisingly fixed order (Tager-Flusberg, 1989). A few of these morphemes, and the ages at which they are typically acquired, are listed in Table 12-3.

Another reason why preschoolers' utterances become longer is that they acquire rules for creating negatives, questions, and compound sentences (Bloom, 1993). The following examples show these advances. In what ways are the 5-year-old's utterances more complex than those of the 2-year-old?

2-year-old: No bite.
5-year-old: Don't bite me.

2-year-old: Mommy go?
5-year-old: Where did Mommy go?

2-year-old: Ball gone. Flush it down.
5-year-old: The ball is gone, because I flushed it and it went down the toilet.

Most psycholinguists believe that by age 5, children have learned almost all the rules of adult syntax (Fenson et al., 1994).

TABLE 12-3
Some Grammatical Morphemes and Typical Age of Their Acquisition

Morpheme	Example	Age
ing	"See Daddy throw*ing*."	22 to 34 months
in	"Doggie *in* box."	22 to 34 months
on	"Baby *on* chair."	22 to 34 months
Plural -*s*	"My book*s*."	22 to 34 months
Past irregular	"Mommy *went*."	24 to 38 months
's	"Baby*'s* cup."	24 to 36 months
a, the	"Throw *the* ball."	26 to 42 months
Past regular: -*ed*	"Mommy *goed*."	26 to 42 months
Third-person regular: -*s*	"The doggie walk*s* fast."	26 to 42 months
Contractions: *'s, 'm, 're, 've, 'd*	"I*'ve* played that already."	28 to 48 months

SOURCE: R. Brown, 1973.

Typical and Atypical Syntactic Development. In some cases, preschool children do not construct sentences in the ways described above. Morphemes may be acquired more slowly; clauses, negatives, and questions may not be used. These difficulties are more frequent in children with mental retardation (McLeavy, Toomey, & Dempsey, 1982), general language delays (Connell, 1987), and hearing impairment (Shames & Wig, 1986). Challenging conditions lead not only to delays in syntax, but also to faulty sentence structures. The following utterances of deaf children, for example, show that syntactic development is not just slowed but disrupted by hearing impairment (Quigley, Power, & Steinkamp, 1977):

Who TV watched?

Tom has pushing the wagon.

John goes to fishing.

Special intervention is likely to be recommended for children who use such atypical sentences.

Syntax and Second-Language Acquisition. Different languages have different structures. One of the most challenging tasks of second-language acquisition is to understand the syntactic differences between two language systems. Some languages are extremely dissimilar in syntax. For example, the Japanese and Korean languages contain no articles, so children speaking these languages have special difficulty learning English, with its preponderance of articles. In Spanish, adjectives follow nouns, so Spanish-speaking children are likely to struggle with English phrases such as "the green crayon." "Crayon green" would make more sense to them.

When children are confronted with two or more distinct syntactic structures, they seek creative solutions to the problem. A common strategy is to learn and use the syntax of just one language—usually the one spoken most often in the home—and apply this structure to any language they speak. For example, children who speak both Spanish and English regularly use Spanish sentence structure when they talk in English (Hakuta, 1986). Since all nouns are preceded by articles in Spanish, they may use these unnecessarily when forming English sentences: "I am going to the school" instead of "I am going to school." Since "no" is the only word used in Spanish to express negation, sentences such as "He no see nothing" are common.

Black English Vernacular also has a different syntax than standard English (e.g., "My sister, she pretty," "He be runnin' home from school," or "He don't like nobody"). Each of these utterances conforms to language rules that children acquire as they interact with family members and peers. These sentences are syntactically correct for these children. Children who speak BEV can, of course, learn standard English syntax. A goal in many preschools and kindergartens is to help children learn standard English as a second language. Most psycholinguists recommend an "additive" rather than "subtractive" approach to language education, in which children add new syntactic rules without giving up their own culture's dialect (D. L. Soto, 1991).

Pragmatics

Children learn language so that they can communicate needs, feelings, and intentions, and thus become active members of a family, peer group, and society. Language is not learned by young children as a set of abstract rules, but as a social and communicative tool to enhance their effectiveness in groups. The most significant language advancement in the preschool years is an ability to use words and sentences to influence other people. The ability to use language socially is called **pragmatics.** Young children gradually discover the power of language. They come to realize that by phrasing requests just so, they can convince parents to delay a bedtime or give a treat. They learn that, with just the right intonation and sentence structure, they can persuade peers to give them toys or grant them entry into play groups. The following vignette (Trawick-Smith, 1992) shows how a slight change in phrasing and intonation accomplishes a play goal for one preschool child:

> A child is engaged in a make-believe conversation on a toy telephone in the dramatic play center of a kindergarten. Another child tries to get the phone away from her.
>
> AIDA: (In an alarmed tone) Cheryl, give me the phone! I have to call the police!
>
> CHERYL: (Gripping the phone defensively and speaking in an annoyed tone) No, Aida! I'm using it!
>
> AIDA: (In an angry voice, tugging on the phone) Come on, Cheryl!
>
> CHERYL: (Pulling the phone away) No!
>
> AIDA: (Pauses a moment, alters her entire demeanor, and speaks in a gentle tone) Cheryl, let's say this is our phone, okay?
>
> CHERYL: (Looks confused. Says nothing.)
>
> AIDA: Alright? This is our phone, okay?
>
> CHERYL: (In a tentative voice) Okay.
>
> AIDA: (Pauses again) And Cheryl, let's say we call the police now on our phone, okay?
>
> CHERYL: Okay. (Hands the phone to Aida)

TABLE 12-4
Some Social Rules of Language in Euro-American Cultures

Rule	Description
Politeness	The speaker listens, responds to questions, and does not make unfriendly demands when talking. *Example:* When speaking to a teacher, a child might request, "Can I have more paint?" rather than demand, "Give me more paint."
Speaking so the listener understands	The speaker adjusts language to the point of view of the listener. The details of the message are clearly spelled out. *Example:* "The bus driver came to my house" instead of "He came over."
Turntaking	The speaker takes a turn talking, then allows the listener to respond. *Example:* "Do you know what?" is followed by a pause for a response.
Talkativeness	The speaker must use just the right amount of language and avoid uncomfortable silences.
Position/Body language	The speaker smiles, establishes eye contact, and maintains a comfortable physical distance from the listener.

Aida has clearly learned the power of language. She uses subtle alterations in intonation and sentence structure to get what she wants from a peer. Note how she changes her request from "*I* have to call the police" to "let's say *we* call the police."

Each culture has rules for the social uses of language. Many of these rules are acquired during the preschool years. Several that are found in Euro-American cultures are presented Table 12-4. In the following sections we will describe some of these rules.

Politeness. A range of politeness rules exists in many Euro-American families (Warren-Leubecker & Tate, 1986), including the following:

- Don't impose
- Be friendly
- Give listeners a turn
- Request, don't demand
- Answer questions when asked

Children in the preschool years not only learn these rules, they apply them most often when conversing with adults or older peers who have higher social status. They are less likely to be polite when speaking with same-age peers, and rarely follow the rules of politeness with younger children (Warren-Leubecker & Tate, 1986). Preschoolers are already tailoring their pragmatic strategies to the social status of listeners.

Speaking So the Listener Understands. Another social rule is that speech must be adapted to match the abilities, interests, and needs of the listener. In the very early years, children often talk *at* one another, not caring whether their messages are getting through. Piaget (1954) referred to such conversations as "collective mono-logues." The following is an example:

JACOB: (Drawing at the art center) I'm making a huge red plane.
HOUDA: (Also drawing, interrupts Jacob) The house is burning up and the people have to get out.
JACOB: Wanna see it? (Shows drawing to Houda)
HOUDA: Get out now everyone!

In this interaction, no effort is made to adapt language to the viewpoint of the listener. Neither child, in fact, pays much attention to or tries to capture the interest of the other during the conversation. During the preschool years, children acquire more **socialized speech** in which they begin to adjust their language to the listener's perspective and level of cognitive ability (Warren-Leubecker & Tate, 1986). They may use simplified language and give more detail when talking to younger children than when talking to older peers or adults (Bloom, 1993).

However, even older preschoolers have much to learn about listeners' perspectives. In one fascinating study, children were videotaped talking to relatives on the telephone and in person (Warren-Leubecker & Tate, 1986). On the phone, they were found to use gestures and refer to things that only they could see (e.g., "Look at this, Grandma"). These behaviors indicate that they were still unable to completely adapt their communications to the perspectives of their listeners.

Turntaking. Turntaking is another basic rule of social language observed in many Euro-American families. In a typical conversation, one speaker talks, then another. In the collective monologues presented earlier, turntaking rules are not in evidence. A number of naturalistic studies of children's play show, however, that turntaking can occur in some conversations in the early years. In a classic study, Garvey and Hogan (1973) found that preschoolers at play engaged in joint conversations 66% of the time. These subjects also responded appropriately to 59% of their peers' comments. Among 5-year-olds, long turntaking chains were discovered: one child would speak, another would answer, the original speaker would respond to that comment, and so on. Such research suggests, then, that children make huge strides in the early years in learning the turntaking rule—especially when they are playing.

Pragmatics and Children With Special Needs. Children who have language delays can still be quite effective in their social communication. For example, research has shown that children with mental retardation—even those who show significant delays in language itself—can still communicate very well with peers and adults (Abbeduto & Rosenberg, 1987). A 5-year-old who is delayed in vocabulary or syntax might still effectively communicate needs, express play ideas, and share humor. Such children often learn turntaking, politeness, and listener-perspective rules at the same age as typically developing children (Ratner, 1989).

Hearing Impairment and Pragmatics. Hearing-impaired children are at risk of poor pragmatics development. Obviously, problems for children with this challenging condition are inattention and an inability to respond to others' initiatives (Shames & Wig, 1986). A peer's invitation to play might go unnoticed, or a teacher's or parent's question may be unheard. Research suggests that some hearing-impaired children who

Hearing-impaired children who learn a manual sign language can interact more effectively in classrooms. Few teachers, however, have learned such a language.

learn a manual sign language, such as American Sign Language (ASL), have richer social interactions with others than those who have not learned such a communication system (Musselman, Lindsay, & Wilson, 1988). Interactions using ASL may have many of the same social features as oral language, such as turntaking and politeness.

The caveat, of course, is that children with hearing impairments must communicate with adults and peers who also use ASL. Although a growing number of families have learned ASL, few teachers and students in preschools and child care centers do so (Quigley & Paul, 1987). Teachers should learn and use the communicative systems of the children in their classes. Hearing children will benefit from inclusion of this "second language," and children with hearing impairments will have a better chance of forming positive peer relations.

Autism and Pragmatics. **Autism** seriously threatens the development of pragmatics. Young children with autistic characteristics are often unresponsive and avoid eye contact with others. They sometimes engage in **echolalia,** a meaningless repetition of others' speech. In almost half of all identified cases, autistic children do not speak at all (Rutter & Schopler, 1987). A number of interventions have shown limited success. Games in which children with autism must seek help from others appear to enhance social language (A. Miller & Miller, 1973). Strategies in which adults encourage—rather than discourage—atypical verbalizations such as echolalia are recommended (Prizant & Duchan, 1981). It is believed that such verbalizations, no matter how ineffective, are important efforts to communicate and therefore should be reinforced. It is important to note that autistic characteristics vary in extremity; many children manifesting these traits can be integrated socially with other children simply by following sound teaching practice.

Pragmatics and Culture. Most research on pragmatics has been conducted with monolingual Euro-American children. Therefore, the rules of language that we have discussed are common in Euro-American families but not necessarily in other cultural groups. Each culture has its own set of rules about how to communicate with others. Professionals who work with young children should recognize and appreciate diversity in pragmatics.

Turntaking Versus Collective Conversation. Many Euro-American families engage in very orderly conversations that involve turntaking: one speaker takes a turn, then another, and so on (J. C. Condon & Yousef, 1975). Some child development researchers have come to view this style of communication as the norm. In fact, children who are unable to wait for their turn to speak are sometimes considered "deficient" in their ability to communicate. Such children are often considered self-centered or lacking impulse control.

Studies of cross-cultural communication patterns reveal that in some families it is the norm for all persons to speak at once. In many African-American, Puerto Rican, and Jewish families, for example, much discourse involves spontaneous and simultaneous talk (Farber, Mindel, & Lazerwitz, 1988; Hale-Benson, 1986; Slonim, 1991). Waiting for a turn, in fact, might result in exclusion altogether from the discussion. It is no wonder that some children have trouble adapting to the typical hand-raising or turntaking routines of American classrooms.

Amount of Language Used. Some cultures are less verbal than others. In fact, in some families it is a social rule of communication that children use few words or remain silent, particularly in the presence of higher-status group members. Mexican-American families are more likely to emphasize physical cues and touch in communication. Western Apache families also have been found to be quieter. This style has led unenlightened Euro-Americans to conclude that Native American children are "strange or rude" (Menyuk & Menyuk, 1988, p. 155). Many Euro-Americans, in contrast, are quite talkative. Care must be taken not to assume that the style of the dominant culture is the norm or the only "correct" way for all children to communicate.

Silence in conversation means different things in different cultures, as the following vignette illustrates:

Two children—Maura, a Euro-American, and Ding Fang, a Chinese American—have just gotten into a disagreement over a toy car in the block area. A teacher, Ms. Miller, intervenes:

MS. MILLER: What's going on over here? It seems like you two are having an argument.

DING FANG: (Looks down, says nothing)

MAURA: (In an angry tone) She took my car. (Now shouting at her peer) I was playing with that, you know!

DING FANG: (Says nothing, does not establish eye contact)

MS. MILLER: Is that right, Ding Fang? Did you take Maura's car?

DING FANG: (Remains silent)

MS. MILLER: Ding Fang? Can you tell me what happened?

DING FANG: (Still silent)

MS. MILLER: Well, you don't seem to want to talk about it. Why don't we come out of the blocks now and do something else. We'll let Maura play here alone.

Ms. Miller has misread the meaning of silence. She assumes that the Chinese-American child is either unwilling to cooperate in solving the conflict or does not care how the matter is settled. She does not understand that in Chinese-American culture, silence is often used to avoid threatening situations or severe conflict. It is likely that this child is, in fact, very troubled about the incident, but is communicating upset in a manner unique to her culture. Ms. Miller has missed the message.

Silence has unique meaning in other cultures, as well (Menyuk & Menyuk, 1988, p. 155). Brazilians and Peruvians, for example, often use silence as a means of greeting guests. Such a welcome might be construed as impolite within Euro-American cultures. Arabs use silence to achieve privacy. For example, an Arab preschooler in a child care center might stop talking as a way of saying "I need to be alone now." Some Euro-Americans, in contrast, are uncomfortable with silence and feel they need to fill in the gaps in conversation (Irujo, 1988).

Body Language. **Body language** is an important component of communication. Misreading the gestures, expressions, or postures of those of other cultures can lead to irritation and discomfort (Ramsey, 1987). Avoiding eye contact is a good example. In some cultures, looking a speaker straight in the eye shows interest and attention. In other cultures, eye contact with people in positions of authority is interpreted as a sign of disrespect. In some African-American, Puerto Rican, or Mexican-American families, for example, children do not look adults directly in the eye, particularly when they are being reprimanded. This is in sharp contrast to some Euro-American families, who view eye contact as evidence that one is listening. More than one Euro-American teacher has been heard getting a child's attention with the imperative, "Look right at me so I can tell that you're paying attention." In some cultures, a "peripheral gaze" is common during conversation. In others, interaction is simply not possible without direct and continuous eye contact (Irujo, 1988).

Smiling is another method of physical communication that varies in social meaning across cultures. Although smiling appears to be a universal expression of positive affect (Eibl-Eibesfeldt, 1979), in some cultures it can mean other things, as well (Irujo, 1988). In the following story, a kindergarten teacher discovers one meaning of a smile for a Japanese-American child:

> During group time, a teacher conducts a discussion of families. Children are taking turns describing their family members. One child has just commented that his grandmother lives with him. The teacher now asks a question of Takie, a Japanese-American child who has been very quiet:
>
> TEACHER: Takie, I believe you live with your grandmother, too.
>
> TAKIE: (Smiles broadly, says nothing)
>
> TEACHER: I can tell by your smile that your grandmother is very special. Can you tell us about her?
>
> TAKIE: (Continues to smile. Tears form in her eyes)
>
> TEACHER: (Sensing that something is wrong) Oh . . . why don't you come sit right here with me.
>
> TAKIE: (Continues smiling and wipes her eyes. Moves over and sits in the teacher's lap.)

The teacher continues the group discussion. Later, she shares the incident with Takie's father. He informs her that Takie's grandmother has just died.

Initially this teacher misread the child's smile as a sign that she was happy and enthused about the group discussion. She quickly discovered, however, that her interpretation was incorrect. This teacher has learned through real experience that some Japanese-American families use a smile to conceal embarrassment, sorrow, and anger (Eckman, 1972).

Cultures also have different rules about the amount of touching that is comfortable or appropriate in communication. In Euro-American and British families, touching is less frequent than in many other cultures. Japanese Americans are even less likely to touch one another, particularly when interacting with members of the opposite sex (Irujo, 1988). In contrast, Puerto Ricans and African Americans are generally more likely to touch one another in their interactions (Hale-Benson, 1986; Slonim, 1991).

Another component of body language is the use of personal space—the distance one speaker stands from another while conversing. Euro-Americans tend to keep a greater distance between themselves and others during interactions, especially when speaking to people with whom they are not well acquainted. African Americans and Puerto Ricans are more likely to stand close to conversation partners. In these groups, the standard conversing distance is the distance for intimate conversation among Euro-Americans. Such differences in the use of personal space have led some Euro-Americans to describe those of other cultures as "too close, too pushy" (Irujo, 1988, p. 144).

LITERACY DEVELOPMENT

Some preschoolers read and write very early. They do not do so in the same way as adults, however. In fact, it is sometimes quite difficult to recognize young children's literacy in the home or classroom. A careful observation in a typical child care center or preschool will reveal that a portion of young children are quite active in writing stories, signs, or labels. Some demonstrate an inventive form of reading. The following story shows how these competencies can, at times, surprise and challenge adults:

CHILD: (Holding up a piece of paper with horizontal lines of scribbles written on it) Look! Read this!

TEACHER: Oh! Interesting! You've done some writing. Why don't you read it to me!

CHILD: You read it!

TEACHER: Well . . . I'd like you to read it to me.

CHILD: (In an annoyed tone) No! You read it!

TEACHER: Since this is your own story, in your own writing, I'd like you to be the one to read it.

CHILD: (Exhaling in exasperation) Alright! It says right here, "No other people allowed in the blocks."

Many very young children truly believe that they can read and write, and expect adults to be able to interpret what they have written (Pflaum, 1986). Do these literacy behaviors represent true reading and writing? Research evidence suggests that these primitive scribbles and make-believe reading acts are directly related to later literacy competence (Sulzby, 1986).

Writing Development

Children's earliest writing looks like scribbling. Samples of this early written work (created by my son when he was 4 years old) are presented in Figure 12-3. Although primitive, these marks on paper stand for ideas or even whole stories (Harste, Woodward, &

FIGURE 12-3
Children's early writing includes scribbles to represent whole stories. By the end of the preschool years, children are using conventional letters with sounds that match some of the words in their stories.

(a)

(b)

(c)

(d)

(e)

Burke, 1984). For example, writing sample A in the figure is a story about a giant who eats up little boys. Over a 2-month period, the young author read and reread the story. In each rereading, the story became more elaborate but had the same basic plot line.

Evidence suggests that these representations are very different from drawing (Harste et al., 1984). In writing sample B, one can easily distinguish between the drawing—an airplane—and the accompanying text—the scribble lines—below it. During the preschool years some children's writing comes to look more and more like adult print (Sulzby, 1986). For example, writing sample C looks very much like adult cursive. Writing sample D demonstrates that children gradually begin to incorporate letters into their early writings. It is not uncommon for early letters to be inserted without regard to the sounds they represent in conventional writing. Children often include letters from their own names to express messages or stories (Clay, 1975; Ferreiro & Teberosky, 1982).

By the end of the preschool years, some children begin to use letters that are associated with sounds in the message or story they are writing (Clay, 1975; Sulzby, 1986). Often these letters stand for whole words or syllables. The letter B might be used to represent the word "baby," for example. In writing sample E in Figure 12-3, the young author has used letters that match sounds in a sign he made for his room: "No people allowed."

Reading

Some children also begin to read very early, as the following story shows:

> A mother and her 4-year-old wait in line at a bank. As the child scans the large room filled with customers and bank employees, he spies a sign announcing the latest interest rates. He walks to the sign, runs his finger along the print, and reads loudly, so that everyone in the bank can hear, "No one is allowed to rob this bank!"

Is this real reading? Research has shown that this behavior is associated with later reading competence (Schickedanz, 1999). Children who are read to and are encouraged to interpret print on signs, cereal boxes, or magazines gradually make attempts to construct meaning from print. Preschoolers' abilities to decode printed messages improve gradually until more conventional reading emerges in the early elementary years.

Schickedanz (1999) has plotted the development of book reading among children. Her proposed stages are presented in Table 12-5. In the first stage, children do not recognize that the words of a book come from print. Young preschoolers focus on the pictures and may even think that the words originate from these. This poses interesting problems for adults who read to them. In some books, occasional pages have pictures but no text. When an adult does not read these pages, a child is likely to grow suspicious and protest, "Read it! Come on!" The child assumes that if there are pictures, there must be a story, so the adult must have some other reason for not reading. (Children learn quickly that adults will pull all kinds of tricks to shorten a story that is too long or is being read just before bedtime!)

In the next stage, children come to understand that the story comes from print (Schickedanz, 1999). They may point to the text or, in an effort at humor, hide the words with their hands so the adult cannot see them. At this stage they may recognize familiar letters: "That letter's in my name!"

TABLE 12-5

Stages of Early Shared Book Reading

Description	Example
The child believes that words of a story come from the pictures.	A child shouts, "read!" even on a page in a book which has only illustrations and no print.
The child notices print and understands that the story comes from the text.	A child says, "This letter's in my name!" or jokingly hides the print so the adult can't read.
The child learns the text of the story by heart.	A child sits and "rereads" a memorized story using the exact language and intonation of an adult reader.
The child begins to "map" the story across the print.	A child tries to find the place in the text where the memorized story is written. The child makes matches—sometimes in error—between syllables and words of the story and segments of print.

SOURCE: Schickedanz, 1982; 1999.

An important next step involves memorizing verbatim the story line of favorite books (Schickedanz, 1999). At this point, children will sit and read aloud independently with such accuracy and adult intonation that unknowing teachers or parents will think they are reading conventionally. Such "by heart" reading allows children to explore their favorite books independently and establish personal relationships with them. Once a particular book is memorized, some children will attempt to match the story line to the printed words. They will run their fingers across the text while retelling the memorized story. If the story and text don't match, they will struggle to solve the problem. Schickedanz offers an example of a child reading *Frosty the Snowman* but erroneously mapping each verbal syllable to a single letter in the title: The child points to the *F* and says "Fro," then points to the *r* and says "sty," and so on. A problem arises when there is a letter *y* left over at the end of this. The child exclaims, "This book's not working right!" (1999, p. 72).

In the final stage of Schickedanz's (1982) profile of early readers, children accurately map the story over the print. Some children will begin to read conventionally at this point, she contends, with very little direct reading instruction.

Cultural Variations in Emergent Literacy

Much of the research done on **emergent literacy** has been conducted with white middle-class children (Schickedanz, 1999). However, not all preschoolers arrive in child care or Head Start with the same knowledge of print. Reading and writing mean different things in different cultures, so children of some cultural groups cannot be expected to conform to profiles drawn from studies of middle-class Euro-Americans.

In a few cultures, children never learn to read and write (UNICEF, 1990). In most families, children do acquire literacy, but reading and writing may be more or less emphasized depending on values and traditions. In traditional African-American families, storytelling is emphasized; parents more often tell stories than read them to their children (Hale, 1994; Heath, 1983). Children's ability to tell meaningful and entertaining stories may be more highly valued than reading competence within these families. In some Native American communities, other forms of expression are emphasized. Ceremonies, art, dance, and story-like lessons that preserve the history and values of the culture are the primary modes of communication.

In some societies, writing is common but the writing implements used are very different from those found in traditional American classrooms. Yup'ik Eskimo children practice "storyknifing," in which a storyteller relates traditional tales or oral family histories while simultaneously carving symbols or pictures in the mud with a knife. Preschool-age children watch, listen, and learn the symbol systems their older peers and siblings use. These early observations of storyknifing are believed to support later formal literacy in school (deMarrais, Nelson, & Baker, 1994).

ASSESSING YOUNG CHILDREN: Preschool Language and Literacy Development

Areas of Development	What to Watch for	Indicators of Atypical Development
Oral language abilities	Accurately utters speech sounds that are typically acquired by the child's age. Articulates clearly enough to be understood by peers. Uses a varied vocabulary to communicate. Speaks in sentences of 4 or 5 words by age 5. Uses morphemes, such as *ing* or plural *s* by, age 4. Uses language in socially appropriate ways.	Poor articulation of speech sounds and an inability to imitate these when presented by an adult. Limited vocabulary. Use of the word *thing* to stand for words the child cannot remember. Absence of morphemes or incorrect uses of these (e.g., "Me go . . ."). Prevalence of short one- or two-word utterances at age 4. Socially inappropriate language (e.g., talking too much).
Literacy skills	Early scribble writing by age 4. Writing part of one's name or other letter writing by age 5. By this same age, an ability to point out print and knowledge that it can stand for ideas. Having favorite books and learning to "read" some of these by heart. By age 5, trying to map memorized stories over the text of favorite books.	An inability to handle or look at books (e.g., inability to turn pages or hold the book upright). A lack of attention and positive response in shared reading with an adult. By age 5, an inability to distinguish print from pictures.

Interpreting Assessment Data: Variations in language and literacy are due to the specific languages spoken in the home and cultural differences in reading preferences. Children will differ in the speech sounds they utter and sentences they speak if they are trying to learn two languages simultaneously. They may learn words and morphemes more slowly if English is not the preferred language of their family. They may be less attentive to children's books and may write less if these are not a regular part of their family life. However, if children cannot communicate verbally with peers or teachers, referral to a speech and language pathologist is recommended. In-class interventions to enhance phonology, grammar, or vocabulary may ameliorate speech deficits. Reading to children in the home or classroom may also address language and literacy problems.

What children read varies across cultures. Some spend more time looking at magazines, catalogs, or other factual, non-narrative texts. Parents interact with their preschoolers in educational ways as they read these materials, much as Euro-American parents do when reading traditional picture books (Pellegrini, Perlmutter, Galda, & Brody, 1990).

There are three interrelated implications of cross-cultural literacy research for teachers:

1. Children and families will come to school with unique and varied attitudes, values, and experiences concerning literacy.
2. Classroom opportunities must be provided for children to express ideas or tell stories using non-print media which are valued within their own cultures.
3. All types of reading material—including non-literature text found in letters, fliers, magazines, and mail-order catalogs—must be included in a culturally sensitive classroom literacy program.

RESEARCH INTO PRACTICE

CRITICAL CONCEPT 1

A major advancement in the preschool years is the acquisition of symbolic thought—a type of thinking in which symbols or internal images are used to represent objects, persons, and events that are not present. Examples of symbolic thought are pretend play, drawing, writing, and speaking.

Application #1

Teachers and caregivers should create classrooms that are rich with symbols. Children should hear much language from both peers and adults and should see print throughout the environment. They should be exposed to the expressive media—art, music, storytelling, literature, and drama—of their own cultures.

Application #2

Preschool children should be given many opportunities to express themselves symbolically. Art, drawing, and writing experiences and musical and dramatic activities will enhance their symbolic thinking.

CRITICAL CONCEPT 2

Symbolic thought is prevalent in the play of young children. When preschoolers engage in sociodramatic play—the imaginative enactment of make-believe roles—much symbolizing can be observed. Children use objects to stand for things that are completely different, and they transform themselves into pretend characters.

Application #1

Teachers and caregivers should create dramatic play centers in the classroom to encourage children to pretend. Such centers should include realistic play props related to home themes or topics in the curriculum. For example, if children are studying transportation, a make-believe boat or airport can be created to encourage curriculum-relevant play.

Application #2

The dramatic play area should also contain non-realistic raw materials, such as wooden rods, boxes, and rubber forms. These materials allow children to use objects to stand for things that are completely different. Such transformations require "symbolic leaps." Transforming a rod into a broom, for example, requires more complex symbolization than using a toy broom as a real one.

Application #3

Teachers and caregivers can intervene in children's play to promote greater symbolization. Encouraging children to take on diverse and highly imaginative roles, to transform objects, and to invent make-believe situations will enhance symbolic thought.

CRITICAL CONCEPT 3

Play differs across cultures. Traditional measures of sociodramatic play may not fully capture the symbolic quality of childhood activities in all families. An example found in many cultural groups is play-work, in which children perform household chores but do so in make-believe ways.

Application #1

Teachers and caregivers should understand and appreciate cultural diversity in play. They should be cautious not to infer play deficits when some children do not appear to engage in make-believe. Careful observation may reveal pretend elements in children's work, storytelling, singing, or other non-play activities.

Application #2

Culturally sensitive dramatic play centers should be created. Dolls representing diverse races should be provided. Thematic centers that reflect distinct cultural experiences might be developed. As examples, a teacher in California designed a Chinese grocery store in her dramatic play area; a caregiver on a reservation created an apartment with food boxes and toy foods reflecting Navajo cuisine; a teacher in Chicago developed two separate apartments in the dramatic play area to replicate a multifamily dwelling. Centers such as these allow children to play out themes related to their own families and communities.

CRITICAL CONCEPT 4

Language advances rapidly during the preschool years. Four interrelated areas of language increase in complexity: phonology, or speech sounds; semantics, or word meanings; syntax, or sentence construction; and pragmatics, or social uses of language.

Application #1

Parents, teachers, and caregivers should provide language-rich environments for young children. Preschool and kindergarten classrooms should be filled with conversation, both among children and with adults. Authentic dialogue, in which children can express ideas of interest to them, will enhance language learning more than artificial language lessons that hold little meaning to children.

Application #2

Teachers and caregivers should evaluate children's language across all four areas of development. They should understand and appreciate typical communication "errors" that are common and necessary in language development. They must also note difficulties that require special services. Children with extensive articulation errors or disfluency, those who have difficulty learning or retrieving words, and those who do not speak in full sentences may require intervention. Most important, children who cannot communicate effectively with peers or adults may need special support.

CRITICAL CONCEPT 5

Bilingual children follow a distinct path in learning language. They acquire unique phonology, semantics, and syntax that include elements of both languages they are learning. These unique language features are logical and rule-governed. Children of diverse cultural backgrounds vary in pragmatics; social rules of communication will differ from one family or community to another.

Application #1

Teachers and caregivers must understand and appreciate the unique language patterns of bilingual children. They must recognize the distinct forms of English that are spoken by children whose preferred languages are, for example, Spanish, Black English Vernacular, or Japanese. Care must be taken not to interpret diverse language patterns as deficits.

Application #2

Bilingual preschool and kindergarten programs are ideal for language development of all children. Two-way programs, in which both the language of the dominant culture and a second language are used in the classroom, will enhance the communicative competence of all students.

Application #3

English-only teachers and caregivers should make an effort to become conversant in the primary languages of all children in their classrooms. Using key phrases in a child's native language shows respect and eases the overwhelming experience of second-language learning.

CRITICAL CONCEPT 6

Many children begin to read and write in the preschool years. However, their efforts are not always recognized by adults. They write by scribbling and read by pretend book-looking. However, these early literacy experiences are the foundation of later reading and writing in school. Literacy experiences vary from one culture or family to another. Not all children come to school with a conventional knowledge of print. However, children of all cultures arrive with skill in personal expression; some families emphasize oral expression, others artistic expression.

Application #1

A writing center should be developed in preschool and kindergarten classrooms. The center should be equipped with such materials as blank books, journals, clipboards, pens and markers, movable alphabets, and a computer. Children should be urged to write in any way they wish; scribble-writing and invented spelling should be accepted and encouraged.

Application #2

Children should be read to daily. Requests to read favorite picture books again and again should be honored so that children will come to know them by heart. Books should be available for children to look at and "read" on their own throughout the day. Children should be encouraged to retell or reread their favorite books.

Application #3

Literacy experiences should be adapted to meet the needs of children of diverse cultures. Bilingual children should be encouraged to write in their preferred language, and books in their native language should be provided. Reading materials should match the family life experiences of all children; non-book reading materials such as magazines, catalogs, and signs should be included. Opportunities for all types of personal expression, including storytelling, drama, and music, should be incorporated.

SUGGESTED ACTIVITIES

1. Observe a preschool classroom in which children of diverse cultural backgrounds are enrolled. Take notes on any sociodramatic play episodes you see, based on descriptions in this chapter. Later, write a report describing this form of play, guided by the following questions:

   a. What kinds of make-believe did you see (e.g., pretend use of objects, role playing, make-believe situations)? Give at least three examples from your observations.

   b. How would you characterize the social interactions you observed during sociodramatic play episodes? Give examples from your observations.

   c. Describe the language you heard during sociodramatic play episodes. Did children assume adult-like intonations and sentences? Did they use pretend voices? How much verbalization occurred?

   d. How did boys and girls differ in their play themes and roles? Did children of different cultural backgrounds play in different ways?

2. Observe a preschool classroom in which children with special needs are enrolled. Select a child who has a challenging condition. Take notes on any socio-

   dramatic play episodes you see the child perform. Later, write a report on your observations, guided by the following questions:

   a. To what degree did the child engage in sociodramatic play? Do you believe the amount of play was related to the child's disability?

   b. How was this child's play alike or different from that of other children? Did the child interact as much with peers? Use as much language? Pretend as much? What other similarities or differences did you notice?

3. Record a 20-minute language sample of an individual preschool child, following these steps:

   a. Have a teacher or parent help you select an interesting subject for your tape. This might be a child with atypical language development, a child who speaks two languages, or a very talkative child who will provide a wealth of verbalizations to analyze.

   b. Find a quiet place to tape. Provide the child with interesting play materials, such as clay, toy figures, or a set of interesting pictures to look at. Engage the child in open-ended conversation.

c. Ask questions to elicit much natural language.

Later, write an analysis of your tape. Discuss how well this child is able to communicate. Comment on any challenges or obstacles the child faces to expressing ideas. Is the child difficult to understand? Is the child's vocabulary limited? Are his or her sentences incomplete? Can the child use language in socially effective ways?

4. Using the tape recorded in activity 3, analyze your subject's phonology. Listen carefully for speech and other sounds. Write an analysis of this area of the child's language, guided by the following questions:

   a. Identify three different "errors" in speech sounds that the child makes. For example, name specific letter substitutions, such as *w* for *r*. Are these errors typical for a child this age, based on the information in the chapter? Are the substitutions regular and understandable?

   b. Do you notice any disfluencies in the child's speech? If so, are they typical for this age, based on the chapter information?

5. Using the tape recorded in activity 3, analyze your subject's semantics. Listen carefully to words the child uses. Write an analysis of this area of the child's language, guided by the following questions:

   a. Does the child appear to have an extensive vocabulary? A limited one? Why do you think so? (Be certain to consider vocabulary in all languages the child speaks!)

   b. Did certain words that the child used impress you? Did the child use any relational words, such as "inside," "outside," "in," "on," and "over"?

   c. Did the child use any words differently from the way adults use them? Did you hear any overgeneralizations, as described in the chapter?

6. Using the tape recorded in activity 3, analyze your subject's syntax. Listen carefully to sentences the child uses. Write an analysis of this area of the child's language, guided by the following questions:

   a. Did the child form questions well? Did the child use negatives? Did he or she form compound sentences? Did you hear any errors in sentence construction? Give examples.

   b. What grammatical morphemes did you hear? (Examples are given in the chapter.)

7. Using the tape recorded in activity 3, analyze your subject's pragmatics. Listen carefully to how effectively the child uses social language. Write an analysis of this area of the child's language, guided by the following questions:

   a. Could the child communicate well with you?

   b. Did the child engage in turntaking in conversation? Did he or she demonstrate politeness in talk? Answer all questions?

   c. To what degree did the child persuade, disagree, explain, or initiate conversations using language? What other social uses of language did you hear?

8. Sit with a child and read a favorite picture book. Note what the child does as you read. Then ask the child to read the book to you. Note what the child does. Later, write a report on the experience, based on the following questions:

   a. Did the child turn pages or in other ways show knowledge of how books work?

   b. Did the child point to print or in other ways show knowledge that the story comes from the text?

   c. Was the child able to "read" the book to you? Did the child read the story "by heart"? How accurately did the child retell/read the story?

9. Interview the parents of two children from distinct cultural backgrounds. Ask questions about literacy in the home. Ask the parents what they read to their children, how often, and in what manner. Ask about their children's reading preferences. Ask whether their children write at home. Inquire about the parents' beliefs concerning the teaching of reading and writing: Should parents try to teach preschoolers to write and read? Write a report of your interview, guided by these questions:

   a. What were significant similarities and differences in the literacy experiences of the two families?

   b. What differences or similarities did you note in attitudes or beliefs about reading and writing and the role of parents in teaching these skills?

   c. To what extent do you attribute differences in the perspectives of these parents to culture?

CHAPTER 13

Social and Emotional Development of Preschoolers

IN THIS CHAPTER WE WILL DISCUSS THE SOCIAL AND EMOTIONAL GROWTH OF CHILDREN BETWEEN THE AGES OF 2 AND 5. During the preschool years, many children become quite self-assured, independent, and social. They acquire the desire and ability to interact with adults and other children. They can persuade peers, gain admission into games or play activities already in progress, and resolve conflicts. Children with social skills are often better liked and have more friends. Such positive peer relationships have been found to predict long-range positive social development and mental health. In fact, having friends and being liked by other children in preschool may be more powerful predictors of later adult happiness than grades in school or scores on achievement tests (Parker, Rubin, Price, & DeRosier, 1995).

Even very young preschoolers display savvy techniques for influencing peers, as the following vignette shows:

> Jason, a 2-year-old, watches as Brendan, also 2, plays with a toy car in the block area of his child care center. He says nothing, but displays an expression of great interest. He seems to say with his eyes, "I want to play with that car. Now, how am I going to get it?" He decides on a very sophisticated approach to obtain the desired toy.
>
> He looks around the play center and spies a smaller, less intricate toy vehicle. He picks this up and offers it to Brendan: "Here. You have this. You have it." As he says this, he holds the toy out toward his peer. Brendan hesitates, then drops the coveted car and accepts Jason's gift. In an instant, Jason seizes the desired toy and pretends to drive it along the floor.

Jason's behaviors demonstrate tremendous social ability and knowledge. Earlier in life he might have resorted to primitive object-attainment strategies common in toddlerhood, such as snatching the toy and running off, or screaming "Give me it! Mine!" Now the child tries a less physical, more social approach. He speculates on what might motivate Brendan to give up the toy—another car. Then, with artfully crafted behaviors and language, he offers it to his peer. The roots of negotiation and compromise can be observed in this simple behavior.

As children get older, their efforts to persuade peers become more savvy and highly linguistic. The following story illustrates a 4-year-old's effort to obtain a needed toy:

Lauren is building with blocks. She discovers that she needs a long block, but Hanna is using all of these. She asks in a friendly voice, "Hanna, can I have one of the long blocks?" Hanna doesn't even bother to look up from her work. "No," she says in an annoyed tone. Lauren pauses, appearing to be studying the situation and thinking through the possible solutions to the problem.

"If you give me a long block, you can be in my club," Lauren says at last. Suddenly, Hanna is quite interested; she looks up from her block-building and asks, "What?"

"Give me long blocks and you can be in my club," Lauren repeats. Hanna smiles. "Okay. You can have them all," she says, pushing her entire pile of blocks over to Lauren.

Realizing that her strategy has paid off, Lauren decides to use it again and again. By the end of the morning, every child in the class is vying for membership in her club!

Lauren has developed a sophisticated—if somewhat manipulative—strategy for getting what she needs. She uses both language and knowledge of peer motivations. For example, she shows that she understands the growing need among her age-mates for peer acceptance and group membership.

This chapter describes these and other social behaviors that emerge during the preschool years. It highlights the emotional characteristics of the preschooler and shows how these enhance—or detract from—human relationships.

EMOTIONAL GROWTH IN THE PRESCHOOL YEARS

Early childhood is a crucial period for the formation of positive feelings toward oneself, others, and the larger world. Children who are nurtured, encouraged, and accepted by adults and peers will be emotionally well adjusted. Children who are abused, neglected, or rejected can suffer social and mental health difficulties. Emotional states in early childhood have a powerful impact on social relationships. Children who are emotionally healthy are better able to enter into positive relationships with both peers and adults.

Initiative Versus Guilt

The work of Erik Erikson (1963, 1982) has long guided teachers, mental health professionals, and parents in understanding the emotional development of young children. Erikson believed that humans must develop through eight "ages" of emotional growth if they are to feel competent and self-fulfilled in their lives (see discussion in

Chapter 3). Each age is characterized by an emotional struggle between two polar internal states, one negative and one positive. During the preschool years, this struggle is between initiative and guilt. Emotionally healthy preschoolers will desire to take action and assert themselves, according to Erikson. They will wish to create, invent, pretend, take risks, and engage in lively and imaginative activities with peers. Erikson (1963) called this urge to make creative efforts *initiative*. When adults encourage such divergent activities and avoid criticism or excessive restriction, a child's sense of initiative will grow. When children are led to believe their efforts are wrong, they develop a sense of *guilt*.

This struggle between initiative and guilt explains why many preschool and kindergarten children are so energetic in pursuit of imaginative play activities. It also explains why some children come to view themselves as "bad" or "naughty." Although feelings of guilt have a positive role in development in that they lead children to assume responsibility for their own behaviors, Erikson argues that overwhelming guilt inhibits emotional growth. Children who are punished or criticized for their efforts will gradually stop trying and will construct understandings of themselves as bad people. Erikson suggests that adults can promote a sense of initiative by creating noncritical environments in which children are allowed to take risks. Encouragement of creative processes with less emphasis on finished products also will facilitate initiative.

Social Initiative

One way initiative manifests itself in the developing child is through energetic interactions with peers. Preschoolers show a growing interest in reaching out to others, making social contacts, and trying out social behaviors. The healthy preschool child, from Erikson's perspective, displays an eagerness to engage others. A child who is burdened by guilt is more hesitant in social interactions and is more likely to be rejected by peers.

Research suggests that **social initiative** is critical for positive peer relations. Children who take initiative in play are better able to sustain peer interactions (Mize & Ladd, 1990) and can more readily enter play groups (Ramsey, 1989a, 1989b). Such children are also better liked by peers and form friendships more easily (Scarlett, 1983). Erikson's interpretation of these findings would be that initiative is necessary for the formation of human relationships. At any age, making friends or becoming intimate necessitates some self-assurance and risk-taking.

Initiative and Self-Concept

Self-concept is defined as an individual's theory of self (Harter, 1990). One's self-concept includes all self-perceptions of one's own competence and characteristics, including ethnic and gender identity. Because it is a theory, it is continually modified and changed with experience. As children grow older, self-concept is refined and clarified. A person with a positive self-concept is said to be happy with or feel good about his or her self-perceptions. When children proudly announce, "Look at how high up I can climb!" or "I have a lot of friends in preschool!" they are displaying healthy views of self. Obviously, a positive self-concept is critical for happiness and fulfillment throughout life.

According to Erikson, positive self-concept is related to feelings of initiative during the preschool years. A child who makes creative efforts in play or work or who actively engages peers will feel successful. It is the process of doing or creating that is crucial; actual skills or accomplishments are less important to young children, from Erikson's viewpoint. Most children with a healthy sense of initiative will feel good about themselves. Only children whose activities are discouraged or harshly criticized by adults will suffer poor self-concept.

Erikson's views are supported by research. Preschoolers do tend to refer to concrete activities and actions—that is, initiatives—in assessing their own competence. Statements such as "I can swing pretty high" and "I can wash my own hair" reflect children's pride in their efforts (Durkin, 1995). Generally, preschool children do have positive self-concepts, as Erikson's theory would suggest. They tend to believe, for example, that they can do almost anything. In one study, even when 4-year-olds had just failed several times to complete a difficult task, they reported that they would be successful on their next try (Stipek, Recchia, & McClintic, 1992). Preschool children have been described as "exceedingly optimistic in self-ratings of their abilities and expectations for success" (Curry & Johnson, 1990, p. 69).

Erikson's explanation of these early, positive self-perceptions would be that children of this age are focusing on attempts or initiatives—that is, on the processes of playing or working—rather than on the outcomes or end products of their efforts. Preschoolers tend to base views of self on whether they try hard, have friends, and are viewed as "good" children (Stipek et al., 1992). If preschoolers make an effort, get positive responses from peers and adults, and don't break rules, they tend to believe they have been successful. How sad it is that such positive self-concepts often disappear around school age!

Social initiative appears to make a unique contribution to positive self-concept. Children who take initiative in interactions with peers and are less dependent on adults have been found to be more self-assured and confident in their abilities (Hartup, 1983; Rubin, 1980). To Erikson, such findings show that self-concept and feelings of initiative are inextricably interrelated.

Initiative and Culture

Erikson observed initiative in preschoolers around the world. Findings of several recent cross-cultural studies, however, suggest that initiative may not be universally valued. Parents in China, for example, have been found to actively socialize children to become cautious, inhibited, and self-restrained—characteristics that are contrary to Erikson's conceptions of initiative (X. Chen, Rubin, & Sun, 1992; Ho, 1986). In fact, Chinese children who are shy or reticent are called "guai," a Mandarin word meaning "well behaved" or "good." Parents' efforts to teach reticence appear to be effective: Chinese children have been found to be more reserved and cautious than those from U.S. cultures (X. Chen et al., 1992). In fact, shy Chinese children tend to be preferred as playmates by peers of their own cultural group. This finding is in sharp contrast to theory and research on shyness in American children (Rubin & Mills, 1988).

Studies of Mexican-American families also reveal that initiative is not a universally valued trait. In several studies, Mexican-American parents have been found to emphasize **affiliative obedience,** defined as a high level of obedience to elders or respected authorities and a low level of self-assertion (Holtzman, Diaz-Guerrero, & Swartz, 1975). Some Mexican-American children have been observed to be collective and dependent upon family members in solving problems and to take less individual initiative in resolving conflicts with peers (Diaz-Guerrero, 1987). Within this cultural group, such behaviors are important adaptations to conditions of hardship and oppression. They lead to mutual interdependence, or **enmeshment,** of family members, which is crucial for survival.

Diaz-Guerrero (1987) raises questions about whether initiative, self-assurance, and guilt are fundamental personality traits at all, or simply patterns of behavior that can vary among individuals depending on the situation. Is it possible, he asks, that children can display initiative in one setting and be hesitant and shy in another? He has observed that Mexican-American children show creative and self-assertive attempts in certain situations, such as when playing with peers in the absence of respected adults. They show more restrained, obedient interactions in other situations, such as during a family meal. He suggests that Mexican-American children living in the United States might be most healthy if they are able to switch between initiative and restrained obedience according to the context.

Professionals working with young children must be cautious, then, not to expect all preschool students to display the high levels of initiative that Erikson described. Children of some cultural groups may have a sense of initiative but choose not to express it fully in some settings, such as at school. Many teachers have had the experience of observing children who are reserved and timid in the classroom engaging in active, noisy social play at home or in the neighborhood.

SOCIAL COMPETENCE

The term **social competence** refers to two interrelated aspects of human development: being liked by others and having skills to interact effectively in social settings. Positive peer relationships and social skills in children during their early years are good predictors of overall happiness and mental health in later life (Hartup & Laursen, 1993; Parker et al., 1995). Children who are disliked by peers, deficient in social abilities, or aggressive and impulsive in their interactions during their preschool years are more likely to become psychologically troubled adults (Rubin, Hymel, LeMare, & Rowden, 1989).

Teachers and parents can assist children in acquiring social skills and making friends. In fact, these may be the most important goals of early childhood education. It is important to keep in mind, however, that social competence is defined differently in different cultures. The social behaviors that predict peer acceptance in one culture may not in another. An active, rough play style, for example, may lead to popularity or rejection, depending on the cultural experiences of playmates. Trying to teach all children precisely the same set of social skills, then, would be a misapplication of the social competence research.

Peer Status: Popular, Rejected, and Neglected Children

Some preschoolers have a very hard time interacting with peers, while others are quite competent at making friends and winning acceptance and respect from their playmates. Researchers regularly use the sociometric interview to assess overall social competence of preschoolers in classrooms. In this technique, children of a particular class are interviewed individually about which peers they like to play with and which they do not. Some children are named often as preferred playmates. Researchers have called these children **popular.** Others are regularly named by their peers as undesirable playmates and are considered to be **rejected.** Children in a third group—**neglected** children—are never named by peers at all (Dodge & Price, 1994). **Sociometric status** refers to the category a particular child is found to occupy in a group. What are the children of each category like? What behaviors do they display in a classroom?

Popular Children. **Popular children** are those who are well liked by peers and who have many friends. These children are named often by peers as desired playmates in sociometric interviews. Characteristics of popular children—drawn from research—are presented in Table 13-1. The table shows why popular children are so well liked. First, they are very active socially (Trawick-Smith, 1992). They often initiate contact with peers and are energetic in directing play activities. Overall, they are leaders who make many play suggestions and structure the activity of others. In the following scenario, Sheila's behaviors illustrate this active social style:

SHEILA: Now, Lauren, it's time to bathe our babies, okay? Can you come over here and help us? Let's bathe 'em 'cause they're very filthy. So let's really scrub 'em. And I'll be the mamma, you be the older sister, okay? Now you come over now, alright?

LAUREN: Alright. (Moves over to Sheila)

SHEILA: Let's say we set up for the party, okay? Some guests are coming at 5 o'clock. (Now addresses Susan) And let's say you come help too, Susan.

susan: (Says nothing, joins Sheila and Lauren)

SHEILA: Now we need to set the table. You have to put the forks just the right way. Here, I'll show you. (Demonstrates how to set the table) Now you do it, okay, Susan? Oh. There's the phone. (To Lauren) Will you answer that, honey?

TABLE 13-1
Characteristics of Popular Children

Characteristic	Description
Socially active	Takes initiative in play and makes many social contacts.
Highly directive	Takes leadership in play and directs the activities of peers.
Linguistically effective	Uses language often and competently to persuade peers or capture and maintain their attention.
Positive in affect	Engages in friendly, supportive, interactions and avoids bossing, bullying, and whining.
Diplomatic	Accepts the suggestions of peers a moderate amount of the time or rejects others' ideas by offering alternatives.
Skilled in conflict resolution	Resolves conflicts in nonaggressive ways that are satisfying to all involved.
Skilled in play group entry	Enters play groups effectively, using interesting and unobtrusive initiatives.
Competent in interpreting social situations	Accurately reads social situations and the characteristics of playmates and selects appropriate behaviors for resolving conflicts.

Sheila is exceedingly active in directing peers. Her playmates seem very pleased to be able to play with her and do as she directs—although they have trouble getting a word in edgewise!

Children who are popular are usually those who can use language effectively in social situations (Hart, Olsen, Robinson, & Mandleco, 1997). In the following vignette, Jeremy demonstrates such verbal skill in persuading a peer to help him build with blocks.

JEREMY: (Addresses nearby child in a friendly tone) Help me build my boat, Alonzo.

ALONZO: (Says nothing. Does not look up from his own blocks.)

JEREMY: (In an angry tone) Alonzo! Help me build it!

ALONZO: (Also angry) No!

JEREMY: (In a friendly tone again) Alonzo, let's say this is our boat. (Points to his block structure) Let's say we build it, alright?

ALONZO: Okay. But I'll do the long blocks. (Helps Jeremy stack blocks)

In this example, Jeremy uses subtle changes in phrasing and intonation to persuade a peer to do what he wants. When his angry demand does not work, he tries a request for joint action: "Let's say we build it, alright?" This tactic leads to success. The child appears to be experimenting with language, trying out options until arriving upon phrasing that works. Such verbal skill is common among well-liked children.

Popular children are friendly and positive in their interactions with peers. They are less aggressive or bossy (Crick, Casas, & Mosher, 1997), and often give positive feedback, attention, and affection to their classmates. Overall, they are very pleasant children to play with. Such popular children can be assertive—they are not "led about" by peers. A moderate amount of the time, they reject the play suggestions or initiatives of their playmates (Trawick-Smith, 1992). When they do reject others' ideas, however, they do so in a tactful manner. Often they will give a reason for rejecting another's idea, and may offer an alternative course of action. This diplomatic style is profiled in the following example:

JOSEPH: (Placing plastic farm animals in a block structure) I'm building a farm here. Let's say this is a farm.

CEDRIC: (Building with blocks) No, this is a museum where paintings are. See, Joseph?

JOSEPH: No! It's a farm!

CEDRIC: No, 'cause there's not enough room for a whole farm. Let's say it's a museum where farm animals can go. They can go to the museum, okay? See? (Begins placing farm animals in his structure)

JOSEPH: Okay. (Joins Cedric's play theme) But those animals might make a mess at the museum!

Here, Cedric has rejected Joseph's suggestion, but has given a reason for rejecting it and offered an alternative play theme. His rebuff of Joseph's ideas was not harsh or hostile and did not result in a disruption of the play.

Popular children are quite competent at resolving conflicts, and they often do so in friendly, non-aggressive ways (Hartup & Laursen, 1993; Trawick-Smith, 1988). They are more likely to compromise when disputes arise, as the next vignette illustrates:

Two 5-year-olds in Kenya are tending cows in a field near their home. One child invents a game to play.

ADISSU: (Grabs a handful of dirt from the ground and throws it at Nicodemu, laughing) Ha! I'll get you all dirty!

NICODEMU: No! I don't want this game.

ADISSU: (Throws another handful) You try to make me dirty, too. You throw at me.

NICODEMU: (In an angry tone) Stop it! It's getting in my eyes.

ADISSU: (Stops and reflects) Well, we can throw at the cows. See? (Tosses a handful of dirt on the grazing farm animals)

NICODEMU: They might run.

ADISSU: No. See? (In a loud, animated voice) Getting the cows! (Throws dirt)

NICODEMU: (Smiles, begins to throw dirt on the animals as well)

Here, Adissu works out a compromise in a dispute over what to play. He adapts his original play suggestion so that the game is acceptable to his peer. He does so without bullying or aggression. Such give-and-take is quite common among popular children.

To be effective with peers, young children must learn how to enter a play group (Putallaz & Wasserman, 1989). Popular children are quite savvy at gaining entrance into play in progress. They have acquired social skills that win their acceptance in groups (Ramsey, 1989a, 1989b). They do not just ask to play—a strategy that has been found to be rarely successful. Instead, they may simply start playing along with peers, making interesting but unobtrusive contributions to the play theme. They often address one of the children by name. These strategies have been found to be very successful among preschool-age children (Ramsey, 1989b).

One last characteristic of popular children is that they can accurately "read" social settings (Dodge & Price, 1994). They seem to be aware of the needs, motives, and behaviors of their peers and of the effects of their own behaviors. They are better able to identify the outcomes of particular social initiatives, for example. They know that pushing or hitting can lead to retaliation, and that some children will do what you ask if you are friendly (Trawick-Smith, 1992). They can more accurately name the intentions of peers (Dodge & Price, 1994). This ability to monitor one's social behaviors and those of others may explain why popular children are able to select those strategies that are most successful: they have come to learn which strategies work well with peers and which do not.

Rejected Children. **Rejected children** are those who are actively avoided by peers. Characteristics of rejected children—drawn from research—are presented in Table 13-2. As shown in the table, rejected children are sometimes disliked because they display **antisocial behaviors** that are extremely obvious and disruptive (Pope, Bierman, & Mumma, 1991). They are often quite aggressive. Interestingly, not

TABLE 13-2
Characteristics of Rejected Children

Characteristic	Description
Negative	Displays a negative, obviously unpleasant affect.
Whiny	Complains, whimpers, or tattles with regularity.
Unpredictably aggressive	Hits, pushes, bites, or verbally assaults peers, often without reason or provocation.
Unskilled at interpreting social situations	Misreads social situations and erroneously assigns hostile intent to benign acts of peers.
Antisocial and isolated from peers	Avoids others and chooses to play alone.

all aggressive children are disliked. It may be that subtle differences in aggression determine a particular child's peer group status in the classroom (Dodge & Price, 1994). For example, children who only display *reactive* aggression—aggression in response to peer mistreatment—are not as likely to be rejected. In contrast, children whose aggression is hostile, unpredictable, and illogical are more likely to be disliked by peers. Indirect, verbal aggressive behaviors such as tattling or name-calling appear to be especially deplored by preschoolers (Bierman, Smoot, & Aumiller, 1993).

It is easy to see why peers stay away from unpredictably hostile classmates. Such children may respond impulsively and unpredictably to the slightest frustration or disagreement with uncontrollable violence. The uncertainty and potential risks of playing with such children tend to offset the benefits of befriending them. The following story illustrates the aggressive and unpredictable behaviors of one rejected child:

Three children are looking at books in the library corner. Each is absorbed in reading; all is quite peaceful for awhile. Without warning, Philip kicks another who has moved too close. He then grabs the child's book.

PHILIP: (Pulling the book from Albert's hands) Give me this.

ALBERT: No. Give it back, Philip!

PHILIP: (Moves toward Albert in a threatening way and uses an angry tone) You better not touch me.

ALBERT: (Covers his head, expecting to be struck)

PHILIP: (Pushes Albert) This is my book. (Now turns to Rubin, who has been watching, and snatches his book as well) You give these to me.

Both Albert and Rubin quickly retreat from the library corner to find a teacher. Philip sits down by himself and continues to read.

In the story, Philip becomes suddenly aggressive for no obvious reason. He bullies both of the other boys, in spite of the fact that such aggression will drive them from the play area. He seems content to be on his own after they have left.

A characteristic of rejected children is an inability to read social situations and to understand the feelings of their peers (Dodge & Price, 1994). For example, rejected children often erroneously interpret the actions of peers as intentional and hostile (Crick & Ladd, 1990), as the following vignette demonstrates:

> Sergio has accidentally bumped into Tamara's child's blocks, toppling a portion of the structure. Tamara immediately attacks, striking her peer several times before a teacher can intervene.

TEACHER: (Alarmed) What's happening here?

TAMARA: He kicked over my blocks.

SERGIO: (In tears) I didn't mean to.

TAMARA: He tried to kick 'em. If he kicks 'em again . . . (turns to Sergio) I'll hit you again!

SERGIO: (Sobs loudly) But it wasn't on purpose!

TAMARA: (Kicking out at Sergio) You better get away from me. Stay outa' my blocks!

Here, Tamara has reacted angrily, and has assumed that the other child's action was deliberate. This tendency to assign negative intentions may explain why rejected children so frequently strike out, seemingly without provocation.

Some rejected children are also isolates. They may choose to play alone and push or hit when others move near them (S. R. Asher & Dodge, 1985). Such children may be most at risk because they are not only difficult to play with, but show no desire to be with peers at all. Many rejected children suffer low self-esteem, although some hold exceptionally unrealistic views of self (Boivin & Begin, 1989). Some rejected children, for example, report that they are very well liked by peers when in fact they are not. This is another sign of their inability to accurately interpret social circumstances.

How do children first come to be rejected? They may begin life with a negative inborn temperament (Hartup & Moore, 1990). They are more likely to have parents who are punitive and authoritarian (Hart, DeWolf, Wozniak, & Burts, 1992). When they come in contact with peers, a vicious circle emerges: Rejected children push, hit, or display negative affect, and their peers move away from them or refuse to play. This rejection may anger them or threaten their positive feelings of self. They respond with even more aggression; their acting-out behavior escalates. Such children are at special risk and are in most need of adult intervention to enhance social relationships (Kupersmidt, Coie, & Dodge, 1990).

Neglected Children. **Neglected children** are those who are largely ignored by their peers, and often by their teachers as well. Characteristics of neglected children—drawn from research—are presented in Table 13-3. As shown in the table, their predominant characteristic is **isolate behavior.** They tend to be loners who rarely initiate contact with others and often retreat when initiatives are directed toward them. Some neglected children choose to be alone (Scarlett, 1983). Many, though not all, neglected children are shy (L. J. Nelson, Hart, Robinson, Olsen, & Rubin, 1997).

Observations of neglected children's interactions with peers reveal that they are quite inept in social settings. They lack the social skills needed to enter a play group or to capture the attention of peers. They have difficulty persuading others. Often they respond inappropriately to others' initiatives, as the following vignette shows:

TABLE 13-3
Characteristics of Neglected Children

Characteristic	Description
Isolated from peers	Plays alone and often retreats when peers approach.
Shy	Exhibits reticence and anxiety in social situations.
Unskilled at entering play groups	Lacks the ability to enter play groups in progress or to join peers in play.
Unskilled in capturing peer attention	Lacks the ability to capture and maintain a peer's attention.
Unskilled in play leadership	Lacks the social skills or initiative to guide peers' play and make play suggestions.

Twana is swinging by herself on an urban playground. Several older children wander over to the swing. They are loud and active.

ROSE: (Laughing, speaking to her peers) Hey, let's swing. (To Twana) We're gonna swing with you, little girl. Alright?

TWANA: (Slows her swinging, looks down, says nothing)

CELESTE: (Speaking to Twana) Little girl, what's your name? You got a name?

TWANA: (Looks down, does not respond)

CELESTE: (Persisting) Can you swing as high as this? Try it. Try this. (Demonstrates)

TWANA: (Gets off the swing and walks to her mother)

ROSE: (Laughs and says to her peers) Don't think she likes us.

MOTHER: Twana, those girls want to play. You go play with them. You can swing with them.

TWANA: (Shakes her head and hides her face under her mother's coat)

In spite of repeated initiatives by the other children, Twana does not respond. She does not appear interested in social interaction, and leaves the area in response to their friendly advances. It is easy to see why peers give up trying to befriend such children and eventually come to ignore them.

A moderate amount of shyness is typical. Most children are shy at one time or another in their early years (Honig, 1987). Even so, most shy children make friends and interact with peers. Children who are shy but socially competent display many social abilities, but only in certain classroom settings or with particular peers. Observations across situations and areas are necessary, then, in assessing **peer neglect** (Broberg, Lamb, & Hwang, 1990). A quiet but friendly social style does not always lead to low peer status. It is those children who never interact with others, and are thus unable to make friends, who are at risk, particularly as they get older (Rubin & Asendorpf, 1993). If a child never initiates contact with peers, adult assistance may be needed.

Neglected children may have been born with a "slow-to-warm-up" temperament that leads to quietness and wariness. Caution and timidity in entering into new relationships may be a fundamental aspect of such children's personalities (Kagan,

Neglected children are often withdrawn and socially anxious.

Snidman, & Arcus, 1993). A circular relationship between temperament and peer interaction emerges: Neglected children may be so quiet and cautious that they are ignored. Since they are not invited to participate in play activities, they miss opportunities to refine social skills and gain confidence in peer relations. They grow comfortable playing in isolation. As they further isolate themselves, they are noticed less and less.

Friendships

Most preschool children have at least one reciprocated friendship with a peer (Matheson & Wu, 1991). Those who maintain long-term friendships tend to be more competent socially (Howes, 1987). A single friendship can insulate a child from some of the negative effects of being rejected or neglected by peers (Hartup & Moore, 1990). It may be that having a friend is reaffirming: it shows children that they can be liked, even if only by one other child. In one study, it was discovered that the number of friends children had in kindergarten was related to how well they adjusted to a new school setting (Ladd, Kochenderfer, & Coleman, 1996).

Friendships are very useful for social skills intervention in preschool. Studies have shown that friendships provide unique social opportunities for children. Conflicts among friends are less heated and more likely to end in compromise (Hartup, Laursen, Stewart, & Eastenson, 1988). A child is more likely to be accepted into a play group when one of the players is a friend (Ramsey, 1989a). Playing with friends enables less effective children to try out new social skills and enjoy greater success. So, an especially opportune time for teachers to facilitate social skills is when children are playing with their friends.

In some cases, preschool friendships are temporary, lasting only the duration of a particular play activity or perhaps extending for a day or two (Howes, 1983). Other friendships are long-lasting (Selman & Demorest, 1984). Some years ago, when I was conducting a study of social competence, I accidentally created a friendship between two 4-year-olds—one a rejected child—by frequently bringing them together in a laboratory play setting. Soon teachers reported that the two children were inseparable in the classroom. Years later, I ran into the mother of one of the children, who reported that they were still close friends in middle school!

Social Participation

Most preschool children—regardless of their status in a classroom—play with peers. However, the level of their **social participation**—the degree of their involvement with others—varies considerably. In her classic research, Mildred Parten (1932) discovered stages of social participation that most young children pass through during the preschool years. These are presented in Table 13-4. In the first of Parten's stages, *unoccupied behavior,* children show little interest in what is going on around them. They do not interact with toys, materials, or peers. Parten proposes that this type of play is most prevalent in toddlerhood, but declines as the social world of the young child broadens after age 3. Parten's second stage, *onlooker behavior,* is distinguished by an interest in what others are doing. Children at this stage often watch their peers play. Although onlooking is not social behavior per se, it is considered an important social advancement. When children begin to show interest in others, they are taking a step toward more involved social participation.

Children show they are interested in peers' activities by increasingly watching or hovering around them, according to Parten. Shortly after this interest emerges, they begin to engage in *parallel play,* the next level of social participation. In parallel play, children engage in activities side-by-side with others. They rarely interact in these activities, however, and often do not even speak to one another. Nevertheless, they show enjoyment of close proximity to their peers. Therefore, parallel play represents significant social experience. The following vignette illustrates parallel play and a teacher's role in encouraging it:

Two 3-year-olds are playing in the sandbox on the playground. Another child stands for a long time watching them. A teacher moves into the area and approaches the onlooking child.

TEACHER: Why don't you make a sand pie, too, Markku? Come with me, I'll help you. (Takes the child's hand and walks to the sandbox)

MARKKU: (Says nothing. Walks with the teacher.)

TABLE 13-4
Parten's Stages of Social Participation

Stage	Description
Unoccupied behavior	Shows little intrests in toys, persons, and activities occurring in the vicinity.
Onlooker behavior	Shows an interest in peers and watches their activities intently. Engages in no social contact.
Parallel play	Engages in activities side-by-side with peers, but rarely converses or interacts.
Associative play	Pursues own individual play themes but interacts often; talks to peers and shares materials.
Cooperative play	Adopts a single, coordinated play theme with peers; plans, negotiates, and differentiates roles in pursuit of a shared goal.

SOURCE: Parten, 1932.

TEACHER: (In an enthused tone) Now I'm going to make a huge pie. (Begins to make a mound of sand)

MARKKU: (Says nothing. Begins to make his own sand mound, occasionally stopping to watch the teacher and other children as they work.)

The teacher continues to converse with Markku and work with the sand. After several minutes, she withdraws from the sandbox. Markku continues to play with the sand and to watch his playmates. No interaction among the children occurs.

The teacher in this vignette is facilitating parallel play. Her intervention leads the onlooking child to a more social level of activity than before: Markku now plays right next to the other children and watches and even copies their actions.

Once children are regularly playing parallel to others, a new form of play can be expected to emerge, according to Parten. At this stage, children begin to engage in *associative play*, in which they pursue their own individual play themes yet interact often. In such activity, children might talk to one another about what they are doing or even share materials, as in the following vignette:

Two 4-year-olds play on the ground near their homes in a village in East India. Meena makes noises and speaks to herself in a pretend voice as she moves a clay elephant along the ground. Sarala is playing with a paper snake. She makes impressive hissing noises and drags the toy along the ground. At first the two children do not speak to one another.

MEENA: (Speaking suddenly) This elephant is so hot in the sun. See? (Points to her clay elephant, then makes a motion showing her elephant is drinking water) See? He's drinking from the river.

SARALA: Yes. My snake is thirsty too. But snakes can't go to the river. (Continues to make her snake slither along)

MEENA: (Places the toy under a structure of sticks) And this is the elephant's house. See? He's going in, but he's not supposed to be in there. (Laughs)

SARALA: (Looks up from her paper snake) Let me see.

MEENA: Here. (Points to the toy under the sticks)

SARALA: Well, my snake needs a house. And she can go inside. Give me those sticks. (Points)

MEENA: (Hands over some sticks, then begins to play with her elephant again)

SARALA: (After fashioning a "house" from sticks, speaks to herself) Now the snake is sleeping. But he wakes up when someone walks by and bites! (Makes a hissing sound)

In the associative play depicted in this vignette, the children play with their own toys but occasionally converse with each other, discussing their individual play activities. They share materials and exchange ideas. Their play is not as yet fully coordinated, however. They have not adopted a single, cooperative theme. They remain very absorbed in their own personal play pursuits.

The last of Parten's stages, *cooperative play,* often emerges in the later preschool years. This form of play represents the most complex form of social participation. Children now adopt a single, coordinated play theme, and they plan, negotiate, and differentiate roles in pursuit of their shared goal. In the following story, associative play is transformed into cooperative play by two older preschoolers:

> Two 4-year-olds are playing with dolls in the dramatic play area. As they each dress and care for their "baby," they speak to one another about their activities.
>
> MIA: (Dressing a doll) I'm getting ready to go shopping. I need to bundle her up 'cause it's cold.
>
> JENNIFER: My baby won't stop crying. (Speaking to her doll) What is it? Are you sick or something?
>
> The two children continue to play out their own themes for several more minutes.
>
> JENNIFER: She's getting real sick, I think. She could spit up or something.
>
> MIA: Maybe she's got to go to the doctor.
>
> JENNIFER: Yeah. She might need some medicine.
>
> MIA: I'm going to the store, alright? And let's say this is our car, okay? (Points to two chairs)
>
> JENNIFER: (In mock urgency) But I need to get to the doctor or the hospital.
>
> MIA: Okay. Let's say you come over and ride with me, alright, Jennifer? And we take your baby to the hospital and then get the groceries.
>
> JENNIFER: Okay. Where do I get in?
>
> As the two children drive to town with their dolls, they discuss the illness and what the doctor will do.

In this interchange, Mia and Jennifer gradually merge their individual but similar play themes into a single, coordinated one. They begin to jointly plan their play and to coordinate their make-believe events, actions, and characters. Their activity moves, then, from associative to cooperative play.

According to Parten, many children begin to engage in frequent cooperative play with peers by age 5. This is not to say that they completely abandon earlier play forms. Even very social children occasionally revisit the onlooker or parallel play stage (Rubin, 1982). However, Parten proposes that the ratio of cooperative play to less social play forms increases in typically developing children.

Positive and Negative Social Behaviors

As we have learned, specific social behaviors will determine whether children are accepted or rejected by peers and whether they make friends. Children who are kind and caring will be well liked. Those who are highly aggressive may not be. How are such behaviors learned? How can parents and teachers promote prosocial interactions and discourage less positive ones?

Altruism and Empathy. Many preschool children display kindness or caring toward other persons in their interactions. Acts such as sharing a toy, helping with a puzzle, and comforting a crying peer are called **altruistic** behaviors. A traditional view has been that very young children are too egocentric to perform these acts (Piaget, 1952b). Research suggests, however, that young children can be very altruistic (Eisenberg et al., 1996). Preschoolers have been observed showing concerned facial expressions and offering help or consolation when a peer begins to cry. Children as young as age 2 have been found to spontaneously share toys and give affection and help without any prompting from adults.

How is altruism learned at such a young age? Each theory of child development (see Chapter 3) holds its own answer to this question. Maturationists would suggest that humans are born with a sense of **empathy,** an ability to feel vicariously others' emotions or physical pain. From this perspective, when children see peers fall and cry, they can almost feel the hurt and sadness themselves. Support for this perspective comes from studies of newborns who have been found to show great upset when they hear others crying (Murray, 1979; Sagi & Hoffman, 1976). A remarkable finding of these studies is that the more a cry resembled the subjects' own crying, the more upset they became. For example, these infants would show greater disturbance when listening to cries of a baby their own age than in response to those of an older child or adult. It is as if these infants could more fully empathize with those who were most similar to them!

Psychoanalysts would propose that early attachment to parents and other caregivers leads to altruism and empathy. If adults are nurturing in their interactions and convey caring and concern, children will integrate these emotional responses into their own personalities (Ekstein, 1978). In contrast, behaviorist and social cognitive learning theorists would suggest that these **prosocial behaviors** are rewarded and modeled by adults. Evidence supporting this view comes from studies showing the power of adult **modeling.** Research has demonstrated, for example, that when adults display sharing and cooperation in classrooms, their students are more likely to demonstrate these behaviors (Radke-Yarrow, Zahn-Waxler, & Chapman, 1982). The effects of prosocial modeling have been found to be most powerful when combined with rewards for prosocial behavior (L. Nelson & Madsen, 1969).

From a cognitive-developmental perspective, children construct understandings of altruism and empathy. As their social experience increases, they come to understand that certain social behaviors lead to desirable responses by others. They discover that kind acts, such as helpfulness and cooperation, bring about caring and acceptance by peers and adults. Programs have been developed to help children make these connections (Ladd & Mize, 1983). In these programs, adults use a variety of methods to help children notice the outcomes of specific social behaviors. Such programs have been found to promote prosocial behavior.

Ecological systems theorists would argue that altruism and empathy can only be fully understood by studying the family, the community, and society as a whole. Microsystem influences are believed to be at work: children in child care or Head Start centers that are of high quality and provide warm, responsive care will display more prosocial behavior (Taylor & Machida, 1994). Exosystem factors may also play a role: families who receive adequate social and mental health services may suffer less stress, and therefore exhibit more positive behaviors in the home. Macrosystem influences are also important: children in societies that value kindness and coopera-

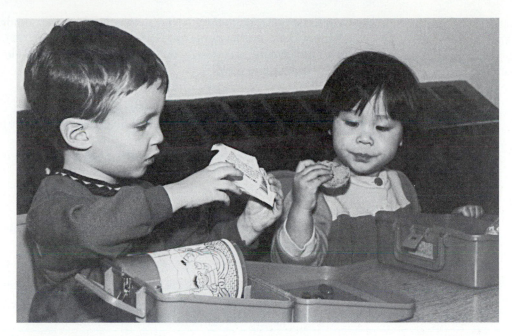

Preschool children often share, help others, and show kindness with no prompting from adults.

tion are more likely to acquire these prosocial behaviors (Konner, 1991; B. B. Whiting & Edwards, 1988).

Implications for working with children can be drawn from all four theories. Teachers can promote altruism by modeling and rewarding kindness in the classroom. They can help children to reflect on the positive outcomes of their altruistic acts (e.g., "Did you see how she smiled when you shared your crayons?"). And they can advocate for family services to relieve stress and enhance kindness in the home.

Aggression. Negative social behaviors can also be observed among some preschool children. The most worrisome of these is **aggression**—defined as any physical or verbal behavior that is intended to harm or threaten another. It is important for teachers and parents to distinguish between aggression and a number of common, non-aggressive behaviors:

1. *Rough-and-tumble play:* Rough play, such as wrestling, play-fighting, and friendly jostling, is usually not considered aggression. In fact, this behavior may lead to social competence (Pellegrini & Perlmutter, 1988).

2. *Teasing play:* Taunting or arguing that is nonliteral and nonhostile is also not usually viewed as aggression. **Teasing play** is very common in the interactions of children of historically under-represented groups (Hale-Benson, 1986; Roopnarine, Johnson, & Hooper, 1994; B. B. Whiting & Edwards, 1988).

3. *Assertiveness:* Sticking up for oneself during disputes is not usually considered aggression. For example, a child who resists having a toy snatched away by tugging it back and shouting "No!" is displaying assertiveness, not aggression.

4. *Conflicts and arguments:* A distinction is generally made between aggression and conflicts and arguments (Hartup & Laursen, 1993). Conflicts, no matter how loud, do not necessarily involve aggression. The following vignette depicts a non-aggressive conflict:

Two 5-year-olds, Marcus and Jamal, are climbing into a cardboard box and rolling down a hill in their neighborhood. An argument erupts.

MARCUS: Let's say this is our cave and we have to hide in it. Hunters are coming, alright? And so we have to hide.

JAMAL: No! Let's just play. (Climbs into the box and rolls down the hill alone)

MARCUS: (In a loud, angry tone) Jamal! No! Don't roll down! This is the cave, alright?

JAMAL: (Ignores Marcus. Drags the box back up to the top of the hill.)

MARCUS: (In an angry tone) No, Jamal! This has to be the cave!

JAMAL: We could say it's a cave that can roll down, alright Marcus? (Laughs) It could be a cave that rolls down.

MARCUS: (Laughs) That's funny. It'll be like . . . a rolling cave. Come on. (Climbs into the box with Jamal and continues to play)

In this play episode, one child becomes angry and shouts at the other. However, no physical or verbal aggression is evident. Marcus and Jamal resolve their conflict independently and in a positive way. Contrast this outcome to that of the next example:

Rachel is building in the block area of her kindergarten. A classmate enters and roughly snatches several of the blocks away.

RACHEL: No! I'm using these. Give them back, Zein.

ZEIN: I need these! I'm building a whole castle.

RACHEL: No! (Snatches one block back)

ZEIN: I hate you. And you're not coming to my birthday party.

RACHEL: (Pushes Zein hard and walks out of the block area)

In this case, aggressive behavior is displayed by both children. Rachel's pushing and Zein's snatching and hateful words would all be viewed as aggressive acts. The important criteria for judging aggressive behavior is whether an action has the effect of hurting another person psychologically or physically.

Professionals who work with young children must be cautious in making judgments about aggressive behavior. True aggression requires immediate adult intervention. However, conflicts or displays of assertiveness may not require adult support. In fact, adult interference could deprive children of opportunities to solve social problems independently.

Adults must also be careful not to misjudge typical play activities of children from diverse cultural backgrounds as aggression. Euro-American teachers have been found to treat culture-specific activities such as teasing or rough-and-tumble play as ag-

TABLE 13-5
Types of
Aggression

Aggression Type	Description
Verbal Aggression	Teasing, name-calling, or other verbal taunts intended to harm others psychologically.
Physical Aggression	Hitting, pushing, biting, or other physical assaults intended to harm others physically.
Reactive	Aggression which is provoked by peers. A reaction to peers' taunts or physical assaults.
Proactive	Aggression which is unprovoked and often unexpected by peers.
Instrumental	Proactive aggression which has a clear goal or purpose, such as obtaining a toy or driving an undesired playmate from a play area.
Bullying	Proactive aggression which has no clear goal and is often displaced and hostile in intent.

SOURCE: Coie, Dodge, Terry, & Wright, 1991; Dodge & Coie, 1987.

gression and to prohibit these within classrooms (Hale-Benson, 1986). Such misinterpretations of play styles can result in barriers to social development for some children.

Researchers find it useful to break down aggression into specific categories, as listed in Table 13-5. Each kind of aggression has a unique impact on others. As shown in the table, some researchers distinguish between *verbal aggression* and *physical aggression*. The former involves taunts, teasing, threats, or cruel statements intended to harm others psychologically, while physical aggression includes biting, hitting, pushing, or kicking (Bierman et al., 1993). Both types of aggression lead to rejection by peers; a hurtful taunt is as distasteful to young children as a punch or kick (Dodge & Coie, 1987)!

Aggressive episodes have been further categorized as either reactive or proactive. *Reactive aggression* involves physical or verbal assaults that are provoked. For example, a child who hits back after being hit is said to be performing reactive aggression. *Proactive aggression* involves unprovoked physical or verbal assaults. Children who are reactive—that is, who only strike out when provoked—tend to be less at risk of being rejected (Dodge & Coie, 1987). It may be that these children are more predictable in their aggressive behavior. They make fine playmates so long as they are not angered or disturbed.

Proactive aggression may be further classified as instrumental aggression or bullying (Coie, Dodge, Terry, & Wright, 1991). *Instrumental aggression* involves acts that have a goal: to get a toy or to chase undesired classmates from a play area, for example. *Bullying,* in contrast, is hostile aggression without a clear purpose. It may stem from rage or upset. It is easy to see why proactive, bullying aggression leads to peer rejection more than any other type. Children who exhibit this behavior tend to be very hostile and unpredictable. Playing with such peers is risky. Sadly, young children who are highly aggressive as preschoolers are very likely to become aggressive older children and adolescents (Bierman et al., 1993; Eron & Huesmann, 1990).

How do children learn these behaviors? Again, each theory of child development offers a unique explanation. Maturationists would suggest that some children are born with an aggressive temperament. Such children may have simply inherited a negative or difficult disposition which inevitably leads to problematic peer relations. Psychoanalytic theorists would also view aggression as part of a child's biological inheritance (Freud, 1930). However, they would propose that the environment—in particular, the child's interpersonal interactions with parents—determines how aggressive drives are expressed. It is the job of adults to redirect aggressive urges toward positive outlets. From this view, active running and jumping or expressive art activities are strategies that may help children "get out" their aggressive urges.

Behaviorists would argue that aggressive behavior is shaped and rewarded by the environment (Bandura, 1962, 1967). This can occur in several ways. First, children observe and emulate aggressive models. For example, those who watch violent television programs may become more aggressive themselves (Paik & Comstock, 1994). Children who are physically punished or abused by parents may more often strike out at peers (Malinosky-Rummel & Hansen, 1993). Second, aggression is rewarded, since children who push and hit peers often get what they want. For example, a child who gets a desired toy by pushing a peer receives a "payoff" for his or her aggression.

Cognitive-developmental theorists would argue that there is an intellectual component to aggression. Aggressive children may be the way they are because they do not *understand* social situations. They may misinterpret the intentions or actions of peers and may be unaware of the consequences of their social initiatives. Such children may not view hitting or pushing as inappropriate, because they cannot see clearly the pain and upset it causes. Further, they may not recognize that aggressive acts lead to peer rejection. This cognitive-developmental explanation has been supported by much research. Aggressive young children have been found to be less able to accurately read social cues (Dodge & Price, 1994) or to make decisions about which behaviors to perform in which situations (Trawick-Smith, 1992). Further, they are more likely to assign hostile intent to the benign acts of peers. For example, when a playmate knocks down their blocks, they are more likely to report that it was done "on purpose" or "to be mean" (Quiggle, Garber, Panak, & Dodge, 1992).

Ecological systems theorists would propose a broader view of aggression. Harsh parental discipline or television watching would not fully explain the problem, from their perspective. Regarding television, they might ask: Why do children in our society watch so much television to begin with? What stresses or lack of child care resources lead parents to utilize TV as the "one-eyed baby-sitter"? Why is children's programming so violent? What marketing trends or profit motivations lead television companies to broadcast damaging programs? What political ideologies dissuade legislators from regulating television programming more fully? A good deal of society-wide soul searching should be done, according to ecological systems theorists, not just finger-pointing at parents who let their children watch too much TV.

Each theoretical perspective is useful in solving problems of aggression. Teachers and parents can model non-aggressive social problem-solving and reward children for doing so. They can further reduce exposure to aggressive models by limiting television viewing. They can encourage children to express anger or upset through positive outlets, such as art or music. They can guide children in reflecting on the outcomes of aggressive acts (e.g., "Look what happened when you hit him. See how he's crying?") Finally, teachers can take political action to change elements within society—such as violent television—that contribute to the problem.

CULTURE AND SOCIAL COMPETENCE

Culture influences children's social interactions, communication patterns, and play interests. Interactions of children of a particular cultural group may be misinterpreted by those who do not understand that culture's unique traditions or interpersonal characteristics. Ogbu (1992) has argued that teachers, in particular, must be cautious not to view social differences as deficits. Variations in social behavior, he proposes, are as much a part of a child's cultural heritage as a family's religious beliefs or holiday celebrations.

Culture and Prosocial Behaviors

Prosocial behaviors, such as altruism and empathy, vary significantly across cultural groups. In a study of six different cultures, B. B. Whiting and Whiting (1975) found great variation in helpfulness and cooperation, for example. Young children in American society scored lowest on measures of these behaviors. The children who scored highest were those of non-Western communities who lived in large families and had parents with extremely challenging workloads. These children were assigned many household tasks, and their work was often critical to the family's survival. Maccoby (1980) has argued that such family circumstances lead children to acquire a "helpful way of life" which will be evident even when adults are not present.

Children in American families are not assigned crucial household work as often. This may be due to a belief that children should enjoy early childhood without the burden of chores. Most American families have more resources than the impoverished non-Western families that Whiting and Whiting studied, so children's work may not be as critical to survival. Helpfulness might not emerge quite as early, then, in the social repertoire of some American preschoolers (Munroe & Munroe, 1977). This does not represent a deficit; it simply means that within some American families, culture has dictated that helpfulness will evolve more gradually in human interactions.

Hale-Benson (1986) has observed more cooperative behavior among African and African-American children, and more competition among children of Euro-American backgrounds. She cites a study showing that children from rural Kenya were more cooperative in playing a board game, for example, than less "traditional" urban African children and those from the United States (Munroe & Munroe, 1977). She proposes that cooperation comes more naturally to children who grow up in cultures where collective thought and action are valued. In many Euro-American families, she contends, individual initiative and competition are the norm.

Classroom Play

How do these cultural differences translate into classroom activity? Traditional African or African-American children might engage in more frequent cooperative play, as defined by Parten (1932). Children from Euro-American cultures might more often pursue individual play interests. Individual ownership may be more important to families of Euro-American cultures. These children might desire more personal space and individual possession of toys and learning materials. Some African-American children may view play items as community property to be spontaneously borrowed and shared. The following story shows how conflicts arise when these social styles clash:

Sonia approaches Robert, who is painting by himself at an easel in a preschool program.

SONIA: (Smiles and stands very close to Robert) You painting a picture, Robert? That's a sun, right? (Points at the painting) What's this? This a boy or something? Is it a boy or a girl?

ROBERT: (Studies his painting intensely. Does not look at Sonia and does not respond.)

SONIA: I could paint that boy . . . paint it, like, a big brother. Alright, Robert? (Grasps a paint brush from the easel)

ROBERT: No! I'm painting, Sonia. Leave me alone!

SONIA: (Begins to paint on Robert's painting) I'll make a boy . . .

ROBERT: (Screaming loudly) No! (Shouts across the room to the teacher) Teacher! Sonia's ruining my painting!

In this story, a misunderstanding has occurred between two children with different social orientations. Robert believes that the easel, brushes, and painting are his alone. He wishes to produce his very own work of art. Sonia sees the easel as community property. In her family, everyone shares toys and works on tasks together. She cannot understand why her peer would not want company in creating a picture.

Access to Peers

Throughout the preceding sections, we have assumed that preschoolers have access to peers they can play with. Studies in countries around the world, however, suggest that this availability of peers varies greatly. In a study of families of 11 different communities, B. B. Whiting and Edwards (1988) conclude that many children of the world stay close to home and play mainly with parents or siblings. They do not, then, form the same kinds of peer relationships as American preschoolers. In fact, some children in non-Western families in this study were found to spend less than half the time that American children do playing with peers. The percentage of time boys and girls from around the world play with peers is presented in Figure 13-1.

Whiting and Edwards also report that work assignments for preschoolers can reduce play time with peers. They observed that in cultures in which the work burden for parents is great, children spend an inordinate amount of time helping out with household chores. Caring for younger siblings, tending livestock, or completing other family tasks may comprise a larger part of a young child's day in such families. These children do often integrate play and work and include peers in their work tasks (Bloch & Adler, 1994). Still, free play time with same-age playmates is often limited.

Without daily peer interactions, social development would take a very different course than that described by Western researchers. Children whose social access is limited might be less outgoing or more hesitant when they do interact with peers. Social skills might not be acquired as early, since opportunities to develop these are lacking. Assessment of social abilities, then, must take into account previous social experiences, which are influenced by cultural values and community circumstances.

Friendliness and Shyness

Friendliness is another dimension of social behavior that varies significantly by culture. Erikson (1963) has described emotionally healthy preschoolers as outgoing and energetic. Parten (1932) has proposed that preschoolers interact with peers more frequently with age. Social initiative has been identified as an important prerequisite

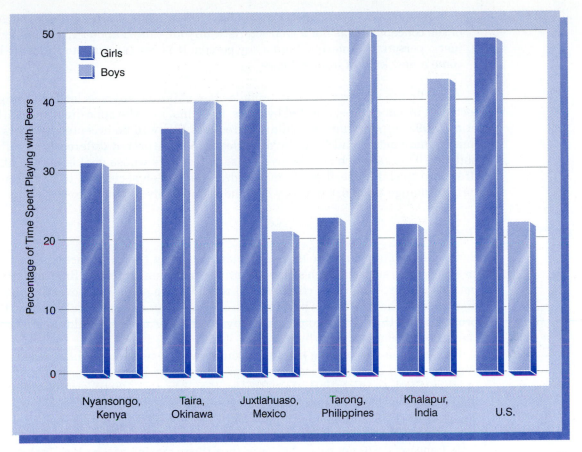

FIGURE 13-1 Children of different cultures vary in the amount of time they spend with peers. Gender differences are also found in most societies.

SOURCE: Extrapolated from data given by B. B. Whiting & Edwards, 1988.

to making friends and being accepted by peers. Yet in some cultures shyness is more typical. Among Chinese parents, in fact, raising withdrawn, cautious children is an important goal of child rearing (Ho, 1986). This may stem from Confucian philosophy, which holds that self-restraint and hesitancy are signs of maturity and accomplishment (X. Chen et al., 1992; King & Bond, 1986). Extreme shyness, which is sometimes considered deviant in Western cultures, is very much accepted and appreciated in China. The following story illustrates this point:

One of my colleagues arrived in the United States several years ago from China to attend graduate school. While pursuing her studies in psychology, she received much positive response from professors and fellow students for her academic competence. She then accepted a position to teach in an American university. Colleagues made friendly comments about her shyness and recommended that she become more outgoing. It was only then that she was confronted with the idea that she was shy. Until that point, she had not thought about herself in this way.

"I never knew I was shy," she confided. "When I was in China, I never heard of the concept. It was not a characteristic anyone talked about. In China, I was just a person. In America, I am a shy person. It is very strange to suddenly become a new kind of human being."

According to research on white middle-class children, shyness leads to being neglected or, in some cases, rejected by peers. In China, just the opposite is true: X. Chen et al. (1992) report that shy children are more likely to be accepted by peers than louder, more active children. Shyness clearly is interpreted differently in different cultures. This research should give pause to teachers whose goal is to turn all children into "social butterflies." Some children have been socialized to be shy, and efforts to change them are not only misguided but likely to be futile.

Rough Play and Teasing

Some children appear to be more rough and active in their interactions with peers. In some cases, such children's play initiatives are misinterpreted. Ramsey (1987) reports that Euro-American children and teachers are sometimes overwhelmed and disturbed by the very rough play of children from other cultures. Hale-Benson (1986) proposes that the active and physical play of African-American children is often misconstrued as aggressive or hyperactive.

Play arguing and teasing have been found to be very common interactions among young children of some African-American, Polynesian, Native American, and Italian families (Bloch & Adler, 1994; Hale-Benson, 1986; Martini, 1994; New, 1994). Such play may involve exchanging insults or telling jokes about peers' families. Making fun of younger peers or siblings is common. Such behaviors, though delivered in jest, can sound horribly antisocial to people from cultures in which such games are not played. Hale-Benson (1986) suggests, however, that these teasing interactions enhance specific areas of social, emotional, and intellectual development. First, they provide an early experience in controlling emotions. The successful player must endure insults or teasing without growing angry or overreacting. Second, teasing behavior involves creativity, verbal competence, and quick thinking. Teachers and caregivers have the difficult task of distinguishing between truly hurtful comments which comprise verbal aggression and playful barbs and insults which may be part of cultural interaction.

Social Interaction and Second-Language Acquisition

One factor that can influence social interactions in preschool peer groups is language diversity. Children who do not speak the language of the majority of classmates in a preschool or child care center may be limited in interactions with peers. In an ethnographic study of peer relationships, Meyer, Klein, and Genishi (1994) described the experiences of four Korean-speaking 3-year-olds who were new to an English-dominant preschool. The researchers observed that the four children first interacted only with each other. They formed friendships with one another almost immediately and were inseparable during free play. They would sit together at group time, speaking to one another in Korean. During their interchanges, they were found to acquire critical play, social, and linguistic competencies. Gradually they began to apply these abilities to interactions with their English-speaking peers.

This study suggests that second-language learners might acquire social skills best by first using their native language to interact with peers who are culturally and linguistically similar to themselves. Had the children of the study been required to speak English or to play with English-speaking children, the authors concluded, they might not have acquired important language and social abilities. It was only after they had refined their social and language competencies that they were able to enter into relationships with children of different backgrounds.

Peer Acceptance and Culture

Since children's social behaviors are often different across cultures, it is reasonable to assume that ethnicity might be a cause for peer rejection. It seems likely that a child in preschool or child care who plays and communicates in very distinct ways would be actively avoided by peers. Research findings on peer acceptance and culture provide a cloudy picture, however. Early studies indicated that young children do show same-race preferences in the selection of friends and playmates (Jarrett & Quay, 1983). These biases appear to become stronger in the elementary years (S. G. Asher, Singleton, & Taylor, 1982). Interestingly, same-race preferences were found to be most prevalent among Euro-American children, and less so among African-American children (D. J. Fox & Jordan, 1973).

More recent research, however, suggests that preschool children may be more accepting of cultural differences and more regularly enter into cross-cultural friendships than early research would suggest. In a large study of young Euro-American, Latino, African-American, and Asian-American children, Howes and Wu (1990) report that peer acceptance was not usually related to ethnicity. Children were liked or not based on other interpersonal attributes. Many cross-ethnic relationships, spanning all cultural groups, were observed in this study.

Why is there a discrepancy in findings between earlier and more recent studies? It would be heartening to think that society has changed, and with it the attitudes of parents and other family members. It is hoped that more children are arriving in

Are preschoolers of historically under-represented groups more likely to be rejected by their Euro-American peers? The research evidence is mixed.

child care or preschool more fully socialized to accept others. Ramsey (1995) suggests that schools might play a role: interventions that enhance children's understanding and interpretation of others' perspectives and behaviors enhance cross-cultural peer relationships.

OTHER SOURCES OF VARIATION IN SOCIAL COMPETENCE

Children's relationships with peers are influenced by many other factors. Disabilities, family stressors, child care, and gender can affect the acquisition of social skills and the formation of friendships.

Social Competence and Challenging Conditions

A number of research studies suggest that children with special needs are likely to be rejected by peers. In fact, some researchers believe that peer rejection and its causes—in particular, hostile, aggressive behavior—are themselves a disability. For example, the condition **serious emotional disturbance (SED)** is defined, in part, as an inability to function effectively in social contexts.

Much research has focused on specific challenging conditions and their effects on social development. Studies suggest that children with hearing and visual impairments are viewed by peers as unfriendly or unable or unwilling to play (Hughes, 1995; Lerner, 1985). Of course, it is the children's impairments that limit their responsiveness to others' initiatives.

By age 5, young children are likely to report negative attitudes toward children with physical disabilities (Sirvis & Caldwell, 1995). Perhaps these negative opinions cause children with physical challenges to be excluded from play and, thus, less socially competent (Coleman, Pullis, & Minnett, 1987). Children with mental retardation or learning disabilities also have been found to be deficient in social skills and more often rejected by classmates (S. B. Vaughn, Hogan, Kouzekanani, & Shapiro, 1990). Autistic children rarely engage in social play; they often show little interest in peers and tend to be rejected as playmates (Welteroth, 1999).

Taken together, these studies paint a bleak prognosis for the social development of children with special needs. Are children with challenging conditions destined to be rejected by peers? Will efforts to facilitate social relationships be futile? Actually, the picture is much more complex—and more positive—than early studies would suggest. Peer rejection varies as a function of the particular exceptionality and its extremity. Handicaps that can actually be observed and understood by young children are less likely to lead to peer rejection (Fallen & Umansky, 1985). Children in wheelchairs, for example, have visible handicaps that are easily explained by parents or teachers, so they are more readily accepted than children who have less obvious impairments. Disorders such as autism are much harder for preschoolers to understand. Autistic children are different in their communication and behavior, which contributes to their rejection by peers. The lack of concrete cues to explain their condition makes it difficult for adults to facilitate their acceptance by peers.

Many children with special needs will not experience peer rejection (Coleman & Minnett, 1992). Several studies have shown, for example, that young children with learning disabilities may have a neutral social status—they are neither the most popular nor the most actively rejected (Dudley-Marling & Edmiason, 1985). One study found that a significant number of children with learning disabilities were actually rated as popular by peers (Perlmutter, Crocker, Corday, & Garstecki, 1983). So, although challenging conditions can impede social relationships in the preschool years, such is not always the case.

Poverty and Family Stressors

Children in poverty are more likely to suffer emotional challenges and, as a result, to be less successful in their relationships with peers (Huston, 1991; McLoyd & Wilson, 1992). Conditions such as poor nutrition and health care may play a role in this problem. Most researchers believe, however, that it is poverty's devastating effect on parenting that explains most poor social outcomes. Parents under the stress of poverty may be less effective, more punitive, and less warm with children (McLoyd, 1990a). They may direct more anger toward their children than do parents who do not suffer economic hardship. These parenting characteristics have a negative impact on social development. Young children whose parents interact with them angrily or negatively are less effective with peers and less competent in understanding emotions and social situations (Garner, Jones, & Miner, 1994; Hart, Ladd, & Burleson, 1990).

The negative effects of poverty may be seen most clearly in the case of dysfunctional families. Children growing up with such problems as domestic violence, abuse, or parental mental health disorders—all more common among poor families—are at special risk in their social development. Children whose mothers are depressed, for example, have been found to be less popular among peers. Social problems among these children are less severe, however, when a mentally healthy adult lives in the home. For example, a child who lives with a depressed mother but also with a healthy father or grandmother might have a greater chance of forming positive peer relations (S. H. Goodman, Brogan, Lynch, & Fielding, 1993).

Child abuse has a devastating effect on children's social development. Abused children have been found to have particularly poor relationships with peers (Salzinger, Feldman, Hammer, & Rosario, 1993). Such children are less liked by playmates and have few friends. This may be due, in part, to their own resistance to peer contact. In one study, it was found that abused children were approached as often by peers as non-abused children were, but were far more likely to reject invitations to play (Haskett & Kistner, 1991). Generally, the social profile of abused preschoolers matches that of other rejected children: they are often negative, unpredictable, and aggressive.

Siblings

Siblings can contribute to positive social development. However, most research focuses on problems in sibling relationships. Sibling rivalry, the trauma of a birth of a brother or sister, and aggression are emphasized in studies and in the popular literature. Ironically, another problem related to siblings which receives much attention is *not* having them: over the years, negative stereotypes have emerged about only children. Many popular parenting books paint a no-win situation: siblings cause conflict and family disharmony, yet children's development is negatively affected without them.

Although problems with siblings certainly exist, the impact of siblings on social development may be more positive than negative. Consider the case of sibling rivalry. It is true that conflicts exist, particularly between same-sex siblings of similar age (Minnett, Vandell, & Santrock, 1983), but this conflict may not be all bad. Older children may gain confidence and leadership ability by directing their younger siblings. Younger children may acquire skills at resisting bullying. Children appear to feel more comfortable in their conflicts with brothers or sisters. Sibling interactions may be ideal contexts for learning to speak one's mind, argue, and resolve disputes. Research suggests that sibling relationships are often cooperative and nurturing (Abramovitch, Pepler, & Corter, 1982). Children learn many social skills, then, from brothers or sisters. Sibling influence is especially important in the many communities of the world in which a sibling is the caretaker or primary playmate (B. B. Whiting & Edwards, 1988).

Parenting guides and the popular literature usually portray the birth of a brother or sister as a traumatic event in the life of a child, but studies have shown that children learn valuable lessons as they adjust to the arrival of a new sibling (Dunn, 1992). A new baby may assist the older child in the process of separating from parents and becoming independent. Children learn to share the affections of their parents. They often acquire nurturing behaviors as they interact with a newborn, particularly in cultures where children are assigned child care responsibilities at a young age (B. B. Whiting & Edwards, 1988).

Does this mean that children who do not have siblings are handicapped in some way? Research dispels the myth that only children are doomed to become self-centered or socially inept. In fact, some studies suggest that only children are advanced in intellectual development, language, and creativity (Blake, 1989; Mellor, 1990). A number of fascinating studies on only children have been recently conducted in China, where there are now incentives for families to have only one son or daughter. Chinese only children have been found to have greater cognitive skills, to perform better in school, and to suffer less anxiety and depression than those with siblings (Wan, Fan, Lin, & Jing, 1994; Yang, Ollendick, Dong, Xia, & Lin, 1995). It appears that siblings are useful, but not necessary, for social development. No research evidence suggests that only children have delayed social abilities or problematic peer relations.

Child Care

If availability of peers influences social development, it stands to reason that young children in child care will show advanced social competence. Many preschoolers in the United States spend over half of their waking time interacting with other children in centers or family child care homes (Children's Defense Fund, 1998). The relationship between child care and social development is not so clear, however. Studies have yielded mixed results. Some studies suggest that children in child care display more prosocial behavior (Clarke-Stewart, 1984; Howes & Olenick, 1986), while others show that such children are more aggressive in their interactions (Haskins, 1985). Some researchers conclude that child care increases both positive and negative social behaviors (Belsky & Steinberg, 1978).

How can these inconsistent findings be explained? More recent research shows that the impact of child care depends on its quality. **Child care quality** has been defined as the degree to which both *structural* and *dynamic* features of care meet the social, emotional, and intellectual needs of young children (Whitebrook, Phillips, & Howes, 1993). Structural features include physical and social characteristics of the center or home—staff-to-child ratio, available play space and toys, and group size. Dynamic features consist of caregiver behaviors—warmth or responsiveness—which promote children's development. Children in centers or family child care homes that are rated as high in quality on both dimensions have been found to be more sociable and positive in play with peers. They also show greater social knowledge and problem-solving abilities (Holloway & Reichhart-Erickson, 1988; Howes, Phillips, & Whitebook, 1992). Children who are in low-quality programs, however, do not show these positive social interactions and, in fact, may be at risk.

The impact of child care on social development depends, then, on quality. Unfortunately, recent research suggests that a large percentage of child care programs in the United States rate quite low on both structural and dynamic dimensions (Cost, Quality, and Child Outcomes Study Team, 1995). Although child care holds promise as a way to resolve serious problems of poor social development, it may also create risks. A national policy is needed in the United States to fund high-quality child care programs in all communities.

Gender and Social Development

Boys and girls can be very different in their social interactions and play. Most parents eventually learn this through experiences like the following:

> A single mother has committed herself to raising her daughter free of sex-stereotyped behaviors and self-perceptions. She carefully selects gender-neutral toys for her child. She encourages her daughter to be active and bold, to make independent decisions. She carefully screens the television shows her daughter watches to be certain she is not exposed to stereotyped role models.
>
> The mother enrolls her daughter in a child care center. After about a month, she visits the center to observe the classroom and her daughter in action. She is somewhat troubled by what she sees. Her daughter plays only with girls during her visit, and their play involves pretending to cook meals, caring for babies, and dressing up in feminine hats and jewelry. At one point, an active 4-year-old boy approaches her daughter's play group with a toy dinosaur. "Dinosaurs are attacking," he calls out. He is quickly rebuffed by the little girls. "We don't need that!" the woman's daughter says, seizing the dinosaur and tossing it to the ground. The boy retreats and the girls resume their play. The mother shakes her head and wonders what went wrong.

Children of all socioeconomic groups and cultures show gender differences in play. By 18 months of age, most children prefer to play with sex-stereotyped toys; boys play with trucks and girls play with dolls (Powlishta, Serbin, & Moller, 1993). As early as 2 years of age, they prefer to play with same-sex peers (Maccoby & Jacklin, 1990). Play styles of boys and girls differ markedly. Boys are usually more active and rough in their play, and girls quieter and more elaborate (Fagot & O'Brien, 1994). These patterns of social interaction and play—often called *sex-typed* or *gender-stereotyped behaviors*—are found in all cultures and societies of the world (B. B. Whiting & Edwards, 1988).

How can these gender differences be explained? How is it that the child in the story above, who was raised in a non-stereotyped home environment, displays such sex-typed behavior? There are two prominent perspectives regarding gender identity and **sex-role stereotyping.** The first perspective is that children acquire sex-typed behaviors because of modeling and reinforcement in the environment (Bandura, 1967). The world is filled with models of stereotyped behavior. Parents may subconsciously act in stereotypical ways, and television regularly depicts men and women in sex-typed roles and interactions. As more and more children are cared for in child care in America, peers become important models. Even very young preschoolers have been found to learn gender-typical social skills and play styles from playmates in the classroom (Maccoby, 1989).

This stereotyped behavior is rewarded in the environment. Parents may reinforce girls to be timid and compliant and boys to be bold and independent. They may do so subconsciously. In one study, for example, parents were found to verbally encourage their children to play with both male and female toys, but their body language gave them away. They moved closer to and became more involved in their children's play when stereotypical toys were selected (Caldera, Huston, & O'Brien, 1989). This may explain why, even in homes where feminist perspectives are taught, children still hold stereotyped views of gender roles (Huston, 1983).

A second perspective of gender differences is that early sex stereotyping stems from cognitive limitations. During the preschool years, children tend to believe that being a boy or girl is determined by clothing, hair, or other physical characteristics (Kohlberg & Ullian, 1974). If you wear a dress you are a girl, or if you have short hair you are a boy, the thinking goes. Once children come to view themselves as male or female, according to this perspective, they actively strive to understand their gender role more fully. They observe the behaviors of models around them and develop a theory of what it is to be a boy or girl. Once a gender theory emerges, they strive to conform to it in their behavior and thinking.

Young children's gender theories are quite rigid and inflexible. Boys tend to play only with trucks; they are often louder and more active than girls. Girls prefer dolls; they are usually quieter and more passive. One reason for such rigid thinking is that society makes stereotyped gender roles so easy to observe and comprehend (Levy & Carter, 1989). Children see that men on TV are more aggressive or have certain kinds of jobs. They see that women play passive, dependent, and nurturing roles. They integrate these characteristics into their theory of boyness or girlness.

If this second perspective is correct, then children should become less stereotyped in their interactions as they develop intellectually. Research shows that this is the case: older and cognitively advanced children have been found to show less rigidly stereotyped beliefs and behaviors than younger or less intellectually competent children (Bigler & Liben, 1992; Stangor & Ruble, 1989).

How do these two perspectives assist professionals in reducing negative gender stereotypes? Based on the first view, care must be taken to avoid modeling or reinforcing stereotypical behaviors in the classroom. At the same time—relying on the second perspective—teachers might provide experiences that help children to construct a non-stereotyped theory of gender. Photographs that depict men and women engaged in non-stereotypic work might be presented and discussed. Children's books that show characters engaged in non-stereotyped play activities might be provided. A focus should be on helping children analyze what it means to be a boy or girl.

ASSESSING YOUNG CHILDREN: Preschool Social and Emotional Development

Areas of Development	What to Watch for	Indicators of Atypical Development
Emotional health	Shows initiative in projects and play activities. Enters readily into play with peers. Shows a positive view of oneself with statements such as "Look how high I can swing" or "I have lots of friends."	Holds back or hesitates in classroom activities or interactions with peers. Expresses feelings of guilt (e.g., "I am a bad boy") or self-doubt ("I can't do it").
Relationships with others	Is liked by at least some other children in the classroom or neighborhood. Forms one or more special friendships. Enters into positive relationships with teachers and other adults.	Shows no interest in interacting with peers. Is actively avoided by peers or ignored completely. Forms no close friendships in school or at home.
Specific social skills	Shows specific social skills, such as getting a peer's attention, entering a play group, or resolving conflicts. Uses language in peer interactions. Shows kindness.	Displays hostile, aggressive behaviors and an inability to solve problems with peers in positive ways. Performs behaviors that peers consider bizarre or disruptive. Shows extreme withdrawal; always chooses to play alone.

Interpreting Assessment Data: Variations in social and emotional development may be due to culture. Some children are less likely to take initiative because dependence and family enmeshment are valued over independence. Children may be quiet and more reluctant to play with peers because their families are less verbal and more cautious and reflective. Some rough play—more common in some cultures than others—may be misinterpreted as aggression by teachers or peers. True rejection by peers or an inability or unwillingness to engage in *any* social interaction is cause for concern, however. Children who are highly aggressive or hostile are at special risk. Such children should be referred for special services as early as such problems are evident. Social intervention strategies such as teaching prosocial skills, social language, and conflict-resolution abilities or nurturing classroom friendships may ameliorate these social problems. The earlier social interventions are provided, the more likely they are to be effective.

RESEARCH INTO PRACTICE

CRITICAL CONCEPT 1

Once preschool children have become attached to caregivers and are autonomous in their actions and thinking, they often begin to show initiative. Initiative is an emotional state that leads children to make creative attempts, take risks, and reach out to peers. Erikson has warned that if children are harshly restricted in their initiatives, they will suffer guilt.

Application #1

Teachers, caregivers, and parents should create play environments in which children feel safe taking risks, trying out new behaviors, and making creative attempts. They should be given opportunities to engage peers in active play. Care should be taken not to stifle initiative. Too many rules or criticism of creative efforts can lead children to suffer guilt.

Application #2

Teachers and caregivers should provide experiences and activities in school that are largely process-oriented; that is, experimentation and self-expression should be emphasized, without regard to end products. Blocks, sculpting and drawing materials, dramatic play, and large motor free play are examples of open-ended activities that inspire initiative. In contrast, art projects that are teacher-directed and require children to produce the same finished product will restrict initiative.

Application #3

Teachers and caregivers should avoid evaluating or comparing children's completed works. Even praise can threaten initiative by giving implicit messages about the efforts of other children. For example, praising one child's painting suggests that there is only one correct way to paint.

CRITICAL CONCEPT 2

Cross-cultural studies have found variation in the degree to which children acquire initiative. Some families discourage individual creative effort and emphasize collective thought and action. Children of such families may be less eager to take risks and to express themselves individually in the child care center or classroom.

Application #1

Teachers and caregivers should understand and appreciate cultural differences in initiative. Care should be taken not to insist that all children take risks or make creative attempts. Caution, ambivalence about individual expression, and a desire to check with others before acting may be a part of some children's cultural heritage.

Application #2

Classroom experiences that focus on group efforts rather than individual initiative may be planned to meet the needs of children of diverse cultural backgrounds. Activities such as collaborative mural painting, joint block building, and cooperative scientific experiments may better match the play styles of children of collective cultures.

CRITICAL CONCEPT 3

Peer acceptance and the formation of friendships are extremely important in the early years. Young children who are not well liked or who are ineffective with peers are at risk. Children who are actively rejected by peers because of aggressive or annoying behavior, and those who are neglected because they are shy or nonsocial, may need special support in forming peer relationships.

Application #1

Teachers and caregivers can intervene in children's play to teach social skills that will lead to peer acceptance. They might model or prompt strategies for joining a play group or getting a peer's attention. They can guide children in resolving disagreements in positive, non-aggressive ways. These interventions are especially important for children who are actively rejected or ignored by peers.

Application #2

Teachers and caregivers can facilitate friendships between pairs of children who are having difficulty forming positive peer relationships. Potential friendships can be identified by observing the play of rejected and neglected children and noting potential classroom friends. Identified pairs of children can then be invited to help prepare snacks or to work on special activities away from the rest of the group. During these experiences, an adult can facilitate positive interactions. Ultimately, lasting friendships may form. Parents might be encouraged to assist in the process by inviting potential friends to their homes after school.

CRITICAL CONCEPT 4

Specific prosocial behaviors contribute to successful relationships with peers. These include cooperative play, altruism, and empathy. Aggression, in contrast, leads to poor peer relations.

Application #1

Cognitive-developmental strategies can be applied in classrooms and centers to teach kindness and reduce aggression. Through intervention, caregivers and teachers can guide children in interpreting the social world. In particular, children can be asked to reflect on the outcomes of both positive and negative social behaviors. During aggressive conflicts, children can be encouraged to think about and discuss the effects of hitting or pushing and the alternatives to solving social problems.

Application #2

Behaviorist and social cognitive learning strategies can also be applied to promote positive social behavior. Children can be praised for positive interactions. Adults can model prosocial behaviors. Negative social models can be reduced by restricting television viewing at home and by eliminating aggressive behaviors by adults in the classroom. Teachers and caregivers should refrain from angry scolding, for example. Parent education programs that promote non-physical, non-aggressive disciplinary methods can be offered.

Application #3

Psychoanalytic strategies can be used to promote positive social development and reduce aggression. Caregivers and teachers can be especially warm, positive, and responsive with children who have problems with aggression. Parents can be encouraged to interact in these ways as well. The purpose of these strategies is to facilitate trust and attachment. Such interactions may lead to positive relationships with adults and children. Once bonds with adults have formed, children may begin to successfully enter into relationships with peers as well.

CRITICAL CONCEPT 5

Social interaction and peer acceptance are influenced by cultural background, gender, disability, and temperament. Children whose patterns of social interaction are considered "different" are sometimes at risk of peer rejection or neglect.

Application #1

Teachers and caregivers must actively facilitate play and social interaction between children with special needs and their typically developing peers. Strategies include facilitating conversations between a child with language delays and a typically developing peer, assisting a hearing child in understanding another child's hearing impairment, and demonstrating positive ways a child with autism can get a classmate's attention.

Application #2

Teachers and caregivers must take an active role in promoting positive relationships and interactions between boys and girls and among children of diverse cultural backgrounds and temperaments. This could include development of an "anti-bias" curriculum in which developmental, cultural, and gender differences are openly discussed and celebrated. Active efforts should be made to ensure diversity in play groups and to reduce rejection on the basis of race, gender, or disability.

SUGGESTED ACTIVITIES

1. Observe children interacting in an early childhood classroom. Identify a child you think is popular, another who is likely to be rejected, and a third who appears to be neglected by peers. (You might ask a teacher to help you select your subjects.) Write a description of each child, guided by the following questions:

   a. Which specific social interactions did you observe in the popular child? The rejected child? The neglected child? How are the three children different in their behaviors? Which social skills described in this chapter were you able to observe in the popular child? Which skills were lacking in the two less effective children?

   b. How did peers respond to each child? What signs did you see of peer rejection or peer neglect?

   c. Based on your observations, what recommendations would you make for social skills intervention?

2. Select two children who are friends. (You will need to ask a teacher to help you identify them.) Observe the two children interacting in a classroom for at least a half-hour period. Write a description of your observations, guided by the following questions:

   a. What signs did you observe that these children are true friends?

   b. Did you observe any disagreements between the two children? If so, how did they resolve them?

   c. How did the two children approach one another to play? To what degree did they allow each other to enter play groups already in progress, if you were able to observe this?

   d. To what degree did the two friends play with other peers? Did they allow other playmates to join them in play activities?

3. Observe an entire classroom of preschool-age children. Watch for examples of the following behaviors reviewed in the chapter: cooperative play, altruism (i.e., kindness, sharing, nurturance), and empathy (i.e., showing concern). Write descriptions of two examples of each of these behaviors. Then write an essay that answers the following question: Based on your observations, why do you believe that children perform these behaviors?

4. Observe an entire classroom of preschool-age children for a full day. Watch for examples of aggression. Write

a description of each example you observe. Then write an essay that answers the following questions:

a. Which of the behaviors were reactive aggression? Which were proactive aggression?

b. Which of the proactive aggressive acts were instrumental? Which were examples of bullying?

c. What seemed to precipitate each aggressive act? To what degree did aggression stem from anger or hostility?

d. Were some children more aggressive than others? How do you explain this?

5. Visit a classroom of preschool children who are from diverse cultural backgrounds. Observe four children—two boys and two girls—of at least two distinct cultural groups. Write an essay about the similarities and differences in social interactions among the children, guided by the following questions:

a. Which specific social behaviors or skills did you observe in all four children?

b. Which specific social behaviors or skills were observed in some of the children but not in others?

c. How would you characterize the relationships between each child and his or her peers? To what degree did you observe differences among children in these relationships?

d. To what degree do you believe differences in social interaction and relationships are due to culture?

e. To what degree are differences due to gender?

6. Visit a preschool in which children with special needs are enrolled. Select two children, one with special needs and one without, to observe. Write an essay about the similarities and differences in social interactions of these children, guided by the following questions:

a. Which similarities and differences did you observe in the social behaviors of the two children?

b. How would you characterize the relationships between each child and his or her peers?

c. What signs did you see of peer rejection or neglect in relations between the child with special needs and his or her peers? What signs of acceptance or popularity did you see?

d. Based on your observations, do you believe children with special needs are at risk of poor social development and negative peer relationships? Why or why not?

CHAPTER 14

Physical Growth and Motor Development in the Primary Years

I N THIS CHAPTER WE WILL DISCUSS CHILDREN'S PHYSICAL GROWTH AND MOTOR DEVELOPMENT DURING THE PRIMARY YEARS—THE PERIOD FROM AGES 6 TO 8. Children of most cultures begin formal schooling during this developmental period. The emphasis of schools in almost all societies is on promoting academic learning. Even in non-industrialized communities, classroom teachers spend the majority of the day providing instruction in traditional subjects, especially language and reading (B. B. Whiting & Edwards, 1988). What appears to be less important to parents, teachers, and even child development researchers is physical growth and motor development during the primary years (Lockman & Thelen, 1993). Many school districts in America have reduced the number of days children spend in physical education each week, and some are eliminating outdoor play altogether (Ross & Pate, 1987).

Trends toward deemphasizing physical growth and activity have serious implications for teachers, as the following story reveals:

A first-grade teacher, Ms. Schreiber, is reading a story to her students during group time. She is having a difficult time holding their attention. This is the first day that a new recess policy has been in effect. Outdoor play time has been significantly reduced and pushed back until later in the school day. The rationale for the new policy is that recess is a waste of instructional time. The superintendent of this particular school system believes that increasing instructional time is the best way to improve scores on achievement tests.

And so, Ms. Schreiber struggles along, reading in an animated voice and reminding students to listen. The children wiggle and talk, until finally she realizes the futility of continuing with the story. She gathers the children together and takes them outdoors. The children run and scream for a short while, then Ms. Schreiber leads them back inside. When she resumes the story, her students are very attentive. Just a few minutes of physical activity has made all the difference!

When she relates this experience to the principal of her school, he is not impressed. In fact, he reprimands her for having violated the new policy.

The teacher in this story has learned that cognitive and motor development are interrelated. Children who are healthy, physically fit, and relaxed will perform well in school. Those who have health problems or are in need of physical exercise will perform poorly.

PHYSICAL APPEARANCE AND STATURE

The rate of physical growth slows considerably in the primary years. Children of this age will usually gain only about 2 inches in height and 4 pounds in weight each year. Initially, boys tend to be taller and heavier than girls, but girls generally catch up to them near the end of the primary-grade period. As legs and torsos become gradually longer and faces thinner, many primary-age children begin to take on a "slimmed down" appearance that contrasts with the roundish body shape of earlier periods.

A trademark of the primary years is the toothless grin. Children at this age lose their "baby teeth," one after the other. Tooth loss is a significant event of this developmental period and predominates peer conversations.

Cultural Variations in Physical Growth

Much variation in growth exists among typically developing children. Furthermore, height and weight vary across cultural groups. Southeast Asian children continue to be shorter, on the average, than Euro-American children (J. E. Brown et al., 1986), while African and African-American children tend to be longer limbed and heavier (Super, 1981). Individual growth trends can differ markedly within each cultural group, however, with some children "shooting up" quickly during this period, others growing more slowly.

Cultural differences in stature among primary-age children are often due to genetics. However, environment plays a role. Children of some cultural groups who live in poverty are smaller in stature because of poor nutrition and health care (Nutritional Status of Minority Children, 1997). For example, Southeast Asian children of poor families tend to be significantly shorter and lighter. Their small stature is believed to result from a combination of genetics and iron deficiency, which is prevalent among low-income families of this cultural group (J. E. Brown et al., 1986).

In a study of black South African children, place of residence was found to influence stature in the primary years (Gaduka, Poole, & Aotaki-Phenice, 1992). Children who were living in their homelands were found to be taller and heavier than those whose families had been relocated to "resettlement communities" during apartheid and those who were living on white-owned farms. These researchers concluded that a complex cluster of community, home, and family factors contributes to general physical development.

Research in China has shown that, in some communities, only children are taller and heavier than those with siblings (Falbo & Poston, 1993). This finding contrasts sharply with research done in the United States, which reports no physical differences between only children and others (Polit, 1982). Why the discrepancy? One explanation is that families with only one child receive special support from the government in China as part of a national policy to reduce the population. Since 1979, Chinese parents having only one child have been awarded certificates entitling them to special nutritional or health care benefits. In this case, then, government policy has affected the physical growth of young children.

Other research shows that children in many non-industrialized countries are taller and heavier if their mothers have obtained a higher level of education (Tucker & Young, 1989). It is clear from these studies that children's stature in the primary years is affected by a complex set of factors which goes beyond health and nutritional influences.

POVERTY AND HEALTH STATUS OF PRIMARY-AGE CHILDREN

Great concern has been expressed around the world about the nutrition and health care of very young children in poverty. Poor prenatal and infant health status, in particular, has been found to predict serious developmental problems later in life (Pollitt, 1994). Are poor health and nutrition as damaging during the primary years? There appears to be a widespread assumption that older children are somehow less vulnerable to these problems. A sign of this belief is the recent reduction in U.S. funding for health and nutritional programs for this age group, such as the National School Lunch Program (Children's Defense Fund, 1998). Research suggests that these programs are crucial to the healthy development of primary-age children. In a large study of families in poverty, Duncan, Brooks-Gunn, and Klebanov (1994) report that elementary school children who do not have an adequate diet or sufficient medical care still suffer serious developmental problems. They are not protected because they have enjoyed good health or nutrition during earlier years. Continuous support is needed—throughout all of childhood—to ensure healthy growth and development.

Illness

Primary-grade children living in poverty are more likely to suffer a number of serious health problems. They are more often afflicted by infectious diseases (Jason & Jarvis, 1987), more regularly diagnosed with chronic conditions, such as asthma (Weitzman, Gortmaker, Walker, & Sobol, 1989), and more frequently found to have dental problems (Klerman, 1991b). Children in poverty miss many more days of school due to physical ailments (Adams & Benson, 1991). Such medical problems are also more common among children of parents who are above the poverty line but have low-wage jobs. This is due, in part, to a lack of medical insurance among these families. There are millions of uninsured children in the United States (Children's Defense Fund, 1998). Such children are four times as likely to have necessary medical procedures delayed, and five times as likely to use the hospital emergency room as their only source of medical care.

These trends are most pronounced for poor children from historically under-represented groups. Children of African-American (J. H. Carter, 1983), Mexican-American (Olvera-Ezzell, Power, Cousins, Guerra, & Trujillo, 1994), and Native American (A. D. Brown & Hernasy, 1983) backgrounds may be at special health risk during the primary years. One reason for this is the existence of cultural barriers to family services (Powell, 1983), as the following story illustrates:

Marcus lives with his young, single mother in a small apartment in a large urban neighborhood. He has a respiratory ailment and spends much time lying in bed. Marcus has missed many days of school already this year. His mother has no health insurance and is frightened to go to a community clinic near her home.

One morning she finds Marcus coughing and wheezing so violently that she becomes afraid. Seeing no other option, she decides to go to Marcus's school, hoping his teacher or a school nurse can help. She asks a neighbor to stay with Marcus and runs to the school, which is several blocks from her home. She enters Marcus's classroom and rushes to the teacher in a panic.

TEACHER: Hello! I'm glad you stopped in. We really need to talk.

MOTHER: (Breathless) Can you . . . can you . . . (Struggles with her words)

TEACHER: (In a concerned tone) Did Marcus not come in with you today? Is he out of school again?

MOTHER: He's sick . . .

TEACHER: We need to talk about all of these absences. He's not learning anything in school, because he's gone so much. Is he really sick all the time, or does he just like staying at home? It really would be good if you'd see to it that he gets here. It's your responsibility as a parent . . .

MOTHER: (Begins to cry)

TEACHER: Oh . . . You seem really upset. Let's sit here a moment. Tell me what's wrong.

The mother finally gets out her story. The teacher arranges for the school nurse to help get Marcus to the clinic. He is diagnosed with asthma. With treatment, he is able to attend school more regularly.

Marcus's family has limited access to health services. His young mother is intimidated by the medical clinic, perhaps because of the complex bureaucracy or the disapproving looks from the staff because of her young age. Even when Marcus is very ill, she is afraid to go. Marcus's teacher has clearly decided that his absences are due to irresponsibility on the part of his mother. At first, the mother's pleas for help go unheeded while the teacher gives a stern lecture. Fortunately, the mother manages to tell of Marcus's problems, and he gets the medical care he needs. Not all families living in poverty are so fortunate.

Nutrition

Children's health is related to good nutrition. Elementary children who eat well will suffer fewer serious illnesses (U.S. Department of Health and Human Services, 1996). In many parts of the world, children do not have enough to eat. Protein deficiency, anemia, and general starvation are still common in some non-industrialized countries (Pollitt, Gorman, Engle, Martorell, & Rivera, 1993). These conditions disrupt healthy development. Children's mental as well as physical and motor competence are impaired by an inadequate diet during the primary years.

Poor nutrition is common among primary-grade children in the United States, as well. Studies of eating habits in the elementary years show that many American children have diets high in saturated fats, salt, and sugar. Over a third of calories consumed by typical elementary school children come from nutritionally poor foods (Berenson et al., 1982). Not surprisingly, problems of inadequate diet are more common among families living in poverty (Olvera-Ezzell et al., 1994).

Certain historically under-represented groups are at special risk of poor nutrition. Mexican-American children, for example, are more likely to be obese in the elementary years than their Euro-American, African-American, and Asian-American peers (Olvera-Ezzell, Power, & Cousins, 1990). This trend is most pronounced for Mexican-American children living in poverty (M. A. Alexander, Blank, & Clark, 1991; Kumanyika, Huffman, Bradshaw, & Paige, 1990). Contributing to obesity among Mexican-American elementary schoolchildren are factors associated with being poor: inadequate diet and lack of health insurance and health care (Olvera-Ezzell et al., 1994). Mothers who believe that they are not in control of their own circumstances are also more likely to have children who are obese.

On the other hand, Mexican-American parents who actively socialize their children to eat healthy foods can significantly reduce the likelihood of obesity. In one study (Olvera-Ezzell et al., 1990), certain parent interventions at mealtime were found to reduce overeating and improve nutrition. Effective parents tailored their interactions to the particular mealtime situation. For example, when coaxing children to try new foods, they were permissive in their responses: "You don't have to eat that, but it's really good!" When they wanted their children to eat healthy foods they were already familiar with, they were more directive: "You need to eat all those vegetables so you will grow." To discourage overeating, they were democratic in their mealtime interchanges: "Do you really think you should eat a big second helping of potatoes?" These strategies reflect the unique socialization beliefs and practices of this cultural group.

Injury

Injury is the leading cause of death among primary-grade children (Peterson, Ewigman, & Kivlahan, 1993). Each year, 30,000 children are permanently disabled due to injuries. Further, 600,000 children are hospitalized annually with injuries; many more visit an emergency room. In the United States, children in poverty—particularly those who live in dangerous urban neighborhoods—suffer more injuries (Rivara & Barber, 1985). Injuries are also more prevalent among children of some historically under-represented groups. Mexican-American children, for example, are more likely to be injured on the playground or in the street (L. M. Olson, Becker, Wiggins, Key, & Samet, 1990).

Vigilant parents and teachers can safeguard children. Poor supervision has been identified as a major reason for preventable accidents involving children (Garbarino, Dubrow, Kostelny, & Pardo, 1992). Risk of injury is highest in single-parent homes, in those in which parents are very young, and in those in which drugs or alcohol are abused (Rivara & Mueller, 1987).

How much supervision is required to keep children safe from injury? In one study, this question was asked of mothers, child protection service workers, and health care providers (Peterson et al., 1993). The consensus among these groups was that preschool-age children should receive constant supervision—that is, they should never be out of the sight of an adult. Early elementary-age children should receive near-constant supervision—no more than 5 minutes without supervision. However, study participants agreed that when children were playing in "high risk" areas, where busy roads or urban hazards are a threat, even primary-age children should receive constant supervision.

Taken together, this research paints a troubling picture of the risks of children living in poverty. While parents and child safety experts recommend constant supervision when children play in high-risk neighborhoods, problems associated with poverty—substance abuse and single or teenage parenthood—can result in insufficient supervision.

Violence

During the time it takes you to read this chapter, one child will die from gunfire in this country. This death rate is equivalent to the loss of an entire classroom of children every 2 days (Children's Defense Fund, 1994). Six million violent crime victimizations were reported in 1990 in the United States; a disproportionate number of these occurred in low-income, urban areas (Reiss & Roth, 1993). Assaults committed by young people under age 15 have increased significantly (Children's Defense Fund, 1994). A growing number of children have been witnesses to or victims of violence (Garbarino et al., 1992; Reiss & Roth, 1993).

By age 5, a majority of children now living in low-income neighborhoods in the United States have encountered a shooting. By adolescence, two-thirds have witnessed a homicide (C. Bell, 1991). Reported cases of child abuse rose from 60,000 in 1974, to 1.1 million in 1980, to 2.4 million in 1988 (U.S. Department of Health and Human Services, 1990). Between 1990 and 1995, numbers of child abuse cases increased in 35 states, with cases in one state growing by over 300% (Children's Defense Fund, 1998)! Although these statistics reflect increased reporting of the problem, it is clear that large numbers of American young people are at risk due to experiences with violence. In no other country in the world is violent criminal behavior more prevalent (van Dijk, Mayhew, & Killias, 1990).

Living in violent communities—"urban war zones," as they have sometimes been called—presents both physical and mental risks. So many children are killed in assaults in such neighborhoods that violent injury and death are now considered major national childhood health problems (Children's Defense Fund, 1994). Children and youth of historically under-represented groups are more likely to be victimized; homicide is the leading cause of death among African Americans under age 24 (Reiss

Children who live in violent neighborhoods live in constant fear.

& Roth, 1993). Figure 14-1 shows the alarming rates of homicide for several cultural groups in the United States.

Violence also takes a great emotional toll (Garbarino et al., 1992). Preschool children exposed to chronic community violence show passive responses: clinging, fearfulness, bed-wetting, and quiet, withdrawn behavior. However, with age, reactions become more overt and problematic in school. Primary-age children from violent communities exhibit more aggression and conduct problems, poor concentration, forgetfulness, and learning difficulties. Regular experiences with violence at this age may lead to serious psychological disorders. Children may undergo major personality changes. Regression—the resumption of bed-wetting or thumb-sucking—is common. Children who live in danger often develop feelings of rage and despair. Many experience "psychic numbing," which causes them to stop caring or feeling (Garbarino et al., 1992, p. 57).

All children who live with violence live in fear. Garbarino et al. (1992) tell the story of one young child who lives in terror in a dangerous neighborhood. When asked why he kept an empty deodorant bottle beside his bed, he ran his finger along the label and read, "Guaranteed 100 percent safe." The intensity of this fear reaction varies according to cultural and family experience. In one study, African-American children—particularly girls—were found to worry more about physical harm than their Euro-American peers (W. K. Silverman, La Greca, & Wasserstein, 1995). Such findings are not surprising, given the high rate of physical assault and homicide in low-income, predominantly African-American neighborhoods.

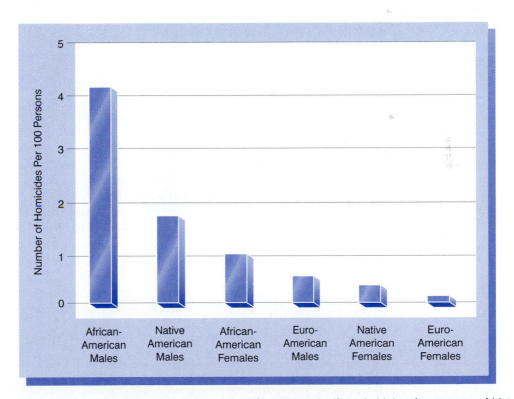

FIGURE 14-1 Homicide rates in the United States are significantly higher for persons of historically under-represented groups. African-American males, in particular, are at risk of violent death.
SOURCE: Extrapolated from data in Reiss and Roth, 1993.

Children's fear of violence is not limited to urban American neighborhoods. Violence causes psychological harm all over the world. In Mozambique, which has been at war throughout its existence, children are regularly killed, kidnapped, and tortured. A growing number of children are orphans whose parents have been killed in the war. In an interview with 35 Mozambiquan children, 24 reported witnessing at least one violent death (Garbarino et al., 1992).

In Cambodia under Pol Pot's Khmer Rouge regime, the horrors of which were documented in the film *The Killing Fields,* children suffered horrible atrocities. Not only were children, their families, and parents killed in great numbers, but children were sometimes recruited as executioners or enforcers, forced to kill others in support of the genocidal restructuring of Khmer society.

Some children are able to cope in spite of such atrocities. These children are called **resilient** because they manage to develop in positive directions under terrible circumstances. Many, however, do not survive intact. Although their physical wounds may heal, their psychological scars remain for life. Children of these communities are often numb and unresponsive—out of touch with the world and the people around them (Garbarino et al., 1992). In every community of the world, fear and injury caused by violence have a devastating effect on development.

Homelessness

A growing problem associated with poverty in America is homelessness. Only a decade ago, the homeless population was composed almost entirely of single men who suffered from mental illness (Zigler & Finn-Stevenson, 1993). Today, children account for the fastest-growing segment of the homeless population (Children Defense Fund, 1998). In some communities, over half of all homeless persons are children (Wood, Valdez, Hayashi, & Shen, 1990).

Living in a car, an abandoned building, or a shelter can have an injurious effect on psychological and physical growth. Homeless children are more likely to be depressed and anxious (Bassuk & Rubin, 1987), and they often display conduct problems and aggression (Axelson & Dail, 1988). Homeless children may also suffer from malnutrition; their health status is generally far poorer than that of children living in poverty who have consistent—if not adequate—housing (Wood et al., 1990). They are more often afflicted by chronic illness and are less likely to be adequately immunized against childhood diseases (Grant, 1989).

It would have been preposterous even 10 years ago to think that homeless children would be living in the streets of America. How could such a problem exist in such an affluent society? It may well be that the actions of policy makers and elected officials have contributed to these sad circumstances. Cuts in federal spending for social services and adequate housing are believed to be responsible for the recent increases in homelessness (Children's Defense Fund, 1998). Professionals who work with young children must become strong advocates for homeless families and their children.

MOTOR DEVELOPMENT IN THE PRIMARY YEARS

In the primary years, children gain greater control over their bodies. The basic large motor skills acquired in the preschool years—running, climbing, jumping, catching, throwing, kicking, and balancing—become refined and coordinated. Primary-grade children can now combine running, stopping, starting, and kicking abilities to play soccer. They

TABLE 14-1
Motor Development Milestones in the Primary Years

Primary children can . . .	by around age . . .
catch a small ball using hands only	6 years
skip using alternate foot	6 years
kick with a mature follow-through of the foot	6 years
hop alternating from one foot to another	6 years
hop accurately into small spaces or squares (as in hopscotch)	6.5 years
swing a bat and strike a ball, rotating the trunk and shifting body weight forward	6.5 years
throw a ball accurately, shifting weight properly and stepping with the foot opposite the throwing arm	6.5 years
balance on one foot without vision	7 years
walk along a narrow balance beam	7 years
perform jumping jacks	7 years
throw a ball or other object 40 to 70 feet	8 years
run between 14 and 18 feet per second	8 years

SOURCE: Cratty, 1986; Gallahue, 1982.

can coordinate movements and balance to ride a two-wheel bicycle. They now use their full bodies in throwing: they can shift body weight to one foot in preparation for a throw, then transfer weight to the other foot as the throw is made. Using this ability, they can excel in catching and throwing games. Specific large motor skills acquired during the primary years, and approximate ages at which they appear, are presented in Table 14-1.

On the average, boys outperform girls on many large motor skills during the primary years (Cratty, 1986). This may be due to boys' greater weight, height, limb length, and muscle tone at this point in development. Also, boys are more likely than girls to be encouraged to excel in physical activities. It is important to note, however, that gender differences in motor competence are not great at this age level, and that, as individuals, many girls are more competent than many boys. Both boys and girls acquire large motor skills at the same rapid rate throughout the elementary years.

Children also show more refined abilities in the use of small muscles in the primary years. They can manipulate markers, crayons, and pencils with greater control and can cut accurately with scissors. They are now able to button, zip, snap, and tie independently, which allows them to accomplish their own dressing and undressing. They can coordinate the use of vision and hands and fingers, which enables them to draw more representational pictures, write their names legibly, and handle and read books. These advances in motor ability are partly due to increases in muscle tone, strength, and coordination, but also to brain growth.

The Body-Brain Connection

Early researchers, such as Arnold Gesell, recognized a connection between the brain and motor ability. However, they viewed motor development as an *outcome* of brain maturation—a physical sign that synapses and nerve cells were forming.

A new theory about the body-brain connection has now been proposed: the **dynamic systems theory** (Lockman & Thelen, 1993) is based on research suggesting that motor action, cognitive development, and behavior are all part of a single, dynamic system in the brain. From this perspective, all of these components influence each other. Movement can foster brain growth, cognitive development, and learning, not just the other way around. This theory holds that physical play and exercise are critical, in part, because they promote learning and academic success.

Here's an example of how this dynamic system works (Sporns & Edelman, 1993): A child climbs on a climber on the playground. As she does this, she activates and coordinates certain neurons—brain cells—which are needed for this action. If she climbs often, these cells will become organized into a *neural cluster*—a collection of connected brain cells which handle climbing. As the child plays, she combines her climbing with other skills—swinging, jumping, and screaming out to her friends. Each of these actions leads eventually to the formation of new neural clusters. Over time, these clusters connect with one another and become an even larger network of cells, called a *neural map*. A neural map is a complex web of cells which connects a whole region of the brain. From this view, the practice and refinement of specific motor abilities leads to brain organization.

According to dynamic systems theory, once the brain is well organized in this way, it is better able to learn all sorts of things. Imagine that a child is crawling through a maze his teacher has created on the playground. As he does this, he creates neural clusters, which helps him to understand space and movement. These same clusters of brain cells may later help him with other spatial tasks in the classroom, like interpreting a map or recognizing or writing letters and words (Bushnell & Boudreau, 1993). When the brain becomes organized in motor play it enhances not only movement, but thinking and learning of all kinds.

If, indeed, brain organization and learning are promoted by movement, it behooves adults to offer active play experiences throughout the primary child's day (Lockman & Thelen, 1993). Denying elementary children—or, for that matter, adolescents or adults—opportunities to move deprives them of key elements in the body-brain system. Children need to jump, run, swing, throw, and balance to become intellectually competent.

MOTOR PLAY AND CULTURE

The ways that children use emerging motor skills in play vary considerably from one culture to another. In some cultures, children play sports at a young age. In others, less competitive play pursuits are common. In spite of cultural variations, certain advancements in motor play during the primary years appear to be universal. Common features of motor play in primary children of all cultures are presented in Table 14-2.

Generally, the somewhat wild and chaotic play actions of preschoolers give way to more organized and rule-governed activities in the primary years (Hughes, 1995; B. B. Whiting & Edwards, 1988). Even the roughest and loudest games can involve teams, role assignments, rules, turntaking, or other evidence of organization.

Children in this developmental period often wish to acquire real skills and become grown up. Their play becomes more and more realistic, then, and skill-centered (Hughes, 1995). The spontaneous make-believe enactments of the preschool years evolve into serious dramatic productions. Wild chasing games develop into more

TABLE 14-2
Elements of Primary Motor Play Found in Most Cultures of the World

Element	Example
Organization and role assignments	In a neighborhood game of war, there are teams, leaders, soldiers, and medics.
Turntaking	In a game of climbing up and jumping off a wall, children announce, one at a time, the kind of jump they will complete and then perform it with peers watching.
Realism	In a game of soccer, children adhere to real adult rules, practice grown-up competencies, and emulate the behavior and language of sports heroes.

SOURCE: F. P. Hughes, 1995.

TABLE 14-3
Types of Motor Play Common Across Cultures

Type of Play	Example
Functional	Children in Polynesia leap off the bank of a stream, competing to see who can land the farthest out in the water.
Rough-and-tumble	Children in Kenya chase one another and throw dirt and sticks on one another as they tend livestock.
Pretend	Two children in Mexico pretend to be grown-up parents as they care for an infant brother in the neighborhood.
Games with rules	A large group of children gather in a village in Nepal for a game of marbles.
Teasing	Children in northern Italy snatch a toy from a younger sister and hide it, taunting, "I wonder where that doll went?"
Rituals	A group of children gather in a park in Chicago and perform jump-rope chants and rhymes passed down from older siblings.

adult-like sporting events which allow children to show off their motor abilities. The emphasis is on practicing real adult competencies.

Several types of motor play are common across cultures in this developmental period. These are presented in Table 14-3. Some of these play activities are more advanced versions of activities observed in the preschool years. Others are unique to this developmental period.

Functional Play

When primary children are released onto the playground after a long morning in school, they can often be observed running, jumping, screaming, and chasing. Many researchers call such open-ended, repetitive motor activity *functional play* (J. E. Johnson, Christie, & Yawkey, 1999). One first-grade teacher has a more down-to-earth name for it: "getting the wiggles out." Functional play appears in infancy and is very common in the preschool years. It is frequently observed in the activities of children in societies around the world (Hughes, 1995; Martini, 1994).

How does this type of play change in the primary grades? Such activity is still loud and wild at this age, but it becomes more organized and skill-oriented. This more organized pattern is illustrated in the following examples, drawn from observations of different cultural groups and communities:

EXAMPLE 1

Two 7-year-old Polynesian children are running under a bridge, emitting high-pitched screams so they can hear their echoes. One child now stops the other.

CHILD A: Wait. Let's try it with just me going under.

CHILD B: No. We need to run together.

CHILD A: I'll go under first and then you.

CHILD B: Yes, okay.

Child A runs through screaming; Child B follows soon after. They giggle at the change in the echoes created by this new approach. They decide to experiment further, first by running faster as they scream, then slower. Then they try whispering as they pass under the bridge, and laugh when they find that no echo is created. (Adapted from Martini, 1994)

EXAMPLE 2

Three 6-year-old African-American children play in an alley in their urban neighborhood in Chicago. They have pulled an old mattress from a dumpster and are using it as a trampoline.

MARCUS: (Jumping on the mattress) Look! I'll do this trick. Like in the circus. (Jumps and lands on his stomach)

ALPHONSE: (Laughing) No. That's not how you do it. My turn!

MICHAEL: Is not! I'm next. I can jump higher. (Climbs onto the mattress as Child A rolls off and begins to jump) Look at this! See how high? (Adapted from Garbarino et al., 1992)

EXAMPLE 3

Two brothers from a small village in Senegal tend cows in a field. One of the children begins to run around, making noises and ducking behind cows to hide from his brother.

BOITSHWARO: Can't catch me!

YAPOYO: I can! (Begins to run after Child A)

BOITSHWARO: (Circles round and round the herd. Laughs at his brother.) You are too slow!

The cows begin to run. The game ends quickly as the boys herd them back into a group.

Each of these games is very different, but all reflect common advancements in functional play. Rules about taking turns are evident in the first two examples. In the second and third examples, children try to display adult-like motor skills: "I'll do this trick. Like in the circus" and "You are too slow!" In spite of the diversity in these activities, all of them show children incorporating similar organization and skill orientation into their actions.

Children in all cultures engage in functional play. However, the frequency of this activity varies significantly from one community to the next. In one study, children in Taiwan were found to engage in almost twice as much functional play as Euro-American children in the United States (Pan, 1994). In another study, low-socioeconomic-status African-American children were found to engage in this type of active play very frequently.

Traditionally, functional play has been considered less sophisticated, socially and cognitively, than make-believe or games with rules. High levels of this type of play have often been interpreted as evidence that some children have play deficits (Smilansky, 1968). For example, the fact that African-American children living in poverty engage in more functional play has caused some researchers to label them as "deficient." A look at the examples provided above shows, however, that functional play in the primary grades can be socially and cognitively challenging. Such play episodes involve rules, social negotiations, and turntaking, just as in a game of kickball.

Elements of make-believe can also be found in functional play (McLoyd, 1986; Trawick-Smith, 1998d). For example, the children in the second example above, who are using a mattress as a trampoline, may be pretending to be acrobats. Hale-Benson (1986) argues that high levels of functional play may relate to the high activity levels found within some cultures and families.

Rough-and-Tumble Play

Rough-and-tumble play is a "cousin" of functional play. As we discussed in earlier chapters, there is evidence that this form of play enhances both physical and social development (Pellegrini, 1995a). How does rough-and-tumble play change in the primary years? As with other play forms, it becomes organized and rule-governed. Parents and teachers who are familiar with this type of play may be doubtful. It takes careful observation to see the structure in such wild interactions.

B. B. Whiting and Edwards (1988) observed explicitly stated rules within the rough-and-tumble play of children of many different cultures. In a community in the United States, primary children's play-fighting is regulated by boxing rules: "gloves" were required, "time-outs" would stop the fighting, and an "I'm sorry" was necessary when a peer got hurt. In Okinawa, primary children's wrestling bouts are very organized, with turntaking, rules, and regulations about not hurting. In Polynesia, children organize their play-fighting into "war games," called *keu tou'a,* which include rules, assignments of leader and follower roles, and teams (Martini, 1994). In East India, children shout, wrestle, and squirt water on each other during the *Holi* holiday. In this society, this holiday is one of the few times of the year when children engage in open-ended, wild activity. Even so, this play is generally more cooperative and less rough than in Western cultures.

The amount of rough-and-tumble play varies from one culture to another. B. B. Whiting and Edwards (1988) found that childhood roughhousing was particularly common among boys in Okinawa, the Philippines, and Mexico. Ramsey (1987) has observed that children of some historically under-represented cultural groups in America have a rougher play style which is sometimes less familiar to Euro-American children and adults. Often this activity is misinterpreted as aggression or "pre-aggression." "It's only a matter of time," one teacher commented as she watched two children wrestle on the playground, "before these two will be fighting."

In fact, rough-and-tumble play rarely leads to actual aggression. Primary children appear to clearly understand the differences between play jostling or wrestling and real fighting (Pellegrini, 1995a). This is true for children around the world. Whiting and Edwards drew this conclusion from their observations of rough play in many different cultures: "It might seem . . . that . . . children are constantly beating one another, but in fact there are surprisingly few incidents of assaulting interactions. . . . There is much evidence of children's genuine concern about hurting others" (1988, p. 254).

Pretend Play

One trend in children's play in the primary years is that make-believe declines as organized games increase (Hughes, 1995). In East India, for example, children at this age are more likely to start a game of marbles or tag than to enact the make-believe game "police and thief" that was a favorite in preschool. In America, second graders will more often organize a kickball or soccer game during recess than initiate a pretend superhero game.

Why does make-believe disappear? Where does it go? In one study, primary-grade children were found to engage in much make-believe when they were given explicit permission to do so (Trawick-Smith, 1993). It is possible that pretend play disappears because it is not sanctioned beyond the preschool years in most societies. Subtle messages from parents and teachers may let children know that this form of play is immature or otherwise inappropriate. In America, a child might be scolded for using math blocks as rocket ships. In Kenya, a child might be told to stop playing and watch the livestock more closely.

What happens to make-believe? Does it simply vanish in early childhood? Many believe that play goes "underground," that it becomes fantasy or secret play (Trawick-Smith, 1998c). An American primary-grade child might daydream or draw fantastic characters on his notebook in school. An African child might secretly pretend to be a mother while caring for her infant brother. I believe that traditional dramatic play equipment, dolls, and toys are removed too early from homes and classrooms. With encouragement, 6-, 7-, and 8-year-olds will pretend in ways that are developmentally useful.

Given the opportunity, what kinds of pretend play will primary-grade children engage in? As with other forms of play, primary make-believe becomes exceedingly structured (Trawick-Smith, 1993). Children's pretending becomes more elaborate than the spontaneous, free-flowing make-believe of the preschool years, taking on many of the characteristics of adult-level theater. Children spend an inordinate amount of time planning their play, developing complex play settings and assigning roles. Sometimes one or another player becomes the director, guiding play organization and directing others' performances (e.g., "Okay, him and me are cops, right? And let's say we chase you in our police car and catch you and lock you up in jail, okay?"). Children often enact real-life settings or re-create the scripts of favorite books, television shows, and movies.

Games with Rules

Games with rules are believed to predominate in children's motor play during the primary years (Hughes, 1995). Children often spontaneously organize their own ball games, races, or besting contests (e.g., "Let's see who can swing the highest without holding on"). Even organized sports are common among primary children in America. It is important to note, however, that the frequency and nature of childhood games vary significantly from one culture to another.

In some cultural groups, games simply are not played. In a study of one small village in Kenya, games were virtually never observed (B. B. Whiting & Edwards, 1988). In another investigation of a small community in Mexico, games were rarely recorded in neighborhood play. Only in school did children of this village participate in organized games. One explanation is that games are not particularly valued within these cultures. Another is that team sports and elaborate games are made impossible by a shortage of players in a village or neighborhood (B. B. Whiting & Edwards, 1988).

In communities in which children do play games, major differences can be found in the content or level of competition of the games that are played. Of course, which games are played will be determined by culture. In America, children play football, T-ball, or soccer. In East India, children play *Kaalla Gjja,* a kind of "follow the leader" game in which all players must imitate precisely the leader's elaborate actions (Roopnarine, Hossain, Gill, & Brophy, 1994). In Polynesia, children organize themselves into games of *Keu toua,* in which one team of children chases another (Martini, 1994). Within some cultural groups, quiet games are the norm: computer and video games in Japan, spinning tops and shooting marbles in Mexico (B. B. Whiting & Edwards, 1988). There are, in fact, as many different varieties of childhood games as there are diverse cultures. Passed down from peers, older siblings, and parents and teachers, games reflect the histories, values, and competencies of the particular society.

One way that games differ is in the amount of competition involved. Among Euro-American and European children, a high degree of competition is common. This likely reflects the attitudes and valued competencies of these cultural groups. Ideals of

Children in many cultures play games with rules and competition.

"rugged individualism" and corporate competition within these societies may underlie the emergence of competitive games in childhood. Sutton-Smith and Roberts (1970) believe that games serve to socialize children to capitalist values of goal-directedness and individual achievement: "In games, children learn all those necessary arts of trickery, deception, harassment, divination, and foul play that their teachers won't teach them" (p. 65). Elkind (1981) warns that intense competition may create undue stress in children, causing their interest in sports and games to decline over time.

In many cultures, intense competition is not a problem because children's games are exceedingly cooperative. Games among children in East India and Polynesia have been described as remarkably noncompetitive (Roopnarine, Hossain, Gill, & Brophy, 1994; Martini, 1994). In a study in Oyugis, a small community in western Kenya, children were found to virtually never argue over the rules of games (B. B. Whiting & Edwards, 1988). This may be because competition and individual achievement are less emphasized in these cultures than in other communities, such as those in the United States, where very many arguments erupt about rules and winning.

Teasing

Teasing becomes an important play form in many societies as children enter the primary years. Some adults view this as negative or antisocial behavior. It is unlikely that primary-grade teachers will rush to encourage teasing games in school! Yet many researchers believe that **teasing play** in childhood is a highly organized, social activity which promotes motor and cognitive development. Hale-Benson (1986) describes a teasing game as a formal rite among older African-American children. Called "playing the dozens," it involves verbal duels between two opponents who trade insults about family members. The contest occurs in the presence of a crowd of peers who encourage and judge the insults with loud reactions.

To play well, a child needs to think quickly and to express taunts and slurs with emotional expression and humor. Most important, children playing the game need to control their emotions; they must not get angry at their opponent's insults. Such control of emotion may be very critical for children living in urban neighborhoods, where rage and hostility are at the heart of many violent acts. Children who learn emotional control through such play may be less likely to become violent when they are older.

Teasing play in Polynesia also reflects a high degree of organization (Martini, 1994). In this culture, teasing is a method of maintaining order and structure in a peer group. A child will tease others as a method of challenging their status and establishing his or her own dominance. Teasing, taunts, and scolding are a form of "status leveling" in which individual children are relegated to lower-status positions in the group. Through the teasing process, clearly identified leaders emerge. Why is leadership so important in Polynesian peer groups? Primary children in this culture have little contact with parents during the day. They do not request help from adults in resolving conflicts or when a minor injury occurs. They rely on their peers. A peer structure which has specific leaders in charge may provide security and comfort to these young children. Thus, teasing is a vital part of peer group organization.

Rituals

Rituals—playful, predictable, often rhythmic routines—are common in the elementary years (Hughes, 1995). The following are familiar examples:

- A child on a climber calls down to his peers in a familiar rhythmic chant: "Nya nya nya-nya nya, you can't catch me!" His peers give chase.

- As two children walk along a sidewalk, one announces, "Step on a crack, break your momma's back!" The two children slow their pace and look down, carefully placing each step.

What is fascinating is that many of these rituals have been part of child culture for generations. They are somehow transmitted to children through the ages, although few parents remember directly teaching them to their children. How do such rituals endure?

Much can be learned about a child's culture by observing rituals (Hughes, 1995). A chant such as "one potato, two potato" to determine who goes first or who obtains a certain object may reflect a Euro-American emphasis on turntaking, competition, and rules. Group chants and jump-rope rhymes, common in the play of African-American children, might reflect a more collective culture (Hale-Benson, 1986), as might the collaborative hopping chants of children in East India (Roopnarine, Hossain, Gill, & Brophy, 1994).

Why do primary-age children perform these repetitive rituals? Perhaps they reflect children's need for order and routine at this age. Rituals may serve the function of socializing children into childhood culture (Hughes, 1995). Learning such chants, sayings, and ritual actions may be a way of establishing membership in a peer group. Children who know the rituals are "in"; those who don't are left out. In essence, the rituals create a special way of interacting or speaking that is exclusively for children.

MODERN THREATS TO MOTOR PLAY

There are threats to motor play in modern life. Technology and even school reform have reduced children's play time.

Television

Children who watch many hours of television engage in less active play. A study in Japan, for example, showed that outdoor motor play time dropped in half during the period that television became popular (Takeuchi, 1994). In the United States, television watching has been linked to obesity in childhood and adolescence (Dietz & Gortmaker, 1985). This may be due to a decline in active play, but also to exposure to commercials that promote foods high in sugars and fats. One study (Klesges, 1993) suggests that children burn fewer calories watching television than when doing nothing at all. In this study, children's metabolic rates slowed to levels lower than those typically found when children are at rest. Metabolic rates slowed significantly more during TV viewing in obese children.

Great variation in television watching is found across individual families. Of course, in some societies television is not available, but in those in which it is available, viewing does not appear to be related to socioeconomic status, parent education, or children's cognitive abilities (Posner & Vandell, 1994). Children of all classes, cultures, and abilities watch TV. Children who spend time in after-school care and those who have older siblings to play with have been found less likely to watch television and more likely to engage in active play (Pinon, Huston, & Wright,

1989). Opportunities to play with other children, as are provided in high-quality after-school programs, may reduce television viewing and related health problems among primary children.

School Policy

Changes in school policies in some communities have threatened opportunities for motor play through reducing or even eliminating recess. Several studies suggest that eliminating active play reduces children's attention in school and their potential for learning (Pellegrini, 1995b). These concerns are voiced by a first-grade teacher whose school district has just changed the recess policy:

> Our school board has been making a big deal out of increasing our "instructional time." They've added minutes to our school day and days to our school year. Several weeks ago, I received notification that outdoor time would no longer be considered instructional time. The memo read, "Since recess time can not be counted in the determination of instructional minutes, outdoor free time must be reduced or eliminated or the school day lengthened."
>
> I argued to my principal, "What do they mean, recess isn't instructional time? In my view there's no greater learning period in the day. Aren't board members concerned about social interaction? Aren't they concerned about health? Don't they understand the connections between the body and the mind? Better they give up math time than recess!" My principal smiled and nodded. He has yet to take action, however, on my concerns.

Perhaps physical education (PE) classes provide adequate exercise to justify reducing recess. However, a recent survey suggests that most schools no longer offer PE on a daily basis (Ross & Pate, 1987). More troubling, one study found that during a typical 30-minute PE class, children actually exercise for less than 2 minutes (G. S. Parcel et al., 1987).

School research suggests that motor development is not a priority among many educators. Troubling trends in poor health and learning may be predicted in communities in which the importance of physical play is not appreciated. The good news is that children in some communities find time to play after school. Figure 14-2 shows the percentage of children who play more than an hour a day after school in various countries in the world.

PHYSICALLY CHALLENGING CONDITIONS

A number of physically challenging conditions affect motor development and physical health in the primary years. These are presented in Table 14-4.

Cerebral Palsy

Children with **cerebral palsy** constitute the largest percentage of elementary students with physical challenges who require special services (Sirvis & Caldwell, 1995). As described in Chapter 10, this condition results from damage to the brain, often from oxygen deprivation during the birth process or trauma in early childhood. Since those areas of the brain responsible for motor coordination are affected, impairment of fine and large motor abilities often results.

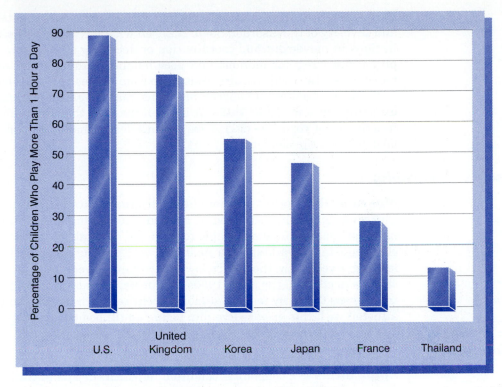

FIGURE 14-2 In both the United States and the United Kingdom, a large percentage of children engage in active play when not in school. In other countries, chores and television may reduce play time.

SOURCE: Extrapolated from data in Takeuchi, 1994.

TABLE 14-4

Challenging Conditions That Affect Motor Development and Physical Health in the Primary Grades

Condition	Description
Cerebral palsy	Increasing limitations in movement and coordination and declining strength in muscles occur. Braces or a wheelchair may be required to move about.
Muscular dystrophy	A steady weakening of skeletal muscles and difficulty climbing stairs and running are common. Eventually, lower extremities may weaken to a point where a wheelchair is needed.
Spina bifida	Sensory impairments or walking difficulty are common. More severe cases can result in paraplegia. Serious health problems, including urinary tract disorders and retention of fluid in the brain, are possible.
Attention deficit/hyperactivity disorder	Extreme activity level and difficulty controlling attention and impulses are common. The disorder is often diagnosed during the elementary grades, as children move from active, play-based settings to quieter, sit-still-and-listen programs in the primary years.

How cerebral palsy manifests itself in the primary years is determined by the type and severity of the disorder. Some children with cerebral palsy show increasing limitations in movement and coordination or declining strength in muscles. Some display jerky, irregular motions and poor balance. Others suffer only fine motor impairments. Many will require assistance from braces or a wheelchair in walking.

Because of motor and speech problems, many children with cerebral palsy have difficulty with academic tasks. It is often the case that limited hand-use or speech functions, not cognitive delays, explain academic challenges for children with cerebral palsy in the elementary years.

Muscular Dystrophy

Muscular dystrophy is a hereditary disorder that also affects motor functioning. The condition is characterized by a steady weakening of skeletal muscles. Children in the primary years may be able to walk and move about the classroom initially, but climbing stairs, walking on a field trip, and playing a running game may be challenging. Eventually, the child's lower extremities weaken to a point where a wheelchair is needed. In the early 1980s the life expectancy of a child with muscular dystrophy was the early teens, but more recent research has shown that many children afflicted with this disease live into young adulthood (Grove, Cusick, & Bigge, 1991).

Spina Bifida

Spina bifida is a congenital condition in which the spinal cord and nerve roots are damaged. Milder forms may involve slight sensory impairments and walking difficulty. More severe cases can result in paraplegia (paralysis of both legs), severe sensory impairment, and incontinence (inability to control the bladder). Serious health problems, including urinary tract disorders and retention of fluid in the brain, are common. Because of this, support for children with spinal bifida in school often requires the involvement of medical, educational, and social services personnel.

Meeting Special Motor Play Needs in School

Many elementary schools have adapted their classroom spaces and curriculum to accommodate children with physical challenges. A child can be given a marker or pen pushed through a rubber ball to assist in drawing or writing. Instead of a traditional desk, an adapted seating device can be provided so that a child can lean or even lie while doing school work. A child can be given a special oversized spoon or a dripless cup to assist in independent eating (Sirvis & Caldwell, 1995).

Less attention has been given to adapting outdoor play spaces for primary-age children with physically challenging conditions. Without such adaptations, children with physical impairments may be unable to engage in motor play and games on the playground. Being denied such opportunities hampers their physical health and social relationships.

New play equipment is being designed to meet the needs of children with physical challenges (Olds, 1987). Accessible playscapes with ramps, support bars, and other devices are becoming more common on school playgrounds. Teachers are acquiring new skills in assisting children in play and motor activity. They can guide them in using equipment, facilitate interaction between children with special needs and peers, and ensure safety. These interventions are necessary so that all children will have opportunities to exercise muscles in play.

ATTENTION DEFICIT/HYPERACTIVITY DISORDER

Children with **attention deficit/hyperactivity disorder (ADHD)** (described in Chapter 10) are extremely active and have difficulty controlling their attention and impulses. Although ADHD can be diagnosed in the preschool years, it is most likely to become a concern for parents and teachers in school during the elementary grades. This is because children move from home settings or active, play-based classrooms in child care or Head Start to quieter, "sit still and listen" programs in the primary years. Children with ADHD are quickly noticed by teachers; these children have difficulty sitting for long periods, attending to learning tasks, and following rules for quietness and impulse control (Barkley, 1990).

What causes ADHD? The most prevalent theory is that the condition results from neurological impairment (Wender, 1987). Studies of brain functioning confirm this (Maugh, 1998; Zametkin et al., 1990). When adults with ADHD are given a PET scan—a medical procedure that measures activity level in the brain—they are found to have significantly slower brain activity than non-ADHD adults. Ironically, hyperactivity might be caused by a sluggish brain! This explains why Ritalin, which is a stimulant, improves the behavior of some children with ADHD. The stimulant speeds up brain processes and may help children become more alert, attentive, and interested.

ADHD and Culture

One theory about ADHD is that it is an artifact of culture (Bogdan & Knoll, 1995; Konner, 1991). From this viewpoint, in societies that value sitting still and being quiet, ADHD is a disability. In communities in which quietness is not an important competency—those in which children do not attend school, for example—ADHD is rarely identified. In fact, in some societies, highly active behavior is believed to be advantageous to survival!

Multicultural scholars have noted with concern that an extremely high percentage of children of color are identified as hyperactive (Janesick, 1995; Morgan, 1976). They suggest that at least a portion of these children do not suffer a *real* disability, but simply do not conform to norms of quietness in American schools. Hale-Benson (1986) points out, for example, that the high activity level and physical style of play among African-American children make them vulnerable to being misdiagnosed as having ADHD.

Perhaps a complex interaction of biological, cultural, and family factors leads to ADHD identification. A good example is the case of hyperactivity among Japanese-American children. Sata (1983) argues that hyperactivity is rarely identified in children of this cultural group. This is not because the disability does not exist, he proposes, but because it is not easily identified in U.S. schools. Japanese-American children with ADHD live in families with quieter styles of interaction. Their behavior may be less active than that of children with ADHD in other cultures. Their activity level—though high by standards of their own culture—may be considered "within the range of normalcy" by the dominant society. Further, Japanese-American parents are more likely to ignore hyperactive behaviors or minimize their significance (Sata, 1983). Hence, they less often disclose problems to teachers or physicians and the condition goes unidentified. It is possible that ADHD is as prevalent in this culture as in others, but that cultural factors diminish the frequency of identification.

ASSESSING YOUNG CHILDREN: Primary-Age Physical and Motor Development

Areas of Development	What to Watch for	Indicators of Atypical Development
Large motor abilities	Large motor skills, such as catching with hands only, throwing, balancing on one foot or a balance beam, and kicking with a mature follow-through, by age 8. Game playing with rules and other highly coordinated motor activities by age 8.	Lack of coordination, balance, and muscle strength. Highly active, impulsive, uncontrollable behavior. Inactivity and obesity. Frequent illness and absence from school.
Perceptual and fine motor abilities	An ability to coordinate small muscles to perform school-related tasks, such as reading and writing. Schematic drawings and sculpting which show greater realism and detail.	An inability to handle school-related implements, such as pencils, books, or scissors. Difficulty in holding or manipulating game-playing materials, such as cards or dice.
Self-help or family life skills	An ability to dress and undress independently and to feed oneself using a fork, knife, and spoon by age 6. Simple cleaning skills and an ability to help with household chores by age 8. Willingness to care for one's classroom and personal cubby or desk.	Poor self-help skills. Dependence on others for dressing, toileting, and caring for one's personal space in the classroom or home.

Interpreting Assessment Data: Culture affects motor development in the primary years. Some children may be less active or physically able and others more so, depending on motor activities in the family. Racial differences in stature and muscle tone exist. Serious motor delays and poor health may indicate serious problems related to poverty and family stress. Poor nutrition, illness, and injury can impede motor growth. Challenging conditions, such as cerebral palsy, muscular dystrophy, and spina bifida, greatly affect motor abilities. These conditions require special services in school. Children who are highly active and inattentive may have attention deficit/hyperactivity disorder. Regardless of cause, motor disabilities can be ameliorated through large- and small-muscle play in the classroom and on the playground. Such play is disappearing in some modern elementary schools. Primary teachers should advocate for physical education, recess, and physical therapy services in schools.

RESEARCH INTO PRACTICE

CRITICAL CONCEPT 1

Although children grow at a slower rate in the primary years than they did in earlier periods of development, they still show significant physical development and acquire important motor skills during this time. There are important connections between motor development, brain growth, and learning. Children who exercise during school may achieve greater brain organization and may be better able to attend to learning tasks. Unfortunately, motor play has declined over time in modern society. School reform efforts have reduced and in some cases eliminated outdoor play time.

Application #1

Teachers must become advocates for outdoor play and motor activity during the primary years. They must defend the importance of physical play in the face of a movement in American education to reduce or eliminate recess.

Application #2

A quiet-active-quiet pattern of interaction should be incorporated into the schedules of primary classrooms. Periods of sitting and listening should be followed by more active experiences. Even brief stretching and exercise sessions or short outdoor mini-breaks during the school day may enhance learning and brain growth.

Application #3

Large motor and fine motor development activities should be integrated into the curriculum. Dance, sculpture, woodworking, and other activities can be related to topics studied in the social studies and science. Aiming games, such as beanbag tossing or bowling, can teach academic skills while enhancing eye-hand coordination.

Application #4

Teachers should collaborate closely with health and physical education teachers to design developmentally appropriate motor play opportunities that relate to the curriculum. In physical education classes, games that relate to social studies, mathematics, and science topics can be introduced.

CRITICAL CONCEPT 2

There is much individual variation in growth during the primary years. Growth patterns also vary across cultures; because of biology or family life experience, average weight and height differ from one cultural group to another. How children use motor skills in play also varies from one culture to another. Some children play highly competitive games with rules; others engage in cooperative pursuits. Rituals and rough-and-tumble play are common in many cultural groups. Children in some communities more often engage in functional play, in which they run, climb, and jump to test their muscles. Teasing may even be considered a form of motor play in some peer groups.

Application #1

Teachers should understand and appreciate diversity in physical growth. Some children will be smaller in stature, less active, or less well coordinated than others. Adaptations must be made in motor play activities to ensure that all children can participate and acquire motor abilities at their individual levels of development.

Application #2

Teachers should provide a variety of play experiences that are relevant to all cultures represented in the classroom. They should be cautious not to misinterpret rough-and-tumble play or teasing as inappropriate. Games with rules should be adapted to address cultural preferences for more or less competition.

Application #3

Teachers and health and physical education teachers can interview parents in order to design a multicultural motor play curriculum. This curriculum may include traditional games and rituals of cultural groups represented in the school or community. Including jump rope chants, sayings, songs, and jokes from children's families and communities will promote cultural understanding and sensitivity.

CRITICAL CONCEPT 3

Poor health status and poverty can inhibit growth. Illness, poor nutrition, injury, violence, and homelessness are all more prevalent among children who live in poverty. These factors can have a devastating effect on physical development.

Application #1

Teachers must help families to access housing, health, and nutritional services for children. If health and safety needs are not met, children cannot learn in school. Writing to local, state, and federal legislators to advocate for family and child services—and encouraging parents to do the same—is part of a teacher's professional role in modern society.

Application #2

Teachers must advocate for safe and affordable before- and after-school care for children who live in dangerous neighborhoods. Care that is well supervised and promotes positive physical and social development is needed.

Application #3

Comprehensive health education programs which include topics of safety and nutrition should be implemented in primary grade classrooms. Parents, family members, and community health professionals should be included in planning such programs. Culturally sensitive activities and projects should be offered. For example, lessons on nutrition should reflect the unique diets and nutritional socialization practices of families served.

CRITICAL CONCEPT 4

Children with physically challenging conditions, such as cerebral palsy, muscular dystrophy, and spina bifida, may be unable to enjoy motor play with peers because of limited access to play equipment and other barriers. Another challenging condition, attention deficit hyperactivity disorder (ADHD), may also limit interactions and play, both in and out of school. Children with this condition are extremely active and have difficulty attending to school tasks. They are more likely to be excluded from play by peers.

Application #1

Schools must adapt indoor and outdoor play spaces to provide access for children with special needs. Special ramps, railings, and climbing apparatus are needed to ensure that children with physically challenging conditions can join the play of peers.

Application #2

Teachers must adapt classroom activities to allow children with ADHD to learn and interact positively with peers. Eliminating extended periods of sitting and tolerating a degree of movement about the classroom are strategies which help children with this condition to be successful in school.

Application #3

Teachers should intervene in children's motor play to promote positive peer relations between children with physically challenging conditions and their typically developing peers. Teachers may suggest activities which all can play. For example, upper-body, non-running games such as beanbag catch or "button-button" can be initiated for children in wheelchairs. As children play, teachers can facilitate conversations and social contact.

SUGGESTED ACTIVITIES

1. Observe a classroom of first, second, or third graders. Take notes on the diversity of stature and activity level of the children. Later, write a report on your observations, guided by the following questions:

   a. To what degree did children's height and weight vary? Did you observe cultural or gender differences in stature?

   b. How well were children able to sit still and attend to classroom activities? Did you see evidence of wiggliness or inattentiveness? Were there variations in the ability to sit still and pay attention?

2. Observe a group of primary children's behavior just before, during, and after recess time at school. Later, write a report on your observations, guided by the following questions:

   a. Describe the behavior of children just before recess. Did you note wiggliness and inattention? What behaviors did you notice the moment children were sent out onto the playground?

   b. What specific motor skills did you observe being exercised (e.g., running, climbing, kicking)?

   c. What kinds of play did you observe on the playground? Did you see functional play? Pretend play? Rough-and-tumble play? Teasing? Rituals?

   d. What evidence did you see of play organization, rules, and realism, as described in this chapter? How common was competition? How common was cooperation?

   e. What were children's reactions when the end of recess was announced? Describe behaviors after play time. Were there differences in activity or attention between the time before recess and the time after recess?

3. Interview a social service professional who serves families in poverty (e.g., a school social worker, a homeless shelter professional). Ask questions about the effects of poverty on children's physical and mental health, nutrition, and safety. Write a report on your interview, guided by the following questions:

   a. Which specific mental health problems does this professional observe among children in poverty?

   b. Which childhood physical health problems does the professional encounter? To what degree do children in poverty get adequate health care? Are children adequately immunized?

   c. Which safety concerns does the professional describe? Is there a risk of injury? Of violence?

   d. To what degree is poor nutrition a problem among the children the professional works with?

4. Observe in a primary classroom that includes a child or children with physically challenging conditions. Later, write a report about your observations, based on the following questions:

   a. In which classroom activities can children with physical challenges participate without difficulty? Which activities are inaccessible to these children?

   b. What adaptations are made in the classroom to meet the needs of children with challenging conditions? Have accommodations been made in physical space? In the curriculum? In the teaching staff?

   c. To what degree are children with challenging conditions able to play outdoors? Do they interact with peers? Do they exercise large muscles?

   d. What adaptations are made in playground equipment or teacher interactions to assist children with physical challenges?

CHAPTER 15

Cognition and Schooling

IN THIS CHAPTER WE WILL EXAMINE THE INTELLECTUAL DEVELOPMENT OF PRIMARY-GRADE CHILDREN. Our major focus will be on how primary cognition influences and is influenced by formal schooling. In almost all cultures in which schools exist, formal education begins sometime between age 5 and 8. Why? In some societies it is a long-standing tradition that children go to school at a certain chronological age. In the United States, for example, age 5 or 6 is considered "school age," the time when classroom instruction is to begin. In many cultural groups, however, chronological age is unimportant. Children are considered ready to learn at whatever point in time they show significant intellectual change. In Taira, Okinawa, parents refer to this as a point when children show they "know what they are doing" or "have sense" (Maretzki & Maretzki, 1963; B. B. Whiting & Edwards, 1988). This usually occurs around age 6 or 7. In one community in Mexico, children are thought to develop "reason" and become "teachable" at around this age (Romney & Romney, 1963).

Of course, psychologists have a more formal explanation for what happens during this period of development. Primary-grade children are entering a new stage of cognitive growth known as the concrete operational period. At this stage, children show new intellectual abilities and a growing capacity to use language. They can now contemplate more than one idea or element of a problem at a time, and can begin to construct understandings of number, historical time, and map space. It is no coincidence, then, that the primary years are almost universally considered a time to begin formal schooling. Tradition, folk wisdom, and psychology all point to this as a period of significant psychological growth.

Nevertheless, children's cognitive growth in the primary years does not mean they think and learn like adults do. Professionals who work with young children must understand both the emerging competencies and the cognitive limitations of this period. Expecting too much of children in school can lead to what David Elkind (1987) calls "miseducation." The following story illustrates the problem:

> A first-grade teacher, Ms. Baker, has arrived at a dreaded point in her school's mathematics curriculum. She has reached a section in the first-grade math text where she is to teach about clocks and time. She has been through this before. Her students rarely understand the concepts and become confused and frustrated. This year is no exception.

MS. BAKER:	(Holding up a model clock) Now, this is 3 o'clock. Can you make your clocks say 3 o'clock? (Watches as children struggle with this problem, moves around helping them) Now. Show me how the clock looks at 3:15. The children look confused.
CELESTE:	What? There's no 15.
SONIA:	No, it's 15 o'clock, so you don't need a 15.
TAYLOR:	Not 15 o'clock, silly. No such thing as that! (Laughs)
MS. BAKER:	No. See, 15 is the number of minutes past 3 o'clock.
TAYLOR:	Like this. (Beings to count the numerals on the clock face) One, two, three . . .
SITA:	I can't do it!
MS. BAKER:	I know. Let's put our clocks down for awhile. Time for a story.

This teacher recognizes that an understanding of clock time is beyond the abilities of her students. In fact, she is aware of research which shows that children may not fully understand some clock concepts until fifth or sixth grade (Friedman & Laycock, 1989). She knows enough not to push children to absorb this lesson. She considers this yet another example of how textbook authors and school district curriculum committees sometimes overestimate what primary-grade children know and are able to do.

SCHOOLING ACROSS CULTURES

Schooling varies from one society to another. In a study of many different cultures around the world, B. B. Whiting and Edwards (1988) found that in some communities education is universal: all children attend school. The United States, the Philippines, and Okinawa are examples. In Kokwet, Kisa, and Kariobangi, Kenya, less than half of all children were in school, whereas in Ngeca, Kenya, over 90% attended. In Nyansongo, Kenya, only boys were found to go to school. Schooling is not, then, a universal part of childhood.

School experiences differ markedly for children who do attend. In Okinawa and the Philippines, school is very informal. Transitions to school are smooth in these communities. Most children are already familiar with classrooms and teachers when they arrive on their first day, since most have been enrolled in nursery schools since they were young. The relaxed, informal atmosphere of primary classrooms resembles their earlier educational experiences. Sometimes teachers in these communities are neighbors or friends of the family. Children have often visited the primary school, having accompanied older siblings on some days as a child care arrangement.

In other societies, adjustment to school is more difficult. For example, a study in a community in Juxtlahuaca, Mexico, found that Mixtec children enter a school which is in a part of town they have never been to and are given instruction in a language different from their own (B. B. Whiting & Edwards, 1988). Teachers and other students treat them poorly, and discrimination is frequent and obvious. Some of these children rebel with bravado or attention-getting behaviors; others become quiet and subservient.

In several small villages in Kenya, teachers—all male—are strict and emotionally distant from their students (B. B. Whiting & Edwards, 1988). Parents in these communities expect schools to require absolute obedience. Interestingly, the parents themselves do not require such compliance from children at home. These parents may have come to view school as the place where conformity and control are first learned.

In some communities, schools emphasize competition and individual achievement, while in others, competitiveness is rare. In Tarong in the Philippines, school achievement is viewed as collective and collaborative. In this community, the only competition is among hamlets, not among individual children.

In schools of all societies, children are evaluated in some way and their achievements and behaviors are labeled "right" or "wrong," "good" or "bad" (B. B. Whiting & Edwards, 1988). This means that, in all communities where there are schools, some children are successful and others are not. Most cultures must deal with a problem called "school failure."

IQ TESTS

How well children do in school is, in part, a function of their overall intelligence. Important advancements in thinking are necessary for children to learn to read, perform arithmetic computations, and understand history. The nature of intelligence has been a subject of much debate among psychologists.

One approach to assessing children's intelligence is to give a test that measures their innate mental capabilities. Two of the most commonly used tests are the Stanford-Binet Intelligence Scale and the Wechsler Intelligence Scales. These are composed of a series of questions which measure verbal and quantitative reasoning and abstract thinking. Intelligence tests are *standardized,* meaning they are administered to large samples of children. Standardization allows test developers to determine how well a "typical" 7-year-old or 16-year-old performs on test items. In grading these tests, an individual child's scores are compared to the scores of other children of the same age. A 6-year-old who can successfully complete test items that the majority of 6-year-olds cannot is considered mentally advanced. Another 6-year-old who failed to answer test items that most 5-year-olds were able to answer is considered delayed.

Scores on an intelligence test are usually expressed as an **intelligence quotient (IQ).** An individual's IQ is computed by dividing the person's mental age by his or her chronological age. Mental age is determined by performance on the test: a child who performs as most 7-year-olds do has a mental age of 7. Chronological age is actual age in years. If a 6-year-old child is determined to have a mental age of 7 on an intelligence test, the child's IQ would be computed this way: 7 (mental age) divided by 6 (chronological age) equals 1.17. For statistical reasons, the score is multiplied by 100, giving an IQ of 117 for this child. Children who score exactly their chronological age would have an IQ of 100, and those who score higher or lower than this would be considered advanced or delayed, respectively. An IQ of 70 or lower might indicate mental retardation; an IQ of 130 or higher could signify giftedness.

Uses of IQ Tests in School

IQ tests are sometimes given to school-age children as part of an assessment to diagnose learning problems or to identify special needs. In the past, a single IQ test might be used to identify mental retardation. Children scoring poorly would be placed in special education classrooms. Likewise, gifted children were often identified using a single IQ test. Fortunately, using a single test score to make such important decisions about children's lives is rare today. Teachers, school psychologists, and parents generally obtain information from a variety of sources, including IQ scores, but also observations, samples of schoolwork, and interviews, when assessing children's intellectual potential.

IQ is highly related to school success (Weinberg, 1989). Proponents of IQ testing would argue that this is because such tests measure innate intellectual potential. From this view, children who score high on IQ tests have biologically determined abilities that allow them to succeed in school.

Analysis and Multicultural Critique of IQ Testing

IQ testing and the idea of innate intelligence have been challenged over the years. Some researchers have argued that there are many different kinds of intelligence which are not measured by traditional IQ tests. Others propose that IQ tests are culturally biased.

Multiple Intelligences. Many believe that there is not a single, general intelligence but **multiple intelligences.** Sternberg and Wagner (1993), for example, have proposed that there are three different kinds of intellectual functioning, that vary among individuals. The first is *componential intelligence,* which is related to basic processes of thinking, attending, and remembering. The second is *contextual intelligence,* which is responsible for adapting thinking processes to changes in the environment. This kind of intelligence is necessary for real-life problem-solving. A child just entering the first grade must not only rely on basic thinking processes to learn, but must accommodate to the new demands of an academic classroom. A child of abusive parents who is placed in a foster home must accommodate thinking and learning to this new home environment. Contextual intelligence is necessary in each case.

Sternberg and Wagner believe that a third type of intelligence, *experiential intelligence,* allows humans to use previous experience in learning. For example, children who have been read to by parents will rely on these early experiences later in learning to read in school. The ability to use personal life history in this way is an example of experiential intelligence. From Sternberg and Wagner's view, a test that fails to measure all three types of intelligence will not give a full picture of mental competence.

Howard Gardner (1993) has categorized intelligences even more fully. He argues that at least seven distinct intellectual competencies can be identified: linguistic, logical-mathematical, spatial, bodily-kinesthetic, musical, interpersonal (social understanding), and intrapersonal (self-understanding). These are described in Table 15-1.

Each form of intelligence is independent, from Gardner's view, and is related to functioning in a particular area of the brain. An important element of Gardner's theory is that different cultures appreciate and enhance different intelligences. In Euro-American cultures, for example, linguistic and logical-mathematical competencies are highly valued, especially in school. Children who are capable in these areas are defined as "intelligent" by mainstream American society. Since traditional IQ tests measure primarily linguistic and logical-mathematical abilities, they are considered important measures of intellectual competence in the United States.

In other cultures, very different intelligences may be emphasized. Hale-Benson (1986) suggests that African-American children are often competent in kinesthetic intelligence—that is, in body control and movement. Also, they excel in social understanding, reflecting the "people-orientation" and "physicality" of their particular

TABLE 15-1
Gardner's Multiple Intelligences

Intelligence	Description
Linguistic intelligence	The ability to use written and oral language. This intelligence is used in storytelling, journalism, and fiction writing.
Logical-mathematical intelligence	The ability to reason well, use logic, and understand and solve problems with numbers. This intelligence is used in such fields as computer programming or chemistry.
Spatial intelligence	The ability to perceive visual-spatial phenomena and to graphically represent and orient oneself to these. This intelligence is used in such fields as architecture or interior design.
Bodily-kinesthetic intelligence	An ability to use one's entire body to express ideas or to produce things. This intelligence is used in athletics, dance, sculpture, and mechanics.
Musical intelligence	The ability to perceive, create, and perform music. This intelligence is used by musical performers, composers, and music critics.
Interpersonal intelligence	An ability to identify and accurately interpret the behaviors, motives, feelings, and intentions of other people. This intelligence is used by community leaders, counselors, and social service workers.
Intrapersonal intelligence	A knowledge of one's own competencies, motivations, self-perceptions, emotions, temperaments, and desires. This intelligence is used to assess strengths and limitations and to make personal life decisions.

SOURCE: H. Gardner, 1983

cultural group. In Puerto Rico, many parents and teachers report special competence in musical intelligence among young children (Trawick-Smith, 1998d). From Gardner's (1993) view, these abilities are every bit as important as linguistic or logical-mathematical skills. However, since these areas of competence are not measured by IQ tests and other traditional assessments of intelligence, such intelligences may not be fully recognized and appreciated in Euro-American schools.

IQ Test Content and Cultural Bias. Other concerns have been raised about IQ tests and cultural diversity. In the United States during the 1960s and 1970s, a growing body of research showed that IQ tests favored middle-class Euro-American children. One reason for this was that concepts and language learned in white middle-class homes were emphasized in these tests (N. Brody, 1990). Another was that IQ tests were being standardized using samples of middle-class Euro-American children—that is, they were developed by being given to many children of this dominant cultural group. Norms for performance were then based on white middle-class scores (Oakland & Parmalee, 1985).

Many studies have verified that IQ tests have favored white middle-class cultural groups. In a classic investigation, Mercer (1972) showed that African-American and Mexican-American children who had performed poorly on traditional IQ tests scored much higher on a culture-free test of intellectual adaptability. In a study on transracial adoption (Scarr, Weinberg, & Waldman, 1993), IQ scores of African-American children who were adopted in infancy by middle-class Euro-American parents were found to be as much as 20 points higher than those of children who were living in their own, non-adoptive African-American families. These researchers explain their findings by noting that IQ tests favor the learning styles, competencies, values, and motivations of the dominant culture.

Since the 1970s, IQ tests have been standardized with more representative samples of children. New tests have been developed with a culture-free content. The Kaufman Assessment Battery for Children (K-ABC), for example, has been standardized using a highly representative sample which includes all cultural groups as well as gifted, emotionally disturbed, and learning-disabled children (Kaufman & Kaufman, 1983). Separate norms are established for African-American and Euro-American children, so scores are based on what is expected for same-aged children of their own cultural group. Test items are often nonverbal and are claimed to be culture-free. Verbal items and responses to them may be presented in almost any language. (An illustration of verbal and nonverbal test items is presented in Figure 15-1.) Administrators of the K-ABC may give prompts or guidance when children miss an item. This addresses a problem of field sensitivity, which we will consider next.

Test Setting, Field Sensitivity, and Culture. Even if the content of IQ tests is culture-free, children of some cultures may still perform poorly on them if the test-

Verbal Test Item: Which does not belong?

                     Spoon   Bowl   Cereal   Cup   Fork

Nonverbal
Alternative: (The test administrator asks, verbally) Which picture does not belong?

Verbal Test Item: Which comes next?

                     2   4   12   48

Nonverbal
Alternative: (The test administrator asks, verbally) Put the pictures in order.

FIGURE 15-1   Verbal and nonverbal test items are shown which resemble those on IQ tests. Modern test developers have tried to use more nonverbal items to reduce racial and linguistic bias.

ing setting favors children of certain groups. In a meta-analysis (a large summary of many different studies), Fuchs and Fuchs (1986) found that when children of color are administered IQ tests in comfortable settings, such as their homes, they score higher than when tested in less familiar environs by adult strangers.

Another test-taking disadvantage that children of some groups may have is field sensitivity. As discussed earlier, children of historically under-represented cultures are more likely to be **field sensitive.** They tend to rely on the entire physical and social environment when solving problems. They more often seek help from others in learning. How does a field-sensitive style affect IQ test performance? Such tests are often delivered individually in stimulus-free rooms so that field-sensitive children cannot rely on peers, teachers, or environmental cues during testing. Research shows that some field-sensitive children will, in vain, study the expressions of the examiner, ask questions, or scan the room while taking tests (Figueroa, 1980). **Field-independent** children, who are disproportionately Euro-American, are often task-oriented and tend to focus less on other people and more on test problems.

The following vignette illustrates how the content of tests, unfamiliarity with testing situations, and learning style can influence IQ test performance of children from historically under-represented groups:

> An African-American girl from rural Mississippi sits in a quiet conference room with an unfamiliar adult. The man is white and speaks in a different kind of accent than she is used to. He asks her to perform tasks as part of an IQ test. The test items make little sense to her. She is puzzled and anxious during the entire experience. There is no one else in the room to get help from. When she asks the adult for assistance, he smiles, shakes his head, and says, "I want you to do this on your own."
>
> At one point, the test administrator shows her a drawing of a late-model car with a wheel missing and asks her to complete the drawing. The child is distracted, however, by the car itself: it is much bigger and newer than any she has seen in her small, rural town. "What kinda car's that?" she asks. The administrator does not answer her question, but repeats the instructions: "Can you finish drawing the car?"
>
> She becomes more confused and anxious. She looks toward the door, hoping her teacher or some children will come in soon. When no one enters, she takes a stab at solving the problem. As she begins to draw, she looks up at the test administrator and studies his face. She wonders, does his smile mean I'm doing it right?

The child in this story is likely to perform less well on this test because of cultural differences in experience and style. She is uneasy about the strange testing room and the unfamiliar examiner. She is confused by the test's content; the items do not relate to her own life. She appears to be field sensitive in that she focuses on everything around her rather than just on the test. Finally, she yearns for help from others, since getting assistance from peers and adults is part of her cognitive style.

PIAGET'S THEORY OF COGNITIVE DEVELOPMENT

A very different view of cognitive development is offered by Piaget (1952b), who was not as concerned with the *outcomes* of intellectual development—as measured by scores on IQ tests—as with the *processes* of intellectual development. He sought to describe the specific steps children go through mentally to learn and to become competent adults. Because his work focuses on how children construct knowledge, it is considered a more practical theory for teachers and parents (R. A. DeVries & Kohlberg, 1990).

Assimilation and Accommodation

As described in Chapter 3, Piaget believed that learning and cognitive advancement at any age is the result of **assimilation** and **accommodation.** The following story illustrates these two mental processes in the primary years:

Antonio, a 7-year-old, is observing fish swim in an aquarium in the science center of his classroom. He begins to wonder how fish can breathe underwater. His teacher, Ms. Tashita, moves to his side.

MS. TASHITA:	You seem to be very interested in the fish.
ANTONIO:	Yeah. But . . . (Stares at the fish intently and looks puzzled)
MS. TASHITA:	What is it? Do you have a question?
ANTONIO:	Yeah. How do they breathe in there? (Taps on the side of the aquarium)
MS. TASHITA:	Well. How do you breathe?
ANTONIO:	(Breathes in and out several times in an exaggerated way) Like this. See? I use my mouth . . . and . . . what are they called?
MS. TASHITA:	Lungs?
ANTONIO:	Yep. And the air goes in and I can breathe. But the fish don't have any air in there. Only water.
MS. TASHITA:	Well, let me explain. Do you know that there is something special in the air that you need to breathe?
ANTONIO:	Yeah. Oxygen, I heard about that. Plants need it, and people too.
MS. TASHITA:	And fish. They need oxygen.
ANTONIO:	But they just breathe the water in. Doesn't the water just get in their lungs? Like this. (Pretends to breathe in water. Makes gurgling noises and laughs.)
MS. TASHITA:	(Laughs) Well, there is oxygen in water. And the fish have something special that helps them take the oxygen out of the water. Not lungs, like people. Fish have gills.
ANTONIO:	Oh! So it's like we take the oxygen out of the air and fish take it out of water. Like that?
MS. TASHITA:	Exactly! You can see the gills near their heads. See? Watch. (Continues to help the child see the gills for several minutes)

The child in this story is engaged in both assimilation and accommodation in coming to an understanding about how fish obtain oxygen. He assimilates information; that is, he integrates this new knowledge into his previous understandings about breathing and oxygen. However, if he only relied on previous knowledge—that is, only assimilated—he would conclude that fish have lungs and breathe water. With questions and prompts from the teacher, and through further observation, he changes his previous understandings a little. He adjusts his ideas about water by adding a new feature: it contains oxygen. He adapts his view of how plants and animals obtain oxygen: gills are another way to get oxygen. This is accommodation.

An important aspect of these processes, from Piaget's view, is that the *child* does the assimilating and accommodating, not the teacher. Learning is internal and personal. The child must play an active role in constructing knowledge; the teacher serves only as a facilitator.

Concrete Operational Thought

Piaget proposed that children between ages 5 and 8 gradually move into a new, distinct stage of intellectual development: the **concrete operational stage.** In this stage they gain freedom from some of the cognitive limitations of previous developmental periods, but they still display some cognitive characteristics of preschool-age children.

Many 7-year-olds can successfully complete the conservation tasks we discussed in Chapter 11. When shown two identical containers holding the same amounts of water, and observing one container being poured into one of a different shape, children of this age will now report that the amounts of water stay the same. Why are children now able to successfully complete such tasks, when only 1 or 2 years before they could not? Piaget explains that they have acquired several important cognitive processes which lead to improvement in problem-solving and learning. These processes are listed in Table 15-2 and described below.

Decentration. Recall that preschoolers tend to focus on only one aspect of a problem at a time. Children in the concrete operational stage, in contrast, are able to coordinate two ideas at once. In the conservation task, above, they can see that the water is *higher* in one container but *wider* in the other. A common response of children at this age would be, "They both have the same amount still, 'cause this container is tall, but this one is real fat." They no longer *center*—that is, fixate—on just one aspect of the problem. They can coordinate ideas of tallness and wideness at the same time.

TABLE 15-2
Intellectual Advancements in the Primary Years

Cognitive Process	Description
Decentration	Children no longer center just on self or on just one aspect or dimension of a problem, but can consider multiple factors simultaneously. For example, they can think about a container as both tall *and* thin and another as short *and* wide.
Reversibility	Children can mentally reverse the steps of a process. For example, they can put a toy back together the way it was before or retrace their steps on a walk.
Causality	Children can understand that actions or events cause things to happen. For example, they can see that throwing a ball harder results in its flying farther or that pushing a peer on the playground causes upset and anger.

SOURCE: Piaget, 1952b.

Piaget used the word **decentration** to describe this kind of thinking. Decentration allows primary-grade children to learn new school-related concepts. In literacy, for example, children come to see that several dimensions of writing must be considered all at once if others are to read what is written. They learn that they must reproduce the correct shapes of letters, but also turn them in the appropriate direction in space (e.g., *b* as opposed to *d*). At the same time, they must attend to the sounds letters represent in conventional writing. While contemplating all of these things, they must simultaneously attend to the idea or story they are relating.

Reversibility. Children in the concrete operational stage can reverse operations; that is, they can mentally or physically reverse the steps of a process to go back to a starting point. How does this kind of thinking help with school learning? **Reversibility** is required in many subject areas. Mathematics is a good example:

A second-grade teacher, Ms. Nagy, sets up a math game in her classroom which requires children to add up points and keep score. As a group of children play, one child accidentally adds too many points to her score sheet and writes down a new, incorrect total: 24. Her peers protest immediately.

ARI: No, Hanna! Not 24! You don't add 5 points! That's wrong!

TINA: (Speaking at the same time) You have to take those off!

HANNA: (Looking confused) What?

TINA: You can't have 5 points.

HANNA: (Still confused) How do I take them off?

MS. NAGY: (Just entering the math center) Sounds like you have a problem with your score.

ARI: Yeah, 'cause Hanna added too many points. Like 5 points. Now we don't know what to do. And I was winning!

MS. NAGY: Okay. If Hanna added 5 points to her score and she shouldn't have, what should she do?

ARI: (Angrily) Tell Hanna she can't play anymore. I was winning!

MS. NAGY: Oh, I think you should all keep playing. What's something else you could do?

HANNA: I know! Add 5 to everybody else. Five points to you and you. (She points to one peer, then the other)

TINA: No, wait. This is how you do it. You take away the five points from Hanna. See? 24, 23, . . . (Now she counts silently to herself) Back to 19. See? That was your score before, 19. (Scribbles out Hanna's total and corrects it)

How did the children in this primary class think through this problem? They relied on reversibility: they discovered that you can reverse addition by subtracting the same amount. Reversibility problems abound in mathematics and many other school subjects.

Causality. In the preschool years, children tend to believe that if two events occur simultaneously, one must cause the other. If a child knocks over a vase and then hears that her father has a fever, she might come to believe her mistake caused her father's illness. In the primary years, children begin to understand cause and effect more accurately. They can often see connections between actions—both their own and others'—and consequences. This is called causal thinking or **causality.**

Piaget notes that children of this age are still struggling to sort out causes and effects. They ask the question "why" quite regularly in an effort to understand causal relationships: "Why are the leaves falling?" "Why is Janelle upset?" Even at this age, great care must still be taken so that children do not misinterpret events. For example, a primary-grade child whose parents are separating should be told explicitly that he or she was not the cause of the separation.

Causal thinking is useful for many learning activities in school. In science experiments, for example, children may be asked to speculate on why ice cubes melt more or less slowly in water of different temperatures, or why the plant that gets no light looks different from the one that does.

Piaget's Theory and Traditional School Subjects

The advancements in cognition described by Piaget allow concrete operational children to gain greater understanding of traditional subjects in school, such as social studies, mathematics, and science.

The Social Studies. In the social studies, an increased knowledge of concepts of time and space allows the early study of history or geography. Piaget (1971) has shown that children only gradually construct an understanding of time in the early years. Preschoolers can make gross estimates of time; they understand that a day is the length of time that the sun shines, and can learn the temporal order of key events (e.g., "My grandmother is picking me up after our nap"). In the concrete operational stage, children begin to accurately reflect on the past. They can understand that time is continuous from past to present to future (Seefeldt, 1998), and can distinguish the long ago from the present. However, they are still challenged by time intervals among events of the past. The following interview with a 6-year-old shows that distinctions between long ago and long, long ago are difficult even for primary-grade children:

RESEARCHER: Tell me what it was like long ago.

CHILD: Long ago? Like when children went to schools that had dirt floors?

RESEARCHER: Sure. Tell me about back then.

CHILD: Well. There was no electricity. And all the people would ride horses.

RESEARCHER: Tell me more.

CHILD: Well, I think back then people would talk like apes.

RESEARCHER: Ah. That *is* long ago.

CHILD: And you know what? There were no electric guitars. (Feigns playing a guitar while making loud guitar noises)

The child in this interview clearly has an understanding of historical time. However, he has difficulty judging the intervals between one historical period and another. Talking like apes and going to a school with a dirt floor are both viewed as having occurred in the same period.

New understandings about time create an emerging interest in the long ago among primary-grade children (Hinitz, 1987; Seefeldt, 1998). Abstract history lessons that require the memorization of dates or complex historical interpretations are beyond the grasp of children of this age. However, early experiences with history, such as school visits by grandparents to talk about the past, or children's books that depict long-ago times, may be very useful for the development of historical understanding.

Piaget (Piaget & Inhelder, 1963) described the gradual acquisition of spatial concepts in early childhood. He found that during the late preschool and early primary years, children think about space in terms of their own movements or actions through it (Hazen, 1982). Their thinking goes, "I know about this space because I walk this way to get to the park" or "I know about this space because I can crawl under it." This conception has been referred to as *action space* (Piaget, Inhelder, & Szeminska, 1960). As children move more fully into the concrete operational stage, they begin to think of space as a whole: directions, locations, and distances are linked together in the child's mind to create a total picture of a familiar area.

Piaget illustrated these ideas by asking children of varying ages to create "maps" of their school and its surroundings out of sand (Piaget et al., 1960). Preoperational children constructed models that highlighted how they move through, in, and out of the school. Such representations reflect action space, from Piaget's view. Concrete operational children added more detail to their maps, including key landmarks. They presented more accurate representations of the area as a whole. These constructions show that children have begun to acquire a conception of **map space.** Other research verifies that primary-grade children can create and interpret simple maps, particularly of familiar areas (Hewes, 1982; Poag, Goodnight, & Cohen, 1985). Figure 15-2 shows young children's maps of their homes.

Although children in the concrete operational stage can think about map space, they are by no means ready for abstract geometry lessons (Seefeldt, 1998). However, early experiences with map space, such as drawing maps of the school and creating models of the community with blocks, may be quite useful for primary children.

Mathematics. In earlier sections we learned that processes such as reversibility and decentration help children learn mathematics. Several other abilities also enhance learning in this area. Piaget noted that children in the concrete operational stage gradually acquire an understanding of number. As described in Chapter 11, he devised an experiment to show this. Children are shown two rows of checkers of equal amount. When one row is spread out or pushed together, the child is asked if the amounts are still the same. Recall that preschoolers regularly answer that the spread-out row now has more. They are fooled by perception. Even when asked to count, children of this age cling to their erroneous beliefs.

Piaget found that children in the concrete operational stage are able to use reason to overcome misleading perceptions. When confronted with this same task, they are now likely to count the checkers or simply state, "Both rows have the same because you didn't take any away." Such solutions indicate that children understand number. When is a complete understanding of number acquired? Possibly not until age 7 or 8. Kamii (1982) notes that even children who can count may not use counting as a tool to solve real problems until third grade! For example, a 6-year-old who has been counting for years may still determine who won a card game by placing the cards in piles and deciding which looks highest. Only in the later primary years do children exclusively use counting and number concepts to solve problems.

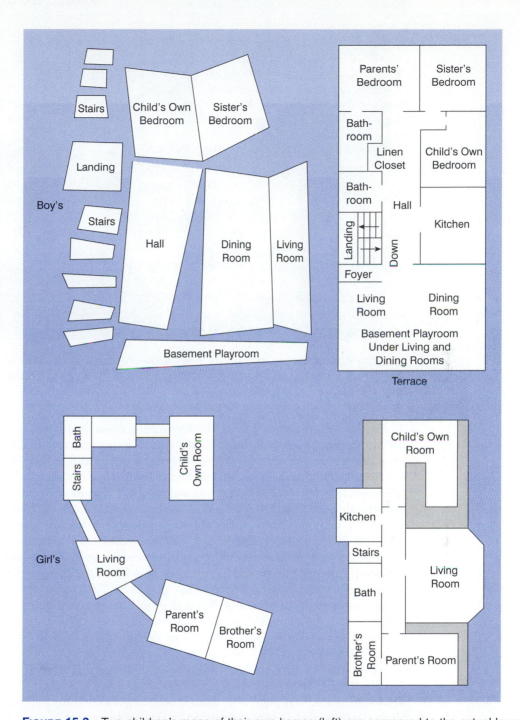

FIGURE 15-2 Two children's maps of their own homes (left) are compared to the actual layouts (right). Although primitive, the children's maps reveal early understanding of map spaces.

SOURCE: Stone, L. J., & Church, J. (1984). *Childhood and adolescence,* 5th ed. (p. 401). New York: Random House. Reprinted by permission.

New cognitive abilities in the primary years allow children to solve more complex mathematical problems. Concrete objects are still needed, however, for children to learn math concepts.

Another mathematics-related competence described by Piaget is **seriation,** the ability to order objects by length. In a classic experiment to test for this skill, Piaget presented children with 8 sticks of varying lengths and asked, "Can you make a row of sticks so that you place the shortest one here (points), then the next tallest, then the next tallest, until you put the very tallest one at the other end?" Very young preschoolers struggle with this task and make many errors. Some simply create interesting designs with the sticks! Four- or 5-year-olds complete the task with much physical trial and error. They might select two sticks at a time, compare the lengths, then place them in the row. Such a process leads to errors, which the child may or may not notice at the end of the task. By age 6 or 7, children exhibit thoughtfulness and careful planning in solving this problem. They scan the entire collection of sticks and select the shortest. Then they search the pile again for the next tallest. Much of their work on the task is internal, with less physical trial and error. When they can complete the task with few or no mistakes, they are said to have fully acquired seriation.

How is this ability related to mathematics learning? Seriation is the foundation for important later math skills, such as *transitive reasoning* (Remember from high school Algebra? If A is greater than B, and B greater than C, then A must be greater than C). Seriation is necessary even in the primary math curriculum. The following ordering activity from a first-grade curriculum guide is an example:

Ask children to stand in a line. Introduce the concepts, "taller," "tallest," "shorter," and "shortest." Then ask children to rearrange themselves in the line so that "the tallest child is on this side of the room and the shortest is on the other side." As children complete the task, ask questions which guide their problem-solving: "How can you figure out where you belong in the line?" or "Are you sure you're in the right spot? How can you check?"

Seriation activities, such as ordering a collection of shells by size or weight, will provide important, early practice at this kind of thinking.

Science. Cognitive advancements in the preoperational stage relate to an understanding of scientific concepts. Piaget (1930) noted that preoperational children lack a full understanding of natural causes. They tend to believe that occurrences in nature are the result of human or human-like agents. When a cloud floats by, for example, they believe it must have been moved by someone or something living, or must be itself alive. A child might claim, "The sun comes out because it wakes up" or "Mommy makes night time so people can sleep" (S. A. Gelman & Kremer, 1991). As children enter the concrete operational stage, however, they begin to overcome this limitation in thinking. They are able to think logically about what causes rain or how and why seeds travel from one place to another. The scientific curriculum can be broadened to topics that were incomprehensible to children only a few years before.

A second advancement in scientific thinking, according to Piaget, is **multiple classification.** Children in the preoperational stage center on only one dimension when they are asked to categorize objects. For example, they might rely only on color, putting all the red shapes in one pile and all the blue ones in another. In contrast, concrete operational children can think about two attributes at once. They can classify by both shape and color, placing all *red* triangles in one pile and all *blue* triangles in another. This multiple classification helps children to mentally organize scientific information.

When encouraged to make a museum in the classroom with objects from nature, for example, second graders create displays of "things from the beach" and "things from the woods." Further, within these categories they might create displays of shells, stones, seeds, and nests. They can simultaneously think about both *where* objects come from and the *form and function* of these objects. With their newfound categorization abilities, concrete operational children can now begin to understand the scientific classification of plants and animals. For example, third graders will no longer categorize animal pictures as either "fish" or "animals," as they might in preschool. Instead, they will place pictures of fish and birds in separate piles *under* the category "animals." This ability to categorize phenomena in a hierarchical structure contributes to later understanding of the standard scientific classifications, such as genus and species.

School and Concrete Learning. The remarkable changes in children's thinking in the primary years have led some teachers to plan very abstract, academic learning activities for this age group. Piaget would have disapproved. He called this developmental period the *concrete* operational stage for an important reason. Children of this age still need the support of concrete objects in order to learn, and attempts to teach classification or number in an abstract way without real objects would be futile and even harmful. To teach about weather or animal classification without concrete observations or experiments would likewise be inappropriate. Attempts to move young children too quickly into abstract thought have been found to lead to a great deal of stress (Hart et al., 1998).

ANALYSIS AND MULTICULTURAL CRITIQUE OF PIAGET'S THEORY

Concerns have been raised about Piaget's theory of concrete operational thought. He has been criticized for overestimating the age at which concrete operational thinking first appears. Also, some believe he does not adequately emphasize the role of culture and social interaction in intellectual development.

Underestimates of Competence

A number of studies have found that children can acquire concrete operational thinking at an earlier age than Piaget proposed. When tasks are altered so that less complex language and more familiar objects are used, even preschoolers have been found to perform concrete operations. For example, some researchers report that with training, 4- and 5-year-olds can successfully perform conservation or seriation tasks (Blevins-Knabe, 1987; R. Gelman, 1982; Zimmerman & Lanaro, 1974).

Several studies have shown that preschoolers can understand natural causes better than Piaget proposed. In one study, children were asked about phenomena that were very familiar to them—flowers and dogs, for example. The questions posed to them were simpler than in Piaget's experiments (e.g., "Do you think people make dogs?" instead of "Where do dogs come from?"). Children as young as age 3 reported that plants or animals came from nature and were not created by humans (S. A. Gelman & Kremer, 1991). In other investigations, researchers have found that 3- and 4-year-olds can perform multiple classification if tasks are presented to them in a clear and simple way (Siegel, McCabe, Brand, & Mathews, 1978; L. Smith, 1989).

Researchers have also shown that primary children can think at higher levels than Piaget suggested. In several studies children were found to engage in *propositional logic,* an advanced kind of thinking that Piaget believed only adolescents or adults could use (Brainerd, 1974; Kodroff & Roberge, 1975). Propositional logic involves the interpretation of if/then statements. When these were presented to children in a simple way and included interesting and familiar objects, even 7- and 8-year-olds could understand and explain them. For example, primary children were asked the following: "If a dog gets wet, it shakes its fur. If a dog shakes its fur, the apartment will get messy. So, if a dog gets wet, then what will happen?" Contrary to what Piaget would have expected, even young primary children could draw the correct conclusion.

Culture and Cognitive Abilities

There is great individual variation in children's cognitive competence in the primary years. Some children are more advanced than Piaget would have predicted, while others develop more slowly. Flavell, Miller, and Miller (1993) suggest that cognitive ability varies more during the primary years than in any other period. One factor that contributes to this variation is culture.

Cultural Differences in Conservation. In a study conducted in West Africa, primary-grade children were found to be unable to perform conservation tasks (Greenfield, 1966). Remarkably, even older children and adolescents in this investigation had not acquired an ability to conserve. In marked contrast, children living in pottery-making families in Mexico were found to conserve surprisingly early in childhood (Price-Williams, Gordon, & Ramirez, 1969). Why the discrepancy in these research findings?

Children of different communities and cultures have different motivations and opportunities to learn skills. In highly cooperative African communities, personal ownership is deemphasized and possessions are more likely to be shared. Because children are accustomed to sharing, disputes over toys or food are less likely. Having the most may not be highly valued in such a family or village, and children who are not accustomed to disagreements over objects and amounts may think about quantity less often. Conservation may be a less important competence in such societies, and thus may emerge later in development (Hale-Benson, 1986; B. B. Whiting & Edwards, 1988).

In contrast, Mexican children from pottery-making families think about quantity every day. In helping family members make pots, children must make many judgments about amount. How much clay is needed to make an urn of a certain size? What amount of water is needed to wet a lump of clay to the correct consistency? Children regularly see quantity transformed during the pottery-making process, and may puzzle over why there appears to be more clay in an unformed lump than in a finished pot. Judgments about quantity and transformations of mass are all important to family livelihood in this society, so these competencies may arise earlier in life.

Cultural Differences in Map Reading.   In some cultures, primary-grade children do not acquire an understanding of map space as Piaget described. In a study in one African community (Dart & Pradhan, 1967), even older children and adolescents were found not to understand maps! This is in sharp contrast to some Euro-American communities, where children have been found to accurately interpret maps in the preschool years (Hazen, 1982). How can these differences be explained? In some cultures, maps are prevalent and important. Families may travel long distances along roads and highways, and children may watch their parents or grandparents study maps of subway systems, interstates, or shopping mall floor plans. Their families may even organize treasure hunts using simple maps during holidays or birthdays. The following is an example of this early map experience:

During a long drive to Disney World, a 4-year-old announces that she is in need of a rest room. "Can you hold it awhile?" her mother implores, having stopped for gas only several minutes before. "No!" the child responds, with convincing urgency. "Why don't you look at the map?" the mother suggests, handing a road map to the child, hoping to distract her from her problem. "We're right about here." She points. "I want you to watch and tell me when we get to this little blue square. See? That's how bathrooms are marked on the map. When we get to that square, we will be at the bathroom."

The child studies the map very seriously and runs her finger along the line that marks the highway, as she has seen her mother do. In moments, she announces, "I think we're here now. Stop, Mom. We're here now." "No, honey," her mother answers, "not yet. We have to go along that highway a little more. See?" She points again. "We haven't reached that little square yet."

"But it's just right here!" the child complains, pointing to the rest area symbol on the map. "It's just a little way." Her mother responds: "Well, on the map it looks like a little way. But a little way on a map is a pretty long way on the real highway." The child reflects on this for several minutes. The rest area finally comes into view. Now the child is even more puzzled. "No, Mom. This isn't the bathroom. It's not blue. The bathrooms are blue, see?" She shows her mother the blue rest area symbol on the map.

Motivation to study maps may never be greater than in such a situation! It is not surprising that children with such family life experiences will construct map space at an early age. In comparison, in some cultures map reading is not important. If motorized transportation is not used, young children may not travel far from their dwellings, much less away from their villages (B. B. Whiting & Edwards, 1988). In some societies, longer trips take place overland, through forests or deserts, rather than on roads, and precise paths of travel may not be as important as general direction. Even a sense of place or home is not critical in every culture. Some nomadic groups, for example, may not have a geographic home. Where they are and where they go is determined by climate or sources of food. In these instances, map reading is simply not relevant, and opportunities to construct map space are minimal.

Cultural Differences in Math. Kamii (1985, 1989), has shown that American children have difficulty learning about place value. For example, a first-grade child will often think that the "1" in the number "16" is just a one, not a ten. So, children of this age struggle when performing multi-digit addition or subtraction problems. Kamii's research was conducted with children living in the United States, however. Other studies have shown that primary children in Korea and China surpass American children in their understanding of number (Fuson & Kwon, 1992; Stevenson, Lee, et al., 1990).

Why the discrepancy? One theory is that language differences lead to advantages for some cultural groups. The Korean language, for example, has number words that clearly identify place value. Korean number words progress in this way: " . . . nine, ten, ten one, ten two, ten three, . . ." The number 2222 is said as "two thousand two hundred two ten two." Because numbers are spoken in this way, it is easier for children to construct an understanding of place value (Fuson & Kwon,

Children learn the most when they receive assistance from others within the "zone of proximal development"—a point at which the solution of a problem is just beyond the child's current level of mastery.

1992). Family attitudes and expectations may also lead to differences in number understanding. In both Korean and Chinese families, parents are found to be more concerned and more demanding about children's performance in math (Stevenson, Lee, et al., 1990).

Cultural experiences, values, and even language explain differences in cognition in the primary years. It is important to point out that cultures are not inferior because they value certain cognitive abilities less or provide fewer experiences to obtain them. The intellectual competence of primary-grade children must be judged in relation to the abilities or knowledge they need to function in their own cultural group.

VYGOTSKY'S VIEW OF LANGUAGE AND SOCIAL INTERACTION

A criticism of Piaget's work has been that it does not place great enough emphasis on language and social interaction, processes which Vygotsky (1962) has argued play a crucial role in school learning. Language, according to Vygotsky, helps to direct children's attention and organize their understandings. Both self-directed speech and the language of others are useful. Primary children often use **self-directed speech** to guide their own thought processes and to work through the steps of a complex problem. Such verbalizations are now internalized: children speak to themselves silently as they think and learn. An important advancement in this period is that children can consciously manipulate this language in their minds. They can say to themselves during school, "Now listen to this, it's really important" or "If you put these two triangles together, you make a rectangle." These are instances of what Vygotsky called **verbal thought.**

The language of others also aids learning. Teachers and peers ask questions or give verbal hints within the **zone of proximal development.** Recall that this zone is a point at which a problem or task is just beyond a child's current level of mastery. Some challenges are *not* in this zone—those that are either completely insurmountable or very easy to overcome. A science experiment, for example, may be so difficult that a teacher actually completes most of it for a child or ends the activity altogether. On the other hand, an experiment may be so simple that a child can perform it easily without any help. A science experience which is moderately challenging and can be completed with indirect assistance, however, is considered to be in the zone of proximal development. Here a teacher can pose an interesting question, point out something that the child has missed, or give a hint. These verbal interventions guide the child in independent discovery.

According to Vygotsky, peers can also assist children who are within the zone of proximal development. In the following vignette, an older peer provides guidance, including much language, to help a younger child solve a problem:

A 6-year-old is gradually constructing an understanding of number, although she still struggles with problems of quantity. So, when she attempts to solve quantification tasks, she is often in the zone of proximal development.

After playing a card game with a slightly older peer, she becomes puzzled about who won. Her playmate shows her how to determine the winner: "You have to line up the cards and count. See?" The child places the cards in one-to-one correspondence along the table and demonstrates counting.

Later, the 6-year-old is confronted with another problem of quantity. She is arguing with another peer about who got the most raisins for a snack. She solves this problem by relying on the words and thinking of the previous peer: "You have to line them up and count." She repeats this instruction, more to herself than to the other child. When they line up the raisins and count them, they find that both have the same number.

As we discussed in earlier chapters, children of some cultural groups may require greater social interaction than others in learning. Those from field-sensitive cultures may be most reliant on external clues, including social input from other people, in learning. Mexican-American and African-American children, for example, have been found to learn more in school when completing group projects and cooperative learning assignments (Rodriquez, 1983).

MEMORY, METACOGNITION, AND SCHOOLING

School success requires not just acquiring knowledge but retaining it for significant periods of time. Children must remember ideas or concepts and build on these during later school experiences. **Memory** is critical for long-term success in school. Several types of memory have been identified. These lie along a continuum from very fleeting recollection to long-term retention. These memory types are described in Table 15-3.

TABLE 15-3
Types of Memory

Type	Description	Example
Sensory memory	Sensations or perceptions are acquired through the senses and stored briefly at a subconscious level.	A child breathes in the rich smells at a farm and stores a recollection of these in the brain for a few minutes.
Short-term memory	Perceptions or information are attended to carefully, then organized and stored in the brain. For a short time, these may be consciously retrieved and pondered.	A child pays special attention to the smells on the farm and consciously stores these in the brain, along with other ideas about the farm experience. Later in the day, the child comments on these to a teacher. A month later, however, the child has no recollection of farm smells.
Long-term memory	Perceptions or information are organized and integrated into semi-permanent recollections that may be retrieved over a long period of time. Information that holds personal meaning and is related to previous ideas or understandings is most likely to be stored in long-term memory.	A child thinks about and talks with parents and other family members about the rich smells of the farm. The child organizes and integrates ideas about these smells into previous, permanent understandings of smells in different contexts.

Types of Memory

Sensory memory refers to brief recollections of experiences involving the senses. If children from an urban neighborhood visit a farm in the country, the rich smell of fertilizer may register briefly and subconsciously in their minds. They may subconsciously hear the steady hum of milking machines in the barn. Such sensory memories disappear in a matter of seconds unless coded or processed in the mind.

If children attend carefully to these sights and sounds, however, they may enter these sensations into a different kind of memory: *short-term memory*. In this type of memory, experiences are stored in the brain for a short period of time. Children organize, make sense of, or in other ways process new information in short-term memory. They can consciously retrieve and reflect on the information at some other time. Upon return to school after the trip to the farm, for example, children can reflect and comment on their observations. Short-term memory vanishes, however, in a relatively short period (Halford, Maybery, O'Hare, & Grant, 1994).

The most important type of memory is *long-term memory*, in which certain images, facts, or concepts are drawn from short-term memory and are permanently stored. Over time, this information is organized and refined. Some have equated long-term memory with knowledge itself. Children are able to construct larger, more complex long-term memories as they get older (Howe, 1995).

Why is some information stored in long-term memory and some not? A prevalent view is that children store in long-term memory that which holds personal meaning and interest—things they are curious about or which captivate them. Furthermore, they are more likely to retain information that they can integrate into their previous knowledge. As a result, facts that are totally meaningless may not be retained because children cannot fit them into what they already know. For example, a child who has no basic concept of time will not retain facts about how clocks work. Teachers must make information both interesting and relevant, then, if they wish their students to retain it.

Metacognition and Memory

As we discussed in earlier chapters, young children gradually acquire **theories of the mind;** that is, they come to understand internal emotional states, motives, and thinking processes. By the primary years, children know what learning and remembering are and can guide and control these in the mind (Lovett & Pillow, 1991). Their ability to think about and regulate internal cognitive processes is called **metacognition.** In the primary years, metacognition enhances children's ability to remember information. They can now consciously guide their own memory processes, using strategies of rehearsal, labeling and organization, and paying attention.

Rehearsal. Children become aware in the primary years that they can remember information for longer periods through **rehearsal.** Several studies have shown that children as young as 6 years repeat facts or skills over and over that they wish to learn (Flavell, Beach, & Chinsky, 1966; Naus, 1982). Whereas kindergartners might learn the names of plants in a terrarium by listening and remembering in a haphazard way, first graders will rehearse these names, saying them aloud or to themselves again and again.

Labeling and Organization. Another way to remember new information is through **labeling and organizing** it in some way in the mind as it is being learned.

A group of preschoolers might do this when learning about animals in science. As they notice similarities and differences among animals, they might mentally create the categories "birds," "fish," and "other animals." As children reach the primary years, they become more sophisticated at placing objects, events, or ideas into mental classifications in order to remember them (Plumert, 1994). They can also create labels for these classifications. For example, in a history activity they might better distinguish objects used long ago from objects used in modern times by creating mental labels (e.g., "things my grandma used" and "things my mom uses").

In one study, children as young as age 5 were found to understand that categorizing and labeling objects would help them in remembering. By age 6, children could even describe why labeling strategies help in memory tasks. As one child puts it, "I say the names of the different things in my mind. The words make pictures in my brain" (Fabricius & Cavalier, 1989, p. 303).

Paying Attention. With age, children become better at **paying attention** to certain important stimuli in the environment. This ability significantly enhances children's ability to remember. Whereas preschoolers attend to almost anything that catches their eye, primary-grade children are better able to focus on one or several relevant phenomena (Bjorkland, 1995). This ability is crucial in school, where children who can comprehend teacher imperatives such as "Pay attention to what I'm about to say" or "Now follow along with me" will be more successful students. An emerging awareness of attention processes helps primary-grade children become more selective in what they learn.

Teaching Metacognition in School. Teachers can help children acquire metacognitive abilities by making informal suggestions for how to remember things. For example, they can suggest rehearsal strategies with statements like "If you say the names of these plants over and over, you'll never forget them." In one study, children whose teachers frequently made these metacognitive suggestions were found to be more competent in remembering facts (Moely et al., 1992). They were also found to more frequently and effectively use metacognitive strategies on their own. Children who were low or average achievers appeared to benefit most from these suggestions. This research suggests that teachers must not only impart information and skills, but also help children learn how thinking and remembering work.

Memory and Culture

What children remember varies from one culture to another. For example, Alaskan native children are more likely to remember labels for various categories of snow than the names of plants and animals that are not indigenous to their homeland. Native American children may more easily remember the governance structure of their tribe than the branches of the government of the United States. Memory problems in schoolchildren may result, in part, from a curriculum that is not wholly relevant to children of diverse backgrounds.

Culture affects not only *what* is remembered, but also *how* it is remembered, as the following story illustrates:

A third-grade teacher tries to help a young African-American child learn addition and subtraction facts. No amount of drilling seems to help. The teacher begins to worry that the child lacks the capacity to remember.

One day the teacher provides jump ropes for his students at recess. The child he has been concerned about quickly organizes a jump rope game. As she jumps, the child chants a complex rhyme that takes many minutes to recite. The teacher is amazed at the child's ability to remember such long and complex verses. (Not to mention her agility with the jump rope!) He begins to reassess his theory about the child's poor memory capacity. In fact, he later reexamines his whole approach to teaching mathematics in the classroom: Is there a way to incorporate such rhythmic games into his math lessons?

Why can the child in this story remember verses but not math facts? According to Hale-Benson (1986), African-American children often have a "performer style"— a mode of thinking and learning that includes movement, dance, and music. Such an orientation comes from a high degree of exposure to creative arts in the community. The child in the story relies on movement and rhyme to recall a jump rope chant. These memory strategies are no less effective than rehearsal, organization, or attention-directing approaches. The teacher in the story wisely considers including these in his teaching.

Research on memory in non-Western cultures confirms that some children and adults remember things in very different ways. In several studies, people of non-Western communities performed poorly on memory tasks in which objects or words were presented in a non-meaningful manner (Cole & Scribner, 1977; Paris & Lindauer, 1982). For example, subjects presented with a list of unrelated, isolated words would later remember very few of the items. Further, instruction in memory strategies such as rehearsal and categorization did not improve these subjects' performance. However, they could remember very well objects or events that were incorporated into songs, chants, stories, dances, woodcarvings, drawings, and other forms of cultural expression. Names of nearby villages, for example, could be recalled when they were presented in a story.

Children of various cultures may even rely on different senses to remember. In one study, African-American children were found to retain information longer when it was received auditorily (Kirk, 1972). In contrast, Mexican-American and Native American children were found to have better visual memory. Members of these cultural groups might remember information longer when it is presented in a visual way, through drawings, photographs, or other graphics.

CULTURE AND SCHOOL SUCCESS

Cognitive development is not the only factor in school success. A wealth of research over several decades has documented that children of some cultural groups in America fare less well in school than others (Okagki & Frensch, 1998). Children of many historically under-represented groups are more likely to perform poorly, with African-American, Mexican-American, Puerto Rican, and Native American children particularly at risk of school failure (Stevenson, Chen, & Uttal, 1990). This risk increases during the school years. In second grade, 15% of Latino and African-American children perform below grade level; by sixth grade, 40% of Latino and 50% of African-American children are below grade level (Norman, 1988). Euro-American children are less likely to fail (Stevenson, Chen, & Uttal, 1990), and children of some Asian-American cultures are most likely to succeed (Okagki & Frensch, 1998).

Why do these cultural variations exist? Poverty is the main explanation. Cultures with high rates of school failure tend to be those with the highest poverty levels. There are other reasons, however, for cultural differences in school success.

Clashes in Cognitive Style

As we discussed earlier, children of different cultures have different cognitive styles—for example, some are field sensitive or are more social in their learning, others less so. These individual variations derive from the rich traditions of families and cultural groups. They also place some children at risk of prejudice and disadvantage in school. Slaughter-Defoe, Nakagawa, Takanishi, and Johnson (1990) cite research suggesting that African-American children have active, expressive styles of learning that clash with the behaviors required for success in dominant-culture classrooms.

Similar findings are reported for Mexican-American (Rodriquez, 1983) and Native American (Wise & Miller, 1983) children. Students of these cultures prefer movement, singing, and conversation in learning, whereas traditional American schools expect quiet sitting, listening, and studying. Children of some Asian-American cultures, on the other hand, show learning styles that are very similar to those of their Euro-American peers (Slaughter-Defoe et al., 1990). Japanese-American children, for example, have been found to demonstrate quiet, studious modes of learning which closely resemble those of white middle-class children (Mordkowitz & Ginsburg, 1987; A. J. Schwartz, 1971). Unfortunately, it may be that school success depends, in part, on whether a child's cultural style matches that of the dominant culture.

Poor Schools and Teaching

One explanation for poor academic performance by some children is that their schools are ineffective. Comer (1985) has noted that schools serving historically under-represented groups are often "hierarchical, authoritarian . . . rigid, and unable to respond" (p. 126) to the needs of diverse groups of children. Teachers and administrators, he contends, unwittingly foster a climate of distrust and alienation.

Teachers may treat children of color differently from students of the dominant culture. Several classic studies were conducted to examine this problem. In one, significant differences were found between teachers' interactions with Mexican-Americans and Euro-American children (Jackson & Cosca, 1974). These teachers directed 35% more praise statements and 21% more questions toward Euro-American students. They also accepted Euro-American children's ideas 40% more often. These figures may not give a full picture of bias, however. This study was conducted in schools identified as "best" within their districts, and teachers were informed ahead of time that they would be observed for possible bias in their responses to children!

In a similar study, teachers were found to interact more frequently with Euro-American children, especially boys (Wahab, 1974). Euro-American girls received the second-highest number of interactions, followed by Mexican-American boys. Mexican-American girls received the least attention in these classrooms. Such trends may exist even when teachers are of historically under-represented groups. Washington (1980, 1982) found that African-American and Euro-American teachers held equally negative attitudes toward African-American children. Irrespective of race, teachers in this study directed more negative classroom behavior toward children of this cultural group. Such studies should give pause to even the most experienced teachers. Professionals who work with young children should carefully monitor their interactions for bias and inequitable distribution of attention.

Family Attitudes Toward School

One widely held belief is that children of historically under-represented groups perform poorly in school because their families do not value education. Research has shown, however, that parents of all cultural groups value schooling and encourage their children to perform well (Okagaki & Frensch, 1998). In fact, one study found African-American and Latino parents to value education more highly than Euro-American parents (Stevenson, Chen, & Uttal, 1990). Both Latino and African-American parents in this investigation reported more positive attitudes toward homework, grades on achievement tests, and a longer school day. Interest in school was high, even among those families living in poverty.

There are families of some cultural groups who may hold less positive attitudes toward Western schooling (Wise & Miller, 1983). Some Native American parents, for example, have been found to view traditional American schools as oppressive or as threatening to cultural traditions and values. Even these parents value their children's education, however. They may be more supportive, however, of family and community education activities or of tribal schools.

CHILDREN WITH SPECIAL NEEDS IN SCHOOL

Since 1975, with the enactment of Public Law 94-142, the Education for All Handicapped Children Act, students with special needs have been integrated into regular classrooms in the public schools. The trend in recent years has been toward even more inclusive classrooms. Even children with severe disabilities are often placed in regular classroom settings (Skrtic, 1995). Primary-grade teachers may work with children with physical challenges, such as sensory or orthopedic impairments, and with children having social and emotional disturbances and autism. It is likely that teachers will have students who face various cognitive challenges.

Approximately 1% of elementary students have mental retardation (G. M. Morrison & Polloway, 1995). Speech and language disorders affect approximately 1–2% of children in the primary years. In most cases, however, the speech or language challenge is related to another, primary disorder. Children with mental retardation and autism, for example, often receive services from a speech and language pathologist (Rice & Schuele, 1995).

Learning Disabilities

The most common yet least understood of cognitive disorders among primary-grade children are **learning disabilities (LD).** Between 3 and 4% of children are learning disabled. The exact number of children affected is difficult to determine due to disagreement about how the disorder is to be defined and identified. One of the most challenging tasks of the primary teacher is to accurately identify children with LD.

Learning disabilities are generally described as impairments in some specific aspect or aspects of learning, such as writing, speaking, or mathematics. A general cognitive delay is not a characteristic, however. In fact, children with LD may be

TABLE 15-4
Some Common
Characteristics of
Children with
Learning
Disabilities

Characteristic	Description
Poor academic achievement	Children with LD often have difficulty in one or several subject areas. Their performance is often uneven; for example, they may excel in math, but struggle with writing.
Perceptual-motor difficulties	Children with LD often have trouble interpreting sensory stimuli and distinguishing left from right. They may exhibit a lack of motor coordination.
Speech and language delays	Children with LD often show delays in language, including slow speech and poor word retrieval.
Faulty memory and logic	Children with LD often have trouble remembering or thinking through problems in school.
Hyperactivity/attention deficits	Some children with LD show extreme degrees of activity in school. They may have great difficulty attending to classroom tasks.

extremely competent in some areas of learning but have difficulty in other areas. For example, a child with LD may be poor in math yet competent in reading.

The prevalent theory is that learning disabilities are caused by neurological impairments. However, persuasive arguments have been offered that environmental factors play a role (Adelman, 1992; B. K. Keogh & Sears, 1991). Although researchers have yet to agree on the cause of LD (S. M. Robinson & Deshler, 1995), most concur that certain characteristics are common among children with the disorder. Several of these characteristics are described in Table 15-4.

Academic Difficulties. Children with LD usually have difficulties in one or more academic areas. A child may show poor reading comprehension or see letters reversed or transposed in written text (sometimes referred to as *dyslexia*). Another child may show mathematics achievement well below his or her grade level. Sometimes a child is delayed in one or several areas, and at grade level or even above in others.

Perceptual-Motor Difficulties. Children with learning disabilities sometimes have perceptual challenges. They may have difficulty accurately interpreting auditory or visual stimuli. They may not hear accurately the instructions for a science activity, or may misinterpret a graph in a math lesson. They may become puzzled about direction, confusing left from right, for example, or may show no regular use of either the left or right hand. Children with LD are sometimes awkward and show poor motor coordination. Their lack of physical competence may cause them to avoid outdoor motor play with peers.

Language and Speech Delays. Some children with learning disabilities have language or speech delays. One child might speak very slowly, another in long, loquacious, rambling sentences. Yet another child with LD might show difficulty in retrieving words. For example, in trying to name a ball, such a child might say, "The . . . the . . . you know . . . that . . . what's it called? . . . the . . . thing."

Faulty Memory or Thinking. Children with LD will sometimes have trouble remembering or paying attention in class, organizing their work, or following tasks or instructions in order. Sometimes teachers will misinterpret these difficulties and claim the child "just doesn't listen" or "never follows directions." On occasion, children with LD become distracted by one small part of a whole, and are therefore unable to see the entire field or "the big picture." For example, a child looking at a topographical globe of the world might center on the bumps on a particular mountain range and attend to nothing else.

Some children with LD have difficulty with change and become upset or angry if routines are disrupted. A child might become surprisingly upset, for example, when discovering one morning that his cubby or desk has been moved to another location.

Hyperactivity/Attentional Deficits. Children with LD are sometimes extremely active and have much difficulty paying attention. Some children are so active that they disrupt the activities of other students in the class. They may have difficulty sitting for even brief periods. They may be unable to attend to even the simplest of instructions.

Some experts believe that LD and **ADHD** (attention deficit/hyperactivity disorder, described in Chapter 14) are essentially the same disability. This is because the two conditions so regularly accompany one another. However, research has shown that ADHD can exist with or without LD. Some children display a full range of LD characteristics; others only show ADHD-related behaviors.

Some characteristics of ADHD are common among younger children. Preschoolers often are wiggly and inattentive, show difficulty following directions, and use less mature syntax and grammar. How is one to determine whether a primary-grade child is simply exhibiting immature characteristics or displaying symptoms of a real disorder? Furthermore, some LD characteristics may be indicators of other disorders, such as underachievement, emotional disturbance, and even mental retardation (S. M. Robinson & Deshler, 1995). Whether a child has LD or some other disorder or is simply immature must be determined by careful observation and assessment.

If a child's challenges are many and severe, some other condition, such as mental retardation, might be suspected. If they are less severe and more specific, LD is a possibility. If a child's challenges do not greatly affect school success or social relationships, immaturity could be the cause.

Gifted and Talented Children

Giftedness is another exceptionality that is associated with cognition. Children are said to be **gifted and talented** if they display a superior intellect and/or talents that are advanced for their chronological age. They often are extremely competent in language, and may grasp complex ideas quickly. They may not benefit from tedious, step-by-step lessons which laboriously break learning down into chunks of information, and may not require drill-and-practice strategies to master concepts. This means that much of a typical school day is unproductive for gifted and talented children (L. K. Silverman, 1995).

One trait of gifted and talented children is a unique learning style. The following story illustrates the idiosyncratic pattern of development for one young child:

A 5-year-old growing up in southern India has not spoken. He appears alert and interested in the world around him, and shows affection toward his family members, but he does not speak. Not one word. Of course, his parents grow worried.

They take him to a clinic, where he is examined by a physician. Nothing appears to be wrong physically. His parents try various techniques to encourage him to talk. They offer rewards and demand that he speak before they will meet his needs. They try speaking in just their native language. (Theirs is a bilingual home, and they hope that simplifying the linguistic environment will help.) None of these strategies work.

Then, one day, the child begins to speak: not just one or two words, but in long, sophisticated sentences. To the surprise and delight of his parents, he speaks eloquently and fluently in both his native language and English. By the end of his sixth year, he can read and write eloquently in both languages.

Children who are gifted and talented face many challenges. They are very much in need of special support in school. They do not always get along well with peers; often they seek the companionship of older children or adults. Gifted children tend to be highly sensitive (Roedel, 1984) and introverted (L. K. Silverman, 1986). They are not always good students; in fact, underachievement is common.

A number of approaches to meeting the needs of children who are gifted and talented have been proposed. Acceleration of the content and pacing of the curriculum is one promising method. Early entrance into kindergarten or skipping grades are extreme examples. This strategy appears to work well, especially for girls (Kerr, 1991). Because gifted and talented children seek the company of older peers, skipping even two or more grade levels has been found to be effective (N. M. Robinson & Noble, 1991).

Developing special gifted classes before, during, or after school is another strategy. Unfortunately, such programs are often limited (many take place only twice per week) or are eliminated altogether during periods of tight budget constraints. Providing enrichment in the regular classroom is the most prevalent (and least costly!) approach. In this method, teachers provide special experiences to challenge the thinking of gifted and talented children in the regular classroom. A problem with this approach is that some teachers confuse enrichment with "MOTS," meaning "more of the same" (L. K. Silverman, 1995, p. 400). Gifted and talented children are simply asked to do *more* worksheets or *more* math problems. Such strategies represent a misunderstanding of the needs of these children.

A growing number of children are now identified as both gifted and learning disabled. One out of six gifted children may have learning disabilities (L. K. Silverman, 1995); they may show specific reading, math, or perceptual challenges (W. K. Silverman, Chitwood, & Waters, 1986). Eliminating rote memory tasks and timed tests—standard fare in most classrooms—and integrating computer technology into the curriculum are strategies which are believed to support the academic achievement of gifted, learning-disabled children (L. K. Silverman, 1989).

Concerns have arisen about the identification of gifted children, since gifted classrooms are often composed exclusively of middle-class Euro-American children rather than being representative of the cultural composition of the community (L. K. Silverman, 1995). One reason for this disparity could be that children of under-represented groups do not always perform well on traditional assessments of giftedness. For example, an African-American child may not perform efficiently on memory or vocabulary tasks because the content of the tasks is not relevant to her life, or a Latino child may not score well on an IQ test because she comes from a field-sensitive culture.

Teachers must use alternate means to determine giftedness among children of diverse cultural backgrounds. Children who show a high degree of competence in

ASSESSING YOUNG CHILDREN: Primary-Age Cognitive Development

Areas of Development	What to Watch for	Indicators of Atypical Development
General congnitive abilities	Shows an ability to understand the perspectives of others. Reverses operations and thinks about more than one aspect of a problem at one time. Categorizes objects using multiple attributes (e.g., size *and* shape). Distinguishes between cause and effect in solving problems. Scores near age level on traditional IQ tests.	Poor performance on tasks that require guessing what others are thinking or feeling. Inability to reverse the steps of a task. Continuing to be fooled by the appearance of things and never relying on logic. An inability to identify the causes of simple events. A score blow 70 on traditional IQ tests.
Specific intellectual skills	Skill in interpreting maps and in distinguishing the long ago from the present. An understanding of how numbers work and an ability to use them to solve real problems. An ability to distinguish natural objects from person-made objects and to place these into simple categories (e.g., plants and animals). A knowledge of what *learning* and *remembering* mean and an ability to regulate these mental processes.	General poor performance on math, science, social studies, and other tasks in school. A lack of ability in just one area of learning (i.e., math), but a high level of competence in other areas. Exceptional intellectual or artistic abilities that are uncharacteristic for one's age level.

Interpreting Assessment Data: There are cultural variations in intellectual or school-related abilities. Children in communities that do not use maps, for example, may be less able in map reading, and those in cultures that emphasize math may be advanced in this area. Children who are generally delayed across all areas of intellectual development may have mental retardation. Those who show poor performance in only one area but are competent in others may have a learning disability. These conditions can be addressed through special services delivered in the classroom. Children who show exceptional intellectual or artistic ability may be gifted/talented. The needs of such children are best met by adding new, more challenging and engaging tasks to the curriculum. Simply asking gifted/talented children to do *more* work is not effective.

movement and the performing arts on the playground or in the neighborhood could be gifted. A child who displays exceptional story- or joke-telling ability may be gifted as well. L. K. Silverman (1995) proposes that children of diverse cultural backgrounds be assessed in the community, not in school. Observations of interactions at church, in the community center, or in work around the home or apartment may be more useful in identifying gifted children from historically underrepresented groups.

RESEARCH INTO PRACTICE

CRITICAL CONCEPT 1

Children's success in school is related, in part, to general intelligence. One measure of intelligence is the intelligence quotient (IQ), which is determined by a score on a standardized test. Concerns have been raised about IQ as an adequate measure of intellectual functioning, however. Some researchers have found that IQ tests only measure one narrow type of intelligence and fail to appreciate others. Others have argued that IQ tests favor children of Euro-American backgrounds. IQ test bias has been a persistent concern in American education.

Application #1

Teachers and parents should use extreme caution in interpreting IQ scores, particularly those for children from historically under-represented groups. They should be aware that IQ tests measure only a narrow range of intellectual abilities and are subject to error. Important educational decisions about children should never be based solely on the results of a single IQ score.

Application #2

Teachers and parents should advocate for more culturally sensitive methods of assessing intellectual competence. These may include recently developed culture-free tests and non-test observational methods. Qualitative observation of children's performance across a range of developmental areas—music, movement, spatial ability, and social competence, for example—will give a broader picture of intellectual functioning.

CRITICAL CONCEPT 2

Piaget has looked at intelligence differently, describing intellectual processes rather than quantifying intelligence with numbers. He has focused as much on how children learn as on what they know. He found that unique thought processes—decentration, reversibility, and causal thinking—emerge in the primary years. These abilities allow children to acquire new knowledge in math, social studies, science, and other academic areas.

Application #1

Teachers can rely on Piaget's descriptions of primary children's thinking to understand and evaluate intellectual development. By asking children to "think out loud" or explain how they solved problems, teachers can assess children's acquisition of such mental processes as decentration, reversibility, and causal thinking.

Application #2

Teachers can apply Piaget's ideas on the acquisition of map space and time concepts in designing activities and materials in the social studies. Based on Piaget's work, they can plan map-drawing or map-interpreting experiences which lead to early understanding of geography. They can assist children in thinking about the long ago and far away by using literature, old photographs, and classroom visits by grandparents.

Application #3

Teachers can apply Piaget's ideas on the acquisition of number, seriation, and transitive reasoning to plan a developmentally appropriate mathematics curriculum. From Piaget's view, providing opportunities for children to make autonomous judgments about amounts, distances, lengths, order, and relationships among objects and events are most important in math learning in the primary grades.

Application #4

Teachers can apply Piaget's ideas on classification and the understanding of natural causes to the planning of a primary-grade science curriculum. Based on Piaget's work, teachers might provide opportunities for children to observe and determine the causes of natural phenomena and to categorize objects in a classroom museum.

Application #5

Teachers should adhere to Piaget's most basic tenet of learning in the primary years: that children construct knowledge through action upon concrete objects. Highly abstract, academic lessons are still inappropriate for children at this age.

CRITICAL CONCEPT 3

Memory improves during the primary years. One ability that enhances memory at this age is metacognition: the awareness of and ability to regulate one's own thought processes. Children begin to control their own thinking at this age; they can choose to attend to some stimuli and not others, for example, and can rehearse information and skills they wish to retain.

Application #1

Primary teachers can initiate memory games in the classroom to help children extend their short- and long-term memories. Examples include the traditional card game "Concentration" and the "Who's missing?" game, in which children try to guess which classmate has secretly left the room.

Application #2

Teachers can suggest strategies that children might use to learn and remember. Hints for remembering, such as "Pay close attention" and "Say these words over to yourself several times," can be understood and utilized by children of this age.

CRITICAL CONCEPT 4

Children of some cultural groups perform less well in school. Racial bias and "clashes" between cognitive styles are contributors. Research shows that cultural differences are minimized when the effect of socioeconomic status is controlled. Children of diverse cultural groups who have the same socioeconomic status will be more alike than different in their performance in the classroom.

Application #1

Teachers must create multifaceted learning environments that meet a wide range of needs. Active, expressive, and artistic learning activities must be planned to address the cognitive styles of children of some cultural groups. Collaborative projects that allow much social interaction and language are necessary to support the learning of field-sensitive students.

Application #2

Teachers must monitor their own classroom behaviors to be certain that they do not show bias in interactions with children. They can ask other professionals to observe their teaching and make note of all comments and questions directed toward individual students in the class. Later, they can examine this feedback to see whether they are directing more attention or praise to certain groups of students—boys or girls, or children of Euro-American backgrounds, for example.

Application #3

Teachers must be cautious not to confuse class and culture. They need to recognize potential negative effects of poverty on children's development, such as ineffective parenting, risks of violence, and poor health. They should also recognize and appreciate the positive effects of culture on development, such as rich traditions, unique learning styles, and strong family ties.

CRITICAL CONCEPT 5

A number of challenging conditions affect intellectual development and school success. Children with learning disabilities and giftedness often require unique instructional intervention.

Application #1

Teachers must recognize the characteristics of children who have intellectual challenges or special needs, including gifted children. Identifying and accessing services for children with special needs is a fundamental role of primary teachers in modern American schools.

Application #2

Primary-grade classrooms must contain activities and materials that match the variety of learning abilities and interests represented in the classroom. Each learning center, group activity, and collaborative project must include graded challenges—varied tasks or problems which reflect all levels of cognitive competence. An art center, for example, must contain complex media to inspire a gifted child to create an elaborate weeklong project; at the same time, it must include simple materials, such as markers and large paper, which a child with mental retardation can use to scribble. Group time must include both extended group story reading for children who can sit for longer periods, and active alternative experiences for those who cannot.

SUGGESTED ACTIVITIES

1. Select two primary-grade children of different ages, and ask each child to complete a categorization task designed by Piaget. Conduct the task with each child separately as follows:

    Present each child with objects or pictures to categorize. These could be "attribute blocks" (multicolored blocks of different sizes and shapes); photographs of different kinds of birds, fish, or other animals; or objects from nature. Present the objects to each child and say, "I'd like you to make separate piles. I'd like you to put the things that are alike together." Take notes on each child's performance, and then write a report based on the following questions:

    a. To what degree did the children use two or more attributes (e.g., size, color, *and* shape) to categorize objects?

    b. Which other strategies did the children use to classify?

    c. How did the two children differ in their performance on the task?

2. Present the same two children with conservation tasks of number and continuous quantity. Conduct the tasks with each child separately as follows (these procedures were described in Chapter 11):

    Conservation of number: Line up eight to ten red and black checkers in one-to-one correspondence so that it is easy to see that there are as many red as black ones. Point to each line and ask the child, "Are there more red checkers, more black checkers, or the same amount of red and black checkers?"

    After the child says aloud that the two lines have the same number of checkers, push one line of checkers into a pile, leaving the other set in a line. Ask the same question as before. Does the child state now that one set has more checkers? If so, ask the child to count both sets, then ask the question again. Challenge the child in other ways: "You said they both had the same number of checkers before, remember? And I didn't add any or take any checkers away. So, . . ." Then repeat the question.

    Conservation of continuous quantity: Fill two identical clear containers (tall, thin laboratory beakers work very well) with water so that both contain exactly the same amount. Point to each container and ask, "Does this container have more water, or does this container have more water, or do they both have the same amount of water?" If the child says one or the other has more, pour a little water out of one; the goal is to get the child to believe the two containers have the same amount.

    Once the child says that the two containers have the same amount of water, pour the water from one of the containers into another, wider container. (The new container should be wide enough that the water levels are now very different.) Now ask the child the same question as before. If the child indicates that one now contains more than the other, ask challenging questions, as in the conservation of number experiment above: "You said they had the same amount before. And I didn't add or take away any water. So, does this container really have more?"

    Write a report on your experiments, guided by the following questions:

    a. Did children perform on these tasks as Piaget would have predicted? In what ways were the two children different in their problem-solving?

    b. What evidence did you see of multidimensional thinking or decentration? Did you observe reversibility?

    c. What can you conclude about young children's thinking? To what degree are they still fooled by perception? What evidence did you see that children are using internal thinking processes?

    d. In what ways were you impressed with these children's problem-solving? In what way was their thinking limited?

3. Ask a primary-grade child to make a map of the school, the home, or neighborhood. As the child draws, ask about the locations and objects depicted on the map, the distances between places, and other map space questions. Later, write a report of your observations, guided by the following questions:

    a. How would you assess the child's performance in map-making? In what ways was the child's map different from the map an adult might draw?

    b. Was the map drawn to scale? Were landmarks depicted? Which details were included in the map? Which important landmarks were omitted?

    c. What can you conclude about the development of map space in children of this age?

4. Present a primary-grade child with 15 straws of various lengths. Tell the child, "Put the straws in order by length. I'll put the longest one here [place the longest straw down] and the shortest here [place the

shortest straw down opposite the longest]. Now you put the rest where they belong in the middle. It's like making steps." Observe the strategies children use to order the straws. Later, write a report guided by the following questions:

a. To what degree did the child use physical trial and error to solve the problem? To what degree was internal reflection used?

b. How would you assess the child's performance in this task? Did the child perform as Piaget would have predicted?

5. Select two children of the same age, gender, and cultural background and present each of them with a memory task. Conduct the task with each child separately as follows:

In front of the first child, lay down 15 small, unusual objects on a table. Have the child name each. Then cover the objects with a towel. Ask the child to name as many objects as can be remembered. Make note of how many the child could recall.

Show the second child the same 15 objects and say, "I'll cover these up in a minute. I want you to remember as many of these as you can. What would be a good way to remember them?" Make note of how many objects the child could remember.

Write a report on these experiences, guided by the following questions:

a. Which child remembered the most objects? Why do you think this was the result?

b. Which memory strategies did the second child name? Were rehearsal, labels and categories, or other techniques used?

c. What can you conclude about metacognition at this age in the primary grades?

6. Conduct the same memory task as in activity 5, only with two children of distinct cultural backgrounds. Conduct the task with each child separately. Tell each child that he or she will be expected to remember the objects. Ask each child, "What would be a good way to remember them?" Then cover the objects with a towel. Take notes on the strategies the children named and which strategies they used to remember the objects. Also note which objects they recalled and the number of objects recalled. Later, write a report on the experience, guided by the following questions:

a. Which memory strategies did the children name? Which memory strategies did they use? What did these strategies reveal about children's metacognition?

b. To what degree did the two children differ in their selection of memory strategies?

c. Did the two children remember the same objects? Did they remember the same number of objects?

d. What can you conclude about cultural differences and similarities in memory?

CHAPTER 16

Language, Literacy, and Schooling

IN THIS CHAPTER WE WILL REVIEW THE DEVELOPMENT OF LANGUAGE AND LITERACY IN PRIMARY-GRADE CHILDREN AND EXPLORE THE RELATIONSHIP BETWEEN THESE AREAS OF DEVELOPMENT AND SCHOOL LIFE. During the preschool years, children of all linguistic and cultural backgrounds learn the basic syntax, semantics, and phonology of the language spoken within their families and communities. Some refinements occur in these areas during the primary years, but the most significant language advancement during this period is in children's ability to use language in a variety of new and different ways.

Children in many cultures must learn a new style of communication: the *language of school*. They must also acquire language that helps them influence peers and make new friends. In most cultures, children learn to read and write conventionally during the primary years. Some children face challenges in learning language and literacy. A child who is delayed in communication abilities may need much adult support in learning the structure and social uses of language. A child who speaks a different language than other students in a classroom must not only learn to speak, read, and write in a new language, but also to use it effectively in peer groups and in school. The following story illustrates this point:

> A 6-year-old Korean child who does not speak English is working at the math center near an English-speaking peer. She tries to get the other child's attention to show him a puzzle she has just completed. She calls out to him in her native language. He looks up briefly with a puzzled expression, then looks down again at the game he is playing.
>
> She tries a new approach. She leans across the table and taps him roughly on the shoulder. He pulls away and calls out across the room to the teacher. "She's bothering me!" he complains. The Korean child, not understanding her peer's words, looks confused.
>
> The teacher approaches. "I think Sook wants to show you something," he says to the English-speaking child. "She's asking you in her own language. See? She's showing you her puzzle." Then, to the Korean child, he says, "If you want to get Robert's attention, you could say, 'Look, Robert!' " He points at Robert as he says this. "Look, Robert!" he repeats. The child appears to understand that this is a way of communicating with peers. "Look, Robert," she imitates. Robert smiles, then returns to his work.

The teacher in this vignette has not only assisted the non-English-speaking child in acquiring vocabulary and language structure, he has also helped her learn a new way of making contact with dominant-culture peers in her classroom. Further, the teacher has assisted a child of the dominant culture in understanding language and communicative differences. Facilitating communication in this way is an important role for teachers in modern multicultural classrooms.

FIRST- AND SECOND-LANGUAGE ACQUISITION

Primary-grade children are remarkably competent in their use of language. A brief experiment will help the reader to appreciate just how linguistically sophisticated 6- and 7-year-olds have become. The following statement was uttered by a primary-grade child. Read it aloud, paying special attention to the various articulators (i.e., tongue, teeth, lips) that are used, and to the rules and word meanings that are applied: "The stone was so huge that I couldn't lift it by myself. So Jeremy had to help, because he's older and bigger." Notice how your tongue, teeth, and lips move in rapid-fire succession from one position to another as you read the statement. You engaged your vocal chords at just the right times, as when you pronounced the *g* sound in "huge." You let air pass through your nose to create important nasal tones such as the *n* sound in "stone" and the *m* sound in "Jeremy." How is it possible that a child only 6 years old can make such precise movements?

While performing this remarkable feat of articulation, the child speaking this utterance is also thinking about word meaning. As you read the passage, did any of the words strike you as particularly complex? Why did the child use "stone" instead of "rock"? "Huge" instead of "big"? These word pairs have subtle differences in meaning. An advancement in the primary years is an ability to differentiate among words that have similar meanings. This child has come to understand that "huge" implies much greater size (and perhaps carries greater emotional impact) than "big." These distinctions require complex analysis, yet the child made these word decisions in a split second!

Note that the child is using pronouns. It would seem that one so young might not yet understand that "it" can stand for "stone" and that "he" can stand for "Jeremy." The child is also applying rules for constructing complex sentences. The agent, action, object, and other critical features of sentences must be expressed in the correct order: "The stone was so huge" rather than "Huge so the stone was." Each sentence the child speaks contains two distinct ideas which must be connected somehow. The child effectively uses conjunctions ("that" and "because") to do this. The child has to follow many rules of word order, such as placing the subject "I" before the verb "lift" and inserting the negative "n't" after the verb "could." Listing all the rules of word order that must be applied in order to speak this one utterance would be a truly mind-boggling task, yet this 6-year-old can apply every one of them correctly in a matter of seconds!

Now imagine that the child who uttered these sentences speaks a completely different native language! Perhaps, in his native tongue, verbs are placed at the ends of sentences. In his own language, he would say, "It I couldn't lift." Suppose that his family's language has no articles. He would be inclined to say, "Stone was so huge." Instead, this child sifts through the two sets of rules in his mind—those from his primary language and those of the new language he is learning—and selects and applies the rules that match the language he is speaking. Many 6-year-olds have learned two languages and can do this with ease!

Primary-grade children have become so proficient in language that only minor refinements are needed for them to possess full adult competence.

Phonology

Children have acquired most of the **phonemes**—that is, speech sounds—of their native language by age 5. They may still have difficulty, however, pronouncing some sounds through the primary years. In English, the sounds *l, r, s, sh,* and *ch* are still very difficult for many 6- and 7-year-olds. It is common for a first-grader to say, "wike" instead of "like" or "wun" in place of "run." These articulation errors usually disappear by age 8. Children whose mispronunciations persist after this period may be in need of special support in school.

Phonology and Second-Language Acquisition. The process of acquiring a second language varies according to family and school circumstances. **Simultaneous second-language learners**—that is, children who are exposed equally to both languages from birth—become quite proficient in both by the end of the preschool years (Arnberg, 1987). These **bilingual** children have learned to distinguish among and produce the unique sounds of the two languages. Even some *trilingual* preschoolers become so proficient at speech sounds that they sound like a native speaker in all three languages (L. W. Hoffman, 1985)!

Successive second-language learning occurs when a child learns a primary language first and a second language later. A common example is a child who spends the first 5 years of life in Puerto Rico and then moves to the United States during the primary years. Because successive bilingual children learn the sound system of their primary language first, they face greater phonological challenges when learning a second language in school. The new speech system may contain sounds that they cannot pronounce or even hear (Reich, 1986).

What do children learning a second language do when confronted with sounds they cannot pronounce? They substitute similar sounds that they do know. Take the example of a Spanish-speaking child learning English. She hears words which contain a hard *s* sound, such as in "rose" and "boys." No such phoneme exists in Spanish, so the child will pronounce these words using a soft *s,* as in "most" and "hoist." In Spanish, *h* is always silent, so this Spanish-speaking child would pronounce the words "horn" and "hello" as "orn" and "ello."

Children who speak non-standard English dialects often engage in the same kinds of substitutions when confronted with standard English word forms in school. In **Black English Vernacular (BEV),** the *th* sound does not exist, so African-American children often say "tink" rather than "think" (Bryen, 1986). Children from Boston and other parts of New England often substitute the *ah* sound for *r,* as in "go pahk the cah" (Berger, 1994).

Children who use a different sound system than that of the dominant culture may be teased or corrected, for the first time, in the primary years (Hemmings & Metz, 1990). Their teachers often insist on standard pronunciations in school. Their peers often mimic their unique speech patterns. It is important for professionals who work with young children to understand that differences in articulation are not deficits. They must also help other students understand this. Substitutions are, in fact, a creative way that children solve the problem of pronouncing unfamiliar speech sounds.

Atypical Phonological Development. Three kinds of phonological difficulties that occur in the primary grades require special services: articulation problems, disfluency, and poor voice quality (Rice & Schuele, 1995). These are summarized in Table 16-1.

Articulation problems relate to an inability to pronounce specific phonemes that are usually acquired by a particular age. For example, a 7-year-old who cannot

TABLE 16-1
Phonological Challenges Identified in the Primary Years

Challenge	Description
Articulation errors	The child has difficulty pronouncing specific phonemes that are usually acquired by a particular age. A 7-year-old, for example, may not clearly pronounce *b, p, m,* or *n*—sounds usually learned very early in childhood.
Disfluency	A child stutters in a manner that interferes with communication. Single phoneme misstarts (*b-b-b-b*), facial grimaces, and struggle behaviors may indicate a need for intervention.
Poor voice quality	A child regularly speaks in a highly nasal or hoarse voice.

clearly pronounce the *b, p, m,* or *n* sounds, which are usually learned very early in childhood, may be identified as having articulation difficulties.

One way to determine the severity of speech errors is to test children for **stimulability** (described in Chapter 12). This involves asking children to imitate the sounds they are not articulating clearly. If children can imitate these sounds, their problem is considered less extensive. If they cannot, intervention may be required. Whether children with phonological impairments are referred for special services will be determined, in part, by whether they are communicating well with peers and teachers in school (Rice & Schuele, 1995). Children whose speech cannot be understood are likely to be referred to a speech and language pathologist, a professional who has received extensive training in identifying and remediating communication problems and disorders. Children who have minor articulation problems but are communicating well with teachers and classmates may not be referred. Their speech may be enhanced informally by the regular teacher in the classroom.

Articulation problems occur for several reasons. They may arise from physiological causes. A child who has a cleft palate—a genetic condition in which the palate did not fully form during prenatal development—may have difficulty making certain speech sounds. A child with cerebral palsy may have trouble coordinating articulators. Chronic **otitis media**—a condition characterized by buildup of fluid behind the eardrum which results in hearing loss—may contribute to articulation problems (Locke, 1980). Sometimes the cause of phonological difficulties is unknown.

Another phonological problem which is identified in the primary years is **disfluency,** or stuttering. All young children stutter. Re-starts or whole-word repetitions are very common in childhood discourse (e.g., "The guy . . . the guy . . . the guy fell . . . down"). So common is this sort of disfluency in the preschool years that speech and language pathologists rarely attempt to treat it at this age (Rice & Schuele, 1995). When, then, should parents and teachers begin to worry about stuttering? In the primary years, children who have severe problems with disfluency will begin to stutter in different ways and with greater frequency. They will engage in more single-sound or single-syllable repetitions, such as "b-b-b-ball." Their stutters will be prolonged and there will be longer hesitations in their speech (Reich, 1986; Yairi, 1983). **Struggle behaviors,** such as facial grimaces and contortions of the mouth, may appear (Rice & Schuele, 1995). Disfluent children stutter more often—ten or more times as frequently, in fact—than typically developing children.

In the primary years, speech and language pathologists will work closely with the families of children who stutter. A common approach is to discourage family members from finishing children's sentences or asking them to start over, since this adult correction can create stress and exacerbate the problem. Informal work with the children themselves is also customary. Usually, speech and language pathologists do not try to directly reduce stuttering or draw a child's attention to the problem. Instead, they provide a comfortable, relaxed setting in which the child may talk, or encourage the teacher to do so in the classroom (Rice & Schuele, 1995).

Poor voice quality is a less common speech disorder identified and treated in the primary years. A teacher may notice that a child is chronically hoarse or has an unusually nasal tone. Such problems may be physiological. Hoarseness can stem from polyps or other growths on the larynx. A cleft palate or cerebral palsy may contribute to nasality. A prompt medical examination is recommended when these characteristics are observed.

The most common source of poor voice quality is vocal abuse. Some children talk so loudly or scream so often they create callouses, called "nodules," on their vocal tissues. If the causes of the abuse are not treated, children may require surgery to have the nodules removed. A speech and language pathologist may work with families to arrange for quieter home experiences and to discourage the child from yelling. Teachers are encouraged to remind children who habitually scream or talk too loud to lower their voices.

Semantics

Children's vocabulary continues to grow throughout childhood. However, the rate at which new words are acquired slows beginning in the primary years. This is not a period of growth, then, but of refining and coordinating word meanings (Pease, Gleason, & Pan, 1989). During this stage, children acquire fuller, more adult definitions for the words they already know. Whereas younger children might think of "big," "huge," and "gigantic" as meaning the same thing, for example, primary-grade children come to understand subtle distinctions among these words (Berger, 1994).

Primary-grade children also begin to construct relationships among the many words they have learned. They create **semantic networks:** internal maps which show connections among words within one's mental dictionary (Aitchison, 1987). For example, children begin to understand that some words are opposites, that some hold the same meaning, and that some have similar but subtly different definitions. They can understand that some words are labels that represent a whole category of other words. For example, they come to see that "mammals" is a broad term that includes "seals," "humans," "dogs," and many other living things.

Semantic networks can be demonstrated most clearly when children are given *free association* tasks. These are tasks in which children are given a word and encouraged to name as many other words as come to mind. When very young children are presented a word—say, "throw"—they usually provide a short list of other terms which follow that word in a sentence: "the ball" or "the beanbag." Around age 7, children respond with longer lists of words which show sophisticated connections in semantics. For example, a child at this age might provide synonyms such as "toss" and "pitch." They might include words for parallel but different activities, such as "catch," "bat," "hit," and "run" (Cronin, 1987; Entwhistle, 1966; K. Nelson, 1974). The increased complexity of primary-age children's free associations is illustrated in Figure 16-1.

Semantics in Bilingual Families. As we learned in Chapter 12, bilingual preschoolers construct one huge vocabulary that consists of words from both languages they are learning. Children of this age who are learning Spanish and English,

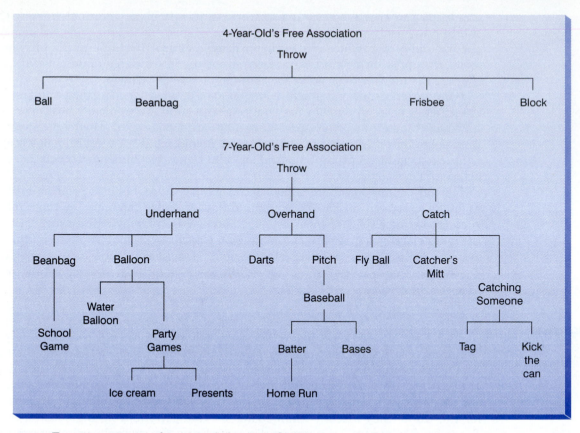

FIGURE 16-1 Two responses to a free association task. Children are asked to name all the words they can think of that go with "throw." The 4-year-old limits responses to things that can be thrown, while the 7-year-old presents a full "semantic network": a complex cluster of many different kinds of related words.

for example, will at first create a mental dictionary of all words learned. They might become confused about which words to use when speaking a particular language. A sign of this confusion is their frequent use of mixed-language utterances, such as "el kitty blanco."

Bilingual primary children begin to differentiate between words from the two languages in their mental dictionary. One factor that influences this process is school, since in some cases the language spoken at school is different from that spoken in the home. In the United States, for example, children who speak both Spanish and English often hear only English spoken in first grade. **Language shock** results when children suddenly discover that their native language is not understood by others. The experience leads some children to more quickly differentiate between the languages they are learning (Arnberg, 1987). "These are the words my peers can understand at school," they learn, "and these are the words they cannot."

Children's experiences with language in the home can also assist them in separating their vocabularies. When one parent speaks one language and the other parent (or perhaps a grandparent) speaks a second language, a child can more readily distinguish the two (Arnberg, 1987; Ramjoue, 1980). In such an environment, the child learns, "these are the words Mom uses and these are different kinds of words Dad uses."

Over the course of the primary years, many children successfully separate their languages. Exactly when this occurs varies as a function of the timing and order of language learning. Are two languages learned simultaneously, or successively? Do both parents speak the native language, or does one speak one language, one the other? The countless variations in home language environment explain the diversity of second-language learners in school.

Each culture has its own vocabulary. Words describing objects, persons, or events which are of critical importance in one culture may not even exist in another. For example, one of my colleagues, who is from Nepal, reports that there are numerous words in English that have no meaning in Nepali. Expressions like "please" and "thank you" have no exact equivalent; in Nepal such sentiments are communicated with facial expressions and gestures. On the other hand, Nepali words such as "ainsselu," "chutro," and "kphal"—names of common berries in Nepal—have no English translation. Some African-American children often use a "street vocabulary" that reflects the artistic and playful features of their culture (Abrahams, 1976). Common terms such as "jiving," or "dissing" often hold little meaning for peers or teachers of another cultural group. Mismatches in semantics create special challenges for children learning a new language.

Atypical Semantic Development. Some children acquire words more slowly. Often delays in semantic development are associated with more general language problems or other challenging conditions (Rice & Schuele, 1995). Children with mental retardation or learning disabilities, for example, may have limited vocabularies or poor word-retrieval skills.

Children with semantic delays may be unable to identify opposites or synonyms or to generate lists of related terms in a free association task. They may even struggle to correctly name pictures or objects. Sometimes children compensate for difficulty in retrieving words by using "thing" to stand for objects they cannot name. A child with delayed semantics who could not retrieve the word "zipper" compensated by saying, "You know . . . that thing you pull up . . . that goes up on the coat."

Some children may have trouble learning **morphemes**—small units of language that hold meaning. For some, endings are challenging. For example, children might say, "Yesterday, my mom play with me" or "There are three ball." Some children become confused over pronouns, and might say, "Me going too" or "Him is my friend."

Speech and language pathologists will often work with children on developing a larger vocabulary or understanding word meanings more fully. A growing number of professionals intervene with children within the classroom setting, designing vocabulary enhancement strategies that relate to the school curriculum. The focus of such an intervention may be, for example, learning new words introduced in a science lesson or a story (Rice & Schuele, 1995).

Syntax

Children are able to construct very complex sentences by only 6 or 7 years of age. They can speak long declaratives or questions that contain negatives and clauses. However, a few syntactic structures are still challenging to them. Passives (e.g., "The cup was dropped by the girl") are acquired only gradually during childhood. Several studies have shown that English-speaking children misinterpret these when they hear them (Bever, 1970; Sudhalter & Braine, 1985). In this research, primary children were asked to match passive sentences to corresponding pictures. For example, they were presented with the sentence, "The farmer was bitten by the cow," then shown two pictures—one of a cow biting a farmer and another of a farmer biting a cow. When asked to point to the picture that corresponded to the sentence, subjects invariably pointed to the drawing of the farmer biting the cow. Why? Children in the primary years are accustomed to straightforward declarative sentences, such as "I hit the ball." In these sentences, the agent performing the action ("I") comes first, then the action ("hit"), and finally the object ("ball"). In passive sentences the object comes first: "The ball was hit by me." Children misinterpret the object to be the agent; that is, in their minds the sentence becomes "The ball hit me."

Syntax and Bilingual Development. When children learn two different languages, they must learn two sets of syntactic rules. At first they may learn only the syntactic rules of their native language. For a time, they may apply these when speaking in the new language as well. For example, a Spanish-speaking child will learn to form some questions in her native language by placing the verb before the subject. So, when speaking English she applies this same rule. She may say, "Saw you the boy?" A child who speaks BEV may use his home and community syntax when speaking standard English in school (Labov, 1971). For example, in standard English, the word "do" is inserted to form certain kinds of questions (e.g., "*Do* you swim?"). This rule does not exist in BEV. So, a BEV-speaking child might initially say, "You swim?"

Some teachers believe that these logical, rule-governed sentences are language "errors" to be corrected, while others view this early syntax as immature or deficient. These beliefs lead to the misunderstanding and sometimes mistreatment of second-language learners in school. Where do such negative attitudes come from? It has been proposed that a hierarchy of languages exists in any culture (Dale, 1976; J. Edwards, 1981). Some languages are viewed more favorably by dominant society, others less so. In America, standard English is highest on this hierarchy, British-English and French-English dialects are next, and BEV, Spanish-English, and Appalachian dialect are lowest. These latter languages are often viewed as unsophisticated, primitive, or "lower class." Such language preferences are easy to observe in schools. Children who are natives of France or Sweden, for example, are not likely to be harshly corrected by teachers for not speaking standard English. In fact, their dialects might even be considered quaint, charming, or cosmopolitan. However, teachers show great concern about BEV or Spanish-English syntax.

Children acquire the syntax of a second language in unique stages, during the primary years (Hakuta, 1986; Wong Fillmore, 1976). For example, Spanish-speakers who are learning English have been found to acquire negatives in the following way (Hakuta, 1986):

Stage 1:   "The man no like cheese"
Stage 2:   "The man not like cheese"
Stage 3:   "The man don't like cheese"
Stage 4:   "The man doesn't like cheese"

This progression shows why correcting the syntax of children who are learning a second language is ill-advised. A child may have just advanced from "no like cheese" to "not like cheese," so a teacher who responds, "No, it's *doesn't*. Can you say that?" fails to acknowledge the child's significant language achievement. Furthermore, the teacher may be suggesting that this new structure is wrong or bad.

Atypical Syntactic Development. Children with special needs are sometimes delayed in syntactic development. Those with mental retardation, learning disabilities, or general language delay may not be able to understand or speak sentences that are typically learned during the preschool years. For example, typically developing primary children can speak and understand embedded clauses. They can interpret and even speak sentences such as "The man who talked to the teacher was angry." Children with language delays may interpret this sentence to mean that *both* the man and the teacher are angry (Rice & Schuele, 1995).

Children with such severe syntactic delays are referred to speech and language pathologists. Again, a recent trend is toward providing services within the regular classroom. A speech and language pathologist may guide a child in using or interpreting complex sentences during group time or in naturalistic interactions with peers.

Metalinguistic Awareness

One advancement in the primary years that greatly enhances language learning is the emergence of **metalinguistic awareness.** This is the ability to think about language itself. Before 6 years of age, children simply speak. Although they may apply the rules of language, structure sentences correctly, and select the right words to convey meaning, they do so subconsciously.

As children enter the primary years, they become more aware of language itself. They can think about and comment on sentence structure, how speech sounds are formed, and the various definitions of words. By age 7, for example, children are able to identify sentences that are grammatically correct or incorrect (Bialystok, 1986). They can critique poorly formed sentences: "No, silly! It should be 'throw the ball,' not 'ball the throw'!"

Primary-grade children are able to define words, not simply use them in sentences (Wehren, DeLisi, & Arnold, 1981). A 6-year-old illustrates this ability when he explains how hot a summer day is: "It's not just 'hot,' because 'hot' doesn't mean hot enough. It's a 'roasting' day. That's better. 'Roasting' means like the stove. It's that hot! A roasting day!"

Primary-grade children can define words by relating them to other words they know. For example, an 8-year-old defined the word "huge" as "very, very big, not just 'big.' It's the opposite of 'teeny tiny.'" These abilities show that children can contemplate word meanings. Children's understanding of word meanings can also be observed in their humor. Consider the classic (if not particularly funny) joke:

What did the big chimney say to the little chimney?
What?
"You're too young to smoke."

Preschoolers might have trouble understanding the joke, but primary-grade children think it is uproariously funny because they now understand that a word can mean two different things. So, they catch the pun.

Children are also more aware of speech sounds in the primary years. One problem they begin to overcome is *missegmentation:* an inability to know where the sounds and words of an utterance are divided. As a child, I used to puzzle over what "donzerly" lights were in the National Anthem. Reich (1986) tells the story of a child who mis-heard a line from a hymn, "Gladly the cross I'd bear," to be "Gladly, the cross-eyed bear." In these examples, children have missegmented utterances. They cannot, as yet, think through the logical sound breaks in sentences. In the primary years, children can contemplate sounds and breaks in language. They can better think through and correct missegmentation errors:

> (A child speaking to her father) Oh! Remember when I was a baby? You said "upyougo," That meant "up," and "you," and "go." Like that. Like "up you go." So, up I'd go (laughs). I get it now.

Awareness of phonology can also be observed in children's humor. Schickedanz, Schickedanz, and Forsyth (1982) provide the following example of a childhood joke. What does it reveal about children's understanding of phonology at this age?

> Knock, knock.
> Who's there?
> Duane.
> Duane who?
> Duane the tub, I'm dwowning!

This joke shows not only that children are aware of the sounds in their language, but also that they have knowledge of typical articulation errors in childhood, such as substituting *w* for *r*.

Metalinguistic awareness is extremely important in second-language acquisition, because when children can reflect on language forms and rules they are better at differentiating between the two languages they are learning (Diaz & Klinger, 1991). Several studies have shown that the process of learning a second language can, in turn, enhance metalinguistic awareness (Cummins, 1987). The struggle to sort out differences between languages may cause bilingual children to think more deeply about language forms and functions.

Pragmatics

Simply speaking the correct language forms is not enough to ensure communication. Children must use words, sounds, and sentences effectively to express ideas and get what they need. They must learn to persuade or argue with peers during a game, converse with adults at a family gathering, explain to a parent that a cherished possession was accidentally broken, or entertain siblings with a scary story. Each of these events requires a very different kind of communication. An argument with a peer may include long, flowing, expressive sentences, while an explanation to an angry parent will call for shorter, concise ones. Each situation is guided by different social rules. A discussion with a parent about a misdeed may require rigid adherence to the turntaking and politeness rules, since it is usually best not to interrupt or be rude when a parent is angry. A holiday gathering may follow different rules. In many families, the turntaking rule all but disappears, as family members talk and joke all at the same time.

During the primary years, children acquire basic social rules of language. They have learned that they must be polite when speaking with adults (Becker, 1986). They say "thank you," make requests instead of demands, and use a pleasant tone when interacting with those in authority. They are able to take turns when speaking to others (Garvey, 1977). The egocentric monologues of the preschool years begin to disappear as children discover the two-way nature of conversations. Primary-grade children are quite competent at **referential communication:** the ability to adjust language to the viewpoint of the listener. They are less likely to nod or make gestures during a phone conversation (Warren-Leubecker & Tate, 1986). They use simpler language when talking to those who are younger (Dunn & Kendrick, 1982), and reduce the complexity of their sentences when they realize that listeners cannot understand them (Warren-Leubecker & Bohannon, 1989).

Social rules of language vary, however, from one culture to another. In some communities collective conversations are the norm. All participants speak spontaneously and simultaneously; turntaking is not considered an important rule (Farber, Mindel, & Lazerwitz, 1988; Slonim, 1991). The rules for politeness vary across cultures. Japanese and Japanese-American children are expected to be exceedingly polite in their conversations with anyone—both adults and peers (Yamamoto & Kubota, 1983). In many Native American and Alaskan Native families, politeness in language is related to the historically defined status of both the speaker and the listener. A very formal, polite style is required when children are speaking to high-status male elders, for example (Blanchard, 1983). In Kenya, polite, respectful interactions toward older siblings are required; older brothers and sisters, in turn, can scold and dominate younger family members. Middle-class American families do not expect children to speak to older siblings in these respectful ways. Bickering and equal-status interchanges are tolerated (B. B. Whiting & Edwards, 1988).

Pragmatics in School. An understanding of the social rules of language is especially important when children enter school. The social rules that govern conversations in the classroom are more numerous and more rigidly enforced than in the home. A number of common school language rules are presented in Table 16-2.

One rule that is common in schools in most cultures is that formal language should be used: children may not use slang in the classroom, and standard language forms are required in all interactions, especially with teachers (DeStefano, 1972). Typical conversation used with peers in the neighborhood will not do, and children who do not speak formally may be corrected by the teacher and even other children.

TABLE 16-2
Rules of Language Use Common in American Schools

Rule	Description
Formal language	Children are expected to speak standard English without slang or informal, artful expression.
Turntaking	Children are required to take turns talking. Handraising and answering questions only when asked are often expected.
Informing/explaining	Children are expected to provide clear, concise information without egocentric "meandering." A succinct, correct answer to questions is often expected.
Requests for information	Children are required to ask clear questions for information. Asking for clarification about assignments or for further explanation of a complex science concept are examples.
Sticking to the main topic	Children are often required to stick to a single topic when talking. Narratives must have a beginning, a middle, and an end.

Formal and informal language styles are referred to as **registers.** In the primary years, children must learn **register switching**—that is, shifting back and forth between these two very different kinds of language. A child must quickly switch from slang or artful expression with peers on the school bus to correct standard forms in answer to a teacher's question during a math lesson. Switching registers is particularly challenging for children who speak different languages and for children who come from historically under-represented groups.

A part of the formal language rule is turntaking and structured conversation. Lessons in school generally are quite orderly: the teacher speaks, the students listen, and a brief time is devoted to questions and answers at the end (Dickinson, 1985). Children must learn when they may speak and the appropriate ways to seek a turn, such as raising one's hand and waiting to be called on. Learning this rule is particularly challenging for children of cultures in which collective conversations are the norm (Schultz, Florio, & Erickson, 1982).

Rules of language in school are shaped by the values, customs, and the status and role assignments of teachers within a particular culture. Not all schools in the world require formal language. B. B. Whiting and Edwards (1988) observed less formal classrooms in Mexico and Okinawa. Their description of a teacher reading a poem in Juxtlahuaca, Mexico, shows that a turntaking rule is not rigidly enforced:

> Before the teacher finishes, Alberto stands up on his bench, waves his hands, and shouts, "Me, teacher, me." The child who is next to him stands up and cries, "Me, teacher, me." Alberto, the other boy, and several others get up and run toward the teacher, surrounding him . . . so that he might give them a part of the poem. (p. 247)

Besides adopting an overall formal style of language in school, children must learn to use language to accomplish new purposes. A child is often expected to *explain* or *inform* with a great deal more clarity than was previously required. Giving a book report or an answer to a question in a science activity must be delivered in an organized, concise way. Egocentric meanderings, common in the preschool years, are now apt to result in correction: "Sandra, please tell us exactly what the book was about."

A particularly challenging form of explaining and informing is responding to right-answer questions (W. S. Hall, Bartlett, & Hughes, 1988). Parents and child care providers often ask preschoolers open-ended questions such as "What did you do in child care today?" or "What are you playing?" In school, teachers often ask children questions that have only one expected, correct answer (e.g., "What are the three ways that seeds travel from one place to another?"). These questions are not departure points for flowing discussion or open-ended conjecture. To be successful in school, the child must answer these directly, concisely, and accurately.

In addition to giving information and answering questions, children must ask questions themselves. However, question-asking has a new purpose in the classroom. No longer do children make inquiries simply to have a curiosity satisfied or a need met; they now ask questions that are vital to school success, such as "Which page do we do for homework?" or "What is the fourth food group again? I forgot." Asking questions is more challenging than it appears, since the child must understand the social rules for making inquiries in school: Be concise. Raise your hand. Ask at the right times. Don't interrupt the teacher. Further, the child must learn to phrase the question so that the teacher will know exactly what information is requested.

Pragmatics, School, and Culture. Children from historically under-represented groups may have more difficulty acquiring the pragmatics required for success in American schools. Conversations in typical classrooms in the United States reflect the communication styles of dominant culture (Dickinson, 1985; Heath, 1988), so children who have learned very different rules of language use may be at a disadvantage. An example of this is the struggle with pragmatics that African-American children often face in school. Hale-Benson (1986) contrasts typical school talk with the unique discourse styles of this cultural group. African-American children often display an open-ended, artful, expressive style. They joke, tell stories, and even tease and argue in playful ways as they converse. Euro-American teachers sometimes view these modes of communication as inappropriate and even threatening. Playful teasing and arguments, for example, are considered disrespectful and immature.

One characteristic of typical African-American discourse is a freedom to verbalize spontaneously. Lein (1975) illustrates this style by describing traditional African-American church services. Throughout a typical service, there is much collective verbalization. Testimonials, singing, and welcoming new members are common. Those who "have the spirit" may shout out or move around. Such interactions are in sharp contrast, Lein notes, to classroom interactions, in which exceedingly long periods of silence are expected and only occasional constrained conversations are allowed. It is easy to see why children from families with such a spontaneous style of interaction would have great difficulty following the turntaking rule in school (Schultz et al., 1982).

Hale-Benson cites research suggesting that African-American children's communication has a *topic-chaining* structure (Michaels, 1980). Conversations flow freely from one subject to another. A single narrative might traverse many different topics

Children of some cultures use a "topic-chaining" structure in conversation. Euro-American teachers do not always understand or appreciate this artful language style.

that are loosely tied together. Conversations in Euro-American communities, in contrast, are more often *topic-centered*. A narrative is likely to have a single theme and a clearly identified beginning, middle, and end. Both conversational styles are expressive; neither is deficient.

Nevertheless, Euro-American teachers often view a topic-chaining structure as a sign of disorganized thinking or poor communication skill. African-American children's free-flowing style clashes with the structured, focused discussions in school. Some teachers vigorously train such children to be more concise and organized in their language and to stick to one topic. Hale-Benson (1986) tells of one teacher who tried to correct African-American discourse style by implementing a new rule that children speak about only one thing during "show and tell." Needless to say, African-American children had great difficulty adhering to the rule.

Perhaps the most challenging school communication rule for children of historically under-represented groups is the formal language requirement. In the classroom, many of these children must switch registers from the more casual, expressive style they use with peers and their family to a language that is concise and conventional. Children who speak a different language or dialect are at a particular disadvantage. To such children, register switching is virtually learning a new language (Heath, 1988)!

For example, a Spanish-speaking child who is just learning English may say, "He don't have a pencil." As described earlier, this is a step forward in language learning; at an earlier time, she may have said, "He no have a pencil." However, a teacher might misinterpret this utterance as informal speech or slang and, thus, a violation of the formal language rule. The teacher might respond, "No. We say it correctly in school. We say, 'He *doesn't* have a pencil.'" Likewise, when an African-American child uses the rule-governed sentence, "He be goin' to the store," the teacher might chastise him for being casual or lazy in his speech.

Most educators have come to believe that helping children learn to switch registers is important for later school success. However, for many children the process takes time, patience, and empathy. Children who come from homes in which only the native language or dialect is spoken will have the greatest difficulty learning the standard English register (Heath, 1988).

Bilingual Education

The term "bilingual education" refers to a variety of strategies in school for assisting children who speak languages different from that of the dominant culture. Bilingual education is used most often in North America to promote the learning of non-English-speaking children. However, concepts and principles of bilingual education have also been used to teach children speaking non-standard English dialects, such as BEV (Roy, 1987).

Several models of bilingual education exist. One, called **immersion,** involves placing children who speak one language into a classroom in which a new, second language is spoken primarily. The expectation is that children will be motivated to learn the second language quickly so that they will be able to communicate with peers and teachers and succeed in school. Unfortunately, some immersion classrooms in the United States have been cynically dubbed "submersion" classrooms because children must "sink or swim" in language learning without special support (Snow, 1987). "Immersion" may be professional jargon to mean that no meaningful assistance is given to non-English-speaking children in school. Most non-English-speaking children in America are simply placed in regular classrooms, where they fail to learn a second language well, do poorly in academic subjects, and drop out of school more often than their English-speaking peers (O'Malley, 1985).

Other bilingual models are designed to enhance children's learning in their native language and at the same time help them acquire the language of dominant culture. In the **maintenance/developmental model,** children are taught primarily in their native language (Ovando & Collier, 1985), so they acquire the same important school-related skills and concepts as dominant-language children. At the same time, they are introduced to English as a Second Language (ESL). In one version of the model, children are enrolled in native-language classrooms throughout the primary years and are given special tutoring from ESL teachers.

The **two-way bilingual education model** is preferred by many educators, not only because it promotes second-language learning, but because it promotes appreciation for all languages (Padilla et al., 1991). In this approach, both the dominant language and the second language are used equally in the instruction of all children. In one two-way bilingual primary program in New England, Latino children and English-speaking Euro-American children learn both Spanish and English together. Spanish is spoken during mathematics, science, and social studies instruction, and English is spoken during reading and writing. In another program, English is exclusively used on one day and Spanish on the next. Two-way bilingual programs have shown promise both in facilitating second-language acquisition among all children and in enhancing appreciation for different languages (Collier, 1989; Padilla et al., 1991).

D. L. Soto (1991) suggests that what is most important in bilingual education is the overall attitude toward languages that is conveyed in the classroom. She notes that some teachers assume a *subtractive* approach to language teaching, in which the goal is to replace a child's native language or dialect with that of dominant culture. Research on Southeast Asian immigrant children in America shows the devastating effect of a subtractive model. Although many children were found to learn English quite well, they lost their ability to effectively communicate with their parents and family members (Wong Fillmore, 1991).

An *additive* approach is more culturally sensitive, Soto argues. In this approach, children add a new language but maintain and refine their native speaking abilities as well. The goal is to expand the child's linguistic repertoire.

Social Strategies in Bilingual Education. Regardless of the type of bilingual education provided, children who do not speak the dominant language of a community will experience a challenging period of transition when they enter school. They often engage in creative social strategies in an attempt to cope with the strangeness of the new classroom environment and to fit in with the dominant-culture peer group (Wong Fillmore, 1976). For example, they may pretend to understand what is being said around them even when they do not. They may smile and nod, join in a group play activity, imitate peers, and utter a few simple words in an effort to make others think they can speak the dominant language.

Sometimes children stay close to dominant-culture friends and emulate their speech or behavior. They may assume that what is being said is related to the immediate situation and make guesses about the meanings of words spoken around them. The following story illustrates these coping strategies:

Thi Liên is a 7-year-old Vietnamese student who speaks very little English. She has enrolled in a classroom in which English is the dominant language. She has made a good friend, Jessica. Although the two cannot understand each other's language, they play well together and have become inseparable. As they walk hand-in-hand along the playground, Cedric approaches them:

THI LIÊN: (Smiles and nods. Says nothing.)

JESSICA: (Speaking to Cedric) Know what? My tooth fell out last night.

CEDRIC: (Begins walking around a tire on the playground as she talks) So? Mine fall out all the time.

JESSICA: (Joins Cedric in walking around the tire. Laughs.) All the time?

THI LIÊN: (Walks on the tire, feigns a laugh) All the time! All the time . . .

JESSICA: (Picks up Thi Liên's chant) All the time . . .

CEDRIC: (Joins in the game, walking around the tire and chanting) All the time . . .

The children continue with the game for many minutes. Thi Liên later reports to her mother that she believes "all the time" is a game you play on the tires.

Thi Liên demonstrates a creative strategy for fitting in. She effectively seeks a common language in play, even when she cannot understand the words of her peers. Through smiling, laughter, and playfulness she has, in all likelihood, convinced her peers that she understands English.

Stages of Production in Bilingual Education. Not all bilingual children are as confident as Thi Liên in speaking. Those who have just entered a bilingual setting are often very quiet and reticent to speak. Over time, as children become familiar with teachers and peers, they advance through stages of vocalization or *production* of the second language (H. Hernandez, 1997; Terrel, 1981). In the *preproduction stage* children in bilingual classrooms are quite silent; they focus on understanding the second language rather than trying to speak it. This is an important period. As they listen, children learn the second language and gradually gain confidence in their ability to speak it. At this early stage, teachers should refrain from asking children to talk, since children's efforts to imitate words or phrases may actually inhibit language acquisition.

In the *transition to production stage,* children demonstrate a readiness to make brief verbalizations in the second language. Next, in the *early production stage* these utterances become longer. Only when they reach the *expansion of production stage* are children able to speak in full sentences or respond in the second language to open-ended questions from teachers or peers. Even at this stage, teachers should not expect perfectly fluent verbal responses. The semantic, syntactical, and phonological features of the child's native language may affect second-language speech even into adulthood. In the final stage, *introduction to written forms,* children show an interest in reading and writing in the second language. Until this point, children are usually encouraged to read and write in their native language. Literacy usually emerges first in the language of a child's own culture (Chamot & O'Malley, 1994; Saunders, 1988).

LITERACY

Children's literacy development resembles the process of oral language learning (N. Hall, 1987). Children actively construct an understanding of print as they strive for authentic communication. Their motivation for reading and writing stems from a desire to acquire meaning from others' writing and to communicate through their own writing. Children of every culture will learn to read and write if they are encouraged by families and teachers and provided with a meaningful, print-rich environment (F. Smith, 1988).

Writing in the Primary Years

Many children have begun to write by the end of the preschool years. Their writing, which may be comprised of scribbles or isolated letters, looks very different from adult text. Vertical lines across paper might represent a whole story, and letters of a child's name might stand for a letter to his or her family. Over time, children's writing looks more and more like adult manuscript or cursive. Chaotic scribbles give way to scribble-writing which runs from the top to the bottom of the page and from left to right, and eventually some letters are incorporated (Sulzby, 1985).

Not all children develop through these scribble stages at an early age. Those who have few opportunities to write or have not observed others writing may continue to scribble-write during the primary years (Ferreiro & Teberosky, 1982). Most children of school age, however, have begun to use conventional letters in their writing. They are then likely to progress through three distinct writing stages before they write conventionally (Clay, 1975; Temple, Nathan, Burris, & Temple, 1988). These stages are summarized in Table 16-3.

Prephonemic Stage. Primary-age children who still write using random letters to stand for stories are said to be in the *prephonemic stage* of writing. An example of a prephonemic composition is presented in Figure 16-2. The child who wrote the story read and reread the text many times over a 4-month period: "Once there were some naughty girls who stole cookies from their friends." The story remained roughly the same on each rereading, suggesting that the letters now represent a permanent idea in the child's mind. However, as can be seen in the figure, the letters have no relationship to the sounds of phonemes in the story. Letters are merely used as "placeholders for meaning" (Temple et al., 1988).

TABLE 16-3

Stages of Writing Development in the Primary Years

Stage	Description
Prephonemic stage	Random letters are used to represent whole words or stories. The letters chosen have no relationship to the sounds in the story, but are "placeholders for meaning."
Phonemic stage	Letters are used that match some of the sounds in the words or stories being written. A letter matching the beginning sound of a word might be used to represent that whole word (e.g., *p* for "people").
Transitional stage	The child spells out words using correct letter sounds. However, writing contains much "invented spelling" in which conventions are not followed. For example, the silent *e* is often omitted, as in "mak" for "make."
Conventional writing	Some children begin writing as adults do during the primary years, using correct spellings and other writing conventions.

FIGURE 16-2
Example of a child's prephonemic writing. The child uses conventional letters selected at random to represent ideas.

Phonemic Stage. Primary-grade children gradually begin using consonants that match some of the sounds in the story they are writing; for example, "Bb" might be used to represent "baby." Often only one or two consonants are used to stand for a complete word. When children do this, they are said to have entered the *phonemic stage*. An example of a phonemic composition is presented in Figure 16-3. The text reads, "Dorothy and the Wizard of Oz." For the first time, the child is showing an understanding that letters represent specific phonemes.

Transitional Stage. During the primary years, children enter a *transitional stage* in which their writing becomes very conventional. During this period, they spell out words using letter sounds and write in full sentences, but they often misspell words, particularly those with unconventional spellings. For example, the word "make" might be spelled "mak," since the final *e* is silent and seems unnecessary to convey meaning. Because of the creative aspect of constructing words, the phrase "invented spelling" has been used to describe this characteristic of children's writing.

One interesting advancement that occurs during the transitional stage is that children discover that breaks between words must somehow be marked. Children use ingenious methods for doing this. One child began using a heavy dot between words (Sulzby, 1981), while another turned the last letter of each word backwards (Pflaum, 1986). A sample of writing in the transitional stage is presented in Figure 16-4.

Many children begin conventional writing by the end of the primary years. Their writing still contains errors in spelling at this age. Children who have been encouraged to write without anxiety over correct form or spelling often become immensely talented authors in middle childhood (Calkins, 1986).

Reading Development

Reading development and writing development are highly interrelated. As children write they learn to read, and vice versa. Among the earliest reading materials are children's own written stories (Chomsky, 1966). Children of many cultures also read picture books. As they are read to or look at books, children construct understand-

ings of print. Sulzby (1985) has described stages of storybook reading through which most primary-grade children develop. These are summarized in Table 16-4.

Picture-Governed Reading. Children begin reading books by studying the pictures and disregarding print. They point to or name persons or objects that are depicted. They do not, in this early period, tell a coherent story from the book. Their "reading" behaviors are disjointed comments about illustrations. Sulzby (1985) called this the *story not formed stage.*

Somewhat later, children who are read to or have much experience with books will tell a full story as they look at the pictures and turn the pages. Their intonation is that of a storyteller. Their stories approximate events in the actual story. Sulzby named this the *story formed stage.* In the *written language–like stage,* children begin to "read" the story by heart; their retellings match the actual text. Their intonation is so similar to that of an adult reader that parents or teachers may believe they are actually reading (Schickedanz, 1999).

During this period, children may begin to notice and comment on print. They may map the story over a portion of print. A child studying the title of the book *The Very Hungry Caterpillar* (Carle, 1969) was observed pointing to each word and trying to read the title. She would begin by saying "The" and pointing to the word "The." (So far, so good!) She would next say the syllable "Ver" and point to "Very" and would say "ry" and point to "Hungry." When she pronounced the syllable "Hun"

FIGURE 16-4 A child has written an angry note to his mother because she would not allow him to go to the mall. His writing is beginning to look conventional. Invented spelling is evident.

and pointed to the word "Caterpillar" she was out of words and quite confused (Schickedanz, 1982). Such puzzlements stimulate children's interest in how print works and move them toward a major advancement in reading development, *print-governed reading.*

Print-Governed Reading. Once children are aware of and curious about print, their reading responses change significantly. Their reading behaviors now center on the text. In the *print watched/refusal to read and aspectual stage,* children show early conventional reading competence. "Refusal to read" refers to the child's ini-

TABLE 16-4
Stages of
Storybook Reading

Stage	Description
Picture-Governed Reading	
Story not formed stage	Children point to and make comments about illustrations. No coherent story is told.
Story formed stage	Children tell a story as they point to illustrations and turn pages. The story often resembles the actual story line of the book.
Written language–like stage	Children "read" a storybook by heart. Their retellings match the actual text. Their reading intonations often resemble those of adult readers.
Print-Governed Reading	
Print watched/refusal to read and aspectual stage	Children begin to point to and study the print as adults read. They are often reluctant to read themselves, preferring to observe the reading process. If they do read independently, they rely on just one aspect of reading, such as phonics or sight vocabulary, to construct meaning from print.
Print watched/holistic stage	Children study print and begin to apply multiple reading strategies in order to construct story meaning. They may use phonics, sight vocabulary, and sentence context. Sometimes these strategies are out of balance, in that the child relies more heavily on one strategy than another.
Independent reading stage	Children are able to read storybooks independently using a variety of reading strategies, including phonics, sentence context, and sight vocabulary. They are able to coordinate these strategies and select those that are appropriate for a particular text.

SOURCE: Sulzby, 1985.

tial reluctance to use words in reading stories. A child might say, "I don't know the words, but I do know the pictures." This period of doubt gives way to aspectual reading, in which the child selects just one aspect of the reading act—perhaps the memory of certain words or phonics—and uses this strategy exclusively in reading the text.

This is the period when some primary-grade children laboriously "sound out" letters without attending to whole words or sentences. Others rely only on whole-word vocabulary and never pay attention to phonics. The following is an example of aspectual reading:

A 6-year-old child with a preference for phonics reading moves along a shelf at a grocery store, sounding out labels of products. He comes to a box of baking soda. He struggles to sound out the letters of the words on the label: "B-A-K-I-N-G." His phonetic reading does not make sense; he has never heard of such a word.

"I give up on that one," he announces to his mother. Then, as an afterthought, he holds the box toward her and asks, "Do you need any baking soda?"

The child in the story is so committed to phonics in reading that he is unable to take advantage of clues from the environment to help decipher a product label. The tendency to center on just one reading strategy is common in early reading development. The particular strategy that a child selects to read may be related to previous experience with print and the method of early reading instruction in school (Hansen & Bowey, 1994). Children taught phonics, for example, may be heavily reliant on phonics in reading.

Sulzby (1986) observed that children eventually enter a *print watched/holistic stage,* in which they use multiple reading strategies—sight vocabulary, sentence context, and phonics—to acquire meaning from print. Early in this stage children are somewhat imbalanced in their use of strategies, however. For example, they may still rely mostly on phonics, but fall back on context clues or sight vocabulary if this initial strategy does not work. Near the end of the primary years, most children have become *independent* readers and are able to apply on their own the particular reading strategies that are most helpful for a certain text. A child who cannot sound out a word will quickly reread the whole sentence in order to acquire context clues, for example. Not all children reach this final stage. Intellectual, emotional, family, and school factors will determine adult reading competence.

Literacy and Culture

Children of different cultures show distinct aptitudes for and dispositions toward literacy. In a small number of cultures in the world, reading and writing do not exist. Some Aboriginal groups in Australia, for example, have never used a written language (Reynolds, 1995). Literacy is important in most societies, although what is written and read, and how literacy is taught, varies significantly.

A growing body of research on the home literacy environments of African-American children illustrates these ideas. Children of low-income African-American families have been found to read books less often than children of other groups (Heath, 1983, 1988). Families of this cultural and class background do read, but primarily as a source of information. Parents and grandparents read mail, newspapers, magazines, funeral announcements, catalogs, and telephone books. They less often read for recreation.

Storytelling, joking, and music are more highly valued by many African-American families. Some parents tell stories to their children more often than they read to them (Hale-Benson, 1986). Neighbors may gather on front porches to share events in the community, relate family experiences, or discuss disputes with their landlord (Heath, 1988). In this cultural group, artful expression replaces written fiction as an outlet for imagination.

Does this mean that these children are deprived of literacy experiences in the home? One study shows that this is not the case (Pellegrini, Perlmutter, Galda, & Brody, 1990). In this research, African-American parents living in poverty were found to help their children learn to read and write, but in different ways than middle-class Euro-American parents do. In the study, mothers were observed reading to their children in the home. When reading narrative books—typical picture books with story lines—they were found to engage in fewer strategies for teaching literacy. Rarely did they ask questions, label illustrations, or summarize plot lines, as middle-class Euro-American mothers typically do. Taken alone, this finding would suggest that children of these families are not well supported in their literacy development.

However, when these mothers read expository books—books containing illustrations and written labels without a plot line—they were as active as middle-class mothers in teaching literacy to their children. The following example, drawn from this research (Pellegrini et al. 1990), illustrates some teaching strategies these mothers used:

MOTHER: (Pointing to text) Chimpanzee.

CHILD: Ooo yeah. Can I see?

MOTHER: What's this? (Points to an illustration of a kitchen sink)

CHILD: Sink. Do that one now.

MOTHER: That's yellow. (Points to boots)

CHILD: My pants are yellow.

Why does reading material make a difference in parent-child literacy interactions? One explanation may be that expository books more closely resemble the kinds of factual reading material—catalogs or church bulletins—that are frequently read within this cultural group. Also, parents may feel more comfortable with expository text, believing this is the kind of reading that is most important within their own culture. The reading of expository books, which involves naming and discussing illustrations, may be more social and active, and more closely match the expressive, interpersonal orientation of many African-American families (Hale-Benson, 1986). Similar findings have been reported in studies of Latino mothers and children (Sulzby & Teale, 1987).

What are the educational implications of research on cultural differences in reading and writing? Literacy programs should be broadened in schools to include all kinds of reading and writing material—magazines, newspaper, catalogs, non-print books, posters, notes, and fliers, as well as books. Also, storytelling, humor, rhyming, chants, singing, and other modes of self-expression should be incorporated.

Biliteracy

Bilingual children must read and write, as well as talk, in two languages. A myth has been that bilingual children take much longer to learn reading and writing. Actually, they acquire literacy in their native language at about the same rate as monolingual children, and follow roughly the same process (Hough & Nurss, 1992). What takes time is learning written communication in a language that is very different from that spoken in the home. The child's native language and that of dominant culture may follow very different oral and graphic rules. It is quite remarkable that children acquire second-language literacy as quickly as they do!

Most experts believe that **biliteracy** begins with the acquisition of verbal skills and early print awareness *within one's native language* (Au, 1993; H. Hernandez, 1997). Literacy abilities that children acquire in their own language have been found to help them when they eventually begin to read or write in a second one (Gunderson, 1991). A next step is the acquisition of *oral* proficiency in the second language. Being able to speak a language to some degree, before you try to read it, makes a great deal of sense. A Spanish-speaking child, for example, would find it very

Once children from bilingual
families have learned to speak a
second language, they have the
additional challenge of learning
to read and write in it as well.

challenging to learn to read or write in English without a solid understanding of this new language. How could she write a coherent English story until she learned to form articles (e.g., "the" and "a," which do not exist in Spanish)? How could she sound out an English word that contained a *v* until she learned the English sound this letter makes (in Spanish, *v* is pronounced "b")? The majority of bilingual education programs stress bilingualism *before* biliteracy.

Only when children acquire a moderate level of bilingualism do most teachers begin to promote reading and writing in the second language. At this point, many challenges still arise. Children may continue to apply the rules of their native language when reading second-language print, as following example highlights:

A third-grade child is reading aloud to a teacher. The text he is reading says, "The old man didn't have enough money for dinner." The child reads it this way: "The old man not have enough money for dinner." The teacher corrects the child: "No. Try reading it again." The child reads the passage in the same way he did before. "Nope," the teacher responds. "Look at this word carefully." He points to the word "didn't" and asks, "What does that say?" The child responds, " 'Didn't.' Oh. I got it now. 'The old man didn't not have enough money for dinner.' " He smiles proudly at his teacher.

Why does the child read in this way? While he is reading English, he is still applying Spanish language rules. The teacher's efforts to correct the child are unsuccessful.

With experience, children begin to note distinctions between rules of their own language and those of a second language. As they do so, they gradually begin to read and write in the new language more conventionally. One advancement that assists in this process is metalinguistic awareness (Cummins, 1987). When children can think about language itself, they can begin to separate the rules of the two languages they are learning. They are able to consciously identify the language in which they are writing and make certain to apply appropriate grammatical rules. Biliteracy involves not only learning to read or write in a second language, but becoming aware of the very nature of literacy itself.

ASSESSING YOUNG CHILDREN: Primary-Age Language and Literacy Development

Areas of Development	What to Watch for	Indicators of Atypical Development
Oral language abilities	Utters speech sounds that are typically acquired by the child's age. Uses an extensive vocabulary and generates many words on free association tasks. Forms complex sentences which include clauses. Is aware of some language rules and can point out when they have been broken. Uses language effectively in social situations and speaks the "language of school."	Poor articulation that leads peers and teachers to misunderstand the child. Limited vocabulary. Use of short sentences that do not include clauses. Inability to use language to solve social problems. Use of socially inappropriate language in certain contexts, particularly school.
Literacy skills	By age 6, uses letters in writing that match some of the sounds in the story. Uses invented spelling by age 7, and more conventional spelling by age 8. Reads books by heart by age 6. Uses at least one conventional reading strategy—phonics, sentence context, or sight vocabulary—by age 8.	Failure to include some conventional letters in writing by age 6. Absence of any conventional spelling by age 8. Inability to acquire any conventional reading strategies—phonics, sight vocabulary, or sentence context—by age 8.

Interpreting Assessment Data: Variations in language and literacy may be due to the specific languages spoken in the home and cultural differences in reading preferences. Children will learn oral language more slowly if they are trying to learn two languages simultaneously. Social language styles may vary depending on cultural tradition. Children whose families converse collectively, for example, may have difficulty learning the turntaking rule at school. Children of some cultures may prefer different kinds of reading material—magazines or mail-order catalogs. Children learning to read in two languages may acquire conventional reading and writing skills more slowly. Those who display poor language and literacy within their preferred language may be at risk, however. Referral to a speech and language pathologist may be necessary. Classroom interventions, using high-quality children's literature and authentic writing activities (e.g., composing letters, family stories, or journal entries), can remediate some literacy problems.

RESEARCH INTO PRACTICE

CRITICAL CONCEPT 1

Most of the rules of one's native language are learned by the primary years. Only minor refinements occur in the structural aspects of speech—phonology, syntax, and semantics. The primary area of oral language growth at this age is pragmatics. Children acquire a sophisticated understanding of social uses of language, including the conventions for talking in school. Most children discover that there are certain ways to ask for help, answer questions, or seek information from a teacher that will lead to academic success. They come to understand that in many classrooms only formal language is acceptable.

Application #1

The focus of oral language teaching in the primary years should be on pragmatics. Children should be provided opportunities to speak in diverse contexts in which varying social rules apply. Children can be encouraged to engage in playful conversations with peers on the playground or in the dramatic play area. Experiences can be planned for children to talk in whole-group settings. Cooperative learning projects can be created to help children learn to persuade one another, negotiate, and exchange ideas. Each of these settings will require that children learn a unique set of social language rules.

Application #2

Teachers should provide whole-group experiences that give children practice in using different kinds of discourse. Children can be invited to tell stories or relate events in their lives. They can be encouraged to present formal reports. They can be given opportunities to ask and answer questions of the teacher and of peers. These experiences will assist children in learning the conventions of "school talk."

CRITICAL CONCEPT 2

For bilingual children, the primary years can be a period of rapid linguistic growth within their second language. They may first apply the structures and rules of their native language when speaking in the new language. For example, a child who speaks both Spanish and English says "The man no like cheese," following rules of Spanish. Eventually, children will be able to separate the two distinct rule systems and speak the second language with accuracy. Special support in school is necessary for this process to occur; a "sink or swim" approach, in which no assistance is provided, may impede linguistic development.

Application #1

Bilingual children should be encouraged to speak in both their native language and the second language they are learning throughout the school day. Thus, language instruction is "additive": children are adding a new language without abandoning the language of their families.

Application #2

Teachers must come to understand, accept, and appreciate early linguistic "errors" among bilingual children. Children should not be harshly corrected for applying rules of their native language when speaking a new, second language. Mistakes are necessary and important in bilingual development.

Application #3

Teachers should advocate for bilingual education programs which give special support to children who do not speak the language of dominant society. Two-way bilingual programs can be created—formally or informally—in which all children in a classroom learn two languages.

CRITICAL CONCEPT 3

Different cultural groups have distinct rules for social language. The styles of discourse of some cultural groups may clash with rules of conversation often required in school. Topic-chaining and collective styles of verbal interaction, for example, may not adhere to the rules for orderly conversations emphasized in the classroom. Informal, non-standard speech styles used in the neighborhood may be viewed as inappropriate by some teachers in American schools. Children of historically under-represented cultures, then, will find school pragmatics particularly challenging to learn.

Application #1

Primary-age children should be provided with opportunities to learn the social rules of school, while at the same time refining their own native discourse patterns. Children might be provided with experiences in giving reports, taking turns talking, and asking questions to seek information in order to promote conventional school talk. At the same time, they can be encouraged to tell stories, provide open-ended accounts of life events, dramatize, and engage in collective conversation using the discourse styles of their own cultures.

Application #2

Primary children should be introduced to the concept of register switching—the ability to change one's language based on the pragmatic rules of a particular context. A group discussion could focus on kinds of language that can be used at home or in the neighborhood but not at school. Older primary children can be encouraged to write a story "in the language of your friends" and then to rewrite it using conventional school language. Such experiences help children to consciously manipulate their language styles in varying contexts.

CRITICAL CONCEPT 4

Some children have language problems in the primary years that require intervention. Articulation errors, disfluency, poor word memory or retrieval, and faulty syntax can all be signs of language disorders.

Application #1

Teachers must be able to identify the characteristics of children with speech and language delays and differentiate these from disfluencies and articulation errors which are typical during the primary years. Identifying these delays and seeking special services for children with special language needs are critical responsibilities of elementary teachers.

Application #2

Teachers should work closely with speech and language pathologists who are serving children with speech and language delays. Incorporating special speech and language games and activities into the regular classroom will enhance communication more effectively—and with less social stigma—than "pull-out" lessons conducted outside of the classroom group.

CRITICAL CONCEPT 5

Literacy growth is rapid in the primary years as children learn to read and write conventionally. Bilingual children will need to learn to read and write in two different languages. By acquiring literacy in their native language first, they will more easily learn to read and write in a second language in later years.

Application #1

Primary-age children should be provided with print-rich classrooms that offer many opportunities to write in meaningful ways. Stories, journal entries, written observations of scientific experiments, and letters to peers or family members are more significant to children than artificial, isolated-skills instruction.

Application #2

Children should be provided with high-quality children's books and other culturally relevant reading materials. They should be read to, but should also be afforded much time to read independently. Signs, posters, sign-up lists, attendance charts, and other types of environmental print also promote reading development. Such meaningful experiences are more potent in promoting literacy than isolated-skills instruction.

Application #3

Bilingual children should be encouraged to learn to read in their native language first. If a teacher does not speak the preferred language of a student in class, a bilingual aid, volunteer, or parent should be invited to assist. Children should be read to and encouraged to write in their native language in various ways. A collection of children's books in the child's native language should be made available. Only when children have shown competence in native-language reading and writing is instruction in the second language appropriate.

SUGGESTED ACTIVITIES

1. Record a 20-minute language sample of an individual primary-age child, following these steps:

    a. Have a teacher or parent help you select an interesting subject for your tape. This might be a child with atypical language development, a child who speaks two languages, or a very talkative child who will provide a wealth of verbalization to analyze.

    b. Find a quiet place to tape. Provide the child with materials that are likely to elicit conversation,

    such as a set of interesting pictures to look at. Engage the child in an open-ended discussion.

    c. Ask questions to elicit much natural language from the child.

    Later, write an analysis of your tape in which you discuss how well the child is able to communicate and comment on any challenges or obstacles the child faces to expressing ideas. Is the child difficult to understand?

Is the child's vocabulary limited? Are the child's sentences incomplete? Can the child use language in socially effective ways?

2. Using the tape recorded in activity 1, analyze your subject's phonology. Listen carefully for speech and other sounds. Write an analysis of this area of the child's language, guided by the following questions:

   a. Are any articulation errors evident? Are these errors typical for a child of this age, based on information in the chapter?

   b. Do you notice any disfluency in the child's speech? Are the disfluencies typical? Is there evidence of "struggle behavior"?

3. Using the tape recorded in activity 1, analyze your subject's semantics. Listen carefully to words the child uses. Write an analysis of this area of the child's language, guided by the following questions:

   a. Does the child appear to have an extensive vocabulary? A limited one? Why do you think so? (Be certain to consider vocabulary in all languages the child speaks!)

   b. Did certain words that the child used impress you?

   c. Did the child have trouble retrieving words or remembering the names of things?

4. Using the tape recorded in activity 1, analyze your subject's syntax. Listen carefully to the sentences the child uses. Write an analysis of this area of the child's language, guided by the following questions:

   a. Did the child use passive forms well? Did the child form compound sentences?

   b. Did you hear any errors in sentence construction? Give examples.

5. Observe the social language of two children in a classroom. Later, write a report on their pragmatics, based on the following questions:

   a. Were the children effective in communicating with and persuading peers? Were both children equally competent in communicating with peers?

   b. What examples did you observe of the rules of school language described in the chapter? Did the two children use polite, formal language? Were they effective in asking or answering questions in class?

   c. Analyze differences between the children in terms of pragmatics.

6. Collect samples of writing from three different children in a primary classroom. Select boys and girls from diverse cultural groups. Choose at least one bilingual child, if possible. Later, write a report about each child's writing development, guided by the following questions:

   a. What stage of writing development do you believe each child is in, based on information from this chapter? Give evidence to support your belief.

   b. Compare and contrast the children's writing. How do the written works differ across individuals? Across cultures? Between genders?

   c. How is the bilingual child's writing distinct (if you were able to select such a child to observe)?

7. Assemble a collection of different kinds of reading materials, such as children's books, books with photographs and no print, mail-order catalogs, magazines, and newspapers. Use these materials to interact with five children of diverse cultural backgrounds, using the following procedure:

   Show each child the materials you have collected and say, "I'd like us to read together. Which of these would you like to read first?" Make note of the child's selection, then engage in joint reading. Encourage the child to read. If the child is reluctant, then read to him or her. When finished reading, ask, "What would you like to read next?" Continue the process until the child is no longer interested in reading with you. Later, write a report about your experiences, guided by the following questions:

   a. Which reading materials were most popular? Which were rarely selected? Were you surprised by some of the choices?

   b. How did reading choices vary across cultural groups? Across gender?

   c. What can you conclude from this experience about children's reading preferences and culture?

CHAPTER 17

Social and Emotional Development in the Primary Years

I N THIS CHAPTER WE WILL ADDRESS CHILDREN'S SOCIAL AND EMOTIONAL DEVEL-
OPMENT IN THE PRIMARY GRADES. The social worlds of primary-age children widen
considerably as they come into contact with larger and more diverse groups of
peers and adults. Children acquire new patterns of social behavior and enter into
unique kinds of relationships. Their emerging intellectual abilities allow them to reflect more fully on their peers' behavior and the meaning of friendship, and they form
opinions about which characteristics of peers they value and which they dislike. They
begin to recognize differences between themselves and others, including racial and
class distinctions.

As they advance intellectually, primary-age children are able to study themselves
more deeply and form opinions about their own competence and self-worth. They can
analyze more accurately what they are good at and not so good at, and can discern
whether they are smarter, faster, and better liked than their peers—or less so. Because
of these advancements, the primary years are a period of great opportunity, but also of
great risk. During this stage, children can come to view themselves as competent and
well liked by friends, family members, and students, achieving a sense of pride in
themselves and their culture. Or, they can suffer self-doubt or feelings of incompetence
and powerlessness, and come to question the worth of their families or cultural heritage. The following story, adapted from the observations of B. B. Whiting and Edwards
(1988), illustrates the potential emotional perils during the primary years:

> Andrés, a Juxtlahuacan child in Mexico has grown up in a supportive ex-
> tended family. His parents and grandparents have encouraged and appreci-
> ated his accomplishments. As one of the oldest children in his village, he has
> always been the fastest, strongest, and smartest among his peers and sib-
> lings. By age 6, he has begun to construct a very positive view of himself; he
> has had no reason to question his own self-worth or ability.
>
> Andrés attends his first day of school in the center of town, far from his
> home. He sits quietly as a raucous scene goes on about him. The teacher is
> asking questions, and the other children in the class are loudly calling out
> the answers. He is overwhelmed by the experience. He does not speak Span-
> ish, the language used exclusively in the school.
>
> He takes a bold step and tries to speak to the teacher in his native lan-
> guage. "I don't understand, teacher," he calls out. His teacher ignores him
> and continues responding to the other children's answers. "Teacher!" he says
> in a loud voice, "I do not understand this." At last the teacher turns to him
> and hisses loudly: "Sh-sh-sh!"

Later, the teacher asks the child to name letters in Spanish. Andrés cannot understand what she is asking and gives a look of confusion. The teacher says something in Spanish that makes the other students laugh, then moves on to ask another student the same question. Although Andrés cannot understand the teacher's language, he recognizes clearly that he has been ridiculed.

At home that night, Andrés is very quiet. When asked about what has occurred on the first day of school, he does not respond. Finally, with prodding from his grandmother, he tries to describe the experience, but breaks down crying: "I can't . . . [sobs] I can't talk well. . . . I just can't talk like everyone else does . . . [sobs]."

His grandmother wraps her arms around him and rocks him.

As a preschooler, the child in the story had enjoyed a very positive view of himself. He had come to believe that he could accomplish anything and that adults and peers would appreciate him unconditionally. Such beliefs are very common during early childhood. His ordeal on his first day of school, however, has threatened his feelings of competence and pride. Over time, such experiences may lead him to conclude that he is inferior or a bad person.

A SENSE OF COMPETENCE

We have discussed Erikson's (1963) theory of emotional development in previous chapters. Recall that according to Erikson, an emotional struggle during the preschool years is to achieve a sense of **initiative.** Preschoolers who have acquired initiative will make creative attempts, take risks, and reach out to peers for interaction and friendship. At this age, they feel pride at simply making a good effort or being creative. This all changes in the primary years. Children of ages 6 to 8 wish to master real skills—the skills possessed by older children and adults. They want to read and write like grownups, to excel at sports and other games, and to be strong and smart (Stipek, 1992). It is not enough to try, from Erikson's view. Primary children want to succeed!

Children who feel they are successful at mastering real skills are said to have a sense of **industry,** more commonly called "competence." Erikson has proposed that children who have genuine successes in their early years and whose accomplishments are accepted and appreciated by adults and peers will develop a sense of competence. The opposite state, called "inferiority," results when children have significant experience with failure. The main psychological work of primary-age children, from Erikson's view, is to come to view themselves as competent persons.

Development of Feelings of Competence

Most preschoolers see themselves as competent. For example, in one study, 4-year-olds who had failed several times to complete a difficult task nevertheless reported that they would be successful on their next try (Stipek, 1992). Curry and Johnson (1990) describe preschoolers as "exceedingly optimistic in self-ratings of their abilities and expectations for academic success" (p. 69). Erikson would explain these positive feelings by noting that children of this age are focusing on attempts and initiatives, not on the outcomes of their efforts. Consider the case of the Juxtlahuacan child, Andrés, in the opening vignette. This child may have held positive views of himself in the preschool years because he tried hard, made friends, and was viewed as a "good boy" by his parents and grandparents. In his early years, it did not matter that he lacked certain skills or knowledge; he made important efforts.

As children approach school age, however, they begin to question their abilities (Eccles, Wigfield, Harold, & Blumenfeld, 1993). What happens during this developmental period to cause this self-doubt? For one thing, primary-age children gain a more accurate understanding of what it means to be "smart" and "good at something." Whereas younger children associate competence with appropriate behavior or hard work, early elementary-age children come to understand that ability at performing school tasks determines "smartness" (Stipek, 1992). Also, children in the early elementary years increasingly compare themselves with peers (Aboud, 1985). This leads them to base judgments about their competence on where they stand within their peer group. As early as age 6, children begin to complain that they cannot run as fast, read as well, or learn math as quickly as others.

A Sense of Competence in School

Primary-age children who attend school are more likely to consider teacher feedback—both positive and negative—in their assessments of self (Barker & Graham, 1987; Pintrich & Blumenfeld, 1985). When a teacher criticizes an elementary-age child's written work, gives a low grade or score on a test, or in other ways provides negative feedback on school performance, the child is likely to feel less competent.

Several common practices in American schools contribute to feelings of inferiority (Stipek & MacIver, 1989). Several of these are summarized in Table 17-1.

TABLE 17-1
Practices in American Schools That Can Threaten Children's Feelings of Competence

School Practice	Example
Evaluative symbols	First graders are given stars, stickers, and grades for performing well on academic work. Children who do not perform well do not earn these rewards.
Public comparison	The number of books children have read is indicated with checkmarks on a huge chart at the front of a second-grade classroom. Some children have many checkmarks, others have few.
Ability grouping	Children are placed into high-, middle-, or low-ability reading groups within a third-grade classroom. All students in the class are aware of which group is "slowest" and which is "smartest."
Whole-group instruction	An entire classroom of children is taught a single mathematics lesson. The teacher calls on students to solve problems on the board in front of the other students. Some children can solve the problems, others can't.
Formal relationships with the teacher	A first-grade teacher welcomes children on the first day of school by presenting a list of rules and expectations. This is in sharp contrast to the smiles and hugs children received on their first day in kindergarten a year ago.

SOURCE: Stipek & MacIver, 1989.

Evaluative Symbols. **Evaluative symbols** predominate American public education. Increasingly, children incorporate symbolic feedback into their assessments of their own competence. In one study (Blumenfeld, Pintrich, & Hamilton, 1986), American elementary children who were asked "How do you know when someone's smart?" regularly named grades as the primary indicator. Poor grades or failure to earn stars, stickers, or happy faces can have a lasting negative impact on children's feelings of competence (Curry & Johnson, 1990).

Public Comparison. Teachers compare their students with one another, both formally and informally, in many American public schools (Stipek, 1992). Charts indicating how many books each child has read or which children have not been behaving appropriately can threaten feelings of competence (Higgins & Parsons, 1983). More subtle forms of comparison can also lead to negative self-judgments (Hallinan & Sorenson, 1983).

The ways teachers interact with children can have an effect. For example, a child may never be called on by the teacher because he or she never gets the right answer or takes too long responding. Over time, the message to the child becomes clear: You are a less competent person.

Ability Grouping. In many schools, children are placed into groups according to ability. Being relegated to a low-ability group can threaten feelings of competence (Hallinan & Sorenson, 1983). One second grader was overheard saying, "I'm in the 'Tigers' group, because I can't sit still and listen, and I talk when the teacher says 'stop' and . . . let's see . . . Oh, I can't read very good either." At a young age, this child can recognize that he has been placed in the "slow group." His feelings of competence are threatened.

Whole-Group Instruction. In many elementary schools around the world, children spend the majority of their time being taught in whole groups. In such classrooms, teachers present the same lesson or ask the same questions to all children, regardless of ability level. Children are expected to provide correct responses in front of their classmates. Since all students are engaged in the same tasks at one time, self-comparison with peers is likely. For example, a child might think, "I couldn't solve that math problem, but Hanna and Ezra could!" For some children, being able to perform as well as peers is not possible (Stipek, 1992).

Formal Relationships With the Teacher. Preschool and day care teachers have been observed to be relatively positive and accepting of their students (Potter, 1982). They tend to respond to processes rather than end products and to accept any effort a child makes as satisfactory. In the elementary years, however, interactions with teachers become more public and formal, more often focusing on whether children behave in prescribed ways, accomplish learning tasks successfully, and complete assignments (Brophy & Evertson, 1987). The transition from the warm, encouraging relationships in child care or preschool to the more formal and evaluative teacher-child relationships can threaten children's feelings of self-worth (Stipek, 1992).

Teachers of young children can redesign the curriculum to reduce threats to their students' feelings of competence. They might offer more small-group or individualized learning projects that emphasize thinking processes rather than right answers, or could reduce the amount of public evaluation and ability grouping. Such steps can contribute to children's positive self-assessments in the primary years.

TYPES OF SELF-ESTEEM

The term **self-esteem** is used to describe a person's overall evaluation of self. A person who has positive feelings of self-worth is said to have high self-esteem, while someone who is unsatisfied with or doubtful about his or her abilities, accomplishments, or interpersonal characteristics is said to have low self-esteem. Erikson (1963) equated a sense of competence with self-esteem in the primary years. From his view, self-esteem is a single psychological trait. Other researchers have challenged this perspective, arguing that two or more types of self-esteem can be differentiated during the primary years (Harter, 1990).

Competence Versus Social Acceptance

In one series of studies, preschool and elementary children were asked to rate themselves on their abilities in many different areas (Harter, 1983; Shavelson & Bolus, 1982). It was discovered that 4- to 7-year-old children differentiated between two basic types of self-esteem: **competence**—that is, being good at things, as Erikson described; and **social acceptance**—that is, being liked as a friend or cared for as a family member. These researchers conclude that these two types of self-evaluation are distinct and somewhat unrelated at this age. Children may believe themselves very competent, for example, but not very well liked. Or they may believe that they have many friends or caring relatives, but doubt their abilities in school. The following story illustrates how some professionals fail to recognize these two distinct types of self-esteem and their importance in development:

A second-grade teacher sits with a group of students in a circle, conducting a self-esteem activity. He asks the children to report things they are very good at and things they would like to learn to do better. The activity is aimed at one child in particular, Twana, who is not doing well in school. The teacher assumes that she suffers low self-esteem, and he hopes the activity will help her to see that she has some worthwhile traits and abilities.

The teacher expects that Twana will have trouble coming up with ideas on what she can do well, so he is prepared to assist her in thinking about her strengths. However, she is actually quite vocal when her turn comes:

TWANA: My grandma says, "You're my favorite little granddaughter" and she loves me all the time. And she is always waiting when I get home from school.

TEACHER: (Gently) That's nice. But we're talking about things we can do well. Can you think of something you do very well?

TWANA: Well, my grandma and my sister are always wanting me to tell them stories and jokes. They love it when I tell my jokes. And, know what? I'm going with my sister and some of the older girls to the community center tonight.

TEACHER: Yes. That's great. Let me ask you a little more about your jokes. Can you tell very funny jokes? Is that something you do well?

TWANA: My grandmother says my jokes are just silly and when I tell her she shakes her head and just puts me right on her lap.

TEACHER: Okay. Well, why don't you think real hard about some things you can do very, very well. We'll give Sarah a turn and come back to you in a minute.

The teacher in this story has developed an activity that focuses only on one type of self-esteem: competence. His interactions are aimed at helping Twana identify things that she can do well. He has failed to recognize social acceptance as an equally important part of a child's self-assessment. Judging by her comments on this other area of self-evaluation, Twana clearly holds a very positive view of herself in terms of acceptance. She feels appreciated and loved unconditionally by her family.

Older primary-age children have been found to have even more highly differentiated and diverse types of self-esteem (Eccles et al., 1993). Seven- and 8-year-olds begin to view themselves as competent or accepted in certain areas but not in others. For example, one child may view herself as very able in math and science but not in reading or athletics. Another may feel very accepted by his family members, but not by peers. Some children may have high estimations of their ability to interact with peers in the neighborhood, but not with peers at school.

The following vignette shows how feelings of competence can vary depending on context:

A first-grade teacher makes a home visit to the family of one of her students. The family has moved recently from Puerto Rico, and their child is just learning to speak English. The teacher is concerned because the child is so quiet and withdrawn. Even on the playground, he stands and watches peers, never joining games or activities. For this reason, he has made no friends and is generally not well liked. She plans to discuss the problem with his mother and grandmother.

When she enters the family apartment, she is shocked by what she sees. Her student is engaged in active play with his cousin and two neighbor children. He is giving directives to the others in his native language with great confidence. He is not the self-doubting, withdrawn child she has observed in school; he is bold, self-assured, and gregarious. She quickly rethinks the reasons for her visit and the approach she will take with this family.

This child's self-esteem in the area of peer acceptance appears to be quite high at home, even though he exhibits much self-doubt at school. The teacher has learned that assessments of self-evaluation must include contexts and activities that extend beyond the classroom.

Feelings of Control

Another distinct area of self-evaluation in the primary years is control (Curry & Johnson, 1990). Children who have acquired a feeling of control are more likely to report that hard work and persistence in solving problems will lead to success. Some psychologists have called this an internal **locus of control,** since such children believe they have the power within themselves to make a difference (Bandura, 1986). Children who have an external locus of control believe that what happens to them is due to external forces beyond their regulation. They are more likely to report that "It doesn't matter how hard I try, the teacher will still give me a bad grade" or "No matter what I say, kids in the class won't like me, because they're mean."

Children gradually acquire an internal or external locus of control during the primary years. As early as the third grade, some children come to hold such fixed views about their lack of control that their success in all endeavors is hampered. Such children often give up trying to perform well in school because they believe failure is inevitable, that improvement is out of their control (Fincham, Hokoda, & Sanders, 1989).

Feelings of Moral Self-Worth

Another dimension of self-esteem is **moral self-worth** (Curry & Johnson, 1990). This refers to children's assessments of their goodness or virtue, as defined by cultural norms. Primary-age children come to view themselves as "good" or "bad" depending on their social experiences. Children with positive self-esteem in this area come to see themselves as proper, worthwhile, and trustworthy friends and family members.

Three virtues of self-worth that are of great importance to children in the primary years are fairness, responsibility, and obedience (Curry & Johnson, 1990; Damon, 1988). Fairness is of great moral concern in the primary classroom. Frequent arguments erupt about inequitable treatment by the teacher or peers, or about the uneven distribution of materials or rewards. Through conflicts over issues of equality, children gradually construct views of themselves as either fair or not so fair.

They also develop a sense of responsibility, which is related to being helpful to teachers, parents, friends, and the community. Parents or teachers often nurture this sense with statements such as "You're such a good helper" or "I could never have cleaned up this kitchen without you." Over time, some children come to view themselves as responsible members of the classroom or household; others will not.

Obedience relates to compliance and respect for adults. A certain degree of obedience is expected of children in all cultures. Children who are relatively compliant over time will evaluate themselves as "nice." Children who are reprimanded regularly in school or at home acquire an opposite view of themselves.

As with other types of self-esteem, children may have positive views of themselves in some areas of moral self-worth and negative views in others. A child may consider himself helpful and nice but not always very obedient. Another may come to feel she is obedient toward adults but not always fair to peers. Children may hold slightly different self-assessments depending on context. For example, some children enjoy positive feelings of self-worth in school settings, but believe themselves to be unkind or unhelpful in the neighborhood.

Integrating the Types of Self-Esteem

Clearly, the development of self-esteem in the primary years is a complex process of self-evaluation. It is quite mind-boggling, in fact, to contemplate the many ways children think about themselves and judge their self-worth at this young age! As we learned, the various types of self-esteem are somewhat disconnected in the primary years (Harter, 1990). Views of self are splintered into distinct self-appraisals in many different areas of life. Figure 17-1 illustrates the specific areas of self-evaluation that have been discussed in this section.

After age 8, children begin to synthesize their various beliefs about self into a single, global self-esteem. It is not until adolescence, however, that an overall, integrated sense of self-worth emerges (Marsh, Smith, & Barnes, 1985).

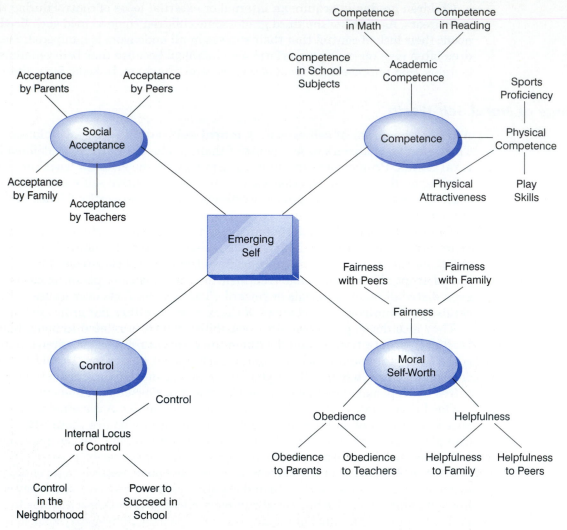

FIGURE 17-1 Self-esteem in the primary years is made up of many separate self-appraisals. During childhood and adolescence, these gradually become integrated into a single, emerging view of self.

SOURCE: Extrapolated from data in Curry & Johnson, 1990; Damon, 1988; Harter, 1983; and Stipek & McIver, 1989.

SELF-ESTEEM AND CULTURE

The sense of self-esteem a child develops in the primary grades is influenced by culture. The worldview, valued competencies, and traditions of a particular cultural group will affect the criteria children use to judge their self-worth.

Inclusive Views of Self

As we discussed in previous chapters, some cultures are more collective in thought and action (Harrison, Wilson, Pine, Chan, & Buriel, 1990). In such cultural groups, extended families tend to work together toward joint goals, and individual family members often sacrifice personal aspirations for the good of the entire household. Accomplishments of a whole village or neighborhood may be valued more than individual achievements.

Children of collective cultures will hold **inclusive views of self:** evaluations of self that are related to accomplishments or competencies of the entire family or community (Harrison et al., 1990). Their personal self-worth is intricately tied to their views about the groups to which they belong. Inclusive views of self have been found to be prevalent among African-American children, for example (Harrison, 1985). The self-esteem of children of this cultural group is likely to be related to family and ethnic pride. African-American children who hold their family, peer group, community and culture in high esteem are more likely to evaluate themselves in positive ways.

School experiences that emphasize personal achievement may promote positive self-esteem among some children, then, but not in others. Children who have inclusive views of self may not derive feelings of competence from learning to read on their own or maintaining a high batting average on the playground. Instead, their self-esteem may be based on pride in family literacy or the success of a whole peer group or team. Feelings of social acceptance may depend on being appreciated by one's entire family or ethnic group.

Children who have inclusive views of self may not acquire feelings of control through individual initiative or self-reliance. Instead, a sense of control may come from a belief that one's family or community is powerful and can overcome adversity. A sense of moral self-worth may be based on the view that one's family, community, and cultural group are fair and responsible. When a child's entire ethnic group is portrayed in the media as "lazy" or "dependent on welfare," self-esteem is threatened.

Children of some cultures have inclusive views of self. Their feelings of competence are tied to the accomplishments of their peer group, family, or community.

Culture, then, shapes the very definition of "self." For children of some groups, proud stories about one's family or the athletic prowess of a neighborhood peer group may be more important indicators of self-esteem than expressions of personal achievement or self-worth.

Cultural Competencies and Criteria for Self-Evaluation

Culture influences the specific criteria children use to evaluate themselves. In the primary years, children make judgments about which abilities are worthwhile or important to learn. Some children may view athletic skill as more important than learning to read, while others believe just the opposite. Some may consider singing or playing a musical instrument to be most critical (Eccles et al., 1993). In order to acquire positive views of self, children must come to believe they are competent at the things they value. A child who believes that reading is very important will derive positive self-esteem from learning to read, while reading achievement will have little effect on a child who does not value this ability.

How do children determine which competencies are important and which are not? Families and culture play a significant role in helping children decide. Parents socialize children to value those competencies that are emphasized within a particular cultural group (Ogbu, 1992). Children then assess their own abilities in these areas. One child may weight storytelling skill more heavily than reading achievement, while another may rely more on social acceptance by peers and family than on grades in school.

The following story, adapted from Blanchard's (1983) observations, shows how professionals do not always recognize that diverse cultural groups adopt unique criteria for judging self-worth:

Karen, a Native American child, has been identified as learning disabled. She is enrolled in a second-grade classroom in a regular public school and is struggling academically. A team of professionals interviews the child's teacher and mother about Karen's classroom and home experiences and her self-esteem. The two offer quite contrasting perspectives on the child's emotional development:

Teacher's comments: Karen is so quiet and withdrawn that she has made no friends. Her struggles with academic work make her stand out among her peers. Her language is a particular problem: she simply can't learn enough English to communicate effectively. I believe her outward smiles and happy demeanor are a just a facade. Inside, I know she's crying. She has a very low opinion of herself.

Mother's assessment: The school calls Karen "learning disabled," but in her family and community we call her "magical." She can draw beautifully. She can draw the old stories better than most adults. Her pictures are on display in our community center. She doesn't speak the language of the school, that's true. But we tell her that English is not as important; Keresan is the language of her people. Words don't matter as much as deeds, anyway. She knows this. She shows us her ideas and her feelings through her actions. Karen is very, very proud of who she is and of her family. She is happy in her real life. Schoolteachers just don't see her in her natural place in the world.

The teacher in this story has assumed that Karen has low self-esteem because she performs poorly in a Western-dominated school. A common misconception among some Euro-American teachers is that children of all cultures base their self-evaluations on criteria defined by the dominant society (M. B. Spencer, 1988; Trawick-Smith & Lisi, 1994). In fact, Karen holds a very positive view of herself that is unrelated to her competence in school. From her mother's reports, she is confident about her abilities in areas that matter within her family and culture. She is a gifted visual artist, and her gift is held in high esteem within her community (Blanchard, 1983). She can communicate in ways that are important to her cultural group: speaking Keresan and using nonverbal expression. Her positive sense of self is related to her successes and acceptance in her own community.

Culture and Feelings of Control

As we have discussed, feelings of control are a part of a child's self-appraisal. A goal of American education has been to instill an internal locus of control—a belief in one's ability to make a difference and to regulate one's own life. Feelings of control vary by culture and gender. In the United States, for example, girls are likely to feel less in control and more helpless than boys (Curry & Johnson, 1990; Dwek, Goetz, & Strauss, 1980). Chinese-American children also tend to have an external locus of control (Sue & Chin, 1983). Children of this cultural group are more likely to believe that successes or failures are governed by fate, luck, or circumstances beyond their control.

Are these findings cause for concern? The results of some studies suggest that an external locus of control can lead to poor achievement and social adjustment (Fincham et al., 1989). However, this trend may not hold for all children. For girls, an external locus of control has been found to be unrelated to school failure (Dwek & Licht, 1980; Parsons, 1983). Chinese-American children who lack feelings of control have, likewise, been found to perform very well in school subjects (Wong, 1988; Yu & Kim, 1983). Sue and Chin (1983) explain these puzzling research findings by proposing that there are two reasons children lack feelings of control in their lives: socialization and prejudice.

Socialization and Control. Some cultures may purposely socialize children to believe in fate and the powerlessness of the individual. In traditional Chinese-American families, for example, children are taught to give over full regulation of their lives to parents and other family elders. According to Yu and Kim (1983), Chinese-American children are often trained to abandon urges for "independence and mastery over one's own fate" (p. 160) and to adopt feelings of absolute deference to adults. It is no wonder that Chinese-American children exhibit an external locus of control in school. Sue and Chin (1983) propose that the effects of these feelings on school achievement are minimal because children *voluntarily* entrust their lives to external persons or circumstances. These beliefs are in accordance with cultural customs.

Girls may, likewise, be socialized to feel they have less individual control over circumstances (Gilligan, 1982). Parents often teach their daughters to be reliant on others in solving problems or making decisions. Thus, girls may come to believe that accomplishments are not due to *individual* initiative, but to the efforts of all persons in a group. Learning a math concept, for example, may not be the result of a child's own actions, but the efforts of everyone—teachers, peers, and parents, working in concert. Gilligan has suggested that what psychologists call "helplessness" in girls may be simply a reliance on and faith in the help of other people.

Sue and Chin (1983) claim that when an external locus of control is a fundamental part of culture and is taught directly by parents, it causes no harm. Another kind of helplessness, they contend, is more damaging to emotional health—that which stems from prejudice.

Prejudice and Control.   Children may have negative experiences which lead them to conclude that they will fail in school or be rejected by peers because of race or gender. They may eventually come to believe that no amount of effort will lead to success. For example, a Puerto Rican child may come to believe that nothing she does in school will lead to success because of teacher prejudice, or a Chinese-American child may be convinced by coaches or peers that, because of his ethnic background, he is not sufficiently aggressive to become an athlete (Sue & Chin, 1983). A Euro-American child may be led to believe that, because she is a girl, her achievement in mathematics is the result of pure luck.

Even positive stereotypes can lead to a reduction in feelings of control. The belief that all Chinese-American children are bright and hardworking is an example. Students of this cultural group are sometimes given good grades simply because of their ethnicity (Sue & Chin, 1983). "You must be a good student if you come from a Chinese-American family," the thinking goes. Children may eventually come to see school success as something that is determined by cultural affiliation, regardless of one's efforts or accomplishments.

Sue and Chin (1983) express concern about feelings of powerlessness that arise from prejudice. It is one thing to *choose* to trust fate, luck, or the guidance of others, they contend; it is quite another to be truly disempowered because of race or gender bias.

Culture and Feelings of Moral Self-Worth

How children judge their moral self-worth can also be shaped by culture. As we discussed earlier, one criterion for determining self-worth is obedience to parents (Damon, 1988). Children come to believe themselves to be "nice" or "well behaved" if they are compliant. How obedient children are expected to be is defined by cultural norms, however, and obedience and respect for adults is required in some cultures more than in others.

In many Japanese-American and Chinese-American families, absolute submission to parents is required (Chao, 1994; Wong, 1988). Piety toward parents, other adults, and ancestors is deeply rooted in ancient tradition. Similarly, African-American parents often command a high degree of respect and obedience from their children. In fact, some African-American parents express disapproval at the more **permissive parenting** styles of Euro-American families (Hale, 1994). Within cultural groups that value obedience, this requirement is likely to be weighted heavily in children's self-evaluations. Even a moderate amount of disrespect toward their family members may, over time, lead to negative views of moral self-worth.

In contrast, some middle-class Euro-American parents are exceedingly permissive (Goodnow & Collins, 1990). Children regularly disobey and argue with adults in these families. Freedom of expression and the individual rights of children are highly valued, so obedience may not be an important criterion when such children judge self-worth.

B. B. Whiting and Edwards (1988) report that in some societies, children are expected to be obedient in some contexts but not in others. In Ngeca, Kenya, for example, children were observed to be very obedient in school. They regularly complied with their teachers' directives and ran errands for them. Some even tended their teachers' gardens! These same children, however, were found to be relatively disobedient at home. They were observed ignoring parents' demands or requests for help. Parents seemed nonchalant about their children's noncompliance. In this cultural group, obedience at school might be an important standard in assessing self-worth, whereas compliance with parents might not.

Responsibility is another criterion children use in self-evaluation. As mentioned earlier, children who believe themselves to be helpful to their family and community tend to develop a positive self-esteem. Expectations for responsibility vary considerably in families, however. The most responsible children tend to be those who live in large non-Western families and whose contributions to the household workload are critical to survival (Hale-Benson, 1986; B. B. Whiting and Whiting, 1975). Middle-class Euro-American children are generally less helpful and perform fewer family tasks.

Children who live in families in which obedience and responsibility are valued and respected will base their self-evaluations on these attributes. Moral self-worth depends on being helpful and respectful. In cultures that do not consider such traits crucial, other criteria will be more heavily weighted.

Self-Esteem, Prejudice, and the Myth of Self-Hatred

Several decades ago in the United States, public concern was raised about the self-esteem of children from historically under-represented groups. It was believed that many children of color, who experienced lives filled with prejudice, hated themselves and wished to be white (Witmer & Kotinsky, 1952). This opinion was based on a series of classic race identification studies, in which children were asked to express their preference for dolls or pictures representing various racial groups (Aboud, 1977; J. T. Spencer, 1970). All children—even children of color—were found to prefer and express more positive attitudes toward white dolls than black or brown ones. These findings were presented by national committees to the Congress, the U.S. Supreme Court, and White House Conferences on Children (Clark, 1952; Joint Commission on the Mental Health of Children, 1970).

Although these concerns were well intentioned, they fostered a new negative racial stereotype: that children of color hate themselves and are to be pitied. I conducted a study that demonstrated this attitude even today among teachers (Trawick-Smith & Lisi, 1994). I presented a photograph of an African-American female child to a group of 22 early childhood professionals. Without giving any background about the child's life, family, or abilities, I asked the teachers to write stories about the child. All but three wrote that the child suffered "low self-esteem," and more than half described the child as "feeling helpless" and "alone." These assessments were based solely on a photograph of the child smiling as she played on the playground! Evidently, some teachers automatically assume that children of color suffer low self-esteem and other emotional problems.

The view that children of color hate themselves has been vigorously challenged. Some believe that too much has been made of the doll-and-picture preference studies. Can it be assumed that children suffer negative views of themselves or their race just because they favor white dolls over black ones? Several studies found no connection between doll identification and self-esteem (McAdoo, 1985; M. B. Spencer & Markstrom-Adams, 1990).

Criticisms have also been raised about the methods used in self-esteem studies (Harrison, 1985). Some argue that the race and attitudes of experimenters may have affected findings. Euro-American researchers may have unconsciously swayed children to express preferences for white dolls or pictures. In doll identification studies, for example, children were found to show greater preference for their own race when researchers were of their own cultural and linguistic background (Annis & Corenblum, 1987; Corenblum & Wilson, 1982). It may be that children respond to doll preference tasks in the way they think researchers expect them to. They may select white dolls if they believe that is the "correct" answer—the one that a white middle-class researcher is looking for.

Many of the self-esteem studies were conducted prior to the late 1960s. The 1960s and early 1970s were a period of great social and political change in the United States. The civil rights movement was gaining momentum, schools were being desegregated, and African-American studies was being incorporated into school curricula. Concepts of "black pride" and "black power" emerged, and "ethnic consciousness" was emphasized (Powell, 1983). In such a climate, it could be predicted that views about self and culture would become more positive. Indeed, many studies in the late 1960s and early 1970s found that children of color—even those who lived in poverty— were found to have self-esteem as high as *or higher than* their Euro-American middle-class peers (Hauser, 1972; M. B. Spencer & Markstrom-Adams, 1990). Some researchers during this period asked children directly about the impact of prejudice (Brigham, 1974; D. T. Campbell, 1976; M. M. Lawrence, 1975; Rosenberg, 1979). Children of color in these studies reported that they were aware of negative attitudes toward their ethnic group in society, but stated that they rejected these biases and held positive views of themselves and their cultures.

How can children who experience prejudice maintain positive views of self? A factor that appears to insulate them from bias and hatred is ethnic pride (McAdoo, 1985; M. B. Spencer & Markstrom-Adams, 1990). Children from historically underrepresented groups who identify proudly with their ethnic heritage and view their communities and families as competent and worthy are more likely to have positive self-esteem (Harrison, 1985). This ethnic pride emerges in the primary years, as children come to understand and appreciate what it means to be African American, Vietnamese, or Native American.

EARLY IDENTITY FORMATION

During childhood and adolescence, children are engaged in **identity formation**— constructing a clear understanding of themselves. According to Erikson (1963), the formation of identity culminates during adolescence, when young people clarify their roles, personal values, characteristics, and competencies. The process of developing an identity involves answering questions such as "Who am I?" "What am I good at?" "What do I believe in?" and "What groups do I belong to?" Many of these questions take a lifetime to answer.

The roots of identity can be traced to a child's early years. Young children come to view themselves as members of a family, as siblings and sons or daughters. Some may see themselves as kindergartners in Public School Number 14 or as members of Ms. Shultz's T-ball team. Piece by piece, the child's picture of self comes into focus. Gender and ethnic identity are two significant self-discoveries that occur during the early years. Children quickly realize that they are boys or girls, and come to understand the behaviors, expectations, and status that accompany each gender. They also come to view themselves as members of an ethnic group. A child in the primary years concludes, for the first time, "I am African American" or "I am Chinese." Some children also discover that they are poor or that their families are better off than others.

Gender Identity

At an early age, children begin to acquire a **gender identity**—that is, they view themselves as boys or girls (Maccoby & Jacklin, 1990). They describe what it means to be a girl or boy, using physical characteristics to define maleness or femaleness (Martin, 1993). Primary-age children come to understand that gender is not determined just by physical appearance. At this age, they begin to view gender as a set of expectations for behavior. A 6-year-old may announce that "boys are rougher and don't cry" or that "girls are quiet and shy."

Initially, children are concerned with the expectations for their *own* gender (Martin, Wood, & Little, 1990). A 6-year-old girl, for example, may hold detailed views of what it means to be a female in her home or school, but less complete understandings of what it means to be a male. By age 8, children have more elaborate perspectives about the roles and expectations of both genders. Their beliefs become extremely stereotyped during this age. They adhere to rigid rules about the "rightness" or "wrongness" of gender-stereotypic behavior (Katz & Ksansnak, 1994). For example, a primary-age child responds in the following way to a story about a boy playing with dolls: "He should only play with things that boys play with. . . . If he doesn't want to play with dolls, then he's right, but if he does want to play with dolls, then he's double wrong" (Maccoby, 1980, p. 236). Double wrong? It is clear from the quotation that a violation of gender rules is more than a minor infringement of primary-grade protocol. This rigidity is pervasive; even children whose parents have struggled to promote nonstereotyped behavior will show stereotyped views at this age (Maccoby, 1989). Such stereotyped beliefs have been found in children in most societies in the world (B. B. Whiting & Edwards, 1988). The good news is that these views become less extreme during later childhood and adolescence (Bigler & Liben, 1992).

Children of all societies are socialized to behave and think as boys or girls. Parents—particularly fathers—encourage the adoption of gender-appropriate roles (Maccoby, 1989), and both mothers and fathers expect boys to follow more rigid rules of gender behavior than girls (Fagot & Leinbach, 1993).

Ethnic Identity

In the primary years, children also begin to construct an **ethnic identity:** a full understanding and appreciation of behaviors, thinking, values, feelings, and competencies of the ethnic group to which they belong. Research suggests that children who understand they are part of a particular group and hold positive opinions of that group are more likely to have high self-esteem (McAdoo, 1985; Phinney & Tarver, 1988; M. B. Spencer & Markstrom-Adams, 1990). Those with this strong ethnic identity are less likely to be psychologically harmed by the experience of prejudice.

Development of Ethnic Identity. When does an ethnic identity form? As early as 4 years of age, most children can identify their own racial or cultural group. By age 7, many become aware of the distinct cultural groups of peers, teachers, and neighbors (Ballard, 1976; Phinney & Rotheram, 1987). In the early primary years, physical characteristics serve as the basis of racial and cultural distinctions (Aboud, 1987). Children at this age use skin color, eyes, hair texture, and other observable traits to define an ethnic group. Not until 8 years of age are children able to identify subtle cultural differences—say, between Chinese-American and Japanese-American, or Apache and Seminole groups (George & Hoppe, 1979).

At first, children can identify people of their own culture. For example, by age 5 they can often name persons who belong to their own race or cultural background (Aboud, 1988; Aboud & Doyle, 1993). Statements such as "You're like me, 'cause you talk just like I do" are indicators of emerging ethnic affiliation. During the later primary years, children acquire the ability to identify those who are from different cultures. For example, an African-American 7-year-old might touch the hair of a Euro-American peer and say, "You don't have hair like Tawana and me. It's all straight like everybody else's."

At an earlier age, children may have believed that their ethnic or cultural membership could change, but during the primary years they begin to understand that these are constant. For example, one 4-year-old child reported that a peer's dark skin could "just wash off" (Ramsey, 1987), and 5-year-olds reported that Italian Canadians could become Canadian Indians simply by changing their clothing (Aboud, 1988). By the mid-primary years, though children report, "You're Mexican. You'll be Mexican when you're a mother," or "Once you have brown color, it just stays there."

Evaluations of Ethnicity. As children come to understand what it means to be a member of a particular cultural group, they also begin to assign a value to that group. Do most children hold positive views of their ethnic heritage? Research findings are mixed. After reviewing a large number of investigations of African-American children's attitudes toward ethnicity, Aboud (1987) found that in 27% of studies, children showed a preference for their own culture, whereas in 57% they showed no preference. In only 16% of studies that he examined did children indicate a preference for Euro-American cultures.

In other studies, positive ethnic attitudes were found for most, but not all, children. In one series of investigations, for example, Euro-American and African-American children and Native American *boys* were found to value their own cultures very highly (Markstrom, 1987; Markstrom & Mullis, 1986). For Native American girls, however, this was not the case. Native American girls, across tribal groups, appear to be at risk of poor ethnic identity (M. B. Spencer & Markstrom-Adams, 1990). Several investigations have shown that preference for one's own race is strongest among children of Euro-American cultures (Hallinan & Teixeira, 1987; Ramsey & Myers, 1990). This may reflect biases in the media and other institutions toward this dominant cultural group.

Variation in Ethnic Identity. Some children identify strongly with their cultural group. When asked, "Who are you?" they will name cultural affiliation as a significant defining characteristic. The following story depicts the strong ethnic identity of some 8-year-olds:

A third-grade teacher, Ms. Flores, conducts a "sharing time" at the beginning of the school day. The topic of basketball has come up. The final game of the National Basketball Association championship series has been played the evening before. Many children wish to share their opinions about the game.

MS. FLORES: So, does anyone else have anything to share? We've talked about basketball quite a bit. Is there anything else you'd like to discuss?

TONY: They only won 'cause of Michael Jordan.

JOSHUA: Yeah. Michael!

ALONZO:	Michael is a black man. He's black just like me and Raymond. Michael is like . . . (laughs) . . . my father . . .
TONY:	What?
ALONZO:	. . . and my brother . . . and my mother (laughs).
JOSHUA:	(Laughing) Michael's no mother!
MS. FLORES:	(Trying to change the topic) Well. What else happened over the weekend?
ALONZO:	Michael's like me, and you, and you (points to peers), but not Sean, and not you . . .
JOSHUA:	And me.
ALONZO:	No, 'cause he's black. We're black people. You're white. That's different, you know.

The children in this story have a clear and positive view of their ethnicity. They are proud that a sports hero shares their cultural background. Alonzo jokingly makes the case that the basketball star and all others in his ethnic group are related, like family members. His comments are reminiscent of Hale-Benson's (1986) observation that "a strong desire exists among black people to be related to each other" (p. 48). Such self-respecting pronouncements of affiliation are indicators of ethnic identity in the primary years.

Other children do not acquire such well-defined views of their ethnicity. Why? Most psychologists believe ethnic identity is nurtured within the family (Thornton, Chatters, Taylor, & Allen, 1990). Parents or grandparents who are committed to imparting cultural pride will strengthen children's feelings of ethnic affiliation. Parents who believe ethnicity plays a minor role in children's development will not promote a strong cultural identity.

Ethnic Socialization. **Socialization** is the process of imparting the competencies, values, and expectations of society to children. **Ethnic socialization,** then, involves teaching the beliefs, abilities, and roles that are unique to one's own cultural group. When parents teach children that it is important to be truthful, they are contributing to their child's socialization. Parents of all cultural groups will wish to impart this message. Examples of ethnic socialization are sharing stories about one's tribal ancestors or teaching the words to a Moslem prayer. These practices teach information that children need in order to participate in a particular cultural group. A primary goal of ethnic socialization is to inspire a sense of ethnic pride and identity.

Parents of historically under-represented groups face significant challenges in the ethnic socialization of their children. On the one hand, they may wish to teach their sons and daughters the values and competencies that will help them get along in dominant society. On the other hand, they may also want to teach their children the traditions of their own cultural group. There is often a dual goal, then, in ethnic socialization. Parents want their children to retain their cultural heritage and, at the same time, learn the knowledge and abilities of mainstream society. Ultimately, many parents wish their children to become *bicultural:* effective members of two distinct cultural groups (Harrison et al., 1990).

One way parents promote ethnic identity is through ethnic socialization messages: statements that guide children in understanding and valuing the uniqueness of their family's cultural heritage. Researchers have identified several kinds of

TABLE 17-2
Common
Socialization
Messages of
African-American
Parents

Type of Message	Example
Achievement and hard work	"Work hard to get a good education."
Moral virtues	"Respect others. Be honest and fair."
Racial pride	"Never be ashamed of your color."
African-American heritage	"Your ancestors had to cope with the cruelty and injustice of slavery."
Acceptance of racial background	"Accept your color; realize you are black."
Positive self-image	"You're as good as anyone else."
Realities of oppression	"Blacks don't have the opportunities that whites have."
Racial equality	"Recognize all races as equal."

SOURCE: Thornton, Chatters, Taylor, & Allen, 1990.

ethnic socialization messages. In a large survey study, African-American parents were asked to write down the beliefs or ideas they teach to children to help them "to know what it is to be black" (Thornton et al., 1990). The most frequent responses are presented in Table 17-2.

As shown in the table, some socialization messages, such as "Be honest and fair," are commonly adopted by families of all cultural groups. Other messages, such as "Blacks don't have the same opportunities that whites have," relate to racial restrictions and bias in society. Some messages refer to historical traditions and heritage: "Black people had to cope with great adversity in the past." Others focus on promoting ethnic identity and pride, such as "Realize you're black" and "Take pride in yourself." Over time, such messages can instill accurate and positive views of culture.

Some parents, even those from historically under-represented groups, do not impart socialization messages. They may view race or culture as unimportant in child rearing, or may worry about the repercussions of instilling positive ethnic views. Some parents are concerned that their children will become arrogant or disrespectful if they acquire ethnic pride, while others are anxious that children will get into trouble with people of dominant culture or become prejudiced themselves (M. B. Spencer, 1983). A range of family stressors—poverty or drug addiction—can also inhibit ethnic socialization (Thornton et al., 1990). Ogbu (1983) warns that children who do not receive an ethnic education from their families are at risk of poor identity development.

Teachers can support children who are at risk of poor ethnic identity. Providing socialization messages in school will complement efforts in the family. It is worthwhile to teach students that all cultural groups have rich, proud histories and traditions and that members of all groups are competent and honorable. An equally important message in school is that prejudice is an evil which persists in society.

PEER RELATIONSHIPS

Peer relationships change significantly in the primary years, for a variety of reasons. First, children are developing intellectually. As they become less egocentric and more other-oriented, they are better able to "put themselves in the shoes" of others and understand their peers' needs and motivations (McKeough, 1992). Children of this age are quite analytical in choosing playmates. They can assess the traits and emotions of peers and make judgments about which characteristics they like and which they don't (Harter & Whitesell, 1989; P. H. Miller & Aloise, 1989).

As children acquire cognitive and social competence, they can solve social problems independently. They can persuade peers (Trawick-Smith, 1993), enter a play group, and strike up a conversation with a stranger (Putallaz & Wasserman, 1989). When conflicts arise, they can contemplate a range of alternative resolutions (Dodge & Price, 1994). In an argument with a friend, for example, they can decide whether to compromise, give a counterargument, give in, or express anger. These growing social understandings cause peer relationships and interactions to become far more complex.

Primary-age children's peer groups are becoming larger and more important in development. At this age, social contacts with family members begin to decline and peer interactions increase (Feiring & Lewis, 1989; Ladd, 1990). Children rely more and more on peers for companionship, advice, and emotional support (Hartup, 1996).

The Peer Group

Children generally belong to one or more **peer groups** during the primary years. Examples of peer groups are one's classmates in school or the children in one's neighborhood. Primary peer groups are more organized than in the preschool years. Each member of a group has a relatively well defined role, with some children viewed as leaders, others as followers (Trawick-Smith, 1993). Some are well liked, others are not. Larger groups often contain subgroups. Small cliques of children form, and some individuals are ostracized from these. Friendships—pairs of children who are mutually attracted—also exist, as they did in the preschool years. The classroom or neighborhood group, then, contains a complex web of interrelationships. Figure 17-2 illustrates graphically the organization of a primary-age peer group.

Each primary peer group to which a child belongs has its own chemistry. Relationships and group status vary from one group to another, depending on composition. A pair of friends in school may not be so close to one another when playing in a neighborhood peer group (Kupersmidt, Griesler, DeRosier, Patterson, & Davis, 1995). A child who is not well liked in the classroom—due to aggression, for example—may be better liked in a neighborhood group composed of more active or aggressive peers (DeRosier, Gillessen, Coie, & Dodge, 1994).

Peer relationships within a group transform over time. The leadership of a group may shift. Children who are initially well liked may gradually come to be rejected, or friendships may dissolve (Dodge, Coie, Petit, & Price, 1990).

FIGURE 17-2

The structure of a primary-age peer group is illustrated graphically. Children are depicted by circles. The strength of relationships is represented by connecting lines. A single line indicates a positive relationship between children who like and respect one another. Double connecting lines indicate friendships. The dotted lines represents a casual association; separate male and female peer groups usually emerge in the primary years. Circles without connecting lines represent neglected or rejected children.

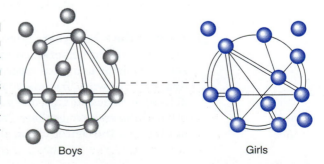

Boys   Girls

Peer Rejection and Reputation

Some children in peer groups are rejected by others. As described in Chapter 13, **peer rejection** is worrisome in preschool; it is even more so in the primary grades. Children who are actively avoided in the elementary grades are likely to exhibit a range of academic and social problems which persist into middle and high school (Parker, Rubin, Price, & DeRosier, 1995).

Reasons for peer rejection in the primary years are more clearly defined than they were in preschool. A 4- or 5-year-old might be shunned because of extreme aggression; "She's mean" might be an explanation a peer gives for avoiding such a child. A 7- or 8-year-old, in contrast, will be avoided for a range of specific behaviors or characteristics. "Spoiled," "bossy," "angry," "fat," "clumsy," and "a tattletale" are terms commonly used to describe why a child is disliked by peers (Rogosch & Newcomb, 1989). Children in the primary years are said to have a "reputation," a detailed collection of traits that determine their peer status (P. Morrison & Masten, 1991).

Negative **peer reputations** take a social and emotional toll. Young children sometimes *become* more and more like what their reputation indicates. A child who has acquired a reputation for being aggressive may become more so, to the point of becoming violent. Another child may become more annoying in school interactions if such behavior is consistent with his reputation among classmates. Sadly, reputations stick with children over time. One study indicates that children's reputations do not become more positive in spite of improvement in their social behaviors (Hetherington, Cox, & Cox, 1979).

Certain clusters of traits are more likely to lead to peer rejection. As in the preschool years, primary-age children who exhibit hostile, aggressive behaviors are more likely to be avoided. Several new causes of rejection also emerge at this age. Some socially withdrawn children, previously overlooked by peers during the preschool years, are now actively rejected (French, 1990). This suggests that shyness and timidity may be less tolerated by primary-age children than by preschoolers (Younger & Daniels, 1992). Children who are regularly victimized by others are also avoided by elementary peer groups (Ladd, Kochenderfer, & Coleman, 1997). These children have been found to exhibit an "anxious vulnerability" which leads to constant assault from bullies. They often acquiesce to the demands of others and cry when attacked. They are often socially anxious and withdrawn.

Neglected Children

Some primary-age children are neglected by their peers. They simply go unnoticed by other children at school or in the neighborhood. As in the preschool years, neglected children tend to be withdrawn (Rubin, Stewart, & Coplan, 1995). The following story depicts a neglected primary-age child:

Early in the school year, a first-grade teacher, Ms. Huels, is conducting a cooperative learning experience in science. Children are to gather in teams and solve problems using balances which she has provided. She encourages her students to join with "friends you'd like to work with." In the midst of a flurry of activity to choose teams, one young child stands alone and quiet. Finally, all the other children have gathered around tables in groups. The quiet child remains standing in the center of the classroom.

MS. HUELS:	(Noticing the quiet child) Uh oh. Have you all forgotten someone?
MANY CHILDREN:	What?
MS. HUELS:	Tyrone doesn't have a group!
MANY CHILDREN:	What?
JAMES:	Tyrone? Who's that?
SABRINA:	(Points to quiet child) It's him.
NICHOLE:	Oh, *that's* Tyrone. (Laughs) I didn't know who it was!
MS. HUELS:	Tyrone needs to join a group.
ARTIS:	He can come here, 'cause he doesn't say anything anyway.
TYRONE:	(Says nothing. Moves over to Artis's group.)

In this story, Tyrone is neglected by his classmates and is not picked as a work partner. In fact, some children do not seem to know his name. A peer announces Tyrone's social reputation with typical primary-grade tact: "he doesn't say anything anyway."

Children may be withdrawn and ignored for different reasons. Children who are reticent show a great interest in the activities of peers but are hesitant to join in. Such children sometimes hover around the fringes of peers' play or work in the classroom and passively watch playground activities. They show interest in peer interactions but lack the confidence to act on their desire for friendship. These children may be at risk emotionally. In one study, reticent children were found to be more anxious than other types of withdrawn children (Coplan, Rubin, Fox, Calkins, & Stewart, 1994).

Other children may be withdrawn because they choose to be. Rather than hover and watch, these children purposely work and play alone (Coplan et al., 1994). Such isolated children do not display the same levels of social anxiety as reticent peers. They may be socially competent, but simply less interested in extensive interaction. This research suggests that being shy, playing alone, and even being ignored by peers do not necessarily lead to negative developmental outcomes. Teachers must give support to reticent children who desire peer contact but lack skills to achieve it. They must also respect a moderate degree of isolated play and shyness as typical.

Friendships

Friendships become more important during the primary years, and children express growing concern about having and keeping friends as they advance through the primary grades (Cassidy & Asher, 1992). Those who have friends are more likely to enjoy school and succeed academically in adolescence (Schneider, Wiener, & Murphy, 1994). Children who do not have friends at this age are more apt to express feelings of loneliness.

An important new role that friendships play is in easing the transition to school (Ladd et al. 1997). Children have been found to use friends as a "secure base" for adjusting to and coping with new school experiences. A child who is starting first grade may be less anxious and more eager to attend if a close friend is in the class.

Teachers can utilize friendships to help new students adjust to their classrooms. They might seat children next to friends from the neighborhood or from preschool in the early weeks of school. They might encourage parents to nurture friendships prior to a new school year by arranging get-togethers at home during the summer. Teachers

Friendships become more exclusive and longer lasting in the primary years.

might give special attention to facilitating at least one friendship for each child in the classroom. Once children have a friend or two, they can more confidently broaden their interactions to other students.

Although children have a growing number of acquaintances in the primary years, the number of true friendships shrinks. By age 8, most children have a small group of true friends. It is not uncommon for girls to have just one best friend during this period (Gilligan, Murphy, & Tappan, 1990).

Friendships are more intimate in the primary years. They provide emotional support and a forum for expressing feelings and disclosing problems (Rottenberg & Sliz, 1988). Children are more demanding of their friends at this age. They change friends less often and suffer greater stress when friends move away or a friendship breaks up (Hartup, 1996). Children are often picky about who their friends are; they select peers who have characteristics they admire. In some cases they choose friends who are like them (Haselager, Hartup, van Lieshout, & Risen-Walraven, 1998), and best friends are often of the same gender, ethnicity, and socioeconomic status.

Peer Relations, Culture, and Class

Does culture or socioeconomic status influence friendships and peer relations in the primary years? Research findings are somewhat mixed. When asked who their friends are, children often name peers from their own ethnic background and sometimes from the same socioeconomic group (Ramsey & Myers, 1990). However, exclusive same-culture friendships and interaction patterns have rarely been observed in primary classrooms. In fact, most studies of multicultural classrooms reveal that cross-ethnic interaction is common (Howes & Wu, 1990; Lederberg, Chapin, Rosenblatt, & Vandell, 1986).

It may be that attitudes vary greatly across individuals in any classroom group. Factors such as previous experience with people of other cultures, family beliefs, and intellectual competence may determine whether ethnicity influences peer relations. Patricia Ramsey (1995) has argued that teachers can facilitate positive attitudes and relationships among children of diverse backgrounds. She proposes that teachers first assess each student's knowledge and attitudes toward culture and class. Then they can plan classroom activities and informal classroom interactions that will support the needs of individual children.

MORAL DEVELOPMENT

Piaget (1932) believed that as young children become less egocentric, they acquire an early sense of morality. They begin to understand and adhere to rules and develop a concern for justice. Most preschool children, he proposed, are *premoral*—they do not adhere to clear rules when making moral decisions or playing games. For example, 4-year-olds playing a marble game might change the rules to better their chances of winning. From Piaget's view, such children should not be considered "bad," since they are not intentionally cheating or being dishonest. They are simply limited in their understanding of rules.

Piaget argued that in the primary years many children exhibit a sense of *moral realism*. At this stage, moral decisions and games are based on fixed rules. In fact, children of this age are quite rule-bound. In a game of marbles, they might now assert, "I don't care if you can't hit any marbles from there. That's where you shoot from. That's the rule." What is right or wrong at this age is determined by unchangeable rules which come from authority figures: parents, other adults, or God.

The final stage of morality—a sense of *moral relativism*—is achieved in adolescence or adulthood, according to Piaget. In this last stage, situations and intentions are taken into account when making moral judgments. When playing a game, a person might agree to bend the rules to assist another who has physical handicaps or to help a younger player win. According to this view, rules are made by people and can be altered for the higher good.

Elaborating on Piaget's stages, Lawrence Kohlberg (1984) identified three levels of **moral development**—*preconventional, conventional,* and *postconventional*—each containing two stages. These are presented in Table 17-3. Kohlberg formulated these levels and stages by presenting special stories to elementary and adolescent children and asking for their response. Each story portrayed a **moral dilemma** such as the following: "A man's wife is dying. Although a drug is available to save her life, it is too expensive for him to afford. In desperation, he steals the medicine."

After describing the dilemma, Kohlberg would ask his subjects, "Was the man wrong to steal the medicine? Why or why not?" The first question was not as important as the second in assessing a subject's moral development, since Kohlberg believed that the *justification* for the moral judgment was more revealing than the judgment itself. One person might say that it is right for the man to steal the medicine because he would not get caught—only a stage 1 answer. Another person might agree that stealing is right because saving a human life is more important than following society's rules—a stage 6 response. The reasoning behind the answer was most critical in evaluating moral development.

TABLE 17-3
Kohlberg's Stages of Moral Development

Levels and Stages	Definitions of Right and Wrong
Level 1: **Preconventional**	**What's right is what you get rewarded for. What's wrong is what you get punished for.**
Stage 1:	What's right is obeying your parents and not getting punished.
Stage 2:	Actions that lead others to like you or reciprocate your kindness are right. The reason for being nice to people is so they will be nice to you.
Level 2: **Conventional**	**Social rules define what's right. Breaking the rules is wrong.**
Stage 3:	What's right is that which pleases others. Actions that others do not approve are wrong.
Stage 4:	What's right is obeying laws that have been set down by those in power in society. What's wrong is breaking society's laws.
Level 3: **Postconventional**	**What's right is determined by higher-order moral principles.**
Stage 5	Rules of society are determined by mutual agreement. Rules that don't work or are destructive may be wrong. Changing the rules can be a morally correct action.
Stage 6	What's right is governed by universal moral principles. Values such as "life is sacred" and "be kind to others" define what is right, not laws created by humans.

SOURCE: Kohlberg, 1984.

Kohlberg found that most elementary-age children respond to moral dilemmas at the preconventional level, at stage 1 or 2 (see Table 17-3). Some adolescents reach the conventional level, at stage 3 or 4. So, Kohlberg believed that relatively little advancement in moral development occurs during childhood.

Critiques of Kohlberg

Although Kohlberg's theory has been supported by an extensive body of research (L. J. Walker, 1984), a number of criticisms, however, have been raised about his work.

Moral Behavior Versus Moral Reasoning. Some believe that Kohlberg's theory does not adequately emphasize the connections between moral thinking and moral behavior (Eisenberg, 1986). Does one necessarily lead to the other? A child who argues that cheating is wrong in a study of moral reasoning might still cheat on a game with peers, and a young gang member who commits drive-by shootings as a desperate effort to belong may still show very advanced levels of moral thinking. Conversely, a toddler who cannot understand moral dilemma stories, much less answer them in sophisticated ways, may nonetheless share a toy with a peer. Moral reasoning and moral action are not the same, and moral actions often do not advance in clearly defined stages, as moral reasoning appears to do. Context, personality, peer relationships, and even biology will affect how children react to real-life moral problems.

Feminist Criticism. Multicultural and feminist scholars have argued that Kohlberg's work reflects the values, social relationships, and interpersonal characteristics of Euro-American males. Gilligan (1982) has suggested that a high rating on Kohlberg's moral dilemma scale requires a male-oriented approach to solving problems. She notes, for example, that male children often present cut-and-dried solutions to moral dilemma stories. They take definitive positions on moral issues, based on rules. Females are more hesitant in offering definitive solutions to these stories. They often refuse to judge rightness and wrongness at all, or seek creative, alternative solutions that are beneficial to everyone involved.

For example, Gilligan found that one girl's response to the dying wife story was to suggest that the man go to a bank for a loan. She offered this solution because she believed that this would help everyone in the story, including the man who owned the drug. Another girl argued that it would be both right and wrong for the man to steal the drug. It would be right to do this to help his wife, she argued, yet it would also be wrong because if the man were to go to jail he would no longer be able to care for his wife. Using traditional research methods, these children might be viewed as lacking moral conviction because of their ambivalence or confusion in solving these problems. Gilligan argues that, to the contrary, a reluctance to take a moral stand may reflect great concern for other people and a need to consider all aspects of a situation fully before making judgments.

Multicultural Criticism. Others have argued that Kohlberg's stages of moral development reflect primarily Western values (Reid, 1984). For example, Kohlberg believed that the most moral arguments are those based on concern for all of humankind. In the dying wife story, a response such as the following would be considered extremely advanced: "The man should steal the medicine, because human life is sacred. It is okay to break rules for the benefit of others."

In some cultural groups, however, concerns about one's own family and community may receive highest priority. Consider the example of a Latino child who lives in a neighborhood in which family and friends have banded together in the face of harsh treatment and racism. The child is taught from a young age to adopt the collective goals of her cultural group. In response to the dying wife story, this child might say, "It's right for the man to steal to save his wife. She is family. She is Puerto Rican. Puerto Rican people stick together." Although Kohlberg might have construed such a justification as self-oriented or less principled, within the child's culture an argument based on the well-being of one's ethnic group might be considered more ethical than one based on the good of all humans (Reid, 1984).

Not surprisingly, then, research has shown variation in the acquisition of moral reasoning across cultures (Nisan, 1987). Although Kohlberg's theory provides a useful framework for observing moral development, variations may be expected across groups and individuals.

SERIOUS EMOTIONAL DISTURBANCE

Typically developing children may exhibit social conflicts with peers or conduct problems in school. Arguments and even physical fights can erupt in primary classrooms. Children may misbehave or disobey teachers and parents. The degree to which such behavior is tolerated varies by culture (B. B. Whiting & Edwards, 1988). In some communities within and outside of the United States, a good deal of misbehavior is accepted. In others, rigid rules of conduct are enforced.

A small number of children are more deeply troubled. They exhibit extreme, negative emotional reactions that go beyond typical misbehavior or peer conflict. They may exhibit disruptive or antisocial behaviors over a long period of time and in many different settings. Sometimes they are very aggressive and, as a result, very challenging to live or work with. At other times they are withdrawn, anxious, and sad. They may regularly complain about physical ailments and avoid going to school (Whelen, 1995). Both types of children—those who outwardly express negative emotions and those who are withdrawn—share a common challenge: they have difficulty entering into satisfying relationships with peers and adults.

Given the variety of emotional and social problems we have described, it is not surprising that professionals cannot agree on a single name for this disorder. Some use the term "social and emotional maladjustment" to categorize children with these challenges. Others adopt the phrase "serious emotional disturbance" to distinguish children whose difficulties are severe enough to require special services in school. This emotional impairment, regardless of its name, is almost always accompanied by poor peer relations (Whelen, 1995).

What causes this **serious emotional disturbance (SED)?** Some believe that children are biologically predisposed to social and emotional problems (Kauffman, 1981). Having a parent or sibling who has suffered an emotional impairment, for example, increases a child's chances of having SED (Cullinan, Epstein, & Lloyd, 1983). Others believe that stressful life experiences cause these problems (Whelen, 1995). Chaotic family lives, abusive parenting, poor attachment, and violence in the community can all contribute to SED.

Classroom Strategies and SED

A number of strategies have been developed to assist children who have SED. A traditional behavior modification approach is often used. In this technique, teachers articulate specific expectations for behavior and then reward children for meeting those expectations. In spite of advancements in special education, behavior modification continues to be the most widely used strategy with children with SED (Knitzer, Steinberg, & Fleisch, 1990; Whelen, 1995). Caution is urged in using this approach. External rewards may impair **intrinsic motivation**—that is, an internal drive to learn or be accepted (Ginsberg & Bronstein, 1993). Furthermore, children of some cultural groups may react less positively to praise (Hitz & Driscoll, 1988).

Other approaches may promote greater self-regulation and intrinsic motivation. In a modified curricular approach, the classroom environment, lessons and activities, and student groupings are altered to reduce stress on children who have SED. Rules for sitting absolutely still or being quiet may be relaxed. Teachers may provide material that is easier for children to read, and projects may be planned that incorporate the personal interests of children with SED. Desks or workstations may be arranged so that children with SED interact with peers who have positive affect or who possess superior social skills. Such changes in the classroom have been found to increase attention to learning tasks by 30% and reduce disruptive behavior by 67% for children with SED (L. Edwards, 1983).

Whelen (1995) proposes a trust-building intervention in which teachers interact with children in ways that build positive relationships. The rationale is that if children who have SED form positive, trusting relationships with adults, they will eventually be able to establish positive peer relations as well. Strategies include *differential acceptance,* in which teachers "receive large doses of hate, aggression, and hostility without reacting in kind to the children who transmit them" (p. 312). Whelen asserts that hostile acts are expressions of pain and anguish caused by years of abuse or family chaos. Responding with anger to such outbursts will only exacerbate children's negative feelings. He recommends firm but non-hostile and non-punitive responses to extreme misbehavior.

ASSESSING YOUNG CHILDREN: Primary-Age Social and Emotional Development

Areas of Development	What to Watch for	Indicators of Atypical Development
Emotional health	Displays a positive view of self across four areas: competence ("I can do it!"), moral self-worth ("I'm a good girl/boy!"), social acceptance ("I have lots of friends!"), and control ("I can do it all by myself!"). Holds positive views of one's family and culture ("I'm glad I'm black!").	Expresses feelings of inferiority ("I can't read like everybody else!"). Stops trying to learn, make friends, or complete tasks independently. Expresses a dislike of one's own ethnicity and a preference for others'.
Relationships with others	Is liked by at least some peers. Forms one or more special friendships. Maintains positive relationships with teachers. Has a positive reputation ("a pretty nice person" or "fun to be with").	Is teased, bullied, or in other ways victimized by peers. Is actively avoided or completely ignored. Has no close friends in school or in the neighborhood. Exhibits hostile aggression toward peers. Shows anxiety and withdrawal.
Specific social skills	Tries alternative solutions to solve social problems. Effectively persuades peers. Compromises and negotiates. Accurately interprets social situations.	Resolves problems with aggression. Chooses to work and play alone. Engages in behaviors that are considered bizarre by peers.

Interpreting Assessment Data: There are cultural differences in social and emotional development. Children of some cultures will evaluate themselves based on their families or cultures. Their self-assessments may be based, for example, on the accomplishments of their parents or community. Some children will base views of self on whether they value their race or ethnic group. Individual achievement may matter less, for example, than having pride in being black or Latino or Asian. Some children will be more or less socially active due to family interactions. Children who have *no* positive relationships with peers may be at risk, however. Those who exhibit extreme aggression or who show great anxiety in social situations may have serious emotional disturbance. Both classroom and family services are required in such cases. Teachers can actively facilitate social skills and peer relationships. Cooperative learning, drama, and outdoor motor play are activities that may promote social development.

In the trust-building strategy, teachers go out of their way to be responsive, warm, and empathic (Whelen, 1995). They show great interest in children's comments or accomplishments, and attempt to understand and ameliorate children's idiosyncratic fears or dislikes. For example, a teacher who notices that a child is anxious about going outdoors during recess might probe for the source of the child's anxiety, rather than expressing intolerance or insisting that the child face the fear. Through conversation the teacher might come to understand that the child fears physical assault from peers. Special accommodations could then be made, such as accompanying the child to the playground for a time or inviting the child and a peer to stay behind in the classroom during recess. The result of the trust-building strategy is that children with SED will bond with the teacher over time. Once this has occurred, the teacher can begin to facilitate peer interactions and friendships.

RESEARCH INTO PRACTICE

CRITICAL CONCEPT 1

The primary years are a period of social and emotional change. As children's cognitive capacity increases at this age, they are able to engage in a great deal more self-reflection. A more accurate and more discerning look at self emerges during this period. Further, children of this age contemplate more fully the meanings of relationships and friendships.

Application #1

Primary-grade classrooms must afford many opportunities for social experience. Children must be able to play, collaborate, and negotiate with peers. Only through authentic social interaction are children able to construct an understanding of the social world and their place within it.

Application #2

Teachers should provide experiences for children to think and talk about themselves and their peers. Group conversations, for example, about individuals' abilities, interests, and unique characteristics will enhance self-reflection. Children's books about the importance of friendship and feelings associated with peer rejection will stimulate thinking about peer relationships.

CRITICAL CONCEPT 2

According to Erikson, emotionally healthy primary-age children acquire a sense of industry or competence—a belief that they are knowledgeable and skilled. Children will enjoy a sense of competence unless they experience harsh evaluation or frequent failure. Children who receive low grades or negative responses from teachers may come to feel inferior.

Application #1

Teachers must provide classroom play and work experiences that lead to true success. Children in the primary years are no longer satisfied with making creative attempts or trying hard; they now seek to master real skills. Activities that challenge their thinking, yet are within their level of ability and lead to real learning, are necessary for children to feel competent.

Application #2

Primary teachers should avoid evaluative symbols. Although grades, stickers, smiling faces, and improvement charts are intended to motivate children, they may have the opposite effect. Evaluative symbols have been linked to poor achievement and negative beliefs about self.

Application #3

Teachers should avoid harsh and public criticism. Classroom interactions should be mainly positive and encouraging. Misbehaviors of individual children should be addressed calmly and privately.

CRITICAL CONCEPT 3

Primary children evaluate themselves in other areas besides competence. They acquire a sense of whether they are accepted by peers, family, and teachers. Some develop an internal locus of control: a feeling that one has the power to regulate one's own life. Others develop an external locus of control: a belief that one is mainly powerless and unable to make a difference. Feelings of moral self-worth—that is, of being a good or bad person—are formed. Hence, children hold many distinct types of self-esteem during the primary years.

Application #1

Teachers should show that they unconditionally care for the children in their classrooms. The following message should be given, even to the most challenging students: "Sometimes I may not care for your behaviors, but I always deeply care about you as a person." By being responsive, showing interest, and being warm, teachers can enhance feelings of acceptance.

Application #2

Teachers should give over to children as much control of the classroom as is possible. Children should be encouraged to solve social or learning problems independently. A group decision-making process can be implemented in which all children in the class participate in selecting projects or topics to study. A group meeting should be held several times a week to air grievances or to raise and solve problems in the classroom. These experiences lead to an internal locus of control in that they help children learn that they have power over their own lives.

Application #3

Teachers should be cautious not to threaten children's feelings of moral self-worth when administering reprimands or other discipline strategies. Statements such as "You are so bad!" are global assaults on self-worth and should be replaced by specific comments about inappropriate behavior, such as "You are so loud and silly that other children can't hear the story." The message should be given that specific behaviors may be unacceptable, but all children are good and honest.

CRITICAL CONCEPT 4

Children of historically under-represented groups may hold slightly different views of themselves. Their self-esteem may be more inclusive in that it is based on pride in their family, ethnic group, and community. Some children may base their self-evaluations on very different criteria than children of the dominant culture. In spite of the experience of prejudice which many children of color face, most acquire positive views of self.

Application #1

Teachers must understand and appreciate cultural diversity in self-evaluation. An inclusive view of self, which is reflected in statements of pride in one's family or community, should be recognized as an important sign of positive self-appraisal in some children.

Application #2

Teachers can redesign typical self-concept activities to accommodate inclusive views of self. Instead of asking children in a group activity to comment on things they do well, teachers might ask, "What are some things that you, your family, or your friends do well?" An activity in which children draw themselves can be modified to allow children to draw their families or neighborhoods. Another useful activity is to ask all children to draw, as a group, a mural of all members of the class.

CRITICAL CONCEPT 5

Group identity is one factor that influences children's views of themselves. Children who understand and are comfortable with their gender are more likely to have positive self-esteem. Those who strongly identify with and are proud of their ethnic heritage are also more likely to hold more positive views of self. Ethnic identity is often a result of ethnic socialization: the conscious effort of parents or other adults to teach children to understand and have pride in their culture.

Application #1

Teachers must create classroom environments in which cultural and gender diversity are celebrated. The first step is to ensure that all children in a class receive the same learning opportunities, encouragements, questions, and contact from the teacher. Teachers can monitor their classroom interactions to make certain that their attention is equitably distributed among all students.

Application #2

The curriculum should reflect an appreciation for all cultures and both genders. Photographs of families of diverse backgrounds should be prevalent. Children's books should be provided which portray competent and likeable characters of both genders and all cultures. The contributions of both male and female scientists, authors, political leaders, and historical figures from all cultural backgrounds should be studied.

Application #3

The unique histories of historically under-represented groups—including experiences of oppression—should be integrated into the curriculum.

CRITICAL CONCEPT 6

Children's peer groups become more complex and organized in the primary years. Popular and less popular children emerge. Friendships are more intimate and more important. Positive peer relationships in the primary years predict later social adjustment and school success.

Application #1

Teachers should provide positive social experiences in the classroom. Sociodramatic play, blocks, outdoor activities, and collaborative projects—which are disappearing in many modern primary classrooms—should be maintained to allow the formation of peer relationships.

Application #2

Teachers should intervene in children's play interactions to support positive peer relations. In particular, they should gently assist rejected or neglected children in entering play groups, getting peers' attention in positive ways, and resolving conflicts.

Application #3

Teachers should facilitate friendships among isolated children. This involves identifying potential friendship pairs and arranging experiences for them to interact in positive ways. Parents can assist by inviting potential friends to visit in their homes.

CRITICAL CONCEPT 7

Children can reflect more competently on moral dilemmas in the primary years. Many base their judgments on whether rules are right or wrong and on a sense of fairness. Cultural and gender variation does exist, however, in how children think about moral problems.

Application #1

Teachers can provide group conversations that encourage children to think about and discuss moral dilemmas. For example, a teacher might tell the classic story of two children who each break a porcelain cup; one of the children does it unintentionally, and the other does it deliberately. The teacher can then ask, "Who is naughtiest?" This activity generates discussions and disagreements and results in advancement in moral reasoning.

Application #2

Teachers can provide group games that allow many real-life discussions about moral dilemmas. Disputes about rules, charges of cheating, and disagreements about who won will contribute to moral development.

Application #3

Teachers should understand and appreciate diversity in moral reasoning. Children may base moral arguments on what's best for family or community, not rules of society as a whole. Other children may not take a stand on moral issues at all, believing that solutions to these dilemmas cannot be so simply decided. Such arguments, which are more common among females and children of historically under-represented groups, reflect advanced forms of reasoning which are not appreciated by traditional measures of moral development.

CRITICAL CONCEPT 8

Some children may suffer serious emotional disturbance (SED) in the primary years, a condition that often leads to peer rejection. A variety of causes and remediation strategies have been proposed. A new strategy for promoting trust and attachment among children with SED has been developed.

Application #1

Teachers must be familiar with and able to identify the characteristics of children with SED. Negative affect, harsh and often aggressive reactions to others, antisocial or withdrawn behavior, and conduct problems in school are common among children with this condition.

Application #2

Teachers, in collaboration with special education personnel, should adapt the classroom to accommodate children with SED. Rules for sitting absolutely still or being quiet may be relaxed. Teachers may provide material that is easier for children to read, and projects may be planned that incorporate personal interests of SED children. Desks or workstations may be arranged so that children with SED interact with peers who have positive affect or who possess superior social skills.

Application #3

Teachers should strive to respond in positive and encouraging ways to children with SED. Patiently accepting a degree of anger and hostility from children with this condition, without responding in kind, may reduce negativism in the classroom.

SUGGESTED ACTIVITIES

1. Interview two boys and two girls of primary age who are of diverse cultural backgrounds. Interviewing each child separately, ask the following self-evaluation questions and write down the child's responses. (These questions are quite sensitive. They should be asked with humor and playfulness, or children may believe they are being evaluated or blamed.)

   a. "What are you good at?" If the child seems confused, change the language of the question, such as "What can you do very well?" After each answer, follow up by asking, "What else do you do well?"

   b. "Name all the people in the world who really like you." After each answer, follow up by asking, "Who else likes you?"

   c. "Let's say there is a new way of reading books called, 'rumpf.' Do you think that if you wanted to be good at rumpf you could be? Why or why not?"

   d. "If you work hard do you always do a good job in school?"

   e. "Are you usually a nice person, a naughty person, or sometimes naughty sometimes nice? Why do you think so?"

   Write a report on children's answers, guided by the following questions:

   a. To what degree did children of different genders and cultures name different areas of competence?

Did girls and boys differ in what they thought they were good at? Did children of different cultural groups vary in the competencies they named?

b. How did children's responses to the "who likes you" question vary? Did some children have longer lists than others? What do you make of this? Did children of different cultural groups vary in the sorts of people they named (e.g., parents, peers, teachers)?

c. Analyze the responses to questions regarding "rumpf" and working hard in school. Were there differences across individuals or groups in the children's answers? What can you conclude about children's feelings of control?

d. What can you conclude from children's comments about being "nice" or "naughty"? Describe variations in children's responses.

2. Interview the same group of children as in activity 1. Again, interview each child separately. Say the following to each child: "People all belong to groups. I belong to a family. I am part of a group of students. I belong to a [name your personal affiliations]. What groups do you belong to?" After each answer, say, "Tell me about that group." Write a report of your observations, guided by the following questions:

a. Which groups did children name? Which were named first? Were any important groups not named?

b. What did children tell you about each group? Did they talk more about some groups than others?

c. How did children of different cultural groups vary in their responses?

d. Did any children name their culture or ethnicity as a group? If so, how would you characterize their cultural descriptions?

3. Observe primary-age children interacting both in a classroom and on the playground. Try to identify rejected and neglected children, as described in this chapter. Also watch for friendships. (Do *not* discuss relationship patterns with the teacher before you observe!) Make careful notes. Later, share your observations with the teacher. Then write a report based on the following questions:

a. How accurate were your speculations about friends and rejected and neglected children? Did the teacher confirm many of your theories? Were you wrong in your categorization of some children or relationships?

b. What evidence did you use to determine friendships?

c. What evidence did you use to identify rejected and neglected children?

d. What recommendations might you give to the teacher for supporting positive peer relationships in this classroom?

4. Present Kohlberg's classic moral dilemma about the dying wife, presented in this chapter, to a boy and a girl of different cultural backgrounds. Write down each child's response to the story and the justifications each child gives for his or her answer. Later, write a report, guided by the following questions:

a. How did the two children differ in their answers to the dilemma? Did they respond at two different levels of moral development (based on Kohlberg's stages)?

b. Did the boy and girl approach the problem differently? Explain. To what degree did you see cultural differences in approaching the problem?

5. In a classroom, observe a child who has been identified as having a serious emotional disturbance. (Such children may be categorized differently in different parts of the country. Sometimes they are labeled "behaviorally disturbed," "emotionally disturbed," or "socially maladjusted.") Take notes on their interactions with peers and teachers. Observe events that precede and follow any disruptive outbursts you observe.

Write a report on your observations, based on the following questions:

a. How would you characterize this child's peer relationships? What behaviors or characteristics appear to help the child interact positively with peers? What behaviors or characteristics seem to inhibit positive peer relations?

b. Did you see evidence that the child had a friend? To what degree was the child accepted by peers (e.g., popular, rejected, ignored)?

c. If there were any outbursts, what events seemed to trigger them? What followed each disruptive event?

d. What unique strategies did the teacher use in working with the child? Did you see examples of the modified curriculum approach or differential acceptance, as described in this chapter?

CHAPTER 18

Parents, Families, and Children: A Multicultural Perspective

A THEME WE HAVE RETURNED TO THROUGHOUT THIS BOOK IS THAT SO-CIAL, PHYSICAL, AND INTELLECTUAL DEVELOPMENT VARY FROM ONE CHILD TO THE NEXT. A major reason for this variation is diversity in parenting and family life. In this chapter, we will review cultural differences in parent-child interactions and family experience.

Families of different cultures adopt unique methods for playing with, carrying, feeding, comforting, educating, and socializing their children, and teachers must understand and appreciate these differences. Interactions with children of one culture may not be appropriate for those of another, as the following vignette reveals:

> An infant care provider, Ms. Tesdal, has just taken a job in a large urban child care center. She has worked in her own family child care home for years and has raised three children of her own. She believes that she really "knows her stuff" when it comes to taking care of babies. She is particularly proud of her ability to soothe babies when they are upset. She can spot the onset of distress and knows many tricks for comforting and distracting children. During her first day of work at the new child care center, however, she begins to doubt her abilities in this area.
>
> She quickly discovers that some infants cannot be consoled through snuggling and physical touch, while for others this is the only technique that works. Her old trick of distracting babies who appear on the verge of upset doesn't seem to work its usual magic. With several of the babies in her center, no amount of animated conversation, jiggling of toys, or other stimulation will dissuade them from crying. One baby, in particular, appears to become even more disturbed by these efforts. Some babies don't cry at all, she finds; they seem resistant to affection, but like to be bounced and played with.
>
> Ms. Tesdal becomes befuddled and frustrated. Nevertheless, she perseveres. Through observation and interviews with parents, she gradually comes to understand how each baby communicates needs and how those needs are best met.

After years of professional experience, this child care provider has learned a valuable new lesson: not all babies interact with adults in the same way. How is it that this lesson escaped her until now? Children in her previous family child care home were of very similar cultural and socioeconomic backgrounds. They were primarily sons and daughters of white middle-class professionals, and their family lives were very much like her own. Her new child care setting includes children of many different cultural and socioeconomic backgrounds. Each baby she now cares for has a different style of communication, a diverse set of needs, and special requirements for having those needs met.

What this caregiver has discovered is that parent-child interactions vary considerably across cultures. Parents of some cultural groups are more likely to console their babies by feeding them. Snuggling, distraction, and other techniques—which she had come to believe were universally effective—are not always a part of some babies' experience. Adult-child interactions are quieter and less active in some cultures. Efforts at stimulation might actually distress these babies further. Infants of some ethnic backgrounds cry very rarely. Their parents may have socialized them to become independent at an earlier age or to express needs less often or less directly.

It is critical for professionals who work with children to understand these diverse patterns of family interaction. Only through a full understanding of parental beliefs, socialization practices, and family relationships can teachers meet the unique needs of individual children.

PARENT BELIEFS ABOUT CHILD DEVELOPMENT

Parent-child interactions are influenced by beliefs about what children are like and how they should be treated at each developmental level (Harrison, Wilson, Pine, Chan, & Buriel, 1990; Okagaki & Frensch, 1998). These beliefs may come from personal experience; often they reflect the values of one's own family. For example, parents who grew up in families that view infants as fragile and vulnerable might be especially protective and nurturing, whereas parents whose families consider babies to be tough and self-reliant might be less so. Parents who were raised to believe that preschool children are old enough to assume household responsibilities are likely to assign chores or child care duties at a very early age. In contrast, those who grew up in homes where the early years were viewed as a carefree time for unrestricted play are likely to have very different expectations for their young children.

Family beliefs vary from one culture to another. Diversity in beliefs about children can be traced to the unique histories and worldviews of individual cultural groups (Garcia Coll, 1990). One factor that has shaped the beliefs of some cultural groups is adversity. Families who have faced prejudice and scarce resources hold beliefs about children that are very different from the beliefs of families in the dominant culture.

Poverty and Beliefs About Children

As we have underlined throughout this book, poverty poses a significant threat to healthy child development. In the face of scarce resources, families make adaptations in their lives. Often beliefs about children shift as parents struggle to meet basic needs.

Poverty and Beliefs About Infants. Levine (1977) has proposed that parents who have scarce resources or live in settings where infant mortality is high will hold very

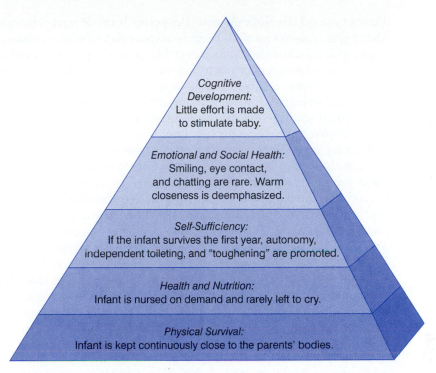

*Cognitive
Development:*
Little effort is made
to stimulate baby.

Emotional and Social Health:
Smiling, eye contact,
and chatting are rare. Warm
closeness is deemphasized.

Self-Sufficiency:
If the infant survives the first year, autonomy,
independent toileting, and "toughening" are promoted.

Health and Nutrition:
Infant is nursed on demand and rarely left to cry.

Physical Survival:
Infant is kept continuously close to the parents' bodies.

FIGURE 18-1 Parents in communities with an infant mortality rate as high as 60% emphasize different goals in child rearing. They show much greater concern for addressing physical survival and health needs, as indicated by the pyramid's broad base. Concerns about children's cognitive development are minimal, as indicated by the pyramid's narrow tip.
SOURCE: Extrapolated from data in Levine, 1977

different beliefs about how babies should be treated. His model of caregiving in high-risk communities is presented in Figure 18-1.

In a study of parents in impoverished African villages, Levine discovered unique beliefs about child rearing. Parents in these communities held physical survival and health as the primary goals of infant care, while intellectual stimulation was considered relatively unimportant. These beliefs, Levine notes, lead to distinct caretaking practices. Breastfeeding or quick attention to crying were common, but teaching interactions were rare. Levine found that these parents also emphasized self-sufficiency. They would attempt to wean children or teach them to walk at an early age.

Garcia Coll (1990) and Hale-Benson (1986) have described similar parenting patterns in low-income African-American families in the United States. Levine concludes that parents in poor communities wish to protect and nurture their children, on the one hand, but help them to become independent, on the other. The message such parents convey to an infant is: "I will do all I can to help get you started in life, but soon you will need to get along on your own."

Other cultural groups in America adopt very different beliefs in the face of poverty. Low-income Mexican-American parents have been found to favor dependence and attachment over self-sufficiency in their child rearing. (Garcia Coll, 1990). These families stress helping children to learn how to get help from others and to rely on family and friends. Poverty influences parental beliefs about infants in a variety of ways, then, depending on cultural values and traditions.

Poverty and Beliefs About Preschoolers. Poverty influences parents' views about preschoolers as well. In some impoverished communities, parents believe that young children should be encouraged to grow up quickly, stand on their own two feet, and contribute immediately to the economic well-being of the family. In some third-world villages, preschoolers as young as age 4 or 5 are assigned child care responsibilities, allowing parents to work outside the home (B. B. Whiting & Edwards, 1988). Children of this age are often expected to tend livestock, weed the garden, and stay on their own for long periods of time.

Poverty may lead to greater expectations for mature behavior. At a very early age, preschoolers may be expected to meet their own personal needs, such as toileting, meal preparation, and personal hygiene. For example, Hale-Benson (1986) has observed that African-American mothers and grandmothers of low socioeconomic status are less tolerant of toileting "accidents" than are middle-class Euro-American parents. Parents in Kariobangi, Kenya, have been found to expect mature behavior and absolute obedience from their preschoolers, particularly boys (B. B. Whiting & Edwards, 1988). The rate of compliance among these young children was discovered to be almost twice as high as that for children living in the United States.

Although some of these parenting practices seem harsh and restrictive, they often stem from concern for the child and the family in the face of brutal economic hardship. Such practices are intended to transform immature preschoolers into self-reliant children who can contribute to the survival of the family.

Poverty and Beliefs About Primary Children. Parental beliefs about primary-aged children are also influenced by experiences of poverty. Expectations for mature behavior and grown-up contributions to family survival may become even greater during this period. Parents who believe that educational attainment is a means to economic well-being and upward mobility may hold high academic ambitions for their children at this age (Okagaki & Frensch, 1998). Hale-Benson (1986), for example, has described African-American families as extremely achievement oriented. Some parents of this cultural group socialize their children to believe that achievement is a way to prosperity, not only for oneself, but for the whole family.

Latino parents have also been found to place great emphasis on learning, performing well on tests in school, and completing homework as means of escaping poverty (C. Chen & Stevenson, 1989). Likewise, Japanese-American and Chinese-American families show positive dispositions toward schoolwork and urge their children to succeed (Okagaki & Frensch, 1998). This achievement orientation stems, in part, from the experience of poverty and a drive to better one's family circumstances.

Oppression and Beliefs About Children

The experience of oppression explains some of the cultural diversity in family life and child rearing (Ogbu, 1992). Ethnic groups which have suffered prejudice, community violence, and even slavery over many generations will adopt unique beliefs about children.

Oppression and Beliefs About Infants. Oppression influences beliefs about how babies are cared for. In families who believe that infants should be "toughened" in preparation for the harsh realities of prejudice, early autonomy and boldness might be major goals. Another family might feel that babies should be taught to seek refuge from racism within the family. In this instance, a caregiving goal might be to create strong family bonds.

Many Puerto Rican parents, as an example, believe that family interdependence and banding together with close friends is the way to survive in the face of prejudice. A typical socialization goal in Puerto Rican families is **enmeshment**—the ability to cooperate with and rely on others. This goal is evident in parent-infant interactions: Puerto Rican mothers have been found to be particularly indulgent in feeding and nurturing babies (Slonim, 1991). In infant care, these families emphasize attachment rather than separation from the family (Garcia Coll, 1990).

As mentioned earlier, oppression has caused many African-American parents to adopt goals of early self-sufficiency and achievement. They more often seek to achieve weaning and toileting at an early age (Bartz & Levine, 1978) and are more likely to believe it appropriate to delay responses to infant cries (P. S. Zeskind, 1983). Their desire is to raise strong individuals who can stand up to the challenges of a biased world.

Oppression and Beliefs About Preschoolers.

Families of historically oppressed groups may hold distinct views about how preschoolers should be raised. In some cultures, children of this age are socialized to stand up to those who would oppress them, to fight back when assailed. For example, in some families it is a goal to teach young children how to defend themselves physically. In one study, African-American mothers and grandmothers were found to be more likely to urge their children to fight back than their Euro-American counterparts (Hale-Benson, 1986). In fact, for these parents and grandparents, the failure to retaliate for an offense could lead to a harsh reprimand or a spanking. These views are in sharp contrast to the dominant society's perspective that childhood aggression is wrong and should be discouraged.

It is easy to see how such family beliefs may clash with typical school regulations against fighting. As a practicing teacher, I have experienced more than one challenging discussion with an angry parent about a "no hitting" rule in the classroom. For some families, fighting back is a way of defending against prejudice, and failing to retaliate is seen as a sign of weakness and results in a loss of dignity.

Other cultural groups socialize their preschoolers to be extremely polite and obedient in order that they might be assimilated into an inhospitable world. Such families emphasize compliance rather than fighting back or speaking one's mind. Mexican-American parents, for example, have been found to emphasize conformity, obedience, and "proper demeanor in public" and to discourage autonomy and self-assertion (Harwood, Miller, & Irizarry, 1995; Knight, Virdin, & Roosa, 1994). Chinese-American parents also have been found to value compliance within the dominant culture (S. A. Miller, 1995). An orientation toward fitting in and "making good" within the dominant society is an effective adaptive strategy which some families use in the face of mistreatment and racial animosity.

Oppression and Beliefs About Primary Children.

Parents' beliefs about primary children are influenced by oppression, as well. This developmental period is a formative one for acquiring a positive view of self, so young children who are confronted with racism in their schools and communities may be at risk. Parents of some families, then, adopt unique socialization goals aimed at offsetting the negative effects of prejudice. Some African-American parents, for example, emphasize racial pride, an understanding of cultural heritage, and the grim realities of racism (Thornton, Chatters, Taylor, & Allen, 1990). Socialization messages such as "You are black and as good as anyone else" predominate in adult-child interactions in this culture.

Parenting Beliefs and Professional Practice

Parenting beliefs arise from unique personal and cultural experiences. These beliefs, which represent the thinking of generations of parents within a particular group, are usually logical and contribute to positive development. They are sometimes misunderstood, however, by those of other cultures. In most cases, it should not be the goal of professionals to change what parents believe. The following story illustrates the difficulties that can arise from an attempt to do so:

Mr. Danforth, a professional in an early intervention program makes regular home visits to low-income parents with infants and preschoolers. His goal is to support families and teach positive parenting skills in order to offset some of the negative effects of poverty. He is facing a challenge from one particular mother, Ms. Gordon, who seems resistant to his parenting suggestions. She does not follow up on his recommendations for playing with her two young children. She continues to swat her toddler on the hand when he touches things he should not. Mr. Danforth decides to address the problem directly at his next visit.

MR. DANFORTH:	I need to talk with you about playing more with your children. Remember, we talked about some games you might play? Have you used any of the toys I left?
MS. GORDON:	(Looks down. Says nothing.)
MR. DANFORTH:	I want to help you teach your children things. If you play these games, they will learn and be ready for school.
MS. GORDON:	(Remains silent)
MR. DANFORTH:	I think if you tried using some of these toys, your children wouldn't get into your other things. You wouldn't have to spank hands anymore.
MS. GORDON:	(No response)
MR. DANFORTH:	What I mean is, when one of your children gets into something, touches something breakable, you could redirect him to toys he could play with. You could say, "Don't touch that. These are your toys over here." What do you think?
MS. GORDON:	(In a very angry tone, tears forming in her eyes) You don't know what's good for my children. I'm their mother, not you!
MR. DANFORTH:	(Looks startled) Well . . .
MS. GORDON:	(Begins to cry) There's a little boy was killed down the street there. (Points out the window) Got shot. What about that?
MR. DANFORTH:	(Remains silent)
MS. GORDON:	I haven't got enough food to eat. There's shooting going on. I just want my children to get by. Want them to live to be grown up. Do you get that?
MR. DANFORTH:	Yes . . .
MS. GORDON:	You're talking about playing and all. I teach my children to survive. Giving them a swat now and then is how I keep them out of trouble. I'm their mother, not you!

Ms. Gordon talks on for many more minutes. While driving to his office after this exchange, Mr. Danforth thinks hard about this parent's message. He comes to see that his approach has been misguided. On a return visit several weeks later, he abandons for now his attempts to teach specific parenting skills. Instead, he focuses on helping Ms. Gordon find additional resources to feed her family.

The home visitor in this story has attempted to impose his own values about child care on a parent of a very different culture and life experience. He misinterprets this mother's disinterest in playing with her children as a lack of concern or knowledge about them. He expects that he can convince her to believe, as he does, that cognitive stimulation and freedom to play are important to children. But these are goals and competencies valued in his world, not hers. It is only when she confronts him with the realities of her life that he comes to see the error of his ways. She behaves as she does for a reason. Learning games seems less important to her than keeping her children out of harm's way in a dangerous neighborhood. Firm discipline may be the only way to ensure the safety of a child who lives in a community filled with violence and racism.

ADULT-CHILD INTERACTIONS

Due to differences in child-rearing beliefs, parents adopt different ways of interacting with their children. Interactions vary across cultural groups in four major ways: communication, responses to crying, teaching, and carrying and holding. These are summarized in Table 18-1.

TABLE 18-1

Cultural Universals and Variations in Parent-Child Interactions

Parenting Interactions	Universals	Variations
Communicating	All parents communicate in some way with their children.	Parents of some cultures use much verbal communication with their children. Others more often communicate through gestures, facial expressions, and physical touch.
Responses to crying	All parents respond in some way to children's crying.	Parents of some cultural groups show distress when their children cry and respond quickly. Others are less concerned by cries and take longer to react. Some use cuddling and feeding as a response; others use a pacifier or physical stimulation.
Teaching	All parents are concerned about the education of their children.	Parents of some cultures believe that teaching is an important part of the parental role. In other cultures, parents believe teachers in school should assume this responsibility.
Carrying and holding	All parents hold and carry their young children.	Some children are bound in slings or cradleboards for much of the day. Others are held in a parent's or grandparent's arms. Some children are held infrequently and move about freely in the home or neighborhood.

Parent Communication

Some characteristics of communication with children are universal (Fernald & Morikawa, 1993). For example, parents in all cultures use exaggerated intonations and unique words and sentences when speaking to their sons and daughters. Such "parentese" includes high-pitched vocalizations and simple sentence structure (Nwokah & Fogel, 1990). Parents of all cultures tend to comment on concrete objects, using many nouns, when they talk to their young children (Markman, 1992). Why do parents around the world do this? Babies, toddlers, and preschoolers are more attentive and smile more frequently when they are spoken to in these ways (Fernald, 1993). Parents of all cultures seem to have an intuitive ability to adapt their speech to children's desires and developmental levels.

There are many cultural differences in adult-to-child language, as well. One example is frequency of verbalization. Some families are very talkative, others quiet. Talkativeness and silence mean very different things in different cultural groups (Irujo, 1988). English-speaking Euro-American parents tend to use lots of language with children. Talkativeness in child-adult interaction has also been observed within Cuban-American and Puerto Rican families (Field & Widmayer, 1981).

In contrast, some Mexican-American, African-American, and Native American parents have been found to be less talkative with children (Zepeda, 1986). Navajo and Hopi parents have been described as particularly quiet (Chisholm, 1983). There are several explanations for why these groups have adopted less verbal interaction patterns. Children of some families may have more passive and less verbal temperaments. Navajo infants and preschoolers, for example, have been found to be timid and quiet. A passive, nonverbal parenting style might be a "good fit" for such children (Garcia Coll, 1990). Also, silence is viewed as a sign of respect in some cul-

Parents in all cultures speak to their children in "parentese"—a simpler form of communication that promotes language development.

tures, and quiet interchanges with children may be an early attempt to impart this concept (Menyuk & Menyuk, 1988).

Quietness within these cultural groups does not mean that there is no communication. Less verbal Hopi mothers communicate quite frequently in nonverbal ways. They may talk less but hold, rub, or bounce young children more (Callaghan, 1981). Nsamenang (1992) provides an example of nonverbal communication in his description of the "gifts-giving game" that West African parents play with their toddlers. In this game, an adult offers a child a toy and then entices the toddler to give it back. As the object is passed back and forth, the adult and child are having a kind of conversation that involves turntaking and rules.

Hale-Benson (1986) has observed a high frequency of physical touch and nonverbal communication between African-American mothers and their children. She proposes that, because of this parenting style, children of this cultural group are particularly proficient in communicating with body movements, expressions, and gestures.

Since Euro-American parents are very verbal in their interactions with children, some teachers have come to conclude that frequent speech is desirable. In fact, programs were developed in the 1960s to "bombard" young children with language and to increase parent language use in the home (E. E. Evans, 1975). Such programs were misguided and did not appreciate diversity of language patterns within families. Further, research suggests that the frequency of verbalization is not related to language ability (Greenbaum & Landau, 1977). Children in quieter cultures still become proficient at language and communication.

Responses to Crying

Crying is the way infants and young children communicate needs, and parents' responses to crying will influence their children's emotional and intellectual development. Parents of different cultures vary in the ways they respond to children's upset. Euro-American mothers have been found to vary considerably in how quickly they respond when their babies cry (Palmer, 1991). Some wait a very long time to respond to infant upset, while others pick up their babies the moment crying begins.

African-American mothers and Cuban-American mothers, in contrast, have been found to more consistently "wait and see" when crying occurs (P. S. Zeskind, 1983). Their response time is generally slower than that of many Euro-American parents. These parents may delay their responses in order to ascertain why their children are crying. An overriding concern among these parents is to give just the right amount of attention, so that children will be neither "spoiled" nor neglected (Garcia Coll, 1990).

In some hunter-gatherer societies in Africa, mothers have been found to respond immediately to even the slightest infant whimper (Levine, 1977; B. B. Whiting & Edwards, 1988). In some cases, these mothers carry their babies throughout the day and sleep with them at night. In these communities, babies were found to virtually never cry!

The methods mothers use to soothe crying children also vary across cultures. African-American parents have been found to prefer using a pacifier or physical stimulation in response to crying, while Euro-American parents more often use physical touch, holding, and breastfeeding (P. S. Zeskind, 1983). Cuban-American mothers were found to use a combination of both a pacifier and cuddling, depending on the circumstances.

Why is there such variation across cultures in responding to cries? It may be that the meaning of crying varies from one cultural group to another. In some populations, crying is viewed as a distress signal and an expression of need. Parents may see their response, then, as an opportunity to nurture attachment and feelings of security. Euro-American mothers, for example, report that infant cries are distressing, arousing, and "sick sounding." Crying induces them to take immediate action (P. S. Zeskind, 1983).

In other groups, cries are not viewed with such urgency and anxiety. Crying is interpreted as a way of expressing a variety of messages, some of which may require a quick response, others not. For example, when crying is perceived as merely a demand for adult attention, parents might be more cautious about responding too quickly. African-American parents report less distress and feelings of urgency when hearing infant cries, and express concern about giving cries too much attention (Garcia Coll, 1990).

Although parents' responses to crying vary, parents of all cultural groups respond in some way to child upset. That babies of all cultures become attached and secure suggests that there is not one correct way to respond to crying.

Teaching Behaviors

Parents vary significantly in the ways they attempt to teach their children (Okagaki & Frensch, 1998). Some parents label objects for their infants and preschoolers children and pose problems and challenges. Others provide educational toys and physical stimulation. Some parents become involved in their children's homework in the primary years. Other parents are less likely to engage in these kinds of activities.

Why is there such variation? In some cultural groups, teaching has been historically valued as a critical component of parenting. Chinese-American mothers, for example, more often report that teaching is primarily the responsibility of the family and parents (M. S. Steward & Steward, 1974). Not surprisingly, mothers of this culture have been observed to be very active in instructing children and providing positive feedback on learning tasks. Jewish-American families also place great value on learning. From the earliest days of life, many Jewish children are provided cognitive stimulation with the goal of enhancing later academic achievement (Farber, Mindel, & Lazerwitz, 1988).

In other cultures, parents are more likely to view teaching as the responsibility of teachers and schools. Euro-American and Mexican-American mothers, for example, have been found to view instruction as only one small part of the parental role (M. S. Steward & Steward, 1974). Teaching activities are not as predominant in interactions with children within these cultures. It is important to note that parents of these cultural groups do value learning. They simply assign the primary teaching role to others—particularly, trained educators within schools.

It is also important to understand that parents of different cultures teach children in different ways. Instruction by Mexican-American mothers, for example, has been found to be more physical; less verbalization and praising are used (Laosa, 1980). In Euro-American families language is more often a part of teaching interactions. No evidence suggests that a nonverbal style of teaching is any less effective than verbal strategies (Garcia Coll, 1990).

Carrying and Holding Practices

Some children are carried around in a parent's arms all day long for the first 6 months of life. Others are rarely held. Still others spend the day in a sling on a parent's back. It is no wonder that babies and even older children have different preferences in how

TABLE 18-2
Variations in Carrying and Holding Practices

Carrying and Holding Method	Description
Arm carrying	Babies are held in the parents' arms, either close to the body or balanced on a hip.
Lap holding	Babies are held in a sitting position in an adult's lap.
Carrying device	Babies are strapped to the front or back of an adult's body by a sling, "snugglie," or backpack.
Swaddling	Babies are wrapped tightly in blankets or sheets, so the arms and legs are held fast.
Cradleboard	Babies are swaddled, as above, and strapped onto a board in an upright position.
Infrequent carrying	Babies are rarely carried, at all, but lie freely in a crib or crawl about.

they are handled by adults. Table 18-2 presents several distinct dimensions of carrying and holding which can differ from one cultural group to another.

Cultural diversity in methods of holding babies has "inspired many misconceptions, stereotypes, and simplistic theories" (Chisholm, 1983, p. 71). For example, carrying practices in which infants are swaddled or bound have often been viewed as detrimental to children's development, and parents using these methods are sometimes portrayed as misguided or neglectful. Likewise, parents who seldom carry their babies are sometimes viewed as negligent. In fact, carrying and holding methods are a function of cultural norms, the practical demands of work and family life, and the temperament of infants themselves.

In America, babies of many cultures are carried in parents' arms. Backpacks and slings are sometimes used for short periods to travel from one place to another. Commonly, infants are cradled or held in a parent's arms close to the chest, balanced on one hip, or bounced or rocked on a knee or lap (Hale-Benson, 1986; B. B. Whiting & Edwards, 1988). Variation exists among ethnic families in America in how often children are carried and the age at which children cease to be carried. African-American babies are held more often during the day and are carried until later in life than Euro-American infants (Hale-Benson, 1986). Mexican-American parents, in contrast, tend to pick up their babies less often than other cultural groups.

In some cultures, devices are used to carry or hold infants for extended periods. Some Hopi and Navajo infants are held through the day on cradleboards. Infants are swaddled on these boards, so that they are unable to move easily any body part but their heads. Although concerns have often been raised about cradleboards, research has shown that this practice has little negative impact on children's physical development (Dennis & Dennis, 1940). Further, although parent-child interchanges are diminished when infants are on the board, rich, full interactions have been found to resume at the end of the day when they are removed (Chisholm, 1983). It has been observed that some Navajo infants have become so attached to cradleboards that they actually cry to be strapped onto them (Konner, 1991)! It would appear that this practice—so often criticized by Western child specialists—is actually comforting and leads to a sense of security.

In societies that have a high mortality rate, babies are more likely to be strapped against their parents' bodies in slings or packs. In families in urban Zambia, for example, babies are carried about in slings on their mothers' backs for much of the day during the first year of life. Most parents gradually reduce the time their children are held in these slings. By age 1, babies are carried far less. Research shows that children who are carried often in slings during the first 6 months of life are actually advanced in development (Goldberg, 1977). These findings challenge the belief that all children must be able to move about freely to grow properly.

How do carrying practices affect teacher-child interactions in school? Some students will seek warm physical contact with peers and teachers. Others, however, will feel less comfortable with physical touch and holding. Professionals can adopt nonphysical methods of showing warmth and caring toward such students.

EXTENDED FAMILIES: GRANDPARENTS, SIBLINGS, FRIENDS, AND FATHERS

A prevalent image in the media is that the "typical" American family consists of children and two parents. In this mythological family, the father goes off to work during the day and the mother remains at home, caring for the children. Such a family structure is becoming rare in modern society. Only 40% of children born in recent years will live with both mother and father until they are 18 (D. Hernandez, 1993). Thirty percent of American children are born to single parents, and in more than half of two-parent families, both parents work outside the home (T. L. Parcel & Menaghan, 1994). The **extended family,** in which parents, grandparents, other relatives, and even friends live together, is growing more and more common (U.S. Bureau of the Census, 1998). The following vignette illustrates the importance of one such arrangement:

A director of a child care center has just enrolled a 6-month-old, Hannah, in his infant program. He meets the baby's young mother only briefly and is struck by her youth. Later he learns that she is only 15 years old. Although the infant seems to be healthy, secure, and developing in a positive way, the director feels that special support needs to be provided for this young mother. He invites her to a meeting to discuss ways he might assist her and to recommend a parent education program.

His meeting with the mother is unsatisfying. She is very quiet and does not establish eye contact. She answers his questions by nodding "yes" or "no." He is dismayed by how little she seems to know about babies. After half an hour, they set up a time to meet again. After this interchange, the director can't help but wonder how Hannah has turned out so well.

The young mother brings her own mother—the baby's grandmother—to the second meeting. The director learns that the three of them all live together in a small apartment. The conversation that follows is markedly different from the first:

DIRECTOR:	(Talking to both the mother and grandmother) Do you play a lot with Hannah? Do you have toys for her to play with?
MOTHER:	(Looks down. Does not answer.)
GRANDMOTHER:	(To the young mother, laughing) Tell him what we do with little Hannah. How we play.
MOTHER:	(Looks only at the grandmother) We don't have too many toys.
GRANDMOTHER:	(Laughing) But we play lots of games. Tell him about "playing faces." That's a game we play. (Looking at the director) My momma played it even with me when I was small. Tell him about that.
MOTHER:	(Still doesn't look at the director) We let little Hannah touch our faces or pull our hair. Then we touch her face. It's like a game.
GRANDMOTHER:	Oh, that little baby will smile and laugh when we play! We say, "Touch your grandma, touch your mama." And then she touches our eyes and gets her little fingers in our hair. And we touch her right back. I tell my daughter, "You have to talk and touch your baby, so she'll get to know you."

As the conversation continues, the director comes to understand why this infant is so secure and healthy. The grandmother is experienced and confident. She has raised her own children and knows how to care for infants. She has clearly been assisting her daughter in learning to become a parent. By the end of this meeting, in fact, the director no longer feels the need to urge this teen mother to take parenting courses. She could get no better instruction, he decides, than from her own mother right at home!

As this story shows, professionals sometimes forget that children come from families of diverse configurations. The director in the story at first assumed that the teenage mother was the sole and primary caregiver of her child. It is only when he meets the grandmother that he understands fully the child-rearing dynamic within this home. He now knows that raising Hannah is a collaboration between the mother and grandmother. He has learned that family support services must include all significant adults in a child's life.

Although many different persons care for children within modern families, parenting research still focuses almost exclusively on mothers. Figure 18-2 presents a new, more inclusive definition of the American family.

Family structure varies by culture and socioeconomic status. A high percentage of children of color and poor children are born to single mothers (Children's Defense Fund, 1998). For example, over half of African-American children live in single-parent households, and only 40% under age 3 live with both parents. A similar pattern is found in Puerto Rican families: 44% of families of this ethnic group are headed by a single parent. Garcia Coll (1990) points out, however, that "so-called single-headed households" are often not this at all. Although a father or mother may not live with a particular family, other non-parent adults do. These individuals—grandparents, other relatives, older siblings, or friends—perform significant family roles, including child caregiving.

Extended families are more common in some ethnic groups. Family extendedness is one way that families of color cope with challenging circumstances (Garcia Coll,

FIGURE 18-2
A new conceptualization of the family: children are cared for by a network of relatives and friends, not just parents. In many cultural groups, significant caregiving responsibilities are shared among non-parents.

1990). African-American, Puerto Rican, Japanese-American, Mexican-American, and Native American families—to name just a few groups—have historically lived in extended families (Lee, Burkham, Zimles, & Ladewski, 1994).

Because children of so many ethnic groups live in extended families, professionals who care for young children must consider the influence of many different family and non-family adults in children's lives. To gain a multicultural perspective on child care, it is necessary to understand the unique roles of such significant persons as grandparents, siblings, friends, and fathers (including those who live outside of the home).

Grandparents

In traditionally under-represented ethnic groups, grandparents are more likely to be directly involved in child-rearing duties (Furstenberg & Cherlin, 1991). For example, African-American grandmothers have been found to be significantly more active in their relationships with their grandchildren than Euro-American grandparents (Pearson, Hunter, Ensminger, & Kellam, 1990). Having a grandmother living in the home appears to be advantageous for young children of color—particularly those in single-parent families. In one study, African-American children who lived with their single mothers and grandmothers were found to be socially better adjusted than children who lived only with their single mothers (Kellam, Ensminger, & Turner, 1977). In fact, children in single-mother/grandmother families showed the same positive development as those raised in traditional mother-father homes.

Grandmothers play several key roles in children's lives. They provide an extra pair of hands in caretaking and other family duties. This is particularly important in families with teenage mothers. Grandmothers provide respite so that their daughters can enjoy some semblance of adolescence, finish school, or pursue career goals (Garcia Coll, Hoffman, & Oh, 1987). Grandmothers also teach parenting skills and provide knowledge about child development to their daughters. In one study, for example, young African-American mothers were found to be more knowledgeable about infant care if their own mothers were involved in caretaking (Stevens, 1984). One way that grandmothers teach their daughters parenting skills is through modeling. African-American grandmothers have been found to be more responsive and less harsh in their discipline strategies than their teenage daughters (Stevens & Duffield, 1986).

An important implication for caregivers is that grandmothers play a role almost equivalent in importance to that of parents within some families. It is critical to include all adults with caregiving responsibilities in parent education programs, parent conferences, and all other means of communication with families.

In many families, grandparents serve as primary caregivers for children.

Siblings

Families from traditionally under-represented groups in the United States generally include larger numbers of children than Caucasian families (Ventura, 1987). Not surprisingly, then, young children of these families are more often played with and cared for by older siblings. In many Puerto Rican, Mexican-American, and African-American households, for example, older siblings are assigned specific child-rearing responsibilities (Hale-Benson, 1986; Sanchez-Ayendez, 1988). This occurs within cultures outside of the United States, as well. In fact, B. B. Whiting and Edwards (1988) report that children living in India, Okinawa, the Philippines, Mexico, and Kenya are more likely to be cared for by older siblings than are children living in suburban America.

Siblings may play a greater role in some families due to scarce resources. Like grandmothers, a teenage brother or sister can lend an extra pair of hands in order to allow a parent to pursue a career or attend to other household duties. Siblings are most involved with younger children in large families. The larger the family, the more likely an older brother or sister is to be assigned direct disciplinary or supervisory responsibilities (Cicirelli, 1982). Across cultures, it appears that girls are more likely to be assigned caretaking roles than boys (B. B. Whiting & Edwards, 1988).

What impact does sibling caretaking have on child development? Older brothers or sisters promote the social development of their siblings (Dunn & McGuire, 1992). This may be because these older siblings are very playful—perhaps more so than parents, who may be struggling with family stressors. Siblings also contribute to ethnic socialization—that is, they teach their younger brothers and sisters the roles and competencies that are important in their particular culture (Slonim, 1991). Siblings also teach younger children new words and concepts (G. H. Brody, Stoneman, & McKinnon, 1982). It is not uncommon for an older sister or brother to label objects, provide toys, and stimulate cognitive development. This teaching role becomes even more pronounced as children get older.

In spite of the fact that in some ethnic groups older siblings assume major child-rearing responsibility, brothers and sisters are rarely included in parenting programs or parent conferences in child care. Professionals might create innovative activities that involve older siblings to a greater extent in early education classrooms.

Friends Who Are Like Family

It is not uncommon for children of historically under-represented groups to have primary caregivers who are non-family members. Describing the phenomenon of strong friendship bonding within the African-American community, Hale-Benson (1986) notes that this bonding leads to shared child rearing. In African-American communities a system of informal adoption has sometimes evolved in which neighbors or friends care for children outside their own family.

A similar pattern of caregiving has been observed in some Native American cultures (Red Horse, 1983). Non-related adults who are of the same culture and community are often invited to join families and to share child care responsibilities. Likewise, in Puerto Rican families, specific persons may be identified as "friends who are like family" (Sanchez-Ayendez, 1988). Although these close friends may have no formal kinship ties, they may be expected to participate in *compadrazgo,* a form of co-parenting in which specific duties for meeting social and economic needs of children are assigned. In times of economic hardship, informal adoptions may occur in which friends assume roles identical to those of birth parents. These *padres de crianza* (parents of courtesy) care for children as if they were their own.

These non-family caregiving relationships are often misunderstood by mainstream American society. The U.S. legal system does not recognize these ties, and well-intentioned social service and education professionals often underestimate their importance. Child care providers and teachers may wish to consider including "friends who are like family" in parent programs and activities.

Fathers

Across cultures, fathers are less involved than mothers in the care of children, particularly infants (B. B. Whiting & Edwards, 1988). When they do interact with their sons or daughters, they are more likely to engage in physical play and less likely to assume diapering, feeding, and bathing responsibilities (Lamb, 1987). Research suggests that fathers may play this subordinate role in child rearing unwillingly. In the United States, fathers report that society condemns their involvement in child care, so they feel uncomfortable in primary caretaking roles (Belsky & Volling, 1987).

Fathers have been found to be more active in child rearing when mothers are not present. When mothers are available, however, they take a backseat. Perhaps this is due to a lack of confidence or deference to mothers' child-rearing skills (Belsky &

Volling, 1987). When they do interact with their sons or daughters, fathers tend to be as warm and sensitive as mothers, and children form critical attachments to them (Easterbrooks, 1989).

Children from some traditionally under-represented groups are more likely to live in mother-headed families. African-American and Puerto Rican children, for example, are much more likely to live without their fathers in the home. Does this circumstance have negative developmental consequences? Hetherington (1993) has found that children whose fathers are absent from the home usually adjust well, particularly if the separation of parents occurs in infancy. Some developmental problems have been observed among boys living in mother-headed households. Social and behavioral problems can emerge later in life; mother-son relationships tend to be more strained. Such problems may be due to the fact that children adjust less well when the same-sex parent is absent (Camara & Resnik, 1988).

If the absent father is accepting and actively involved with a child, however, these problems diminish. Hetherington (1993) found that children who enjoyed regular positive interactions with their outside-the-home fathers were better adjusted than those whose fathers were unavailable. The presence of a non-father male role model was found to have a similarly positive effect. Children who were rejected by both their father *and* stepfather were particularly at risk.

Whether or not fathers live within the home, they must be considered important caregivers, especially for boys, and teachers and child care providers should make every effort to include them (or other significant male role models) in parent programs and conferences. Creativity may be necessary when family disharmony and legal custody issues arise. It should never be assumed, however, that because fathers are not living in the home they do not matter in children's lives.

FOSTER PARENTS

More than half a million children in America have been removed from their families by child protection agencies and placed in temporary foster homes (Children's Defense Fund, 1998). The primary reason is abuse and neglect by parents. Victims of child abuse, for example, are usually placed with foster parents until successful family interventions have been implemented or permanent adoptions arranged. Some children who are placed in foster homes develop well. Foster care can be preferable to continued exposure to the psychological or physical dangers of an abusive family.

However, concerns have been raised about the negative effects of foster care on young children (Lindsey, 1991). Foster care is often not a temporary arrangement, as it was designed to be, and almost 20% of children currently in foster care have been there for at least 6 years (Children's Defense Fund, 1998). Some children have spent their entire childhoods in the foster care system, often moving from one foster home to another. This movement from home to home is especially difficult for infants who are forming attachments to caregivers.

Lindsey (1991) has noted that hasty decisions to place children in foster homes may result partly from a misunderstanding of cultural differences in family life. Grandparents and other extended family members are often overlooked as important alternative caregivers for children who must be removed from their homes. An illiterate grandmother of an abused child, for example, may not be considered a viable alternative guardian by social services professionals (Berger, 1994). Extended family members may be better caregivers for children than foster parents. They may be eligible to receive more social and mental health services than foster parents (Lindsey, 1991). Further, children may already be attached to grandparents or other relatives.

RESEARCH INTO PRACTICE

CRITICAL CONCEPT 1

Children vary in development partly because they have different family experiences. Culture often shapes how children are raised. Families in one culture may view children as fragile and needing protection; families in another may view children as resilient and bold. So, very different approaches to caring for children emerge.

Application #1

Teachers and child care providers must learn as much as they can about the beliefs, routines, and traditions of families of the children they serve. Understanding parenting and family life experiences can provide insight into children's development and lead to appreciation of diverse styles of playing and learning.

Application #2

Before children begin school, teachers and caregivers can conduct face-to-face interviews with family members to learn about expectations for behavior, discipline techniques, communicative styles, and methods of soothing, feeding, and carrying children. Some family interaction patterns can be replicated in the classroom. For example, a teacher might use more physical and less verbal methods of encouraging a child whose family interacts in these ways. Some family practices, such as physical punishment, may not be compatible with teacher beliefs or school policies. Differences in viewpoints should be openly discussed so that consensus about goals and approaches can be achieved.

CRITICAL CONCEPT 2

Family structures differ as well. What constitutes a family in one culture may be quite different in another. Sometimes grandparents, siblings, and even friends live in the home and assume child-rearing responsibilities. Sometimes fathers do not live in the home and yet still play a critical role. The rich variety of family characteristics reflects the ways that distinct cultural groups have adapted to challenges and life experiences throughout history.

Application #1

In most cases, both parents should be involved in the programs and activities of the school or center. This is important even when one parent lives outside the child's home. Special effort should be made to communicate with absent fathers and encourage their involvement in the classroom. In the case of an unharmonious relationship between parents, separate parent-teacher conferences can be scheduled.

Application #2

Care must be taken to understand legal issues related to divorce or separation of parents. Some parents may be denied contact with their children by the courts; others may have limited custody. Involving both parents is extremely important; however, in light of the many complex legal issues that arise in modern family life, teachers and caregivers should proceed cautiously toward this goal.

Application #3

Teachers and caregivers should be cautious not to assume that living in a single-parent family will impede children's development. In fact, they should be aware that mother-only homes may not be true single-parent families at all, since grandparents and other relatives may play a positive role in child rearing and family life. The positive influences on child development of all family members should be appreciated.

Application #4

Grandparents who play primary caregiving roles should be involved in school or center activities and programs. They can be invited to participate in parent-teacher conferences and should be included in discussions of classroom problems. They also can be asked to work with children in the classroom. All students will benefit from multi-generational interactions.

Application #5

Other family members and friends who have primary caregiving roles should be involved in school or center activities and programs, as well. Older siblings might be encouraged to work with children in the classroom. Aunts, uncles, and even "friends who are like family" can be invited to attend conferences and parent education programs—especially if they are significant caregivers.

Application #6

The curriculum in early childhood education should reflect the diverse family configurations of modern society. Children's books, photographs, and curriculum materials should show a variety of types of families. Many different kinds of households, such as those headed by mothers and grandmothers, by fathers only, by mothers and friends, and even by mothers and older siblings, should be portrayed throughout the curriculum. Discussions of families should center on caring relationships rather than on blood relations or marital status.

SUGGESTED ACTIVITIES

1. Identify two families with babies who are of distinct cultural backgrounds. Interview parents or other caregivers living in the home regarding child-rearing beliefs and methods. Ask questions about response to crying, carrying practices, and teaching interactions, as described in this chapter. Also ask about the roles of all those living in the home who have child care responsibilities, including siblings, relatives, and friends. Write a report on these interviews, guided by the following questions:

   a. How do these two families differ in infant care beliefs and practices? How are they alike?

   b. To what degree does culture affect similarities and differences in caregiving? Does family structure have an influence? Does the specific role of the caregiver (i.e., parent, grandparent, relative) affect his or her practices and beliefs?

   c. Who cares for children in these families? How do caretaking roles vary across these individuals?

For example: Do mothers differ from fathers in their interactions? Do grandparents differ from siblings?

d. Do parents or significant caregivers of these infants live outside the home? What role do these individuals play in infant care?

2. Identify two families with preschoolers who are of distinct cultural backgrounds. Interview parents or other caregivers living in the home regarding socialization practices. Ask questions about what kinds of child behavior they believe are acceptable in the home and in child care. Ask what they do when children misbehave. Ask about whether they believe children should be independent and self-assertive or dependent and obedient. Ask other questions that are inspired by ideas in this chapter. Write a report on your findings, guided by the following questions:

a. How do these two families differ in socialization beliefs and practices? How are they alike?

b. To what degree does culture affect similarities and differences in preschool socialization? Does family structure have an influence? Does the specific role of the caregiver (i.e., parent, grandparent, relative) affect his or her practices and beliefs?

c. What can you conclude from your interviews about goals for and beliefs about preschoolers in these two families?

3. Identify two families with primary children who are of distinct cultural backgrounds. Interview parents or other caregivers living in the home regarding the importance of school and what strategies they use in the home to promote academic success. Also ask whether they believe schools are sufficiently sensitive to their family's culture. (Note: All families have a culture, even those of Euro-American backgrounds!) Ask about what out-of-school strategies they use to instill cultural pride. Ask other questions that are inspired by the ideas in this chapter. Write

a report on your findings, guided by the following questions:

a. How do these two families differ in their beliefs and attitudes about school? What are the sources of these beliefs?

b. To what degree does culture affect similarities and differences in beliefs? To what degree do parents and family members believe schools are sensitive to their culture?

c. How active are parents or caregivers in ethnic socialization? What socialization messages do they give to their children to instill ethnic pride?

d. What can you conclude from your interviews about the attitudes and beliefs about primary children in these two families?

4. Interview a director of a child care center or a principal of an elementary school. Ask about the families of children served. Inquire about who lives in children's homes and what the caregiving responsibilities are of various family members. Ask about how these various caregivers are involved in the center or school. Write a report on this interview, guided by the following questions:

a. Discuss the various family configurations which the director or principal describes. Of the families served, how many are single-parent families? How many are two-parent families? How many families have non-parent adults living in the home? Do any families served by the school or center have non-relatives living in the home?

b. What important roles do non-parents play in children's development, from the administrator's perspective?

c. To what degree are non-parent caregivers involved in parent activities and conferences at the center or school? What are the challenges, as the administrator sees them, to full involvement of these individuals?

Glossary

accommodation Jean Piaget's term for a mental process in which previously existing understandings and thought structures are modified to make room for new ideas and phenomena within the environment.

achievement motivation A drive to learn and perform well in school.

action research Informal research conducted by teachers to answer pressing questions related to teaching, learning, and children's development.

affiliative obedience Respect and deference to elders in one's family or community; emphasized more in some cultures than in others.

aggression Any action that has the intent of harming another either physically or psychologically. Some aggression is instrumental—that is, it is performed to accomplish a goal. Pushing and snatching a toy is an example. Some aggression is hostile and proactive. Hitting out of anger, without provocation or purpose, is an example.

altruism A propensity toward being kind and helping others.

amniocentesis A test to detect genetic disorders before birth. The procedure involves extracting with a needle a small amount of fluid from the amniotic sac that surrounds the developing fetus.

amnion A protective, fluid-filled sac that forms around the embryo during prenatal development.

anecdotal records A qualitative research method—often used in the classroom—in which children's behavior is observed and recorded in a rich narrative.

antisocial behavior Behavior which alienates others or leads to peer rejection. Antisocial behavior includes aggression, whining, name-calling, and disruptive activity.

articulation problems Difficulty in producing word sounds. Articulation problems are considered a disorder if they interfere with effective communication.

articulators Organs of the body that are responsible for speech production, including the tongue, teeth, lungs, vocal cords, and lips.

assimilation Jean Piaget's term for a mental process in which new information is integrated into previous understandings or thought structures.

at-risk children Children who are in jeopardy, psychologically or physically. Certain family and neighborhood factors, such as drug abuse, violence, parental depression, and child abuse, put children at risk.

attachment The psychological process by which infants form emotional bonds with significant others, especially parents. Infants become attached to adults who are nurturing and responsive.

attachment patterns Diversity in how children become attached to parents across various cultural groups. In some cultures, children are more often insecurely attached; in others, secure attachment is more prevalent.

attention deficit/hyperactivity disorder (ADHD) A disorder of childhood that is characterized by high activity level, impulsiveness, and an inability to pay attention. Often leads to poor peer relations and school performance.

atypical development Development that does not follow a typical course because of delays, deficits, or environmental obstacles.

autism An often severe childhood condition characterized by social isolation, delayed development, and atypical and unpredictable behavior.

autonomy Erik Erikson's term for an emotional state in which children strive to be independent and separate from parents and caregivers. Among emotionally healthy children, this state is acquired in toddlerhood. Shame and doubt are negative feelings which can threaten autonomy.

axon A long fiber on a nerve cell which sends a signal to the next cell.

babbling The playful vocalization of babies which appears at around 6 months of age.

behaviorist theory A theory of human development which holds that all that children become is shaped by the environment. B. F. Skinner was a prominent behaviorist thinker.

bilingualism The ability to speak two different languages.

biliteracy The ability to read and write in two different languages.

Black English Vernacular (BEV) A form of English spoken by African Americans. The language has its own rules, and is as expressive and sophisticated as any other language.

body language The use of gestures, expressions, and movement to express ideas or needs. In some cultures, body language is a more important mode of communication than oral language.

book babble Distinct babbling sounds which infants produce when they are being read to.

case study A qualitative research method often used by teachers in classrooms. The method involves gathering in-depth information on an individual child or family and writing an extensive narrative profiling development.

categorization A mental activity—described by Piaget—in which children put objects that are alike together. Early categorization is based on one characteristic (e.g., size, color, or shape). As children get older they can categorize with two or more traits (e.g., placing shapes of the same color together).

causality A capacity to understand cause and effect. Infants and preschoolers have limited causal thinking—that is, they have difficulty determining what causes what. Primary children construct a fuller understanding of agents, actions, and consequences.

centration An inability to think about more than one object or element of a problem at a time. This is a common characteristic of preschoolers.

cephalocaudal growth gradient The tendency of children to grow and develop from the head down.

cerebral palsy A condition caused by an injury, illness, or defect in the central nervous system, resulting in motor impairment and muscle weakness. Some children with this challenging condition require support in movement and play.

child abuse and neglect A circumstance in which parents or other family members physically or psychologically assault a child or fail to meet the child's basic needs.

child care quality The overall quality of the interactions and environment of child care centers and family child care homes. *Structural* quality elements include adult-child ratio and amount of available play space. *Dynamic* quality elements include positive social interaction and responsiveness and warmth in caregivers.

chorionic villus biopsy A relatively new procedure in which genetic disorders are detected by sampling fetal tissue as early as 6 weeks' gestation.

chromosomes Chemical structures within the nucleus of cells that transmit genetic information. Traits are passed from ancestors to offspring through chromosomes.

circular reactions Repetitive actions performed by young babies which show a lack of causal thinking. For example, an infant will wiggle or bang a rattle, feel the interesting sensation, and repeat the action over and over. The infant has no understanding of which is the cause and which is the effect; the action and the sensation simply go together in the infant's mind.

classical conditioning A strategy for shaping behavior by which a neutral stimulus is paired with a desirable one. Following the training, a subject responds in the same way to the neutral stimulus as to the desirable one. Pavlov provided an example: A dog salivates when shown food. When a bell is rung when food is presented, the dog will eventually salivate at the sound of the bell alone.

cognitive development Development of mental capacity, including problem-solving and language.

cognitive-developmental theory A theory of human development that holds that knowledge is actively constructed by the child, and that active problem-solving, social interaction, and language are necessary for learning.

collective conversation A style of communication in which all speakers talk at the same time with little turntaking. In many cultures, collective conversations are more prevalent than orderly, one-at-a-time discourse.

competence That part of self-esteem related to perceptions about abilities and skills. Children with a sense of competence believe they are smart and able in school subjects, athletics, or the arts.

concrete operational stage One of Jean Piaget's stages of cognitive development in which a child can use logic to solve problems that involve concrete objects. Most elementary schoolchildren are in this stage.

conservation An understanding that amounts (i.e., volume, continuous quantity, number) stay the same even when their appearance changes. For example, a child who can conserve understands that an amount of water does not change just because it is poured into a container with a different shape. This knowledge is usually acquired in the early primary years.

construction play Play in which children build things. Playing with blocks is an example.

correlational study A type of research in which two traits are measured and then their relationship is examined. An example is a study of the relationship between social behavior and grades in school.

cross-sectional study Research in which a trait is studied by examining children of many different ages at one time. Developmental trends are determined by comparing children of one age group to those of another.

culture The unique collection of beliefs, practices, traditions, valued competencies, worldviews, and histories that characterize a particular group of people.

decentration The process of acquiring an ability to think about more than one object or element of a problem at one time. In the elementary years, children are said to *decenter*, to move away from the unidimensional thinking of the preschool years.

deferred imitation The ability to watch another person perform a behavior, then imitate it many hours or even days later. Toddlers often engage in deferred imitation by reenacting the behaviors of family members in child care.

dendrite A collection of short fibers on a nerve cell which receive a signal from the axon of another nerve cell.

difficult temperament An inherited disposition toward irritability and negative affect. The difficult child is often easily upset and displays a regular, negative affect.

disfluency Stuttering. Some disfluency is common in the preschool years. In the elementary years, disfluency that includes facial grimaces and single-sound stutters may be considered a speech disorder.

DNA (deoxyribonucleic acid) Long, double-stranded molecules that make up chromosomes. Genetic information is carried in DNA within cells.

dominant gene A gene for one trait that will overpower a gene for another trait. For example, a gene for brown eyes will overpower a gene for blue eyes, resulting in brown eye color. The brown gene is dominant and the blue gene is recessive.

Down syndrome A genetic condition caused by an extra chromosome in the twenty-first chromosome pair; leads to physical challenges, mental retardation, and a shortened life span.

drug and substance abuse The use of legal or illegal drugs to an extent that threatens the health and positive behavior of the user and the development of the user's offspring. Drug and substance abuse contributes to poor prenatal development, ineffective parenting, and child abuse.

dynamic systems theory of motor development A theory which holds that motor development and brain growth are interrelated.

early intervention A program aimed at enhancing the development of infants, toddlers, and preschoolers, particularly those with special needs. Early intervention may include education, family support, and nutritional and health services.

easy temperament An inherited disposition to be pleasant and easygoing. The easy child adjusts well to new people and situations and displays a positive affect.

echolalia A language behavior in which a child repeats words, syllables, or sounds spoken by others, as if echoing them. Echolalia is common among children with autism or mental retardation.

ecological systems theory A theory of human development which holds that interactions among family, school, neighborhood, society, and the larger culture influence children's learning and behavior. The theory suggests that individual development does not occur in a psychological vacuum, but is affected by larger society.

ego Freud's term for that part of the personality which is rational and regulates and redirects the instinctual impulses of the id.

egocentric speech Verbalizations in which the child does not take the perspective of the listener.

egocentrism A type of thinking, characteristic of young children, in which the perspectives and feelings of others are not understood. Egocentric thought limits children's abilities to see beyond their own needs and desires.

embryo A prenatal human organism from 2 to 6 weeks after conception. All major organs and body structures are formed during the embryonic period.

emergent literacy The natural acquisition of early reading and writing processes in young children who have had rich experiences with print. Preschoolers' spontaneous scribble-writing or "by heart" book reading are examples.

emotions theories Perspectives on how emotions are acquired in infancy and childhood. Two distinct viewpoints are prevalent. The *discrete emotions theory* holds that feelings such as happiness, distress, and interest are "prewired" at birth and unfold during infancy. Discrete emotions may be observed in the facial expressions of very young infants, from this view. The *cognitive/attachment theory* holds that emotions are constructed gradually through interactions with other people.

empathy An ability to feel and sympathize with the experiences of others. Empathic children show concern when others are hurt, and smile when they watch peers at play. The roots of empathy may be present at birth.

enmeshment The process of family bonding, in which children are taught to be dependent on and care for their parents, siblings, and other relatives and friends. Enmeshment is a primary goal of socialization in some cultural groups.

ethnic group A group of people who share a common culture—that is, who share the same beliefs, practices, traditions, valued competencies, worldviews, and histories. Examples include Vietnamese, Mexican Americans, German Americans, Puerto Ricans, and Iranians.

ethnic identity Individuals' perceptions and evaluations of the ethnic group to which they belong. A positive ethnic identity can protect children from the negative effects of racism.

ethnic socialization The process of teaching children to understand and value the beliefs, competencies, role expectations, and unique histories of their ethnic group.

ethnography A type of research in which investigators spend significant time working or living with a group—a classroom, a family, or a community, for example. Based on these experiences, they write qualitative descriptions of behavior and development.

evaluative symbols Methods of evaluating children's work, such as grades, stickers, and charts for good behavior. Such methods can threaten self-esteem and intrinsic motivation to learn.

event sampling A method of observing children in which a teacher or researcher records the number of times a particular behavior or event occurs. Frequencies of these behaviors or events are then tallied and studied.

exosystem In ecological systems theory, that layer of environmental influences on children's development which includes the local community.

A social service agency, health clinic, and town government are examples.

experimental study Research in which a treatment, such as an education intervention, a nutritional program, or a parent education, is administered to subjects. This research design often uses an experimental group which receives the treatment and a control group which does not, and compares the outcomes of the two groups.

expressive jargon A form of babbling in which infants string together long chains of sounds in language-like utterances. The intonations of expressive jargon match adult intonation and give an impression that the baby is speaking an impressive second language.

extended family A family which includes children, parents, grandparents, and possibly aunts, uncles, and even "friends who are like family." Extended family households are common in historically under-represented cultural groups. This family configuration is a way to cope in the face of hardship and prejudice.

extrinsic motivation Motivation to achieve which comes from the outside environment. Learning a skill only to obtain external rewards or praise from others is an example.

fetal alcohol syndrome A condition caused by a mother's heavy use of alcohol during pregnancy. The condition threatens the health of the fetus and jeopardizes development after birth. Babies with this condition are often retarded and physically deformed.

fetus A prenatal human organism from the third month to birth. Organs and body structures which were formed during the embryonic period are further refined in the fetal stage.

field independent A style of thinking in which a person can learn and solve problems without the support of cues from the external environment. Children from Euro-American backgrounds are often field independent in that they are better able to solve problems without hints, prompts, or other outside assistance.

field sensitive A style of thinking in which a person is dependent on

cues from the external environment in learning or solving problems. Children from historically under-represented groups are often field sensitive in that they rely on information from the immediate environment and other people for learning.

fine motor development The development of skills involving small muscles in the hands and fingers. Fine motor development in the preschool years leads to refinement of such skills as drawing, writing, painting, puzzle making, and block building.

fontanelle The soft membrane which separates the cranial bones in the head of a fetus and newborn.

forceps Surgical tongs used to speed delivery by pulling the baby from the birth canal.

formal operational stage The most advanced of Jean Piaget's stages of cognitive development, in which an adolescent or adult can think abstractly and hypothetically.

friendship The reciprocal preference of two peers to play with or spend time with each other. Friendship in childhood is often measured by a sociometric interview in which children are asked whom they prefer to play with.

friends who are like family Close friends within a neighborhood or village who are informally adopted as family members.

functional play Play that involves active, repetitive motor actions. Banging objects, running and screaming, swinging, and jumping are examples.

games with rules A predominant form of play during the primary years. Children in all cultures play games; the games differ as a function of cultural values and socialization practices.

gender identity An individual's perceptions and evaluations of his or her gender. A positive gender identity can protect children from the effects of sexism and sex-role stereotyping.

gene A segment of a DNA molecule which determines the characteristics of a developing human.

general language delay A condition in which a child's language lags

behind that of other children of the same age. This is a broad term often used to describe disorders of many different origins. Brain dysfunction may be one cause.

genetic counseling A variety of emotional, educational, and medical services provided to couples at risk of bearing children with genetic disorders. Services include genetic testing for couples of high-risk families or cultures and counseling for parents who will give birth to infants with disorders.

gifted and talented children Children who have been identified as exceptionally intelligent or competent in language, music, or other areas of development.

gross motor development The development of skills using the large muscles in the legs and arms. Large muscle development leads to refinement of such abilities as running, climbing, jumping, throwing, and catching.

habituation A psychological process in which infants become so familiar with objects or events that they show disinterest in them. Habituation has been utilized to show what babies know. A child who displays disinterest in one object but excitement at a slightly different one must be able to differentiate between the two.

hearing impairment A condition characterized by deafness or severely limited auditory perception.

heritability ratio A mathematical estimate of the role of genetics in determining intelligence. Researchers who believe that less than half of intelligence is explained by genetics, for example, may propose a heritability ratio of .45.

id Freud's term for the part of personality that contains instinctual urges. The id strives for immediate gratification but is modulated by the ego and the superego.

identify formation The process of coming to understand the beliefs, roles, and competencies which define oneself.

immersion model of bilingual education A model for educating bilingual children that involves teaching exclusively in the language of the dominant society. The method has been called "submersion" because it often plunges children into a foreign language environment in which they must sink or swim.

inclusive views of self A self-appraisal which is based on perceptions and evaluations of one's family, community, and culture rather than on individual accomplishment. Children of historically under-represented groups are more likely to have inclusive views of self than children of Euro-American cultures.

industry Erik Erikson's term for a feeling of competence which is acquired by many children in the primary years. Successful experiences in and out of school will lead to feelings of mastery; failure will result in the opposite emotional state—inferiority.

infant mortality An indicator of the relative number of infants who die before childhood within a community or society; often expressed as the frequency of deaths per 1,000 live births.

initiative Erik Erikson's term for an emotional state in which preschool-age children make creative attempts, take risks, and reach out to peers. If children's initiatives are thwarted, they may suffer the opposite emotional state: guilt.

injury Accidental physical harm which is a leading cause of disability and death in young children. Injury is more common in low-income urban neighborhoods.

insecure attachment A condition in which an infant or young child does not form a strong bond with a parent, family member, or significant other. There are two types of insecure attachment. *Avoidant* insecure attachment is characterized by a child's avoidance of contact with a parent before or after a separation. *Ambivalent* insecure attachment is characterized by alternately clingy then angry and rejecting behavior by the child after separation.

intelligence quotient (IQ) A measure of intelligence which is based on performance on an intelligence test. Such a test is standardized to show the expected performance for a given age level. IQ scores for children are computed by comparing

their actual performance to that typical of children their age.

intrinsic motivation Motivation to achieve which comes from within. A child who learns because of the joy it brings is intrinsically motivated. External rewards and praise have been found to threaten intrinsic motivation.

irreversibility An inability, common among preschoolers, to reverse the direction of thinking or action. For example, children with irreversibility will have difficulty going back exactly the way they came on a walk on the playground.

isolate behavior The active avoidance of contact with peers in play settings. Distinct from peer rejection, isolate behavior is self-chosen segregation from others.

kinship Close, supportive relationships with relatives or non-relatives. Para-kinship ties are bonds with people who have no formal blood relations but are "like family."

labeling and organizing Cognitive strategies for learning and remembering things. Using these strategies, children organize information into categories in their minds and assign labels to these categories. They remember information longer when they do this.

labor The process of giving birth, which occurs in three stages: dilation, birth of the baby, and expulsion of the placenta.

Lamaze childbirth method A Western method for preparing mothers for childbirth which includes providing information, teaching relaxation exercises, and providing support during labor and delivery.

language differences Variations in language due to cultural or linguistic background. Some children in the United States do not speak English. Even among English speakers, there is variation in dialect. Each language or dialect is rule-governed and as expressive as any other language. Such differences should not be construed as deficits.

language shock Feelings of surprise experienced by bilingual children when they learn for the first time that others cannot understand their native language.

learned helplessness A belief that one is helpless and has no control over life events. Learned helplessness is related to continued experiences with failure.

learning disabilities A disability characterized by poor performance in one or more academic areas. The condition may also result in poor perceptual and motor coordination, language delays, attention problems, and poor peer relations. One theory is that learning disabilities result from minimal brain damage.

Leboyer childbirth method A Western method of childbirth in which the birthing room is made quiet, warm, and dark to ease the newborn's transition into the world. Providing the baby with a warm bath after delivery is a prominent feature of the method.

locus of control A belief about the degree of control one has over life events. An *internal* locus of control is a belief that one has much power in determining successful outcomes in school and in life. An *external* locus of control is a belief that outcomes are determined by outside forces and hence are beyond one's control.

longitudinal studies Research in which a group of children is studied over a long period of time in order to observe changes in behavior and development at various ages.

low-birth-weight infant A baby who is born weighing less than 5.5 pounds. Low-birth-weight babies are at risk of health and learning problems later in life, particularly if they are born in poverty.

macrosystem In ecological systems theory, that layer of environmental influences on children's development which includes cultural traditions, the political and economic system, and the prevalent ideology of society as a whole. The macrosystem affects other local systems, such as the school and the family. For example, the political beliefs of the U.S. electorate, which are part of the macrosystem, affect the services and supports that are made available to children and their families.

maintenance/developmental model of bilingual education A model of bilingual education in which children are taught mainly in their native language. They are gradually taught English as a second language.

map space An understanding of directions, distance, and the relationships among landmarks on maps.

maturationist theory A theory of human development which holds that all that children become is predetermined by genetics. From this perspective, development is simply the unfolding of traits inherited from ancestors.

memory A capacity to learn and retain information for a period of time. Sensory memory is fleeting recollection of sensory experiences and is quickly lost. Short-term memory is information which is consciously stored and can be retrieved for a limited time. Information in short-term memory can be integrated into long-term memory, which may be retrieved over a long duration.

mental retardation A broad term to describe a condition of poor general intellectual functioning and impairment in adaptive behavior. Mental retardation can have many causes, including genetic disorders and injury to the central nervous system.

mesosystem In ecological systems theory, that layer of environmental influences on development which is comprised of relationships among persons or organizations that have daily contact with the child. Parent-teacher communications and collaborations between child care and public school professionals are examples of relationships that lie within the mesosystem.

metacognition The capacity to think about and regulate one's own thinking and learning processes. Knowing what it means to remember something and using a special strategy, such as rehearsal, to remember it are examples.

metalinguistic awareness The capacity to think about and regulate language processes. Acquired during the primary years, this ability allows children to attend to the rules of language. Metalinguistic awareness assists children in learning to read, write, and speak a second language.

microsystem In ecological systems theory, that layer of environmental influences on development which includes all persons and institutions that have direct contact with a child. The family, the classroom, and the community center are examples.

midwife A non-relative who supports a mother through the labor and delivery process. In some societies a midwife is one of the most respected members of the village or community.

modeling The process by which children observe the actions of others, integrate those actions into their repertoire, and perform them at some later time.

moral development Advancement through stages of moral reasoning. According to Lawrence Kohlberg, humans progress through stages of moral development that are based on cognitive competence. These stages include premorality, moral realism, and moral relativism.

moral dilemmas Hypothetical stories told to children to evaluate their moral reasoning. An example is the Lawrence Kohlberg's classic story of a man who must decide whether to steal medicine to save his wife's life.

moral self-worth That type of self-esteem which is related to perceptions about being fair, honest, or kind.

morphemes Small units of language that hold meaning, such as plural "-s," past-tense "-ed," or the "-ing" ending. Morphemes are learned in a predictable sequence in the toddler and preschool years.

movement consistency The capacity to use specific motor skills, such as running and throwing, in play.

movement constancy An ability to adapt basic motor skills, such as running and throwing, to meet varying environmental challenges. For example, a child must alter basic throwing in order to toss a ball to a peer standing far away.

multiple classification An ability to categorize objects using more than one characteristic. Placing all blue triangles in one pile and all red triangles in a different one is an example.

multiple intelligences Howard Gardner's term to describe seven distinct kinds of intellectual competence in humans: linguistic, musical, logical-mathematical, spatial, kinesthetic, intrapersonal (self-understanding), and interpersonal (social understanding).

muscular dystrophy A genetic disorder that leads to the progressive deterioration of motor functioning and the breakdown of muscle tissue.

myelin An insulating sheath, formed during infancy and early childhood, that grows around nerve cells and results in more accurate and rapid transmission of neural messages.

myth of self-hatred A well-intentioned misconception held by many social scientists in past decades that children from historically underrepresented groups hated themselves and wished to be members of the dominant culture.

myth of single-parent families A misconception that children in father-absent families are raised by a single parent, when in fact grandparents, aunts and uncles, older children, and even friends often reside with such families and contribute to child care.

neglected children Children who are ignored or forgotten by peers. They are rarely named at all in a classroom sociometric interview.

Neonatal Behavior Assessment Scale (NBAS) A rating system that assesses newborn functioning, measuring reflexes and such neonatal behaviors as responsiveness and irritability.

neonate A newborn baby.

neurons Nerve cells that transmit messages from the brain to the body.

neurotransmitters Chemicals secreted from neurons which are responsible for transmitting messages from one cell to another in the nervous system.

nonconceptual speech An early form of language—described by Vygotsky—in which children utter words or phrases without thinking about what they mean.

nonverbal thought A kind of early thought—described by Vygotsky—in which children observe or perform actions on objects without using any language.

normative charts Graphic representations of the stages or milestones children pass through as they develop. Many normative charts are based on observations of white middle-class children in America.

nuclear family A family unit which consists only of parents and their children. In many cultures and communities, nuclear family households are rare; multigenerational and single-parent living arrangements are more common.

obesity A condition in which a person weighs significantly more than is typical for a particular height, gender, and age. Obesity can cause health problems and contributes to peer rejection.

object permanence An understanding that objects still exist even if they cannot be seen. Young infants lack object permanence; to them, if an object is out of sight it does not exist.

operant conditioning A form of training inspired by B. F. Skinner and other behaviorists in which a desired behavior is immediately rewarded.

otitis media A condition in which fluid buildup and inflammation of the middle ear lead to conductive hearing loss. Often the condition causes fluctuating hearing loss in which afflicted children can hear on some occasions and not on others.

overgeneralization A language characteristic of toddlers and preschoolers in which a word is used to describe more objects, events, or ideas than are appropriate. For example, a child uses the word "car" to stand for cars, trucks, vans, and buses.

overrestriction A language characteristic of toddlers and preschoolers in which a word is used to describe fewer objects, events, or ideas than are appropriate. For example, a child uses the word "shoes" to mean only his or her own shoes.

ovum The developing human, during its first two weeks after conception. It is a rapidly growing, shapeless mass of cells.

paying attention A cognitive strategy in which children direct their attention to important stimuli in the environment. By controlling and guiding attention, children can learn that information which is most important in school.

peer group A group of children who share a common play environment, such as a classroom, apartment, or playground. Peer groups have a structure that includes popular and unpopular children, leaders and followers, and friendships. This structure becomes more rigid as children get older.

peer neglect A condition of being ignored by others in a peer group. Quiet and withdrawn children are often neglected by peers.

peer rejection A condition of being actively avoided or ostracized by others in a peer group. Aggressive children and children with special needs are at risk of being rejected.

peer reputation A negative characterization of a child by peers which is so persistent that the child eventually internalizes it. A child with a reputation of being a "tattle tale," for example, may begin to act in ways consistent with that characterization.

perceptual development The growing capacity to use vision, hearing, touch, taste, and smell to interpret the environment.

perceptual/motor coordination An ability to coordinate the use of muscles and senses in play or problem-solving.

permissive parenting A style of parenting in which children are encouraged to behave as they choose with little intervention.

phonemes Individual speech sounds used in language.

phonology The part of language which involves speech sounds. The articulation of specific phonemes as well as intonation and fluency are included.

pincer grasp An advanced form of grasping in which the thumb and forefinger are used to hold small objects. The pincer grasp is acquired at around age 1.

placenta An organ that allows the developing fetus to receive nutrients from the mother. It separates the bloodstream of the fetus from that of the mother but permits nutrients and waste products to be exchanged.

play Spontaneous and joyful activity which is performed for its intrinsic reward. Children of all cultures play; games vary according to cultural traditions and socialization practices.

play-work A type of play in which children integrate play activities with family chores, found in many African societies.

poor voice quality A condition characterized by a nasal or hoarse voice sound.

popular children Children who are nominated as preferred playmates in sociometric interviews. Popular children are often highly social, verbally competent, and creative.

positive reinforcement A method used by behaviorists to shape the behaviors of young children which involves providing praise or a reward following desirable behavior.

poverty A condition in which families live without adequate resources. Poverty often includes poor nutrition, lack of health care and family services, and inadequate housing or homelessness. Poverty has a devastating effect on children's development.

pragmatics The social uses of language. Children who are skilled at pragmatics can use language to persuade peers or adults, ask and answer questions in school, and request entry into a play group.

premature birth A birth in which a child is born at least 3 weeks before the end of the 38- to 42-week gestation period or weighs less than 5.5 pounds at the time of delivery.

prenatal development The development of the human organism after conception and before birth.

preoperational stage According to Jean Piaget, preschoolers are in this stage of cognitive development, which is characterized by an inability to use logic in solving problems. Unidimensional thinking, egocentrism, irreversibility, and perception-based reasoning are typical in this period.

pretend play A form of play in which children take on imaginative roles and play out make-believe themes. Pretend play emerges in toddlerhood. Children around the world engage in pretend play.

preterm infant A baby born more than 3 weeks before the projected due date. A premature baby is also likely to be a low-birth-weight baby.

primary circular reactions Repetitive motor actions which are performed using one's own body. Examples are wiggling limbs and cooing. These emerge at about 1 month of age.

productive language Actual vocalizing or speaking; language which is produced, not just understood.

prosocial behavior Behaviors such as sharing, cooperating, and nurturing which are performed in kindness without the inducement of external reward.

protective factors Factors in children's lives that may protect them, to some degree, from the negative effects of poverty, discrimination, and community violence. Such factors include attachment to parents and family, a positive temperament, intellectual competence, and early childhood education programs.

proximodistal growth gradient The tendency of children to grow from the center of the body outward toward the extremities.

psychoanalytic theory A theory of human development that is concerned with the formation of personality. Psychoanalysts believe that development is characterized by tensions between instinctual urges and the demands of the outside world, and that resolution of these tensions is needed to become a healthy adult.

qualitative research Research that involves narrative description of behaviors and development rather than counting or quantifying observations. The purpose of qualitative work is to provide a rich, "thick" description of children.

quantitative methods Research methods in which children are observed and their behaviors are counted or rated numerically. The numbers that are obtained are then entered into computer programs and analyzed statistically.

race A broad category of humans that share a common genetic heritage. Asians, blacks, Native Americans, Caucasians, and Latinos are examples. Cultures exist within races. Latinos include Mexicans, Puerto Ricans, etc. Native Americans include Algonquins, Seminoles, etc.

rapid eye movement (REM) sleep An important state of sleep characterized by eye movements, accelerated heart rate and respiration, and much brain wave activity.

reaction time The period of time it takes a child to respond motorically to a stimulus.

receptive language Language which can be understood by a child but not necessarily spoken. Receptive language usually precedes productive language in young children.

recessive gene A gene for one trait which will be overpowered by a gene for another trait. For example, a gene for blue eyes will be overpowered by a gene for brown eyes, resulting in brown eye color. The brown gene is dominant and the blue gene is recessive.

referential communication An ability to adapt language to the viewpoints, understandings, and language competencies of the listener. Using simpler language to talk to a younger sibling is an example.

reflexes Involuntary motor reactions to stimuli during early infancy. Examples include the rooting, sucking, startle, and walking reflexes, which are present at birth and disappear around age 6 months.

register A particular style of language which is used in certain contexts but not others. The informal language of the neighborhood and the formal language of school are examples.

register switching The ability to effectively switch from one language register to another in different situations. An example is found in the child who switches from informal speech spoken in the neighborhood to the formal language of school.

rehearsal A strategy for remembering and learning that involves repeating material verbally or practicing actions over and over so they are retained.

rejected children Children who are named as undesirable playmates in a sociometric interview or are actively avoided by peers in a classroom.

resiliency A state of being protected psychologically, even in the face of harsh or dangerous elements in the environment. Children who live in poverty, in dangerous neighborhoods, or with the threat of abuse and still develop in positive ways are said to be resilient.

reversibility An ability to reverse an operation either physically or mentally. Primary-grade children are often capable of reversibility. They can watch water poured from one cup to another and can mentally pour it back into the original container. They can reverse their steps on a walk, returning by the same path they originally followed.

risk factors Conditions that may lead to poor development, such as poverty, violence, poor housing, family disharmony, and child abuse.

rough-and-tumble play A form of play in which children wrestle, push, tickle, and swat at one another, sometimes in mock violence, with no intent to do real harm. This form of play is common in all cultures and is important in social and motor development.

scaffolding A process by which adults provide supportive structures to help children learn and play. Scaffolding occurs at a time when children are faced with a challenge that they can solve independently with a simple hint, question, or prompt from an adult.

scanning A visual ability to look over all the features of an object and to get a complete picture of what it is like. Infants become more proficient at scanning in the first months of life.

secondary circular reactions Repetitive actions in infancy which are performed on toys or other objects. Banging a rattle is an example. These usually emerge between 4 and 8 months of age.

secure attachment A category of attachment in which an infant has securely bonded to a parent or significant other. Secure attachment is measured by observing what children do when separated from parents. Securely attached children show some distress upon separation, but quickly reestablish warm interactions when reunited.

self-concept A person's overall view of self, which includes perceptions about traits, abilities, gender, and ethnic affiliation. As children acquire a self concept they strive to answer the question, Who *am* I?

self-directed speech A verbal behavior—described by Vygotsky—in which children talk to themselves in order to guide their own learning, such as labeling objects, narrating actions, or telling oneself to pay attention or remember.

self-esteem The complex collection of self-appraisals that make up a child's overall evaluation of self worth. It is widely believed that there are many types of self-esteem. Children have different self-perceptions depending on the context or the particular trait being considered. It is not until adolescence that these differentiated self-assessments are integrated into an overall view of self. As children acquire self-esteem, they answer the question, Am I a worthwhile person?

semantic networks A complex organization of words and word meanings within the brain of language learners. Semantic networks become more intricate in the primary years, when words of like meaning are clustered together in a "mental dictionary."

semantics That part of language which has to do with the meanings of words and parts of words.

sensorimotor stage One of Jean Piaget's stages of cognitive development which encompasses the period of infancy. To a young baby at this stage, thinking is limited to using actions and perceptions to explore the world and have needs met. In the later phases of this stage, children begin to use symbols and use more internalized problem-solving.

separation anxiety A fear of being separated from primary caregivers or left alone. This anxiety appears between 6 and 8 months and lasts until at least 14 months.

seriation An ability to order objects logically by size, such as placing sticks in a row from shortest to longest. Children acquire seriation skills as they enter the primary years.

serious emotional disturbance (SED) A broad term used to describe children with a range of social and emotional challenges. Such children are often aggressive, antisocial, and emotionally troubled.

sex-role stereotyping The tendency to rigidly conform to traditional definitions of gender roles. Sex-role stereotyping includes articulated beliefs about how boys and girls should behave, as well as uncompromising adherence to gender-role expectations in play and social interactions.

shyness A tendency to be quiet, reserved, and anxious around others. Shyness may have its roots in both genetics and culture.

sibling caretakers Children who are given primary responsibility for caring for younger siblings. In some cultures, children as young as age 5 assume this role.

sickle-cell anemia A genetic disorder which results in defective blood cells and causes a range of medical problems, most often found in persons of African or African-American background.

simultaneous second-language learning The process by which a child in a bilingual family learns two languages at the same time, beginning at birth.

slow-to-warm-up temperament An inherited disposition to be wary and reticent. A slow-to-warm-up child may be socially anxious and slow to form relationships with new people.

small-for-dates Babies who are smaller than expected for their gestational age. Small-for-dates are often full-term babies that are small due to health or nutritional deficiencies.

social acceptance That type of self-esteem which is related to perceptions about how well one is liked by peers and adults.

social cognition An ability to read social situations and to interpret the feelings, motives, and intentions of others.

social cognitive learning theory A theory of human development—related to behaviorism—which holds that much of what children become they have emulated from models in their lives. From this perspective, adults should model those behaviors they want children to acquire. An old adage reflects this theory: "Children are more likely to do what adults do than what adults tell them to do."

social competence The degree to which a person is well accepted by peers, makes friends, and interacts with others in effective ways.

social initiative A social and emotional trait that leads a person to actively make contact with other human beings. Some children exhibit this trait; they interact often with peers. Other children do not display social initiative; they are more withdrawn and quiet.

socialization The process by which adults within a family or community transmit to children the values, traditions, role expectations, and competencies of the culture.

socialized speech Verbalizations in which the speaker takes into account the perspectives of the listener.

social participation The degree of interaction and collaboration in children's play. Levels of social participation include onlooking, isolate play, parallel play, and cooperative play.

social referencing The process by which an infant or child acquires information on emotions by watching the facial expressions of others. A child will study a parent's face, for example, to determine whether there is cause for worry in a new situation.

sociocultural theory A theory of human development, posited by Lev Vygotsky, which holds that social interaction and language are most important for learning. According to this theory, peers, parents, teachers, and others in society "scaffold" children's development by asking questions, arguing, giving hints, or in other ways guiding problem-solving.

sociodramatic play A form of pretend play in which children coordinate make-believe roles and play themes with peers.

socioeconomic status (SES) A measure of a family's overall economic and social status. The most common way to assess SES is to examine the level of education, income, place of residence, and occupation of primary wage earners.

sociometric status A child's relative status in a group of peers. Some children are popular; others are rejected or neglected. Status is often measured by a sociometric interview, in which children are asked whom they prefer to play with.

spina bifida A congenital malformation of the spine which can lead to paralysis of the lower extremities, loss of perceptual and motor functioning, and loss of bowel and bladder control.

stages of reading The stages of understanding print and competence with books that characterize emergent reading in the early years.

stages of writing The stages of written expression—from early scribble-writing to conventional spelling—that characterize emergent writing in the early years.

stimulability The ability of children to imitate accurately speech sounds which they do not produce accurately when they are speaking their natural language. Stimulability is used to test severity of articulation errors; children who can imitate the sounds accurately are believed to be less at risk.

stranger anxiety A fear of strangers or even familiar persons who are not primary caregivers. This anxiety often appears between 6 and 8 months and lasts throughout toddlerhood.

strange situation procedure A research technique used to assess the quality of attachment of young children to their caregivers. The procedure involves observing the responses of a child under a number of conditions, including the departure of a parent and the arrival of a stranger.

struggle behaviors Facial grimaces and other signs of difficulty in producing speech sounds which are common among children who are disfluent.

successive second-language learning The process of learning a second language after acquiring a primary or native language, often later in life.

sudden infant death syndrome (SIDS) A condition in which an infant stops breathing without cause, usually during the night. A leading cause of death among infants under age 1.

superego The part of the mind that comprises the conscience, according to Freud. The values and mores of one's culture are included in the superego.

symbolic thought A type of thinking in which mental images are used to imagine, solve problems, and communicate. Language, writing, and pretend play all require symbolic thought.

synapse A juncture between the axon of one neuron and the dendrites of another, through which neural messages are transmitted.

syntax That part of language that involves word order and the construction of sentences; often called *grammar.*

tacit knowledge of language A subconscious ability to apply complex language rules without thinking about them. Young children adhere to almost all the rules of adult language, but cannot think or talk about them until much later in life.

teasing play A form of play in which children taunt one another. This play form is prevalent in some cultures but not others, and is viewed as useful for learning self-control.

telegraphic speech Early utterances of young children which contain only the key words required for meaning. Less important words, such as articles and morphemes, are omitted, as in "Throw ball."

temperament A general emotional disposition which is consistently observed throughout development. Three basic classifications are *easy, difficult,* and *slow-to-warm-up.* Additional temperaments, such as boldness, timidity, sociability, and high activity level, have been identified in very young infants. These temperament types tend to persist into adulthood in many children.

teratogen Environmental agents, such as drugs, radiation, or illness, which threaten the development of the fetus.

theories of the mind Theories formulated by young children about how the mind works. A number of different theories of the mind are acquired in the preschool and primary grades, including theories about learning and knowing, intentions and motives, and feelings.

time sampling A research method in which teachers or researchers observe children at regular intervals and record interactions that occur within that time frame. The observer can, thus, determine the frequency of these interactions over time.

tracking The ability to visually follow a moving object with one's eyes. Tracking becomes quite proficient in the first few months of infancy.

transductive reasoning A type of thinking, common in the preschool years, in which two unrelated events are interpreted as if one caused the other. For example, a child who breaks a dish and then sneezes may conclude that the accident caused the sneeze.

trust Erik Erikson's term for an emotional state in which children feel secure and know that basic needs will be met by primary caregivers. Threats to a feeling of trust, such as child abuse or neglect, will lead infants to mistrust the world and the people in it.

two-way model of bilingual education A model of bilingual education in which all children in a classroom—even those of the dominant culture—learn two different languages.

two-word utterances The very earliest sentences spoken in toddlerhood, composed of two words which convey a whole idea. The two words usually express the agent and an action, or an action and the object of the action.

umbilical cord A cord leading from the developing fetus to the mother, through which nutrients and waste products pass.

unidimensional thought A type of thinking, prevalent in the preschool years, in which a child is unable to think about more than one object or element of a problem at one time.

verbal thought A kind of advanced thought—described by Vygotsky—in which language and thinking are integrated. In this kind of thinking, verbal labels or self-directed speech support one's learning.

violence A serious threat to the physical and psychological well-being of young children. Violent crime is most prevalent in low-income neighborhoods. Families of color are more likely to be affected by violence than Euro-American families.

visual cliff A research apparatus designed to show that babies have depth perception. Babies are enticed to crawl over a clear plastic surface that appears to be a deep drop-off; if they do not, depth perception can be inferred.

visual impairment A condition characterized by blindness or severely limited vision.

zone of proximal development Vygotsky's term to describe that part of a task which is just beyond the child's current level of mastery. It is the point at which a simple prompt, hint, or question from an adult or older peer will allow the child to solve the problem independently. Vygotsky believed that this was the ideal time for adults to intervene to promote development.

References

Aaronson, D., & Ferres, S. (1987). The impact of language differences on language processing: An example from Chinese-English bilingualism. In P. Homel, M. Palij, & D. Aaronson (Eds.), *Childhood bilingualism: Aspects of linguistic, cognitive, and social development.* Hillsdale, NJ: Erlbaum.

Abbeduto, L., & Rosenberg, S. (1987). Linguistic communication and mental retardation. In S. Rosenberg (Ed.), *Advances in applied linguistics* (Vol. 1, pp. 33–97). Cambridge: Cambridge University Press.

Aboud, F. (1977). Interest in ethnic information: A cross-cultural developmental study. *Canadian Journal of Behavioral Science, 9,* 134–146.

Aboud, F. (1985). The development of a social comparison process in children. *Child Development, 56,* 682–688.

Aboud, F. (1987). The development of ethnic self-identification and attitudes. In J. S. Phinney & M. J. Rotheram (Eds.), *Children's ethnic socialization: Pluralism and development* (pp. 32–55). Newbury Park, CA: Sage.

Aboud, F. (1988). *Children and prejudice.* New York: Basil Blackwell.

Aboud, F., & Doyle, A. B. (1993). The early development of ethnic identity and attitudes. In M. E. Bernal & G. P. Knight (Eds.), *Ethnic identity: 1. Formation and transmission among Hispanics and other minorities* (pp. 46–59). Albany: SUNY Press.

Abrahams, R. D. (1976). *Talking black.* Rowley, MA: Newbury House.

Abramovitch, R., Pepler, D., & Corter, C. (1982). Patterns of sibling interaction among preschool-age children. In M. Lamb & B. Sutton-Smith (Eds.), *Sibling relationships: Their nature and significance across the life span.* Hillsdale, NJ: Erlbaum.

Adams, P. F., & Benson, V. (1991). *Current estimates from the National Health Interview Survey* (pp. 92–109). Hyattsville, MD: National Center for Health Statistics.

Adelman, H. S. (1992). The classification problem. In W. Stainback & S. Stainback (Eds.), *Controversial issues confronting special education* (pp. 377–469). Boston: Allyn & Bacon.

Adelson, E., & Fraiberg, S. (1974). Gross motor development in infants blind from birth. *Child Development, 45,* 114–126.

Ainsworth, M. D. S. (1977). Infant development and mother-infant interaction among Ganda and American families. In P. H. Leiderman, S. R. Tulkin, & A. Rosenfeld (Eds.), *Culture and infancy: Variations in the human experience.* New York: Academic Press.

Ainsworth, M. D. S., Blehar, M. C., Waters, E., & Wall, S. (1978). *Patterns of attachment.* Hillsdale, NJ: Erlbaum.

Aitchison, J. (1987). *Words in the mind: An introduction to the mental lexicon.* London: Basil Blackwell.

Aldis, O. (1975). *Play fighting.* New York: Academic Press.

Alexander, G. R., Weiss, J., & Hulsey, T. C. (1991). Preterm birth prevention: An evaluation of programs in the United States. *Birth, 18,* 160–169.

Alexander, M. A., Blank, J. S., & Clark, L. (1991). Obesity in Mexican-American preschool children: A population group at risk. *Public Health Nursing, 8,* 53–58.

Amaro, H., Zuckerman, B., & Cabral, H. (1989). Drug use among adolescent mothers: Profile of risk. *Pediatrics, 84,* 144–151.

American Psychiatric Association. (1994). *Diagnostic and statistical manual of mental disorders* (4th ed.). Washington, DC: Author.

Amiel-Tison, C. (1985). Pediatric contribution to the present knowledge on the neurobehavioral status of infants at birth. In J. Mehler & R. Fox (Eds.), *Neonate cognition* (pp. 365–380). Hillsdale, NJ: Erlbaum.

Anderson, N. H., & Cuneo, D. O. (1978). The height and width rule in children's judgements of quantity. *Journal of Experimental Psychology: General, 47,* Serial No. 198.

Anderson, R. M., Giachello, A. L., & Aday, L. A. (1986). Access of Hispanics to health care and cuts in services. *Public Health Reports, 101,* 238–252.

Anisfeld, E., Casper, V., Nozyce, M., & Cunningham, N. (1990). Does infant carrying promote attachment? An experimental study of the effects of increased physical contact on the development of attachment. *Child Development, 61,* 1617–1627.

Annis, R. C., & Corenblum, B. (1987). Effect of test language and experimenter race on Canadian Indian children's racial and self-identity. *Journal of Social Psychology, 126,* 761–773.

Anthony, J. C., & Petronis, K. R. (1989). Cocaine and heroin dependence compared: Evidence from an epidemiologic field survey. *American Journal of Public Health, 79,* 1409–1410.

Aries, P. (1962). *Centuries of childhood.* New York: Vintage.

Arnberg, L. (1987). *Raising children bilingually: The preschool years.* Philadelphia: Multicultural Matters Ltd.

Asher, S. G., Singleton, L. C., & Taylor, A. J. (1982). *Acceptance versus friendships: A longitudinal study of racial integration.* Paper presented at the American Educational Research Association.

Asher, S. R., & Dodge, K. A. (1985). Identifying children who are rejected by their peers. *Developmental Psychology, 22,* 444–449.

Aslin, R. N. (1987). Motor aspects of visual development in infancy. In P. Salapatek and L. Cohen (Eds.), *Handbook of infant perception* (Vol. 1, pp. 43–114). Orlando: Academic Press.

Aslin, R. N. (1988). Visual perception in early infancy. In A. Yonas (Ed.), *Perceptual development in infancy.* Hillsdale, NJ: Erlbaum.

Au, K. (1993). *Literacy instruction in multicultural settings.* Fort Worth: Harcourt Brace Jovanovich.

Avis, J., & Harris, P. L. (1991). Belief-desire reasoning among Baka children: Evidence for a universal conception of mind. *Child Development, 62,* 460–467.

Axelson, L., & Dail, P. (1988). The changing character of homeless in the United States. *Family Relations, 10,* 463–469.

Azrin, N., & Foxx, R. (1974). *Mrs. James potty trains Mickey.* New York: Simon & Schuster.

Ballard, R. (1976). Ethnicity: Theory and experience. *New Community, 5,* 196–202.

Balogh, R. D., & Porter, R. H. (1986). Olfactory preferences resulting from mere exposure in human neonates. *Infant Behavior and Development, 9,* 395–401.

Bamford, F. N., Bannister, R., Benjamin, C. N., Hillier, V. F., Ward, B. S., & Moore, W. M. O. (1990). Sleep in the first year of life. *Developmental and child neurology, 32,* 718–734.

Bandura, A. (1962). Social learning through imitation. In M. R. Jones (Ed.), *Nebraska symposium on motivation.* Lincoln: University of Nebraska.

Bandura, A. (1965). Influence of model's reinforcement contingencies on the acquisition of imitative responses. *Journal of Personality and Social Psychology, 1,* 589–595.

Bandura, A. (1967). The role of modeling processes in personality development. In W. W. Hartup & N. I. Smothergill (Eds.), *The young child: Reviews of research.* Washington, DC: National Association for the Education of Young Children.

Bandura, A. (1986). *Social foundations of thought and action.* Upper Saddle River, NJ: Prentice-Hall.

Bandura, A. (1989). Social cognitive theory. *Annals of Child Development, 6,* 1–60.

Banks, J. A. (1995). The historical reconstruction of knowledge about race: Implications for transforming learning. *Educational Researcher, 24*(2), 15–25.

Barden, R. C., Ford, M. E., Jensen, A., Rogers-Salyer, M. E., & Salyer, K. (1989). Effects of craniofacial deformity in infancy on the quality of mother-infant interactions. *Child Development, 60,* 819–824.

Barker, G., & Graham, S. (1987). Developmental study of praise and blame as attributional cues. *Journal of Educational Psychology, 79,* 62–66.

Barkley, R. A. (1990). Attention deficit disorders: History, definition, and diagnosis. In M. Lewis & S. M. Miller (Eds.), *Handbook of developmental psychopathology* (pp. 65–76). New York: Plenum.

Barrett, D. E., Radke-Yarrow, M., & Klein, R. E. (1982). Chronic malnutrition and behavior: Effects of early caloric supplementation on social and emotional functioning at school age. *Developmental Psychology, 18,* 541–556.

Barron-Cohen, S. (1997). Autism and symbolic play. *British Journal of Developmental Psychology, 5,* 139–148.

Barron-Cohen, S., Leslie, A. M., & Frith, U. (1985). Does the autistic child have a theory of the mind? *Cognition, 21,* 37–46.

Bartz, K. W., & Levine, E. S. (1978). Child rearing by black parents: A description and comparison to Anglo and Chicano parents. *Journal of Marriage and the Family,* November, 709–719.

Bassuk, E., & Rubin, L. (1987). Homeless children: A neglected population. *American Journal of Orthopsychiatry, 57,* 2.

Bates, E., O'Connell, B., & Shore, C. (1987). Language and communication in infancy. In J. D. Osofsky (Ed.), *Handbook of infant development* (2nd ed., pp. 149–203). New York: Wiley.

Bauer, P. J., & Hertsgaard, L. A. (1993). Increasing steps in recall events in 13.5- and 16.5-month-olds. *Child Development, 64,* 1204–1223.

Baumrind, D. (1994). The social context of child maltreatment. *Family Relations, 43,* 360–368.

Bayley, N. (1969). *Bayley Scales of Infant Development.* New York: Psychological Corporation.

Becker, J. (1986). Bossy and nice requests: Children's production and interpretation. *Merrill-Palmer Quarterly, 32,* 393–413.

Beckman, P. (1991). Comparison of mothers' and fathers' perceptions of the effect of young children with and without disabilities. *American Journal on Mental Retardation, 95,* 585–595.

Beckwith, L., & Rodning, C. (1991). Intellectual functioning in children born preterm: Recent research. In L. Okagaki & R. J. Sternberg (Eds.), *Directors of development: Influences on the development of children's thinking.* Hillsdale, NJ: Erlbaum.

Behrman, R. E. (Ed.). (1995). *The future of children: Low birth weight* (pp. 19–34). Los Angeles: Center for the Future of Children.

Bell, C. (1991). Traumatic stress and children in danger. *Journal of Health Care for the Poor and Underserved, 2,* 175–188.

Bell, S. M. (1970). The development of the concept of object as related to infant-mother attachment. *Child Development, 41,* 291–311.

Bell, S. M., & Ainsworth, M. D. S. (1972). Infant crying and maternal responsiveness. *Child Development, 43,* 1171–1190.

Belsky, J., & Rovine, M. (1987). Temperament and attachment security in the strange situation. *Child Development, 58,* 787–795.

Belsky, J., & Steinberg, L. D. (1978). The effects of day care: A critical review. *Child Development, 49,* 929–949.

Belsky, J., & Volling, B. L. (1987). Mothering, fathering, and marital interaction in the family triad during infancy: Exploring family systems processes. In P. Berman & F. Pedersen (Eds.), *Men's transition to parenthood* (pp. 37–63). Hillsdale, NJ: Erlbaum.

Bench, J. (1969). Audio-frequency and audio-discrimination in the human neonate. *International Audiology, 8,* 615–625.

Bereiter, C., & Engelmann, S. (1966). *Teaching the culturally disadvantaged child in preschool.* Upper Saddle River, NJ: Prentice-Hall.

Berenson, G., Frank, G., Hunter, S., Srinivasan, S., Voors, A., & Webber, L. (1982). Cardiovascular risk factors in children: Should they concern the pediatrician? *American Journal of Diseases of Children, 136,* 855–862.

Berger, K. S. (1994). *The developing person through the life span.* New York: Worth.

Berk, L. E. (1997). *Child development* (3rd ed.). Needham Heights, MA: Allyn & Bacon.

Berk, L. E., & Winsler, A. (1995). *Scaffolding children's learning: Vygotsky and early childhood education.* Washington, DC: National Association for the Education of Young Children.

Bertenthal, B. I., & Campos, J. (1990). A systems approach to the organizing effect of self-produced locomotion during infancy. In C. Rovee-Collier & L. P. Lipsitt (Eds.), *Advances in infancy research* (Vol. 6). Norwood, NJ: Ablex.

Bever, T. G. (1970). The cognitive basis for linguistic structures. In J. R. Hayes (Ed.), *Cognition and the development of language.* New York: Wiley.

Bhushan, V., Paneth, N., & Kiely, J. L. (1993). Impact of improved survival of very low birthweight infants on recent secular trends in the prevalence of cerebral palsy. *Pediatrics, 91,* 1094–1100.

Bialystok, E. (1986). Factors in the growth of linguistic awareness. *Child Development, 57,* 498–510.

Bierman, K. L., Smoot, D. L., & Aumiller, K. (1993). Characteristics of aggressive-rejected, aggressive nonrejected, and rejected nonaggressive boys. *Child Development, 64,* 139–151.

Bigler, R. S., & Liben, L. S. (1992). Cognitive mechanisms in children's gender stereotyping. *Child Development, 63,* 1351–1363.

Bjorkland, D. F. (1995). *Children's thinking: Developmental function and individual differences.* Pacific Grove, CA: Brooks/Cole.

Blake, J. (1989). *Family size and achievement.* Berkeley: University of California Press.

Blanchard, E. L. (1983). The psychosocial development of Native American children. In G. J. Powell (Ed.), *The psychosocial development of minority children.* New York: Brunner/Mazel.

Blevins-Knabe, B. (1987). Development of the ability to insert into a series. *Journal of Genetic Psychology, 148,* 427–441.

Bloch, M. N., & Adler, S. M. (1994). African children's play and the emergence of the sexual division of labor. In J. L. Roopnarine, J. E., Johnson & F. R. Hooper (Eds.), *Children's play in diverse cultures* (pp. 148–178). Albany: SUNY Press.

Bloom, L. (1993). *The transition from infancy to language: Acquiring the power of expression.* Cambridge, England: Cambridge University Press.

Blumenfeld, P., Pintrich, P., & Hamilton, V. (1986). Children's conceptions of ability, effort, and conduct. *American Educational Research Journal, 29,* 95–104.

Bodrova, E., & Leong, D. (1996). *Tools of the mind: The Vygoskian approach to early childhood education.* Upper Saddle River, NJ: Merrill/Prentice Hall.

Bogdan, R., & Knoll, J. (1995). The sociology of disability. In E. L. Meyen & T. M. Skrtic (Eds.), *Special education and student disability* (pp. 675–712). Denver: Love.

Boismier, J. D. (1977). Visual stimulation and wake-sleep behavior in human neonates. *Developmental Psychobiology, 10,* 219–227.

Boivin, M., & Begin, G. (1989). Peer status and self-perception among early elementary school children: The case of rejected children. *Child Development, 60,* 591–596.

Borke, H. (1975). Piaget's mountain revisited: Changes in the egocentric landscape. *Developmental Psychology, 11,* 240–243.

Bornstein, M. H. (1992). Perception cross the life span. In M. H. Bornstein & M. H. Lamb (Eds.), *Developmental psychology: An advanced textbook* (3rd ed., pp. 155–210). Hillsdale: Erlbaum.

Bornstein, M. H. (Ed.). (1995). *Handbook of parenting.* Mahwah, NJ: Erlbaum.

Borovsky, D., & Rovee-Collier, C. (1990). Contextual constraints on memory retrieval at 6 months. *Child Development, 61,* 1569–1583.

Bower, T. G. R. (1975). *The perceptual world of the child.* Cambridge: Harvard University Press.

Bowlby, J. (1969). *Attachment and loss: Vol. 2. Separation, anxiety, and anger.* New York: Basic Books.

Boyce, W. T., Schaeffer, C., Harrison, H. R., Haffner, W. H. J., Lewis, M., & Wright, A. L. (1986). Social and cultural factors in pregnancy complications among Navajo women. *American Journal of Epidemiology, 25,* 217–235.

Boykin, A. W. (1978). Psychological/behavioral verve in academic/task performance. *Journal of Negro Education, 47,* 343–354.

Boykin, A. W., & Toms, F. D. (1985). Black child socialization: A conceptual framework. In H. P. McAdoo & J. L. McAdoo (Eds.), *Black children: Social, educational, and parental environments.* Newbury Park, CA: Sage.

Bradley, R. H., Whiteside, L., Mundfrom, D. J., Casey, P. H., Kelleher, K. J., & Pope, S. K. (1994). Early indications of resilience and their relation to experiences in the home environments of low birth weight, premature children living in poverty. *Child Development, 65,* 346–360.

Bradley, R. M. (1972). Development of taste bud and gustatory papillae in human fetuses. In J. F. Bosma (Ed.), *The third symposium on oral sensation and perception: The mouth of the infant* (pp. 137–162). Springfield, IL: Thomas.

Braillargeon, R. Graber, M., Decops, J., & Black, J. (1990). Why do young infants fail to search for hidden objects? *Cognition, 36,* 255–284.

Brainerd, C. J. (1974). Training and transfer of transitivity, conservation, and class inclusion. *Child Development, 27,* 114–116.

Brazelton, T. B. (1962). A child-oriented approach to toileting. *Pediatrics, 29,* 121–127.

Brazelton, T. B., Koslowski, B., & Tronick, E. (1971). Study of neonatal behavior in Zambian and American neonates. *Journal of the American Academy of Child Psychiatry, 15,* 97–107.

Brazelton, T. B., Nugent, K. J., & Lester, B. M. (1987). Neonatal behavioral assessment scale. In J. D. Osofsky (Ed.), *Handbook of infant development* (pp. 780–817). New York: Wiley.

Bricker, D., Carlson, L., & Schwartz, R. (1981). A discussion of early intervention for infants with Down syndrome. *Pediatrics, 67,* 45–46.

Bridges, A. (1986). Actions and things: What adults talk about to 1-year-olds. In I. Kucjaz & M. D. Barrett (Eds.), *The devel-opment of word meaning* (pp. 114–136). New York: Springer-Verlag.

Brigham, J. C. (1974). Views of black and white children concerning the distribution of personality characteristics. *Journal of Personality, 42,* 144–158.

Brill, B. (1986). Motor development and cultural attitudes. In H. T. A. Whiting & M. G. Wade (Eds.), *Themes in motor development.* Dordrecht, The Netherlands: Martinus Nijhoff.

Broberg, A., Lamb, M. E., & Hwang, P. (1990). Inhibition: Its stability and correlates in 16- to 40-month-olds. *Child Development, 61,* 1153–1163.

Brody, G. H., Stoneman, Z., & McKinnon, C. E. (1982). Role asymmetries in interactions among school-aged children, their younger siblings, and friends. *Child Development, 53,* 1364–1370.

Brody, N. (1990). *Intelligence* (2nd ed.). San Diego: Academic Press.

Bronfenbrenner, U. (1979). *The ecology of human development: Experiments by nature and design.* Cambridge: Harvard University Press.

Bronson, G. W. (1990). Changes in infants' visual scanning across the 2- to 14-week period. *Journal of Experimental Child Psychology, 49,* 101–125.

Bronson, G. W. (1991). Infant differences in rate of visual encoding. *Child Development, 62,* 44–54.

Brookhart, H., & Hock, E. E. (1976). The effects of experimental context and experiential background on infants' behavior toward their mothers and a stranger. *Child Development, 47,* 333–340.

Brooks-Gunn, J., Klebanov, P. K., Liaw, F., & Spiker, D. (1993). Enhancing the development of low birthweight, premature infants. *Child Development, 64,* 736–753.

Brophy, J., & Evertson, C. (1987). Context variables in teaching. *Educational Psychologist, 12,* 310–316.

Brown, A. D., & Hernasy, M. A. (1983). The impact of culture on the health of American Indian children. In G. J. Powell (Ed.), *The psychosocial development of minority children* (pp. 39–48). New York: Brunner/Mazel.

Brown, J. E. (1995). *Nutrition now.* Saint Paul, MN: West.

Brown, J. E., Serdula, M., Cairns, K., Godes, J. R., Jacobs, D. R., Elmer, P., & Trowbridge, F. L. (1986). Ethnic group differences in nutritional status of young children from low-income areas of an urban county. *American Journal of Clinical Nutrition, 44,* 938–944.

Brown, R. (1973). *A first language: The early stages.* Cambridge, MA: Harvard University Press.

Brownell, C. A., & Carringer, M. S. (1990). Changes in cooperation and self-other differentiation during the second year. *Child Development, 61,* 1164–1175.

Brozek, J., & Schurch, B. (Eds.). (1984). *Malnutrition and behavior: Critical assessment of key issues.* Lausanne, Switzerland: Nestle Foundation.

Bruner, J. (1984). Vygotsky's zone of proximal development: The hidden agenda. In B. Rogoff & J. Wertsch (Eds.), *Children's learning in the zone of proximal development. New Directions in Child Development, No. 12.* San Francisco: Jossey Bass.

Bryen, D. N. (1986). *Inquiries into child language.* Boston: Allyn & Bacon.

Bushnell, E., & Boudreau, J. P. (1993). Motor development and the mind: The potential of motor abilities as a determinant of aspects of perceptual development. *Child Development, 64,* 1005–1021.

Caldera, Y. M., Huston, A. C., & O'Brien, M. (1989). Social interactions and play patterns of parents and toddlers with feminine, masculine, and neutral toys. *Child Development, 60*(1), 70–76.

Calkins, L. M. (1986). *The art of teaching writing.* Portsmouth, NH: Heinemann.

Callaghan, J. W. (1981). A comparison of Anglo, Hopi, and Navajo mothers and infants. In T. M. Field, A. M. Sostek, P. Vietze, & P. H. Leiderman (Eds.), *Culture and early interaction* (pp. 115–131). Hillsdale, NJ: Erlbaum.

Camara, K. A., & Resnick, G. (1988). Interparental conflict and cooperation: Factors moderating children's post-divorce adjustment. In E. M. Hetherington & J. D. Arasteh (Eds.), *Impact of divorce, single parenting, and stepparenting on children* (pp. 169–195). Hillsdale, NJ: Erlbaum.

Campbell, D. T. (1976). Stereotypes and the perception of group differences. *American Psychologist, 22,* 817–829.

Campbell, F. A., & Ramey, C. T. (1994). Effects of early intervention on intellectual and academic achievement. *Child Development, 65,* 684–698.

Carle, E. (1969). *The very hungry caterpillar.* Cleveland: Collins-World.

Caron, A., Caron, R., & MacLean, D. (1988). Infant discrimination of naturalistic emotional expressions. *Child Development, 59,* 604–616.

Carter, A. S., Mayes, L. C., & Pajer, K. A. (1990). The role of dyadic affect in play and infant sex in predicting infant response to the still-face situation. *Child Development, 61,* 764–773.

Carter, J. H. (1983). Vision or sight: Health concerns for Afro-American children. In G. J. Powell (Ed.), *The psychosocial development of minority children.* New York: Brunner/Mazel.

Caspi, A., Henry, B., McGee, R. O., Moffitt, T. E., & Silva, P. A. (1995). Tempermental origins of child and adolescent behavior problems: From age 3 to age 15. *Child Development, 66,* 58–66.

Cassidy, J., & Asher, S. R. (1992). Loneliness and peer relations in young children. *Child Development, 63,* 350–365.

Cassidy, J., & Berlin, L. J. (1994). The insecure/ambivalent pattern of attachment: Theory and research. *Child Development, 65,* 971–991.

Casto, G., & Mastropieri, M. (1986). The efficacy of early intervention programs: A meta-analysis. *Exceptional Children, 52,* 417–424.

Catherwood, D. (1993). The robustness of infant haptic memory. *Child Development, 64,* 702–710.

Caughy, M. O., DiPietro, J. A., & Strobino, D. M. (1994). Day-care participation as a protective factor in the cognitive development of low-income children. *Child Development, 65,* 457–471.

Ceci, S. (1991). How much does schooling influence general intelligence and its cognitive components? A reassessment of the evidence. *Developmental Psychology, 27,* 703–722.

Cernoch, J. M., & Porter, R. H. (1985). Recognition of maternal axillary odors by infants. *Child Development, 56,* 1593–1598.

Chamot, A. U., & O'Malley, J. (1994). *The CALLA handbook.* Reading, MA: Addison Wesley.

Chao, R. K. (1994). Beyond parental control and authoritarian parenting style: Understanding Chinese parenting through the cultural notion of training. *Child Development, 65,* 1111–1119.

Charlesworth, R. (1989). Behind before they start? Deciding how to deal with the risk of kindergarten failure. *Young Children, 44*(3), 5–13.

Chavez, A., & Martinez, C. (1979). Consequences of insufficient nutrition on child character and behavior. In D. A. Levitsky (Ed.), *Malnutrition, environment, and behavior* (pp. 238–255). Ithaca, NY: Cornell University Press.

Chavez, L. R., Cornelius, W. A., & Jones, O. W. (1986). Utilization of health services by Mexican immigrant women in San Diego. *Women and Health, 11,* 3–20.

Chen, C., & Stevenson, H. (1989). Homework: A cross-cultural examination. *Child Development, 60,* 551–561.

Chen, S.-J., & Miyake, K. (1986). Japanese studies of infant development. In H. Stevenson, H. Azuma, & K. Hakuta (Eds.), *Child development and education in Japan.* New York: Freeman.

Chen, X., Rubin, K. H., & Sun, Y. (1992). Social reputation and peer relationships in Chinese and Canadian children: A cross-cultural study. *Child Development, 63,* 1336–1343.

Cherlin, A. J., & Furstenberg, F. F. (1986). *The new American grandparent.* New York: Basic.

Chess, S., & Thomas, A. (1987). *Origins and evolution of behavior disorders from infancy to early adult life.* Cambridge: Harvard University Press.

Chess, S., & Thomas, A. (1990). Continuities and discontinuities in development. In L. S. Robins & M. Rutter (Eds.), *Straight and devious pathways from childhood to adulthood* (pp. 98–114). New York: Cambridge University Press.

Children's Defense Fund. (1994). *Cease fire in the war against children.* Washington, DC: Author.

Children's Defense Fund. (1998). *The state of America's children: Yearbook 1998.* Washington, DC: Author.

Chisholm, J. S. (1983). *Navajo infancy.* New York: Aldine.

Chomsky, C. (1966). Write now, read later. In C. Cazden (Ed.), *Language in early childhood education.* Washington, DC: National Association for the Education of Young Children.

Christie, J. F. (1994). Literacy play interventions: A review of empirical research. *Advances in Early Education and Day Care, 6,* 3–24.

Christie, J. F. (1983). The effects of play tutoring on young children's cognitive performance. *Journal of Educational Research, 76,* 326–330.

Chugani, H. T. (1997). Neuroimaging of developmental nonlinearity and developmental pathologies. In R. W. Thatcher, G. R., J. Lyon, R. Rumsey, & N. Krasnegor (Eds.), *Developmental neuroimaging: Mapping the development of brain and behavior.* San Diego: Academic Press.

Cicchetti, D., & Beeghly, M. (1990). *Children with Down syndrome: A developmental perspective.* Cambridge, England: Cambridge University Press.

Cicirelli, V. G. (1982). Sibling influence throughout the life span. In M. E. Lamb & B. Sutton-Smith (Eds.), *Sibling relationships* (pp. 73–106). Hillsdale, NJ: Erlbaum.

Cizek, G. H. (1995). Crunchy granola and the hegemony of narrative. *Educational Researcher, 24*(2), 15–17.

Clark, K. B. (1952). The effects of prejudice and discrimination on personality formation. In H. Witmer & R. Kotinsky (Eds.), *Personality in the making.* New York: Harper.

Clarke-Stewart, K. A. (1984). Day care: A new context for research and development. In M. Perlmutter (Ed.), *The Minnesota symposium on child psychology* (Vol. 17, pp. 61–100). Hillsdale, NJ: Erlbaum.

Clarke-Stewart, K. A. (1988). "The effects of infant day care reconsidered" reconsidered. *Early Childhood Research Quarterly, 3,* 293–318.

Clay, M. (1975). *What did I write?* Portsmouth, NH: Heinemann.

Coie, J. D., Dodge, K. A., Terry, R., & Wright, V. (1991). The role of aggression in peer relations: An analysis of aggression episodes in boys' play groups. *Child Development, 62,* 812–826.

Cole, M., & Scribner, S. (1974). *Culture and thought: A psychological introduction.* New York: Wiley.

Cole, M., & Scribner, S. (1977). Cross-cultural studies of memory and cognition. In R. V. Kail & J. W. Hagen (Eds.), *Perspectives on the development of memory and cognition* (pp. 239–271). Hillsdale, NJ: Erlbaum.

Coleman, J. M., & Minnett, A. M. (1992). Learning disabilities and social competence: A social ecological perspective. *Exceptional Children, 59,* 234–246.

Coleman, J. M., Pullis, M. E., & Minnett, A. M. (1987). Studying mildly handicapped children's adjustment to mainstreaming: A systematic approach. *Remedial and Special Education, 8,* 19–30.

Collier, V. (1989, March). *Academic achievement, attitudes, and occupation among graduates of two-way bilingual classes.* Paper presented at the American Educational Research Association, San Francisco.

Colombo, J., & Mitchell, D. W. (1991). Individual differences in early visual attention: Fixation time and information processing. In J. Colombo & J. W. Fagen (Eds.), *Individual differences in infancy: Reliability, stability, and prediction* (pp. 193–227). Hillsdale, NJ: Erlbaum.

Comer, J. P. (1985). Empowering black children's educational environments. In H. P. McAdoo & J. L. McAdoo (Eds.), *Black children: Social, educational, and parental environments* (pp. 123–138). Newbury Park, CA: Sage.

Condon, J. C., & Yousef, F. S. (1975). *An introduction to intercultural communication.* Indianapolis: Bobs-Merrill.

Condon, W. S., & Sander, L. W. (1974). Neonate movement is synchronized with adult speech. *Science, 183,* 99–101.

Connell, P. (1987). An effect of modeling and imitation teaching procedures on children with and without specific language impairment. *Journal of Speech and Hearing Research, 30,* 105–113.

Cooper, R. P., & Aslin, R. N. (1990). Preference for infant-directed speech in the first month after birth. *Child Development, 61,* 1584–1595.

Coplan, R. J., Rubin, K. H., Fox, N. A., Calkins, S. D., & Stewart, S. L. (1994). Being alone, playing alone, and acting alone: Distinguishing among reticence and passive and active solitude in young

children. *Child Development, 65,* 129–137.

Corenblum, B., & Wilson, A. E. (1982). Ethnic preference and identification among Canadian Indian and white children: Replication and extension. *Canadian Journal of Behavioral Science, 14,* 50–59.

Cost, Quality, and Child Outcomes Study Team. (1995). *Cost, quality, and child outcomes in child care centers: Public report* (2nd ed.). Denver: Economics Department, University of Colorado.

Cratty, B. J. (1986). *Perceptual and motor development in infants and children.* Upper Saddle River, NJ: Merrill/Prentice Hall.

Crick, N. R., Casas, J. F., & Mosher, M. (1997). Relational and overt aggression in preschool. *Developmental Psychology, 33,* 579–588.

Crick, N. R., & Ladd, G. W. (1987, April). *Children's perceptions of the consequences of aggressive behavior: Do the ends justify the means?* Paper presented at the biennial meeting of the Society for Research in Child Development, Baltimore.

Crick, N. R., & Ladd, G. W. (1990). Children's perceptions of the outcomes of social strategies. *Developmental Psychology, 26,* 612–620.

Cronin, V. (1987, April). *Word association and reading.* Paper presented at the biennial meeting of the Society for Research in Child Development, Baltimore.

Crook, C. K. (1987). Taste and olfaction. In P. Salapatek and L. Cohen (Eds.), *Handbook of infant perception* (Vol. 1, pp. 237–264). Orlando: Academic Press.

Cullinan, D., Epstein, M. H., & Lloyd, J. W. (1983). *Behavior disorders of children and adolescents.* Upper Saddle River, NJ: Merrill/Prentice Hall.

Cummins, J. (1987). Bilingualism language proficiency and metalinguistic development. In P. Homel, M. Palij, & D. Aaronson, (Eds.), *Childhood bilingualism: Aspects of linguistic, cognitive, and social development* (pp. 57–74). Hillsdale, NJ: Erlbaum.

Cuneo, D. O. (1980). A general strategy for quantity judgements. *Child Development, 50,* 170–179.

Cunningham, A. S., Jelliffe, D. B., & Jelliffe, E. F. P. (1991). Breastfeeding and health in the 1980s. *Journal of Pediatrics, 118,* 659–666.

Cunningham, C. C., Glenn, S. M., Wilkinson, P., & Sloper, P. (1985). Mental ability, symbolic play, and receptive and expressive language of young children with Down's syndrome. *Journal of Child Psychology and Psychiatry, 26,* 255–265.

Curry, N. E., & Johnson, C. N. (1990). *Beyond self-esteem: Developing a genuine sense of human value.* Washington, DC:

National Association for the Education of Young Children.

Dale, P. S. (1976). *Language development: Structure and function.* New York: Holt, Rinehart, & Winston.

Damon, W. (1988). *The moral child.* New York: Free Press.

Dansky, J. L. (1980). Make-believe: A mediator of the relationship between play and creativity. *Child Development, 51,* 576–579.

Dart, F. E., & Pradhan, P. L. (1967). Cross-cultural teaching of science. *Science, 155,* 649–656.

Dasen, P. R. (1984). The cross-cultural study of intelligence. *International Journal of Psychology, 19,* 407–434.

Davidoff, J. B. (1975). *Differences in visual perception: The individual eye.* New York: Academic Press.

Dawson, G., & Fischer, K. W. (1994). *Human behavior and the developing brain.* New York: Guilford.

De Boysson-Bardies, B., Sagart, L., & Durand, C. (1984). Discernible differences in the babbling of infants according to target language. *Journal of Child Language, 11,* 1–16.

DeCasper, A. J., & Fifer, W. P. (1980). Of human bonding: Newborns prefer their mother's voice. *Science, 208,* 1174–1176.

deMarrais, K. B., Nelson, P. A., & Baker, J. H. (1994). Meaning in mud: Yup'ik Eskimo girls at play. In J. L. Roopnarine, J. E. Johnson & F. H. Hooper (Eds.), *Children's play in diverse cultures* (pp. 179–209). Albany: SUNY Press.

deMause, L. (1974). The evolution of children. In L. DeMause (Ed.), *The history of childhood.* New York: Psychohistory Press.

Dennis, W., & Dennis, M. G. (1940). The effects of cradling practices upon the onset of walking in Hopi children. *Journal of Genetic Psychology, 56,* 77–86.

Denzin, N. K., & Lincoln, Y. S. (1994). *Handbook of qualitative research.* Thousand Oaks, CA: Sage.

Derman-Sparks, L. D. (1989). *Anti-bias curriculum: Tools for empowering young children.* Washington, DC: National Association for the Education of Young Children.

DeRosier, M. E., Gillessen, A. H., Coie, J. D., & Dodge, K. A. (1994). Group social context and children's aggressive behavior. *Child Development, 65,* 1068–1080.

DeStefano, J. (1972). Social variation in language: Implications for teaching reading to black ghetto children. In J. A. Figurel (Ed.), *Better reading in urban schools* (pp. 18–24). Newark, DE: International Reading Association.

De Vos, G. (1954). A comparison of the personality differences in two generations of

Japanese-Americans by means of the Rorschach Test. *Nagoya Journal of Medical Science, 17,* 153–265.

DeVries, M. W., & DeVries, M. R. (1977). The cultural relativity of toilet training readiness: A perspective from East Africa. *Pediatrics, 60,* 170–177.

DeVries, M. W., & Sameroff, A. J. (1984). Culture and temperament: Influences on infant temperament in three East-African societies. *American Journal of Orthopsychiatry, 54,* 83–96.

DeVries, R. A., & Kohlberg, L. (1990). *Constructivist early education: Overview and comparison with other programs.* Washington, DC: National Association for the Education of Young Children.

Diaz, R. M., & Klinger, C. (1991). Toward an explanatory model of the interaction between bilingualism and cognitive development. In E. Bialystok (Ed.), *Language processing in bilingual children* (pp. 181–197). Cambridge, England: Cambridge University Press.

Diaz-Guerrero, R. (1987). Historical sociocultural premises and ethnic socialization. In J. S. Phinney & M. J. Rotheram (Eds.), *Children's ethnic socialization.* Newbury Park, CA: Sage.

Dickinson, D. K. (1985). Creating and using formal occasions in the classroom. *Anthropology and Education Quarterly, 16,* 47–62.

Dickinson, D. K. (1994). Features of early childhood classroom environments that support development and literacy. In J. Duchan, L. Hewitt, & R. Sonnenmeir (Eds.), *Pragmatics: From theory to practice* (pp. 185–201). Upper Saddle River, NJ: Prentice Hall.

Dietz, W., & Gortmaker, S. (1985). Do we fatten our children at the television set? Obesity and television viewing in children and adolescents. *Pediatrics, 75,* 807–812.

Di Leo, J. H. (1982). Graphic activity of young children: Development and creativity. In L. Lasky & R. Mukerji (Eds.), *Art: Basic for young children.* Washington, DC: National Association for the Education of Young Children.

Dockrell, J., Campbell, R., & Neilson, I. (1980). Conservation accidents revisited. *International Journal of Behavioral Development, 3,* 423–439.

Dodge, K. A., & Coie, J. D. (1987). Social information processing factors in reactive and proactive aggression in children's peer groups. *Journal of Personality and Social Psychology, 53,* 1146–1158.

Dodge, K. A., Coie, J. D., Pettit, G. S., & Price, J. M. (1990). Peer status and aggression in boys' groups: Developmental and contextual analysis. *Child Development, 61,* 1289–1309.

Dodge, K. A., & Price, J. M. (1994). On the relation between social information processing and socially competent behavior in early school-aged children. *Child Development, 65,* 1385–1398.

D'Odorico, L. (1984). Nonsegmental features in prelinguistic communications. *Journal of Child Language, 11,* 17–27.

Dowling, P. T., & Fisher, M. (1987). Maternal factors and low birthweight infants: A comparison of blacks with Mexican-Americans. *Journal of Family Practice, 25,* 153–158.

Dudley-Marling, D. D., & Edmiason, R. (1985). Social status of learning disabled children and adolescents. *Learning Disability Quarterly, 8,* 189–204.

Duncan, G. J., Brooks-Gunn, J., & Klebanov, P. K. (1994). Economic deprivation and early childhood development. *Child Development, 65,* 296–318.

Dunn, J. (1992). Siblings and development. *Current Directions in Psychological Sciences, 1,* 6–9.

Dunn, J., & Kendrick, C. (1979). Interactions between young siblings in the context of family relationships. In M. Lewis & L. Rosenblum (Ed.), *The child and its family* (pp. 230–246). New York: Plenum.

Dunn, J., & McGuire, P. (1992). Sibling and peer relationships in childhood. *Journal of Child Psychology and Psychiatry, 33,* 67–105.

DuPaul, G. J., & Barkley, R. A. (1993). Behavioral contributions to pharmacotherapy: The utility of behavioral methodology in the medical treatment of children with attention deficit hyperactivity disorder. *Behavior Therapy, 24,* 47–64.

Durkin, K. (1995). *Developmental social psychology.* Cambridge, MA: Blackwell.

Dwek, C. S., Goetz, T. E., & Strauss, N. L. (1980). Sex differences in learned helplessness: An experimental and naturalistic study of failure generalization and its mediators. *Journal of Personality and Social Psychology, 38,* 441–452.

Dwek, C. S., & Licht, B. G. (1980). Learned helplessness and intellectual achievement. In J. Garber & M. E. P. Seligmann (Eds.), *Human helplessness theory and applications* (pp. 197–221). New York: Academic Press.

Easterbrooks, M. A. (1989). Quality of attachment to mother and to father: Effects of perinatal risk status. *Child Development, 60,* 825–830.

Eaton, W. O., & Yu, A. P. (1989). Are sex differences in child motor activity level a function of sex differences in maturational status? *Child Development, 60,* 1005–1011.

Eaves, L. J., Eysenck, H. J., & Martin, N. G. (1989). *Genes, culture, and personality.* London: Academic Press.

Eccles, J., Wigfield, A., Harold, R. D., & Blumenfeld, P. (1993). Age and gender differences in children's self- and task-perceptions during elementary school. *Child Development, 64,* 830–847.

Eckerman, C. O., Whatley, J. L., & Kutz, S. L. (1975). Growth of social play with peers during the second year of life. *Developmental Psychology, 11,* 42–49.

Eckman, P. (1972). Universals and cultural differences in facial expressions of emotion. In J. K. Cole (Ed.), *Nebraska symposium on motivation* (pp. 46–52). Lincoln: University of Nebraska Press.

Edwards, J. (1981). *Ratings of black, white, and Acadian children's speech patterns.* Unpublished manuscript, Mount St. Vincent University, Halifax, Nova Scotia.

Edwards, L. (1983). Curriculum modifications as a strategy for helping regular classroom behavior disordered students. In E. Meyen, G. Vergason, & R. Whelan (Eds.), *Promising practices for exceptional children: Curriculum implications* (pp. 87–104). Denver: Love.

Eibl-Eibesfeldt, I. (1979). Universals in human expressive behavior. In A. Wolfgang (Ed.), *Nonverbal behavior: Applications and cultural implications* (pp. 124–129). New York: Academic Press.

Eilers R. E., & Minifie, F. D. (1975). Fricative discrimination in early infancy. *Journal of Speech and Hearing Research, 18,* 158–167.

Eimas, P. D., & Tartter, V. C. (1979). The development of speech perception. In H. W. Reese & L. P. Lipsitt (Eds.), *Advances in child development and behavior* (Vol. 13, pp. 155–193). New York: Academic Press.

Eisenberg, N. (1986). *Altruistic emotion, cognition, and behavior.* Hillsdale, NJ: Erlbaum.

Eisenberg, N., Fabes, R. A., Murphy, B., Karbon, M., Smith, M., & Maszk, P. (1996). The relations of children's dispositional empathy-related responding to their emotionality, regulation, and social functioning. *Developmental Psychology, 32,* 195–209.

Ekman, P. (1994). Strong evidence for universals in facial expressions: A reply to Russell's mistaken critique. *Psychological Bulletin, 115,* 268–287.

Ekstein, R. (1978). Psychoanalysis, sympathy, and altruism. In L. Wispe (Ed.), *Altruism, sympathy, and helping* (pp. 237–250). New York: Academic Press.

Elkind, D. (1981). *The hurried child.* Reading, MA: Addison-Wesley.

Elkind, D. (1987). *Miseducation: Preschoolers at risk.* New York: Knopf.

Entwistle, D. R. (1966). *Word association responses of young children.* Baltimore: Johns Hopkins University.

Erikson, E. H. (1963). *Childhood and society* (2nd ed.). New York: Norton.

Erikson, E. H. (1982). *The life cycle completed: A review.* New York: Norton.

Erikson, M. F., Sroufe, L. A., & Egeland, B. (1985). The relation between quality of attachment and behavior problems in preschool in a high-risk sample. In I. Bretherton & E. Waters (Eds.), Growing points for attachment theory and research (pp. 147–166). *Monographs of the Society for Research in Child Development, 50,* Serial No. 209.

Eron, L. D., & Huesmann, L. R. (1990). The stability of aggressive behavior: Even unto the third generation. In M. Lewis & S. M. Miller (Eds.), *Handbook of developmental psychopathology* (pp. 147–156). New York: Plenum.

Eskanazi, B., Prehn, A. W., & Christianson, R. E. (1995). Passive and active maternal smoking as measured by serum cotinine: The effect on birthweight. *American Journal of Public Health, 85,* 395–398.

Eskes, T. K. A. (1992). Home deliveries in the Netherlands: Perinatal mortality and morbidity. *International Journal of Gynecology and Obstetrics, 38,* 161–169.

Esposito, B. G., & Koorland, M. A. (1989). Play behavior of hearing impaired children: Integrated and segregated settings. *Exceptional Children, 55,* 412–419.

Evans, E. E. (1975). *Contemporary influences in early childhood education.* New York: Holt, Rinehart, & Winston.

Evans, H. J. (1981). Abnormalities and cigarette smoking. *Lancet, 1,* 627–634.

Fabricius, W. V., & Cavalier, L. (1989). The role of causal theories about memory in young children's memory strategy choice. *Child Development, 60,* 298–308.

Fagot, B., & Leinbach, M. D. (1993). Gender role development in young children. *Developmental Review, 13,* 205–224.

Fagot, B., & O'Brien, M. (1994). Activity level in young children. *Merrill Palmer Quarterly, 40,* 378–398.

Fajardo, B. F., & Freedman, D. G. (1981). Maternal rhythmicity in three American cultures. In T. Field, M. Sostek, P. Vietze & P. H. Leiderman (Eds.), *Culture and early interaction* (pp. 133–146). Hillsdale, NJ: Erlbaum.

Falbo, T., & Poston, D. L. (1993). The academic, personality, and physical outcomes of only children in China. *Child Development, 64,* 18–35.

Fallen, N. H., & Umansky, W. (1985). *Young children with special needs* (2nd ed.). Upper Saddle River, NJ: Merrill/Prentice Hall.

Fantz, R. L. (1961). The origin of form perception. *Scientific American, 204,* 66–72.

Fantz, R. L. (1963). Pattern vision in newborn infants. *Science, 140,* 296–297.

Fantz, R. L., Fagan, J., & Miranda, S. (1975). Early visual selectivity. In L. Cohen & P. Slapatek (Eds.), *Infant perception: From sensation to cognition* (pp. 249–341). New York: Academic Press.

Farber, B., Mindel, C. H., & Lazerwitz, B. (1988). The Jewish American family. In C. H. Mindel, R. W. Habenstein, & R. Wright (Eds.), *Ethnic families in America: Patterns and variations* (pp. 400–437). New York: Elsevier.

Feiring, C., & Lewis, M. (1989). The social network of girls and boys from early through middle childhood. In D. Belle (Ed.), *Children's social networks and social supports.* New York: Wiley.

Fenson, L., Dale, P. S., Reznick, J. S., Bates, E., Thal, D. J., & Pethick, S. J. (1994). Variability in early communicative development. *Monographs of the Society for Research in Child Development, 59,* no. 5 (Serial No. 242).

Fenson, L., Cameron, M., & Kennedy, M. (1988). Role of perception and conceptual similarity in category matching at age two years. *Child Development, 59,* 897–907.

Fernald, A. (1993). Approval and disapproval: Infant responsiveness to vocal affect in familiar and unfamiliar languages. *Child Development, 64,* 657–674.

Fernald, A., & Morikawa, H. (1993). Common themes and cultural variations in Japanese and American mothers' speech to infants. *Child Development, 64,* 637–656.

Ferreiro, E., & Teberosky, A. (1982). *Literacy before schooling.* Exeter, NH: Heinemann.

Field, T. M., & Widmayer. (1981). Mother-infant interactions among lower SES black, Cuban, Puerto Rican, and South American immigrants. In T. M. Field, A. M. Sostek, P. Vietze & P. H. Leiderman (Eds.), *Culture and early interactions* (pp. 41–60). Hillsdale, NJ: Erlbaum.

Figueroa, R. A. (1980). Field dependence, ethnicity, and cognitive styles. *Hispanic Journal of Behavioral Science, 2,* 10.

Fincham, F. D., Hokoda, A., & Sanders, R. S. (1989). Learned helplessness, test anxiety, and academic achievement: A longitudinal analysis. *Child Development, 60,* 138–145.

Flavell, J. (1985). *Cognitive development.* Hillsdale, NJ: Erlbaum.

Flavell, J. (1992). Cognitive development: Past, present, and future. *Developmental Psychology, 28,* 998–1006.

Flavell, J., Beach, D., & Chinsky, J. (1966). Spontaneous and verbal rehearsal in a memory task as a function of age. *Child Development, 37,* 283–299.

Flavell, J., Green, H. L., & Flavell, E. R. (1995). Young children's knowledge about thinking. *Monographs of the Society for Research in Child Development, 60,* no. 1 (Serial No. 243).

Flavell, J., Miller, P. H., & Miller, S. A. (1993). *Cognitive development.* Hillsdale, NJ: Erlbaum.

Flavell, J., Zhang, X.-D., Zou, H., Dong, Q., & Qi, S. (1983). A comparison of the appearance-reality distinction in the People's Republic of China and the United States. *Cognitive Psychology, 15,* 459–466.

Floyd, R. L., Rimer, B. K., Giovino, G. A., Mullen, P. D., & Sullivan, S. E. (1993). A review of smoking in pregnancy. *Annual Review of Public Health, 14,* 379–411.

Fox, D. J., & Jordan, V. B. (1973). Racial preferences and identification of black American, Chinese, and white children. *Genetic Psychology Monographs, 88,* 229–286.

Fox, N. A., Kimmerly, N. L., & Schafer, W. D. (1991). Attachment to mother/attachment to father: A meta-analysis. *Child Development, 62,* 210–225.

Fraiberg, S. (1977). *Insights from the blind: Comparative studies of blind and sighted infants.* New York: Basic Books.

Fraiberg, S. (1978). *Insights from the blind.* London: Souvenir Press.

Fraser, A. M., Brockert, J. E., & Ward, R. H. (1995). Association of young maternal age with adverse reproductive outcomes. *New England Journal of Medicine, 332,* 113–117.

Freedman, D. G. (1974). *Human infancy: An evolutionary perspective.* Hillsdale, NJ: Erlbaum.

Freedman, D. G. (1979). Ethnic differences in babies. *Human Nature, 2,* 36–43.

French, D. C. (1990). Heterogeneity of peer-rejected girls. *Child Development, 61,* 2028–2031.

Freud, S. (1930). *Civilization and its discontents.* London: Hogarth.

Freud, S. (1938). The history of the psychoanalytic movement. In A. A. Brill (Ed.), *The basic writings of Sigmund Freud.* New York: Modern Library.

Freund, L. S. (1989). Maternal regulation of children's problem solving behavior and its impact on children's performance. *Child Development, 61,* 113–126.

Friedman, W. J., & Laycock, F. (1989). Children's analog and digital clock knowledge. *Child Development, 60,* 357–371.

Frodi, A. M., & Senchak, M. (1990). Verbal and behavioral responsiveness to the cries of atypical infants. *Child Development, 61,* 76–84.

Frost, J. L., & Klein, B. L. (1979). *Children's play and playgrounds.* Boston: Allyn & Bacon.

Fuchs, D., & Fuchs, L. S. (1986). Test procedure bias: A meta-analysis of examiner familiarity effects. *Review of Educational Research, 56,* 243–262.

Furstenberg, F. F., & Cherlin, A. J. (1991). *Divided families: What happens to children when parents part.* Cambridge: Harvard University Press.

Fuson, K. C., & Kwon, Y. (1992). Korean children's understanding of multidigit addition and subtraction. *Child Development, 63,* 491–506.

Gaduka, I. N., Poole, D. A., & Aotaki-Phenice, L. (1992). A comparative study of black South African children from three different contexts. *Child Development, 63,* 500–525.

Gallahue, D. L. (1982). *Understanding motor development.* New York: Wiley.

Gandini, L. (1997a). Foundations of the Reggio Emilia approach. In J. Hendrick (Ed.), *First steps toward teaching the Reggio way* (pp. 14–23). Upper Saddle River, NJ: Merrill/Prentice Hall.

Gandini, L. (1997b). The Reggio Emilia story: History and organization. In J. Hendrick (Ed.), *First steps toward teaching the Reggio Emilia way* (pp. 2–13). Upper Saddle River, NJ: Merrill/Prentice Hall.

Gandour, M. J. (1989). Activity level as a dimension of temperament in toddlers. *Child Development, 60,* 1092–1098.

Garbarino, J., Dubrow, N., Kostelny, K., & Pardo, C. (1992). *Children in danger.* San Francisco: Jossey Bass.

Garbarino, J., & Kostelny, K. (1992). Neighborhood and community influences on parenting. In T. Luster & L. Okagaki (Eds.), *Parenting: An ecological perspective.* Hillsdale, NJ: Erlbaum.

Garbarino, J., & Kostelny, K. (1996). The effects of political violence on Palestinian children's behavior problems: A risk accumulation model. *Child Development, 67,* 33–46.

Garcia Coll, C. T. (1990). Developmental outcome of minority infants: A process-oriented look into our beginnings. *Child Development, 61,* 270–289.

Garcia Coll, C. T., Emmons, L., Vohr, B. R., Ward, A. M., Brann, B. S., Shawl, P. W., Mayfield, S. R., & Oh, W. (1988). Behavioral responsiveness in preterm infants with intraventricular hemorrhage. *Pediatrics, 81,* 412–418.

Garcia Coll, C. T., Hoffman, J., & Oh, W. (1987). The social ecology and early parenting of Caucasian adolescent mothers. *Child Development, 14,* 147–154.

Garcia Coll, C. T., Meyer, E. C., & Brillon, L. (1995). Ethnic and minority parenting. In M. H. Bornstein (Ed.), *Handbook of parenting* (Vol. 2, pp. 189–209). Mahwah, NJ: Erlbaum.

Garcia Coll, C. T., Sepkoski, C., & Lester, B. M. (1981). Cultural and biomedical correlates of neonatal behavior. *Developmental Psychobiology, 14,* 147–154.

Gardner, D., Harris, P. L., Ohmoto, M., & Hamazaki, T. (1988). Japanese children's understanding of real and apparent emotion. *International Journal of Behavior Development, 11,* 203–218.

Gardner, H. (1993). *Multiple intelligences: The theory in practice.* New York: Basic Books.

Garner, P. W., Jones, D. C., & Miner, J. L. (1994). Social competence among low-income preschoolers: Emotion socialization practices and social cognitive correlates. *Child Development, 65,* 622–637.

Garvey, C. (1977). Play with language and speech. In S. Ervin-Tripp & C. Mitchell-Kernan (Eds.), *Child discourse.* New York: Academic Press.

Garvey, C., & Hogan, R. (1973). Social speech and social interaction: Egocentrism revisited. *Child Development, 44,* 562–568.

Garvey, C., & Kramer, T. L. (1989). The language of social pretend play. *Developmental Review, 9,* 364–382.

Gelman, R. (1982). Accessing one-to-one correspondence: Still another paper about conservation. *British Journal of Psychology, 73,* 209–220.

Gelman, S. A., & Kremer, K. E. (1991). Understanding natural cause: Children's explanations of how objects and their properties originate. *Child Development, 62,* 396–414.

George, D. M., & Hoppe, R. A. (1979). Racial identification, preference, and self-concept. *Journal of Cross-Cultural Psychology, 10,* 85–100.

Gesell, A. (1933). The maturation and patterning of behavior. In C. Murchison (Ed.), *Handbook of child psychology.* Worcester, MA: Clark University Press.

Gesell, A., & Ilg, F. L. (1949). *Child development.* New York: Harper and Row.

Gesell, A., & Thompson, H. (1929). Learning and growth in identical infant twins: An experiment by the method of co-twin control. *Genetic Psychology Monographs, 6,* 1–125.

Gibson, E. J., & Walk, R. D. (1960, April). The visual cliff. *Scientific American,* 64–71.

Gilligan, C. (1982). *In a different voice: Sex differences in the expression of moral judgement.* Cambridge: Harvard University Press.

Gilligan, C., Brown, L. M., & Rogers, A. G. (1990). Psyche imbedded: A place for body, relationships, and culture in personality formation. In A. J. Rabin, R. A. Zucker, R. A. Emmons, & S. Frank (Eds.), *Studying persons and lives.* New York: Springer.

Gilligan, C., Murphy, J. M., & Tappan, M. B. (1990). Moral development beyond adolescence. In C. N. Alexander & E. J. Langer (Eds.), *Higher stages of human development* (pp. 41–116). New York: Oxford University Press.

Ginsberg, G. S., & Bronstein, P. (1993). Family factors related to children's intrinsic/extrinsic motivational orientation and academic performance. *Child Development, 64,* 1461–1474.

Gleitman, L. R., & Gleitman, H. (1992). A picture is worth a thousand words, but that's the problem: The role of syntax in vocabulary development. *Current Directions in Psychological Science, 1,* 31–35.

Glenn, S. M., Cunningham, C. C., & Joyce, P. F. (1981). A study of auditory preferences in nonhandicapped infants and infants with Down syndrome. *Child Development, 52,* 1303–1307.

Goldberg, S. (1977). Infant development and mother-infant interaction in urban Zambia. In P. H. Leiderman, S. R. Tulkin, & A. Rosenfeld (Eds.), *Culture and infancy: Variations in the human experience.* New York: Academic Press.

Goldberg, S., Brachfeld, S., & DiVitto, B. (1980). Feeding, fussing and play: Parent-infant interaction in the first year as a function of prematurity and perinatal medical problems. In T. M. Field (Ed.), *High risk infants and children* (pp. 133–153). New York: Academic Press.

Goldberg, S., Markovitch, S., MacGregor, D., & Lojkasek, M. (1986). Family responses to developmentally delayed preschoolers. *American Journal of Mental Deficiency, 90,* 610–617.

Goldin-Meadow, S., & Morford, M. (1985). Gesture in early language: Studies of deaf and hearing children. *Merrill-Palmer Quarterly, 31,* 134–176.

Goldin-Meadow, S., Mylander, C., & Butcher, C. (1995). The resilience of combinatorial structure at the word level: Morphology in self-styled gesture systems. *Cognition, 56,* 195–262.

Goldsmith, H. H. (1987). What is temperament? Four approaches. *Child Development, 58,* 505–529.

Goldsmith, H. H., & Campos, J. J. (1990). The structure of temperamental fear and pleasure in infants: A psychometric perspective. *Child Development, 61,* 1944–1964.

Goodman, R. M. (1986). *Planning for a healthy baby.* New York: Oxford University Press.

Goodman, S. H., Brogan, D., Lynch, M. E., & Fielding, B. (1993). Social and emotional competence in children of depressed mothers. *Child Development, 64,* 516–532.

Goodnow, J., & Collins, W. (1990). *Development according to parents: The nature, sources, and consequences of parent ideas.* Hillsdale, NJ: Erlbaum.

Gopnik, A., & Choi, S. (1990). Do linguistic differences lead to cognitive differences? *First Language, 10,* 199–215.

Gottesman, I. I., & Goldsmith, H. H. (1994). Developmental psychopathology of antisocial behavior: Inserting genes into its ontogenesis and epigenesis. In C. A. Nelson (Ed.), *The Minnesota Symposium on Child Psychology* (Vol. 27, pp. 69–104). Hillsdale, NJ: Erlbaum.

Grant, R. (1989). *Assessing the damage: The impact of shelter experience on homeless young children.* New York: Association to Benefit Children.

Grantham-McGregor, S., Powell, C., Walker, S., Chang, S., & Fletcher, P. (1994). The long-term follow-up of severely malnourished children who participated in an intervention program. *Child Development, 65,* 428–439.

Green, J. A., Jones, L. E., & Gustafson, G. E. (1987). Perception of cries by parents and nonparents: Relation to cry acoustics. *Developmental Psychology, 23,* 370–382.

Greenbaum, C. W., & Landau, R. (1982). The infant's exposure to talk by familiar people: Mothers, fathers, and siblings in different environments. In M. Lewis & I. Rosenblum (Eds.), *The social network of the developing child* (pp. 50–102). New York: Plenum.

Greenfield, P. M. (1966). On culture and conservation. In J. S. Bruner, R. P. Olver & P. M. Greenfield (Eds.), *Studies in cognitive development* (pp. 35–59). New York: Wiley.

Greenfield, P. M. (1995). Profile: On teaching, culture, ethnicity, race, and development. *Society for Research in Child Development Newsletter* (Winter), 3–4, 12.

Griffith, D. R., Azuma, S. D., & Chasnoff, I. J. (1994). The year outcome of children exposed prenatally to drugs. *Journal of the Academy of Child and Adolescent Psychiatry, 33,* 20–27.

Grove, N., Cusick, B., & Bigge, J. (1991). Conditions resulting in physical disabilities. In J. Bigge (Ed.), *Teaching individuals with physical and multiple disabilities* (pp. 1–15). Upper Saddle River, NJ: Merrill/Prentice Hall.

Gunderson, L. (1991). *ESL literacy instruction: A guidebook to theory and practice.* Upper Saddle River, NJ: Regents/Prentice Hall.

Gunnar, M. R. (1996). *Quality of care and buffering of stress physiology: Its potential for protecting the developing human brain.* Minneapolis: University of Minnesota Institute of Child Development.

Guntheroth, W. G., Lohmann, R., & Spiers, P. S. (1990). Risk of sudden infant death syndrome in subsequent siblings. *Journal of Pediatrics, 116,* 4.

Guthrie, H. (1986). *Introductory nutrition.* St Louis: Times Mirror/Mosby.

Hack, M., Klein, N. K., & Taylor, H. G. (1995). Long-term developmental outcomes of low birth weight infants. *The future of children: Low birth weight* (pp. 176–197). Los Altos, CA: The David and Lucille Packard Foundation.

Haglund, B., & Cnattingious, S. (1990). Cigarette smoking as a risk factor for sudden infant death syndrome: A population-based study. *American Journal of Public Health, 80,* 29–32.

Haith, M. M. (1990). Sensory and perceptual processes in early infancy. *Merrill-Palmer Quarterly, 36,* 1–27.

Hakuta, K. (1986). *Mirror of language: The debate on bilingualism.* New York: Basic Books.

Hale, J. (1994). *Unbank the fire: Visions for the education of African-American children.* Baltimore: Johns Hopkins University Press.

Hale-Benson, J. E. (1986). *Black children: Their roots, culture, and learning styles.* Baltimore: Johns Hopkins University Press.

Halford, G. S., Maybery, M. T., O'Hare, A. W., & Grant, P. (1994). The development of memory and processing capacity. *Child Development, 65,* 1338–1356.

Hall, G. S. (1893). *The content of children's minds.* New York: Kellog.

Hall, N. (1987). *The emergent literacy.* Portsmouth, NH: Heinemann.

Hall, W. S., Bartlett, E., & Hughes, A. T. (1988). Patterns of information requests. In D. Slaughter (Ed.), *Black children and poverty: A developmental perspective* (pp. 11–28). San Francisco: Jossey-Bass.

Hallinan, M., & Sorenson, A. (1983). The formation and stability of instructional groups. *American Sociological Review, 48,* 838–851.

Hallinan, M., & Teixeira, R. A. (1987). Opportunities and constraints: Black-white differences in the formation of interracial friendships. *Child Development, 58,* 1358–1371.

Hansen, J., & Bowey, A. B. (1994). Phonological analysis skills, verbal working memory, and reading ability in second-grade children. *Child Development, 65,* 938–950.

Harris, J. C. (1995). *Developmental neuropsychiatry.* New York: Oxford University Press.

Harris, S. (1986). Evaluation of a curriculum to support literacy growth in young children. *Early Childhood Research Quarterly, 1,* 333–348.

Harrison, A. O. (1985). The black family's socializing environment: Self-esteem and ethnic attitude among black children. In H. P. McAdoo & J. L. McAdoo (Eds.), *Black children: Social, educational, and parental environments* (pp. 174–193). Newbury Park, NJ: Sage.

Harrison, A. O., Wilson, M. N., Pine, C. J., Chan, S. Q., & Buriel, R. (1990). Family ecologies of ethnic minority children. *Child Development, 61,* 347–362.

Harste, J., Woodward, V., & Burke, C. (1984). *Language stories and literacy lessons.* Portsmouth, NH: Heinemann.

Hart, C. H., Burts, C., Durland, M. A., Charlesworth, R., DeWolf, M., & Fleege, P. O. (1998). Stress behaviors and activity type participation of preschoolers in more and less developmentally-appropriate classrooms: SES and sex differences. *Journal for Research in Childhood Education, 12,* 176–197.

Hart, C. H., Burts, D. C., & Charlesworth, R. (1997). Integrated developmentally appropriate practice: From theory and research to practice. In C. H. Hart, D. C. Burts, & R. Charlesworth (Eds.), *Integrated curriculum and developmentally appropriate practice: Birth to age eight.* Albany: SUNY Press.

Hart, C. H., DeWolf, D. M., Wozniak, P., & Burts, D. (1992). Maternal and paternal disciplinary styles: Relations with preschoolers' playground behavior orientations and peer status. *Child Development, 63,* 879–892.

Hart, C. H., Ladd, G. W., & Burleson, B. R. (1990). Children's expectations of the outcomes of social strategies: Relations with sociometric status and maternal disciplinary styles. *Child Development, 61,* 127–137.

Hart, C. H., Olsen, S. F., Robinson, C. C., & Mandleco, B. L. (1997). The development of social and communicative competence in childhood: Review and a model of personal, familial, and extrafamilial processes. *Communication Yearbook, 20,* 305–373.

Harter, S. (1983). Developmental perspectives on the self-system. In E. M. Hetherington (Ed.), *Handbook of child psychology* (Vol. 4, pp. 275–386). New York: Wiley.

Harter, S. (1990). Causes, correlates, and the functional role of global self-worth: A life span perspective. In R. J. Sternberg & J. Kolligan (Eds.), *Competence considered* (pp. 67–97). New Haven: Yale University Press.

Harter, S., & Whitesell, N. R. (1989). Developmental changes in children's understanding of single, multiple, and blended emotion concepts. In C. Saarni & P. L. Harris (Eds.), *Children's understanding of emotion* (pp. 105–139). Cambridge, England: Cambridge University Press.

Hartup, W. W. (1983). Peer relations. In P. H. Mussen (Ed.), *Handbook of child psychology* (Vol. 4, pp. 120–163). New York: Wiley.

Hartup, W. W. (1996). The company they keep: Friendships and their developmental significance. *Child Development, 67,* 1–13.

Hartup, W. W., & Laursen, B. (1993). Conflict and context in peer relations. In C. H. Hart (Ed.), *Children on playgrounds: Research perspectives and applications* (pp. 44–84). Albany: SUNY Press.

Hartup, W. W., Laursen, B., Stewart, M. A., & Eastenson, A. (1988). Conflict and friendship relations of young children. *Child Development, 59,* 1590–1600.

Hartup, W. W., & Moore, S. G. (1990). Early peer relations: Developmental significance and prognostic implications. *Early Childhood Research Quarterly, 5,* 1–17.

Harwood, R. L. (1992). The influence of culturally derived values on Anglo and Puerto Rican mothers' perceptions of attachment behavior. *Child Development, 63,* 822–839.

Harwood, R. L., Miller, J. G., & Irizarry, N. L. (1995). *Culture and attachment: Perceptions of the child in context.* New York: Guilford.

Haselager, G. J. T., Hartup, W. W., van Lieshout, C. F. M., & Risen-Walraven,

J. M. A. (1998). Similarities between friends and nonfriends in middle childhood. *Child Developemnt, 69,* 1198–1208.

Haskett, M. E., & Kistner, J. A. (1991). Social interactions and peer perceptions of young physically abused children. *Child Development, 62,* 979–990.

Haskins, R. (1985). Public aggression among children with varying day-care experience. *Child Development, 56,* 698–703.

Hauser, S. T. (1972). Black and white identity development: Aspects and perspectives. *Journal of Youth and Adolescence, 1*(2), 113–130.

Hawley, T. L., & Disney, E. R. (1992). Crack's children: The consequences of maternal cocaine abuse. *Social Policy Report of the Society for Research in Human Development, 6*(4), 1–23.

Hazen, N. (1982). Spatial exploration and spatial knowledge: Individual and developmental differences in very young children. *Child Development, 53,* 826–833.

Heath, S. B. (1983). *Ways with words: Language, life, and work in communities and classrooms.* Cambridge, England: Cambridge University Press.

Heath, S. B. (1988). Language socialization. In D. Slaughter (Ed.), *Black children and poverty: A developmental perspective* (pp. 11–28). San Francisco: Jossey-Bass.

Hemmings, A., & Metz, M. H. (1990). Real teaching: How high school teachers negotiate societal, local, community, and student pressures when they define their work. In R. Page & L. Valli (Eds.), *Curriculum differentiation: Interpretive studies in the U.S. secondary schools* (pp. 290–356). Albany: SUNY Press.

Hernandez, D. (1993). *America's children.* New York: Russell Sage Foundation.

Hernandez, H. (1997). *Teaching in multicultural classrooms: A teacher's guide to content, process, and context.* Upper Saddle River, NJ: Merrill/Prentice Hall.

Herrnstein, R. J., & Murray, C. (1994). *The bell curve: Intelligence and class structure in American life.* New York: Free Press.

Hetherington, E. M. (1989). Coping with family transition: Winners, losers, and survivors. *Child Development, 60,* 1–14.

Hetherington, E. M. (1993). Overview of the Virginia Longitudinal Study of Divorce and Remarriage. *Journal of Family Psychology, 7,* 39–56.

Hetherington, E. M., Cox, M., & Cox, M. (1979). Play and social interaction in children following divorce. *Journal of Social Issues, 35,* 26–49.

Hewes, D. W. (1982). Preschool geography: Developing a sense of self in time and space. *Journal of Geography, 31,* 94–97.

Hicks, L. E., Langham, R. A., & Takenaka, J. (1982). Cognitive and health measures following early nutritional supplementation: A sibling study. *American Journal of Public Health, 72,* 1110–1118.

Higgins, E., & Parsons, J. (1983). Social cognition and the social life of the child: Stages as subcultures. In E. T. Higgins, D. N. Ruble & W. W. Hartup (Eds.), *Social cognition and social development* (pp. 15–62). New York: Cambridge University Press.

Hinitz, B. F. (1987). Social studies in early childhood education. In C. Seefeldt (Ed.), *The early childhood curriculum: A review of current research* (pp. 237–255). New York: Teachers College Press.

Hitz, R., & Driscoll, A. (1988). Praise or encouragement. New insights into praise: Implications for early childhood teachers. *Young Children, 43*(5), 6–13.

Ho, D. Y. F. (1986). Chinese pattern of socialization: A critical review. In M. H. Bond (Ed.), *The psychology of Chinese people* (pp. 1–37). Oxford: Oxford University Press.

Ho, D. Y. F. (1994). Cognitive socialization in Confucian heritage cultures. In P. M. Greenfield & R. R. Cocking (Eds.), *Cross-cultural roots of minority child development* (pp. 285–314). Hillsdale, NJ: Erlbaum.

Hock, E., McBride, S., & Gnezda, M. T. (1989). Maternal separation anxiety: Mother-infant separation from the maternal perspective. *Child Development, 60,* 793–802.

Hoffman, H. J., & Hillman, L. S. (1992). Epidemiology of the sudden infant death syndrome. *Clinics in perinatology, 19*(4), 717–737.

Hoffman, L. W. (1975). The value of children to parents and the decrease in family size. *Proceedings of the American Philosophical Society, 117,* 430–438.

Hoffman, L. W. (1984). Work, family, and the socialization of the child. In R. D. Parke (Ed.), *Review of child development research* (Vol. 7, pp. 223–282). Chicago: University of Chicago Press.

Hoffman, L. W. (1985). The changing genetics/socialization balance. *Journal of Social Issues, 41,* 127–148.

Holloway, S. D., & Reichhart-Erikson, M. (1988). The relationship of day care quality and free-play behavior and social problem-solving skills. *Early Childhood Research Quarterly, 3,* 39–53.

Holtzman, W. H., Diaz-Guerrero, R., & Swartz, J. D. (1975). *Personality in two cultures.* Austin: University of Texas Press.

Honig, A. S. (1987). The shy child. *Young Children, 42*(4), 54–64.

Hough, R. A., & Nurss, J. R. (1992). Language and literacy for the limited English proficient child. In L. O. Ollila & M. L. Mayfield (Eds.), *Emerging literacy* (pp. 42–70). Boston: Allyn & Bacon.

Howe, M. L. (1995). Interference effects in young children's long-term retention. *Developmental Psychology, 31,* 579–596.

Howes, C. (1983). Patterns of friendship. *Child Development, 54,* 1041–1053.

Howes, C. (1987). Peer interaction of young children. *Monographs of the Society for Research in Child Development, 53*(1), Serial No. 217.

Howes, C., & Olenick, M. (1986). Family and child care influences on toddlers' compliance. *Child Development, 57,* 202–216.

Howes, C., Phillips, D., & Whitebook, M. (1992). Thresholds of quality in child care centers and children's social and emotional development. *Child Development, 63,* 449–460.

Howes, C., & Wu, F. (1990). Peer interactions and friendships in an ethnically diverse school setting. *Child Development, 61,* 537–541.

Huffman, L. C., Bryan, Y. E., Pederson, F. A., Lester, B. M., Newman, J. D., & Carmen, R. (1994). Infant cry acoustics and maternal ratings of temperament. *Infant Behavior and Development, 17,* 45–53.

Hughes, F. P. (1995). *Children, play and development.* Boston: Allyn & Bacon.

Hull, J. N., & Simpson, P. S. (1985). *Breastfeeding across cultures.* New York: Academic Press.

Humphry, R. A., & Hock, E. (1989). Infants with colic: A study of maternal stress and anxiety. *Infant Mental Health Journal, 10,* 263–272.

Huntington, L., Hans, S. L., & Zeskind, P. S. (1990). The relationship among cry characteristics, demographic variables, and developing test scores in infants prenatally exposed to methadone. *Infant Behavior and Development, 13,* 533–538.

Huston, A. C. (1983). Sex-typing. In M. Hetherington (Ed.), *Handbook of child psychology* (Vol. 4, pp. 387–468). New York: Wiley.

Huston, A. C. (Ed.). (1991). *Children in poverty: Child development and public policy.* New York: Cambridge University Press.

Huston, A. C., McLoyd, V. C., & Garcia Coll, C. T. (1994). Children and poverty: Issues in contemporary research. *Child Development, 65,* 275–282.

Hymel, S., Rubin, K., Rowden, L., & LeMare, L. (1990). Children's peer relationships: Longitudinal prediction of internalizing and externalizing problems from middle to late childhood. *Child Development, 61,* 2004–2021.

Ilg, F. L., & Ames, L. B. (1965). *School readiness: Behavioral tests used at the Gesell Institute.* New York: Harper and Row.

Ingram, D. (1976). *Phonological disability in children.* London: Edward Arnold.

Irujo, S. (1988). An introduction to intercultural differences and similarities in nonverbal communication. In J. S. Wurzel (Ed.), *Toward multiculturalism: A reader in multicultural education.* Yarmouth, ME: Intercultural Press.

Irwin, O. C. (1952). Speech development in the young child: 2. Some factors related to the speech development of the infant and young child. *Journal of Speech and Hearing Disorders, 17,* 269–279.

Isabella, R. A. (1993). Origins of attachment: Maternal interactive behavior across the first year. *Child Development, 64,* 605–621.

Isabella, R. A., & Belsky, J. (1991). Interactional synchrony and the origins of infant-mother attachment. *Child Development, 62,* 373–384.

Izard, C. E., & Harris, P. (1995). In D. Ciccetti & D. J. Cohen (Eds.), *Developmental psychology: Vol. 1. Theory and methods* (pp. 467–503). New York: Wiley.

Jacklin, C. N. (1989). Females and males: Issues of gender. *American Psychologist, 44(2),* 127–133.

Jackson, G., & Cosca, C. (1974). The inequality of educational opportunity in the Southwest: An observational study of ethnically mixed classrooms. *American Educational Research Journal, 11,* 219–229.

Jackson-Maldonado, D., Thal, D., Bates, E., Marchman, V., & Gutierrez-Clellan, V. (1993). Early lexical development in Spanish-speaking infants and toddlers. *Journal of Child Language, 20,* 523–549.

Janesick, V. J. (1995). Our multicultural society. In E. L. Meyen & T. M. Skrtic (Eds.), *Special education and student disability* (pp. 713–728). Denver: Love.

Janzen, L., & Nanson, J. (1993, March). *Neuropsychological evaluation of preschoolers with fetal alcohol syndrome.* Paper presented at the biennial meeting of the Society for Research in Child Development, New Orleans.

Jarrett, O., & Quay, L. (1983, April). *Cross-racial acceptance and best friend choices in racially balanced kindergarten and first-grade classrooms.* Paper presented at the biennial meeting of the Society for Research in Child Development, Detroit.

Jason, J. M., & Jarvis, W. R. (1987). Infectious disease: Preventable causes of infant mortality. *Pediatrics, 80,* 335–341.

Jensen, A. R. (1969). How much can we boost IQ and scholastic achievement? *Harvard Educational Review, 39(1),* 1–123.

Jensen, J. V. (1962). Effects of childhood bilingualism. *Elementary English, 39,* 132–143.

John, R. (1988). The Native American family. In C. H. Mindel, R. W. Habenstein & R. Wright (Eds.), *Ethnic families in America: Patterns and variations.* New York: Elsevier.

Johnson, J. E., Christie, J. F., & Yawkey, T. D. (1999). *Play and early childhood development* (2nd ed.). Glenview, IL: Scott, Foresman.

Johnson, S. F., McCarter, R. J., & Ferencz, C. (1987). Changes in alcohol, cigarette, and recreational drug use during pregnancy: Implications for interventions. *American Journal of Epidemiology, 126,* 695–702.

Joint Commission on Mental Health of Children. (1970). *Crisis in child mental health: Challenge for the 1970s.* New York: Harper and Row.

Jones, D. C., Swift, D. J., & Johnson, M. A. (1988). Nondeliberate memory for a novel event among preschoolers. *Developmental Psychology, 24,* 641–645.

Jordan, B. (1983). *Childbirth and culture.* New York: Academic Press.

Jusczyk, P. W., Cutler, A., & Redaz, N. J. (1993). Infants' preference for the stress patterns of English words. *Child Development, 64,* 675–687.

Kacergis, M. A., & Adams, G. R. (1979). Implications of sex-typed childrearing practices, toys, and mass media materials in restricting occupational choices of women. *Family Coordinator, 28,* 368–375.

Kagan, J. (1977). The uses of cross-cultural research in early development. In P. H. Leiderman, S. R. Tulkin, & A. Rosenfeld (Eds.), *Culture and infancy: Variations in the human experience* (pp. 271–286). New York: Academic Press.

Kagan, J. (1994). *Galen's prophecy.* New York: Basic Books.

Kagan, J., Arcus, D., Snidman, N., Feng, W. Y., Hendler, J., & Greene, S. (1994). Reactivity in infants: A cross-national comparison. *Developmental Psychology, 30,* 342–345.

Kagan, J., Kearsley, R. B., & Zelazo, P. R. (1978). *Infancy: Its place in human development.* Cambridge: Harvard University Press.

Kagan, J., Reznick, J. S., & Gibbons, J. (1989). Inhibited and uninhibited types of children. *Child Development, 60,* 838–845.

Kagan, J., Snidman, N., & Arcus, D. (1993). On the temperamental categories of inhibited and uninhibited children. In K. H. Rubin and J. Asendorpf (Eds.), *Social withdrawal, inhibition, and shyness in children* (pp. 19–28). Hillsdale, NJ: Erlbaum.

Kalyan-Masih, V. (1985). Cognitive performance and cognitive style. *International Journal of Behavioral Development, 8,* 39–54.

Kamii, C. (1982). *Number in preschool and kindergarten: Implications of Piaget's theory.* Washington, DC: National Association for the Education of Young Children.

Kamii, C. (1985). *Young children reinvent arithmetic.* New York: Teachers College Press.

Kamii, C. (1989). *Young children continue to invent arithmetic: 2nd grade.* New York: Teachers College Press.

Kaplan, P. S. (1996). *Pathways for exceptional children.* St Paul, MN: West.

Kaplan-Sanoff, M., Brewster, A., Stillwell, J., & Bergen, D. (1988). The relationship of play to physical/motor development and to children with special needs. In D. Bergen (Ed.), *Play as a medium for learning and development.* Portsmouth, NH: Heinemann.

Katz, P. S., & Ksansnak, K. R. (1994). Developmental aspects of gender role flexibility and traditionality in middle childhood and adolescence. *Developmental Psychology, 30,* 272–282.

Kauffman, J. M. (1981). *Characteristics of children's behavior disorders.* Upper Saddle River, NJ: Merrill/Prentice Hall.

Kaufman, A. S., & Kaufman, N. L. (1983). *Kaughman Assessment Battery for Children: Interpretive manual.* Circle Pines, MN: American Guidance Service.

Kaye, K., & Marcus, J. (1981). Infant imitation: The sensory-motor agenda. *Developmental Psychology, 17,* 258–265.

Kellam, S. G., Ensminger, M. E., & Turner, R. J. (1977). Family structure and the mental health of children. *Archives of General Psychiatry, 34,* 1012–1022.

Kelly, M. L., & Tseng, H. (1992). Cultural differences in child rearing: A comparison of immigrant Chinese and Caucasian American mothers. *Journal of Cross-Cultural Psychology, 23,* 444–455.

Keogh, B. K., & Sears, S. (1991). Learning disabilities from a developmental perspective. Early identification and prediction. In B. Y. L. Wong (Ed.), *Learning about learning disabilities* (pp. 80–154). Upper Saddle River, NJ: Merrill/Prentice Hall.

Keogh, J. (1977). The study of movement skill development. *Quest* (Monograph No. 28), 76–80.

Kerr, B. A. (1991). *Handbook for counseling the gifted and talented.* Alexandria, VA: Counseling Association.

Kessen, W. (1965). *The child.* New York: Wiley.

King, A. Y. C., & Bond, M. H. (1986). The Confucian paradigm of man: A sociological view. In W. S. Tseng & D. Y. H. Wu (Eds.), *Chinese culture and mental health* (pp. 29–45). New York: Academic Press.

Kirk, S. A. (1972). Ethnic differences in psycholinguistic abilities. *Exceptional Children, 39,* 112–118.

Kisilevsky, B. S., & Muir, D. W. (1984). Neonatal habituation and dishabituation to tactile stimulation during sleep. *Developmental Psychology, 20,* 367–373.

Kisilevsky, B. S., Muir, D. W., & Low, J. A. (1992). Maturation of human fetal responses to vibroacoustic stimulation. *Child Development, 63,* 1497–1508.

Klerman, L. (1991a). *Alive and well? A research and policy review of health programs for poor young children.* New York: National Center for Children in Poverty.

Klerman, L. (1991b). The health of poor children: Problems and programs. In H. Huston (Ed.), *Children in poverty.* New York: Cambridge University Press.

Klesges, R. C. (1993). Parental influences on children's eating behavior and relative weight. *Journal of Applied Behavioral Analysis, 16,* 371–378.

Knight, G. P., Virdin, L. M., & Roosa, M. (1994). Socialization and family correlates of mental health outcomes among Hispanic and Anglo American children: Consideration of cross-ethnic scalar equivalence. *Child Development, 65,* 212–224.

Knitzer, J., Steinberg, Z., & Fleisch, B. (1990). *At the schoolhouse door.* New York: Bank Street College of Education.

Kochanska, G., & Radke-Yarrow, M. (1992). Inhibition in toddlerhood and the dynamics of the child's interaction with an unfamiliar peer at age 5. *Child Development, 63,* 325–335.

Kodroff, J. K., & Roberge, J. J. (1975). Developmental analysis of the conditional reasoning abilities of primary-grade children. *Developmental Psychology, 11,* 21–28.

Kohlberg, L. (1984). *Essays on moral development: Vol. 2. The psychology of moral development.* San Francisco: Harper and Row.

Kohlberg, L., & Ullian, D. Z. (1974). Stages in the development of psychosexual concepts and attitudes. In R. C. Friedman, R. M. Richart & R. L. Vande-Wiele (Eds.), *Sex differences in behavior* (pp. 224–249). New York: Wiley.

Konner, M. (1977). Evolution of human behavior development. In P. H. Leiderman, S. R. Tulkin, & A. Rosenfeld (Eds.), *Culture and infancy: Variations in the human experience.* New York: Academic Press.

Konner, M. (1991). *Childhood.* Boston: Little, Brown.

Kopp, C. B., & Krakow, J. B. (1982). *Child development in the social context.* Reading, MA: Addison-Wesley.

Korner, A. F., & Thoman, E. B. (1972). The relative efficacy of contact and vestibular-proprioceptive stimulation in soothing neonates. *Child Development, 43,* 443–453.

Kotelchuck, M. (1984). WIC participation and pregnancy outcomes: Massachusetts Statewide Evaluation Project. *American Journal of Public Health, 74,* 1084–1092.

Kropp, J. P., & Haynes, O. M. (1987). Abusive and nonabusive mothers' ability to identify general and specific emotion signals of infants. *Child Development, 58,* 187–190.

Kumanyika, S. K., Huffman, S. L., Bradshaw, M. E., & Paige, D. (1990). Stature and weight status of children in an urban kindergarten population. *Pediatrics, 85,* 783–790.

Kupersmidt, J. B., Coie, J. D., & Dodge, K. A. (1990). Predicting disorder from peer social problems. In S. R. Asher & J. D. Coie (Eds.), *Peer rejection in childhood.* New York: Cambridge University Press.

Kupersmidt, J. B., Griesler, P. C., DeRosier, M. E., Patterson, C. J., & Davis, P. W. (1995). Childhood aggression and peer relations in the context of family and neighborhood factors. *Child Development, 66,* 360–375.

Labov, W. (1971). Stages in the acquisition of standard English. In W. Labov (Ed.), *Readings in American dialectology* (pp. 1–43). New York: Appleton-Century-Crofts.

Ladd, G. W. (1990). Having friends, keeping friends, making friends, and being liked by peers in the classroom: Predictors of children's early school adjustment? *Child Development, 61,* 1081–1101.

Ladd, G. W., Kochenderfer, B. J., & Coleman, C. C. (1996). Friendship quality as a predictor of young children's early school adjustment. *Child Development, 67,* 1103–1118.

Ladd, G. W., Kochenderfer, B. J., & Coleman, C. C. (1997). Classroom peer acceptance, friendship, and victimization: Distinct relational systems that contribute uniquely to children's school adjustment? *Child Development, 68,* 1181–1197.

Ladd, G. W., & Mize, J. (1983). A cognitive-social learning model of social skill training. *Psychological Review, 90,* 127–157.

Lally, J. R. (1994). *Infant / toddler caregiving: A guide to culturally sensitive care.* Sacramento: California State Department of Education.

Lamaze, F. (1958). *Painless childbirth.* London: Burke.

Lamb, M. E. (1981). The development of father-infant relationships. In M. E. Lamb (Ed.), *Nontraditional families: Parenting and child development* (pp. 1–46). Hillsdale, NJ: Erlbaum.

Lamb, M. E. (1987). *The father's role: Cross-cultural perspectives.* Hillsdale, NJ: Erlbaum.

Landau, R. (1982). Infant crying and fussing. *Journal of Cross-cultural Psychology, 13,* 427–443.

Landau-Stanton, J., & Clements, C. D. (1993). *AIDS health and mental health: A primary sourcebook.* New York: Brunner/Mazel.

Landry, S. H., & Chapieski, M. L. (1989). Joint attention and infant toy exploration: Effects of Down syndrome and prematurity. *Child Development, 60,* 103–118.

Laosa, L. M. (1980). Maternal teaching strategies in Chicano and Anglo-American families: The influence of culture and education on maternal behavior. *Child Development, 51,* 759–765.

Larroque, B., Kaminski, M., Dehaene, P., Subtil, D., Delfosse, M. J., & Querleu, D. (1995). Moderate prenatal alcohol exposure and psychomotor development. *American Journal of Public Health, 85,* 1654–1661.

Larson, M. C., Gunnar, M. R., & Hertsgaard, L. (1991). The effects of morning naps, car trips, and maternal separation on adrenocortical activity in human infants. *Child Development, 62,* 362–372.

Lawrence, M. M. (1975). *Young inner city families: Development of ego under stress.* New York: Behavior.

Lawrence, R. (1991). Breastfeeding trends: A cause for action. *Pediatrics, 88,* 867–868.

Layton, T., & Sharifi, H. (1979). Meaning and structure of Down's syndrome and nonretarded children's spontaneous speech. *American Journal of Mental Deficiency, 83,* 439–445.

Leboyer, F. (1975). *Birth without violence.* New York: Random House.

Lederberg, A. R., Chapin, S. L., Rosenblatt, V., & Vandell, D. L. (1986). Ethnic, gender, and age preferences among deaf and hearing preschool peers. *Child Development, 57,* 375–386.

Lederberg, A. R., & Mobley, C. E. (1990). The effect of hearing impairment on the quality of attachment and mother-toddler interactions. *Child Development, 61,* 1596–1604.

Lee, V. E., Burkham, D. T., Zimles, H., & Ladewski, B. (1994). Family structure and its effect on behavioral and emotional problems of adolescence. *Journal of Research on Adolsescence, 4,* 129–142.

Lefly, H. P. (1976). Acculturation, childrearing, and self-esteem in two North American Indian tribes. *Ethos, 5,* 385–401.

Lein, L. (1975). Black American migrant children: Their speech at home and school. *Council on Anthropology and Education Quarterly, 6,* 1–11.

Leonard, L. (1982). Specific language impairment. In S. Rosenberg (Ed.), *Handbook of applied psycholinguistics* (pp. 94–108). Hillsdale, NJ: Erlbaum.

Lerner, J. W. (1985). *Learning disabilities: Theories, diagnosis, and teaching strategies.* Boston: Houghton Mifflin.

Leslie, A. M. (1987). Pretense and representation: The origins of theory of mind. *Psychological Review, 94,* 412–426.

Leslie, A. M., & Frith, U. (1987). Metarepresentation and autism: How not to lose one's marbles. *Cognition, 27,* 291–294.

Lester, B. M. (1987). Prediction of developmental outcome from acoustic cry analysis in term and preterm infants. *Pediatrics, 80,* 529–534.

Lester, B. M., & Brazelton, T. B. (1982). Cross-cultural assessment of neonatal behavior. In H. Stevenson & D. Wagner (Eds.), *Cultural perspectives on child development* (pp. 20–53). San Francisco: Freeman.

Levine, R. A. (1977). Child rearing as cultural adaptation. In P. H. Leiderman, S. R. Tulkin, & A. Rosenfeld (Eds.), *Culture and infancy: Variations in the human experience.* New York: Academic Press.

Levy, G. D., & Carter, D. B. (1989). Gender schema, gender constancy, and gender role knowledge: The roles of cognitive factors in preschoolers' gender-role stereo-type attributions. *Developmental Psychology, 25,* 444–449.

Lewis, M., Feiring, C., McGuiffog, C., & Jaskir, J. (1984). Predicting pathology in six-year-olds from early social relations. *Child Development, 55,* 123–136.

Lewis, V., & Boucher, L. (1988). Spontaneous, instructed, and elicited play in relatively able autistic children. *British Journal of Developmental Psychology, 6,* 325–339.

Lewkowicz, D. J. (1996). Infants' response to the audible and visible properties of the human face. *Developmental Pscychology, 32,* 347–366.

Li, A. K. F. (1985). Toward more elaborate pretend play. *Mental Retardation, 23,* 131–136.

Lieberman, E., & Ryan, K. J. (1989). Birth-day choices. *New England Journal of Medicine, 321,* 1824–1825.

Lieberman, E., Weston, D. R., & Pawl, J. H. (1991). Preventive intervention and out-come with anxiously attached dyads. *Child Development, 62,* 199–209.

Lienhardt, G. (1961). *Divinity and experi-ence: The religion of the Dinka.* Oxford: Clarendon Press.

Lillard, A. S. (1995, March). *Children's un-derstanding of pretense intentions.* Paper presented at the biennial meeting of the Society for Research in Child Develop-ment, Indianapolis.

Lindsey, D. (1991). Factors affecting the fos-ter care placement decision: An analysis of national survey data. *American Jour-nal of Orthopsychiatry, 61,* 272–281.

Lipsitt, L. P., Engen, T., & Kaye, H. (1963). Developmental changes in the olfactory threshold of the neonate. *Child Develop-ment, 34,* 371–376.

Locke, J. (1980). The inference of speech per-ception in the phonologically disordered child: Part I. A rationale, some criteria, the conventional tests. Part II. Some clin-ically novel procedures, their use, some findings. *Journal of Hearing and Speech Disorders, 45,* 431–468.

Lockman, J. J., & Thelen, E. (1993). Devel-opmental biodynamics: Brain, body, be-havior connections. *Child Development, 64,* 953–959.

Lockman, J. J., & Wright, M. H. (1989, April). *Relating objects and surfaces dur-ing infancy: A longitudinal study.* Poster presented at the biennial meeting of the Society for Research in Child Develop-ment, Kansas City, MO.

Logan, O. L. (1991). *Motherwit: An Alabama midwife's story.* New York: Plume.

Lollis, S. P. (1990). Effects of maternal be-havior on toddler behavior during sepa-ration. *Child Development, 61,* 99–103.

Lorenz, K. (1971). *Studies in animal and hu-man behavior* (Vol. 2). Cambridge: Har-vard University Press.

Losonsky, G. M., Santosham, M., Sehgal, V. M., Zwahlen, A., & Moxon, E. R. (1984). Hemophilus influenza disease in the White Mountain Apaches. *Pediatric Infectious Disease, 3,* 539–547.

Lovett, S. B., & Pillow, B. H. (1991, April). *The development of the comprehension-memory distinction.* Paper presented at the biennial meeting of the Society for Research in Child Development, Seattle.

Lowenfeld, V. (1947). *Creative and mental growth.* New York: Macmillan.

Lowrey, G. H. (1986). *Growth and develop-ment of children.* Chicago: Year Book Medical Publishers.

Lozoff, B. (1989). Nutrition and behavior. *American Psychologist, 44,* 231–236.

Lozoff, B. (1990). Has iron deficiency been shown to cause altered behavior in in-fants? In J. Dobbing (Ed.), *Brain, behav-iour, and iron in the infant diet* (pp. 107–131). London: Springer-Verlag.

Ludeman, P. M. (1991). Generalized discrim-ination of positive facial expressions by 7- and 10-month-old infants. *Child Develop-ment, 62,* 55–67.

Lyons-Ruth, K., Connell, D. B., Grunebaum, H. U., & Botein, S. (1990). Infants at so-cial risk: Maternal depression and family support services as mediators in infant development and security of attachment. *Child Development, 61,* 85–98.

Maccoby, E. M. (1980). *Social development: Psychological growth and the parent-child relationship.* New York: Harcourt Brace Jovanovich.

Maccoby, E. M. (1989, August). *Gender and relationships: A developmental account.* Paper presented at the biennial meeting of the Society for Research in Child De-velopment, New Orleans.

Maccoby, E. M., & Jacklin, C. N. (1990). Gender segregation in childhood. In H. Reese (Ed.), *Advances in child develop-ment and behavior* (pp. 161–206). New York: Academic Press.

MacDonald, K., & Parke, R. D. (1986). Parent-child physical play: The effect of sex and age of children and parents. *Sex Roles, 15,* 367–378.

MacGowan, R. J., MacGowan, C. A., Serdula, M. K., Lane, J. M., Joesoef, R. M., & Cook, F. H. (1991). Breastfeeding among women attending women, infants, and children clinics in Georgia, 1987. *Pedi-atrics, 87,* 361–366.

Makin, J. W., & Porter, R. H. (1989). Attrac-tiveness of lactating females' breast odors to neonates. *Child Development, 60,* 803–810.

Malatesta, C. Z., Culver, C., Tesman, J. R., & Shepard, B. (1989). The development of emotion expression during the first 2 years of life. *Monographs of the Society for Research in Child Development, 54,* Serial No. 219.

Malina, R. M. (1982). Motor development in the early years. In S. G. Moore & C. R. Cooper (Eds.), *The young child: Reviews of research* (Vol. 3, pp. 211–229). Wash-ington, DC: National Association for the Education of Young Children.

Malinosky-Rummel, R., & Hansen, D. J. (1993). Long-term consequences of child-hood physical abuse. *Psychological Bul-letin, 114,* 68–79.

Malone, D. M., Stoneman, Z., & Langone, J. (1994). Contextual variation of corre-spondences among measures of play and developmental level of preschool children with cognitive delays. *Journal of Early Intervention, 18,* 199–215.

Maretzki, T. W., & Maretzki, H. (1963). Taira: An Okinawan Village. In B. B. Whiting (Ed.), *In six cultures: Studies of child rear-ing* (pp. 73–157). New York: Wiley.

Markides, K. S., & McFarland, C. (1985). A note on recent trends in the infant mortality-socioeconomic status relation-ship. *Social Forces, 61,* 268–276.

Markman, E. M. (1992). Constraints on word learning: Speculations about their na-ture, origins, and domain specificity. In M. R. Gunnar & M. P. Maratsos (Eds.), *Minnesota symposium on child psychol-ogy, 25,* 59–101. Hillsdale, NJ: Erlbaum.

Markstrom, C. A. (1987, April). *A comparison of psychosocial maturity between four eth-nic groups during middle adolescence.* Paper presented at the biennial meeting of the Society for Research in Child De-velopment, Baltimore.

Markstrom, C. A., & Mullis, R. L. (1986). Ethnic differences in the imaginary audi-ence. *Journal of Adolescent Research, 1,* 289–301.

Marschark, M. (1993). *Psychological develop-ment of deaf children.* New York: Oxford University Press.

Marsh, H., Smith, I., & Barnes, J. (1985). Multidimensional self-concepts: Rela-tionships with sex and academic achieve-ment. *Journal of Educational Psychol-ogy, 77,* 581–596.

Martin, C. L. (1993). New directions in in-vestigating children's gender knowledge. *Developmental Review, 13,* 184–204.

Martin, C. L., Wood, C. H., & Little, J. K. (1990). The development of gender stereotype components. *Child Develop-ment, 61,* 1891–1904.

Martini, M. (1994). Peer interactions in Polynesia: A view from the Marquesas. In J. L. Roopnarine, J. E. Johnson & F. H. Hooper (Eds.), *Children's play in diverse cultures* (pp. 73–103). Albany: SUNY Press.

Matheson, C., & Wu, F. (1991, April). *Friend-ship and social pretend play.* Paper pre-sented at the biennial meeting of the So-ciety for Research in Child Development, Seattle.

Maugh, T. H. (1998). Researchers make key attention deficit disorder finding. *Hartford Courant*, November 24, 7.

Mauldon, J., & Luker, K. (1996). The effects of contraceptive education on method use at first intercourse. *Family Planning Perspectives, 28,* 19–24, 41.

McAdoo, H. P. (1985). Racial attitude and self-concept of young black children over time. In H. P. McAdoo & J. L. McAdoo (Eds.), *Black children: Social, educational, and parental environments* (pp. 213–242). Newbury Park: Sage.

McCall, R. B., & Carringer, M. S. (1993). A meta-analysis of infant habituation and recognition memory performance as predictors of later IQ. *Child Development, 64,* 57–79.

McCune, L. (1995). A normative study of representational play at the transition to language stage. *Developmental Psychology, 31,* 198–206.

McKenzie, B. E., Skouteris, H., Day, R. H., Hartman, B., & Yonas, A. (1993). Effective action by infants to contact objects by reaching and leaning. *Child Development, 64,* 415–419.

McKeough, A. (1992). A neo-structural analysis of children's narrative and its development. In R. Case (Ed.), *The mind's staircase: Exploring the conceptual underpinning of children's thought and knowledge* (pp. 58–114). Hillsdale, NJ: Erlbaum.

McLeavy, B., Toomey, J., & Dempsey, P. (1982). Nonretarded and mentally retarded children's control over syntactic structures. *American Journal of Mental Deficiencies, 86,* 485–494.

McLoyd, V. C. (1986). Social class and pretend play. In A. W. Gottfried & C. C. Brown (Eds.), *Play interactions: The contribution of play materials and parental involvement to children's development* (pp. 175–196). Lexington, MA: Heath.

McLoyd, V. C. (1990a). The impact of economic hardship on black families and children: Psychological distress, parenting, and socioemotional development. *Child Development, 61,* 311–346.

McLoyd, V. C. (1990b). Minority children: Introduction to the special issue. *Child Development, 61,* 263–266.

McLoyd, V. C., & Randolph, S. (1985). The conduct and publication of research on Afro-American children: A content analysis. *Human Development, 27,* 65–75.

McLoyd, V. C., & Wilson, L. (1992). Telling them like it is: The role of economic and environmental factors in single mothers' discussions with their children. *American Journal of Community Psychology, 20,* 419–444.

Mejia, D. (1983). The development of Mexican-American children. In G. J. Powell (Ed.), *The psychosocial development of minority children.* New York: Brunner/Mazel.

Meadow, K. P. (1980). *Deafness and child development.* Berkeley: University of California Press.

Mellor, S. (1990). How do only children differ from other children? *Journal of Genetic Psychology, 151,* 221–230.

Menn, L. (1989). Phonological development: Sounds and sound patterns. In J. B. Gleason (Ed.), *The development of language* (pp. 59–100). Upper Saddle River, NJ: Merrill/Prentice Hall.

Menyuk, P., & Menyuk, D. (1988). Communicative competence: A historical and cultural perspective. In J. S. Wurzel (Ed.), *Toward multiculturalism: A reader in multicultural education.* Yarmouth, ME: Intercultural Press.

Mercer, J. (1972, September). IQ: The lethal label. *Psychology Today,* 44–47.

Meyer, C. A., Klein, E. L., & Genishi, C. (1994). Peer relationships among 4 preschool second language learners in "small-group time." *Early Childhood Research Quarterly, 9,* 61–86.

Michaels, S. (1980, March). *Sharing time: An oral preparation for literacy.* Paper presented at the Ethnography in Education Research Forum, University of Pennsylvania, Philadelphia.

Michelsson, K., Rinne, A., & Paajanen, S. (1990). Crying, feeding, and sleeping patterns in 1 to 12 month old infants. *Child Care, Health, and Development, 116,* 99–111.

Millar, W. S., Weir, C. G., & Supramaniam, G. (1992). The influence of perinatal risk status on contingency learning in 6- to 13-month-old infants. *Child Development, 63,* 304–313.

Miller, A., & Miller, E. (1973). Cognitive developmental training with elevated boards and sign language. *Journal of Autism and Childhood Schizophrenia, 3,* 65–85.

Miller, L. B., & Bizzell, R. P. (1983). Long-term effects of four preschool programs: Sixth, seventh, and eighth grades. *Child Development, 54,* 727–741.

Miller, P. H., & Aloise, P. A. (1989). Young children's understanding of psychological causes of behavior: An overview. *Child Development, 60,* 257–285.

Miller, S. A. (1995). Parents' attributes for their children's behavior. *Child Development, 66,* 1557–1584.

Miller-Jones, D. (1988). The study of African-American children's development: Contributions to reformulating developmental paradigms. In D. T. Slaughter (Ed.), *Black children and poverty: A developmental perspective* (pp. 75–92). San Francisco: Jossey Bass.

Milunski, A. (1977). *Know your genes.* Boston: Houghton Mifflin.

Milunsky, A. (1989). *Choices, not chance.* Boston: Little Brown.

Minnett, A., Vandell, D., & Santrock, J. (1983). The effects of sibling status on sibling interaction. *Child Development, 54,* 1064–1072.

Misciones, J. L., Marvin, R. S., O'Brien, R. G., & Green, M. T. (1978). A developmental study of preschool children's understanding of the words "know" and "guess." *Child Development,* 49, 1107–1113.

Mitchell, E. A., Ford, R. P. K., & Steward, A. (1993). Smoking and sudden infant death syndrome. *Pediatrics, 91,* 893–896.

Mitchell, P. R., & Kent, R. D. (1990). Phonetic variation in multi-syllable babbling. *Journal of Child Language, 17,* 247–265.

Mitchell-Copeland, J., Denham, S. A., & DeMulder, E. K. (1997). Q-Sort Assessment of Child-Teacher Relationships and social competence in the preschool. *Early Education and Development, 8,* 135–157.

Miyake, K., Chen, S., & Campos, J. J. (1985). Infant temperament, mother's mode of interaction, and attachment in Japan: An interim report. In I. Bretherton & E. Waters (Eds.), Growing points of attachment theory and research. *Monographs of the Society for Research in Child Development, 50,* Serial No. 209.

Mize, J., & Ladd, G. W. (1990). A cognitive-social learning approach to social skills training with low-status preschool children. *Developmental Psychology, 26,* 388–397.

Moely, R. E., Hart, S. S., Leal, L., Santulli, K. A., Rao, N., Johnson, T., & Hamilton, L. B. (1992). The teacher's role in facilitating memory and study strategy development in the elementary school. *Child Development, 63,* 653–672.

Molfese, D. L., Freeman, R. B., & Polermo, D. S. (1975). The ontogeny of brain lateralization for speech and nonspeech stimuli. *Brain and Language, 2,* 356–368.

Moore, K. L. (1989). *Before we are born: Basic embryology and birth defects* (3rd ed). Philadelphia: Saunders.

Moore, K. L., & Pursaud, T. V. (1993). *The developing human: Clinically oriented embryology.* Philadelphia: Saunders.

Mordkowitz, E. R., & Ginsburg, H. P. (1987). The academic socialization of successful Asian-American college students. *Quarterly Newsletter of the Laboratory of Comparative Human Cognition, 9,* 85–91.

Morelli, G. A. (1986). *Social development of 1-, 2-, and 3-year-old Efe and Lese children within the Ituri Forest of Northeastern Zaire.* Doctoral dissertation, Department of Psychology, University of Massachusetts, Amherst, MA.

Morgan, H. (1976). Neonatal precocity and the black experience. *Negro Educational Review, 27,* 129–134.

Morrison, G. M., & Polloway, E. A. (1995). In E. L. Meyen & T. M. Skrtic (Eds.), *Special education and student disability* (pp. 213–270). Denver: Love.

Morrison, P., & Masten, A. S. (1991). Peer reputation in middle childhood as a predictor of adaptation in adolescence: A seven-year follow-up. *Child Development, 62,* 991–1007.

Moss, M., Colombo, J., Mitchell, D. W., & Horowitz, F. D. (1988). Neonatal behavioral organization and visual processing at three months. *Child Development, 59,* 1211–1220.

Muller, E., Hollien, H., & Murry, T. (1974). Perceptual responses to infant crying: Identification of cry types. *Journal of Child Language, 1,* 89–95.

Munroe, R., & Munroe, R. (1977). Cooperation and competition among East-African and American children. *Journal of Social Psychology, 101,* 145–146.

Murray, A. D. (1979). Infant crying as an elicitor of parental behavior: An examination of two models. *Psychological Bulletin, 85,* 191–215.

Murray, A. D. (1985). Aversiveness is in the mind of the beholder. In B. M. Lester & C. F. Z. Boukydis (Eds.), *Infant crying* (pp. 217–239). New York: Plenum.

Musselman, C., Lindsay, P., & Wilson, A. (1988). An evaluation of trends in preschool programming for hearing-impaired children. *Journal of Speech and Hearing Disorders, 53,* 71–88.

Musselwhite, C. R. (1986). *Adaptive play for special needs children: Strategies to enhance communication and learning.* London: Taylor and Francis.

Myers, G. D. (1985). Motor behavior of kindergartners during physical education and free play. In J. Frost & S. Sunderlin (Eds.), *When children play.* Wheaton, MD: Association for Childhood Education International.

NAEYC [National Association for the Education of Young Children]. (1996). NAEYC position statement: Responding to linguistic and cultural diversity. *Young Children, 51*(2), 4–12.

Naus, M. J. (1982). Memory development in the young reader: The combined effects of knowledge base and memory processing. In W. Otto & S. White (Eds.), *Reading expository text* (pp. 273–302). New York: Academic Press.

Nelson, K. (1974). Variations in children's concepts by age and category. *Child Development, 45,* 577–584.

Nelson, K. (1988). Constraints on word learning. *Cognitive Development, 3,* 221–246.

Nelson, L., & Madsen, M. C. (1969). Cooperation and competition in 4-year-olds as a function of reward contingency and subculture. *Developmental Psychology, 1,* 340–344.

Nelson, L. J., Hart, C. H., Robinson, C. C., Olsen, S. F., & Rubin, K. (1997, April). *Relations between sociometric status and three subtypes of withdrawn behavior in preschool children: A multi-method perspective.* Paper presented at the Biennial Meeting of the Society for Research in Child Development, Washington, DC.

New, R. S. (1994). Child's play—una cosa naturale: An Italian perspective. In J. L. Roopnarine, J. E. Johnson & F. H. Hooper (Eds.), *Children's play in diverse cultures* (pp. 123–147). Albany: SUNY Press.

Nisan, M. (1987). Moral norms and social conventions: A cross-cultural comparison. *Developmental Psychology, 23,* 719–725.

Nobles, (1974). Africanicity: Its role in black families. *Black Scholar, 5,* 10–17.

Norman, C. (1988). Math education: A mixed picture. *Science, 24,* 408–409.

Nsamenang, A. B. (1992). *Human development in cultural context: A third world perspective.* Newbury Park, CA: Sage.

Nutritional Status of Minority Children. (1997). *Morbidity and Mortality Weekly Report, 36,* 366–369.

Nwokah, E. E., & Fogel, A. (1990). *Cross-cultural differences in baby-talk to infants: The missing link?* Unpublished manuscript, Purdue University.

Nyiti, R. M. (1982). The validity of cultural differences explanations for cross-cultural variations in the rate of Piagetian cognitive development. In P. Wagner & H. Stevenson (Eds.), *Cultural perspectives in child development* (pp. 58–86). New York: Freeman.

Oakland, T. D., & Parmalee, R. (1985). Mental measurement of minority group children. In B. B. Wolman (Ed.), *Handbook of intelligence* (pp. 699–736). New York: Wiley.

Odom, S., & Bricker, D. (Eds.) (1993). *Integrating young children with disabilities into community programs.* Baltimore: Paul H. Brooks.

Ogbu, J. U. (1983). Socialization: A cultural ecological approach. In K. Borman (Ed.), *The social life of children in a changing society* (pp. 253–267). Hillsdale, NJ: Erlbaum.

Ogbu, J. U. (1988). Cultural diversity and human development. In D. Slaughter (Ed.), *Black children and poverty: A developmental perspective* (pp. 11–28). San Francisco: Jossey-Bass.

Ogbu, J. U. (1992). Understanding cultural diversity and learning. *Educational Researcher, 21,*(8), 5–14.

Ogbu, J. U. (1994). From cultural differences to differences in cultural frame of reference. In P. M. Greenfield & R. R. Cocking (Eds.), *Cross-cultural roots of minority child development* (pp. 365–391). Hillsdale, NJ: Erlbaum.

Ogura, T., Yamasjota, Y., Murase, T., & Dale, P. S. (1993). *Some preliminary findings from the Japanese early communicative development inventory.* Paper presented at the International Congress for the Study of Child Language, Triste, Italy.

Okagaki, L., & Frensch, P. A. (1998). Parenting and children's school achievement: A multiethnic perspective. *American Educational Research Journal, 35*(1), 123–144.

Olds, A. R. (1987). Designing space for children. In C. S. Weinstein & T. G. David (Eds.), *Spaces for children: The built environment and child development.* New York: Plenum Press.

Olsho, L. W., Koch, E. G., Carter, E. A., Halpin, C. F., & Spetner, N. B. (1988). Pure tone sensitivity in human infants. *Journal of the Acoustical Society of America, 84,* 1316–1324.

Olson, H. C., Sampson, P. D., Barr, H., Steissguth, A. P., & Bookstein, F. L. (1992). Prenatal exposure to alcohol and school problems in late childhood: A longitudinal prospective study. *Development and Psychopathology, 4,* 341–359.

Olson, L. M., Becker, T. M., Wiggins, C. L., Key, C. R., & Samet, J. M. (1990). Injury mortality in American Indian, Hispanic, and non-Hispanic white children in New Mexico. *Social Sciences Medicine, 30,* 479–486.

Olvera-Ezzell, N., Power, T. G., & Cousins, J. H. (1990). Maternal socialization of children's eating habits: Strategies used by obese Mexican-American mothers. *Child Development, 61,* 395–400.

Olvera-Ezzell, N., Power, T. G., Cousins, J. H., Guerra, A. M., & Trujillo, M. (1994). The development of health knowledge in low-income Mexican-American children. *Child Development, 65,* 416–427.

O'Malley, J. M. (1985). *Children's English and services study: Language minority children with limited English proficiency.* Rosslyn, VA: InterAmerica Research Associates.

Ovando, C., & Collier, V. (1985). *Bilingual and ESL classrooms.* New York: McGraw Hill.

Owens, R. E. (1994). Development of language, communication, and speech. In G. H. Shames, E. H. Wigg, & W. A. Second (Eds.), *Human communication disorders.* New York: Macmillan.

Padilla, A. M., Linholm, K. J., Chen, A., Duran, R., Hukata, K., Lambert, W., & Tucker, G. R. (1991). The English-only movement: Myths, reality, and implications for psychology. *American Psychologist, 46,* 120–131.

Paik, H., & Comstock, C. (1994). The effects of television violence on anti-social behavior: A meta-analysis. *Communication Research, 21,* 516–546.

Palmer, J. T. (1991, April). *Maternal responses to infant cries: Effects of context and acoustical properties of crying.* Paper presented at the biennial meeting of the Society for Research in Child Development, Seattle.

Pan, H.-L. W. (1994). Children's play in Taiwan. In J. L. Roopnarine, J. E. Johnson, & F. H. Hooper (Eds.), *Children's play in diverse cultures* (pp. 31–50). Albany: SUNY Press.

Paneth, N. S. (1995). The problem of low birth weight. In R. E. Behrman (Ed.), *The future of children: Low birth weight* (pp. 19–34). Los Angeles: Center for the Future of Children.

Parcel, G. S., Simons-Morton, B. G., O'Hara, N. M., Baranowski, T., Kolbe, J. J., & Bee, D. E. (1987). School promotion of healthful diet and exercise behavior: An integration of organizational change and social learning theory intervention. *Journal of School Health, 57,* 150–156.

Parcel, T. L., & Menaghan, E. G. (1994). *Parents' jobs and children's lives.* New York: Aldine de Gruyter.

Paris, S. G., & Lindauer, B. K. (1977). Constructive processes in children's comprehension and memory. In R. V. Kail & W. Hagen (Eds.), *Perspectives on the development of memory and cognition* (pp. 35–60). Hillsdale, NJ: Erlbaum.

Parker, J. G., Rubin, K. H., Price, J. M., & DeRosier, M. E. (1995). Peer relationships, child development, and adjustment. In D. Cicchetti & D. J. Cohen (Eds.), *Developmental psychopathology: Vol. 2. Risk, disorder, and adaptation* (pp. 96–161). New York: Wiley.

Parsons, J. E. (1983). Expectancies, values, and academic behaviors. In J. T. Spence (Ed.), *Achievement and achievement motives* (pp. 75–146). San Francisco: W. H. Freeman.

Parten, M. B. (1932). Social participation among preschool children. *Journal of Abnormal and Social Psychology, 27,* 243–269.

Pearson, J. L., Hunter, A. G., Ensminger, M. E., & Kellam, S. G. (1990). Black grandmothers in multigenerational households: Diversity in family structure and parenting involvement in the Woodlawn Community. *Child Development, 61,* 434–442.

Pease, D. M., Gleason, J. B., & Pan, B. A. (1989). Gaining meaning: Semantic development. In J. B. Gleason (Ed.), *The development of language* (pp. 101–134). Upper Saddle River, NJ: Merrill/Prentice Hall.

Pederson, D. R., Moran, G., Sitko, C., Campbell, K., Ghesquire, K., & Acton, H. (1990). Maternal sensitivity and the security of infant-mother attachment. *Child Development, 61,* 1974–1983.

Pellegrini, A. D. (1995a). Boys' rough and tumble play and social competence: Contemporaneous and longitudinal rela-

tions. In A. Pellegrini (Ed.), *The future of play research* (pp. 107–126). Albany: SUNY Press.

Pellegrini, A. D. (1995b). *Recess.* Albany: SUNY Press.

Pellegrini, A. D., & Perlmutter, J. C. (1988). Rough-and-tumble play on the elementary school yard. *Young Children, 43*(2), 14–17.

Pellegrini, A. D., Perlmutter, J. C., Galda, L., & Brody, G. H. (1990). Joint reading between black Head Start children and their mothers. *Child Development, 61,* 443–453.

Pepler, D. J., & Ross, H. S. (1981). The effects of play on convergent and divergent problem solving. *Child Development, 52,* 1202–1210.

Perlman, M. Claris, O., Hao, Y., Pandid, P., Whyte, H., Chipman, M., & Liu, P. (1995). Secular changes in the outcomes to 18 to 24 months of age of extremely low birth weight infants. *Journal of Pediatrics, 126,* 75–87.

Perlmutter, B. F., Crocker, J., Corday, D., & Garstecki, D. (1983). Sociometric status and related personality characteristics of mainstreamed and learning disabled adolescents. *Learning Disability Quarterly, 6,* 20–30.

Perner, J., Frith, U., Leslie, A. M., & Leekam, S. R. (1989). Exploration of the autistic child's theory of the mind: Knowledge, belief, and communication. *Child Development, 60,* 689–700.

Perner, J., Ruffman, T., & Leekam, S. R. (1994). Theory of mind is contagious: You catch it from your sibs. *Child Development, 65,* 1228–1238.

Perris, E. E., Myers, N. A., & Clifton, R. K. (1990). Long-term memory for a single infancy experience. *Child Development, 61,* 1796–1807.

Perry, D. (1996). Incubated in terror: Neurodevelopmental factors in the "cycle of violence." In J. D. Osovsky (Ed.), *Children youth and violence: Searching for solutions.* New York: Guilford.

Peterson, L., Ewigman, B., & Kivlahan, C. (1993). Judgements regarding appropriate child supervision to prevent injury: The role of environmental risk and child age. *Child Development, 64,* 934–950.

Petitto, L. A., & Marentette, P. F. (1991). Babbling in the manual mode: Evidence for the ontogeny of language. *Science, 251,* 1493–1496.

Pflaum, S. W. (1986). *The development of language and literacy in young children.* Upper Saddle River, NJ: Merrill/Prentice Hall.

Phillips, D. A., Voran, M., Kisker, E., Howes, C., & Whitebook, M. (1994). Child care for children in poverty: Opportunity or inequity? *Child Development, 65,* 472–492.

Phinney, J. S., & Rotheram, M. J. (1987). Children's ethnic socialization: Themes

and implications. In J. S. Phinney & M. J. Rotheram (Eds.), *Children's ethnic socialization: Pluralism and development* (pp. 274–292). Newbury Park, CA: Sage.

Phinney, J. S., & Tarver, S. (1988). Ethnic identity search and commitment in black and white eighth graders. *Journal of Early Adolescence, 8,* 265–277.

Piaget, J. (1930). *The child's conception of physical causality.* London: Routledge & Kegan Paul.

Piaget, J. (1932). *The moral judgement of the child.* New York: Free Press.

Piaget, J. (1952a). *The child's conception of number.* London: Routledge and Kegan Paul.

Piaget, J. (1952b). *The origins of intelligence.* New York: International Universities Press.

Piaget, J. (1954). *The construction of reality in the child.* New York: Basic Books.

Piaget, J. (1959). *Language and thought of the child.* London: Routledge and Kegan Paul.

Piaget, J. (1962). *Play, dreams, and imitation in childhood.* New York: Norton.

Piaget, J. (1965). *The child's conception of number.* New York: Norton.

Piaget, J. (1970). *The child's conception of time.* New York: Basic Books.

Piaget, J. (1971). *The construction of reality in the child.* New York: Ballantine.

Piaget J., & Inhelder, B. (1963). *The child's conception of space.* London: Routledge & Kegan Paul.

Piaget, J., Inhelder, B., & Szeminska, A. (1960). *The child's conception of geometry.* New York: Basic Books.

Pickens, J. (1994). Perception of auditory-visual distance relations by 5-month-old infants. *Developmental Psychology, 30,* 537–544.

Pine, J. M., Lieven, V. M., & Rowland, C. F. (1997). Stylistic variation at the "single-word" stage: Relations between maternal speech characteristics and children's vocabulary composition and usage. *Child Development, 68,* 807–819.

Pinon, M. F., Huston, A. C., & Wright, J. C. (1989). Family ecology and child characteristics that predict young children's educational television viewing. *Child Development, 60,* 846–856.

Pintrich, P., & Blumenfeld, P. (1985). Classroom experience and children's self-perceptions of ability, effort, and conduct. *Journal of Educational Psychology, 77,* 646–657.

Pizzo, P. A., & Wilfert, M. (Eds.). (1994). *Pediatric AIDS: The challenge of HIV in infants, children, and adolescents.* Baltimore: Williams and Wilkins.

Plonim, R. (1995). Genetics and children's experiences in the family. *Journal of Child Psychology and Psychiatry, 36,* 33–68.

Plumert, J. M. (1994). Flexibility in children's use of spatial and categorical organizational strategies in recall. *Developmental Psychology, 30,* 738–747.

Poag, C. K., Goodnight, J. A., & Cohen, R. (1985). The environments of children: From home to school. In R. Cohen (Ed.), *The development of spatial cognition* (pp. 71–114). Hillsdale, NJ: Erlbaum.

Poest, C. A., Williams, J. R., Witt, D. D., & Atwood, M. E. (1992). Challenge me to move: Large muscle development in young children. *Young Children, 45*(5), 4–10.

Polit, D. (1982). *Effects of family size.* Bethesda, MD: National Institutes of Health.

Pollack, L. A. (1983). *Forgotten children.* London: Cambridge University Press.

Pollitt, E. (1994). Poverty and child development: Relevance of research in developing countries to the United States. *Child Development, 65,* 283–296.

Pollitt, E., Gorman, K. S., Engle, P. L., Martorell, R., & Rivera, J. (1993). Early supplementary feeding and cognition: Effects over two decades. *Monographs of the Society for Research in Child Development, 58,* Serial No. 235.

Pope, A. W., Bierman, K. L., & Mumma, G. H. (1991). Aggression, hyperactivity, and inattention-immaturity: Behavior dimensions associated with peer rejection in elementary school boys. *Developmental Psychology, 27,* 663–671.

Posner, J. K., & Vandell, D. L. (1994). Low-income children's after-school care: Are there beneficial effects of after-school programs? *Child Development, 65,* 440–456.

Potter, E. (1982, March). *Demands upon children regarding quality of achievement: Standard setting in preschool classrooms.* Paper presented at the American Educational Research Association, New York.

Powell, G. J. (Ed.). (1983). *The psychosocial development of minority children.* New York: Brunner/Mazel.

Powlishta, K. Serbin, L., & Moller, L. (1993). The stability of individual differences in gender typing: Implications for understanding gender segregation. *Sex Roles, 28,* 723–737.

Price-Williams, D. R., Gordon, W., & Ramirez, M. (1969). Skill and conservation. *Developmental Psychology, 1,* 769.

Prizant, B., & Duchan, J. (1981). The functions of echolalia in autistic children. *Journal of Speech and Hearing Disorders, 46,* 241–249.

Putallaz, M., & Wasserman, A. (1989). Children's naturalistic entry behavior and sociometric status: A developmental perspective. *Developmental Psychology, 25,* 297–305.

Quiggle, N. L., Garber, J., Panak, W. F., & Dodge, K. A. (1992). Social information processing in aggressive and depressed children. *Child Development, 63,* 1305–1320.

Quigley, S., & Paul, P. (1987). Deafness and language development. In S. Rosenberg (Ed.), *Advances in applied psycholinguistics* (Vol. 1, pp. 109–121). Cambridge: Cambridge University Press.

Quigley, S., Power, B., & Steinkamp, M. (1977). The language structure of deaf children. *Volta Review, 79,* 80.

Quilligan, J. E. (1995). Obstetrics and gynecology. *Journal of the American Medical Association, 273,* 1760–1791.

Radke-Yarrow, M., Zahn-Waxler, C., & Chapman, M. (1982). Children's prosocial dispositions and behaviors. In P. H. Mussen (Ed.), *Handbook of child psychology* (Vol. 4, pp. 469–545). New York: Wiley.

Ramey, C. T., & Landesman-Ramey, S. (1996). *Prevention of intellectual disabilities: Early intervention to improve cognitive development.* Birmingham: University of Alabama Civitan International Research Center.

Ramjoue, B. (1980). *Guidelines for children's bilingualism.* Paris: Association of American Wives of Europeans.

Ramsey, P. G. (1987). *Teaching and learning in a diverse world: Multicultural education for young children.* New York: Teachers College Press.

Ramsey, P. G. (1989a, April). *Friendships, groups, and entries: Changing social dynamics in early childhood classrooms.* Paper presented at the biennial meeting of the Society for Research in Child Development, Kansas City, MO.

Ramsey, P. G. (1989b, April). *Successful and unsuccessful entry attempts: An analysis of behavioral and contextual factors.* Paper presented at the biennial meeting of the Society for Research in Child Development, Kansas City, MO.

Ramsey, P. G. (1995). Growing up with the contradictions of race and class. *Young Children, 50*(6), 18–22.

Ramsey, P. G., & Myers, L. C. (1990). Young children's responses to racial differences: Relations among cognitive, affective, and behavioral dimensions. *Journal of Applied Developmental Psychology, 11,* 49–67.

Ratner, N. B. (1989). Atypical language development. In J. B. Gleason (Ed.), *The development of language* (pp. 369–406). Upper Saddle River, NJ: Merrill/Prentice Hall.

Red Horse, J. (1983). Indian values and experiences. In G. J. Powell (Ed.), *The psychosocial development of minority children.* New York: Brunner/Mazel.

Reich, P. A. (1986). *Language development.* Upper Saddle River, NJ: Merrill/Prentice Hall.

Reid, B. V. (1984). An anthropological reinterpretation of Kohlberg's stages of moral development. *Human Development, 27,* 56–74.

Reiser, J., Yonas, A., & Wikner, K. (1976). Radial localization of odors by human neonates. *Child Development, 47,* 856–859.

Reiss, A. J., & Roth, J. A. (Eds.). (1993). *Understanding and preventing violence.* Washington, DC: National Academy Press.

Reynolds, R. (1995). *Education of Aboriginal groups in Australia.* Unpublished manuscript, Eastern Connecticut State University.

Rheingold, H., & Hay, D. F. (1976). Sharing in the second year of life. *Child Development, 47,* 1148–1158.

Rice, M. L. (1987). *Preschool children's fast mapping of words.* Paper presented at the Fourth Congress of the International Association for the Study of Language, Lund, Sweden.

Rice, M. L., & Schuele, C. M. (1995). Speech and language impairments. In E. L. Meyen & T. M. Skrtic (Eds.), *Special education and student disability* (pp. 339–376). Denver: Love.

Richman, A. L., Miller, P. M., & Levine, R. A. (1992). Cultural and educational variations in maternal responsiveness. *Developmental Psychology, 28,* 614–621.

Rivara, F. P., & Barber, M. (1985). Demographic analysis of childhood pedestrian injuries. *Pediatrics, 76,* 375–381.

Rivara, F. P., & Mueller, B. A. (1987). The epidemiology and causes of childhood injuries. *Journal of Social Issues, 43,* 13–31.

Robins, L. N., & Mills, J. L. (1993). *Effects of in utero exposure to street drugs.* Washington, DC: National Institute of Child Health and Human Development.

Robinson, N. M., & Noble, K. D. (1991). Social-emotional development and adjustment of gifted children. In M. C. Wang, M. C. Reynolds, & H. J. Walberg (Eds.), *Handbook of special education: Research and practice* (pp. 29–50). New York: Pergamon Press.

Robinson, S. M., & Deshler, D. D. (1995). Learning disabled. In E. L. Meyen & T. M. Skrtic (Eds.), *Special education and student disability* (pp. 171–212). Denver: Love.

Rodriquez, A. (1983). Educational policy and cultural plurality. In G. J. Powell (Ed.), *The psychosocial development of minority children* (pp. 499–514). New York: Brunner/Mazel.

Rodriguez, C., & Moore, N. B. (1995). Perceptions of pregnant/parenting teens. *Adolescence, 30,* 685–706.

Roedel, W. C. (1984). Vulnerabilities of highly gifted children. *Roeper Review, 6,* 127–130.

Roffwarg, H. P., Muzio, J. N., & Dement, W. C. (1966). Ontogenetic development of the human sleep-dream cycle. *Science, 152,* 604–619.

Rogoff, B. (1990). *Apprenticeship in thinking.* New York: Oxford University Press.

Rogoff, B. (1994). Observing sociocultural activity on three planes: Participatory appropriation, guided participation, apprenticeship. In A. Alvarez, P. del Rio, & J. V. Wertsch (Eds.), *Perspectives in sociocultural research.* Cambridge: Cambridge University Press.

Rogoff, B., Mistry, A., Goncu, A., & Mosier, C. (1993). Guided participation in cultural activity by toddlers and caregivers. *Monographs of the Society for Research in Child Development, 58,* Serial No. 236.

Rogosch, F. A., & Newcomb, A. F. (1989). Children's perceptions of peer reputations and their social reputations among peers. *Child Development, 60,* 597–610.

Romney, K., & Romney, R. (1963). The Mextecans of Juxtlahuaca, Mexico. In B. B. Whiting (Ed.), *In six cultures: Studies of child rearing* (pp. 25–41). New York: John Wiley.

Roopnarine, J. L., Hossain, Z., Gill, P., & Brophy, H. (1994). Play in the East Indian context. In J. L. Roopnarine, J. E. Johnson, & F. H. Hooper (Eds.), *Children's play in diverse cultures* (pp. 9–30). Albany: SUNY Press.

Roopnarine, J. L., Johnson, J. E., & Hooper, F. H. (1994). *Children's play in diverse cultures.* Albany: SUNY Press.

Roosa, M. W. (1984). Maternal age, social class, and the obstetric performance of teenagers. *Journal of Youth and Adolescence, 13,* 365–374.

Rose, S. A., Feldman, J. F., & Wallace, I. F. (1992). Infant information processing in relation to six-year cognitive outcomes. *Child Development, 63,* 1126–1141.

Rosen, C. S., Schwebel, D. C., & Singer, J. L. (1997). Preschoolers attributions of mental states in pretense. *Child Development, 68,* 1133–1142.

Rosen, W. D., Adamson, L. B., & Bakeman, R. (1992). An experimental investigation of social referencing: Mothers' messages and gender differences. *Developmental Psychology, 28,* 1172–1178.

Rosenberg, M. (1979). *Conceiving the self.* New York: Basic Books.

Rosenblith, J. F. (1992). *In the beginning.* Thousand Oaks, CA: Sage.

Rosenstein, D., & Oster, H. (1988). Differential facial responses to four basic tastes. *Child Development, 59,* 1555–1568.

Ross, J. G., & Pate, R. R. (1987). The national children and youth fitness study: II. A summary of findings. *Journal of Physical Education, Recreation, and Dance, 58,* 51–56.

Rosser, P. L., & Rudolph, S. M. (1989). Black American infants: The Howard University Normative Study. In J. K. Nuegent, B. M. Lester, & T. B. Brazelton (Eds.), *The cultural context of infancy: Vol. 1. Biology, culture and infant development.* Norwood, NH: Ablex.

Rottenberg, K. J., & Sliz, D. (1988). Children's restrictive disclosure to friends. *Merrill-Palmer Quarterly, 34,* 203–215.

Rovee-Collier, C., Griesler, P. C., & Earley, L. A. (1985). Contextual determinants of retrieval in 3-month-old infants. *Learning and Motivation, 16,* 139–157.

Roy, J. D. (1987). The linguistic and sociolinguistic position of Black English as related to situation and social class. In P. Homel, M. Palij, & D. Aaronson (Eds.), *Childhood bilingualism: Aspects of linguistic, cognitive, and social development* (pp. 231–243). Hillsdale, NJ: Erlbaum.

Rubin, K. H. (1980). Fantasy play: Its role in the development of social skills and social cognition. In K. H. Rubin (Ed.), *Children's play.* San Francisco: Jossey-Bass.

Rubin, K. H. (1982). Nonsocial play in preschoolers: Necessary evil? *Child Development, 53,* 651–657.

Rubin, K. H., & Asendorpf, J. (1993). Social withdrawal, inhibition, and shyness in childhood: Conceptual and definitional issues. In K. H. Rubin & J. Asendorpf (Eds.), *Social withdrawal, inhibition, and shyness in children* (pp. 3–17). Hillsdale, NJ: Erlbaum.

Rubin, K. H., Fein, G. G., & Vandenberg, B. (1983). Play. In E. M. Hetherington (Ed.) & P. H. Mussen (Series Ed.), *Handbook of child psychology: Vol. 4. Socialization, personality, and social development.* New York: Wiley.

Rubin, K. H., Hymel, S., LeMare, R. S. L., & Rowden, L. (1989). Children experiencing social difficulties: Sociometric neglect reconsidered. *Canadian Journal of Behavioral Science, 21,* 94–111.

Rubin, K. H., Maioni, T. L., & Hornung, M. (1976). Free play behaviors in middle and lower class preschoolers: Parten and Piaget revisited. *Child Development, 47,* 414–419.

Rubin, K. H., & Mills, R. S. L. (1988). The many faces of social isolation in childhood. *Journal of Consulting and Clinical Psychology, 6,* 916–924.

Rubin, K. H., Stewart, S. L., & Coplan, R. J. (1995). Social withdrawal in childhood: Conceptual and empirical perspectives. In T. H. Ollendick & R. J. Prinz (Eds.), *Advances in clinical child psychology* (Vol. 17, pp. 157–196). New York: Plenum.

Rutter, M. (1987). Continuities and discontinuities from infancy. In J. Osofsky (Ed.), *Handbook of infant development* (pp. 87–104). New York: Wiley.

Rutter, M., & Schopler, E. (1987). Autism and pervasive developmental disorders: Concepts and diagnostic issues. *Journal of Autism and Developmental Disorders, 17,* 159–186.

Ryan, A. S., Rush, D., Krieger, F. W., & Lewandowski, G. E. (1991). Recent declines in breastfeeding in the United States. *Pediatrics, 88,* 719–727.

Sagi, A., & Hoffman, M. (1976). Emphatic distress in the newborn. *Developmental Psychology, 12,* 175–176.

Sagi, A., van Ijzendoorn, M. H., & Koren-Karie, O. (1991). Primary appraisal of the strange situation: A cross-cultural analysis of preseparation episodes. *Developmental Psychology, 27,* 587–596.

Sahler, O. J. Z. (1983). Adolescent mothers: How nurturant is their parenting? In E. R. McAnarney (Ed.), *Premature adolescent pregnancy and parenthood* (pp. 37–59). New York: Grune and Stratton.

Salzinger, S., Feldman, R. S., Hammer, M., & Rosario, M. (1993). The effects of physical abuse on children's social relationships. *Child Development, 64,* 169–187.

Sanchez-Ayendez, M. (1988). The Puerto Rican American family. In C. H. Mindel, R. W. Habenstein & R. Wright (Eds.), *Ethnic families in America: Patterns and variations.* New York: Elsevier.

Sanders, K. M., & Harper, L. V. (1976). Free play fantasy behavior in preschool children: Relations among gender, age, season, and location. *Child Development, 47,* 1182–1185.

Sansavini, A., Bertoncini, J., & Giovanelli, G. (1997). Newborns discriminate the rhythm of multisyllabic stessed words. *Developmental Psychology, 23,* 3–12.

Sata, L. S. (1983). Mental health issues of Japanese-American children. In G. J. Powell (Ed.), *The psychosocial development of minority children* (pp. 362–372). New York: Brunner/Mazel.

Saudino, K. J., & Eaton, W. O. (1989, July). *Heredity and infant activity level.* Paper presented to the International Society for the Study of Behavioral Development, Jybaskyla, Finland.

Saunders, G. (1988). *Studies in bilingual development.* Hillsdale, NJ: Erlbaum.

Scafidi, F. A., Field, T. M., Schanberg, S. M., Bauer, C. R., Vega-Lahr, N., Garcia, R., Power, J., Nystrom, G., & Kuhn, C. M. (1986). Effects of tactile/kinesthetic stimulation on the clinical course and sleep/wake behavior of preterm neonates. *Infant Behavior and Development, 9,* 91–105.

Scarlett, W. G. (1983). Social isolation from agemates among nursery school children. In M. Donaldson, R. Grieve, & C. Pratt (Eds.), *Early childhood development and education.* New York: Guilford.

Scarr, S. (1993). Biological and cultural diversity: The legacy of Darwin for development. *Child Development, 64,* 1333–1353.

Scarr, S., Weinberg, R. A., & Waldman, I. D. (1993). IQ correlations in transracial adoptive families. *Intelligence, 17,* 541–555.

Schaal, B. (1986). Presumed olfactory exchanges between mother and neonate in humans. In J. S. Cimus & J. Cosnier (Eds.), *Ethology and psychology* (pp. 101–110). Toulouse: Privat, I. E. C.

Schaffer, H. R., & Emerson, P. E. (1964). The development of social attachments in infancy. *Monographs of the Society for Research in Child Development, 29,* Serial No. 94.

Schiamberg, L. B. (1988). *Child and adolescent development.* Upper Saddle River, NJ: Merrill/Prentice Hall.

Schickedanz, J. A. (1982). "Hey! This book's not working right!" In J. F. Brown (Ed.), *Curriculum planning for young children.* Washington, DC: National Association for the Education of Young Children.

Schickedanz, J. A. (1999). *More than ABCs: The early stages of reading and writing* (2nd ed.). Washington, DC: National Association for the Education of Young Children.

Schickedanz, J. A., Schickedanz, D. I., & Forsyth, P. D. (1982). *Toward understanding children.* Boston: Little, Brown.

Schlesinger, H. S., & Meadow, K. P. (1972). *Sound and sign: Childhood deafness and mental health.* Berkeley: University of California Press.

Schneider, B. H., Wiener, J., & Murphy, K. (1994). Children's friendships: The giant step beyond peer relations. *Journal of Social and Personal Relationships, 11,* 323–340.

Schultz, J., Florio, S., & Erickson, R. (1982). Where's the floor? Aspects of the cultural organization of social relationships in communication at home and in school. In P. Gilmore & A. Glatthorn (Eds.), *Children in and out of school: Ethnography and education.* Washington, DC: Center for Applied Linguistics.

Schutter, L. S., & Brinker, R. P. (1992). Conjuring a new category of disability from prenatal cocaine exposure: Are the infants unique biological or caretaking casualties? *Topics in Early Childhood Special Education, 11,* 84–111.

Schwartz, A. J. (1971). The culturally advantaged: A study of Japanese-American pupils. *Sociology and Social Research, 55,* 341–353.

Schwartz, R. G., & Leonard, L. B. (1982). Do children pick and choose? An examination of phonological selection and avoidance in early lexical acquisition. *Journal of Child Language, 9,* 319–336.

Schweinhart, L. J., & Weikart, D. P. (1996). *Lasting difference: The High/Scope preschool curriculum comparison study through age 23.* Ypsilanti, MI: High/Scope Press.

Schweinhart, L. J., Weikart, D. P., & Larner, M. B. (1986). Consequences of three preschool curriculum models through age 15. *Early Childhood Research Quarterly, 1,* 15–45.

Seefeldt, C. (1987). The visual arts. In C. Seefeldt (Ed.), *The early childhood curriculum: A review of current research.* New York: Teachers College Press.

Seefeldt, C. (1998). Social studies in the integrated curriculum. In C. H. Hart, D. C., Burts & R. Charlesworth (Eds.), *Integrated curriculum and developmentally appropriate practice.* Albany: SUNY Press.

Selman, R. L., & Demorest, A. P. (1984). Observing troubled children's interpersonal negotiational strategies: Implications of and for a developmental model. *Child Development, 55,* 288–304.

Serpell, R. (1979). How specific are perceptual skills? A cross-cultural study of pattern reproduction. *British Journal of Psychology, 70,* 365–380.

Shames, G. H., & Wig, E. H. (1986). *Human communication disorders.* Upper Saddle River, NJ: Merrill/Prentice Hall.

Shatz, M., Grimm, H., Wilcox, S. A., & Niemeier-Wind, K. (1989, April). *The uses of modal expression in conversation between German and American mothers and their two-year-olds.* Paper presented at the biennial meeting of the Society for Research in Child Development, Kansas City, MO.

Shavelson, R. J., & Bolus, R. (1982). Self-concept: The interplay of theory and methods. *Journal of Educational Psychology, 74,* 3–17.

Shepard, L., & Smith, M. L. (1989). *Flunking grades: Research and policies on retention.* Bristo, PA: Taylor and Francis.

Shirley, M. M. (1933). *The first two years.* Minneapolis: University of Minnesota Press.

Shonkoff, J. P., Hauser-Cram, P., Krauss, M. W., & Upshur, C. C. (1992). Development of infants with disabilities and their families. *Monographs of the Society for Research in Child Development, 57,* Serial No. 230.

Shore, N. (1977). *Rethinking the brain: New insights into early development.* New York: Families and Work Institute.

Siegel, L. S., McCabe, A. E., Brand, J., & Mathews, J. (1978). Evidence for the understanding of class inclusion reasoning in preschool children: Linguistic factors and training effects. *Child Development, 49,* 688–693.

Siegler, R. S. (1986). *Children's thinking.* Upper Saddle River, NJ: Prentice-Hall.

Silverman, L. K. (1986). Parenting young gifted children. In J. R. Whitmore (Ed.), *Intellectual giftedness in young children* (pp. 73–87). New York: Haworth.

Silverman, L. K. (1989). Invisible gifts, invisible handicaps. *Roeper Review, 22,* 37–42.

Silverman, L. K. (1995). Gifted and talented students. In E. L. Meyen & T. M. Skrtic (Eds.), *Special education and student disability* (pp. 377–414). Denver: Love.

Silverman, W. K., Chitwood, D. G., & Waters, J. L. (1986). Parents as identifiers of the gifted. *Topics in Early Childhood Special Education, 6*(1), 23–38.

Silverman, W. K., La Greca, A. M., & Wasserstein, S. W. (1995). What do children worry about? Worries and their relation to anxiety. *Child Development, 66,* 671–686.

Sirvis, R. P., & Caldwell, T. H. (1995). Physical disabilities and chronic health impairments. In E. L. Meyen & T. M. Skrtic (Eds.), *Special education and student disability* (pp. 533–564). Denver: Love.

Skinner, B. F. (1948). *Walden two.* New York: Macmillan.

Skinner, B. F. (1957). *Verbal behavior.* Upper Saddle River, NJ: Prentice-Hall.

Skrtic, T. M. (1995). The crisis in professional knowledge. In E. L. Meyen & T. M. Skrtic (Eds.), *Special education and student disability* (pp. 567–608). Denver: Love.

Slaughter-Defoe, D. T., Nakagawa, K., Takanishi, R., & Johnson, D. J. (1990). Toward cultural/ecological perspectives on schooling and achievement in African- and Asian-American children. *Child Development, 61,* 363–383.

Slonim, M. B. (1991). *Children, culture, and ethnicity: Evaluating and understanding the impact.* New York: Garland.

Small, M. Y. (1990). *Cognitive development.* San Diego: Harcourt Brace Jonvanovich.

Smilansky, S. (1968). *The effects of sociodramatic play on disadvantaged preschool children.* New York: Wiley.

Smilansky, S., & Shefatya, L. (1990). *Facilitating play: A medium for promoting cognitive, socioemotional, and academic development in young children.* Gaithersburg, MD: Psychosocial & Educational Publications.

Smith, F. (1988). *Understanding reading.* Hillsdale, NJ: Erlbaum.

Smith, L. (1989). A model of perceptual classification in children and adults. *Psychological Review, 96,* 125–144.

Smith, M. E. (1926). An investigation of the development of the sentence and the extent of vocabulary in young children. *University of Iowa Studies in Child Welfare, 3,* 5.

Smith, P. K. (1997). *Play fighting and fighting: How do they relate?* Lisbon: ICCP.

Snow, C. (1987). *Common terms in second language education: Center for Language and Research.* Los Angeles: University of California.

Sorce, J. F., Emde, R. N., Campos, J., & Klinnert, M. D. (1985). Maternal emotional signalling: Its effect on the visual cliff behavior of 1-year-olds. *Developmental Psychology, 21,* 195–200.

Soto, D. L. (1991). Understanding bilingual/bicultural young children. *Young Children, 46*(2), 30–36.

Soto, L. D., & Negron, L. (1994). Mainland Puerto Rican children. In J. L. Roopnarine,

J. E. Johnson, & F. H. Hooper (Eds.), *Children's play in diverse cultures*. Albany: SUNY Press.

Spencer, J. T. (1970). *The effects of systematic social and token reinforcement on the modification of racial and color-concept attitudes in preschool-aged children*. Unpublished master's thesis, University of Kansas.

Spencer, M. B. (1983). Children's cultural values and parental child rearing strategies. *Developmental Review, 4,* 351–370.

Spencer, M. B. (1985). Racial variations in achievement prediction: The school as a conduit for macrostructural cultural tension. In H. P. McAdoo & J. L. McAdoo (Eds.), *Black children: Social educational, and parental environments* (pp. 85–112). Newbury Park: Sage.

Spencer, M. B. (1988). Self-concept development. In D. Slaughter (Ed.), *Black children and poverty: A developmental perspective* (pp. 59–74). San Francisco: Jossey-Bass.

Spencer, M. B. (1990). Development of minority children: An introduction. *Child Development, 61,* 267–269.

Spencer, M. B., & Markstrom-Adams, C. (1990). Identity processes among racial and ethnic minority children in America. *Child Development, 61,* 290–310.

Spiers, P. S., & Guntheroff, W. G. (1994). Recommendations to avoid the prone sleeping position and recent statistics for Sudden Infant Death Syndrome in the United States. *Archives of Pediatric and Adolescent Medicine, 148,* 141–146.

Spiker, D., Ferguson, J., & Brooks-Gunn, J. (1993). Enhancing maternal interactive behavior and child social competence in low birth weight, premature infants. *Child Development, 64,* 754–769.

Spock, B., & Rothenberg, M. B. (1985). *Dr. Spock's baby and child care*. New York: Dutton.

Sporns, O., & Edelman, G. M. (1993). Solving Bernstein's problem: A proposal for the development of coordinated movement by selection. *Child Development, 64,* 960–981.

Sroufe, L. A. (1985). Attachment classification from the perspective of infant-caregiver relationships and infant temperament. *Child Development, 56,* 1–14.

Sroufe, L. A., Fox, N., & Pancake, V. R. (1983). Attachment and dependency in developmental perspective. *Child Development, 54,* 1615–1627.

Stack, D. M., & Muir, D. W. (1992). Adult tactile stimulation during face-to-face interactions modulates five-month-olds' affect and attention. *Child Development, 63,* 1509–1525.

Stangor, C., & Ruble, D. N. (1989). Differential influences of gender schemata and gender constancy on children's informa-tion processing and behavior. *Social Cognition, 7,* 353–372.

Staples, R. (1988). The black American family. In C. H. Mindel, R. W. Habenstein, & R. Wright (Eds.), *Ethnic families in America: Patterns and variations*. New York: Elsevier.

Stechler, G., & Halton, A. (1982). Prenatal influences on human development. In B. Wolman (Ed.), *Handbook of developmental psychology* (pp. 175–189). Upper Saddle River, NJ: Prentice-Hall.

Sternberg, R. J., & Wagner, R. K. (1993). The g-ocentric view of intelligence and job performance is wrong. *Directions in Psychological Science, 2,* 1–5.

Stevens, J. H. (1984). Black grandmothers' and black adolescent mothers' knowledge about parenting. *Developmental Psychology, 20,* 1017–1025.

Stevens, J. H., & Duffield, B. N. (1986). Age and parenting skill among black women in poverty. *Early Childhood Research Quarterly, 1,* 221–235.

Stevenson, H. W., Chen, C., & Uttal, D. H. (1990). Beliefs and achievement: A study of black, white, and Hispanic children. *Child Development, 61,* 508–523.

Stevenson, H. W., Lee, S., Chen, C., Lummis, M., Stigler, J., Fan, L., & Ge, F. (1990). Mathematics achievement of children in China and the United States. *Child Development, 61,* 1053–1066.

Steward, J. F., Popkin, B. M., Guilkey, D. K., Akin, J. S., Adair, L., & Flieger, W. (1991). Influences on the extent of breastfeeding. *Demography, 28,* 181–199.

Steward, M. S., & Steward, D. S. (1973). The observation of Anglo-, Mexican-, and Chinese-American mothers teaching their young sons. *Child Development, 44,* 239–337.

Steward, M. S., & Steward, D. S. (1974). Effect of social distance on teaching strategies of Anglo-American and Mexican-American mothers. *Developmental Psychology, 10,* 797–807.

Stipek, D. (1992). The child at school. In M. H. Bornstein & M. E. Lamb (Eds.), *Developmental psychology: An advanced textbook* (579–625). Hillside, NJ: Erlbaum.

Stipek, D., & MacIver, D. (1989). Developmental change in children's assessment of intellectual competence. *Child Development, 60,* 521–538.

Stipek, D., Recchia, S., & McClintic, S. (1992). Self-evaluations in young children. *Monographs of the Society for Research in Child Development, 57,* no. 1 (Serial No. 226).

Streissguth, A. P., Martin, D. C., Barr, H. M., Sandman, B. M., Kirchner, M., & Darby, T. (1984). Intrauterine alcohol and nicotine exposure: Attention and reaction time in 4-year-old children. *Developmental Psychology, 20,* 533–541.

Sudhalter, V., & Braine, M. D. S. (1985). How does comprehension of passives develop? *Journal of Child Language, 12,* 455–470.

Sue, S., & Chin, R. (1983). The mental health of Chinese-American children: Stressors and resources. In G. J. Powell (Ed.), *The psychosocial development of minority children* (pp. 385–400). New York: Brunner/Mazel.

Sulzby, E. (1981). *Kindergartners begin to read their own compositions: Beginning readers' developing knowledge about written languages project*. Washington, DC: National Council of Teachers of English.

Sulzby, E. (1985). Children's emergent reading of favorite storybooks: A developmental study. *Reading Research Quarterly, 20,* 458–481.

Sulzby, E. (1986). Children's elicitation and use of metalinguistic knowledge about words during literacy interactions. In D. B. Yaden & S. Templeton (Eds.), *Metalinguistic awareness and beginning literacy*. Portsmouth, NH: Heinemann.

Sulzby, E., & Teale, W. (1987). *Young children's storybook reading: Longitudinal study of parent-child interaction and children's independent functioning. Final Report to the Spencer Foundation*. Ann Arbor: University of Michigan.

Super, C. M. (1981). Cross-cultural research on infancy. In H. C. Triandis & A. Heron (Eds.), *Handbook of cross-cultural psychology: Developmental psychology* (Vol. 4, pp. 17–53). Boston: Allyn & Bacon.

Super, C. M., & Harkness, S. (1982). The infant's niche in rural Kenya and metropolitan America. In L. Adler (Ed.), *Issues in cross-cultural research* (pp. 47–56). New York: Academic Press.

Surwillo, W. W. (1971). Human reaction time and period of the EEG in relation to development. *Psychophysiology, 8,* 468–482.

Sutton-Smith, B. (1983). One hundred years of change in play research. *Association for the Anthropological Study of Play Newsletter, 9*(2), 13–17.

Sutton-Smith, B., & Roberts, J. M. (1970). The cross-cultural and psychological study of games. In G. Luschen (Ed.), *The cross-cultural analysis of games* (pp. 64–98). Champaign, IL: Stipes.

Svejda, M., & Campos, J. (1982). *The mother's voice as a regulator of the infant's behavior*. Paper presented at the International Conference on Infant Studies, Austin, Texas.

Tager-Flusberg, H. (1989). Putting words together: Morphology and syntax in the preschool years. In J. B. Gleason (Ed.), *The development of language* (pp. 135–166). Upper Saddle River, NJ: Merrill/Prentice Hall.

Tait, P. (1973). Behavior of young blind children in a controlled play setting. *Perception and Motor Skills, 34,* 963–969.

Takeuchi, M. (1994). Children's play in Japan. In J. L. Roopnarine, J. E. Johnson, & F. H. Hooper (Eds.), *Children's play in diverse cultures* (pp. 51–72). Albany: SUNY Press.

Tallal, P. (1987). Developmental language disorders. In *Learning disabilities: A report to the U.S. Congress*. Washington, DC: Interagency Committee on Learning Disabilities.

Tanner, J. M. (1990). *Fetus into man: Physical growth from conception to maturity* (3rd ed.). Cambridge: Harvard University Press.

Tavecchio, L. W. C., & Ijzendoorn, M. H. (1987). *Attachment in social networks: Contributions to the Bowlby-Ainsworth attachment theory*. Amsterdam: Elsevier.

Taylor, A. R., & Machida, S. (1994, April). *Parental involvement: Perspectives of Head Start parents and teachers*. Paper presented at the American Educational Research Association, New Orleans.

Teale, W. H. (1984). Reading to young children: Its significance for literacy development. In H. Goelman & F. Smith (Eds.), *Awakening to literacy* (pp. 110–121). Portsmouth, NH: Heinemann.

Temple, C. Nathan, R., Burris, N., & Temple, F. (1988). *The beginnings of writing*. Newton, MA: Allyn & Bacon.

Terrel, T. D. (1981). The natural approach to bilingual education. In *Schooling and language minority students: A theoretical framework* (pp. 117–146). Los Angeles: Evaluation, Dissemination, and Assessment Center, School of Education, California State University, Los Angeles.

Teti, D. M., & Ablard, K. E. (1989). Security of attachment and infant-sibling relationships. *Child Development, 60,* 1519–1528.

Thelen, E., & Ulrich, B. D. (1991). Hidden skills. *Monographs of the Society for Research in Child Development, 56,* Serial No. 223.

Thomas, A., & Chess, S. (1977). *Temperament and development*. New York: Brunner/Mazel.

Thomas, A., & Chess, S. (1984). Genesis and evaluation of behavioral disorders: From infancy to early adult life. *American Journal of Psychiatry, 141,* 1–9.

Thomas, R. M. (1992). *Comparing theories of child development* (3rd ed.). Belmont, CA: Wadsworth.

Thompson, R. A. (1988). The effects of infant day care through the prism of attachment theory: A critical appraisal. *Early Childhood Research Quarterly, 3,* 273–282.

Thompson, R. A., & Limber, S. P. (1990). Social anxiety in infancy: Stranger and separation anxiety. In H. Leitenberg (Ed.), *Handbook of social anxiety*. New York: Plenum.

Thornton, M. C., Chatters, L. M., Taylor, R. J., & Allen, W. (1990). Sociodemographic and environmental correlates of racial socialization by black parents. *Child Development, 61,* 401–409.

Tobin, J. J., Wu, D. Y. H., & Davidson, D. H. (1989). *Preschool in three cultures: Japan, China, and the United States*. New Haven, CT: Yale University Press.

Tomasello, M., & Mervis, C. B. (1994). Commentary: The instrument is great, but measuring comprehension is still a problem. In L. Fenson, P. S. Dale, J. S. Reznick, E. Bates, D. J. Thal, & S. J. Pethick (Eds.), Variability in early communicative development. *Monographs of the Society for Research in Child Development, 59,* Serial No. 242.

Trawick-Smith, J. (1988). Let's say you're the baby, OK?: Play leadership and following behavior in young children. *Young Children, 43*(5), 51–59.

Trawick-Smith, J. (1990). Effects of realistic vs. non-realistic play materials on young children's symbolic transformation of objects. *Journal of Research in Childhood Education, 5,* 27–36.

Trawick-Smith, J. (1991). The significance of toddler pretend play in child care. *Early Child Development and Care, 68,* 79–98.

Trawick-Smith, J. (1992). A descriptive study of persuasive preschool children: How they get others to do what they want. *Early Childhood Research Quarterly, 7*(1), 95–115.

Trawick-Smith, J. (1993, April). *A content analysis of the Early Childhood Research Quarterly*. Paper presented at the annual meeting of the American Educational Research Association, Atlanta.

Trawick-Smith, J. (1994). *Interactions in the classroom: Facilitating play in the early years*. Upper Saddle River, NJ: Merrill/Prentice Hall.

Trawick-Smith, J. (1998a). An analysis of metaplay in the preschool years. *Early Childhood Research Quarterly, 13,* 433–452.

Trawick-Smith, J. (1998b, April). *A cultural-ecological model of children's play: Lessons from Puerto Rican children*. Paper present at the annual meeting of the American Educational Research Association, San Diego.

Trawick-Smith, J. (1998c). School-based play and social interactions. In D. Fromberg & D. Bergen (Eds.), *Play from birth to 12: Contexts, perspectives, and meanings*. New York: Garland.

Trawick-Smith, J. (1998d, March). *A sociocultural model of children's play: Observations of Puerto Rican children on the island and the mainland*. Paper presented at the annual meeting of the American Educational Research Association, San Diego.

Trawick-Smith, J., & Lisi, P. (1994). Infusing multicultural perspectives in an early childhood development course: Effects on the knowledge and attitudes of inservice teachers. *Journal of Early Childhood Teacher Education, 15,* 8–12.

Trehub, S. E. (1976). The discrimination of foreign speech sound contrasts by infants and adults. *Child Development, 47,* 466–472.

Tucker, K., & Young, F. W. (1989). Household structure and child nutrition. *Social Indicators Research, 2,* 201–221.

Turner, P. J. (1993). Attachment to mother and behavior with adults in preschool. *British Journal of Developmental Psychology, 11,* 75–89.

UNICEF. (1990). *Children and development in the 1990s: A UNICEF sourcebook*. New York: United Nations.

U.S. Bureau of the Census. (1994). *Current population reports*. Washington, DC: Author.

U.S. Bureau of the Census. (1998). *Statistical abstract of the United States*. Washington, DC: Government Printing Office.

U.S. Department of Education. (1995). *The educational progress of Hispanic Students*. Washington, DC: Author.

U.S. Department of Health and Human Services. (1986). *Health United States*. Hyattsville, MD: Public Health Service.

U.S. Department of Health and Human Services. (1990). *Health United States*. Hyattsville, MD: Public Health Service.

U.S. Department of Health and Human Services. (1996). *Trends in the well-being of America's children and youth*. Washington, DC: Author.

U.S. Department of Health, Education, and Welfare. (1979). *Smoking and health: A report of the surgeon general*. Washington, DC: Government Printing Office.

Valenzuela, M. (1990). Attachment in chronically underweight young children. *Child Development, 61,* 1984–1996.

van Dijk, J. J. M., Mayhew, P., & Killias, M. (1990). *Experiences of crime across the world: Key findings from the 1989 International Crime Survey*. Deventer, The Netherlands: Kluwer Law and Taxation Publishers.

van Ijzendoorn, M. H., Goldberg, S., Kroonenberg, P. M., & Frenkel, O. J. (1992). The relative effects of maternal and child problems on the quality of attachment: A meta-analysis of attachment in clinical samples. *Child Development, 63,* 840–858.

van Ijzendoorn, M. H., & Kroonenberg, P. M. (1988). Cross-cultural patterns of attachment: A meta-analysis of the strange situation. *Child Development, 59,* 147–156.

Vaughn, B., Lefever, G., Seifer, R., & Barglow, P. (1989). Attachment behavior, attachment security, and temperament during infancy. *Child Development, 60,* 728–737.

Vaughn, S. B., Hogan, A., Kouzekanani, K., & Shapiro, S. (1990). Peer acceptance of learning disabled children prior to identification. *Journal of Educational Psychology, 82,* 101–106.

Ventura, S. J. (1987). Births of Hispanic parentage, 1983 and 1984. *Monthly Vital Statistics Report, 36,* 1–19.

Vygotsky, L. S. (1962). *Thought and language.* Cambridge, MA: MIT Press.

Vygotsky, L. S. (1976). Play and its role in the mental development of the child. In J. Bruner, A. Jolly, & K. Sylva (Eds.), *Play: Its role in development and evolution.* New York: Basic Books.

Vygotsky, L. S. (1978). *Mind and society: The development of higher mental processes.* Cambridge: Harvard University Press.

Wahab, Z. (1974). *Teacher-pupil transaction in bi-racial classrooms: Implications for instruction.* Paper presented at the Pacific Sociological Association, San Jose, CA.

Walker, D., Greenwood, C., Haret, B., & Carta J. (1994). Prediction of school outcomes based on early language production and socioeconomic factors. *Child Development, 65,* 606–621.

Walker, L. J. (1984). Sex differences in the development of moral reasoning: A critical review. *Child Development, 55,* 677–691.

Wallis, C. (1986, January 20). Cocaine babies. *Time,* 20.

Wan, C., Fan, C., Lin, G., & Jing, Q. (1994). Comparison of personality traits of only and sibling children in Bejing. *Journal of Genetic Psychology, 155,* 377–389.

Warren-Leubecker, A., & Bohannon, J. N. (1989). Pragmatics: Language in social contexts. In J. B. Gleason (Ed.), *The development of language* (pp. 327–368). Upper Saddle River, NJ: Merrill/Prentice Hall.

Warren-Leubecker, A., & Tate, C. (1986, October). *Is preschoolers' speech egocentric?* Paper presented at the Boston University Conference on Language Development, Boston, MA.

Washington, V. (1980). Teachers in integrated classrooms: Profiles of attitudes, perceptions, and behavior. *Elementary School Journal, 80,* 192–201.

Washington, V. (1982). Racial differences in teacher perceptions of first and fourth grade pupils on selected characteristics. *Journal of Negro Education, 51,* 60–72.

Watson, J. B. (1929). *Psychological care of the infant and child.* New York: Norton.

Watson, M. M., & Jackowitz, E. R. (1984). Agents and recipient objects in the development of early symbolic play. *Child Development, 55,* 1091–1097.

Wegman, M. E. (1994). Annual summary of vital statistics—1993. *Pediatrics, 94,* 792–803.

Wehren, A., DeLisi, R., & Arnold, M. (1981). The development of noun definition. *Journal of Child Language, 8,* 165–175.

Weinberg, R. (1989). Intelligence and IQ: Landmark issues and great debates. *American Psychologist, 44,* 98–104.

Weinraub, M., & Lewis, M. The determinants of children's responses to separation. *Monographs of the Society for Research in Child Development, 42,* Serial No. 172.

Weitzman, M., Gortmaker, S., Walker, D. K., & Sobol, A. (1989). Social and environmental risks for childhood asthma. *American Journal of Diseases of Children, 143,* 436.

Welteroth, S. (1999). Play, special children, and special circumstances. In J. E. Johnson, J. F. Christie, & T. D. Yawkey (Eds.), *Play and early childhood development* (pp. 154–188). New York: Longman.

Wender, P. H. (1987). *The hyperactive child, adolescent, and adult: Attention deficit disorder through the life-span.* New York: Oxford University Press.

Werner, E. E. (1990). Protective factors and individual resilience. In S. J. Meisels & J. P. Shonkoff (Eds.), *Handbook of early childhood intervention* (pp. 57–83). Cambridge, England: Cambridge University Press.

Werner, E. E., & Smith, R. S. (1992). *Overcoming the odds: High-risk children from birth to adulthood.* New York: Cornell University Press.

Whelan, R. J. (1995). Emotional disturbance. In E. L. Meyen & T. M. Skrtic (Eds.), *Special education and student disability* (pp. 271–338). Denver: Love.

White, K., Bush, D., & Casto, G. (1985). Learning from reviews of early intervention. *Journal of Special Education, 19,* 417–428.

White, S. (1989). Backchannels across culture: A study of Americans and Japanese. *Language and Society, 18,* 59–76.

Whitebrook, M., Phillips, D., & Howes, C. (1993). *National child care staffing study revisited.* Oakland, CA: Child Care Employee Project.

Whiting, B. B., & Edwards, C. P. (1988). *Children of different worlds.* Cambridge: Harvard University Press.

Whiting, B. B., & Whiting, J. W. M. (1975). *Children of six cultures: A psycho-cultural analysis.* Cambridge: Harvard University Press.

Whiting, J. W. M. (1977). A model for psychocultural research. In P. H. Leiderman, S. R. Tulkin, & A. Rosenfeld (Eds.), *Culture and infancy: Variations in the human experience.* New York: Academic Press.

Whitney, M. P., & Thoman, E. B. (1994). Sleep in premature and full-term infants from 24-hour home recordings. *Infant Behavior and Development, 17,* 223–234.

Wicks-Nelson, R., & Israel, A. C. (1997). *Behavior disorders of childhood.* Upper Saddle River, NJ: Merrill/Prentice Hall.

Widmayer, S. M., Peterson, L. M., Larner, M., Carnahan, S., Calderon, A., Wingerd, J., & Marshall, R. (1990). Predictors of Haitian-American infant development at twelve months. *Child Development, 61,* 410–415.

Wiesenfeld, A. R., Malatesta, C. Z., & DeLoache, J. S. (1981). Differential parental response to familiar and unfamiliar infant distress signals. *Infant Behavior and Development, 4,* 281–295.

Williams, D. C., & Kantor, R. (1997). The challenge of Reggio Emilia's research: One teacher's reflections. In J. Hendrick (Ed.), *First steps toward teaching the Reggio Emilia way* (pp. 112–126). Upper Saddle River, NJ: Merrill/Prentice Hall.

Williams, H. G. (1983). *Perceptual and motor development.* Upper Saddle River, NJ: Prentice-Hall.

Winick, B. (1981). Food and the fetus. *American Scientist, 1,* 76–81.

Wise, F., & Miller, N. B. (1983). The mental health of the American Indian child. In G. J. Powell (Ed.), *The psychosocial development of minority children.* New York: Brunner/Mazel.

Witmer, H. L., & Kotinsky, R. (1952). *Personality in the making: The report on the Midcentury White House Conference on Children.* New York: Harper Row.

Wolff, P. H. (1966). The causes, controls, and organization of behavior in the neonate. *Psychological Issues, 5,* 1–105.

Wolff, P. H. (1969). The natural history of crying and other vocalizations in early infancy. In B. M. Foss (Ed.), *Determinants of infant behavior: IV. Proceedings of the Fourth Tavistock Study Group on Mother-Infant Interaction* (pp. 81–109).

Wong, M. G. (1988). The Chinese American family. In C. H. Mindel, R. W. Habenstein & R. Wright (Eds.), *Ethnic families in America: Patterns and variations* (pp. 230–257). New York: Elsevier.

Wong Fillmore, L. (1976). *The second time around: Cognitive and social strategies in second language acquisition.* Doctoral dissertation, Stanford University.

Wong Fillmore, L. (1991, April). *Asian-Americans and bilingualism.* Paper presented at the biennial meeting of the Society for Research in Child Development, Seattle.

Wood, D. L., Valdez, R. B., Hayashi, T., & Shen, A. (1990). Health of homeless children and housed poor children. *Pediatrics, 86,* 858–866.

Wright, J. L., & Samaras, A. S. (1986). Play worlds and microworlds. In P. F. Campbell & G. G. Fein (Eds.), *Young children and microcomputers.* Reston, VA: Reston.

Yairi, E. (1983). The onset of stuttering in 2- and 3-year-old children: A preliminary report. *Journal of Speech and Hearing Disorders, 48,* 171–177.

Yamamoto, J., & Iga, M. (1983). Emotional growth of Japanese-American children. In G. J. Powell (Ed.), *The psychosocial de-*

velopment of minority children (pp. 167–180). New York: Brunner/Mazel.

Yamamoto, J., & Kubota, M. (1983). Emotional development of Japanese-American children. In G. J. Powell (Ed.), *The psychosocial development of minority children* (pp. 237–247). New York: Brunner/Mazel.

Yang, B., Ollendick, T. H., Dong, Q., Xia, Y., & Lin, L. (1995). Only children and children with siblings in the Peoples Republic of China. *Child Development, 66,* 1301–1311.

Yip, R. (1990). The epidemiology of childhood iron deficiency. In J. Dobbing (Ed.), *Brain, behaviour, and iron in the infant diet* (pp. 27–42). London: Springer-Verlag.

Younger, A. J., & Daniels, T. M. (1992). Children's reasons for nominating their peers as withdrawn: Passive withdrawal versus active isolation? *Developmental Psychology, 28,* 955–960.

Yu, K. H., & Kim, L. I. C. (1983). The growth and development of Korean-American children. In G. J. Powell (Ed.), *The psychosocial development of minority children* (pp. 147–158). New York: Brunner/Mazel.

Zametkin, A. J., Nordahl, T. E., Gross, M., King, A. C. Semple, W. E., Rumsey, J. Hamberger, S., & Cohen, R. M. (1990). Cerebral glucose metabolism in adults with hyperactivity of childhood onset. *New England Journal of Medicine, 323,* 1361–1366.

Zepeda, M. (1986, April). *Early caregiving in a Mexican origin population.* Paper presented at the International Conference on Infant Studies, Los Angeles.

Zeskind, E. F., Sale, J., Maio, M. L., Huntington, L., & Weiseman, J. R. (1985). Adult perceptions of pain and hunger cries: A synchrony of arousal. *Child Development, 56,* 549–554.

Zeskind, P. S. (1983). Cross-cultural differences in maternal perceptions of low- and high-risk infants. *Child Development, 54,* 1119–1128.

Zigler, E. F., & Finn-Stevenson, M. (1993). *Children in a changing world: Development and social issues.* Pacific Grove, CA: Brooks/Cole.

Zigler, E. F., & Weiss, H. (1985). Family support systems: An ecological approach to child development. In R. N. Rapoport (Ed.), *Children, youth, and families.* Cambridge: Cambridge University Press.

Zimmerman, B. J., & Lanaro, P. (1974). Acquiring and retaining conservation of length through modeling and reversibility cues. *Merrill-Palmer Quarterly, 20,* 145–161.

Zuckerman, D. M., & Zuckerman, B. S. (1985). Television's impact on children. *Pediatrics, 75,* 233–240.

Name Index

Subject Index